D1336757

JONATHAN D. SMELE

The "Russian" Civil Wars, 1916–1926

Ten Years That Shook the World

HURST & COMPANY, LONDON

First published in the United Kingdom in 2015 by
C. Hurst & Co. (Publishers) Ltd.,
41 Great Russell Street, London, WC1B 3PL
© Jonathan D. Smele, 2015
All rights reserved.
Printed in India

The right of Jonathan D. Smele to be identified as the author
of this publication is asserted by him in accordance with the
Copyright, Designs and Patents Act, 1988.

A Cataloguing-in-Publication data record for this book
is available from the British Library.

ISBN: 978-1-84904-424-0

This book is printed using paper from registered sustainable
and managed sources.

www.hurstpublishers.com

For Lola

CONTENTS

NOTES FOR THE READER

At midnight on 31 January 1918, in accordance with a decree signed by V.I. Lenin a few days earlier, the new, revolutionary Soviet government, Sovnarkom—which had replaced the liberal–socialist Russian Provisional Government that eight months earlier had stepped into the gap left by the toppled Tsar, and which had already laid claim to sovereign control of most of the old Russian Empire—also revolutionized time in that former imperial space. Sovnarkom adopted, for what was soon to become the Russian Soviet Federative Socialist Republic (RSFSR), the Gregorian ("new style") calendar that had prevailed further west in Europe since its adoption by Pope Gregory XIII in 1582, and which, in the early twentieth century, was thirteen days ahead of the Julian ("old style") calendar that until that date had been in use in Orthodox Russia (where the Church authorities still anathematized this "new style" calendar as a Catholic fallacy). The day following 31 January 1918 consequently (and to the acute consternation of many Orthodox souls, who feared they had lost almost a fortnight of their lives) became 14 February 1918 in Soviet Russia. In this volume, in a certainly hopeless search for clarity, dates of events in areas of what had been the Russian Empire prior to the change in the calendar are given in the old style. Dates of events in those areas after the change of calendar are given in new style. It should be noted, however, that many of the Russian military, political, cultural, and (of course) religious forces that opposed the Soviet regime during and after the "Russian" Civil Wars refused to recognize this heretical breach with the one true Church and continued to use the Julian calendar throughout (and beyond) the civil-war period. Hence chronological confusions still abound. (Curiously, it should be acknowledged, Lenin's decree specified that the new calendar, "as used by almost all civilized people," was for "lay use" only, thereby explicitly exempting the Church, which, logic suggests, Lenin regarded as uncivilized.) Dates of events outside the former Russian Empire are always given according to the Gregorian calendar, although the amoebic nature of states, quondam states, and mutative borders in this turbulent era will certainly have introduced yet more inconsistencies and errors here also.

In this volume, all Russian words (including names) have been transliterated according to the Library of Congress (LoC) system, except for other Anglicized versions of personal names that gained general acceptance prior to the widespread adoption of the LoC system of transliteration, often as a consequence of their bearer's domestication or frequent publication in the West (chiefly, for example, for our purposes, "Trotsky," not "Trotskii," "Kerensky" not "Kerenskii," and "Wrangel" not "Vrangel'"), although a more accurate transliteration of publications by (or about) such individuals in Russian has of course been employed in the footnotes and bibliography. But early twentieth-century Russia was a multinational empire—indeed, it was the multinational empire of the modern era. Consequently, of the figures who came to prominence in it, many were not Russian at all—which is part of the point of this book—even if they sided with ostensibly "Russian" political and/or military formations. In this regard, it might be worth mentioning that even the bearers of the names most familiar to those with only a cursory acquaintance with the "Russian" Civil Wars had a very heterogenous mix of recent forebears. Thus on the side of the Reds we find V.I. Lenin (who had recent Tatar, German, and Jewish ancestors); L.D. Trotsky (from a family of non-devout Jews); J.V. Stalin (a Georgian); Feliks Dzierżyński (Polish, and destined for life as a Catholic priest before his politicization); M.K. Frunze (half-Moldavian); commander-in-chief of the Red Army Jukums Vācietis (a Latvian); and myriad others. And, on the White side (generally presumed to be the acme of pure and aristocratic Russian revolt against Bolshevik internationalism), we find: General A.I. Denikin (half-Polish, son of a former serf); P.N. Wrangel (of German and Swedish heritage); L.D. Kornilov (a Cossack); E.K. Miller (Baltic German); N.N. Iudenich (patently of Jewish heritage); and Admiral A.V. Kolchak (descended, through his father's line, from a Bosnian/Turkish family). We need not speak here, obviously, of the many leaders of nationalist forces that opposed the Bolsheviks in these multi- and inter-ethnic wars, which have previously—and erroneously—been described as "Russian."

In deference to this trope, the personal names of non-Russians mentioned in this book have been rendered, for the most part (and unless their families had been entirely Russianized), according to the most common transliteration of their names from the Latvian, Ukrainian, Polish, etc. rather than the Russian/ Russified version: therefore, for example, the aforementioned "Vācietis," not "Vatsetis"; and "Dzierżyński" not "Dzerzhinskii" (although the line has been drawn at the likes of Mihail Frunză, which seems too anachronistic). This at least has the advantage of conveying the multinational (even international) nature of the wars that wracked "Russia" in the revolutionary era, even if it is not in line with what the subjects themselves might have preferred. Probably, it has to be said, on the Red side most would not have preferred it. Many Leftist, non-Russian Bolsheviks and socialists of the old empire welcomed—and, indeed, invited—their Russification (or, as they perceived it, "internationalization"), as a necessary process that would release them and their peoples from the parochial concerns of "small nationalities" that were destined to die out in some sort of Darwinian struggle. It is worth recording too that German was chosen as the *lingua franca* of what we have learned to call the "Russian-dominated" Communist International (the Komintern). It is worth remembering here, also, that there were very many Red enthusiasts of the universalist language of Esperanto—none other than the first *de facto* Soviet commander-in-chief of what was becoming the Red Army, N.V. Krylenko, for one. It is also widely known that, later in his career, the largely Russianized Georgian we know as Josef Stalin (Ioseb Besarionis je Juašvili) would persecute Esperantists for cultivating "the language of spies," but prior to the revolution he had actually tried to teach himself that experimental, international tongue. The Esperantists' symbol, a five-pointed green star, also provided the model for the red version that became associated with the Soviet armed forces, according to one of the many contending accounts of that device's origins.

Personal names are one thing, place names are another—and they are a minefield (historically, politically, literally) for those in search of clarity and equity. Herein, due to their familiarity, exceptions have been made for Moscow and St Petersburg and (for purely aesthetic reasons) Yalta, but the line has been drawn at Archangel/Arkhangel'sk in rendering English versions of Russian place names. More consequential is that place names can be piquant political and ethnic markers. During a kaleidoscopic series of civil wars, and an immense imperial collapse, such as that endured by Russia and its borderlands in the period after 1917 (not to mention the overlapping disintegration of its German, Austrian, and Turkish neighbors, as well as the contemporaneous upheavals afflicting Persia, Mongolia, and China), they become multiply significant. (Indeed, in so far as a name employed might be read by an interlocutor—often toting a big gun—as betraying some hostile political or national intent, it could be a matter of life or death.) Thus many of the places mentioned in this volume were called by two or three or four or more different names (usually as a consequence of national differences and military conquests) even before the Soviet government began renaming towns and cities (and even mountains and other natural and man-made features, not to mention satellites) in honor of "heroes of the revolution." For example, Lwów (Polish), L'vov (Russian), L'viv (Ukrainian), Lemberg (German), and Liov (Romanian) were all current during the revolutionary period as the name for the largest city in Western Ukraine (which the Poles called Eastern Galicia)—and a place that will be frequently mentioned in this volume even though it had never been part of the Russian Empire. For the sake of consistency, I have here, in general, and not without regret, become all too often a Russianizer, giving the Russian version of a place name in the first instance, sometimes followed, for clarification, by the chief native form: for example, Kiev (Kyiv) for what is now the capital of Ukraine; or presenting the historical name followed by its current name when that might enhance clarity. However, there were about 100 or 200 "nationalities" (depending on definitions of ethnicity) in what, up until the revolutionary period, was called "Russia," and at least half as many linguistic groups. I am certain that I have not done justice to all of them—or even to most of them. So, please excuse the inevitable inconsistencies. Hopefully, though, meaning will be clear, while the complexity of the problem will be illustrated through my failures. That is the point, in fact.

Finally, in this regard (and emblematically for something that might seem otherwise to be so straightforward), the city that is now, once again, St Petersburg (and, from 1924 to 1991, was called Leningrad), is generally herein referred to as "Petrograd." This was the confusing and confused name adopted for it by the tsarist government upon the outbreak of war in August 1914, so that the name of the Russian capital should not sound too "German." This was in naked defiance of the fact that, in 1703, the city had actually been christened with the Dutch name "Sankt-Peterburg" by its founder, Peter the Great, according to his infatuation with all things Netherlandish. Mystifying here, also, is that this renaming was chosen, in August–September 1914, to express sympathy with the Dutch territories that, in those months, were, of course, being only threatened—though never invaded—by the Germans. In a more sensible repudiation of these official onomastic gymnastics, through war, revolution, and civil war, the inhabitants of Peter's perfect city persisted in referring to it, familiarly, as "Piter"—which is not German, Dutch, or even Russian. It is slang. What, indeed, is in a name?

ACKNOWLEDGEMENTS

Astonishingly, three of the most acclaimed and influential books on the Russian Revolutions and Civil Wars, in any language, have been written by scholars affiliated with the University of Glasgow—whose inspiring George Gilbert Scott tower dominates the city's skyline from almost every angle. I was extraordinarily fortunate that, a long, long time ago, two of those authors, Evan Mawdsley and Jimmy White, taught me, as a postgraduate student, at what was then known as the university's Institute of Soviet and East European Studies. To this day, that contrasting scholarly pair continue to inspire and inform me in their very different ways. The third, Geoffrey Swain, recently retired from the Alec Nove Chair of Russian History at Glasgow, has also been a friend and an inspiration for many years, and kindly commented on a draft of this book, which was probably saved from several disasters by his interventions. Thanks are also due to Evan (and his current publishers, Birlinn, of Edinburgh) for allowing me to reproduce the maps from his seminal *The Russian Civil War* (originally published by Allen & Unwin in 1987). Acknowledgement is also due to Nik Cornish (www.stavka.org.uk), who supplied most of the photographs. I am grateful also to my home department, at Queen Mary, University of London, for providing the sabbatical leave that allowed me to spend a year at home in Glasgow, just a few minutes' walk from the magnificent collections on Russian and Soviet history of Glasgow University Library, working on this book—and its companion *Historical Dictionary of the "Russian" Civil Wars, 1916–1926*, 2 vols (Lanham: Scarecrow Press, 2015).

GLOSSARY, ACRONYMS, AND ABBREVIATIONS

AFSR	The Armed Forces of South Russia: the White army commanded by General A.I. Denikin.
All-Russian Central Executive Committee	See VTsIK.
ataman	A Cossack leader; cf. hetman.
Basmachi	The term, first deployed in Soviet times, to describe Muslim rebels in Central Asia. It has some pejorative overtones (of banditry), but has become standard.
Bolsheviks	Members of the RSDLP(b)/RKP(b).
Borotbists	*Borotbisty*: the popular name for the Ukrainian Party of Socialists-Revolutionary Borotbists (Communist). Literally, *Borotbisty* means "Fighters."
cadet	The Russian term for a pupil at an officer training school (sometimes also rendered as "junker").
Cheka	Chrezvychainaia Komissiia: the Russian acronym for the short form of the "Extraordinary Commission [for Combating Counter-Revolution and Sabotage]" (formally, the "All-Russian Commission": Vserossiiskaia Chrezvychaynaia Komissiia po Bor'be s Kontrrevoliutsiei i Sabotazhem), the Bolsheviks' political police (established in December 1917).
Chekist	A member of the Cheka.
commissar	An official of either the Provisional Government or the Soviet government charged with a particular task. The term was derived from the *commissaires* of the era of the French Revolution.

Cossack	Originally a population group of eastern Slavs who settled Russia's steppe frontier, from the fourteenth to the seventeenth centuries, and who prospered largely by raiding and looting. By the nineteenth century, the term denoted a member of a military caste living in the borderlands of the Russian Empire in a separate Host that received certain privileges from the state in return for military service.
druzhina	A militia or small military unit, a squadron.
FER	The Far Eastern Republic.
front	In imperial Russian and Soviet usage, a group of armies (or what might be called an army corps).
genshtabisty	Graduates of the Imperial Russian (Nicholas) Academy of the General Staff.
Glavkom	Main commander of the Red Army.
guberniia	A province (pl. *gubernii*).
hetman	A Ukrainian Cossack leader.
Host	A Cossack group, based on a geographical nomenclature (e.g. the Don Cossack Host, the Kuban Cossack Host). The Russian term is *voisko*.
junker	See cadet.
Kadets	Members of the Constitutional Democratic Party (also known as the Party of the People's Freedom), Russia's main liberal party after 1905.
Komandarm	Army Commander of the Red Army.
kombedy	Komitety [Derevenskoi]Bednoty: Committees of the Village Poor, established by the Soviet government in May 1918 to facilitate the collection of grain from the countryside and to foster class warfare among the peasants.
Komintern	The Communist International (often rendered as "Comintern"), founded in Moscow in March 1919.
Komuch	Komitet Chlenov Uchreditelnogo sobraniia: the Committee of Members of the Constituent Assembly, the anti-Bolshevik government established at Samara in June 1918, consisting predominantly of members of the PSR.
krasnoarmeets	Red Army soldier (pl. *krasnoarmeetsy*)

krug	A Cossack assembly or council (literally, "a circle").
kursant	An officer cadet in the Red Army.
left-bank Ukraine	That part of Ukraine on the left (eastern) bank of the River Dnepr, absorbed into the Russian state after 1654. The region was sometimes referred to (by Russians) as "Little Russia."
Left-SR	A member of the Party of Left Socialists-Revolutionaries.
Mensheviks	Those members of the RSDLP who opposed the Bolsheviks, on issues of ideology and party organization.
military district	A region, usually made up of several *gubernii* (provinces) responsible for mobilizing, training, and supplying troops in imperial Russia and Soviet Russia.
NEP	New Economic Policy: the term denotes the series of measures introduced by Sovnarkom from March 1921 that relaxed state control over the economy and encouraged (limited) private enterprise. It replaced War Communism.
oblastnik	A proponent of regionalism (*oblastnichestvo*), especially Siberian regionalism.
October Manifesto	Nicholas II's pronouncement of 17 October 1905, promising a legislative assembly and the extension of civil rights.
Octobrists	A right-liberal party founded in 1905, which advocated working within the terms of the October Manifesto.
otaman	During the civil war, this was the title accorded to a division, corps, or army group commander in the Ukrainian Army. Originally it was the title of the elected leader of the Zaporozhian Cossack Host.
Pale of Settlement	The fifteen provinces along the western marches of the Russian Empire where most Russian Jews were obliged, by law, to live.
People's Commissar	A member of Sovnarkom, a Soviet cabinet minister.
pervopokhodniki	Veterans of the Volunteer Army's First Kuban (Ice) March.
pogrom	A violent attack on Jewish settlements.

prodotriad	A grain confiscation brigade of the Soviet regime.
prodrazverstka	The Bolsheviks' system of requisitioning foodstuffs during the period of War Communism.
prodrazchet	The Bolsheviks' system of taxing agricultural production during the NEP.
PSR	The Party of Socialists-Revolutionaries (SRs).
rada	A Ukrainian term, meaning "council," as in the Ukrainian Central Rada. The term was also adopted by the assembly of the generally pro-Ukrainian Kuban Cossack Host. (Other Hosts used the term *krug*).
revkom	A Bolshevik revolutionary committee, often prefaced by an abbreviated form of its location (e.g. Sibrevkom, the Siberian Revolutionary Committee): an extraordinary military-civilian administrative organ established to oversee a region's transition to Soviet power.
revvoensovet	Revolutionary Military Council—an army council, answerable to the central *Revvoensovet* of the Republic (RVSR).
right-bank Ukraine	That part of Ukraine, on the right (western) bank of the River Dnepr, that had been annexed by Russia during the late eighteenth century (in the second and third partitions of Poland). The region was sometimes referred to (by Russians) as "the south-western provinces."
RKP(b)	The Russian Communist Party (Bolshevik): the Bolsheviks' official party name from 8 March 1918.
RSDLP	Russian Social Democratic Labor Party: the party organization of the Russian followers of Karl Marx, which, after 1903, was divided into factions of Bolsheviks and Mensheviks.
RSDLP(b)	Russian Social Democratic Labor Party (Bolsheviks): the name used by V.I. Lenin's party from 1912 to 8 March 1918, when it became the RKP(b).
RSFSR	The Russian Soviet Federated Socialist Republic: the Soviet state during most of the civil-war period.
ROVS	The Russian All-Military Union, the White émigré military organization founded by General P.N. Wrangel in 1924.

RVSR	See *revvoensovet*.
Sovnarkom	Sovet Narodnykh Komissarov (Council of People's Commissars): the first Soviet government, founded on 26 October 1917 and chaired by V.I. Lenin.
SR	A member of the PSR.
SSR	Soviet Socialist Republic—a Soviet state allied to the RSFSR (and subsequently incorporated into the USSR).
stanitsa	A Cossack village.
State Duma	Gosudarstvennaia Duma: the legislative assembly, first elected in 1906, following Nicholas II's October Manifesto.
stavka	An army headquarters.
steppe	The mostly treeless, grassy plain covering much of southern and south-eastern Russia.
taiga	The chiefly coniferous forest stretching across northern Russia, between the steppe and the tundra.
uezd	A subdivision of a province (*guberniia*); a district.
UNR	The Ukrainian National (sometimes People's) Republic.
USSR	The Union of Soviet Socialist Republics.
village commune	The fundamental institution of peasant self-government throughout much of European Russia. Russian peasants tended to call it the *mir* (literally 'the peace' or 'the world,' or even 'the universe').
volost'	A county: the unit of local administration, established by the Emancipation edict of 1861, that united between *c.*300 and *c.*2,000 people, often from a number of settlements and village communes.
Volunteers	Members of the anti-Bolshevik Volunteer Army, established by General M.V. Alekseev at Novocherkassk in November 1917.
VSNKh	Vysshii sovet narodnogo khoziastva: the Supreme Council of the National Economy: a powerful body within the RSFSR.
VTsIK	Vserossiiskii Tsentral'nyi Ispol'nitelnyi Komitet: the All-Russian Central Executive Committee, elected at the All-Russian Congress of Soviets as the executive

	branch of the Soviet government. It might be described as the Soviet parliament.
War Communism	The term used (retrospectively) by V.I. Lenin to denote the series of economic measures employed by the Bolsheviks during the civil wars, including wholesale nationalization of industry and the forced requisitioning of food (*prodrazverstka*).
zemstvo	Officially, Zemskoe Uchrezhdenie: an elected local assembly (pl. *zemstva*), at *uezd* and *guberniia* levels, of representatives of all classes, established by the reform of 1 January 1864.

LIST OF MAPS

LIST OF PHOTOGRAPHS

Photo 1: Men of the 7th Infantry Division of the Armed Forces of South Russia in British uniforms (Russian State Archive of Film and Photography, Krasnogorsk).

Photo 2: General M.V. Alekseev in his open coffin: Ekaterinodar, October 1918 (Russian State Archive of Film and Photography, Krasnogorsk).

Photo 3: Kalmyk cavalry of the Don Army (Andrei Simonov Collection).

Photo 4: Colonel V.G. Buizin, commander of the Partisan Regiment General Alekseev, with his wife, V.I. Buizina, who served as his adjutant. Note her four wound stripes (Russian State Archive of Film and Photography, Krasnogorsk).

Photo 5: Austro-Hungarian troops hanging Ukrainian dissidents: summer 1918 (Central Museum of the Armed Forces, Moscow).

Photo 6: Czech legionnaires entrenched (Nik Cornish Collection).

Photo 7: General A.I. Denikin (rear seat, left) converses with his chief of staff, General I.P. Romanovskii: Taganrog, 1919 (Russian State Archive of Film and Photography, Krasnogorsk).

Photo 8: General A.I. Denikin (back to camera) having issued the Moscow Directive before Tsaritsyn Cathedral, 3 July 1919. On horse, with sword raised in tribute, is General K.K. Mamontov; on foot, saluting, in black Circassian uniform, is General P.N. Wrangel (Russian State Archive of Film and Photography, Krasnogorsk).

Photo 9: General F.C. Poole arriving at Novocherkassk (23 November 1918) and saluting General A.I. Denikin (Central Museum of the Armed Forces, Moscow).

Photo 10: General E.K. Miller (with sword) converses with General W.E. Ironside: Arkhangel'sk 1919 (Nik Cornish Collection).

Photo 11: M.I. Kalinin (left) and S.M. Budennyi in the rear seat of a staff car: Polish front, August 1920 (Russian State Archive of Film and Photography, Krasnogorsk).

Photo 12: Nestor Makhno. To his right, in sailor's cap, is Fedir Shchus' (Russian State Archive of Film and Photography, Krasnogorsk).

Photo 13: On board a vessel of a Red Military Flotilla (Central Museum of the Armed Forces, Moscow).

Photo 14: Men of Colonel A.P. Liven's Volunteer Detachment in German uniforms: Latvia, 1919 (Nik Cornish Collection).

Photo 15: Red armoured car unit (Central Museum of the Armed Forces, Moscow).

Photo 16: Red Army men with a captured Mk.5 tank: Poland, 1920. Note the *budenovki* helmets (Russian State Archive of Film and Photography, Krasnogorsk).

Photo 17: Red Gunners with a 122mm Krupp Howitzer, built under licence in tsarist Russia (Central Museum of the Armed Forces, Moscow).

Photo 18: Red Army infantry: Eastern Front, 1919 (Central Museum of the Armed Forces, Moscow).

Photo 19: Tachankas of the Red 2nd Cavalry Army, 1920 (Central Museum of the Armed Forces, Moscow).

Photo 20: Makhnovists. Left to right: Efim Taranovskii, Fedir Shchus' and 'Kuzhin' (Russian State Archive of Film and Photography, Krasnogorsk).

Photo 21: L.D. Trotsky and (third from left) Ia.M. Sverdlov present honours to a Red Army unit outside the Bolshoi Theater: Moscow, 1919 (Russian State Archive of Film and Photography, Krasnogorsk).

Photo 22: White armoured cars at Tsaritsyn, August 1919. Left to right: "The Eagle-eyed", "The Brave", "The Mighty". Note British instructors, in shorts (Russian State Archive of Film and Photography, Krasnogorsk).

Photo 23: The White armoured train "United Russia" (Russian State Archive of Film and Photography, Krasnogorsk).

Photo 24: R.F. Ungern von Sternberg under guard: Novonikolaevsk, September 1921 (Central Museum of the Armed Forces, Moscow).

Photo 25: General P.N. Wrangel with Circassian bodyguards: Tsaritsyn, 1919 (Russian State Archive of Film and Photography, Krasnogorsk).

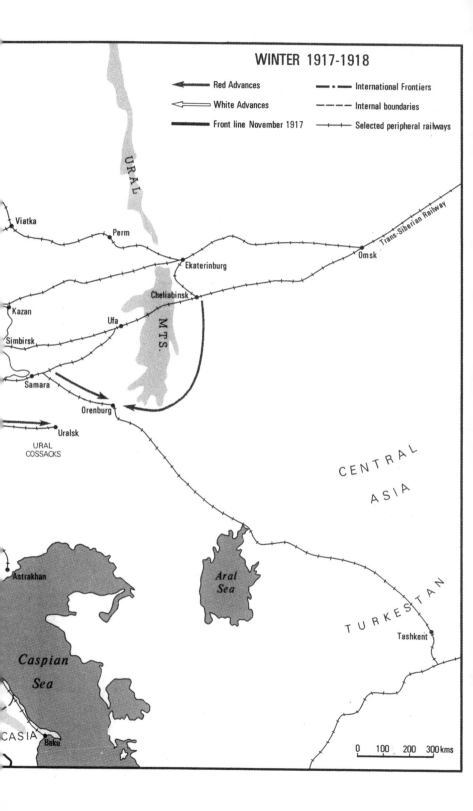

WINTER 1917-1918

Red Advances
White Advances
Front line November 1917

International Frontiers
Internal boundaries
Selected peripheral railways

URAL

Viatka
Perm
Ekaterinburg
Omsk

Trans-Siberian Railway

Kazan
Cheliabinsk
Ufa
Simbirsk

M T S.

Samara
Orenburg

Uralsk

URAL
COSSACKS

CENTRAL
ASIA

Astrakhan

Aral
Sea

TURKESTAN

Tashkent

Caspian
Sea

CASIA Baku

0   100   200   300 kms

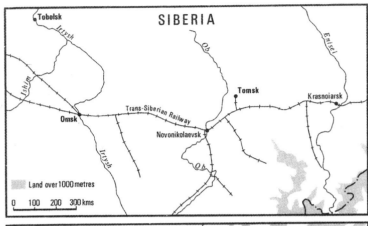

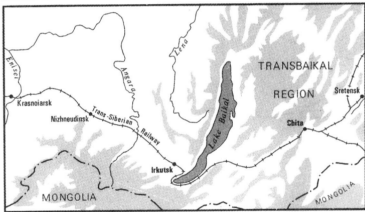

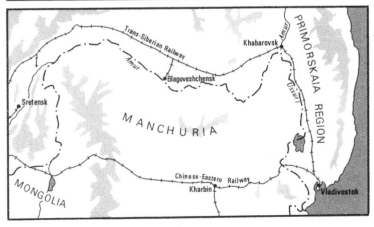

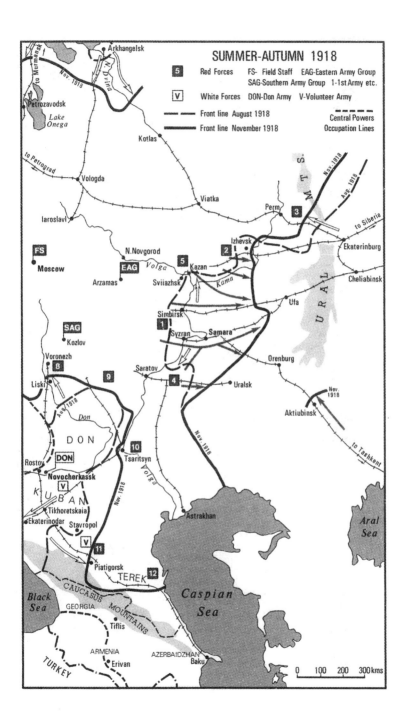

SUMMER-AUTUMN 1918

5	Red Forces	FS- Field Staff	EAG-Eastern Army Group
			SAG-Southern Army Group 1-1st Army etc.
V	White Forces	DON-Don Army V-Volunteer Army

– – – Front line August 1918

—— Front line November 1918

– – – Central Powers Occupation Lines

to Murmansk

Nov. 1918

Arkhangelsk

N. Dvina

Petrozavodsk

Lake Onega

Kotlas

to Petrograd

Vologda

Viatka

Perm

3

Nov. 1918

Aug. 1918

to Siberia

Iaroslavl

Izhevsk

Ekaterinburg

FS

Moscow

N.Novgorod

2

EAG

Volga

Kazan

5

Kama

Ufa

Cheliabinsk

Arzamas

Sviiazhsk

U R A L

M T S.

Simbirsk

1

Syzran

Samara

SAG

Kozlov

Saratov

Orenburg

Voronezh

8

9

4

Uralsk

Liski

Aug 1918

Nov. 1918

Aktiubinsk

Don

to Tashkent

D O N

10

Tsaritsyn

Rostov

DON

Volga

Novocherkassk

V

K U B A N

Tikhoretskaia

Astrakhan

Ekaterinodar

Stavropol

Aral Sea

V

11

Piatigorsk

TEREK

12

CAUCASUS

Caspian Sea

Black Sea

MOUNTAINS

GEORGIA

Tiflis

ARMENIA

AZERBAIDZHAN

Baku

TURKEY

Erivan

0   100   200   300 kms

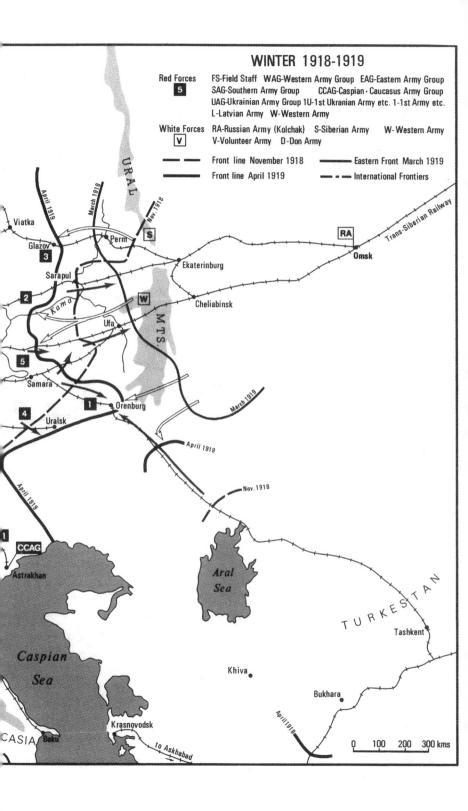

WINTER 1918-1919

Red Forces
5

White Forces
V

FS-Field Staff WAG-Western Army Group EAG-Eastern Army Group
SAG-Southern Army Group   CCAG-Caspian·Caucasus Army Group
UAG-Ukrainian Army Group 1U-1st Ukranian Army etc. 1-1st Army etc.
L-Latvian Army W-Western Army

RA-Russian Army (Kolchak) S-Siberian Army   W-Western Army
V-Volunteer Army   D-Don Army

— — — Front line November 1918   ———— Eastern Front March 1919
———— Front line April 1919   —··—·· International Frontiers

URAL

April 1919
March 1919
Nov. 1918

Trans-Siberian Railway

Viatka

Glazov
3

Perm
S

RA

Omsk

Ekaterinburg

Sarapul

2

Kama

W

Cheliabinsk

Ufa

M
T
S.

5

Samara

March 1919

1 Orenburg

4 Uralsk

April 1919

April 1919

Nov. 1918

April 1919

1
CCAG

Astrakhan

Aral
Sea

T
U
R
K
E
S
T
A
N

TURKESTAN

Tashkent

Caspian
Sea

Khiva

Bukhara

Krasnovodsk

April 1919

CASIA Baku

to Askhabad

0   100   200   300 kms

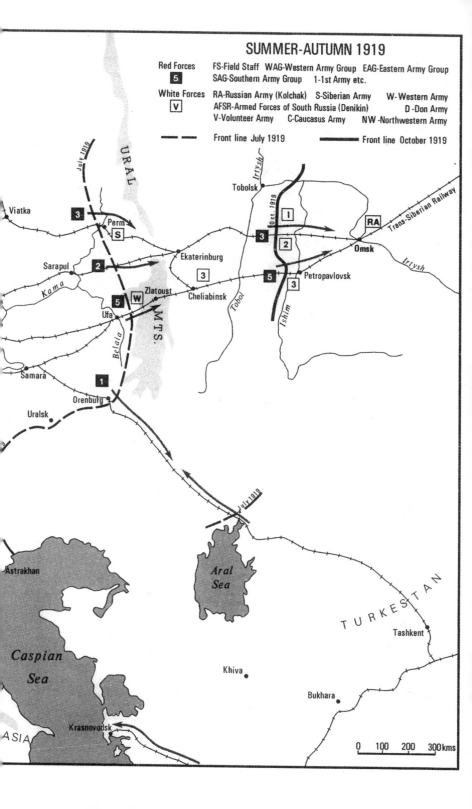

SUMMER-AUTUMN 1919

Red Forces   FS-Field Staff   WAG-Western Army Group   EAG-Eastern Army Group
▪5▪   SAG-Southern Army Group   1-1st Army etc.

White Forces   RA-Russian Army (Kolchak)   S-Siberian Army   W-Western Army
▢V▢   AFSR-Armed Forces of South Russia (Denikin)   D-Don Army
               V-Volunteer Army   C-Caucasus Army   NW-Northwestern Army

– – –   Front line July 1919   ▬▬▬   Front line October 1919

URAL

July 1919

Viatka

▪3▪   Perm
      ▢S▢

Tobolsk

Irtysh

Oct. 1919

▢1▢

RA   Trans-Siberian Railway

▪3▪

▢2▢

Ekaterinburg

Omsk

Sarapul   ▪2▪

Kama

▢3▢

Irtysh

Cheliabinsk

Tobol

▪5▪

▢3▢   Petropavlovsk

Zlatoust
▪5▪ ▢W▢

Ufa

Belaia

M T S.

Ishim

Samara

▪1▪

Orenburg

Uralsk

July 1919

Astrakhan

Aral
Sea

T U R K E S T A N

Tashkent

Caspian
Sea

Khiva

Bukhara

ASIA

Krasnovodsk

0   100   200   300kms

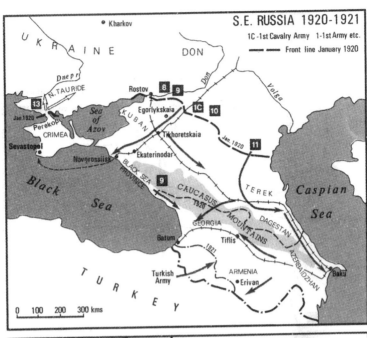

S.E. RUSSIA 1920-1921

1C -1st Cavalry Army   1-1st Army etc.

Front line January 1920

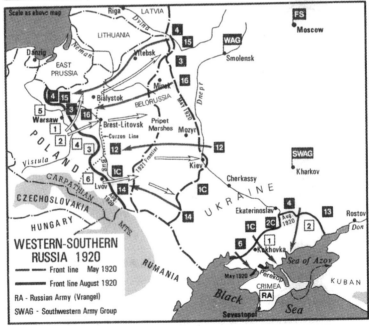

WESTERN-SOUTHERN RUSSIA 1920

Front line   May 1920

Front line August 1920

RA - Russian Army (Vrangel)

SWAG - Southwestern Army Group

INTRODUCTION

A WORLD WAR CONDENSED

In a survey of "Western Historiography of the Russian Civil War," one of the pioneer Western historians of the subject asserted that "the Civil War was not merely an appendage of the revolution, but on the contrary, it was its most significant and decisive component."[1] This inspiring remark has helped fashion what follows: an attempt to build upon that premise in order to establish that the ascent of V.I. Lenin's Bolshevik Party to power during the October Revolution of 1917, which is usually located at the center of any account of the period, was but one stage—albeit an especially important one, though not even the first of that magnitude—in a continuum of crises, wars, revolutions, and civil wars that ebbed and flowed across the collapsing Russian Empire for a decade. Thus the important role in all this of Lenin's party is not denied: there is no intention here of endorsing the post-Soviet, "triumphalist" school of historiography that (with eyes fixed firmly on Stalin) sought to purge the record of communism's many achievements in the twentieth century—of throwing out, in Alan Wood's memorable phrase, "The Bolsheviks, the baby and the bathwater."[2] Yet while seconding Wood's avowal, elsewhere, that it is to the revolutionary events in Russia that we can trace the origins of "The post-Versailles settlement in Europe, the rise of Fascism in Italy and Nazism in Germany, the Spanish Civil War, the Second World War, the Jewish Holocaust, the Chinese Revolution, the Cold War, the Korean War, the Berlin Wall, the Cuban missile crisis, America's anti-communist incendiarism in Vietnam" and so much more that has shaped what we are,[3] at the fulcrum of the current study is the contention that it was not the events on the streets of

1

the Russian capital that, in the course of ten days, set these events in motion. Rather, it was the reverberations of a complex series of overlapping struggles across a period of ten years that "shook the world."

The allusion being made here is of course to an uncommonly august predecessor: the famous account of the October Revolution that the American communist journalist John Reed penned, entitled *Ten Days that Shook the World*, which was published soon after the heady events it described and not long before he died.[4] The gathering excitement and expectations aroused by the revolutionary events that "Jack" Reed portrayed in the Russian capital and in Moscow, as the Bolsheviks gained strength, and then took power from an enervated Provisional Government of moderate-socialist and liberal politicians and held on to it (against very many odds), is the feature of the American radical's work that is most often remarked upon; and rightly remembered. But other passages of that seminal book are equally, if not more, illuminating. As, on the night of 24–5 October 1917, political squabbles raged furiously at the Second All-Russian Congress of Soviets at the Tauride Palace in Petrograd—and thus as the Bolshevik coup was completed—and as crowds surged into the Winter Palace to arrest ministers cowering in an ante-chamber to its famous Malachite Room (and to drink dry the wine cellars beneath), Reed noted that, strangely, across most of the rest of this architecturally and spatially dramatic but quite compact capital:

> all was quiet; hundreds of thousands of people retired at a prudent hour, got up early, and went to work. In Petrograd [on the following morning] the street-cars were running, the stores and restaurants open, theatres going, an exhibition of paintings advertised ... All the complex routine of common life—humdrum even in war-time—proceeded as usual. Nothing is so astounding as the vitality of the social organism—how it persists, feeding itself, clothing itself, amusing itself, in the face of the worst calamities ...[5]

Admittedly, Reed describes this unusual quietude as having a rather "superficial" ambiance about it. But whatever might have been the popular mood of those "ten days," over the next ten years very few such moments of even superficial tranquility would be afforded to even fewer people anywhere in what had been the boundless Russian Empire and was becoming the USSR, as they endured a decade of unprecedentedly brutal and extensive calamities and civil wars.

* * *

As the author of a recent popular survey of the period averred, the internecine conflicts that concern us here "dwarfed all others" of the civil war-strewn twentieth century, both "in scope and significance."[6] Few would dispute that the "scope" of what has traditionally been termed the "Russian Civil War" was stupendously extensive: after all, it was waged across (and beyond) the borders of a collapsing and then reconfiguring empire that enveloped fully one-sixth of the land surface of the globe; and it involved not only the 160 million or so inhabitants of that multitudinous and multinational imperium, as well as millions of the inhabitants of neighboring states into which the conflicts leached, but also interventionist forces of contending First World War combatants of both the Allies and the Central Powers, from across Europe and beyond (including colonial units of the British and French empires and armies from the United States, Japan, and China). Having germinated in the mulch of a global conflict, the hitherto so-called "Russian Civil War" was a world war condensed. Australians and other Antipodeans, it must be recorded, disembarked at Arkhangel'sk! It was also, then, truly a world turned upside down.

The cost, or intensity, of the "Russian Civil War" was also unparalleled (except, perhaps, by the still unaccounted "cost" of the vicious wars in China from 1927 to 1949): between 1917 and 1921, at least 10,500,000 people lost their lives during the struggles with which we are dealing here; many millions more were maimed, orphaned, or widowed; and at least two million former subjects of the tsar were pressed into an exile from which most would never voluntarily return—except, in some cases, as ill-fitted and usually (but not always) unlikely auxiliaries to Hitler's invading forces during the Second World War.[7] As the most active fronts of the "Russian Civil War" began to die down in 1921–22, at least another five million people then perished in a horrendous famine across the Volga–Urals region, the North Caucasus, and Ukraine that had been precipitated, in large part, by the previous years of civil war-induced upheaval. And several tens of thousands, at least, of others were then killed in battles and uprisings—mostly in Transcaucasia and Central Asia—before the upheavals reached a temporary quietude around 1926. Consequently, the first complete ("All-Union") Soviet-era census, which was conducted in that year, identified 147,027,915 citizens of the USSR, where, without world war, revolution, and civil wars (and taking into account the loss of the former imperial lands of Finland, Poland, Bessarabia, and other territories), it might have expected to have found at least 175,000,000, and perhaps more.[8]

In addition to the physical losses, the psychological scars all this inflicted on the participants in the "Russian Civil War" (and their descendants)—be they victors or vanquished—remain incalculable, for this was, without a doubt, the greatest cataclysm to engulf Russia since, in 1237–40, the Mongols surged through the Caspian Gate to overrun Kievan Rus' and sack the cities of what had been one of the richest and most sophisticated societies in Christendom. It took Russia half a millennium to recover from that catastrophic event. It could be argued that, a century after the events with which we are here concerned, the Russian Republic and the other successor states to the USSR are still coming to terms with them as well.

The historical "significance" of the "Russian Civil War," as our afore-cited author posits, is unchallengeable—not least in that, in so many senses, it marked a transition from one historical epoch to another. Thus although this was the last major conflict in Europe that featured such picturesque (to modern eyes) spectacles as mass cavalry charges and regimental colors routinely unfurled, "rallied 'round," defended to the death, or triumphantly captured on the field of battle, it also saw the dun-dressed armored train come into its own (short-lived) era, as well as the equally brutal and even more portentous equipage of tanks, armored cars, and military aircraft.[9] Poison gas too was sometimes employed during these struggles; and, in this conflict, mass terror, ethnic cleansing, and other recognizably twentieth-century weapons of psychological warfare also made their first sizable debuts;[10] while propaganda—especially on the Red side—became an art. More broadly, the "Russian Civil War" (for now, we shall still call it that) and the revolution from which it partly sprouted witnessed the opening salvos of a clash of ideologies—communism and capitalism (leavened with hefty admixtures of nationalism, proto-fascism, and antisemitism)—of world-historical import that anticipated many of the attendant terrors of the twentieth century. Indeed, some recent scholarship has drawn attention to Nazism's alleged "roots" in the right-wing, anti-Bolshevik Russian ideologies that developed in the course of the civil war.[11]

On the other hand, *pace* our afore-cited author's assertion alluded to above, its chronological distance from our present age has, to a significant degree, diminished the generally perceived "significance" of the "Russian Civil War," at least in what we must still call the West (for the want of a better noun to encompass those parts of the world that were not, for most of the twentieth century, under the dominance of Soviet Russia). Our Russian "Civil War," for example, has certainly been eclipsed in the popular imagination by its Spanish counterpart of 1936–39. Apart from the passage of time, this may perhaps be accounted for by the peninsular events' easy association (however exaggerated for TV history) with the ubiquitous Nazis on the one hand; and, on the other, with the romantic images conjured up by the involvement in Spain's convulsions of poets, painters, and what we now term "public intellectuals" who became famous in the English-, French-, and Spanish-speaking worlds. In the West, no artistic or literary conjugation of the "Russian Civil War" has the harrowing presence of a "Guernica" or the questioning ache of a *Homage to Catalonia* (or even the problematic popularity of *For Whom the Bell Tolls*), and there was no immediate literary martyr to match the murdered Federico García Lorca. It was all very different in the Soviet Union, though, as some of the references in what follows will seek to explain.

But the events that are the subject of this study have very many artistic and cultural representations of massive profundity and influence that have actually pricked—or more than that—the consciousness of anybody interested in what Europe is. It is certain, for example, that nobody can pretend to approach an understanding of the brutalities of the twentieth-century history of that continent, let alone the evolution of its modern literature, who has not absorbed the perspectives on the "Russian Civil War," which encapsulated the horrors to come, offered by Isaak Babel's *Red Cavalry* (1926), Mikhail Bulgakov's *White Guard* (1926), and Mikhail Sholokhov's *Quiet Don* (1928–40). Moreover—and on a lighter note—apart from its obvious "stars," such as Lenin, Trotsky, Winston Churchill, and Woodrow Wilson, the "Russian Civil War" had bit-parts for foreign players as diverse, fascinating, and influential as Arthur Ransome, W. Somerset Maugham, and the aforementioned John Reed, as well as Emma Goldman, Alexander Berkman, Ernest Shackleton, Fridtjof Nansen, Tomáš Masaryk, Charles de Gaulle, Oskar Niedermayer (the "German Lawrence of Arabia"), Josip Tito, Béla Kun, Jaroslav Hašek; and the men who would be seen as inspirations for such enduringly effective literary creations as Rudyard Kipling's "Stalky" (General Lionel Dunsterville), John Buchan's "Richard Hannay" (General W. Edmund Ironside), and Ian Fleming's "James Bond" (Sidney Reilly); not to mention the man (Captain Merian C. Cooper) who would co-direct and fly a plane in the indelible 1933 film *King Kong* (dir. Merian C. Cooper and Ernest B. Schoedsack), but who had earlier helped found and flown with American volunteers of the Kościuszko Squadron in support of Poland in the Soviet–Polish War, was shot down behind Red lines in 1920, and found himself being interrogated by none other than the aforementioned Isaak Babel. (Cooper then escaped and was awarded Poland's highest military honor for bravery, the *Virtuti Militari*.)[12] However, probably the only time that the Russian Civil War has broadly impinged upon Anglo-American public consciousness was during the later scenes of the Warner Brothers' mostly lamentable, but admirably snowy, film version (dir. David Lean, 1965) of Boris Pasternak's *Doctor Zhivago* (1957), which was largely shot in Finland.

Until such lessons are learned, it will always surprise most Westerners to discover, for example, that a quite hard-edged portrait of a relatively minor (but, in Stalin's Russia, much-lauded) Red Army commander of the civil-war era, V.I. Chapaev, in *Chapayev* (dir. G.N. and S.D. Vasil'ev, 1934), was by far the most successful and popular Soviet film of the 1930s and 1940s in the USSR. "We," in the meantime, were gawking at *Gone with the Wind*—about which, surely, we should no longer give a damn. Also interesting is that the most expensive Russian film ever produced at the time of its release, 2008's *Admiral'* (dir. Andrei Kravchuk), focused (fuzzily) on the White "Supreme Ruler" of the civil war.[13] But certainly, for the properly focused historian of the twentieth century, the imagistic ascendancy of the civil war in Spain over that in "Russia" bears little relation to those conflicts' relative historical significance. Indeed, it is worth wondering whether there ever would have been a Spanish Civil War without its "Russian" precursor.[14]

It is commonplace—although no less true for all that—to allow that the Bolsheviks' victory in what, for the moment, we will continue to term the "Russian Civil War" (continuing to use inverted commas) begat the Soviet Union and all that it entailed for subsequent world events. Unsurprisingly, such a rationale was given for the publication of their work by the authors of the two best surveys of the conflict to appear in English while the Soviet Union was still extant and the outcome of the Cold War remained contested.[15] However, such an approach—albeit most judicious at the time—might lead nowadays to the unspoken supposition that the "Russian Civil War" somehow lost its "significance" with the collapse of the Soviet Union it had birthed. In fact, quite the opposite is the case: the demise of the USSR has not diminished the significance of the "Russian Civil War" one iota, still less rendered it obsolete or undeserving of study. On the contrary, the events that took place in the period from around 1989 to 1991 and their volcanic reverberations across the former Soviet space have very greatly enriched, necessitated, and energized historical investigations of the conflict, as they have made it unchallengeably clear that any approach to the "Russian Civil War" that places the Red versus White struggle within that matrix too starkly in its foreground is missing the point. As Geoffrey Swain sagely noted, from the vantage point of observers in the twenty-first century such a perspective provides a very unsound and not at all useful basis for appreciating the apparently adamantine Soviet Union as the "fragile state" it really was—and one which imploded so spectacularly, and unbelievably quickly, at the end of the twentieth century.[16] In sum, to comprehend the rapidity and complexity of the Soviet Union's unravelling and demise, and the untold difficulties that have flowed from those events—that the conflicts experienced in and around Russia and its neighbors since the late 1980s were, in the words of Ronald G. Suny, "the revenge of the past"—it is essential to grasp the international and intra-national intricacies of the Soviet Union's very troubled gestation and difficult birth.[17] In brief, as will become apparent from the following chapters, this was not simply a "Russian Civil War": it was a compound compendium of overlapping wars and conflicts in a disintegrating *imperium*, involving not only (and very frequently not even mainly) Russians but also the non-Russian majority of the former Russian Empire, as well as the peoples of the former empire's neighbors, from Finland, Poland, and Romania through Turkey, Iran, and Afghanistan to China, Mongolia, and Korea. Hence the title of this book: *The "Russian" Civil Wars*.[18] Also, as will become very apparent from what follows, the "Russian" Civil Wars feature many bizarre bedfellows—relationships misshaped and multiply tangled in layers of baffling and intractable complexity—and allegiances fleeting and shifting. Indeed, it is the almost wilful perversity of the currents and eddies of the "Russian" Civil Wars that lends the subject its particular flavor, its distinct contribution to the course of European and world history, and its fascination.[19]

Furthermore, as another estimable post-Soviet, English-language survey of the period posits among its many *raisons d'être*, the collapse of the Soviet Union, and the brief and transitory period of *glasnost'* that preceded it, have provided an important new impetus and opportunity for the study of the "Russian" Civil Wars, through the opening of archives across Russia and the former republics of the USSR and the publication of an immense number of scholarly (but very often not so scholarly) secondary works and collections of primary materials.[20] The "Russian" Civil Wars may have been half-forgotten in the West, but in today's Russian Federation, especially, the publication and republication of works about it—particularly those dealing with the anti-Bolshevik forces that were largely off-limits to researchers in Soviet times—is an astonishingly big business. Moreover, writing in 1994, the author of that still especially insightful survey could have little anticipated the immense flood of sources on the "Russian" Civil Wars that has since become available to historians through the Internet. Much of that material—contentious and problematic as it may be—stems from enterprising non-Russian investigators of the period, although much more of it stems from equally enterprising historians in Russia: their often immensely exacting excursions into the history of the Russian Army, the Red Army, and the White Armies are producing online resources of as yet (and probably for ever more) indigestible dimensions.[21] Another aim of this volume, then, is to provide a preliminary, of-the-moment, but inevitably incomplete, integration of these lodes of new sources into the canon.[22]

* * *

Finally, another purpose of this book is to raise questions about the chronology that has traditionally been attributed to the conflicts under study. The first and last chapters of this volume seek to demonstrate that neither the dates traditionally ascribed as signifying the outbreak of the conflicts (May–June 1918, or sometimes October 1917), nor those generally attached to their end (November 1920 or, more often, March 1921 and, rarely, October 1922) are at all satisfactory or accurate. In history, as in life, beginnings and endings are rarely clear-cut. They tend, rather, to be foggy notions, with events melding and morphing into one another: conveniently named historical epochs cannot truly be made to click together, like Lego bricks, to construct a seamless narrative. In the case of revolutionary Russia, this was certainly the case; and thus this study of the "Russian" Civil Wars sets out, deliberately, to re-blur the boundaries between world war, revolution, civil war, and the subsequent period of the early 1920s (during which the new Soviet state has generally been portrayed as being at peace, as the Bolsheviks developed their New Economic Policy).[23] Herein it is instead suggested that the wars that wracked the collapsing Russian Empire and emerging Soviet Union can be said to have begun in the summer of 1916 and to have ended only in the summer of 1926, precisely a decade later. It is certainly clear that, whatever the economic retreats and concessions (especially to the peasantry) the Bolshevik government may have made under NEP after March 1921, Lenin and his colleagues still regarded themselves as being very much involved in wars in the years after that date. Moreover, many of those wars began and ended in the same place—Central Asia—and the beginnings and endings of them shared a common characteristic: the wars opened and (in the *longue durée*, perhaps, only temporarily) closed, not with battles between Reds and Whites, but with colonial and religio-cultural conflicts in which Russians (once Orthodox, then militantly atheistic) battled Muslims.

Before turning to the conflict of 1916, however, some background is necessary. From it should emerge an understanding of why it was that events perceived at the time as merely another of the outbreaks of discontent in the distant Muslim reaches of the tsar's realm that had had to be quelled periodically, time and again, over the previous century, in fact portended the opening salvos of an epochal cataclysm. This was, indeed, a new *smuta* ("Time of Troubles"): ten years that would shake not just Russia, but the world.[24]

Russia's Century of Decline: From Alexander I to Nicholas the Last

When Russia celebrated the tercentenary of Romanov rule in 1913, the incumbent Tsar, Nicholas II, was not sitting altogether comfortably on his throne. A hundred years earlier, in contrast, his august ancestor, Tsar Alexander I, had emerged from the Napoleonic Wars, having expelled the Anti-Christ from Moscow and then driven Bonaparte back across Europe, with an empire and a reputation so mightily enhanced that he was regarded as the arbiter of continental affairs (albeit he was frequently manipulated by the Austrian Chancellor, Prince Metternich). Alexander's successor, Nicholas I, further embossed and burnished that repute; and, as guardian of the conservative principles of "Orthodoxy, Autocracy, and Nationality," and as the bane of revolutionaries across the continent, earned the muscular title of the "Gendarme of Europe." Thereafter, however, from the humiliation in the Crimean War of 1854–56 (during which Nicholas died) to the national disgrace of defeat against Japan in 1904–5, not to mention diplomatic debasements at the Congress of Berlin in 1878 and during the Bosnian crisis of 1908–9, Russia's international renown steadily and seemingly inexorably diminished.[25] It will suffice to note that, with regard to the essential problem of that age, the "Eastern Question," in 1833, at the Treaty of Unkiar Skelessi (Hünkâr İskelesi) the Russians had established what bordered on a protectorate over the Ottoman Empire, but in 1912 were forced meekly (albeit reluctantly) to accept the appointment of a German military governor of Constantinople.[26]

Domestically, Nicholas II's predecessors had fared little better in the previous century. The semi-constitutionalist and semi-Jacobin uprising of young army officers and their friends (known thereafter as the Decembrists) in late 1825 was easily crushed by Nicholas I, but, as a harbinger of later revolutions, it was far from forgotten.[27] Indeed, sympathizers of the martyred Dekiabristy (five of whom were hanged and hundreds more imprisoned or exiled) were very active in the swiftly ensuing November Uprising in Poland of 1830 and also formed the core of the intellectual and literary flowering of Russia's cultural "Golden Age"—Pushkin, Lermontov, Chaadaev, Herzen, *et al.*—that was to spawn tsarism's revolutionary nemesis: the intelligentsia.[28] Equally, Nicholas I's son and successor to the throne (in 1855), Alexander II, emancipated the serfs in 1861, overhauled Russian local government, education, and the legal system and reformed the army, but at the same time earned the disdain of his Polish subjects and Russian liberals and radicals alike for the bloody suppression of Warsaw's January Uprising of 1863, and engendered the irreconcilable detestation of the throne by the empire's first generation of socialists, who were enraged by the limited aims and contentious outcomes of the so-called "Great Reforms" of the 1860s. It mattered not a jot to such irreconcilable foes of the Tsar that he was en route to giving written assent to a scheme for a limited democratic constitution on the last day of his life: on 1 March 1881, Alexander II, the "Tsar Liberator," was duly assassinated by a bomb-wielding terrorist. His son and successor, Alexander III, steeled by that catastrophe and coached by the high priest of Russian conservatism, Count K.P. Pobedonostsev, thereafter ministered an era of retrenchment and counter-reform, but despite the Tsar's and his mentor's wishes, Old Russia could not be quarantined from the encroachments of the modern world, as the empire experienced a hugely impressive but also socially, politically, and emotionally destabilizing era of ultra-rapid industrialization in the 1890s. Moreover, Alexander III, despite being a remarkably robust man in many ways, was to die unexpectedly and suddenly in 1894. His son and successor, the young and febrile Nikolai Aleksandrovich, while also under the sway of Pobedonostsev, proved weaker-willed, yet at the same time, oddly, more stubbornly independent, than his father.[29]

This new Tsar, Nicholas II, might later be dubbed by his opponents "Nicholas the Bloody" (*Krovavyi*), but that reflected not his fearsomeness—he was no recognizable relation to Ivan the Terrible (*Groznyi*)—but his habit of quashing with arbitrary, insensate, and often unmeant cruelty even moderate and sensible critics of his regime. Nicholas's nadir in this respect, of course, was "Bloody Sunday": the infamous slaughter of a thousand or more peaceful demonstrators by Cossacks on the streets of St Petersburg in January 1905 that precipitated the outbreak of a long-gathering revolutionary storm.[30] Nicholas then hesitated and, at the height of the ensuing 1905 Revolution, which saw huge disturbances across the whole of his empire, culminating in the revolutionaries almost seizing control of Moscow and St Petersburg at the end of the year, as Russia reeled from its defeat against Japan in the Far East in September, offered concessions to his opponents in an imperial manifesto of 17 October 1905. But as they then witnessed the Tsar, having made peace with Japan, shamelessly clawing back what he had reluctantly conceded in a forlorn effort to stem the revolution (the new parliament, the State Duma, for example, was emasculated by an illegal tampering with its electoral law as early as June 1907), even many Russian liberals and progressives, who might otherwise have aspired to constructive partnership with their emperor, found themselves instead in sympathy with revolutionary socialists who predicted that this Tsar would be "Nicholas the Last."

Troublingly, and much against his better judgment—and certainly against the urges of Pobedonostsev, who once proclaimed that all would be well in the world if only people would "stop inventing things"—Nicholas had also overseen during his reign a period of national economic growth unprecedented in world history in its speed and intensity. Indeed, during the 1890s, under the stewardship of the preternaturally talented and far-sighted Minister of Finance, Sergei Witte, and funded by massive foreign investments, Russia underwent an accelerated and concentrated industrial revolution that, apart from all else, witnessed the construction of the engineering miracle of the age, the Trans-Siberian Railroad, linking Europe, overland, with the Pacific. Then, from 1906, Nicholas's last intelligent, energetic, and in many ways progressive prime minister, P.A. Stolypin, while overseeing a brutal period of repression against those radicals who had encouraged and led the violence of 1905, also introduced a very radical (if cumbersomely bureaucratic) program of land reform that, given time, might have solved or at least ameliorated one of the key social problems in Russia.[31] At issue here was the fact that the emancipation edict of 1861 may have provided a stop-gap to tumults in the Russian countryside, but in other ways it accentuated pressure on land ownership across European Russia. The pressing "land question" was then exacerbated by a doubling of the empire's rural population in the half century after 1861 (chiefly, it seems, a consequence of declining infant mortality), which was addressed but not solved by efforts to tempt migration to Siberia after 1892. These efforts were redoubled by Stolypin after 1906, for he, as much as any of his predecessors, balked at the notion of transferring lands from the nobles' estates into the peasant land fund. Yet despite initial successes and the transformation of virgin lands in Western Siberia into a tremendously productive center of dairy farming, rates of success here were diminishing almost as dangerously as were peasant applications to sign up to the new land reform and quit the commune.[32] So, in sum, time was short.

Then it got shorter. Prime Minister Stolypin was assassinated in 1911; world war was looming; and Nicholas II's span of attention was equally attenuated. He would clearly have been delighted to spend more time with his family, but tsars do not resign from office. Moreover, after Stolypin had gone, no minister of similar robustness or independent spirit was permitted thereafter to replace him. Thus the Tsar and his wife, the Empress Alexandra, lacked sensible guidance in ruling an empire that was unrecognizably different from that Alexander I had been bequeathed when he had unwittingly helped to assassinate his father, Paul I, in March 1801. The royal couple did not fall quite so unthinkingly under the sway of the infamous Rasputin as has popularly been imagined, yet the devilish machinations of that former mystic were certainly malign and, through a fatal combination of his perverse patronage and the royal couple's other-worldly indifference, a gaggle of self-serving nonentities packed the imperial Russian Council of Ministers after 1911.[33]

As Nicholas's alternately timorous and tyrannical tsardom diverged, tragically, from the colossal model established by Peter the Great, Russia's industrial might (despite occasional slumps) did, at least, continue to expand in the last pre-war years. But then, so too did that of the other Powers—notably imperial Germany, Russia's chief contender for influence in the Near East (as the Ottoman Empire began terminally to crumble during the Balkan Wars of 1912–13) and the ally of Russia's rival in the Balkans, the unstable, irretrievably declining, and dangerously desperate Austro-Hungarian Empire.[34] Moreover, late-imperial Russia's second industrial boom (dating from around 1909) was fed by a continent-wide arms race that only sharpened the perilous international tensions of the time. And, of course, industrialization—particularly at the giddy and unprecedented tempo experienced in Russia—induced domestic crises of urbanization, proletarization, impoverishment, and social degradation of a hitherto unimagined toxicity that dredged a dual division across Russia between the new working class and their would-be liberal benefactors, and between the liberals and the government.[35] Out of all this emerged, predictably, a wave of increasingly politicized industrial strikes in Russia's highly concentrated new industrial centers (around St Petersburg and Moscow, the Don basin in Eastern Ukraine, Poland, the Baltic, and Baku), beginning with protests against the shooting of hundreds of striking workers and their families in the gold mines of Eastern Siberia in April 1912 (the "Lena Goldfields Massacre") and culminating in a general strike in St Petersburg in July 1914. In that month the Russian capital seemed about to burst into revolution.[36]

End Days of Tsardom: Russia's War, August 1914–February 1917

That painful and potentially revolutionary boil was lanced with the outbreak of a European war in July–August 1914 that had been precipitated by the latest Balkan crisis, stemming from the assassination of the heir to the Austrian throne, Archduke Franz Ferdinand, at the hands of Bosnian Serb terrorists on 28 June 1914 at Sarajevo. As Europe tottered into war, and as was the case across the continent, young Russian men in their millions volunteered for the colors or were more-or-less happily drafted and marched off to the front in the name of "God, Emperor, and Country." In St Petersburg, though, this was particularly remarkable: among the throng of would-be recruits genuflecting in the great square, beneath the huge column commemorating Alexander I, as Nicholas offered his blessing from the balcony of the Winter Palace, were many of the strikers and *barricadiers* of just a few days earlier. A quite remarkable *union sacrée* was thus forged, as all but one of the opposition parties in the State Duma offered their more-or-less unconditional support for the war and pledged to shelve their political agendas until victory had been achieved.[37]

Nevertheless, when Nicholas I plunged his realm into what was to become the First World War by mobilizing the Russian Army against Germany and its allies in support of Serbia at the climax of the "July Crisis," he was taking a huge risk—with his empire, with his throne, with his dynasty, and with his own life and the lives of his closest family members. We now know that it was also a gamble with the future of Europe and the world. It was a gamble that, on every count, he lost.[38] The loyalty of the Russian Army and the willingness of volunteers and recruits to it to make the sacrifices demanded of them—like the eagerness of most of the hitherto faithless political opposition to bury the hatchet and to support the regime for the course of the war—were, of course, predicated on the hope (and even expectation) of victory. But victory, although far from being altogether unsavored, was one of many commodities in short supply in Russia during the First World War.

* * *

Clichéd accounts of Russia's military performance during the First World War as being one of unremitting failure, in which half-naked and unshod *muzhiki* (peasants) battled Howitzers with hand-axes, wooden stakes, and pitchforks, are no longer tenable: 1914 and 1915 were undoubtedly bad years for Nicholas's empire, but thereafter, at the front, things got better. Mistakes were certainly made by the Russian command (as they were made by the directors of all armies entering this unprecedented struggle), notably in the disastrous invasion of East Prussia of August–September 1914 (although, equally, that early campaign disrupted Germany's Schlieffen Plan and, on the Western Front, probably saved Paris). Also, being isolated from its allies by the Central Powers' closure of the entrances to the Black Sea and the Baltic, Russia definitely faced unique wartime problems of communications and supply (although Vladivostok and Arkhangel'sk remained open, when not occluded by ice, and the completion of the Petrograd–Murmansk railway in late 1916 eased matters further). But it should be very firmly emphasized: by early 1917, the Russian Army was holding its own against Germany (indeed, in the last of its major pre-revolutionary operations, it recaptured and held Riga in December 1916); it had also periodically bested the Austrians (notably in the Brusilov Offensive of June–September 1916); and, on the Caucasus Front, it had strung together a laudable series of victories against the Turks (at Ardahan and Sarikamish in December 1914, at Van in May and September 1915, and at Erzurum, Trabzon, and Erzincan in February, April, and July 1916 respectively). The collapse of Romania, in late 1916, was certainly a setback (compounding what was already a logistical nightmare, by adding over 350 miles to the extent of the Eastern Front, and by depriving Russia of a rare and potentially useful ally in the East); but, at a conference at Chantilly in November 1916, the Tsar's command nevertheless expressed confidence that the Russian Army could participate effectively in the simultaneous offensives the Allies had planned for the coming year, to crush the Central Powers.

Such assured optimism from St Petersburg rested not only on hopes that the Americans might soon enter the war on the Allied side, but on the solid evidence that, contrary to enduring popular impressions, the Russian economy had not entirely collapsed during the war. In fact, under the aegis of a Special Council for State Defense, enthusiastically supported by a network of War-Industries Committees and other public-minded organizations, the monthly output of rifles by Russia's factories had increased more than tenfold since 1914 and the output of shells by twice that. There were gaps, but they could be bridged, if not totally plugged, by the Allied aid that was promised by the conference that convened in Petrograd in January 1917 (and that could now flow more directly to the Eastern Front along the newly opened railway linking Murmansk and the Russian capital).[39]

On the other hand, it has to be conceded that, long before the Eastern Front had stabilized—and long before the Russians began to hold their own against their prime opponent—utterly unacceptable losses had been incurred and tsarism had been mortally wounded: in the "Great Retreat" of April–September 1915, all of Poland and Lithuania and much of Courland had been abandoned to the Germans; and, by the end of 1916, Russian casualties had passed the 1.5 million mark (around 700,000 of these being military casualties), with three times that number wounded and a further 3 million prisoners in enemy hands. Such an unprecedentedly catastrophic war record inevitably sapped faith in the imperial regime, at all levels of Russian society, and reinforces the notion that there was an etiological connection between world war and revolution in Russia. Nevertheless, what was fatal to tsarism was not the situation at the front, but the crisis in the rear. That crisis, by January 1917, was not being managed at all; rather, it was reaching breaking point.

The British historian Bob McKean conceptualized this neatly in describing how the First World War precipitously accelerated four underlying and pre-existing trends in pre-revolutionary Russian society.[40] First, deemed McKean, the social disruption caused by industrialization and modernization was compounded by new wartime stresses associated with mass mobilizations and an inconceivably colossal refugee crisis,[41] while former bulwarks of the regime, such as the officer corps and the state bureaucracy, were diluted by an influx of new, socially diverse recruits (to replace fallen officers and to assist overstretched government agencies).[42] Secondly, the already overheated domestic economy—although it might (just about) have been capable of supplying the front—was incapable of also meeting domestic demands (particularly in the food- and fuel-hungry north), as imports were blocked, agricultural production fell, and the railway system proved capable of meeting only military demands.[43] Thirdly, the popular sense of injustice that had been simmering in Nicholas's Russia since the tragic 1896 events on Khodynka field reached boiling point, as unimaginable sacrifices were made at the front for war aims only dimly, if at all, understood by Russia's "peasants in uniform"; meanwhile, in the rear, unscrupulous businessmen made vast fortunes from government spending on arms and equipment.[44] And, finally, the person of the Tsar himself—never a beloved ruler, or man, in the popular mind and already besmirched by association with his German-born wife and the reported pro-German "dark forces" surrounding Rasputin and elements of the Petersburg Court—was further sullied by his assumption of supreme command of the Russian Army in August 1915, thereby attracting censure for every setback experienced by his troops.[45]

Thus by the time the State Duma reconvened for its meeting of 1 November 1916, the *union sacrée* of July–August 1914 was long forgotten, as deputies from the Left (such as P.N. Miliukov, leader of the radical-liberal Kadets) to the Right (including V.V. Shul'gin, a future ideologue of the White movement), took turns to lambast the "stupidity or treason" of Nicholas and his ministers in their conduct of the war.[46] Meanwhile, the head of the right-liberal Octobrist Party, A.I. Guchkov, not very discreetly canvassed political and military opinion regarding the possibility of a palace coup.[47] What might have come of such conspiratorial cabals remains a matter of conjecture, but talk of them—even when partly hushed—could only have adumbrated all the more starkly the precipitous decline of Nicholas's reputation among the Russian elite.[48] Thus when disturbances in bread queues in the capital in late February 1917 flared up (seemingly stirred by rumors of an impending flour famine), alongside a mass demonstration of locked-out workers from the giant Putilov armament plant (who were, in turn, joined by socialist demonstrators marking International Women's Day), and when angry crowds thronging the main streets of the capital reached the quarter-million mark on 26 February, and—especially—when, on 27 February, units of the Petrograd garrison (inspired by the rebellion of the Ukrainian Volynskii Regiment) mutinied and confined or even shot their officers, to transform that unfocused street revolt into a revolution, those who might previously have advised the Tsar to stand firm acted quite differently: on 1–2 March 1917, as the leaders of a putative Provisional Government (drawn from self-selected members of the State Duma) and a hastily convened Soviet of Workers' and Soldiers' Deputies (led by self-selected radical socialists) met in Petrograd to debate the way forward, an enervated and isolated Nicholas, on his train home from the front (embarrassingly sidetracked at provincial Pskov by striking railwaymen), received the advice from almost every senior commander of the Russian Army that he should immediately vacate the throne. "Nicholas the Last" quickly acceded and abdicated, signing the necessary document at 3.05 p.m. on 2 March 1917. He had at first been inclined to pass the throne to his son, Aleksei, but the poor boy was a physically weak and very sickly hemophiliac. Nicholas therefore changed his mind and, instead, abdicated for himself and—illegally—for his rightful heir.[49] Next in line for the Romanov throne, at that point apparently only temporarily unoccupied, was Nicholas's younger brother, Mikhail Aleksandrovich. But he, on 3 March 1917, unexpectedly refused the succession when offered it by the emergent Provisional Government.[50] Russia's February Revolution was thereby consecrated in confusion. Its even more confounding civil wars were already commencing.

1

1916–18

THE BEGINNINGS OF THE "RUSSIAN" CIVIL WARS

Despite what has already been noted above, there is also a very strong case for dating the outbreak of the "Russian" Civil Wars to the extensive anti-Russian uprising in Central Asia during the summer of 1916, as a large number of the tsar's Muslim subjects, in a rebellion that anticipated the later Basmachi movement, resisted forced mobilization into labor battalions to service the Russian Army and the armaments industry (although this was merely the most overt assault on local sensibilities that had been repeatedly affronted by the waves of non-Muslim settlers that had been moving into the region for half a century). As the author of the pioneering—and, so far, sole—English-language study of these events noted, "the revolt of 1916 sounded the first rumble of the oncoming disaster and in it there participated in one form or another the eleven million native peoples of Russian Central Asia." Moreover, although the 1916 revolt was brutally suppressed, it broke out again in the summer of 1917; and, in the same region, enlivened by recent events, in September of that year, the Executive Committee of the Tashkent Soviet proclaimed Soviet power more than a month before the Bolsheviks' action in Petrograd. Thus, as Edward Sokol had it, "the Revolt of 1916 was both the prelude to the Revolution in Russia proper and the catalytic agent which hastened the alignment of forces in Russian Central Asia," the most long-contested theater of the "Russian" Civil Wars over the next decade.[1]

The origins of the Central Asian revolt of 1916 can be traced to the Russian colonial penetration of the region in the late nineteenth century. The empire had been pressing into what was to become the Turkestan Region (*krai*) since Peter the Great had sent a force towards Khiva in 1717, but it had only been fully integrated into the tsars' realm following a series of annexations from the mid-1860s to the mid-1880s that had incorporated lands as far south as Ferghana, while protectorates had been established in 1873 over the still nominally independent (but territorially reduced) khanates of Bukhara and Khiva. Meanwhile, the Kokand khanate had been dissolved following an anti-Russian uprising in 1875. To these lands were added the Transcaspian region, conquered by Generals M.D. Skobelev and M.N. Annenkov between 1881 and 1885.[2]

The first motor of these expansions was the securing of the cotton-rich valleys of the irrigated regions of southern Turkestan, in order to feed Russia's booming textile industry (as supplies from the United States became unreliable during and after the American Civil War). The second was St Petersburg's playing of the Great Game, as its military and economic presence in these regions placed pressure on British possessions and protectorates in India, Persia, and Afghanistan—thereby unsettling the power still roundly reviled for causing Russia's humiliation in the Crimea in the 1850s and at the Congress of Berlin in 1878 (when Alexander II had been forced to renounce many of the prizes won, at huge cost, in the Russo-Turkish War of 1877–78).[3] However, as Russian settlers followed the imperial flag into Turkestan, particularly during the resettlement campaigns sponsored by Sergei Witte in the 1890s and Prime Minister Petr Stolypin after 1906, and facilitated by the completion of the Orenburg–Tashkent railway in 1906, various complex economic and political problems ensued: clashes over land rights and water rights between the natives and incoming settlers, for example, and, especially, conflicts between nomads and Russian farmers, as well as resentment of the semi-military, colonial government imposed upon the region by St Petersburg. No other region of the Russian Empire had, over such a lengthy period of time, endured such discriminatory rule as that of the Turkestan governor-generalship and, for the historian Daniel Brower, the 1916 revolt was nothing less than "a judgement on the empire's half century of colonial rule" in Central Asia.[4] The development of a major cotton industry in the irrigated southern valleys of the region brought some benefits to the local population, but it was a fragile affair, subject to huge fluctuations in world cotton prices (chiefly fixed in the United States) that frequently resulted in economic crises in Central Asia: a bumper crop in Louisiana could spell disaster for Ferghana. Economic problems were exacerbated by the First World War, with cotton prices falling and the price of consumer goods spiraling, while the forced mobilization of horses by the military authorities was also greatly resented.

The trigger for the revolt, however, was the decision of the Russian *stavka* (high command), authorized by Nicholas II on 25 June 1916, that such was the shortage of manpower in industry and military support services in European Russia that 390,000 men aged between nineteen and forty-three were to be mobilized for war work from the hitherto exempt *inorodtsy* (native peoples, literally "foreigners") of Central Asia. They would formally be members of the armed forces but would be assigned work in "the construction of defensive fortifications and military communications in frontline areas and also for any other work necessary for national defense."[5] When the order was publicized in Central Asia, between 30 June and 8 July 1918, according to the whims of tsarist administrators and without adequate preparation and explanation (and in the midst of the very labor-intensive cotton harvest), confusion and panic ensued: in particular, rumors spread that the men would be sent to fight at the front (some of them against Muslim Turkey). Within a few days much of the region had risen in protest and revolt, from Ural'sk in the west to Ferghana in the east, with a particularly large demonstration in Tashkent on 11 July, while railway tracks and telegraph lines were extensively sabotaged across the region and government offices raided in order to prevent the enforced movement of those scheduled to be mobilized. So widespread was the disorder and violence that, on 17 July 1916, the entire Turkestan region was declared to be under martial law and General A.N. Kuropatkin, the former war minister of the empire (1898–1904), who was renowned as the Russian Army's chief expert on Asian affairs, was sent from the German front to command the Turkestan Military District.[6]

However, although the revolt of the Sarts (the settled native population) was quickly contained, disorder spread rapidly to the nomads of the Kazakh and Turkoman steppe. Very soon, as one historian of the empire noted, with 15,000-strong bands of rebels sweeping across the region, "to some extent, the insurrection acquired the character of a 'Holy War' against the Russian infidels, and of an anti-colonial struggle for independence," especially in Semirech'e, where many Russian incomers had settled.[7] For almost the first time, moreover, Kazakh leaders overcame clan rivalries to host regional assemblies that would debate and discuss strategy. All this was dealt with abruptly, and mercilessly, by the imperial authorities. The commander of all forces deployed in the suppression of the uprising (and governor-general of Vernyi) was Colonel P.P. Ivanov—who later, in 1918, promoted and renamed General

Ivanov-Rinov, became the ataman of the Siberian Cossack Host and commander-in-chief of the anti-Bolshevik Siberian Army. A survivor of Ivanov's "pacification" of a rebel area in Jizzakh province (now in eastern Uzbekistan) recalled how:

> Ivanov gave the order to shoot, to set fires and to confiscate household goods and agricultural tools. The units entered the villages, burned goods and shot anyone they encountered. Women were raped and other bestial events took place. In the villages they burned the crops in the fields and harvested grain was confiscated. The people fled to the city and into the steppe, abandoning their homes. Famine ensued. Women fled, leaving their children behind. Refugees starved in the distant steppe lands and in the towns.[8]

Such actions were encouraged by orders from General Kuropatkin, who demanded the confiscation of goods from areas that had rebelled. In accordance with his prescripts and recommendations, in the Turkoman area alone half of all cattle and nomad tents were taken, along with 780 horses, 4,800 camels, 175,000 sheep, and 2,500 cattle.[9] Soviet figures indicate that across the entire region 88,000 "rebels" were killed and a further 250,000 fled (chiefly from Semirech'e) into China, together amounting to 20 percent of the native Central Asian population. In addition, 50 percent of the local population's horses, 55 percent of their camels, 39 percent of their cattle, and 58 percent of their sheep and goats were killed or confiscated. In contrast, just over 3,000 Russian settlers and soldiers were killed.[10] Visitors to the region reported scenes of utter devastation. Even in 1919, three years after the rising, the geologist P.S. Nazarov was shocked at what he saw on the road from Tokmak to the village of Samsonovka:

> I kept passing large Russian settlements on the road, and in all of them half the population was drunk; then Kirghiz villages completely ruined and razed literally to the ground—villages where, but three short years previously, there had been busy bazaars and farms surrounded with gardens and fields of luzerne. Now on every side a desert. It seemed incredible that it was possible in so short a time to wipe whole villages off the face of the earth, with their well-developed system of farming. It was with only the most attentive search that I could find the short stumps of their trees and remains of their irrigation canals ...
>
> The destruction of the *aryks* or irrigation canals in this district quickly reduced a highly developed farming district into a desert and blotted out all traces of cultivation and settlement ...
>
> After the suppression of the rebellion it was the turn of the Russian settlers to get some of their own back at the expense of the Kirghiz, to loot their *auls*, drive off their cattle and take away their property but in doing this they made no discrimina-

tion between the rebels and the peaceful Kirghiz who had remained true to the Russian allegiance. All were indiscriminately robbed, plundered and killed, including many who had fought on the Russian side.[11]

Contemporary Bolshevik interpretations of the 1916 rising tended to portray it as a progressive, anti-imperialist movement that aimed at national liberation. In this they were helped by the fact that some of the rebel leaders subsequently joined the Bolshevik Party (Tokash Bokin, for example). However, as those natives who had fled to the hills and steppe and across the borders into Persia, Afghanistan, and China began to return in 1917 and 1918, with their resentment of Russians and Russian rule reinforced by the tsarist terror of 1916, Soviet commentators had to find more nuanced arguments, for the scene was being set for the clashes between natives and local Soviet organizations that would characterize the next decade of the civil wars in Central Asia. Conflict would first be ignited by the Muslim intelligentsia's establishment of an anti-Soviet government at Kokand (the "Kokand Autonomy") on 29 November 1917 (crushed by Red Guards with the slaughter of thousands of *inorodtsy* on 18–22 February 1918). It would then develop into a region-wide guerrilla resistance, the Basmachi movement, strongly influenced by the Muslim clergy, which the Red Army, as we shall see, would only be able (at great cost) to tame, but never entirely extinguish, by 1926. Prominent and numerous among the Basmachi, unsurprisingly, were those who had fought the Russians in 1916—Junaïd-khan, for example—and who had lost their livelihoods and their families to the "pacification" of Ivanov-Rinov and his ilk. Whether this would have happened without the February Revolution is unknowable, but the breakdown of authority across the Russian Empire that accompanied the collapse of tsarism in early 1917 greatly facilitated the rise of the *basmachestvo*, and the 1916 uprising in Central Asia can therefore be considered as the outbreak of the "Russian" Civil Wars.

Impermanent Revolution and the Phony Civil War: March–August 1917

Considerable scholarly attention has been devoted to the issue of whether or not the events of 1905 in Russia constituted a revolution.[12] In contrast, opinion seems set and unanimous that the events of February 1917 were indeed a revolution—after all, the Tsar was gone! Historical conclusions differ sharply, however, regarding important matters of ownership of and agency in the February Revolution.[13] And clearly, in 1917 and during the subsequent civil wars, the outcome and meaning of the events of February 1917 were among the many matters much contested. No wonder: for, in fact, an essential feature of the process of removing "Nicholas the Last" was that nobody got the revolution they wanted in February 1917. Hence, the events of February–March of the first revolutionary year should properly be regarded as an impermanent—or unfinished—revolution, and the months of uncertainty that followed as a dress rehearsal for the civil wars: with nothing settled in February, duels surrounding many of the same issues that would later be decided on the battlefield were staged in Petrograd and across the collapsing empire, albeit more peaceably and in a more choreographed fashion than would be the case once the main drama opened. Equally, many of the lead actors of the sanguinary civil-war years would "enter stage left" or "enter stage right" in 1917—for now as troupes, not troops—or would heckle from the wings, as the Petrograd Soviet and the Provisional Government contested, center-stage, what became known as "dual power."[14] But, for the moment, the duelists and their seconds were, for the most part, firing blanks. It was a phony civil war.[15]

The artificiality of the proceedings of February and their issue endured while key players came to terms with the fact that the revolution and the sudden collapse of tsarism had failed to deliver what each of them had either expected or desired.[16] Most liberals—and certainly most of Miliukov's Kadets, who would subsequently form the political leadership corps of the White movement in the civil wars—desired a constitutional monarchy. So too, albeit sometimes reluctantly, did most of the military leaders who had advised Nicholas to abdicate—and certainly the future White commanders Admiral A.V. Kolchak and Generals A.I. Denikin and L.G. Kornilov. However, Nicholas did not know the script and wrong-footed his prompters by their abdicating not only for himself but also for his son and heir, the Tsarevich Aleksei, while the next Romanov in the line of succession, Nicholas's younger brother Grand Duke Mikhail Aleksandrovich, missed his cue and refused the throne when offered it by the Provisional Government on 3 March 1917.[17] Russian liberals—even radical ones, like most Kadets—generally cleaved to the idea of a constitutional monarchy for the sake of continuity and out of a realistic calculation that, in a democratic system, their weak and stunted constituency, the Russian middle class, would deliver to them only a tiny fraction of the popular vote. Hence, while unconditionally supporting the principle that Russia's future form of government should be decided by a Constituent Assembly (to which the Provisional Government should lead the country), the Kadets spent most of 1917 attempting to delay the summoning of that very assembly.[18]

All this, in turn, also rather complicated the calculation of Russia's revolutionary socialist parties. Particularly wrong-footed were the mainstream social democrats, the Mensheviks, who immediately concluded that February was Marx's predicted "bourgeois revolution," from which, in due course (and with the requisite prompts and direction from the socialist intellectuals) the Russian bourgeoisie would somehow, unthinkingly, edge the country toward socialism. And where the Mensheviks led in 1917, the vastly more popular but less well-organized and much less well-led Party of Socialists-Revolutionaries tended to follow—not least because at the heart of its ideology and party program was a commitment to a solution of Russia's land problems through universal socialization of the land (under the aegis of the village commune, the *mir*, beloved of misty-eyed Populists since the era of Alexander Herzen) that was so unrealistic that most of their party leaders, by 1917, no longer stood by it (including none other than the chairman of the All-Russian Peasant Soviet, N.D. Avkesent'ev, who was to be prominent during the democratic counter-revolution of 1918). Even those SR luminaries who (in principle) did stand by land socialization, such as V.M. Chernov, found its practical implementation during wartime problematic and untimely, even while occupying the post of minister of agriculture in the Provisional Government from May to September 1917. Chernov was so enraged by the propensity of his SR partners in government in 1917 to stymie any scheme he put forward to at least edge toward the general ("Black") repartition of the land (*chernyi peredel*) that the peasants desired that he eventually resigned.[19] Thus unable to get what they wanted alone, Mensheviks, SRs, and Kadets, throughout most of 1917, found themselves attached to (and usually in) a series of coalition governments with each other.[20] The contortions provoked by these uncomfortable—if never less than lively—*pas de trois* threatened to drag the theater of February into farce.

* * *

Adding to the coalition partners' unease were their miscalculations regarding the impact the revolution had upon the war. (This was a feature of 1917 Russian politics that was to meld into and dominate the opening phases of the civil wars.) The Kadets had anticipated that the removal of Nicholas and the tsarist Court would rekindle a mood of national unity and a renewed commitment to the Allied cause. It did not, although the front line in the east was at least held until the army attempted an ill-fated advance in June 1917 that was intended to take pressure off the Western Front and to prove that revolutionary Russia was a force to be reckoned with. The failed June offensive—"Russian democracy's fatal blunder," in the words of its chronicler[21]—precipitated the collapse of the Russian Army as a fighting force: by 19 October, the Minister of War himself, A.I. Verkhovskii, was counselling the Provisional Government that the army could no longer fight or even feed or clothe itself, that it should be demobilized and a peace sought with the enemy.[22] Part of the reason for that collapse was, contrarily, the SR–Menshevik war policy, which they now termed "revolutionary defensism." This approach to the conundrum of how socialists should operate in the midst of an imperialist war entailed a commitment to defending revolutionary Russia, by force of arms, from the predations of imperial Germany and its allies, while at the same time conducting a vigorous campaign in favor of a general peace, "without annexations or indemnities," as the Petrograd Soviet put it in its "Declaration to the Peoples of the World" of 14 March 1917. The Kadets, who perhaps more realistically calculated that Russia could have a revolution or could have defensism but could not have both, were wary of this policy from the beginning.[23] In April, their unease revealed itself in a note circulated to the Allies by Miliukov, as foreign minister of the Provisional Government, in which the Kadet leader committed post-tsarist Russia to the agreed war aims of the Allies (which, of course, involved territorial conquest, including the dismemberment of the Ottoman Empire, from which Russia would gain Constantinople and the Straits), even as the Soviet was preparing to dispatch its own "Argonauts of peace" to the Allied capitals to agitate for a revision of war aims and a generally negotiated end to the war.[24]

Miliukov paid with his job (and, historically, much of his reputation) for so affronting the sensibilities of the Soviet. Following the consternation induced by publication of the infamous "Miliukov Note," he resigned from office on 5 May 1917, but the Kadets remained, for the most part, committed to resisting revolutionary change in society and, especially, the army for as long as the war was being fought, consistently backing calls for an end to the soldiers' committees and other post-February democratic innovations and demanding the re-establishment of "order"—at the front and in the rear. This led the increasingly illiberal Kadet party into nefarious plots aimed at the forging of what was euphemistically referred to as a "firm power" (*tverdaia vlast'*), meaning a military dictatorship. Initially, the conspirators' sights were set on Admiral A.V. Kolchak, the young, sternly charismatic and very successful commander of the Black Sea Fleet (and later "supreme ruler" of the Whites in the civil war); soon, though, the newly installed commander of the Russian Army, General L.G. Kornilov (in 1917–18 commander of the Whites' Volunteer Army in South Russia) became their favorite—cheered to the rafters at a state conference in Moscow in mid-August to which he had been borne, from the railway station, on the shoulders of his admirers.[25]

Despite these machinations, the majority (that is, the party centers and right wings) of the PSR and the Mensheviks were anxious to keep the Kadets in government (apart from anything else, it was hoped the liberals' presence might assuage the qualms that Allied diplomats and generals, as well as the Russian General Staff, had about dealing with socialists). They stuck to their guns on this even when, on 2 July 1917, the Kadets walked out of the coalition in protest at the socialists' intention to grant autonomy to Ukraine (presaging the centrality of the "nationalities question" in the coming civil wars), while mass demonstrations took place across Petrograd, with workers and soldiers demanding, precisely, the creation of a Soviet (that is, all-socialist) government: famously, Viktor Chernov was almost lynched by a mob unable to understand why the leader of the PSR should demur when the populace was insisting that he should "take power, you son-of-a-bitch when it is offered to you."[26]

The majority socialists' timidity during these "July Days" would eventually cost them dearly. That, however, was obscured for a few weeks in the summer of 1917, as the Provisional Government offered a diversion by blaming the Bolsheviks for the disorders at Petrograd (and the synchronous collapse of the front), alleging that V.I. Lenin and his party, some of whom had been ferried back to Russia from Switzerland on a "sealed train" provided by Germany, were paid agents of the Kaiser and releasing documents (from 5 July 1917 onwards) that seemed to substantiate claims that the Bolsheviks were fifth columnists working for Berlin. We now know, in the unqualified conclusion of the most detailed investigation of this affair, that the materials in the possession of the Provisional Government actually contained "no evidence" that funds had been transferred into the Bolsheviks' coffers from Berlin.[27] In the rumor-rife atmosphere of the Russian capital of July–August 1917, though, anything seemed possible. Even so, it being widely held in the post-February euphoria that there were "no enemies on the Left," the spectacle of a "revolutionary" government, in which socialists participated, banning a fellow socialist party, arresting its leaders, occupying its headquarters, and calling in the Cossacks left a very bitter taste.

Civil War Unproclaimed, August 1917–January 1918

The Russian democrats' dyspepsia was to become acute with the country's second great crisis of the summer of 1917 when, in the aftermath of what appeared to be a failed military coup by General Kornilov—forces he had ordered to march on the capital were persuaded to desist by revolutionary agitators and Red Guards sent out to meet them by the Petrograd Soviet—it emerged that the commander was not acting alone but (or so it appeared) in partnership with the socialist Prime Minister, A.F. Kerensky. This event, the "Kornilov affair," remains the most deeply controversial aspect of the history of the Russian revolutions of 1917, with a variety of schools of thought contending over the extent to which Kerensky was complicit in the general's plans and protracted debates ensuing as to precisely what Kornilov's intentions were: did he mean to crush the Soviet, or to crush the government?[28]

Much about the Kornilov affair still remains murky. It can confidently be asserted, though, that this praetorian intervention was crucial to the events of 1917 and that it marked the overture of the civil wars proper.[29] Not least, the Kornilov affair irretrievably blackened the reputation of Alexander Kerensky: the man who through his feverish activity and sheer ubiquity had personified February. Kerensky was the "first love of the revolution," in the words of his best biographer,[30] but, having identified himself so closely with the June offensive, he was already vulnerable to criticism in the aftermath of its failure, and now, post-Kornilov, he found himself rudely abused by the Right and Left alike. For the latter, he was a traitor to the cause of the revolution who had flirted with the reactionaries; for the former, he was a windbag and a betrayer of his country, who, through his base enslavement to socialism and narrow class interests, had laid low the one hope of Russia's salvation, General Kornilov. Both sides of the political spectrum, as well as many Allied politicians and military leaders, held that Kerensky had placed his personal ambitions above any higher cause.[31] So, the Prime Minister's demise was also the agony of the Provisional Government, which Kerensky, newly self-crowned as "minister-president," now entirely personified. A further coalition was eventually cobbled together, but it was populated by rather second-rate ministers whose authority was rivalled by a gathering of notables hastily summoned by Kerensky, the Provisional Council of the Republic (the "Pre-Parliament"), that was really supposed to bolster it. In fact, from early September onwards, in the wake of the Kornilov affair, with Bolshevik majorities holding sway in the Petrograd Soviet and its Moscow equivalent from early September, with the Mensheviks and the PSR wracked by splits, while Bolshevik-led Red Guards patrolled the streets of Russia's cities, and with the Kornilovites girding themselves for a second thrust, the battle lines of the impending conflicts had been sharply drawn. Kerensky would later entitle the book he wrote about the Kornilov affair *The Prelude to Bolshevism*.[32] He might have as deftly dubbed it *The Prelude to the Civil Wars*.

* * *

None of the above is meant to imply that the eventual victors of (most of) the civil wars—the Bolsheviks, renamed the Russian Communist Party (Bolsheviks), RKP(b), in 1918—were getting things entirely their own way in 1917. The party, which had developed under the leadership of V.I. Lenin from a minority faction of the tiny Russian Social Democratic Labor Party (RSDLP), after a split in 1903 over rather arcane organizational matters, was as, if not more, unclear about where it stood on the key post-February issues as were its rivals. Indeed, it was not entirely sure it wanted to be a separate party: when Lenin arrived back in Petrograd on 3 April 1917, after a decade abroad, one of the events his solicitous colleagues had organized to welcome him was a joint meeting with the Mensheviks, which many Bolsheviks clearly viewed as a precursor to reunion. This could have been awkward, given Lenin's hostility to his rivals.[33] After all, during his trip across Europe—on the legendary German-supplied "sealed train"—Lenin had prepared a new policy document for his followers, the "April Theses," which insisted, among other things, that the Bolsheviks reconstitute themselves as a Communist Party immutably separate from other social democrats; that, in what remained an "imperialist" war, "not the slightest concession to 'revolutionary defencism' is permissible" (and a new Communist International should be established to fight for that principle against those socialists who supported the war); that there should be "no support for the Provisional Government" (and the "utter falsity of its promises should be made clear"); and that, instead, power in Russia should pass to a "republic of Soviets of Workers', Agricultural Labourers' and Peasants' Deputies" that would be established "throughout the country, from top to bottom."[34]

Many Bolsheviks found this perplexing. L.B. Kamenev, for example, long a close associate of Lenin, had been offering conditional support since early March 1917 to the Provisional Government and to its foreign policy in the pages of *Pravda*, the party newspaper (as had Kamenev's editorial collaborator, Josef Stalin). On the other hand, there were a significant number of anarchists and leftist Mensheviks (Mensheviks-Internationalists) in Petrograd who supported a lot of what Lenin had to say. One of them, N.N. Sukhanov, left a wonderful portrait of the beard-stroking befuddlement that Lenin's pronouncements occasioned among his Bolshevik "generals" as he was welcomed at the party headquarters—the commandeered mansion of Nicholas II's former lover (the ballerina Mathilda Kshesinskaia)—late in the evening of 4 April 1917.[35] Thus although Lenin's April pronouncement might be regarded as a declaration of civil war, and although it landed like a bombshell among the thereto-comradely euphoria of post-February Petrograd (albeit among only the more fanatical cognoscenti of Russian socialism's many schisms), the battle-lines were not yet clearly drawn.[36] Indeed, Lenin soon became aware that he had arguments to win within the Bolshevik ranks before such a campaign could be considered, although he was aided in preparing for this intra-party struggle by the manner in which the upsurge in popular radicalism, demanding that the Provisional Government press ahead with radical land reform and labor policies and that a more decisive stance should be taken on the war, was largely in tune with his prognostications. Moreover, and most importantly, it is now abundantly clear just how responsive, as an organization, the Bolshevik Party was to the increasingly radical mood of "the street" and how elections to its local and national bodies moved party opinion in line with Lenin as 1917 progressed.[37]

That popular radicalism was, of course, expressed in the aforementioned July Days. The extent to which the Bolshevik Party was responsible for "organizing" those events remains a matter of debate—not least because the almost elemental sweep of the crowds across the capital was not really "organized" at all, in any formal sense, although individual party members, particularly ultraradicals and anarchists associated with the party's Military Organization, probably did play a part in stoking the disorders.[38] The impact of the July Days and the ensuing scandal over the "Bolshevik–German conspiracy" on Lenin, however, was clear. The Bolshevik leader concluded that, thereafter, there really could be no compromise with the other major socialist parties, and for a while, he even dropped the slogan "All Power to the Soviets" from his repertoire, in desperation over how the SR and Menshevik-dominated organs had acted.[39] He would only reprise it once the Kornilov affair had delivered Bolshevik majorities in key Soviets and, even then, would harbor some doubts about the utility of the Soviets as instruments for seizing and defending power in a socialist revolution.[40] Having been forced to flee the capital during the post-July Days government crackdown, in a series of letters sent to the party Central Committee from his hiding place in Finland in mid-September 1917 Lenin would demand that, in the light of recent events (chiefly the Kornilov affair), "the Bolsheviks can and *must* take state power into their own hands" and insisted that "the Bolsheviks will form a government that *no one* will overthrow." Moreover, not only did he insist that it would be foolish to wait for the election of the Constituent Assembly and naïve to allow matters to depend upon a "'formal' Bolshevik majority" (presumably across all Russia), he also disparaged the ongoing Democratic Conference the socialist parties had summoned in Petrograd.[41] In addition, upon returning to Petrograd in early October, at a series of party meetings Lenin would also dismiss those who spoke in favor of coordinating a revolt with the forthcoming Second All-Russian Congress of Soviets, and even as late as the evening of 24 October 1917, as delegates to that congress were gathering, he (still in hiding in a northern suburb of the city, so as to evade the Provisional Government's police) would dispatch an urgent note to the Bolshevik Central Committee arguing that the important thing was to take power, not to take power in the name of the congress. This, he urged, would be to act "not in opposition to the soviets but on their behalf."[42]

Once again, Lenin did not get things all his own way: his September letters were read by the Central Committee and then a single copy of them was quietly filed away (all other copies of these incendiary missives were destroyed); the Central Committee decision of 10 October 1917 to put "an armed rising on the order of the day" had to be revisited on 16 October because nothing at all had been done; and a Central Committee "Military Revolutionary Center" (established on 16 October) seems never to have met. When power was seized, the action was coordinated more by the Petrograd Soviet—or, at least, its Military-Revolutionary Committee, dominated by L.D. Trotsky, who had (unlike Lenin) favored coordination with the congress of soviets—than by party bodies.[43] Moreover, the decision to seize power was opposed by several leading Bolsheviks, including Kamenev and G.E. Zinov'ev (who actually published their dissent, in advance of the revolution, in a non-Bolshevik newspaper). Finally, even after power had been seized and a new, exclusively Bolshevik government, Sovnarkom (the "Council of People's Commissars"), had been established on 26 October 1917, Lenin had to fight tooth and nail over the following ten days against the insistence of party colleagues that SRs and Mensheviks be permitted to join it in a new, "all-socialist" coalition.[44]

In deliberately wrecking the ensuing talks (sponsored by Vikzhel, the powerful railway workers' union) of 30 October to 4 November 1917 that were aimed at fostering such a coalition, Lenin acted with a single-minded determination that bordered on deviousness. This has led Geoffrey Swain to characterize Lenin's machinations as launching a "civil war within democracy, a Red versus Green civil war of Bolsheviks against SRs."[45] To conclude that Lenin launched such a civil war, however, presumes that civil war flowed from

Lenin's actions. But what if Lenin's actions were a tactical maneuver in a civil war that was already under way? Of course, Swain is correct that "no generals had rallied to Kerensky" in the latter's forlorn attempt to oppose the October Revolution, but his assertion that "the collapse of Kornilov's rebellion had removed the danger of ... a White versus Red civil war" is misleading.[46] After all, Kornilov and his supporters were not dead. Indeed, although the fighting had not yet started, the Kornilovites were re-equipping and girding themselves to re-engage.

* * *

So, when, then, did the "Russian" Civil Wars begin? We can safely dismiss the argument that our conflicts commenced in the summer of 1918, with the revolt of the Czechoslovak Legion on the Volga and in Western Siberia. That canard was propagated by Soviet historians with the aim of establishing that the so-called post-October "Triumphal March of Soviet Power" had not met serious domestic resistance (and was therefore, by implication, legitimate) and that civil war had to be "imported" into Russia by foreign intervention-ists. This was an odd position for them to adopt, given that the author of that triumphalist phrase, Lenin, had a propensity to predict and then describe events stemming from the seizure of power in late 1917 precisely as "civil war." It is odder yet that one finds the assertion repeated in very recent works on the period.[47] The Czechoslovak Legion's revolt and what flowed from it, in the shape of the democratic counter-revolution, was certainly of huge significance in the civil wars (as will be discussed below), but it was signifi-cant as the second or third phase or movement in an ongoing series of strug-gles, rather than as the curtain raiser of the main event. Given the prior Allied and Austro-German and Turkish interferences and interventions in the affairs of what had been the Russian Empire, it can also be concluded with some certainty that "The first phase of the internationalisation of the Russian Civil War" was not "marked in May and June 1918 by the uprising of the Czech[s]."[48]

More interesting is a recent essay, by Rex Wade, that is specifically con-cerned with the issue of Russia's metamorphosis from a state of revolution to one of civil war. In it, Wade moves the focus of the chronology back to the first days of 1918, specifically 5–6 January of that year.[49] On those days, the long-awaited Constituent Assembly met, with the PSR as the largest single party (and, in union with their non-Russian sister parties, in an absolute majority of around 60 percent) and with the Bolsheviks garnering around 24 percent of the vote. When the Assembly refused to neuter itself by voting in favor of a Lenin-authored Bolshevik resolution that would have confirmed the existence of Soviet power, confined the Assembly to overseeing the general principles of establishing a Soviet federation, and endorsed the major legislative acts already passed by the Bolshevik-dominated government, it was summarily closed by Red Guards on the orders of the Bolshevik leadership.[50] For Wade:

> The basic proposition is simple: the period from February 1917 to January 1918 has a certain internal coherence which gives a unity to the period and marks it as a single period, "The Russian Revolution", whereas the action of dispersing the Constituent Assembly fundamentally changed that and ushered in "The Civil War", something very different from what had preceded.[51]

Wade then posits five examples of what distinguished this caesura, this "fundamental break in the revolutionary process and transition to civil war": a realization by the Bolsheviks' opponents that Lenin's party would not allow itself to be voted out of office, thereby inspiring armed opposition; the Bolsheviks' concomitant commitment "to rule by force and to the development of an authoritarian political system"; the realization by leaders of the non-Russian regions of the old empire that their own previous commitment to a federal state was no longer viable and that they would be forced to go it alone; a move away by the Soviet government from the flurry of social and economic decrees it had enacted immediately post-October, which was dominated by measures that had been "widely discussed and were supported by most political parties in 1917, especially the socialist ones," toward ordinances that were peculiarly the Bolsheviks' own and were largely concerned with preparing the Soviet state, militarily and economically, for civil war; and finally, the coincidental timing of the opening of the peace negotiations at Brest-Litovsk that were to prove so fundamentally divisive.[52]

Wade's arguments are extremely insightful in many respects, and are certainly deserving of careful consideration, although the claim that the Bolsheviks were committed in perpetuity to authoritarianism from 6 January 1918 is very contentious—it could equally be argued, for example, that they were making a considered defensive action to protect a popular government, whose rule had been legitimized by the elections to the Second All-Russian Congress of Soviets (which the Bolsheviks had won).[53] The very important Polish and Finnish exceptions to Wade's second point might also be weighted heavier,[54] although it holds true for the equally important case of Ukraine[55] and (just about) for the almost as vital Transcaucasia.[56] And, regarding the fifth point, more pertinent surely was that it was only immediately after the closure of the

Constituent Assembly that Lenin felt able to begin arguing for a separate peace between Soviet Russia and the Central Powers—a matter on which he had hitherto remained silent. That was a really abrupt disjunction.[57]

Two further matters, though, make Wade's dating of the mutation from revolution to civil war to around 5–6 January 1918 problematic. First, although deeply significant to socialist intellectuals in Russia at the time and ever after, as well as to their sympathizers abroad and to historians of the Russian Revolution (who were often one and the same),[58] on the ground, in Petrograd and the other urban centers of Russia at the time, the closure of the Constituent Assembly passed without much comment—or, still less, widespread protest, or even a period of mourning. Indeed, popular reactions to the event seem to have been the very definition of indifference. The quotidian mood was poignantly reflected in observations made by the first character introduced in the most celebrated Russian poem of the era, Alexander Blok's "The Twelve," which depicts the petrified streets of post-October Petrograd:

> From building to building
> Stretches a cable
> On the cable's a placard:
> "All Power to the Constituent Assembly!"
> An old woman keens and weeps beneath it.
> She just can't understand what it means.
> Why such a huge scrap of cloth
> For such a placard?
> It would make so many footwraps for the boys,
> So many are without clothes or shoes ...[59]

Still less likely to leap to the defense of the Assembly were the more politicized denizens of the frozen and in every manner—including psephologically—"unnatural city."[60] The SRs may have won the elections nationally, but that masked crucial urban lodes of Bolshevik popularity: in Petrograd, the Bolsheviks won 45 percent of the vote and in Moscow 50 percent; in the army as a whole they matched the SRs on 41 percent of the vote, but on the Western Front and the Northern Front, closest to the capital, their share was over 60 percent and in the pivotal rear garrisons it bettered 80 percent in both Petrograd and Moscow. In the Baltic Fleet the party's share was also close to 60 percent.[61] Of course, the SRs' major strength was in the villages, but although they received an overwhelming majority of peasant votes, such support remained largely in the abstract and was inherently difficult to mobilize, as peasant populations were scattered, illiterate, and usually unconcerned with formal political structures. As one authority on the Russian peasantry has explained:

There was no mass reaction to the closure of the Constituent Assembly ... The SR intelligentsia had always been mistaken in their belief that the peasants shared their veneration for the Constituent Assembly ... [T]o the mass of the peasants ... it was only a distant thing in the city, dominated by the "chiefs" of the various parties, which they did not understand, and was quite unlike their own political organizations.[62]

The peasants, unsurprisingly, had far more material concerns: specifically land reform and the division among themselves (in a so-called "Black Repartition") of the estate lands they had been denied in the settlement accompanying the Emancipation of the Serfs in 1861. But that had already been settled in their favor by the Sovnarkom's "Decree on Land" of 26 October 1917—a "Bolshevik" document largely plagiarized from the SR program's espousal of the immediate break up of large estates and the redistribution of land to the peasants that the SRs themselves had hesitated to realize in 1917. Thereafter, the SRs really had nothing to offer the peasantry.[63]

A second problem with Wade's chronology of the passage from revolution to civil war is that although, indubitably, by far the majority of the fighting occurred after the closure of the Constituent Assembly, some intense and important battles preceded that event—and some of them were clearly the ripening seeds of yet larger conflicts to come. Of these, the clashes between Red Guards and officer cadets in Petrograd (the "Junker Revolt") and in Moscow during the last days of October 1917 are perhaps the best known (although similar events occurred elsewhere, notably at Irkutsk in the first weeks of November) and might be regarded as the precursor to the larger Red-versus-White struggles of 1918 to 1920. Also well known is the so-called "Kerensky–Krasnov" uprising of late October 1917, in which 500–700 Don Cossacks at Ostrov accepted the deposed premier's mission to recapture Petrograd and got as far as Pulkovo and Tsarskoe Selo before being rebuffed by the revolutionaries. This event, however, is best not regarded as a precursor of subsequent civil war struggles between the Bolsheviks and the Cossacks, as the latter were very reluctant recruits to the cause of resurrecting the Provisional Government and rapidly abandoned the tarnished Kerensky.[64]

The Bolshevik–Cossack struggle is, indeed, far better predicted by immediate post-October events further from the Russian center and often ignored in Western works on the period: notably the beginning of the anti-Soviet "Dutov uprising" of the Orenburg Cossack Host, in the southern Urals, on 26 October 1917, and the capture of Rostov-on-Don, by forces of the Don Cossack Host, on 2 December 1917. At the same time, in the Far East, on 18 November 1917, the first clashes also occurred, at Verkhneudinsk, between Red forces and one of the most infamous figures of the entire civil war, "Ataman" G.M. Semenov.[65] These events definitely set in chain subsequent wars between the Soviet government and the Cossacks—wars that were to culminate in a murderous process of "de-Cossackization" inflicted on the vanquished by the Red victors a full decade before Stalin's better-known de-kulakization campaign. The Cossacks' immediate post-October actions were countered, moreover, by the Sovnarkom appeal "To the Entire Population" of 25 November 1917, placing those areas of the Urals and the Don where "counter-revolutionary detachments have revealed themselves" under a state of siege and signaling something that looks very much like the onset of civil war.[66]

It might be tempting, then, to concur with Evan Mawdsley that "The Russian Civil War ... began in the autumn of 1917. To be precise, it began on 25 October[,] during the evening," with the Bolshevik seizure of power in Petrograd.[67] Even that, however, might be too late a date—and not only on the perhaps pedantic grounds that Estonian Bolsheviks under Jaan Anvelt had actually proclaimed Soviet power at Revel (now Tallinn, the Estonian capital) a day or so earlier, on 23–4 October 1917. Rather, if a date for the outbreak of the Red–White civil war in Russia has to be identified one might best choose the misleadingly stilted, but in retrospect portentous, climax to the "Kornilov affair" on 2 September 1917. On that day (during a week in which Bolshevik majorities were recorded in the Soviets of Petrograd, Moscow, and Krasnoiarsk), General Kornilov, commander-in-chief of the Russian Army, was formally arrested and was thereafter incarcerated at Mogilev and then Bykhov (Bykhaw), together with his chief supporters and co-conspirators in the Kornilov affair: Generals A.I. Denikin, I.G. Erdeli, A.S. Lukomskii, S.L. Markov, I.P. Romanovskii, and others.[68]

As much as marking the end of what we have already termed the prelude to the civil war, however, this marked the opening passage of the first movement of the Red–White civil war proper, for although the "Bykhov generals," as they became known, who were to become the leadership corps of the future White army in South Russia, were formally incarcerated on the orders of Kerensky, they were placed in the charge of the new commander-in-chief, General Alekseev. He saw his task not as imprisoning the plotters until a trial for treason could be arranged, but as protecting them while more careful plans were laid to realize the aims of the very action for which they had been arrested. Over the following weeks, the Bykhov group was in steady communication with Alekseev on the subject of establishing a network of volunteer officers' organizations devoted to a continuation of the war and a loosely defined commitment to the restoration of "order," while Alekseev himself (having resigned as commander of the army as soon as 11 September 1917) set about readying—financially, militarily, and motivationally—officers and officer cadets in Petrograd and Moscow to oppose, or move against, the anticipated deepening of the revolution. On 30 October 1917 the men of this "Alekseev Organization," having failed in their efforts to quell the October Revolution, were ordered by Alekseev to follow him southward to Novocherkassk, the Don capital, to rendezvous with the Bykhov generals, who (with the assistance of General N.N. Dukhonin, Alekseev's successor as commander-in-chief) had been allowed to slip away from their place of detention to also make their way to the Cossack capital. The first officer-volunteers ("eagles," as the Whites affectionately termed them) arrived with Alekseev at Novocherkassk on 2 November 1917 and were joined soon afterwards by some of the leading lights of the Kadet party. Thus the "rank and file" (although, at this early stage, many of the rankers were officers) and the commanding staff of the Volunteer Army, as well as its political leadership—in sum, the heart and soul of the "White cause"—were united on the Don in the weeks immediately subsequent to the October Revolution. However, this union was forged, it should be emphasized, according to a scheme that had actually been established two months earlier.[69] In the light of this, the tense used by Lenin in the following sentences written on 29 September 1917 is worth noticing:

> During the past half year of our revolution, we have experienced very strong spontaneous outbursts (April 20–21, July 3–4) in which the proletariat came very close to starting a civil war. On the other hand, the Kornilov revolt was a military conspiracy supported by the landowners and capitalists led by the Cadet Party, a conspiracy by which the bourgeoisie has actually begun a civil war.[70]

Lenin was right regarding chronology, but very wrong in another respect: for, in fact, on the Don, neither the Kornilovites nor the Kadets were much welcomed by the Cossacks—throughout November and the first half of December 1917, men of the nascent Volunteer Army were even forbidden by Ataman Kaledin from bearing arms in public at Novocherkassk. What was underway, then, was not "a civil war" but something much more multifaceted and multifarious than that.

The "Russian" Civil Wars and their Antecedents

It is now no longer so very unusual to refer to the events that sprang from the collapse of tsarism and the attendant revolutions of 1917 as, in the plural, the

Russian Civil Wars. A recent chapter on the subject by David Stone used precisely that title;[71] and this was also the designation offered in 1997 by Vladimir Brovkin, as the subtitle of a collection of essays he edited.[72] In 2001, Rex Wade was more tentative, offering a chapter on "The Civil War(s)" in a book that deployed only the singular in its title.[73] In the volume before you, all such precautions and parentheses will be dispensed with. The scope of this study will establish beyond disputation that what wracked Russia from 1916 to 1926 were, in the plural, civil wars (although within that title, the reader should understand, are encompassed national wars, international wars, inter-ethnic wars and conflicts, wars of national liberation, and local adjuncts of the ongoing world struggle).

Moreover, this volume is designed to question the designation of those wars as "Russian." Of course, most of the conflicts that are traditionally described as contributing to the "Russian Civil War" occurred across territories that had, prior to the revolutions of 1917, been part of the Russian Empire, but not all of them: Czechoslovakia, Romania, Turkey, Persia, Xinjiang (Sinkiang, or Chinese Turkestan), Mongolia, and Manchuria were also drawn into the struggles, while certainly Finland and debatably Poland, to which the conflicts indubitably spread, had never been fully absorbed into the Russian *imperium* in the first place.[74] The very striking apogee of this transnational and multi-ethnic aspect of the subject was that one of the most contested cities of the civil war period was L'vov (formerly Austrian Lemberg), which had never been part of the Russian Empire (although it was briefly occupied by Russian forces in 1914–15) and which was fought over in 1918–19 chiefly by Poland and Ukraine (who called it Lwów and L'viv, respectively), although mischievous Romania (where the city was known as Liov) also staked its claim.[75] The Red Army also besieged L'vov in August 1920, during the Soviet–Polish War, but did not quite capture it.

In addition, as the example of L'vov again reveals—although we could just as well refer to Vil'na/Vil'no/Wilna/Wilno/Vilnius—a good deal of the fighting within the bounds of the former empire occurred between Russians of various political hues (Red, White, Green, etc.) and non-Russian former subjects of the tsar—from Ukrainians, Belorussians, Balts, and Poles to Georgians, Armenians, Tatars, Kazakhs, and Bashkirs—while some of the most fierce campaigns were waged between the non-Russian minorities of the ex-empire: the Armenian–Azerbaijan War, the Georgian–Armenian War, the Georgian–Ossetian Conflict, the Landeswehr War, the Polish–Lithuanian War, and the Ukrainian–Polish War are the chief examples, although there are many more. Cossacks too, although more a social caste rather than a true ethnos, also featured prominently in the ranks of both the Red and White armies and in Ukrainian nationalist forces. And Jews, of course, were attacked by all sides (although, equally, Jewish brigades could be found among the Red and White armies and, despite its reputation for antisemitism, even in the ranks of the anarchist Revolutionary Insurgent Army of Ukraine, as well as high up in that force's political machinery).

A further stratum of complexity is added by the issue of religion. If one can argue (as will be done below) that the end date of the civil wars is virtually impossible to pin down because anti-Bolshevik rebels in Central Asia, the Basmachi, continued armed resistance to Soviet rule well into the 1930s, the significance of religion in the Russian Civil Wars cannot be denied—certainly for the rebels, whose central pillar of identity was their adherence to Islam, and also, perversely, on the part of the Soviet leaders, who saw the eradication of the mullahs' power as a *sine qua non* of national liberation across the Muslim world and as a central plank of their anti-imperialist strategy.[76] Of course, the Russian Orthodox Church was also a target of Bolshevik militant atheists, and it is undoubtedly significant that as soon as the party felt strong enough to engage with that organization it did so: as the civil wars wound down in 1921–22, the Church was still regarded as having too tight a grip on the populace to attack head on, but the Soviet government instead sought to weaken it (and to blacken its name when it resisted) through the confiscation of its wealth in the name of famine relief.[77]

Yet, however bitter and bloody the materialists were in Moscow's confrontations with the Church authorities, nothing could dissuade believers in Warsaw from the conviction, as Red Army forces approached the Vistula in August 1920, that this was but the latest battle in the centuries-long campaign of the Russian Orthodox to crush the Polish outpost of Roman Catholicism. (Although, to complicate matters further, the Polish authorities added a dose of antisemitism to their propaganda attacks on the invader.)[78] On the other hand, in a region such as Transcaucasia, where centuries-old religious conflicts between Christians and Muslims were so ingrained that they could produce, at Baku in 1918, two of the most sanguinary slaughters of the civil war era (the "March Days" butchery of Azeris by Armenians and the "September Days" massacre of Armenians by Azeris), in the civil-war period Christian Georgia enjoyed remarkably harmonious relations with Muslim Azerbaijan while waging war against Christian Armenia for control of the provinces of Lori and Javakheti and the Borchalo district.[79]

One more interesting and unusual aspect of the "Russian" Civil Wars was the part that foreign contingents played in the fighting. The prominent part played in the anti-Bolshevik movement in 1918 by the Czechoslovak Legion is well known and will be examined below, as will the equally important contribution made to the establishment of the Soviet state by the Latvian Riflemen of the Red Army.[80] But intermingled with Red forces from the summer of 1918 onwards were also many contingents of so-called "Internationalists." This was the name applied to individuals and groups who fought on the side of the Red Army but who had been born outside of the Russian Empire. There were some five million foreigners on Russian soil by 1917 (almost half of them prisoners of war and many others displaced persons of one sort or another) and some tens of thousands of them (but certainly not the 200,000 cited in a generally more reliable late Soviet source)[81] were recruited to Soviet forces in the course of the civil wars, many of them from the pool of POWs who were released from camps upon the conclusion of the Treaty of Brest-Litovsk (3 March 1918) and chiefly, by nationality, Germans, Austrians, Magyars, Czechs, and Slovaks, although the 100,000 Chinese and Korean laborers that had been employed by the tsarist regime during the First World War also provided many volunteers. Among the latter were the 450-strong Chinese Battalion of the Tiraspol' Detachment (which fought against Romanian forces in Bessarabia in early 1918, under the command of I.E. Iakir), the Red Chinese (Zen Fu-chen) Detachment (which fought in the Urals in 1918–19), and the Chinese Platoon of the Kiev Military District (which was active in 1919). A contemporary Soviet source claimed that the number of Chinese in the Red Army was between 2,000 and 3,000 in 1919.[82]

The role of Internationalists in the Red Army is still one of the most difficult aspects of the "Russian" Civil Wars to evaluate, as both Soviet historians and émigrés tended (for very different reasons) to exaggerate their importance: for the former, the Internationalists—the subject of no less than 600 books published in Soviet Russia to the mid-1980s, according to one source[83]—symbolized the international proletarian revolution; for the latter, although their observations tended to appear more often in the form of pejorative asides than heavy tomes of documents and memoirs, they symbolized the illegitimacy and alien nature of Bolshevik rule in Russia.[84] The picture was further complicated by the move under Stalin, from the mid-1930s onwards, to denigrate the Internationalists and to promote the Russian-ness of the Reds. However, the best treatment in English of the Internationalists finds that perhaps Stalin had a point, for only the Latvian Riflemen had a notable military impact on the civil wars.[85] Indeed, as many members of the loosely organized Internationalists detachments of the Red Army left Russia following the end of the world war, in May 1919 the Field Staff of the RVSR (Revolutionary-Military Council of the Republic) put the strength of "all registered international units serving with the Red Army" at only 15,000–18,000 men.[86] Perhaps the most significant aspect of the entire business was that many Internationalists returned home to play a prominent part in the founding of their domestic communist parties—for example, Béla Kun in Hungary and Josip Broz aka Tito in Yugoslavia (although Tito's active service in Russia as an Internationalist seems to have been minimal). After working as a commissar with the 5th Red Army on the Eastern Front from 1918 to 1920, Jaroslav Hašek returned to Prague to spread subversion by a different means, authoring the stories that would become his satirical masterpiece *Osudy Dobrého Vojáka Svejka za Svetové Války* ("The Good Soldier Schweik," 1921–23).[87]

Finally, far less numerous (although of sometimes great prominence) were those non-Russian members of the pre-revolutionary emigration who were sucked back into the sphere of the maelstrom of the "Russian" Civil Wars by the events of the revolution. Some returned by choice and are better known by history (leaders of the various revolutionary parties, for example); some are less well known and were forced to return, notably from Britain and the United States, as London and Washington used the abdication of the Tsar to purge themselves of aliens regarded as to one degree or another undesirable.[88]

The events that stemmed from the collapse of tsarism, therefore, were far more than a "Russian" civil war. That they have generally been portrayed as such is perhaps unsurprising, given the numerical predominance of Russians within the former empire: of the 125,666,500 subjects of the tsar identified in the first census of his empire in 1897, 55,667,500 (44 percent) were (by language) Russians, alongside 22,380,600 Ukrainians and 5,885,500 Belorussians, with closely related tongues of the eastern Slavic group (accounting for 18 and 5 percent of the population respectively); 7,931,300 (6 percent) were Poles; 5,063,200 (4 percent) were Jews; 4,285,800 (3 percent) were Kazakhs and Kirghiz; and 3,767,500 (3 percent) were Tatars.[89] No other linguistic or national group exceeded two million, although culturally, commercially, and politically the empire's minorities generally punched far above their weight (especially the large number of Baltic Germans serving in the tsarist army and bureaucracy) and, in sum, the "minorities" were, of course, in a majority.[90]

That the civil-war role of non-Russians has to some extent been under-explored might also, in part (and understandably), be explained by the severe linguistic and logistical challenges of seeking more comprehensiveness. But that is not quite the whole story, as the fact that even fine studies of the civil war that place non-Russians in the foreground have titles that may mask their content.[91] This happens, ultimately, because of a linguistic quirk, whereby English-speakers are ill-served. In the Russian language, there are two adjectives that connote "Russian": *russkii*, meaning things relating to the history, culture, and language of things ethnically Russian (derived from the ancient Kievan Rus'); and *rossiiskii* (possibly derived from a corrupted Polish form and, for a while in the twentieth century, supplanted by *sovetskii*), describing things relating to the wider Russian/Soviet empire/state. Thus the second of these appellations is more appropriate when describing the "Russian" Civil Wars, but is deprived of its subtle and precise meaning in English translation.[92]

Finally, even within the areas of the old empire that were populated, in the main, by Russians, the struggle was multifaceted, involving not only the Bolshevik "Reds" against the conservative and militaristic "Whites" of popular renown, but layer upon layer of internecine conflicts and wars within wars: behind the major front lines of the civil wars, as they emerged in 1918–19, socialists fought each other—with ideas, guns, and bombs—and simultaneously battled anarchists and left-liberals who competed for the favors of the same constituency, while White officers sought to contain or coerce right-liberal and progressive (but anti-socialist) forces that had joined the anti-Bolshevik struggle on their side. Moreover, these contests within the Bolshevik and anti-Bolshevik camps were again more acute in the even more confused years of 1917–18, before the front lines became fixed—a period which, as will be made clear below, might be regarded as key in determining the eventual outcome of the struggle. After all, it was in 1917–18 that Lenin first made his mark on Red strategy in the civil wars by waging a successful campaign, against the majority of his party that opposed it, to accept a separate peace with Germany; while, in the anti-Bolshevik camp, the democratic counter-revolution briefly flared and offered a socialist alternative to Bolshevism in those years, but was then extinguished, as the White military and their liberal–conservative political allies smothered the Mensheviks, Socialists-Revolutionaries, and Popular Socialists.

These, then, were wars in which Russians fought Russians, Russians fought non-Russians, non-Russians fought non-Russians, republicans fought monarchists, socialists fought socialists, Christians fought Muslims, towns fought the countryside, family fought family, and brother fought brother. It was also a war of man against nature: as we have seen, of the 10,500,000 or so who lost their lives in the conflicts, the overwhelming majority (perhaps as many as 80 percent) died from hunger, cold, and disease (especially the pandemics of typhus and Spanish Flu) that were attendant upon the social and economic Gomorrah of the civil wars. Thus, as already noted, the period had as many echoes of Russia's turbulent and chaotic "Time of Troubles" (the *smuta*) of the early seventeenth century as it had parallels with other more antiseptic, politico-ideological civil wars of the twentieth century.[93]

From World War to Civil War: Smoke and Mirrors

This anomie, however, was not solely caused by the civil wars: to a significant although incalculable degree, the civil wars themselves (and the death, disease, depravity, and destruction that accompanied them) were outgrowths of a greater struggle, the First World War, which had prepared the soil from 1914 to 1918 for the bitter harvest reaped after 1918 across Eastern Europe, Russia, Transcaucasia, Central Asia, Siberia, and the Russian Far East, in an upheaval far removed in geographical scope from the cockpit of the Western Front but intimately linked to it.[94] As such, the "Russian" Civil Wars constituted not a separate volume in the history of the country, but the closing chapters of what historians have come to term, after Peter Holquist, "Russia's Continuum of Crisis"[95]—successive waves of war, revolution, and socio-economic collapse, accompanied by convulsions in settlement, mass psychology, and cultural norms that, among other things, sanctified violence and habitualized quotidian upheavals and sometimes quite unhinged (while equally liberating) artistic experimentation.[96] However, despite the pioneering effort of Geoff Eley to recast our understanding of the end days of the war in the east as a universal crisis of empire and a process of state-building,[97] the continuities between the world war and the Russian Civil Wars have not yet fully infiltrated scholarly works on the latter.[98] This remains the case despite, on a level less superficial than it might initially appear, the clear lineage dating back to the world war of some of the emblematic military units of the civil wars: for example, the Czechoslovak Legion (the most puissant of all anti-Bolshevik forces in 1918) had its origins in the Czech *druzhina* of tsarist times and the Latvian Riflemen (the Bolsheviks' Praetorian guard of 1918) were also birthed on the Eastern Front of Nicholas II's army, not Trotsky's (as were the Whites' equally fêted Kornilovtsy).[99]

The umbilical link between the First World War and the "Russian" Civil Wars is also apparent in an issue that was fundamental to the birth of the struggle: one that divided inhabitants of the former empire in the months before and after October 1917 (reasserting the continuum thesis) and defined contending successors to the Romanovs and the Provisional Government more clearly than might otherwise have been the case (yet, simultaneously, further muddied the waters of the "Russian" Civil Wars). This was the question of foreign intervention in Russia, which pre-dated October (in that Allied military missions had strong presences in the country during the world war) and colored all post-October events.[100] That much has long been understood in both Western and Soviet accounts of the civil wars. Contemporary Bolshevik propaganda, for example, generally portrayed the White leaders as nothing more than the puppets of Uncle Sam, John Bull, and the Mikado;[101] while, at its crudest, Soviet historiography "reduced the Civil War to three 'Entente Campaigns,'" as an imperialist conspiracy "fitted in with the Bolshevik world outlook."[102] Equally, White propaganda leaflets of the time (when not regurgitating racial slurs about Jews, Magyars, and Chinese, or denigrating the Soviet government as an abhorrent ochlocracy) routinely painted Lenin and Trotsky as the lapdogs of the Kaiser and claimed that the Red Army was "led by German officers"—even after the collapse of imperial Germany in October–November 1918.[103] And, following the Red victory in the civil wars, White memoirists would habitually ascribe their movement's defeat to betrayal by the Allies—a view that still held currency among émigré apologists for the Whites in post-Soviet times.[104]

* * *

Whatever the shortcomings of both the Reds and Whites' partisan and partial analyses (and they are legion), they at least have the considerable merit of reminding us of a facet of the civil wars—and foreign intervention in them—that has largely been obscured in Western historiography, but which was key in the crucial months of 1917–18. This was the issue, faced by all putative combatants—in nascent civil wars that were very much an adjunct of the wider, world war—of "orientation" (*orientatsiia*): for all the peoples of the old empire, after all, foreign intervention—real and anticipated, demanded or abjured—came in more than one guise. Specifically, it could be Allied or it could be "German."[105] There was, usually, a choice (albeit one that might have been offered by Hobson).[106] Thus some Ukrainian nationalists looked to the Central Powers (notably during the Hetmanate government of P.P. Skoropadskii of April–December 1918, although this had roots in the pro-Ukrainian policies sponsored in Berlin and Vienna during and even before the First

World War)[107] and found support in this among diverse Russians: some predictable (the renegade White commander Colonel P.R. Bermondt-Avalov, for example, and the right-liberal, anti-Bolshevik, underground National Center); others less so (such as the despairing liberal P.N. Miliukov, whose pro-Entente credentials had been impeccable before 1918). Of course, a lot depended on proximity and chance: thus, like Kiev, the Don Cossack Host sought accommodation with Berlin in 1918, as invading Austro-German forces approached Rostov, Taganrog, and Novocherkassk, while the more distant and thus buffered Kuban Cossack Host did not, and offered succor instead (at least initially) to the staunchly pro-Ally, anti-Bolshevik Volunteer Army.[108] Finnish nationalists, like the Hetman's Ukrainians, invited German intervention in early 1918, and on 9 October of that year went a step further by inviting Prince Frederick of Hesse, brother-in-law of Kaiser Wilhelm II, to accept the throne of a new Kingdom of Finland. In this, the Finns were aping the Lithuanians, whose national council (the Taryba) had earlier offered the throne of a new Kingdom of Lithuania to Duke Wilhelm of Urach. (He accepted the offer on 13 July 1918, and took the name King Mindaugas II, but was not crowned.)[109] Meanwhile, Archduke Wilhelm Franz von Habsburg, who was redubbed Vasil' Vishivanii ("Vasil' the Emboidered") for his habit of wearing Ukrainian shirts under his military uniform, schemed to have himself crowned king of Ukraine, and had some support in that country (notably from Andrei Sheptyts'kii, the Metropolitan archbishop of the Ukrainian Greek Catholic Church).[110]

Non-Bolshevik socialists across the old empire (including supporters of the Ukrainian National Republic that Skoropadskii had toppled in April 1918) were generally appalled by these machinations and opposed the pro-"German" orientation, although Mensheviks (whose affinities and historical contacts with the German socialist movement were hard to set aside) tended to be less pro-Allied than were members of the Party of Socialists-Revolutionaries. That, in part, explains why the Mensheviks who governed the newly independent Democratic Republic of Georgia from May 1918 accepted a German protectorate over their country (at the Treaty of Poti, 28 May 1918),[111] although the chief inspiration of this move was to seek a bulwark against the incursion on to Georgian territory of the forces of Germany's ally, the Ottoman Empire, which at that time was engaged (in collaboration with its Azeri partners) in overrunning the newfound Armenian Democratic Republic. For their part, hemmed in between Muslim Turkey and Azerbaijan and a Georgia that claimed much of its territory (and in late 1918 was willing to go to war to secure it), the Armenians knew that their only hope was a so-called "Wilso-nian" settlement to borders in eastern Anatolia and thus cleaved to the Allied cause that promised them such an extension of territory, but were ultimately betrayed by all sides.[112]

Although it was the variant that perhaps had the best chance of toppling the Soviet regime (had Berlin desired that outcome, rather than finding the perpetuation of Lenin's rule to be useful),[113] and certainly the one that had the deepest impact on the opening exchanges of the civil wars, the "German ori-entation" of 1918 has now largely been forgotten. This is in large part because, of course, the Germans lost the world war and those Russians, Ukrainians, Georgians, Cossacks, and others who had adopted that *orientatsiia* found themselves in an awkward position vis-à-vis the victors and had no desire after the event to broadcast their earlier, ill-fated choices. The fact that German expansionist policies in the East in 1918 have been cited as the progenitor of the later Nazi thrust for *Lebensraum* has also deterred those who were com-plicit in it from trumpeting the fact, as this subject became a very hot histori-cal potato from the 1950s onwards.[114]

At the time, in 1918, the "German orientation" was equally abhorrent to the Party of Left Socialists-Revolutionaries, who had split from the PSR to become the Bolsheviks' allies in coalition government from December 1917 but who then resigned from Sovnarkom in March 1918 in protest at the sign-ing of the Soviet–German Treaty of Brest-Litovsk.[115] In June–July 1918 they were involved in the assassination of both the German ambassador to the RSFSR (Count Wilhelm von Mirbach) and Berlin's military governor of Ukraine (General E.G.H. von Eichhorn) and also staged an armed uprising in Moscow, while the Left-SRs' adherent, Colonel M.A. Murav'ev, who was effectively commander-in-chief of the Red Army at this point, led a synchro-nous revolt against Soviet power at Simbirsk, on the Volga, and issued a dec-laration of war against the Central Powers: another civil war within the civil wars. Moreover, the Left-SRs had many allies within the Bolshevik Party itself, chiefly in the shape of the Left Bolsheviks around N.I. Bukharin, who were equally appalled at the prospect of treating with the Kaiser and thereby betray-ing the revolutionary movement in Germany, but who in the end could not shift Lenin from his determination to save the "healthy baby" of the Russian Revolution, even if that meant depriving (if not aborting) the German infant, as Germany was "only just pregnant with revolution."[116] So, on 3 March 1918, the Treaty of Brest-Litovsk was signed. Under its terms, Soviet Russia became, in effect, an ally (potentially a vassal) of imperial Germany and the other Central Powers.[117]

This hardly resolved the issue of *orientatsiia*, however. Although Lenin had finally won a vote in favor of accepting the German terms for peace at the Bolshevik Central Committee meeting of 23 February 1918, he had only done so by threatening to resign from Sovnarkom unless he got his way and even then won the support of only a minority of those present: eight voted in favor of peace, four against, and four (including Trotsky) abstained.[118] Moreover, even then it is clear that without party secretary Ia.M. Sverdlov's careful gerrymandering of elections to the Fourth (Extraordinary) All-Russian Congress of Soviets (14–16 March 1918), to ensure a Leninist majority, and without the pressure brought to bear upon those local committees selecting Bolshevik delegates to adhere to the principle of "democratic centralism," the treaty would not have been ratified.[119] Moreover, so unabashedly plunderous were the terms of the Brest-Litovsk treaty that it voided itself of any moral force and all its signatories immediately chose to ignore it: "Peace had been signed, but a *de facto* war continued."[120] Very soon the German Army had advanced beyond the agreed demarcation line in the north-west, occupying Polotsk, Orsha, and Bobruisk, while the Turks mustered an Army of Islam to capture Transcaucasia and set off toward Erevan and Baku.[121] Meanwhile, the Soviet government continued to organize the foundations of a Red Army—the new forces were described as "Screens," rather than armies, but this fooled nobody—and sought to scupper rather than dock the Black Sea Fleet; while anarchists, Left-SRs, and renegade Left Bolsheviks dispatched guerilla forces, weapons, and funds across the new border into Ukraine to galvanize opposition to the Austro-German occupation.[122]

Not that the Left Bolsheviks and their ilk would have been any more comfortable with an "Allied orientation." When, on 22 February 1918, just a day before the decision was taken to treat with Germany, the Bolsheviks received a note via the French military mission in Russia that formally offered Allied aid to resist the Central Powers (whose forces, for the previous week, had been advancing toward Petrograd), Bukharin was indignant. Minutes of the Bolshevik Central Committee meeting of that day record him as insisting that "the 'allies' have a plan here to turn Russia into one of their colonies" and pointing out that "it is unthinkable to accept support from imperialists of any sort." Lenin was not present at the meeting, but—even while arguing in favor of signing a treaty with Germany—he submitted a note instructing his comrades to "Please add my vote in favour of taking potatoes and weapons from the Anglo-French imperialists robbers."[123]

As for Trotsky, even after the ratification of the treaty with Germany (which he was very unwilling to accept), the People's Commissar for Foreign Affairs himself was only too happy also to keep lines open to the Allies, notably in the shape of the British agent in Moscow, R.H. Bruce Lockhart, with whom he was on excellent terms.[124] Lockhart's statement in his memoirs that "right up until the end of June [1918], there was a reasonable prospect of arriving at a *modus vivendi*" between Moscow and the Allies[125] is a slight exaggeration and is contradicted by the documentary record: quite suddenly, on 20 May 1918, after almost three months of attempting to convince Whitehall that the Brest-Litovsk treaty was meaningless and that Germany and Soviet Russia would inevitably come to blows (thereby opening the way for Allied intervention in Russia with the consent of the Soviet government), Lockhart performed a U-turn, conceding that:

> On this point I admit frankly that [the] situation has so changed that Bolshevik consent is no longer as important a consideration as before. Our great danger is not [the] Bolsheviks ... but [the pro-]German counter-revolution.[126]

Yet, further to confound traditional assumptions regarding the parameters of "the Russian Civil Wars" and the Allied intervention in them, is worth emphasizing that, nevertheless, at least up until that point (mid-May), Allied intervention in Russia with the consent of Moscow had remained a possibility; and that the Bolsheviks—or, at least, very many Bolsheviks and perhaps a majority of them—were not fully committed to a pro-German *orientatsiia*.[127] That much was made graphically clear when, on 6 March 1918, three days after the signing of the Treaty of Brest-Litovsk, the first contingent of Allied "interventionist" forces (130 men of the Royal Marines) went ashore at Murmansk—not with all guns blazing but with the written permission of the Bolshevik chairman of the local Soviet, who had taken care to seek the endorsement of none other than Trotsky before requesting their disembarkation from the Royal Navy's HMS *Glory* (with which the Russian battleship *Chesma* exchanged formal salutes) in order to ensure that stockpiled military stores in the port did not fall into the hands of the Germans or their White Finnish allies. Trotsky soon changed his mind,[128] but the local Soviet authorities at Murmansk were more flexible and the surprising fact remains that, although the relationship was an uneasy one (and notwithstanding some typical bluster by Lenin about the "counter-revolutionaries" at the head of the Murmansk Soviet),[129] in April–May 1918 British marines were engaged in joint operations with Red Guards to ward off advances toward Murmansk by White Finnish raiders (supported by anti-Bolshevik Russians) and anticipated German U-boat attacks on Pechenga.[130]

Meanwhile in Moscow, as if to personify the panoply of possibilities still open during the spring of 1918, the British intelligence officer George Hill was actively organizing groups of socialist and anarchist partisans in Russia to send into German-dominated Ukraine to inspire and assist in peasant resistance to the requisitioning policies of the Central Powers, while at the same time (with the title of "inspector of aviation") assisting Trotsky in organizing the fledgling Red Army and reporting directly to the newly installed People's Commissar for Military Affairs.[131] Alongside Hill, by 26 March 1918, some forty Allied officers had been assigned to work with the Red Army, following discussions between Trotsky and General J.G. Lavergne of the French Military Mission.[132] Around the same time, in contrast, at Petrograd and Helsingfors, the British naval attaché Captain Francis Cromie was evading the attentions of Red Guards and White Finns so as to scupper vessels both wanted to protect (before they could be captured by the advancing Germans).[133] In the light of these twisted tales, it perhaps does not seem quite so surreal that the British intelligence officer at Tashkent, Colonel F.M. Bailey, disguised as an Austrian POW, would later find himself in employment with a local Cheka unit that was hunting down "the British spy Bailey"![134] This, truly, was a war of smoke and mirrors.

2

1918–19

THE TRIUMPHAL MARCH OF REACTION

After these initial perturbations and contortions, from around May–June 1918, the political and military battle lines of the "Russian" Civil Wars would begin to become less fluid. There would still be very many exceptions, however, and some of these are worth exploring to illustrate the taxing, yet fascinating, complexity of the fissiparous loyalties and unfixed enmities that characterized these many conflicts.

Thus, although the Party of Socialists-Revolutionaries countenanced armed struggle against the Soviet regime—and, as we shall see, in the summer of 1918, set about waging war against the Bolsheviks, in what became known as the "democratic counter-revolution"—some members of the PSR (the "Narod" group) would cross the front lines in late 1918, deserting the anti-Bolshevik camp as it became dominated by the often reactionary Whites, to offer conditional support to the Bolsheviks; but in 1922, members of the PSR Central Committee would appear in a Moscow court, in what amounted to one of the first show trials of the Soviet era, charged with counter-revolutionary crimes.[1] Meanwhile, in February 1919, Bashkir forces that had been organized in the homelands of that Turkic people on the western slopes of the Urals would follow a similar path in deserting the Whites' Siberian Army to, to support instead the Red Army on the Eastern Front, and were rewarded for their efforts with the creation on 23 March 1919 of the first autonomous region within the new Soviet state (the RSFSR), the Bashkir Autonomous

Soviet Socialist Republic.[2] But they would later witness Moscow favoring local Tatars, the Bashkirs' rivals in the region, prompting the most eminent Bashkir leader, Ahmed Zeki (Togan) Validov, to flee in 1920, to Central Asia where he joined the anti-Bolshevik Basmachi.[3] Likewise, supposed Bolshevik allies in Central Asia, such as the former Turkish minister of war Enver Pasha, would also desert Red forces, in 1922, to rally the anti-Bolshevik Basmachi against them.[4] Meanwhile, Nestor Makhno's anarchist Revolutionary-Insurgent Army of Ukraine would occasionally ally with the Red Army, but would just as often find itself pilloried, outlawed, and attacked by Trotsky; thus, after playing a leading role in defeating the Whites in Southern Russia in 1920, many of its leaders (Mikhail Brova, Petr Gavrilenko, Semen Karetnik, D.I. Popov, Trofim Vdovichenko, C. Zhivoder, and others) were ambushed and summarily executed by the Cheka, just a few days after the evacuation of White forces from the peninsula—although, just to add one more carapace of complexity and confusion, one Makhnovist who escaped, L.N. Zin'kovskii, would subsequently return to Soviet Russia to become a much-feared and much-decorated Chekist.[5]

Within the Soviet camp, Mensheviks would switch from hostile to benevolent neutrality and back again in their attitude to the Bolsheviks during the civil wars, but many would work throughout the 1920s in the Soviet administration, only to find themselves rewarded with arrest and exile following the farcical trial of their banned party's former members in 1931.[6] Within the White camp, especially in the East, former friends might join enemy plots as the civil wars progressed.[7] Also, in all White-held areas, tensions became increasingly acute between the Russian leadership of the movement and their Cossack allies, who were variously accused of banditry (Ataman G.M. Semenov of the Transbaikal Cossack Host) and separatism (Ataman A.P. Filimonov of the Kuban Cossack Host).[8] Meanwhile, that the Red zone was wracked with peasant uprisings (especially from late 1920) might not be so surprising, as the entire Bolshevik ethos was urban, but in February–March 1921 the Soviet government was simultaneously challenged militarily by its once most fervent advocates, the Kronstadt sailors, and politically attacked by its proletarian conscience, the Workers' Opposition, as mass strikes of workers across the "Red citadel" of Petrograd brought the city to its knees.[9]

In a full account of the "Russian" Civil Wars, there could be an all but limitless list of unhappy and odd bedfellows. Among the Allied interventionists, the commander of the American Expeditionary Force in Siberia, General William S. Graves, clearly regarded his purported partners, the Japanese army, as the root of all evil in the Far East,[10] while Colonel P.J. Woods of the British interventionist force, the so-called "King of Karelia," was not alone in regarding local White forces as being the fundamental cause of anti-Bolshevism's downfall in North Russia. (Woods' Karelian regiment, meanwhile, went from assisting British forces in clearing their territory of White Finns in 1918 to allying with the latter against the Bolsheviks from the summer of 1919, as the Allies withdrew.)[11] Meanwhile in Transcaucasia in 1918–19, mindful of the impression their activities in the region might have in restless India (currently disturbed by Mahatma Gandhi's non-cooperation movement), in the bitter Azeri–Armenian disputes over the Karabakh (Qarabağ) and Zangezur (Siunik) regions the British interventionist forces tended usually, and perversely, to favor the Muslim Azeris (who had largely refused to fight against the Ottoman Empire in the First World War and had welcomed the Turkish invasion of their territory in 1918) over the Christian Armenians (who, despite their grievances against Russia—not least the fact that, in 1903, the properties of the Armenian Apostolic Church had been purloined by the Russian Orthodox Church—had provided many thousands of volunteers for the Allied cause during the First World War and had staunchly resisted the invasion of Transcaucasia by Turkey's Army of Islam in 1918).[12]

Perhaps, though, the most instructive example of the extraordinary mutability of choices (albeit between varieties of "evil") that remained open to contending forces throughout the civil wars occurred in Ukraine. Although formally united (through the Act of Zluka of 22 January 1919), when faced with annihilation in 1919–20 the Western Ukrainian People's Republic (WUPR) (which had developed, after November 1918, on formerly Austrian territory) and the Ukrainian National Republic (UNR) (founded in November 1917, at Kiev, on formerly Russian territory) sought salvation by means that could not have been more starkly contrasting: Evhen Petrushevych, leader of the WUPR, advocated an alliance with the Whites; Simon Petliura, leader of the UNR, opted, instead, for a formal military alliance with Poland (the Treaty of Warsaw, 21–4 April 1920), the heavy price of which was a recognition of Polish sovereignty over Western Ukraine (Eastern Galicia)—the issue that had been at the heart of the WUPR–Polish (Ukrainian–Polish) War of the previous two years—thereby condemning the WUPR to death.[13] In contrast, independent Lithuania sought aid in its own territorial contest with Poland (the Polish–Lithuanian War) through a treaty with the RSFSR (the Treaty of Moscow, 12 July 1920), which recognized Lithuanian claims to Vil'na/Wilno/Vilnius. In fact, as the Red Army was defeated in the ongoing

Soviet–Polish War, and following the "Żeligowski Mutiny" of October 1920 (which was staged, covertly, on behalf of Warsaw by local Polish forces), the city was eventually captured by the Poles, and Lithuania was divorced from its claimed capital for the next twenty years. Had the Reds won the Soviet–Polish War and held on to the city, on the other hand, it is almost certain that it (and all Lithuania) would have been Sovietized as rapidly as Ukraine, Transcaucasia, and Central Asia. Lithuania, in that scenario, would have had no true independence at all, demonstrating that there can be victory in defeat.[14] After all, where the Soviet government, for tactical purposes, tolerated difference in the civil wars, it tended not to do so for very long after strategic victory had been secured. For example, east of Lake Baikal, a nominally independent Far Eastern Republic (FER), with a coalition socialist government, was founded on 6 April 1920 as a buffer between the Red Army and forces of the Japanese intervention. But when the latter agreed to withdraw from the region in late October 1922, the People's Convention (parliament) of the FER voted with unseemly haste for union with the RSFSR on 14 November 1922—a move sealed on the following day by a decree of VTsIK.[15]

The ever-shifting sands of civil-war allegiances would become hardly more settled after the conflicts ended, but again there would be important and interesting exceptions. Of course, most White émigrés remained inveterate enemies of the Soviet regime—no more so than the adherents of the Russian All-Military Union (Russkii Obshche Voinskii Soiuz, ROVS), founded in September 1924 by the last White leader, General P.N. Wrangel. Yet successive presidents of ROVS (Generals A.T. Kutepov and E.K. Miller) were abducted by the Soviet intelligence services after being betrayed by their own subordinates who were working for the Soviet intelligence services, while the organization's Paris headquarters was comprehensively bugged on behalf of the NKVD by its landlord, none other than S.N. Tret'iakov—a former minister in the White governments of Kolchak's Siberia and Wrangel's Crimea in 1919–20. In 1918, Tret'iakov had been a founder of the National Center, which followed the "German orientation"; in 1944, he was executed as a Soviet spy by the Gestapo![16] Such unsettlingly odd occurrences might be ascribed to personal factors (greed, fear, jealousy, foolishness, madness, etc.), or to provocation and diversionary plots on the part of the crafty Cheka. A prime example of the latter was the devious Operation "Trust," which netted the former SR terrorist and civil-war anti-Bolshevik leader Boris Savinkov, in August 1924, and the British "Ace of Spies," Sydney Reilly, in September 1925, by convincing them that an extensive network of anti-Bolshevik agents awaited their return to Russia, when all that actually awaited them was a cell in the Lubianka and an untimely death.[17] But ideology too could come into play: émigré adherents of the notion of *Smenovekhovtsvo* ("Changing Landmarks") in the 1920s were convinced, not without reason, that the Soviet government had legitimized its rule and that returning to Soviet Russia offered the best future for their countrymen. Among the returnees were none other than former luminaries of the White regime in Siberia such as N.V. Ustrialov and Iu.V. Kliuchnikov. The former (director of the Russian Press Bureau in Kolchak's Omsk) became professor of economic geography at the Moscow Institute of Transport Engineers; the latter (director of the Ministry of Foreign Affairs at Omsk), mutated into an advisor to the People's Commissariat for Foreign Affairs of the USSR.[18] Of course, neither survived the purges (Ustrialov was executed in September 1937, Kliuchnikov in January 1938), but then neither did hundreds of senior officers of the imperial Russian Army who had thrown in their lot with the Bolsheviks from the start to serve as military specialists (*voenspetsy*) in the civil-war Red Army: the tortured, and then slaughtered, *komandarmy* ("army commanders") M.N. Tukhachevskii, A.I. Kork, S.D. Kharlamov, M.S. Matiiasevich, V.I. Motornyi, D.N. Nadezhnyi, V.A. Ol'derogge, A.V. Novikov, F.F. Novitskii, S.A. Pugachev, N.I. Rattel', A.E. Snesarev, A.A. Svechin, P.P. Sytin, and A.I. Verkhovskii represented only the tip of a very large and very bloody iceberg in the 1930s.[19]

Poignantly, by then the revenge of the past had also already arranged a very different fate for one of the most prominent White generals of the civil war, Ia.A. Slashchov. He was known as "Slashchov-Krymskii" for having held the Perekop isthmus against Red assaults in early 1920, thereby preserving the Crimea as a haven for the White armies that had failed—just—to capture Moscow. Having been retired from active service on health grounds in August 1920, "Slashchov of the Crimea" went into emigration, but quarreled with the White leader, General Wrangel, and, in November 1921, returned from Constantinople to Soviet Russia. He was conveyed to Moscow on the private train of none other than the Cheka boss Feliks Dzierżyński, and subsequently taught at prestigious military schools in the Soviet capital. But, on 11 January 1929, Slashchov-Krymskii was shot dead in his Moscow apartment by one Lazar Kolenberg. Apparently, this Kolenberg was seeking vengeance on behalf of his brother, who had been executed in the Crimea in 1920 on Slashchov's orders. After all, to the civil-war Reds, Slashchov was known as "the hangman." Kolenberg was tried but walked free from court, with suspicions voiced ever since that he was an agent of the Cheka's successor, the OGPU.[20]

Finally, to confound all neat refractions of the "Russian" Civil Wars as a clear-cut contest between "socialists" and "reactionaries," just as Slashchov had departed Constantinople there arrived in the Turkish capital, to join the improvised and impoverished government-in-exile of General Wrangel, none other than the former propagandist, activist, and champion of revolutionary terrorism V.I. Burtsev—a man once described by no lesser authority than Alexander III as the most dangerous enemy of the Russian state and one who, in 1897, had been arrested in the British Museum on a charge of incitement to tsaricide.[21]

Only once fully aware of the many such problems associated with establishing firm lines of demarcation in any of the political and military struggles at the heart of the "Russian" Civil Wars should the historian proceed to attempt a narrative and analysis of them. With that in mind ...

Opening Campaigns: Ukraine, the Don, and the Kuban

Although, as we have seen, Russia had been in a state of civil war for at least several months before they were signed—and arguably for an entire year, or even for almost two years before that—it was the treaties of Brest-Litovsk that the Central Powers concluded first with the Ukrainian National Republic (27 January 1918) and then Soviet Russia (3 March 1918) that largely determined the warp and weft of the actual fighting in 1918. With the Reds' suppression of the aforementioned uprising of the Orenburg Cossacks in January 1918, their quelling of an uprising of Polish forces in Belorussia (the "Dowbór-Muśnicki uprising"), their dispersal of a popularly elected Siberian Regional Duma at Tomsk (26–7 January 1918), and their rebuffing of an incursion into Transbaikalia of Ataman G.M. Semenov's Special Manchurian Detachment (from 29 January 1918), those alarming foci of various subsequent anti-Bolshevik efforts were—albeit only for the time being—contained. Thus, up until the spring of 1918, the initial flashpoints of the conflict were in Ukraine and neighboring reaches of the Don *oblast'* and the North Caucasus.

In December 1917, Ukraine itself had experienced an invasion of Soviet forces (chiefly Red Guards and hastily organized shock battalions of Baltic sailors), which were dispatched toward Kiev by rail, nominally as the army of the first Ukrainian Soviet Socialist Republic (based at Khar'kov since 25 December 1917, as pro-Soviet forces had been driven out of Kiev by Ukrainian units loyal to the newly proclaimed Ukrainian National Republic).[22] The Bolsheviks' reason for launching this attack—apart from the fact that the UNR's government, the General Secretariat of the Rada ("Council"), consisted of non-Bolshevik Ukrainian socialists who were not always popular among the usually Russian or Russianized (and sometimes Bolshevized) workers of the Ukrainian cities, especially in the east of that country—was that it was disorganizing the front against the Central Powers (through attempting to bring under its own control Ukrainized regiments of the former imperial Army), was allowing the organization on its territory of anti-Bolshevik, White forces (what the Soviet government termed the "Cadet–Kaledin plot"), and was providing shelter also for Alekseev's group, the nascent Volunteer Army, on the Don.[23] It was to be an uneven battle. Former units of the imperial Russian Army on Ukrainian soil had been in the process of Ukrainization for several months by this point, but the process was incomplete and a separate command structure had not yet emerged. Moreover, although some nationalists had called for the establishment of a Ukrainian Army, most of the Rada socialists—both SRs and social democrats—who otherwise differed on a number of matters, were united by their initial opposition to a standing army and had developed, instead, the hazy idea of a popular militia. When more-or-less spontaneous formations of "Free Cossacks" began to appear in the Ukrainian villages, however, the Rada leaders at first sought to ban them, fearing they would provide an armed force for the wealthier elements in the countryside.[24] Various volunteer units were, nevertheless, hastily assembled—or, usually, assembled themselves—to oppose the Soviet invasion, but these—notably the 300 "Kruty Heroes" (students and cadets subsequently regarded as glorious martyrs in independent Ukraine)—were easily swept aside (and largely slaughtered) by the Reds; and, on 26–7 January 1918, the Soviet army, commanded by the Left-SR Colonel M.A. Murav'ev, entered Kiev.[25] At that point, "the Ukrainian cabinet literally disappeared," noted one historian: "Meetings held in war minister Nemolvolsky's office were attended only by Prime Minister Holubovich, Khristiuk (interior), Tkachenko (justice) and the former secretary for military affairs, Porsh." The other seven cabinet ministers were nowhere to be found.[26]

According to an account by the US consul in Kiev, at least 3,000 people lost their lives in the fighting for the city and as many again were injured. Before they retreated from the city, Ukrainian forces executed hundreds of captured Bolsheviks and deserters from their own ranks, he reported, while:

> For the first two days of Bolshevik occupation there were hundreds of executions, or more properly speaking murders. It is estimated that 300 or 400 officers were shot down on the streets or taken to a park near the former residence of the governor where they were killed.[27]

In total, according to one Ukrainian source, somewhere between 2,000 and 5,000 people may have been executed by the occupying Soviet army.[28] Actually, to call Muarav'ev's men an "army" is to abuse that word. Even according to a contemporary Bolshevik: "They were oddly dressed, totally undisciplined people, covered from head to toe with every conceivable type of weapon—from rifles to sabres to hand-guns and grenades. Arguments and fights constantly flared up among their commanders."[29] It was not merely for effect that Mikhail Bulgakov opened his masterful novel, *The White Guard*, concerning the chaotic civil war in Kiev, with the harrowing remark that "Great and terrible was the year 1918, of the revolution the second."[30]

In these weeks, equally improvised—but better-led and better-armed—Red detachments also captured most of Ukraine's major cities, including Ekaterinoslav (28 December 1917), Poltava (5–6 January 1918), and Odessa (16–17 January) and also took the Crimean cities of Yalta and Feodosiia (11 January), although they were driven out of Bessarabia by Romanian troops (who captured Kishinev on 13 January 1918).[31] Meanwhile, in the south-east, another Red front was opened by a second Ukrainian Soviet government, the Donetsk Krivoi Rog Soviet Republic. Its hastily fashioned army, led by the talented Bolshevik commander V.A. Antonov-Ovseenko, captured Rostov-on-Don (23–4 February 1918) from its White defenders, having already taken the Don Cossack capital, Novocherkassk (29 January 1918). The last act was of huge symbolic importance and had some lasting consequences. First, the Don Cossacks' failure—indeed, the apparent unwillingness of most of the partially Bolshevized and wholly war-weary Host—to defend their capital so desponded their leader, Ataman A.M. Kaledin, that he committed suicide, shooting himself through the heart in his rooms at the Ataman's Palace in the city as the Reds entered Novocherkassk. Secondly, it persuaded General Kornilov that the only hope of saving the newly created Volunteer Army, which had been organized at Novocherkassk, was to withdraw from the Don into the North Caucasus. Thus was initiated the legendary "First Kuban (Ice) March" of the Volunteers, which was not only to provide one of the foundation myths—or, at least, partial myths—of the White movement but was to determine the geographical constraints of the Whites' strategy in the South for the next year.

From February to April 1918, a few thousand Volunteers—almost all of them officers or officer cadets—dragging almost as many civilian refugees along with them, with a few heavy cannon and carts laden with the wounded and sick, set off into the icy steppe lands of the North Caucasus, where at least 100,000 loosely organized Red Guards (the detritus of the Caucasus Front of the imperial Russian Army and its rear garrisons) awaited them. In fifty days the Volunteers fought forty battles and suffered horrendous casualties before uniting with the Kuban Cossacks of Ataman A.P. Filimanov and General V.L. Pokrovskii at Novodmitrievsk *stanitsa*, raising their complement to around 6,000. This encouraged Kornilov to launch a do-or-die assault on Ekaterinodar, the Kuban capital: Kornilov, however, whose headquarters was hit by a shell, was among the hundreds of Whites who perished, as 18,000 Red defenders beat off the Volunteers' repeated assaults over 10–13 April. The loss of so potent and (because of his stance in 1917) symbolic a leader as Kornilov was a heavy blow to the Volunteers, and the siege of Ekaterinodar was immediately lifted, leaving the city for the time being as the center of the Kuban Soviet Republic (from 30 May 1918, the Kuban–Black Sea Soviet Republic). Soon, though, encouraging news would arrive from the north, where the Don Cossacks had finally risen against Soviet rule and had been joined by 2,000 crack troops, under General M.G. Drozdovskii, that had undertaken a 2,000-mile march across southern Ukraine from the Romanian Front to join the Volunteers.[32]

Indeed, hardly had Kiev and the Don been secured by them in February 1918 than, as a consequence of the terms of the Brest-Litovsk treaties, the tide turned forcefully against the Reds. Under the agreed terms, Moscow was forced to recognize the UNR, obliging the withdrawal of Soviet forces from Ukraine (although of what provinces of the former empire "Ukraine" consisted was not clear) and Crimea. Kiev was consequently abandoned on 2 March 1918, while the 450,000-strong forces of the Austro-German intervention invested Eastern (that is, formally Russian) Ukraine, and an anticipatory uprising of the Don Cossack Host (from 27 March 1918) and the creation of a Cossack Don Army (with an attendant new civilian administration, the Don Republic) forced Antonov-Ovseenko's army to withdraw northwards.

* * *

The Brest-Litovsk treaty of 3 March 1918 had also determined that Moscow should desist from opposing the German occupation of the Baltic provinces: German forces, having captured the Latvian capital of Riga in mid-August 1917, reached the Estonian capital, Revel (Tallinn), on 24–5 February 1918. In the Baltic theater, the presence of powerful German forces not only forestalled the plans of local Bolsheviks (most of them ethnic Russians) to Sovietize the region and unite with Soviet Russia, but also rendered ineffective the proclamations of independence issued by local nationalists and their people's councils: the Lithuanian Taryba proclaimed independence on 16 February 1918, and the Estonian Maapäev (heir to the Autonomous Governorate of Estonia of 1917) did so on 24 February 1918. However, the real effort to win independence would have to await Germany's defeat in the First World War.[33]

The Finnish Civil War

By contrast, further north in Finland, where the Germans had influence but not power, Berlin's assistance facilitated an early and decisive White Finnish victory in the Finnish Civil War.[34] This conflict, which lasted from around 21 January (new style) to 15 May 1918, was closely entwined with the events of the emergent struggles within the former Russian Empire (although, formally, the Grand Duchy of Finland had never been part of that entity but rather the personal domain of the tsar). It was fought between forces loyal to the Social Democratic Party of Finland, which declared a Finnish Socialist Workers' Republic, and conservative "White Finns." The former received some moral and material support from Soviet Russia; the latter received significant armed assistance from the Central Powers.

The war had its roots in the collapse of order in the former Grand Duchy of Finland following the February Revolution, in a grave economic crisis precipitated by that (although prior to February 1917 Finland had profited from the war), and the consequent organization of contending Red and White Guards units on the streets. Although the Social Democrats, led by Oskari Tokoi, gained an initial majority in the Finnish Diet, following a period of near anarchy over the summer and new parliamentary elections in October 1917, conservative forces took control, provoking a general strike among Finland's workers the following month. There were numerous armed clashes in the towns of southern Finland, which served as the prelude to a full-scale and very brutal civil war.[35] Meanwhile, on 6 December 1917, the Finnish Senate proposed Finnish independence in order to forestall Soviet Russian intervention in Finnish affairs. Subsequently, Finnish independence was recognized by Sovnarkom on 18 December 1917—apparently with the false expectation that the Finnish social democrats would soon reassert their control.

As the White Guards, now commanded by the former tsarist general C.G.E Mannerheim, were incorporated into a new Finnish White Army, based at Vaasa, on the Gulf of Bothnia, tensions rose. The Red Guards, initially commanded by Ali Aaltonen (and subsequently by Eero Haapalainen, Eino Rahja, and Kullervo Manner) and based at Helsinki (Helsingfors), refused to recognize the legitimacy of the new (White) force and the civil war proper began. Initially, the front ran in a line from just north of Pori and Tampere and Kouvola and Viipuri through Karelia to the Russian border, with the Reds controlling the more industrialized and agriculturally prosperous south, while the Whites commanded the poorer north (as well as enclaves around Turku and to the east and west of Helsinki). However, most fighting took place in the following weeks along the railways, with the Reds' prime objective being to cut the Whites' east–west rail connection, which they attempted but failed to achieve north of Tampere during the Battle of Vilppula in February 1918.

Estimates as to the number of forces serving on each side vary, but figures of around 50,000 during the early stages of the war to over 90,000 at its peak are often quoted. The Reds were mostly volunteers, drawn from the industrial proletariat and agricultural laboring classes; the Whites attracted more landowners, independent farmers, and members of the bourgeoisie (as well as representatives of the economically powerful Swedish upper classes), but their army was numerically dominated by conscripted Finns of the lower classes, chiefly peasants.[36] These latter seem mostly to have accepted mobilization as a means to survive during a period of economic chaos, but many also feared that the Finnish Reds would abandon Finnish independence and unite with Soviet Russia.

In fact, Soviet interference in the Finnish conflict was not very significant.[37] Although there were more than 60,000 Russian forces in Finland in January 1918, most refused to become involved (only some 7,000 men joined the Finnish Reds—constituting little more than 5 percent of their complement—and fewer than 4,000 saw service at the front), and by late March 1918 most had returned to Russia. Moreover, Article IV of the Treaty of Brest-Litovsk, of 3 March 1918, obliged Soviet Russia to withdraw its troops from Finland and to cease agitation and interference within the country. In contrast, the Whites enjoyed the advantage of the large number of former tsarist officers serving in their ranks (as well as nearly 100 Swedish officer volunteers and 1,000 more Swedish other ranks, as well as numerous Estonian volunteers) and the 1,300-strong, elite Jäger force that had been trained in Germany since 1915 (and which had seen action against the imperial Russian Army on the Eastern Front during the First World War). The latter formed the shock troops of the White Finns and facilitated the training of other forces.

Once peace terms had been secured with Soviet Russia at Brest-Litovsk, imperial Germany also sent immediate armed assistance to the White Finns: on 5 March 1918, a German naval squadron landed on the Åland Islands; on 3 April 1918, the 10,000-strong Baltic Sea Division (led by the impetuous

General Rüdiger von der Goltz) landed west of Helsinki at Hangö (Hanko); and, on 7 April 1918, the 3,000-strong Brandenstein Detachment landed on the south-east coast and overran the town of Loviisa. German forces then closed on Helsinki, which fell to them on 12–13 April 1918, before moving north to capture Hyvinkää and Riihimäki on 21–22 April, followed by Hämeenlinna on 26 April 1918.[38] Unable to counter this intervention in their rear, the untrained, ill-disciplined, internationally isolated and poorly led Finnish Reds thereafter suffered a series of crushing defeats by the Whites, notably surrendering the chief industrial city of Tampere following brutal street battles in and around the city from 28 March to 6 April 1918, and Viipuri on 29 April 1918. Most of the Red leadership (the so-called People's Delegation of Finland) had fled Helsinki on 25 April, making their way to Petrograd, via Viipuri, while the few remaining Red forces retreated into south-west Finland, where their last redoubts fell by 5 May 1918. Other Red enclaves in Karelia were mopped up by 14–15 May, and the White leadership duly celebrated its victory with a huge parade in Helsinki on 16 May 1918.

According to figures produced by the Finnish National Archives, during the course of the war 5,199 Reds and 3,414 Whites were killed in action, 7,370 Reds and 1,424 Whites were executed, and 11,652 Reds and four Whites died in prison camps.[39] The very large proportion of casualties that fell victim to political terror on both sides, or (disproportionally) to neglect in White prison camps in the months following the war, thereafter created a legacy of bitterness and festering division in Finnish society that took many decades to expunge. Meanwhile, the White victors' reliance on Germany, formalized by a proposed military alliance in the summer of 1918 and the Finnish Senate's invitation on 9 October 1918 to Prince Frederick of Hesse to reign over a putative Kingdom of Finland, damaged the country's relations with the Allies following Germany's defeat in the First World War.[40] Perhaps more immediately important however, from our point of view, was that, as a consequence of the defeat of the Finnish Reds, the Bolsheviks had been deprived of a strategically useful ally on the Baltic and were faced, instead, with another potential White enemy, whose border lay only some 25 miles from the center of Petrograd.[41]

Compliance or Resistance? The Intervention of the Central Powers: Ukraine, the Baltic, and Transcaucasia

In stark contrast to the case of Finland, in Ukraine, where from early March 1918 onwards German power was all too obvious, local nationalist forces would only be tolerated by Berlin if they were abjectly obeisant: the socialist politicians of the Council of People's Ministers of the UNR were not only not that but were organizationally incapable of delivering the supplies of grain and other foodstuffs so desperately required by the Central Powers (especially by starving Austria–Hungary, where strikes and riots in Vienna made the matter especially pressing) and demanded under the terms of the first (Ukrainian) Treaty of Brest-Litovsk.[42] Consequently, they were briskly swept aside by a coup d'état on 29 April 1918 that was engineered by the supreme commander of German forces in Ukraine, Field Marshal E.G.H. von Eichhorn, and the German commandant of Kiev, General Wilhelm Groener. With the sanction of the local branch of the Union of Landlords to provide a cloak of legitimacy, the German interventionists rapidly replaced the UNR with a more compliant and conservative regime under a former guards officer of the imperial Russian Army (and aide-de-camp to Nicholas II), General P.P. Skoropadskii, who proclaimed himself "Hetman." This so-called Ukrainian State (*Ukrain'ska Derzhava*), with which the Soviet government was obliged by the Germans to make peace (by an agreement signed at Kiev on 12 June 1918), provided an unusual *entr'acte* in the Soviet–Ukrainian War: led by an entirely Russianized general of the high imperial nobility, who spoke little Ukrainian and who was surrounded by Russian generals and politicians (including many Kadets and Octobrists), it jarringly bedecked itself with the pseudo-Cossack trappings of a semi-mythologized Ukrainian national reawakening—uniforms, flags, titles, and ranks not heard of since the seventeenth century (and some of them not even then) could be espied on the boulevards of rechristened Kyiv—yet the regime was patently a German puppet.[43] The Ukrainian socialist parties, which had won an overwhelming majority of the votes cast across the region in the elections to the Constituent Assembly a few months earlier, refused almost to a man to cooperate with the new regime (which had rapidly abolished all the political and social reforms of the UNR, banned strikes, and resurrected censorship) and instead rallied around a new Ukrainian National Union, chaired from 18 September 1918 by the popular Ukrainian author and social democrat Volodymyr Vynnychenko (the former head of the General Secretariat of the Ukrainian Central Rada that had begotten the UNR). This organization arranged or supported a number of uprisings against the Hetmanate, including one in the Kiev region in June 1917 that involved some 30,000 people.

During Skoropadskii's administration, it was estimated by the Austrian foreign minister that Ukraine delivered 51,428 railway carloads of grain and other materials to the Central Powers, although that might have been an underestimate if smuggled goods are taken into account: one historian placed the true figure at 75,000 carloads (or 1,500,000 tons).[44] These expropriations, which of course caused widespread resentment among the peasantry and among the socialist intelligentsia, more than outweighed any efforts towards state-building that the Ukrainian State might have managed during its existence. Thus when Austria and then Germany collapsed in November 1918, having failed in a tardy attempt to patch together a coalition cabinet that might tempt the Allies to support him, Skoropadskii (disguised as a wounded German officer) caught the first train to Berlin and his ephemeral regime disintegrated.[45] It was replaced by a resurrected UNR in the shape of a five-man Ukrainian Directory, which had gathered at the Free Cossack base of Bila Tserkva (50 miles south of Kiev) and was dominated by the charismatic Symon Petliura and Vynnychenko. They were both founder members of the Ukrainian Social Democratic Labor Party, but nevertheless differed on numerous political issues, thereby allowing local Ukrainian military figures to assume the role of power brokers, notably Lieutenant Evhen Konovalets, commander of the Galician-Bukovina Battalion (*kurin*) of the Ukrainian Sich Riflemen.[46] This largely rendered stillborn the Directory's radical legislation on the nationalization of industry, the seizure of private estates, and so forth.

* * *

A similar pattern characterized events in the Baltic, where nationalist governments were created in the former Russian imperial provinces that covered what we now regard as Estonia, Latvia, and Lithuania. These regimes were dominated by chiefly liberal politicians, who had been scorned and sometimes persecuted or even imprisoned by the occupying Germans, but not eliminated. Consequently (and just as the Allies had hoped), the collapse of the Central Powers during the autumn of 1918 did not facilitate an immediate Red flood into a vacuum along the former western marches of the old empire—not least because German forces remained *in situ*, while within days of the Armistice (and in advance of any request for assistance for the emerging Baltic States) the British government had determined that if the new regimes should show signs of stability they should be supported "with military material."[47] When requests for assistance were received, in late November 1918, Arthur Balfour (Secretary of State for Foreign Affairs) spelt out British policy on Russia:

> For us no alternative is open at present than to use such troops as we possess to the best advantage; where we have no troops, to supply arms and money; and in the case of the Baltic provinces, to protect, as far as we can, the nascent nationalities by the use of our fleet.[48]

Thus, a week earlier, on 22 November 1918, Rear Admiral Edwyn Sinclair had received orders to proceed to the Baltic with a squadron of cruisers, destroyers, and minesweepers. Soon, from the holds of Sinclair's vessels, 5,000 rifles were handed over to the nationalist government of Konstantin Päts at Revel, while Royal Navy cruisers and battleships bombarded Red lines around Narva and ferried hundreds of anti-Bolshevik Finnish volunteers across the Gulf of Finland to Estonia.[49]

Such subsequent Red victories as were—eventually—to prevail in these north-western and south-western reaches of the former empire would clearly have to be hard fought and hard won. Moreover, although these victories would eventually prove lastingly effective in Ukraine—chiefly because the Allies remained bitingly suspicious of Kiev, as a consequence of its 1918 flirtations with Berlin (and were not even appeased by the Directory's ditching of its social-ist members in early 1919)[50]—they would not be so lasting in the Baltic, where wars of independence against Soviet Russia (as well as against local Germans, in the case of Estonia and Latvia, and the Poles in the case of Lithuania) were won by new liberal-republican regimes strongly backed by the Allies.

* * *

A similar pattern was followed in Transcaucasia, where a collapsing world war front over the winter of 1917–18 likewise complicated matters. There, on 15 November 1917, in the aftermath of the October Revolution, the Tiflis-based Transcaucasian Commissariat (heir to the Provisional Government's Special Transcaucasian Committee, Ozavkom) pronounced the autonomy of Transcaucasia and proceeded to seal a separate armistice with the Turks at Erzincan, on 5 December 1918. That agreement was remarkably favorable to the Armenians and Georgians in its (provisional) territorial terms; but the Turks were merely biding their time and those terms, unsurprisingly, were overturned by the final Treaty of Brest-Litovsk of 3 March 1918. However, Russian forces in the region also approached the final stages of disintegration in the aftermath of that settlement, so that regional leaders were obliged to take advantage of that opportunity to establish a Transcaucasian Sejm (parliament) on 26 March 1918, which on 9 April of that year declared the full independence from Russia of a Transcaucasian Democratic Republic. This loose federation of Azeris, Georgians, and Armenians (which, like the UNR, had a predominantly socialist complexion) would (again like the UNR) not outlast the incursion of decidedly anti-socialist enemy troops into the region, which began with the invasion of the Turkish Army of Islam in May–June

1918, although in this case hostilities were more inter-ethnic and inter-confessional than political.[51]

Subsequently, Azeris and Armenians, in particular, engaged in bouts of mutual bloodletting as circumstances allowed, but the presence of the Turks at least deterred any attempt by local Bolsheviks to Sovietize the region, while not extinguishing the independent democratic republics of Armenia, Georgia, and Azerbaijan that emerged in Transcaucasia from late May 1918 onwards. Indeed, just as the Germans had chased the Bolsheviks out of Revel, Riga, and Kiev, the Turkish invasion facilitated the final crushing of the forces of the Russian- (or, at least, Russianized-) and Bolshevik-dominated leadership of the Baku Commune in September 1918. This short-lived polity had held power in the Azeri capital from 13 April to 31 July 1918, in opposition first to the Transcaucasian Federation and then to the newly proclaimed Democratic Republic of Azerbaijan (whose government was consequently forced to settle, initially, in Tiflis). The Commune was dominated by Armenian, Georgian, and Russian parties and activists, consisting (initially) of eighty-five Left-SRs and other members of the PSR, forty-eight Bolsheviks, thirty-six Dashnaks, eighteen members of the Muslim Democratic Party (Musavat), and thirteen Mensheviks, and was led by the Bolshevik S.G. Shaumian. It faced numerous difficulties: notably, food shortages, isolation from Soviet Russia, inter-ethnic (especially Armenian–Azeri) tensions and massacres, and the advance on Baku of the Army of Islam and its Azeri allies. On 5 June 1918, its small and disorganized Baku Red Army repulsed a Turkish attack, but a subsequent offensive against the Turks' headquarters at Ganja (also the temporary capital of the Armenian republic) failed. In light of this, the Dashnaks, Mensheviks, and SRs decided to invite into the city the British expeditionary force (Dunsterforce), which had moved up from Persia, scraping a vote in favor of this action through the Baku Soviet on 25 July 1918.[52] The Bolsheviks then resigned from the Soviet leadership and the Commune ceased to exist. It was replaced, on 1 August 1918, by a Menshevik–SR–Dashnak coalition: the ambitiously named Central Caspian Dictatorship (Tsentrokaspyi).[53]

However, Tsentrokaspyi, despite its British support, was entirely unable to keep the Turks out of Baku, which fell to the Army of Islam on 15 September 1918. The Turkish tenure of what was then the oil-producing capital of the world was, though, never secure and turned out to be brief, allowing the opposing Armenian and Bolshevik forces to retire and regroup. Consequently, when the Ottoman Empire collapsed in October–November 1918, though mutually hostile (and in the case of the Armenians and Azeris, already in a state of war), the Transcaucasian republics were sufficiently puissant and prepared to be able to reassert their independence and to resist (for the next two years) the incursion from the north of either their Red or White opponents.[54]

That such a breathing space was enjoyed by the Transcaucasians was, in large part, a consequence of the preoccupation with each other in 1918–19 of the Red and White forces massing to the immediate north of the shelter offered to Baku, Tiflis, and Yerevan by the precipitous barrier of the Caucasus mountains. As we shall see, as soon as their hands were free (from April 1920 onwards), having defeated the Whites, Soviet forces would pour into Transcaucasia along the Black Sea and Caspian littorals and through passes in the Caucasus range that carried the Georgian Military Highway and other routes. But, for the time being, Azeris, Armenians, and Georgians were untroubled by the incursion of external forces as they assaulted each other, although the population of the North Caucasus certainly was very often troubled.[55]

The Second Kuban Campaign of the Volunteer Army and the Don Rebellion

The Volunteer Army's spirited but doomed First Kuban Campaign, as we know, had ended in defeat to Red forces before the Kuban capital of Ekaterinodar. In that campaign, General Kornilov, the Whites' and all Rightist elements' totem since the events of August 1917, lost his life to a stray shell. Having regrouped back on the Don, where in March–April 1918 a rising of the Don Cossack Host, in anticipation of the arrival of Austro-German interventionists, had driven Red forces from the southern reaches of the Cossacks' territory, including the Host's capital of Novocherkassk and the industrial centers of Rostov and Taganrog, a Second Kuban Campaign was then launched. It commenced on 23 June 1918 (under General A.I. Denikin) and aimed, again, to capture Ekaterinodar, while at the same time conveniently quarantining the pro-Allied Volunteers from encountering the Austro-German interventionists that were, by then, investing regions adjacent to the Don region. (German forces had entered Rostov-on-Don itself during the first week of May 1918.) This time the southward advance of the Volunteers went well, with combined cavalry and infantry attacks snaring a string of railway towns from Rostov to Belaia Glina. In the fighting, General Markov—another of the Bykhov generals—was fatally wounded by an artillery shell on 25 June, but subsequently 30,000 Reds were crushed at Tikhoretskaia on 15 July 1918, thereby severing the remaining Soviet forces' rail communications with the north, before the Volunteers triumphantly entered Ekaterinodar on

15 August. On 26 August 1918, the key Black Sea port of Novorossiisk also fell to the Whites, allowing new recruits to be ferried across from the Crimea (among them, significantly, General P.N. Wrangel). The Second Kuban Campaign concluded with a series of grinding battles against the massive but ill-organized Red Army of the North Caucasus and its seasoned ally, the Taman (Red) Army around Armavir and Stavropol', the latter falling to Wrangel's Kuban Cavalry on 15 November 1918. This time, though, among the 30,000 White casualties was the revered General Drozdovskii, who immediately entered the pantheon of anti-Bolshevik martyrs as various regiments were renamed in his honor.

The Volunteers were triumphant, but exhausted and much depleted, with some units (including Wrangel's 1st Cavalry Division) suffering 100 percent casualties in the course of the campaign and most at least 50 percent. For their part, the Reds had endured one of the most notable collapses in discipline among Soviet forces in the entire civil war (capped by the rebellion of Colonel I.L. Sorokin at Piatigorsk in October).[56] That all this coincided with the collapse of the Central Powers and the end of the world war seemed doubly auspicious to the Volunteers' leadership, which was now concentrated in the hands of General Denikin (Alekseev having, on 8 October 1918, succumbed to cancer and a horrible roster of other diseases and joined the roll call of dead leaders of the Volunteers).

Synchronously, with the withdrawal of almost half a million Austro-German forces from south-east Ukraine and the Don borders following the Armistice,[57] that region too came into the White orbit. Don Cossack efforts to overthrow Soviet power had begun soon after the Volunteers had departed for the Kuban in February 1918. The Bolsheviks had arrested and executed Ataman A.M. Nazarov, Kaledin's successor, along with several other Cossack generals, but this seemed only to enrage the Host, which, under its energetic and inspirational new Ataman, General P.N. Krasnov, drove Red forces from its capital, Novocherkassk, on 6 May 1918 and inspired rebellion all across the Don territory. Any Bolshevik who fell into the Cossacks' hands could expect short shrift: the chairman of the Don Soviet Republic F.G. Podtelkov and seventy-nine of his associates were summarily executed at Krasnokutskaia *stanitsa* on 11 May 1918, for example.[58] However, the reappearance of the Volunteers close to the Don aroused predictable tensions between the White leadership and the Don Cossacks, largely on account of the latter's collaboration with the Germans since the Don uprising. Yet, at least for the time being, these were brushed aside as the potential value of the Cossacks to the White cause was demonstrated by the Host authorities' ability to mobilize no less than 50,000 men by August 1918 and by the advance north-eastwards of a group of forces of the Don Army, under General K.K. Mamontov, which threatened, from mid-October 1918, to engulf, on the lower Volga, the "Red Verdun" of Tsaritsyn—the strategically vital hub through which grain and oil supplies to the Soviet north moved from the North Caucasus and from Baku and which was also the key conduit for Moscow's aid to its isolated Turkestan Group in Central Asia.[59] Thus, as the First World War closed (and, consequently, the Black Sea was opened to allow Denikin easier communications with the outside world, and specifically with the Allies), the remnants of Red forces in the North Caucasus, although now boasting the title of a full Red Army (the 11th Red Army), were almost completely isolated. Faced with imminent and total destruction, they disintegrated. A few thousand men (of what had once been a nominal Red Army presence of 120,000) managed to withdraw, chiefly towards the isolated and distant Soviet stronghold of Astrakhan, as the remainder braced themselves for destruction in the desolate plains of Kalmykia.

Apart from the superior military skills and discipline of White forces in the North Caucasus, as well as their patently stronger *esprit de corps* and devotion to their leaders (including those aforementioned iconic figures—Kornilov, Alekseev, Markov, Drozhdovstkii *et al.*—who had perished in 1918), one reason for the collapse of the forces of the North Caucasus Soviet Republic had been that, from May 1918 onwards, Moscow's attentions had been chiefly focused elsewhere—specifically, towards the middle Volga. Moreover, whereas the Volunteers (although, in a sense, building an army from scratch) were able to slot into place the personnel, practices, and *esprit* of the old army, Red forces were really being constructed from scratch in 1918, with many fewer such shortcuts available, with a variety of "revolutionary" approaches to the notion of army-building demanding a voice, and amid a spirit of distaste for all things military or militarist that was hardly conducive to the formation of what became one of the most formidable practitioners of the military art ever witnessed, the Red Army.

The Revolt of the Czechoslovak Legion and the Democratic Counter-Revolution

The emergency in eastern Russia that chiefly inspired the regularization of the Red Army was sparked by the revolt of the Czechoslovak Legion in late May 1918. The 35,000-strong Czechoslovak Legion, consisting of former prisoners of war (captured from the Austro-Hungarian Army) and some Czechs and Slovaks who had long resided in Russia, had been formed on a volunteer basis (as a *druzhina*) during the world war and had seen action in 1917 (notably at the Battle of Zborov in July 1917).[60] In January 1918 the Legion had been formally incorporated into the French Army and on 26 March that year had secured the agreement of the new Soviet government (anxious to be rid of a potential Allied fifth column) that it should leave Russia, via Vladivostok. The Legionnaires mostly wanted nothing more than to be transported out of Russia, and around the world, in order to continue their efforts for the Allied cause (and Czechoslovakian independence) on the Western Front. Throughout May 1918, however, clashes had occurred across the Volga–Urals–West Siberian stretch of the Trans-Siberian Railroad (the Legion's escape route to the east) between the heavily armed Czechs, who were nervous of being handed over to the Central Powers in the wake of the Brest-Litovsk treaty, and the equally querulous local Soviet authorities, goaded on by intemperate orders from Trotsky: apparently unaware, or uninterested, in the fact that hard-pressed local Soviet authorities had no means whatsoever of disarming the Czechs, the recently installed People's Commissar for Military Affairs ordered that they should seize the arms of the Legion and threatened those who refused to obey such inappropriate instructions with the death penalty.[61]

Although they were generally too fearful to interfere with the Czech echelons—which were positively and purposively bristling with arms, as they passed through their stations—by this time the Soviet authorities in Penza and Samara, as much as Trotsky in Moscow, wondered whether it was really such a good idea after all to dispatch these phalanxes of Allied soldiers across the Urals into areas where anti-Bolshevik Cossacks, from Orenburg to Transbaikalia, were already challenging Soviet power. This murky soup of mutual distrust was then seasoned and stirred by those with an interest in causing a rupture between the Soviet authorities and the Czechs: including Allied agents (who had been plotting for such an outcome since the mission to Petrograd in late 1917 of W. Somerset Maugham) and committed anti-Bolsheviks (such as General M.K. Diterikhs and the mercurial Radola Gajda) among the Czech command.[62] The Legionnaires themselves, as later events would demonstrate, had no wish other than to get out of Russia and to display their mettle to the Allies on the Western Front, so as to win independence for their homelands. However, following a murderous clash at Cheliabinsk on 14 May 1918, between eastbound Czechs and westbound Magyars (former POWs, who were being repatriated from camps in Siberia and Central Asia according to the terms of the Brest-Litovsk treaty), things reached boiling point, and the Legion—already primed temperamentally (if not, fully, organizationally) for action—seized the Trans-Siberian line from Samara on the Volga into Western Siberia within a few days; and, by the end of June 1918, had the eastern terminus of Vladivostok in its hands. Still, the prime concern for the Legionnaires was the securing of their own exit from the Russian quagmire, but in the chaos that was Russia in 1918, things could not be that simple.

Had the Czechoslovak revolt remained a self-contained and essentially alien phenomenon, it is possible that some sort of accommodation between the Legion's leaders and the Soviet regime might have been arrived at, or that the nascent Red Army might have chased the rebels out of Russia.[63] However, in eastern Russia, Siberia and the Far East, the revolt of the Czechoslovak Legion instead provided a nourishing environment in which the already planted seeds of domestic counter-revolution might germinate. Thus, as the revolt flowed eastwards, there emerged from the Volga–Urals–Siberian soils in which Bolshevism had never firmly taken root—the PSR, after all, had won huge majorities east of the Volga in the elections to the Constituent Assembly[64]—a string of challengers to Soviet authority (and mutual rivals to local and putative all-Russian authority), stretching from the Volga to the Pacific Ocean. At Samara, on 8 June 1918, the rule was proclaimed of a Committee of Members of the Constituent Assembly (Komuch); at Ekaterinburg, from 25 July 1918, there gathered a Provisional *Oblast'* Government of the Urals (formally constituted on 25 August 1918); and at Omsk there appeared a Western Siberian Commissariat (26 May 1918), which soon gave way to a rather more conservative (although it still, initially, contained socialists) Provisional Siberian Government (23 June 1918).[65] Actually, both the WSC and the PSG were scions of a Provisional Government of Autonomous Siberia, the regional government long dreamed of by Siberian regionalists (*oblastniki*) that had been elected by delegates of the Siberian Regional Duma at Tomsk, on 26–7 January 1918, before its aforementioned dispersal by Red Guards. Having left its "sleepers" in Siberia, the leadership of the PGAS had fled to the Far East, where it too re-emerged, somewhat incongruously (Vladivostok is around 3,500 miles from Tomsk), in the wake of the Czechs' action, to proclaim its all-Siberian authority at Vladivostok in July 1918.[66]

This so-called "democratic counter-revolution" in the east had significant local roots, symbolized by the presence in the PSG, in particular, of political and social activists of long standing who described themselves as adherents of the Siberian regionalist movement (*oblastnichestvo*) that dated back to the late nineteenth century, when, inspired by the activities of the archaeologist and ethnographer N.M. Iadrintsev and seeking to emulate the success of the anti-colonial American War of Independence, radical Siberian students (albeit mostly based in St Petersburg) had sought to establish a separate identity for their homeland as something other than a Russian colony.[67] However, in the charged post-October and post-Brest-Litovsk atmosphere, national politics, national parties, national concerns, and national ambitions soon impinged upon local affairs and many of the PSG *oblastniki* (among them the Prime Minister, P.V. Vologodskii, and the Finance Minister, I.A. Mikhailov) soon shed their skin-deep regionalism. In this regard, the forced closure of the popularly elected Siberian Regional Duma (Sibobduma) by the PSG on 16 August 1918 was symptomatic, although the fact of the matter was that even most true regionalists (including the now aged associate of Iadrintsev and doyen of the movement, G.N. Potanin) regarded the Sibobduma as a fifth column of the PSR that would always sacrifice Siberian interests before the altar of the metropolitan Russian party's all-Russian concerns.[68] Sibobduma sympathizers within the PSG, though, felt that their colleagues were using the regionalist cloak to conceal their own movement to the Right and their merger with the local Kadets, who made no secret of their centrist, statist, and nationalist predilections.[69] Certainly, any regional sympathies Siberian Kadets may have entertained were expunged over the summer of 1918 by the arrival in the region of emissaries of the underground anti-Bolshevik organizations in Moscow that the Kadets had joined in the spring of 1918. A prime mover in this regard was the Kadet Central Committee member (and Vologodskii's eventual successor as prime minister of the White government in Siberia) V.N. Pepeliaev, of the National Center. Having been roughed up by sailors at Kronshtadt, during a brief tenure there as commissar to Kotlin Island of the Provisional Government in 1917, and having then assisted Alekseev in the general's gathering of officers and cadets to face down the revolution in October 1917, Pepeliaev was sent east in the summer of the following year to found and lead the Eastern Section of the Central Committee of the Kadets that was—rather awkwardly for the Siberians—entirely devoted to the all-Russian national cause.[70]

In this struggle within the Siberian anti-Bolshevik camp, between regionalists and centrists, the emerging Siberian Army—although sporting white-and-green cockades and arm patches, as a symbol of Siberia's snows and forests—invariably offered its support to the Whites, not the Siberians, in 1918. This force was, after all, essentially an outgrowth of what remained of the structures of the imperial Russian Army's West Siberian Military District, with much of its personnel and organization intact. Even its Siberian Cossack contingents (who were far less differentiated culturally and historically from the Russians than were their counterparts on the Don, the Kuban, and the Terek) had no truck with regionalism, or even notions of Cossack autonomy, and would serve the Whites most loyally: indeed, one could say that the Siberian Cossack leadership was more White than many of the Whites (they certainly had little sympathy with the Kadets).[71] Portents here were offered by the involvement of the Siberian Army in the "Novoselov affair" in September 1918, when the regionalists' attempts to increase their number within the PSG resulted in the murder of their candidate for office (A.E. Novoselov, the *oblastnik* author and Minister of Internal Affairs in the PGAS) by Cossacks of the Omsk garrison, commanded by V.I. Volkov (and probably orchestrated by I.A. Mikhailov).[72] This praetorian intervention in many ways echoed the Kornilov affair of a year earlier; but, if anything, it was more successful. In the Omsk affair, the military were able to prevent the deepening of the revolution: a full-scale coup d'état would not occur for another eight weeks, but it is arguable that the death of Novoselov (which occasioned no more than a perfunctory investigation by the authorities and no official apportionment of guilt) marked the end of the democratic counter-revolution in Siberia.[73]

* * *

A markedly similar course of events was being played out in anti-Bolshevik camps elsewhere, albeit at different tempos. In isolated Central Asia, for example, the process extended over the greater part of a year, as the SR–Menshevik Transcaspian Provisional Government that had been established following an anti-Bolshevik Ashkhabad uprising of 11–12 July 1918 (sponsored by British forces across the Persian border at Meshed) gave way to a far more conservative Committee of Social Salvation in January 1919 which, in July 1919 accepted its incorporation into the White orbit of General Denikin's authority.[74] In Northern Russia, meanwhile, the democratic counter-revolution had adopted the countenance of a regime rather more Leftist than had been the case in Siberia—the Supreme Administration of North Russia, led by the veteran Populist N.D. Chaikovskii—but one that, oddly, was even more a creation of the Allies than the PSG: Chaikovskii's cabinet had assumed power at Arkhangel'sk on 2 August 1918, on the basis of a program inspired by the anti-Bolshevik Union for the Regeneration of Russia, but unashamedly with the connivance and intervention of British forces that had landed at the port on that day to support a military coup against the local Soviet. Within weeks, on 6 September 1918, tiring of the socialist ministers' schemes, the local military, led by a Colonel G.E. Chaplin, had toppled the Supreme Administration. Members of the Allied military missions seem to have initially encouraged this act, but then had second thoughts: Chaikovskii was freed from his incarceration in the island monastery of Solovetskii and was permitted to establish a new government, the Provisional Government of the Northern Region. Nevertheless, it was thereafter the White's Northern Army that had control of events in the Northern region and Chaikovskii, one of the totemic individuals of Russian democrats for the past half century, was obliged to retire. Eventually, Chaikovskii took his leave of the anti-Bolshevik North and went instead to Paris (to join the Russian Political Conference there, in its forlorn and frustrating endeavors to gain admission for Russian representatives to the deliberations of the Allies). On the day of Chaikovskii's departure, 1 January 1919, there duly arrived at Arkhangel'sk General E.K. Miller, who was to become military governor of the region for the remainder of the civil war in the North.[75] They must have passed each other in the harbor: socialist democracy was leaving Russia as White militarism disembarked.

* * *

Back in the east, having cowed its domestic socialist and regionalist opponents with the implicit threat of offering them a one-way ticket to join Novoselov in the "Kingdom of the Irtysh,"[76] and having buttressed its international standing by dispatching its Prime Minister, P.V. Vologodskii, to secure the support of Allied forces in the Far East,[77] the PSG prepared to take on its detested regional rival, Komuch, at a "state conference" at Ufa. This gathering was mooted as a forum of conciliation within the anti-Bolshevik camp, but was actually much less—and, at the same time, much more—than that.

The rivalry between the PSG and Komuch operated at several levels, but was driven, from Omsk's point of view, by the fact that the Samara regime was almost uniformly led by members of the PSR.[78] Moreover, these were members of the PSR who, for the most part, even remained unencumbered by ties to the Union of Regeneration and other cross-party bodies that were working to resurrect the coalition politics of 1917: instead, they sought their own unilateral and independent (socialist) authority. Worse still, they regarded a legitimate aim of the struggle against Soviet power to be the resurrection of the Constituent Assembly elected in November 1917 that—with its SR majority, sizable Bolshevik caucus, and all but invisible non-socialist contingent—would formalize socialist dominance of a future Russian state. This was anathema to the leaders of the PSG (now dominated, in Vologodskii's absence, by the mercurial—his enemies would say scheming—I.A. Mikhailov) and was a red rag to the reactionary bulls of the Siberian military.

So, although the Ufa State Conference duly convened (from 8 to 23 September 1918)—and, compared to its raucous and divisive precursor at Moscow in August 1917, convened in apparent harmony—it, and its outcome, were a sham. There were reported to be 160–70 delegates present, from a variety of political parties, social organizations, and local and minority-nationality authorities, but neither of the chief protagonists was sincere in its offerings: both Komuch and the PSG had been forced to the negotiating table by the Allies' threats of withdrawing support and by fears aroused upon the advance of Soviet forces across the Volga in September 1918 (see below). What emerged from the conference—a coalition regime, the Ufa Directory, claiming all-Russian authority—was hailed as a triumph for the Union of Regeneration, good sense, and good compromise, but it was none of these. For Komuch and its allies, the SRs elected as members of the Directory (N.D. Avksent'ev and V.M. Zenzinov) had long since sacrificed their *bona fides* as party members (and even as socialists) in favor of their predilection for coalition with the Kadets (both, of course, were founder members and mainstays of the URR), while the very existence of the regime was an affront to Komuch's claim to be the true government of all Russia, on the basis of the democratic credentials of its members accorded by their election to the Constituent Assembly in 1917.[79] Needless to say, the extreme Right and the military looked upon the whole affair with a mixture of disdain and alarm, but even eminent Kadets who had been committed to the creation of a coalition directory were dismayed by this one: for them, there were too many members (five, not the three his party had endorsed by joining the National Center and the Union of Regeneration), noted N.I. Astrov, and its military member had insufficient power (and was, to compound the sin, the notorious friend of the socialists V.G. Boldyrev, not a hardliner, such as General Alekseev, that he had been promised). Finally, and most damningly, Astrov charged, the Ufa conference had admitted the possibility of a reconvention of the Constituent Assembly of 1917: "I shall not enter into a debate as to whether that assembly was good or bad," he remonstrated in a letter from South Russia, abruptly refusing to accept the seat on the Ufa Directory that had been reserved for him, "I shall merely point out that it simply does not exist and to build an all-Russian government on the basis of it is the grandest of illusions."[80] He had a point.

So, just as in February 1917, in Petrograd, nobody had got the revolution they wanted, in September 1918, at Ufa, nobody got the counter-revolution they wanted. But time was now moving faster: the progeny of February, the Provisional Government, lasted eight months; the offspring of Ufa, the Directory, lasted barely eight weeks. Its demise was definitely hastened by the Directors' decision to relocate immediately to Omsk, the capital of the PSG and the headquarters of the Siberian Army. Its SR members were not so naïve as to fail to recognize that this relocation was implicitly perilous: "We must put our heads in the lion's mouth," N.D. Avksent'ev informed critics of the move. "Either it will eat us or we will choke it."[81] But, given the situation at the front, where Soviet forces were approaching the western slopes of the Urals by late September 1918, it was probably necessary. Yet nobody was surprised when, on 18 November 1918, the Siberian lion duly swallowed the meek Directory in a coup d'état organized by local Kadets, Cossacks, and leaders of the Siberian Army (with at least the tacit encouragement of the British Military Mission at Omsk).[82] In its stead was established a military dictatorship led by a "supreme ruler,"[83] Admiral A.V. Kolchak, which promised the restoration of order, the merciless expunging of Bolshevism in all its forms from Russian life, the re-establishment of a "Russia, One and Indivisible," and a prioritization of the needs of the army.[84]

This was just the sort of menu for which the Russian military and political Right had been hungering since the abortive Kornilov coup of August 1917. Whether it was a recipe for either political or military success remained to be seen, but in the short term, at least, the signs were positive: the abducted Directors meekly accepted their fate (and in the case of the socialists were quietly ushered into exile); swayed by their pro-Kolchak commanders, the men of the Czechoslovak Legion (who were generally supportive of the PSR and socialism in general) declined to intervene again in Russian politics in order to resurrect the Directory; the dregs of Komuch (in the guise of a Congress of Members of the Constituent Assembly) were mopped up and imprisoned at Ekaterinburg or fled; a Bolshevik-inspired uprising against the new Kolchak government, in mid-December 1918, was a shambles, with the local party subsequently decimated; and, after an initial bluster of protest, Ataman Semenov, now based threateningly astride the Trans-Siberian Railroad at Chita, reluctantly subordinated himself to Kolchak.[85] The accession of the Supreme Ruler was immediately greeted with great warmth by the heads of Cossack hosts east of the Urals, by the command of the Siberian Army, local councils of trade and industry, and so on, and, subsequently, as the news spread, by their equivalents elsewhere, including (on 18 February 1919) the *krug* (assembly) of the Don Cossack Host.[86] Even the Allies refrained from openly criticizing the brazen toppling of a semi-democratic regime that at least one of them had been on the point of recognizing as the legitimate government of Russia.[87]

Militarily, too, as fall turned to winter on the Urals front, the omens for the Siberian Whites were good. The politicking and horse-trading that characterized the eastern anti-Bolshevik camp in the summer and early fall of 1918 had, for the most part, played itself out far from the front line, in the relatively peaceful haven of Western Siberia and the Urals from which the Bolsheviks had fled in May–June of that year: hence the contrast with the more unabashedly militaristic character of the anti-Bolshevik movement in South Russia described above. Yet it was the eastern military too that, ultimately, were to call the shots. The Siberian Army, augmented by refugee officers who had chosen to move east (some of them having deserted from Komuch's People's Army en route), rather than south to join the Volunteers, had swelled to a complement of almost 40,000 by September 1918. This force, latterly commanded by the talented but hubristic Radola Gajda (recently precipitously promoted from captain in the Montenegrin army to major-general in the White forces) was then deployed (with its headquarters at Ekaterinburg) to replace the retiring Czechoslovak Legion in the northern Urals, to face Bolshevik formations around Perm'. It would capture that important regional and industrial center, to great acclaim, on 24–5 December 1918.[88] Since June 1918, however, the bulk of anti-Bolshevik military endeavors in eastern Russia had fallen to formations of the Czechoslovak Legion and units fashioned into a People's Army by Komuch that took to the field alongside the Czechs on the Volga.

Komuch's People's Army grew from a dense web of underground officer groups that had existed since early 1918 in the Volga Military District, as the new and febrile Soviet authorities struggled to assert control of these peripheral (and, in terms of the Constituent Assembly elections in 1917, solidly SR) provinces. With the revolt of the Czechoslovak Legion, these anti-Bolshevik cells emerged, in early June 1918, under the command of Colonel N.A. Galkin (supported by a staff led by the SR Colonel V.I. Lebedev and Komuch member B.B. Fortunatov). Following negotiations with Major Stanislav Čeček, commander of the Legion's 1st Division, a joint Czech–Komuch Volga Front was soon established, centered on Samara, which, in a series of lightening operations, succeeded in driving Red forces from the important regional centers of Ufa (5 July 1918), Simbirsk (22 July 1918), and Kazan' (7 August 1918). The last of these victories was of particular significance: on the one hand, at Kazan' had been stored about half of the Imperial Russian Gold Reserve, which now fell into the hands of the anti-Bolsheviks in the east;[89] on the other, as Trotsky recognized from his vantage point at Sviiazsk (on the opposite bank of the Volga), with Kazan' in their hands and with Red forces in such disarray—actually in "a state of psychological collapse," as the war commissar put it, dodging bullets while threatening left and right to execute commissars and commanders who failed to rally their troops—the road to Moscow lay wide open before the People's Army and "the fate of the revolution was hanging by a thread."[90]

The causes of Trotsky's discomfort are not difficult to fathom. The collapse of Red efforts in the east since May–June 1918 had been hastened by the aforementioned revolt at Simbirsk against Soviet power (in the name of continuing the war against Germany) that had been staged on 10–11 July 1918 by none other than the commander of the Reds' recently organized Eastern Front, the Left-SR M.A. Murav'ev.[91] This had been accompanied by a disastrous collapse in morale among key units, particularly the exhausted 4th Regiment of the Latvian Riflemen, hitherto among the most effective of Red forces, which in mid-July simply abandoned Syzran' and refused to advance on Simbirsk.[92] Worryingly for the Soviet command, all this coincided not only with the uprising against the creeping authoritarianism of the Bolsheviks that was staged in Moscow on 6 July 1918 by their former partners in Sovnarkom, the Party of Left Socialists-Revolutionaries (who were also strongly opposed to the treaty with Germany), but with a series of revolts organized at Iaroslavl' and surrounding towns engineered by B.V. Savinkov—the enigmatic former SR terrorist and (in 1917) champion of Kornilov, who was now in command of an extensive network of (partly Allied-financed) anti-Bolshevik officer organizations across Russia that he called the Union for Defense of the Fatherland and Freedom.[93] That these widespread revolts were followed by Allied landings at ports as disparate as Vladivostok, Krasnovodsk, and Arkhangel'sk in early August and by the arrival of representatives of Norperforce at Ashkhabad (10 August 1918) and of Dunsterforce at Baku (14 August 1918), then by the assassination of the Cheka boss Moisei Uritskii by SR terrorists at Petrograd on 30 August 1918, and the attempted assassination of Lenin that same day in Moscow, could hardly have calmed the Bolsheviks' nerves. Indeed, the Soviet government responded by unleashing a wave of Red Terror in Moscow that claimed hundreds of the lives of its domestic opponents (and alleged and potential opponents) within a few days. The Bolshevik leadership then revealed the existence of the so-called "Lockhart Plot"—the Cheka's uncovering of the contacts Allied diplomats in Moscow had forged with the anti-Bolshevik underground, and their plans for joint action against the Soviet government, and for subverting the Latvian Riflemen—which completely ruptured Bolshevik relations with the Allies. These events should be borne in mind as an essential background to the frantic battles on the Eastern Front in the autumn of 1918.[94]

These, though, were really symptoms of the Reds' malaise, rather than its root cause. That root cause lay in the fact that it was only during the summer of 1918, on the Eastern Front, as these alarming events unfolded, that the Red Army in the form that was eventually to prevail in the civil wars was somewhat belatedly busy being born.

The Birth of the Red Army

The gestation of the Red Army lasted, appropriately, nine months. It began in November–December 1917, with the efforts of the first Soviet commander-in-chief, Ensign N.V. Krylenko, to disorganize the old army (so as to neutralize real and potential nests of counter-revolution), and gave issue on the Volga in August–September 1918. Krylenko's efforts towards creating a revolutionary force first involved him standing by as a revolutionary mob at Mogilev lynched his predecessor as main army commander, General N.N. Dukhonin. It then entailed an avalanche of decrees canceling all ranks and titles, permitting the election of officers, expanding the competences of soldiers' committees, and ordering the demobilization of one class of conscript after another, and culminated in the order for a general demobilization of the old army on 29 January 1918.[95] There were ideological factors at work here too, naturally: before October, like most socialists, the Bolsheviks generally despised militarism and regarded the standing army as the chief instrument of state oppression of the individual and of the organized working class. For them, especially those consolidating around N.I. Bukharin, A.S. Bubnov, and V.M. Smirnov as the nucleus of the Left Bolsheviks within the party, one of the essential purposes of the revolution was to destroy the army and replace it with an accountable and democratic militia system.[96] As advocates of the untapped potential for revolutionary creativity of the proletariat, the Left further considered that any subsequent conflict, either domestic or international, would be conducted according to quite different principles of organization and strategy—a concept they dubbed "revolutionary war"—in which what would count would not be military training or experience but the unstoppable and incorruptible élan of the workers-in-arms.

The initial "troops" (*otriady*) of volunteers organized by Bolsheviks, in and around Petrograd and other cities in early 1918, conformed to this romantic ideal. As one of these organizers recalled: "They were usually not like regular army units, but were guerrilla troops in the full sense of the word. They bore original and sometimes fantastic names. Thus, there was a troop that called itself 'The Ruthless', and another that took the name 'The Wolf Pack'."[97] The former tsarist general (and subsequent Soviet commander) F.F. Novitskii quizzically observed this phenomenon:

> The Red Army. Crop-headed fellows with service caps on the backs of their heads, wearing unbuttoned soldiers' greatcoats and rifles slung over their right shoulders, trudging along the pavements of Petrograd in a noisy crowd ... Sentries at their posts of duty, sitting on stools or on the thresholds of porches, their rifles between their knees, peacefully chatting with passers-by ... This is what the workers' and peasants' army looks like ... We who are used to the well-drilled movements, the order and discipline of the old army cannot reconcile ourselves to this lack of discipline, this sloppiness of the revolutionary soldiers.

Yet, sensibly, Novitskii recognized that the embryo of something vital was there before him:

> Nevertheless, I observe these new phenomena with great interest, and I find in them much that is original, distinctive and colourful, and I receive many impressions that reconcile me to them and impel me to adopt a more thoughtful and serious attitude towards them. You smile? You think I am joking? Not at all. I say this with absolute conviction. Of course the present profile of the Red Army pains the eyes of a professional soldier, but in all this outward disorganization there is nevertheless something revolutionary, a sort of contemporary style.

And, at least, he concluded, "this is not the old army in a decayed condition," as it was post-February 1917:

> I saw and observed the old army closely in those memorable days when it had already disintegrated, when discipline had vanished, when well-drilled units turned into a disorderly mob. And that was something quite different from the disorder that we see today. Outwardly, the two things may seem identical—untidy dress, lack of respect for rank, careless performance of military duties: but *that* was the disorderliness of an order that had broken down, whereas *this* is the disorderliness of a structure that has not yet been put together. *There* one smelt decay, one tasted death: *here* we have the chaos of a new, clumsy process of construction and of uncompleted, not yet finally established forms.[98]

This was at the same time uncommonly prescient regarding the potential of the revolutionary army and all too accurate regarding its current prowess. The Bolsheviks' major problem, though, was that too few volunteers were coming forward. The People's Commissar for Military Affairs N.I. Podvoiskii had expected 300,000 willing recruits in February 1918, but only around 20,000 were mustered (a third of them from Petrograd).[99]

Nevertheless, the disastrous showing of these meager Red volunteer forces during the Soviet–German "Eleven-Days' War" of February–March 1918, as the Germans pressed north-eastwards (virtually unopposed) to compel the Soviet government to sign a formal peace treaty at Brest-Litovsk on 3 March 1918, together with the simultaneous expulsion of Soviet forces from Kiev, did not immediately disabuse the Left of their rose-tinted visions of revolutionary warfare.[100] But it certainly seems to have had that impact upon Trotsky, who in the aftermath of the treaty was named as People's Commissar for Military Affairs on 14 March 1918. Or, rather, as the German Army sliced through Soviet defenses as if they did not exist—and, for the most part, they were non-existent—Trotsky was not only obliged to discount (for the time being) as unrealistic any hope that such a naked display of imperialist bullying might rouse the specter of revolution in Berlin and Vienna, but also confirmed in him the confidence to prioritize—in the task of building more effective defenses—issues of order, routine, hierarchy, and discipline that were central to his character and style as a revolutionary. These character traits would remain with him, at the very forefront of his conduct—personal and professional—throughout the rest of his life.[101] Thus, on 19 March 1918, Trotsky opened a speech to the Moscow Soviet with the exhortation, "Comrades! Our Soviet Socialist Republic needs a well-organized army," and went on to assert that:

> While we were fighting with the Kaledinites we could successfully remain content with units which had been put together in haste. Now, however, in order to cope with the creative work of reviving the country ... in order to ensure the security of the Soviet Republic under conditions of international counter-revolutionary encirclement, such units are already inadequate. *We need a properly and freshly organized army!*[102]

This imprecation was subsequently expanded upon in the notes penned in 1920 by N.I. Bukharin and E.A. Preobrazhenskii, entitled *Azbuka kommunizm* ("The ABC of Communism"), a guide to the 1918 program of the RKP(b). Struggling to justify the party's newfound commitment to the establishment of a standing army, the authors of this seminal text muddied the water by initially claiming that the former demands of all socialist parties for the abolition of such armed forces were made only under the bourgeois order and were "only applicable for the very brief period during which the pre-existing bourgeois standing army is being broken up," which was clearly not what Lenin had had in mind in his aforementioned appeals to the party of April and September 1917.[103] The Left Bolshevik editors of the *Azbuka* were on much safer and more comfortable ground, though, in explaining why a standing army was necessary in the existing Soviet republic:

> It is necessary to remember that socialism cannot gain the victory in simultaneously in all countries of the world. Some countries will, of course, lag behind the others in the matter of abolishing class and of realizing socialism. In such circumstances, the countries in which the bourgeoisie has been overthrown ... may have to fight or be prepared to fight against the bourgeoisies of those States in which the dictatorship of the proletariat has not yet been established; or they may have to give armed assistance to the proletariat of those lands in which the dictatorship of the working class has been inaugurated but in which the struggle with the bourgeoisie has not yet been carried to a successful issue.

In other words, they continued: "Other socialists, though they recognized the inevitability of a forcible transformation effected by the armed workers, failed nevertheless to foresee that this armed struggle would be long drawn out, that Europe would have to pass through a phase, not only of socialist revolutions, but also of socialist wars."[104] If we substitute the words "revolutionary wars" for "socialist wars" in the foregoing, we may understand how it was that, despite lingering qualms, stalwarts of Left Bolshevism such as Bukharin and Preobrazhenskii, who had been in such trenchant opposition to Lenin over the Treaty of Brest-Litovsk, were able to re-accommodate themselves to the party by the summer of 1918, as circumstances now offered them the general, anti-imperialist conflagration they had wished for some months earlier. For the Bolshevik Left, the creation of the Red Army could be justified on the grounds that, without it, "It is perfectly clear that the Russian workers and peasants would have been crushed by the forces of reaction at home and abroad."[105] This, though, was *post facto* justification, written from hindsight in 1920; in 1918, there remained some bitter pills yet to be swallowed by the Bolsheviks, especially those of the Left.

In an address of 28 March 1918 to a Moscow city conference of the RKP(b) (subsequently published as a pamphlet, under the self-explanatory title *Work, Discipline and Order will Save the Soviet Republic*), Trotsky focused on what he euphemistically termed the "ticklish matter" and "sore point" in party discussions that, for him, had to be at the heart of the new army:

the question of drawing military specialists, that is, to speak plainly, former officers and generals, into the work of creating and administering the Army. All the fundamental, leading institutions of the Army are now so constructed that they consist of one military specialist and two political commissars. This is the basic pattern of the Army's leading organs.

It followed, for Trotsky, that:

Given the present regime in the Army—I say this here quite openly—the principle of election is politically purposeless and technically inexpedient, and it has been, in practice, abolished by decree.[106]

To indicate that he meant business, on 31 March 1918 Trotsky appointed to the Supreme Military Council (SMC) of the Red Army none other than Rear Admiral D.N. Verderevskii, who had been Minister of Marine in the last configuration of the Provisional Government of 1917, and who had been placed under arrest by the Bolsheviks during the October Revolution together with other of Kerensky's ministers found cowering in the Malachite Room of the Winter Palace.[107] Within a few weeks, more than 8,000 former officers were serving in the Red ranks, and, by the end of 1918, 30,000 of them were employed—not as "officers" but, to spare Bolshevik blushes, as "military specialists" (*voenspetsy*)—a disproportionate number of them being graduates of the imperial Academy of the General Staff.[108] There were, of course, cases of treachery and mass desertion by *voenspetsy* (notably when virtually the entire faculty of the Academy of the General Staff itself went over to the enemy on the Volga during the summer of 1918), which fed the fires of opprobrium that leftist party radicals felt for this "treachery" to proletarian principles. Also, Trotsky's wish, expressed in an article of 31 December 1918 eulogizing "The Military Specialists and the Red Army," that he was returning to the topic "for the last time, I hope," was not realized: residual Left Bolshevik resentment at such confounding of revolutionary purity remained widespread (and was voiced with great bitterness at a conference of Bolshevik army delegates in late March 1919).[109] Critics of the employment of *voenspetsy* could point out that it had, after all, been stated in the Sovnarkom decree of 3 January 1918, which first mentioned the creation of such a force, that "The Red Army of Workers and Peasants will be formed from the most conscious and organized elements of the working masses"—a definition that hardly encompassed the employment of the military elite of tsarist Russia.[110] Debates around this issue would become particularly vitriolic and divisive at the Eighth Congress of the Bolshevik Party in March 1919, where concessions had to be made to Trotsky's opponents in order to defuse a sizable "Military Opposition" within the

RKP(b). This loosely organized group was demanding that military commissars be afforded a greater role in decision-making within the army and that party institutions should assume a larger role in directing a Red Army that was increasingly manned by conscripted peasants.[111] And, even as late as 1920, in an otherwise predictably positive review of Red Army institutions, Bukharin and Preobrazhenskii felt obliged to record in their aforementioned *Azbuka* that "The utilization of the officers of the old army involved difficulties which were grave, and which have not yet been overcome," as "their utilization entailed terrible dangers, for it occasionally involved widespread treachery on the part of the officers, and enormous sacrifices of the Red soldiers, who were betrayed and handed over in masses to the enemy."[112] Although it was claimed at the time, by Trotsky, that only five out of eighty-two *voenspetsy* army commanders ever deserted,[113] a more recent investigation of materials in the Russian archives has established that some 549 highly valued general staff officers (*genshtabisty*) deserted from the Red Army in the period from 1918 to 1921, and that, in total, almost one in three *voenspetsy* managed to flee to the "enemy."[114] Yet, despite this debilitating and dangerous hemorrhage, and despite the lingering qualms of the Leftists, at least the principle of utilizing officers and experts had been firmly established, and the majority of officers employed in the Red Army (including 613 *genshtabisty*) remained, however steadfastly or reluctantly, at their posts. As Trotsky noted in January 1919:

> We have often cited betrayals and defections of command personnel to the enemy camp. There were many such defections, mainly on the part of officers who held less prominent positions. However, we rarely speak about how many whole regiments were destroyed because of the lack of combat training of command personnel, because of the fact that the regimental commander was unable to adjust communications, did not set up an ambush or field guard, did not understand an order, or could not read a map. If we ask what until now has done us the most harm—the betrayal of former officers or the lack of training of many new officers—I would personally find it difficult to answer this.[115]

One senses a certain coyness here on Trotsky's part. He knew he had won the argument, but did not scour his critics too deeply. This was quite uncharacteristic of a man who, in general, liked to beat his opponents into a pulp with words, perhaps indicating just how contentious this issue was.

Contributing to Trotsky's uncharacteristically reserved attitude here, moreover, was that during the so-called "Tsaritsyn Affair" of the fall of 1918, in a clash over command in the campaign against the advance of the Don Cossacks—between those who generally valued the *voenspetsy* (such as Trotsky) and those who instinctively distrusted them (in this case, J.V. Stalin and K.E. Voroshilov)—the war commissar had already won a key battle of wills (and, critically, the support of Lenin) to establish that, unless compelling evidence could be produced to indicate otherwise, the expertise and loyalty of the *voenspetsy* should be acknowledged and their orders obeyed.[116] That expertise and loyalty was a factor weighing heavily in the balance of forces that won the Red Army so many victories in the civil wars: the Whites, although perhaps correctly calculating that most *voenspetsy* were serving "for a crust of bread" or for other such materialistic matters and were secretly wishing for the collapse of Soviet power, were certainly wrong so frequently to dismiss the service they provided as thereby inherently negligible.[117]

Finally, Left Bolshevik (and Left-SR) irritations were at least partly salved by a second, truly revolutionary aspect of the new army: the appointment of military commissars to all units. Although this office was based on the far-distant precedent of a similarly named institution at the time of the French revolutionary wars, and while the Provisional Government of 1917 had also named its special plenipotentiaries at the front and in the regions "commissars," the military (or political) commissar of the Red forces was something new and something else. It was, in fact, one of the key martial innovations of the Reds during the civil wars. According to an order, signed by Trotsky on 6 April 1918:

> The military commissar is the direct political organ of Soviet power in the army. His post is one of exceptional importance. Commissars are appointed from among irreproachable revolutionaries, capable of remaining under the most difficult circumstances, the embodiment of revolutionary duty ... The military commissar must see to it that the army does not become disassociated from the Soviet system as a whole and that particular military institutions do not become centres of conspiracy or instruments to be used against the workers and peasants. The commissar takes part in all the work of the military leaders, receives reports and dispatches along with them, and counter-signs orders. War Councils will give effect only to such orders as have been signed not only by military leaders but also by at least one military commissar. All work is done with the cognizance of the commissar, but leadership in the specifically military sphere is the task not of the commissar but the military specialist working shoulder to shoulder with him. The commissar is not responsible for the expediency of purely military, operational, combat orders ... In the event that he disapproves of a purely military instruction, the commissar is not to delay its application, but merely to report his disapproval of it to the War Council immediately above him.[118]

Two days later, with the aim of standardizing the activities of military commissars across the country (and of ensuring control over them), on 8 April

1918 the People's Commissariat for Military Affairs proclaimed the formation of the All-Russian Bureau of Military Commissars (Vsebiurvoenkom).

In terms of army administration, the aforementioned Supreme Military Council was at the apex of a still nebulous command hierarchy of what was becoming, in the first half of 1918, the "Worker–Peasant Red Army": this new, revolutionary armed force had been first mentioned by (a similar) name in a Sovnarkom decree of 3 January 1918 ("On the Formation of Workers' and Peasants' Red Army"), but did not begin to become a living reality until its founding units were mustered from 23 February of that year (a date subsequently celebrated as "Red Army Day" in Soviet Russia). The Supreme Military Council itself replaced the improvised Revolutionary Field Staff, which at Krylenko's behest had managed affairs at the front since 27 November 1917, retreating from Mogilev to Orel during the Soviet–German Eleven-Days' War and disbanding there on 12 March 1918. The SMC was established by an order of Sovnarkom of 4 March 1918, and given the tasks of providing strategic leadership to the armed forces of the Soviet Republic and overseeing the building of the Red Army. It initially consisted of several senior military specialists, watched over by two military commissars, but, having moved with the rest of the Soviet central administration from Petrograd to Moscow (fearing capture by the still advancing Germans and White Finns), its composition was expanded from 19 March 1918 to include all senior military commanders and their deputies, the quartermaster-general and representatives of the operational staffs, military intelligence sections, and so on of the Red fronts and armies. Also, from 19 March 1918, the institution was chaired by the people's commissar for military affairs (that is, from 28 March 1918, by Trotsky) and the role of commissars within it was then annulled, but the most important figure within the establishment was its director, the former tsarist officer Major-General M.D. Bonch-Bruevich, who was Trotsky's closely trusted aide.[119] The institution was abolished on 6 September 1918 and was replaced by the Revvoensovet (Revolutionary Military Soviet, or Council) of the Republic (RVSR), which restored some of the influence of senior commissars.

Thus the new Red Army had some central, strategic direction (greatly aided by the fact that the Soviet government had inherited, wholesale, the central administrative apparatus and personnel of the old army—from telegraphists to typewriters).[120] The Whites were far less fortunate in this respect, having to rely upon the meager resources of the outlying military districts of tsarist times to which they had been confined. From May 1918, the nascent Red Army could also begin to draw upon a steadier stream of recruits, as a general mobilization was instituted and the volunteer principle was abandoned, although the registration of those eligible was rudimentary and the non-appearance and desertion of mobilized men remained a problem (see below, pp. 89–91). The new Soviet force retained, however, certain damaging dualities and even introduced new ones. Thus an element of administrative and command confusion was inculcated by the fact that the All-Russian Main Staff (Vseroglavshtab), created on 8 May 1918 (to replace the former All-Russian Collegium for the Formation of the Red Army, the main Directorate of the General Staff, and other bodies), was subordinated not to the SMC but to the Collegium of the People's Commissariat for Military Affairs. This confusion would only be overcome, at the height of the blows inflicted on the Reds by Czechoslovak and Komuch forces on the Volga, by measures flowing from the VTsIK proclamation of 2 September 1918, "On Declaring the Soviet Republic to be an Armed Camp," including the creation for the first time of a post of main commander-in-chief (2 September 1918) and the subordination of Vseroglavshtab (from 6 September 1918) to the newly formed RVSR.[121] Henceforth, all Red fronts, armies, and military organizations and institutions, at the front and in the rear, operational and administrative, were subordinated to the RVSR, which included a revamped Field Staff among its departments and remained the highest military authority of Soviet Russia throughout the civil-war years.[122] On 11 September 1918, the RVSR then devised a formal structure for the entire Red Army, which was initially divided into five armies, each with eleven divisions of between six and nine regiments (plus reserve units), grouped around three fronts (the Northern Front, the Eastern Front, and the Southern Front) and the Western Fortified Area.[123]

The coordinating organs of the Red Army were then topped-off, following a VTsIK decree of 30 November 1918, with the formation of the Council of Workers' and Peasants' Defense (from April 1920, the Council of Labor and Defense, the STO).[124] This body, which was chaired (*ex officio*) by Lenin and included Trotsky (as chair of the RVSR, although he was rarely available to attend its meetings), Stalin (as the representative of VTsIK), and several people's commissars of the most interested commissariats, was created by Sovnarkom but was coequal to it, as STO directives were considered to be the equivalent of state laws.[125] It played no part in the formation of military strategy, but STO sought instead to direct and coordinate the work of all economic commissariats with all institutions having a stake in the defense of Soviet Russia and had subordinate organizations at provincial, district, and even village level (although few of the last of these made any meaningful contribution). In the circumstances of a confusion of civil wars, it managed that task with relative success.

* * *

More—and potentially even more damaging—confusions, however, surrounded the very purpose of the new Red Army, which again contributed directly to the crisis on the Volga in the summer of 1918. The issue here was whether the object of the new force was to fight the Central Powers and thereby (implicitly) to continue the world war, or to defend the revolution against the incipient internal counter-revolution. Most of the *voenspetsy*, it is certain, initially regarded the new army as a rejuvenated instrument of national defense against Germany, Austria–Hungary, Bulgaria, and Turkey and would not have agreed to serve in it on other terms. Once recruited, though, as Evan Mawdsley put it, this acted for officers "as a bridge—a one-way bridge—to the service of the Soviet regime and to battles on the 'internal' front."[126] Inducements to cross that bridge appeared, initially, in the form of carrots (the lingering post-Brest-Litovsk hope that Soviet Russia might yet rejoin the Allied cause) and, later, sticks (the introduction of compulsory military service for former officers on 29 July 1918 and the use of their families as hostages against their loyalty). Admixtures of inertia, potential poverty, and a bizarre sort of professional pride in not allowing political ructions to disturb the armed services also played their parts.[127] Many military specialists, though, required few inducements to join what, quite early on in the civil wars, began to look increasingly like the national army of Russia (or whatever it was that was going to replace the old empire).[128] A.F. Il'in-Zhenevskii, then working in the War Commissariat, recalled that (apparently sometime in February–March 1918): "I was visited by a relation of my wife's, a former officer, who said that he too wanted to take part in the defence of Petrograd. 'I must tell you straight,' he said, 'that by conviction I am a monarchist, but I can't let the Finns take Petrograd.'" The tsarist officer was duly assigned to a construction team. "The next time I saw him he literally roared with laughter," Il'in-Zenevskii continued: "'Do you know where you sent me?' he said. 'In that construction team we are all monarchists. I've fallen in with my own set, as it were.'"[129]

Resolving the issues of command and control, moreover, did not entirely clarify the issue of strategic purpose. Initially, from March to June 1918, most of the new Soviet regime's efforts were directed westwards, towards the creation of defensive "screens" to protect Petrograd (the Northern Screen) and

Moscow (the Western Screen) against anticipated further incursions by the Germans and Austrians. It was in that direction—to the west—that were deployed the early volunteers for the Red Army, from January to March of 1918, and the conscripts (although there were disappointingly few of them) who came forward following a Sovnarkom decree proclaiming Universal Military Training (*Vsevobuch*) on 22 April 1918, and the introduction of conscription on 29 May 1918.[130] After that, for several months inertia determined that undue weight, in terms of the deployment of men and equipment, was still given to the west: in short, during and following the Czechoslovak revolt in May–June 1918, the Red Army was simply facing the wrong way, which contributed significantly to the disastrous defeats of July–August of that year along the Volga and in Siberia. As Trotsky bluntly recorded in a report from Sviiashk to the Supreme Military Council of 7–9 August 1918, "The slow rate of arrival of reinforcements constituted the principal, direct cause of the Kazan' catastrophe."[131]

This circumstance gravely alarmed the new commander of the Eastern Front, Colonel Jukums Vācietis—one of the very first of the *genshtabisty* to side with the Bolsheviks after the October revolution[132]—who set to work making more effective (in contrast to the piecemeal efforts of April–May) the mobilization in June 1918 of men of the 1883–97 age groups of the Volga–Urals region (from fifty-one districts, in all). More effective again was a general mobilization across the Soviet zone of the 1898 and then the 1893–97 age groups that was organized in September 1918, to meet the threat on the Volga (which saw many committed Bolshevik workers sent east from the industrial towns of central Russia). Between 25 July and 18 August 1918, against the advice of Bonch-Bruevich (who remained overly obsessed with the Germans, though these actually had their hands too full in attempting to occupy and exploit Ukraine to allow for schemes involving attacks on Russia), more than 30,000 men were transferred from the northern and western screens to the Eastern Front. Thus by October 1918 the Eastern Front (now composed, from north to south, of the 3rd, 2nd, 5th, 1st, and 4th Red Armies) mustered a total of 103,000 men. It was also given priority for the supply of heavy guns and machine-guns and many vessels were transferred from the Baltic Fleet, through the Mariinsk Canal System, to create a crucially effective Volga Military Flotilla. It was these forces that, in operations we may with hindsight deem to have been key to the eventual outcome of the civil wars, recaptured Kazan' on 10 August 1918 (the 5th Red Army) and Simbirsk on 12 August 1918 (the 1st Red Army). On 7–8 October 1918, Samara too, Komuch's capital, fell to the Reds.[133]

In the midst of these events, on 2 September 1918, Vācietis was promoted to main commander-in-chief (*glavkom*) of the Red Army (and Bonch-Bruevich was quietly shunted aside).[134] Also, as we have seen, the command structure beneath the *glavkom* was re-forged, with the creation on 6 September 1918 of the RVSR, chaired by Trotsky, to coordinate operational and administrative affairs. The practices that were tried and tested in the east were then reproduced elsewhere: Red armies were grouped into fronts;[135] *revvoensovets* were established for each army (from 12 December 1918); military commissars were assigned to shadow commanders and to offer ideological guidance and motivation to Red forces; and regular units finally displaced almost all irregular ("partisan") formations. The structure of the Red Army that would eventually emerge victorious from the wars was thus essentially in place before the end of the first year of serious struggle. Moreover, with control of the heartland of the old empire firmly established, the Soviet regime was able to draw upon the stocks of supplies meant for the old army—supplies that had had to be stretched to breaking point in 1916–17 to maintain a force of some 10 million but would provide rich pickings for a Red Army that would never put in the field more than 5 percent of such a figure.

Yet, for the Reds, in late 1918 victory remained a long way off. The sudden collapse of the Central Powers in October–November of that year offered opportunities: it deprived the Allies, for example, of their justification for the allegedly non-political intervention in Russia and inspired dreams of journeys home for those troops unlucky enough to be caught in the Russian mire (especially for the Czechoslovaks, who had a newly independent homeland awaiting them from 28 October 1918); and it deprived nationalists, from Estonia to Azerbaijan, of the protection they had hitherto enjoyed (albeit accidentally) in the shape of the forces of the Central Powers (consequently, Red forces had recaptured Narva and Pskov before the end of November 1918). But, by December 1918, surveying the view from Moscow, it would not have escaped Trotsky's attention that almost all the North Caucasus was in the hands of the Volunteers. Meanwhile, in the North, White forces were preparing to advance down rail and river corridors toward Petrograd and Moscow. In the North West, the lingering presence of the Germans (whose regular forces were disintegrating, but only to reform into a variety of militant, anti-Soviet *Freikorps*) and the arrival of Allied missions in the Baltic theater—to say nothing of the Royal Navy, which proceeded to bombard Narva—was providing a mighty fillip to White formations based within a day or two's march from Petrograd.[136]

Even in the east there were causes for concern: at Simbirsk and Syzran' major rail bridges across the Volga had been dynamited and destroyed by the retreating forces of Komuch and the Czechs in September 1918, leaving only the rail crossing at Kazan' (150 miles further north, on the Moscow–Ekaterinburg line) as a route to the east and severely hampering any further push along the Samara–Ufa track. Ufa was eventually reached by Red forces, on 29–31 December 1918, but it had been a difficult task to supply units moving toward the southern Urals passes. Moreover, the Reds' progress beyond the Volga was far from uncontested. First, around the armory and factory towns of Izhevsk and Votkinsk, 15,000 workers who had risen against Soviet rule in August 1918 had clung on there until November, and had then retreated eastwards through Red lines towards Perm', en masse and in good order, to join Kolchak's forces.[137] Then, the Reds' vanguard (chiefly of the 1st Red Army) revealed themselves to be close enough to exhaustion to fall into a trap laid by General V.O. Kappel' at Belebei, which allowed 15,000 more former Komuch troops to escape encirclement and retreat eastwards.[138] Further north, the failure to provide relief and furlough for men who had been in the front line for six long months witnessed an even more dramatic disintegration of the 3rd Red Army, which surrendered Perm' to the Siberian Army on 25 December 1918, having retreated 150 miles in less than a month. The White victors at Perm' were jubilant: "People believed, or wanted to believe, that the future was now clear, bright and of unlimited happiness," recalled General G.I. Klerzhe, who was there.[139] Back at Omsk, the naïve Colonel D.A. Lebedev, whom Admiral Kolchak had been unwise enough to raise to chief of staff of his newly proclaimed Russian Army, was even more gung-ho: he confided to an American visitor that the Perm' victory presaged not just the reunification of the Russian Empire, but "the realization of the old dream of a Russian Constantinople."[140] This was of course madness, but there were nevertheless plenty of reasons to hope, in Omsk, Ekaterinodar, and Arkhangel'sk, that 1919 would be the year of the Whites, and in the Baltic and Transcaucasian capitals that it would be the year of the national minorities: if the winter of 1917–18 could be characterized by Lenin as witnessing "The Triumphal March of Soviet Power," the winter of 1918–19 could surely be described as "The Triumphal March of Reaction" or "The Triumphal March of Nationalism."

* * *

At the heart of problems facing all sides in the civil wars were issues of the recruitment, retention, and desertion of soldiers. By late 1918, the Red Army was still a long way from solving them, but was further advanced toward a solution than were most of its rivals, and signs were apparent that a solution acceptable to both sides of this bargaining process—the citizens and the state—was possible. Back in June 1918, the Bolsheviks had attempted to mobilize all workers and all "non-exploiting" peasants aged 21–25 years in fifty-one districts of the Volga and the Urals to deal with the revolt of the Czechoslovak Legion, but in the absence of a functioning central draft organization and lists of those eligible, local and impromptu *levées* had to be relied upon and the results were meager. Hardly more was achieved by a country-wide draft on 11 September 1918, while even by early 1919 drafts were widely evaded: for example, in May 1919, a month after a draft was initiated, Tambov had produced precisely twenty-four recruits of the 5,165 anticipated, and by the time this round of mobilizations was called off in June 1919, just 24,364 of 140,000 expected recruits had been secured.[141] In his examination of this phenomenon, Erik Landis describes "hundreds of thousands" of deserters taking up arms in the Red rear and of this so-called "green army" severely compromising the stability of Red fronts from around April to September 1919.[142] According to one pioneering Western study of the phenomenon of desertion, the rate of flight was so great throughout the civil wars that, ultimately, the Reds were only able to triumph over their enemies by dint of the larger pool of men they could draw upon.[143]

There is certainly something in that argument, yet a more recent investigation concludes that, gradually, retention rates were improving in the Red Army. In the most insightful examination of this process to date, Josh Sanborn dates the beginning of it to a decree passed at the Fifth All-Russian Congress of Soviets on 10 July 1918 that linked citizenship to military service and obliged all healthy men aged between eighteen and forty to make themselves available for recruitment.[144] Improvements thereafter he attributes to the Soviet state building an apparatus that could be seen to apportion the burden of mobilization at least reasonably fairly among its citizens—the crucial factor being that the system was one that was central, not local, and therefore perceived to be less open to petty rivalries, jealousies, and abuses.[145] In sum, Sanborn concluded, the Bolsheviks "created a state-sponsored discourse that finally incorporated the idea that soldiers acquired rights when they performed their national duty." In particular, they were assured that their families would be cared for and that they, as soldiers, would be respected by the state and would acquire privileges above those granted to other citizens.[146] Tied to this, though, was a degree of flexibility in the approach of the state. The Red

Army could, of course, unleash terror against those who disobeyed or deserted—Trotsky infamously urged that on many occasions and, in August 1918, was dispatching telegrams to Lenin requesting that front commanders be better supplied with revolvers in order to execute miscreants.[147] Also, by April 1919 the Anti-Desertion Commission had established numerous branches at local level, which organized armed patrols to comb the countryside and snare runaways and had the power to confiscate property from the families of known deserters and those suspected of assisting or harboring them.[148] But, as Sanborn notes, commanders actually used a "two-pronged" approach to desertion. This was reflected in an order by Lenin of December 1918 in which, while describing deserters as "heinous and shameful" and representative of "the depraved and ignorant," he nevertheless offered a two-week amnesty for those absentees who returned to their units. This was accompanied by a nationwide propaganda campaign to convince shirkers and deserters that they could not hide and would be punished, while the Red Army Central Desertion Commission urged that repression be mixed with "proof of concern for the families of Red Army soldiers."[149] Finally, particularly effective seems to have been an intensive and extensive "verification" campaign throughout 1919, during which all those men of draft age in the Soviet zone were required to attend meetings at which their eligibility for military service would be checked. This was never applied universally, but in the second half of 1919, 2,239,604 men attended such meetings and 272,211 of them were then enrolled in the armed forces. By August 1920, a further 470,106 men were recruited by this means. Thus, noted Sanborn, "a military service consensus had been reached and conscription normalized."[150] Certainly the White forces never came close to emulating this—although their failure to do so had as much to do with the more primitive and sparse systems of communication and administration in the peripheral areas in which they operated than, necessarily, ignorance of the importance of such systems of social control. On the Red side, the results were clear: a Red Army of 800,000 men in January 1919 would become one of three million by January 1920.[151]

1918–19: Post-Armistice Campaigns in the Baltic and Ukraine

Just as it had been factors stemming from the climax of the First World War, particularly the Austro-German intervention in Russia, that determined the shape and pattern of the opening stages of the civil war in 1917–18, it was the end of the world war, and the termination of the Austro-German intervention, that determined the warp and weft of conflicts waged across the former Russian Empire from late 1918 into early 1919. This was true in the southeast, where the withdrawal of German forces deprived the Don Cossacks of any alternative *orientatsiia* and soon corralled them into an uneasy union with the pro-Allied Volunteers; and it was true also in the east, where the most consequential shift was the effective withdrawal from the scene of the Czechoslovak Legion from November to December 1918.[152] It was most immediately the case, though—and in an array of starkly contrasting senses—in the west, where the fate of Ukraine and the emergent Baltic States was intimately tied to the fate of the Kaiser and forces loyal to him that had been in occupation of those regions.

* * *

While not ignoring the obvious dangers posed by the fact that, henceforth, the Allies would have their hands free to deal with Bolshevik Russia, as the Central Powers crumbled in early November 1918, Lenin delivered a generally optimistic address on "The Anniversary of the Revolution" to the (Extraordinary) Sixth All-Russian Congress of Soviets (6–9 November 1918) at Moscow. Noting that "Germany is on fire and Austria is all ablaze," the Soviet leader insisted that: "Our slogan must be: Put every effort into the fight once more, and remember that we are coming up to the last, decisive fight, not for the Russian revolution alone, but for the world socialist revolution."[153] But where to fight? Despite the presence of the Royal Navy in the Baltic, the north-west looked like a good bet.

For reasons that remain unclear—perhaps Mannerheim's realm seemed too large, or too powerful, or too peripheral to the direct route to Europe—an offensive against Finland, though discussed by the Red command, was deemed unpropitious.[154] The Belorussian–Lithuanian region, though, was given some priority by Moscow and local Bolsheviks had some traction there (and had formed good relations with the soldiers' councils, *Soldatenräte*, springing up in German forces opposed to the reactionary propensities of the *Freikorps*)— indeed, they had seized power in Vilnius before the Red Army arrived in January 1919 and a Western Front was established in February. But predominantly Jewish-Polish-Russian Vilnius was not representative of Lithuania, which in turn shared little with Belorussia (other than a common history of being lumped together as the "Western Provinces" by the Russians). An attempt to combine them in a Lithuanian–Belorussian SSR (Litbel) in February 1919 consequently faltered and Litbel was disestablished in August 1919, when the hastily fashioned Belorussian–Lithuanian Red Army was forced to abandon even Minsk to the other active power in the region, Poland, which was clearly too puissant for the Bolsheviks to confront at this point (and which, the indications from the ongoing Paris Peace Conference made clear, had Allied support). Poland also had long-term designs on Vilnius, which it had seized in April 1919—and thereby inadvertently provided a cushion behind which, at Kovno (Kaunas), the Lithuanian provisional government (the Taryba) could inculcate independence. Confrontation here would have to wait another year.[155]

Between Lithuania and Finland lay the other putative Baltic States of Estonia and Latvia, against both of which the Red Army attempted to put Lenin's words into action, but with—for a variety of reasons—little more success. In late November 1918, the 7th Red Army captured Pskov and Narva (which had been abandoned by German forces) and an Estonian Workers' Commune under Jaan Anvelt was established at the latter city as a Soviet government for Estland. However, Revel (Tallinn) remained tantalizingly out of reach, with a provisional national government there, the Maapäev, shored up by a combination of popular support (as it distributed the estates of Baltic German barons to the Estonian peasantry) and the presence of the Royal Navy. While holding off the Reds, the new Estonian commander-in-chief, Colonel Johan Laidoner, began reorganizing Estonian forces and recruiting men in numbers. By May 1919, the Estonian Army was some 75,000 strong. It was, moreover, leavened with more than 1,000 Swedish and Finnish volunteers, enjoyed the tactical support of White Russian forces in the region (the Pskov Volunteer Corps), and was permitted by the German command to make use of weapons, uniforms, and other equipment abandoned by its retreating forces. In the face of such a broad alliance, redubbing the 7th Red Army the Estonian Red Army in February 1919 did not much help the Soviet cause—it was soon reconfigured again within the 7th Red Army in June 1919—and the Estonian Workers' Commune (having abandoned Narva on 19 January 1919 and thereafter living a fugitive existence at Vyra, Pskov, Luga, and Staraia Russa) was disestablished that same month.[156] The Estonian–Soviet front then stabilized along the river Narova (Narva), south from Narva and through Lake Chud (Peipus/Peipsi), which provided a natural and defensible eastern frontier for Estonia.[157]

Further south, the provisional Latvian national government that had been formed from the Latvian People's Council (Tautas Padome), although proclaimed (on 18 November 1918) in a Riga covered by the guns of British warships, was blessed with no such natural defenses and had major problems to confront, in the shape of a powerful pro-Bolshevik workers' movement (especially among the proletarian population, both Russian and Latvian, of Riga and other urban centers) and the distractive presence of German *Frei-korps*, with which it was soon in open conflict (in the so-called Landeswehr War). Taking advantage of this (and the large number of Latvians, especially Latvian Riflemen, in its own formations)[158] the Soviet command created the (Red) Army of Soviet Latvia from elements of the 7th Red Army, which ploughed, unresisted, through Tartu (Dorpat) and Valk, as their German garrisons fled, and captured Riga on 3 January 1919. They there installed a Latvian Soviet Socialist Republic (proclaimed on 17 December 1918 and already recognized by the RSFSR), confining the nationalist regime to a small enclave around Liepāja (Libau). However, the Latvian Soviet regime (led by the zealous Bolshevik jurist Pēteris Stučka) proved spectacularly unpopular. Particularly contested by the local populace were Stučka's efforts to introduce early forms of collective farming in the countryside. Ideologically rigid Latvian Bolsheviks, remarking that, in their provinces, serfs had been liberated without land in 1816–18 (and were thereby proletarianized), whereas Russian peasants had received land allotments in the emancipation of 1861 (thereby inculcating a petty-bourgeois attachment to private property), held that a direct move to socialist forms of production was tenable in Latvia. They were wrong. Moreover, the corollary of the Latvian Bolsheviks' didacticism was that they felt no inclination whatsoever to collaborate with non-Bolshevik socialists—even the local Left-SRs were shunned. Indeed, Stučka's regime instituted a wide-ranging terror against all enemies, real and perceived.

According to one witness in Riga, the son of a tsarist general, "The first executions took place about a month after the Reds entered the town. During the night, in a forest outside Riga called Bickern wood, thirteen well-known citizens were shot."[159] This was followed by a period of "financial terror," as the Latvian SSR attempted to ruin the bourgeoisie through "the abolition of money" and a variety of taxes (extortions).[160] When combined with the disastrous impact of Bolshevik policies in the countryside, the results were dreadful and predictable:

> Riga, the fair and flourishing city of former days now presented the appearance of a dying town ... Everywhere the town gave the impression that a malignant, all destroying plague had swept over it. In the quarters where the well-to-do bourgeoisie had lived, the windows and doors of many houses stood wide open. The houses had been abandoned by their owners and stood empty ... Even the animals had deserted the streets ... Not a bird fluttered in the air, not a cock crew. As for the dogs and cats, the faithful companions of every human community, they seem to have all run away or crept into hiding, for none was to be seen.[161]

This was symptomatic of a wider malaise: in general, the national communist leaderships of the Soviet republics established, at Moscow's behest, to coat the pill of Sovietization with a sugary national façade in the wake of the Western Front's advance actually proved less flexible than Moscow with regard to reaching accommodations with local nationalists, even those of a socialist stamp. They tended to regard merger with a larger state entity (Soviet Russia) as representing not a retrograde subjugation but a progressive internationalization and, in general, followed not Lenin's but Rosa Luxemburg's line on the national question, thus abhorring the notion of national self-determination. Pointedly, even as Lenin was attempting to persuade them to at least allow non-Bolshevik socialist parties to contest elections in the newly occupied regions, Luxemburg was named as honorary president of the RKP(b)'s very influential Central Bureau of Communist Organizations of the Occupied Territories which prepared cadres to create new governments in the Baltic region, as the Red Army's Western Front advanced.[162]

Meanwhile, and doubly dangerously for the Reds' efforts, the Latvian Riflemen's revolutionary zeal waned after a year in action, allowing combined attacks from the small army of the nationalist regime (which had secured Allied support) and, more effectively, from German and White Russian forces in the Baltic region (notably the 30,000-strong Iron Division of General Rüdiger von der Goltz) to drive the Latvian SSR from Riga on 22 May 1919.[163] (Von der Goltz, fresh from a major contribution to the White victory in the Finnish Civil War, had already expelled the nationalist government of Kārlis Ulmanis from Liepāja on 16 April 1919, and established a puppet pro-German regime under Pastor Andrievs Niedra.) The Latvian Soviet government, lacking reserves as well as popular support, was able to hold out in part of Latgale, but only until that region too was re-conquered by Latvian and Polish forces in early 1920 (the Latvians having been revived by the Allies' disarming of von der Goltz) and the Latvian SSR was disestablished on 13 January 1920.[164]

Thus what had looked, in the period from November 1918 to February 1919, to have been the realization of Lenin's predicted westward march of the revolution in the Baltic theater, had by May–June 1919 resulted in the repulse and expulsion of Red forces all along the Western Front. Who would emerge as the victors to the west of that front was not yet clear: the Maapäev's relations with Russian Whites tended to cool dramatically with each mile further from Revel that the Reds retreated, and conflict there would only be extinguished once the emerging White North West Army was defeated by the Red

Army in late 1919 and, exhausted, was disarmed by the Estonians in January 1920; the Latvian government would not extinguish its unwelcome German guests' hopes of a Baltikum tied to Berlin until their final factotum, Colonel P.R. Bermondt-Avalov and his Western Volunteer Army, was driven from Riga on 11 November 1919; and only a full-scale Polish–Lithuanian War in September–October 1920 would resolve (temporarily) the Vilnius question. But, from the summer of 1919 onwards, one thing was clear: in the Baltic theater, the Red Army would not be the victor. It would take Hitler and another world crisis, a generation later, to secure that.

* * *

In Ukraine, by contrast, Soviet prospects looked brighter in early 1919. This was somewhat surprising, in that the country was so much larger than the Baltic provinces (Ukraine, by any reasonable measure of what might constitute its contested borders, was larger than France) and very populous (accounting for just over 20 million people in 1919, almost a fifth of the former empire's population). Crucial here was that although Ukraine had, like the Baltic, been subjected to German occupation prior to November 1918, there was a subtle difference: rather than scorn or imprison would-be nationalist rulers (as had been the case in Estonia and Latvia), in Ukraine the Germans had propped up a puppet nationalist regime, the Ukrainian State of Hetman Skoropadskii—a fact that was thereafter to color Allied attitudes toward the Ukrainian national movement in shades very unflattering to Kiev. It seemed not to register in London, Paris, or Washington that Skoropadskii's regime had been deeply unpopular among the population—that Ukrainian peasants had suffered as the Hetman's officials sought to implement the requisitioning policies of the grain-hungry Central Powers—while, in addition to the Ukrainian socialists' enmity towards Skoropadskii, the liberal and nationalist intelligentsia (those of them not in the Hetman's prisons) were angered and embarrassed by the dominant position that Russians assumed in the Hetmanite army and Skoropadskii's government.[165] It seemed also not to have mattered among governing circles in Britain, France, or the United States that, having overthrown Skoropadskii in November–December 1918, in early 1919 the newly reinstalled Ukrainian National Republic, in order to appease the Allies, was polite enough to purge itself of the socialist elements of its Council of People's Ministers. Nothing, it seemed, could atone for the UNR having signed a peace with the Central Powers in February 1918—even before such treachery had been committed by the Bolsheviks.[166]

Furthermore, as the Allied leaders gathered at Paris to deal with the aftermath of the First World War and attempted to prevent its repetition, many counseled that, whatever the abstract justice of the Ukrainian national cause, geopolitical realities determined that to remain free of Russian dominance (Red or White), Kiev would always have to look to Germany; better, then, so as to avert another war to contain Berlin's continental ambitions, that Ukraine remain within the Russian orbit (especially as hopes were still high at this point that the future of Russia was not Red).

Poland was a different matter—the new Polish (Second) Republic was accorded pride of place in the Allies' schemes to construct a *cordon sanitaire* around Russia for as long as Russia harbored the Bolshevik contagion—but support for a strong Poland implied yet further unwelcome brickbats launched against Kiev regarding the issue of Western Ukraine/Eastern Galicia: this was a knotty and embarrassing problem from the Allies' point of view and one from which a solution would only deliver them once Warsaw was contesting the outcome with Moscow and not with Kiev.[167] Of course, this was not the sole reason for the difficulties faced by the UNR in defending itself against the Soviet forces massing to its north in late 1918. Other reasons included the debilitating distraction of the conflict with Poland over the former Habsburg crownland north of the Carpathians (the former Kingdom of Galicia and Lodomeria), after Warsaw contested by force of arms the declaration of a Western Ukrainian People's Republic at L'viv (Lemberg) following the local Ukrainians' November Uprising of 1918. This led to the Ukrainian–Polish War that raged until a ceasefire was brokered by the Allies in May 1919, but rumbled on until the WUNR was abandoned by the UNR in April 1920.[168] Less extensive, but nevertheless debilitating, were Ukraine's battles with Romania over the Khotyn region. On 9 April 1918 Khotyn, along with the rest of Bessarabia, had been formally united with Romania by a vote of its parliament (the Sfatul Țării), although the region was at that point occupied by Austrian and German troops and Romanian forces only arrived in November 1918, in the wake of the Central Powers' defeat in the First World War. On 23 January 1919, the Ukrainian population of Khotyn drove these forces from the city (killing the Romanian General Stan Poetaș in the process) and established an interim government (the Khotyn Directory) under M. Liskun that sought union with the neighboring UNR. The latter, however, at a critical point of the Soviet–Ukrainian War, could not afford to become embroiled in conflict with Romania—still less could the WUPR, to Khotyn's north, which was then in the midst of the Ukrainian–Polish War—and Romanian forces re-occupied the area on 1 February 1919. Ukrainian sources suggest that some 55,000 Ukrainians then fled eastwards across the Dnestr River into the UNR and that at least 15,000 of those who did not flee were slaughtered by the Romanians.[169]

Also enervating to Ukrainian efforts toward statehood was the very weakly developed sense of nationalism in the territories it claimed as "Ukrainian."[170] Despite the inculcation of Ukrainian nationalism by successive generations of intellectuals during the nineteenth century, few of the region's numerically predominant peasant population seem yet to have absorbed the notion of a distinct Ukrainian identity by the early twentieth century,[171] while in the country's cities Ukrainians tended to be greatly outnumbered by Russians and Poles (who also dominated the public life in the civil service, education, and other professions) and Jews (who were prominent in commerce and intellectual life): even in Kiev only around 18 percent of the population were Ukrainians in the civil-war era and many—perhaps most—of those were Russianized.[172] Consequently, and tellingly, in elections to city councils in July 1917, overtly Ukrainian parties had won just 12.6 percent of the vote in towns with a population under 50,000 and only 9.5 percent of the vote in those with a population higher than 50,000.[173]

Important too was the general atmosphere of chaos and disorder that pervaded the much-contested Ukrainian lands in the civil-war years, creating conditions that even a deep-rooted and long-established regime would have struggled to master: according to one count, Kiev changed hands no fewer than sixteen times in the maelstrom of the civil wars[174] while the shifting sands of Ukraine's politics were exemplified by the peculiar progress of the commander of an independent peasant army, Ataman Nykyfor Hryhoriiv. Having initially aligned his powerful guerilla force with Hetman Skoropadskii in 1918, this outrageous freebooter then joined the Ukrainian Army in November–December 1918 to help topple Skoropadskii's Ukrainian State, but subsequently deserted with his forces to the Reds when forbidden by UNR commander (Symon Petliura) from attacking the French interventionists at Odessa, only thereafter to revolt against the Reds and suggest to the anarchist commander Nestor Makhno that their armies should ally themselves with General Denikin![175] Finally, Ukrainian nationalists suffered as a consequence of many Russians' refusal to recognize them as an ethnically distinct group. There was often among Russians a not very carefully hidden agenda here, relating to Ukraine's vital economic and strategic importance to Russia as the supplier of most of the former empire's coal and iron, as a land-bridge to central Europe, and as the holder of the longest Black Sea coastline.[176] But the sincerity with which such Russian views of Ukrainians as being not really different—unlike Estonians, or Latvians, or Georgians or Armenians, who were at least offered some grudging recognition as "others," even by the Whitest of Whites—is attested by the fact that even at times when common sense dictated they should offer, at minimum, a simulacrum of sympathy to Ukrainian national feelings, White leaders simply could not bring themselves to do it. Thus upon entering Kiev in August 1919, almost the first thing General Denikin did was to address a grossly insulting speech to "the people of Little Russia."[177] Nothing could have been better calculated to drive what remained of the UNR and its Ukrainian Army into the arms of Poland, which was precisely what ensued.[178] But the fact was that adherence to the Russian national cause was what made Denikin and his followers "White": to have sullied such principles through political calculations was unthinkable in general, but especially in the case of Ukraine—which had, after all, a millennium earlier, been the site of the foundation of the first "Russian state," Kievan Rus', and whose capital, Kiev, was deeply revered, even by Muscovites, as the "Mother of Russian cities."[179]

For all these reasons, it is clear that the situation domestically and internationally in 1918–19 did not favor Ukrainian independence.[180] Perhaps chief among them, however, may have been that the Ukrainian national movement elicited only negative or at best mixed responses from the Allies, certainly in comparison to the very positive regard in which were held the autocephalous aspirations of Poland and the Baltic States—all of which would achieve independence in the civil-war period, despite the existence of many domestic obstacles to their ambitions that were at least as formidable as those that confronted Ukraine. The direct upshot of this was that when, with the Straits now open, Allied forces began to land at Odessa from 23 to 27 November 1918, they regarded the regime in Kiev with a suspicion that bordered on hostility. Consequently, although comparatively large numbers of Allied forces were disembarked at Odessa—three French divisions (including many African troops) and three Greek divisions, a total of between 40,000 and 50,000 men—they were all withdrawn within six months and the interventionists would never afford local Ukrainian anti-Bolsheviks anything like the material assistance, in terms of tanks, aircraft, and weaponry, that was made available in other theaters.[181] This, of course, was a situation from which only the enemies of Ukrainian independence could benefit, be they Polish, White, or—in the first (and, eventually, last) instance—Red.

* * *

The intervention in South Russia of 1918–19 had two further consequences, both of which boded ill for the anti-Bolshevik movement. The first, which need not delay us here, was a serious mutiny in the French fleet in the Black Sea during the withdrawal of April 1919. This remains a contentious matter, as debates have raged ever since as to the causes of the revolt: the Soviet government attributed it to successful Bolshevik propaganda, while most Western historians cited the sailors' discontent with the delay of their demobilization, rotten rations, and so forth. Either way, anti-Bolsheviks within Russia would note that thereafter the French presence in their struggle declined steeply—a process that would not be reversed. Nevertheless, it is a subject which is really part of the history of the intervention rather than the "Russian" Civil Wars, although it does reinforce their international dimensions.

The second consequence of the briefly reinforced Allied presence in southwest Russia was that it facilitated (and encouraged) the Jassy Conference. This was a meeting of twenty-one prominent anti-Bolshevik politicians (among them P.N. Miliukov, V.I. Gurko, V.V. Shul'gin, A.V. Krivoshein, and S.N. Tret'iakov) and military leaders (including Generals A.N. Grishin-Almazov and D.G. Shcherbachev of the Volunteer Army) that took place at the temporary Romanian capital of Jassy (Iaşi) from 16 to 23 November 1918 and then reconvened at Odessa from 25 November to 6 December 1918. Encouraged by the French and other Allied missions in Romania and Ukraine (notably by the possibly bogus French vice-consul in Kiev, Captain Emile Henno) and by supporters of the Union for the Regeneration of Russia, the conference, which was also attended by representatives of the National Center and the Kiev-based (and right-Kadet-dominated) State Unity Council of Russia (some delegates representing more than one of these anti-Bolshevik groupings) aimed to unify the various anti-Bolshevik forces in Russia and to provide them with political guidance. However, despite the Allies' indication that only a unified opposition to the Soviet government might receive their financial and military assistance, the delegates could not agree on a common program and no candidate discussed as a potential (provisional) military dictator by a meeting of fourteen delegates on 21 November 1918 could be agreed upon (although General A.I. Denikin gained the most support, with nine votes, followed by the Grand Duke Nikolai Nikolaevich, who gained four). Indeed, there was no agreement that a temporary military dictatorship might be the best solution for defeating the Bolsheviks, with some right-wing delegates favoring the restoration of the monarchy and moderates supporting a civilian Directory. Votes were passed, though, in favor of Allied intervention in Russia (and delegations were sent to meet Allied military leaders in Constantinople and to liaise with Allied governments in London and Paris) and in support of the indivisibility of the former Russian Empire (although most delegates accepted the loss of Poland). The National Center seemed to have achieved most success in gaining endorsement of its program, but in fact more leftist elements remained unreconciled to its support for military dictatorship and remained adamant that the only legal all-Russian authority was the recently established Ufa Directory; and, in any case, the results of votes won at the conference were merely symbolic and had no legally binding authority over the participants. Unsurprisingly, Allied observers were less than impressed with the endless bickering and politicking of the various delegates and it was not without just cause that the conference was later adjudged to have been a "fiasco" by historians of the anti-Bolshevik movement.[182]

* * *

Meanwhile, Soviet forces (specifically the 1st and 2nd Ukrainian Insurgent Divisions) had begun probing the defenses of the Hetmanite Army and its German allies as early as September 1918, and by 26 November 1918 had captured Iambol', Ryl'sk, and other towns. On 30 November 1918, a united Ukrainian Soviet Army was formed, under the command of V.A. Antonov-Ovseenko, which then pressed on towards Chernigov, Kiev, and Khar'kov, capturing the last of these centers on 3 January 1919. The next day, the Revvoensovet of the Republic formed the Ukrainian Front, whose forces captured Kiev from the irregulars of the improvised Ukrainian Army of the UNR by 5 February 1919. The UNR government was then obliged to resettle at provincial Kamenets-Podol'sk, far in the Ukrainian south-west. Further battles in March–April 1919 entirely shattered the Ukrainian Army, which in May 1919 was pushed across the River Zbruch into former Austrian territory, where it united with the more disciplined Galician Army of the WUPR (just in time to suffer further blows from Polish forces from the north-west).[183] Thus by late April 1919, all of what had been formerly Russian Ukraine, including the Black Sea coast and Crimea, had been conquered by the Reds.

However—and just as had been the case in the Baltic theater—the insistence of the leaders of the re-established Ukrainian Soviet Socialist Republic (proclaimed at Khar'kov in January 1919, as a successor to the Provisional Workers' and Peasants' Government of Ukraine proclaimed earlier at Kursk on 20 November 1918), on the immediate introduction of radical socialist measures (including Committees of the Village Poor to counter the perceived dominance of rich peasants in Ukraine and, as in the Latvian SSR, prototype collective farms, as well as almost 2,000 state farms to run the sugar-beet industry) soon set the countryside against them. Meanwhile, the radical Ukrainian intelligentsia was alienated by the reluctance of local Soviet leaders, notably Christian Rakovski, to work with non-Bolshevik revolutionary groups in Ukraine, especially the Borotbists. A host of peasant rebellions against Soviet power consequently erupted across Ukraine, which were barely contained by a hastily instituted and Moscow-enforced moderation of policy and the formation of a coalition government of the Ukrainian SSR with the *Borotbisty*. Moreover, by progressing, against the inclinations of Glavkom Vācietis, across the Dnepr into south-west Ukraine, Antonov-Ovseenko had badly overstretched his thin resources. In fact, he was obliged to rely upon unstable alliances with a variety of unreliable Ukrainian warlords (*otomany*) and was unable to counter the sudden revolt against Soviet Russian power of the 20,000-strong Trans-Dnepr Brigade of the aforementioned Otaman Hryhoriiv, who on 8 May 1919 proclaimed a "Soviet Ukraine without Communists" and briefly, before his sudden demise at the hands of Makhno, had control of most of Kherson and Ekaterinoslav *gubernii*. Hryhoriiv was a complex and possibly unbalanced character, but his rebellion was motivated by a quite sound analysis of what forced requisitioning and Cheka execution squads meant for his peasant supporters in Ukraine: he was genuinely popular and his revolt was echoed by a number of other such actions across the country.[184]

On the positive side, for Moscow, the Red push across the Dnepr, and Hryhoriiv's impressive sallies against White and Allied troops that had briefly brought him control of a stretch of the Black Sea littoral, had at least persuaded the French interventionists not to dally at Odessa and in the Crimea, from which all Allied forces had been withdrawn by late April 1919.[185] But, on the negative side, once Hryhoriiv turned, Moscow and Khar'kov were rudely awakened from dreams of crossing the Dnestr to occupy Bessarabia and then to relieve pressure on the doomed Hungarian Soviet Republic that had been established by Béla Kun in Budapest (from 21 March 1919). Indeed, despite the foundation a Third International (the Komintern) at Moscow in March 1919, which was dedicated to unyielding struggle for a worldwide Soviet republic, the ambitions Lenin had voiced in November 1918 now seemed very premature.[186] Significantly, the stranglehold of the Allied blockade of Soviet Russia—a new "Great Wall of China," Lenin had termed it back in November 1918—was still sufficiently intact (if not visible from space) that only a pitiful handful of foreign delegates made it to Moscow for the Komintern's inauguration. Meanwhile, Rosa Luxemburg, the secular saint of the national communists who had stalled just a stone's throw from German territory in their march toward her, was now two months dead—brutally murdered by counter-revolutionaries on the eve of a communist uprising in Berlin in January 1919 that, deprived of aid from the east, was also doomed to failure. Indeed, it might be argued that these events represented the death *in utero* of the Komintern. At the same time, not only having proved unable to spread Soviet power through the Baltic into Germany but also having established only a tenuous grip on Ukraine, the Soviet government was now facing stern challenges from its own domestic counter-revolution, as pincers of the White forces closed on Petrograd and Moscow from the east, south-east, north, and north-west.

* * *

In the struggles of the Baltic States for independence, the political agenda of the Bolsheviks' opponents was fairly transparent from the outset: in Estonia, Latvia, and Lithuania, liberal politicians, with generally pro-peasant agendas, took charge from early on and proclaimed separation from Russia and a commitment to liberal democracy through the (eventual) summoning of constitutional assemblies.[187] In 1919 Ukraine, in the shape of the UNR and the WUPR, the Bolsheviks' political challenge came chiefly from SRs, social-democrats, and (in the case of the WUPR) radical liberals, many of whom had become nationalists almost against their will in the resistance to Soviet Russian (and Austro-German and White Russian) incursions and interference,[188] and whose agendas prioritized pro-labor policies and radical land reform but, of course, also included a commitment to national independence. By contrast, what was represented politically by the Bolsheviks' White opponents of the next stage of the civil wars—the Volunteers and Kolchakovites, who, until early 1919, had been swarming menacingly around the Russian periphery— was difficult to judge at the time and remains, to this day, somewhat obscure. Their immediate martial intent, on the other hand, was quite clear.

3

1919–20

WHITE THRUSTS, RED RIPOSTES

Both of the major White leaders of 1918–20, Admiral A.V. Kolchak and General A.I. Denikin, elaborated political programs in 1919 that might—despite the generally held perceptions of the Whites as "reactionaries"—broadly be described as "liberal." In their pronouncements, Kolchak and Denikin committed themselves, repeatedly and clearly, to resuscitating local governments, to respecting the right of the non-Russian peoples to self-determination (short of secession), to respecting the rights of trade unions, and to radical land reform and vowed that, upon victory in the civil war, they would summon a new national assembly to determine the future constitution of the Russian state. Kolchak, whose Omsk government was more stable, rooted, and fully developed than the rather nebulous and peripatetic Special Council that advised Denikin, tended to take the lead in such matters,[1] but both the main White military camps had stout phalanxes of Kadet auxiliaries to add flesh to the bones of their declarations on politics and to staff their press agencies, advisory councils, and bureaus of propaganda.[2] Moreover, there is little doubt that, personally, both Denikin and Kolchak held genuinely progressive views on a range of issues, including the necessity of radical land reform in Russia—the key issue of the previous century—and that both were entirely sincere in their protestations that they had no personal desire to hang on to political power for a moment longer than it would take to drive Lenin from the Kremlin. Also, although the document that established the Kolchak dictatorship

("The Statute on the Provisional Structure of State Power in Russia") made no provision for its termination, the admiral put on public record, in a speech at Ekaterinburg in February 1919, for example, a solemn (if yet slightly indefinite) pledge that he would not retain power "for a single day longer than the interests of the country demand," and asserted that "in the future the only admissible form of government in Russia will be a democratic one." And, "once the normal conditions of life have been established, once law and order rule in the country," he promised, "then it will be possible to set about the convocation of a National Assembly."[3] These declarations reaped some rewards: in May 1919, for example, the Big Four at Paris were sufficiently impressed with Kolchak's democratic credentials that they would consider recognizing his regime as the government of all Russia.[4]

But however well drafted—and there was never a shortage of Kadet lawyers in Omsk or Ekaterinodar to do such a job—or well intentioned, there was always something flimsy, half-baked, and unconvincing about White politics; and a lingering sense prevailed that neither Denikin nor Kolchak was much interested in the details of the political concerns that had been agitating Russia since—and, indeed, long before—February 1917. Moreover, however egalitarian were the personal beliefs and intentions of the major White leaders, who were far from the clichéd caricatures of pince-nez-adorned, sadistic fops of Bolshevik propaganda,[5] this could not disperse the stench of restorationism that suffused their camps, which were heavily populated with the former elite of the Russian Empire or would-be elitist *arrivistes* who craved such status. British officers with the mission in South Russia, for example, who had been invited to a banquet held by the local branch of the Union of Landowners at Novocherkassk, soon sensed that they were among "a hot-bed of monarchists" and were deeply embarrassed when one of the guests (a cousin of Nicholas Romanov) ordered the orchestra to play "God Save the Tsar," the old imperial anthem that had been banned since the February Revolution.[6]

Consequently, although Denikin's land laws and labor legislation might have promised fair treatment to peasants and workers, the populace of the territory occupied by the Volunteers invariably felt the whip and wrath of returning landlords and factory bosses who had been driven out by the widespread seizures of private property that had accompanied the spread of Soviet power in 1917–18, and who now sought revenge and recompense.[7] The same rule applied in the east, as Kolchak's forces advanced from Siberia (where large, landed estates were almost unknown) across the Urals to the Volga region (beyond which they became general)—despite the fact that Kolchak himself was clearly committed to a progressive land reform resembling that attempted in Russia in the aftermath of the 1905 Revolution and that Omsk's Ministry of Agriculture was teeming with former associates of the reforming prime minister of those days, P.A. Stolypin.[8] Most telling of all was that Kolchak's "Decree on Land" was not issued until April 1919, when his army's move towards European Russia necessitated such action.[9] Similarly, on the second great issue of the day—national self-determination—he also remained silent until the spring of 1919, when the focus of Paris on the Whites' intentions prompted action—or, at least, more promises.[10]

A variety of explanations might be adduced for such prevarication. A generous reading of White policy would emphasize that the movement was genuinely committed to a stance of non-predetermination—one that, disinterestedly, inhibited (even forbade) the introduction of significant reforms during the armed struggle: such acts, according to the doctrine routinely espoused by the Whites (even as they lambasted the similarly hamstrung Provisional Government of 1917 for its inertia), would have to await the decisions of a new constituent assembly (Kolchak, as quoted above, preferred to term it a "national assembly") once the Bolsheviks had been defeated. A less generous exposition of the "White idea" could cite cynical distortions and maskings of their true aims by the Whites, in order to secure peasant recruits to man their armies and Allied weapons to equip them, while attempting to hoodwink any too trusting members of the national minorities into accepting that promises of self-determination emanating from Omsk and Ekaterinodar were real.[11]

The Whites' variously evasive and contradictory stance on the nationalities question was particularly damaging to their cause given that, especially in southern and north-western "Russia," they tended to be operating from bases in lands where Russians were in a minority and non-Russians were using the post-imperial and post-world war hiatus to fashion their independence. Thus Denikin would occasionally sing the praises of self-determination, yet more often espouse the cause of a "Russia, One and Indivisible," while engaging in a prolonged border war (the "Sochi Conflict") with the Democratic Republic of Georgia,[12] while also directly insulting the Ukrainians (as we have seen).[13] He would also offer up such alarming suggestions regarding the proper delineation of a new Polish–Russian border that Piłsudski would call a halt to his army's operations in the spring of 1919 and then enter secret peace talks with Moscow that would facilitate the redeployment of 40,000 men from the Red Army's Western Front to its "Southern Front, Against Denikin" in the fall of that year.[14] Another instructive example was the case of Daghestan and its neighbors in the Caucasus, who had united in an autonomous Mountain Republic. This regime had initially been dissolved by the Bolshevik-dominated Terek Soviet Republic at Vladikavkaz in the spring of 1918, but had re-established itself as Soviet power crumbled in the North Caucasus later that year, then had repulsed a new Soviet offensive in April 1919, only to find that when Denikin's forces subsequently occupied the North Caucasus and then Daghestan, it had to flee again—this time from the Whites.[15]

In Siberia, Kolchak had less immediate concerns with the non-Russian nationalities, who were not present in sufficient numbers within his realm to cause harm (although the desertion from his front line around Ufa, in February 1919, of 6,500 Bashkir combatants who had despaired of their treatment by the Whites was a sizable blow and left a big hole in the front line).[16] However, as Supreme Ruler his pronouncements on the issue had national and international connotations and consequences, and here it was revealing that Kolchak should choose the case of Finland, which was already independent and certainly unrecoverable, to dig in his heels: when General Mannerheim, in July 1919, offered a deal whereby his 100,000-strong army would capture Petrograd for the Whites in return for some not inconsiderable but hardly outrageous returns (recognition of Finnish independence, the secession to Finland of Pechenga, self-determination for Karelia, free navigation through Lake Ladoga for Finnish merchant vessels, etc.), Kolchak adamantly refused to agree a deal. His advisor, George Guins, would plead with him that "the prime aim must be the defeat of the Bolsheviks and only second the putting back together of Russia,"[17] but the admiral would not recognize the logic of such an approach. For Kolchak, Russia could not be saved from the Bolsheviks if it was in pieces, because Russia in pieces was not Russia.

So, both generous and cynical approaches to White politics have elements of truth to them. Over and above such considerations, however, it has to be conceded that—for what they regarded as the purest of motives—the White leaders disdained all politics: their contempt for what they, as officers, regarded as an unwholesome and ungentlemanly pursuit was at least honest, if misguided, and was certainly reinforced by the depressing experience of 1917, when all of Russia seemed to have turned into a vast, endless, clamorous, and pointless political meeting.[18]

The Whites' distaste for politics, and especially class-based politics, knitted perfectly with the claim of their Kadet allies to be, as a party, "above class" and "above politics" (although, again, a cynic might point out that the Kadets were calculating here that there was no strong bourgeois class in Russia that might support their liberal platform) and with that party's historical tendency to place nation above all else. Moreover, the particular circumstances of post-world war Europe at the moment, over the winter of 1918–19, that the White movement reached maturity strongly reinforced this predilection. The White leaders were all too well aware that although there were ranks of irreconcilable anti-Bolsheviks in and around the governments in London, Paris, and Washington, there were many Allied politicians who did not fear the Soviet government, or who hoped to use Russia's discomfort to their own countries' advantage, or who were genuinely overwhelmed by war-weariness. In these circumstances, the end of the world war might not prove advantageous: consequently, a Kolchak supporter in the Russian Far East recorded his impressions of the sight of British Tommies celebrating the armistice to have been "not particularly joyous," as civil wars waged on in Russia; the admiral's secretary, the aforementioned Guins, would reflect that the collapse of Germany had been "fatal to the anti-Bolshevik struggle"; and one of his generals would assert that from 11 November 1918 onwards "Kolchak had no Allies."[19] Consequently, if Kolchak and his supporters were to win what they desired above all else—the admittance of Russia to the family of Allied "victor nations," a seat at the forthcoming peace conference, and the opportunity to ensure their country was properly rewarded for the very considerable part it had played in the world war—the lesson was clear. A few days after having assumed the mantle of "Supreme Ruler" in November 1918, Kolchak spelled that lesson out:

> The day is dawning when the inexorable course of events will demand victory of us; upon this victory or defeat will depend our life or death, our success or failure, our freedom or ignoble slavery. The hour of the great international peace conference is now near and if, by that hour, we are not victorious then we will lose our right to a vote at the conference of victor nations and our freedom will be decided upon without us.[20]

Kolchak's calculations were correct. In November–December 1918, nothing was done by the Allies to dissuade Romania from snatching Bessarabia from its German occupiers (to reverse the settlement of the Treaty of Bucharest of 1812).[21] Then, at meetings during 12–19 January 1919, in Paris, the Council of Ten established that no Russian representatives would be afforded a seat among them. Days later, in accordance with a scheme devised by Lloyd George and Robert Borden, the Prime Minister of Canada, an invitation was sent out by radio (from a transmitter atop the Eiffel Tower) suggesting that all warring parties in "Russia" should meet at a separate peace conference at Prinkipo, off

Constantinople, in the Sea of Marmara. When informed of the latter, Kolchak was aghast and spluttered, "Good God! Can you believe it? An invitation to peace with the Bolsheviks!"[22] Had he been told some weeks later, in early March 1919, that a senior American diplomat, William C. Bullitt, was at that moment being entertained in Moscow, was parlaying in a semi-official manner with Lenin, and was offering very generous terms to end the intervention, Kolchak's language might have been less temperate.[23] Indeed, such news might have occasioned one of the violent fits of anger in Kolchak that his advisors had learned to fear, as the admiral slashed at his furniture with a penknife, smashed items on his desk and threw them around his office.[24] Then, in April, news broke of a scheme approved in Paris for supplying food relief and medicine to the peoples of Russia, including those in the Soviet zone. Kolchak's precise response to news of this initiative of Fridtjof Nansen is unrecorded, but he would probably have found himself in unusual accord with Trotsky, who, surveying the scene on 13 April 1919, commented that "We have before us a case of betrayal of the minor brigands by the major ones."[25]

In the light of all this, it seems sensible to conclude that analyses of the Whites' defeat in the civil wars that focus on their tardy, half-hearted, and haphazard attempts to win political support are—however accurate in such a portrayal—ultimately misguided. "All for the Army," as the mantra went at Omsk, was probably a reasonable response to the circumstances of the time; and, from the moment he took power, Kolchak set about putting that imprecation into action.

Kolchak's Spring Offensive

Admiral Kolchak's deep concerns regarding the impression his ambitiously redubbed Russian Army's battlefield performances might have in the conference chambers and chancelleries of the Allied capitals had their most striking impact upon the timing of the White advance from the east in 1919. In essence, Kolchak's spring offensive was scheduled for the earliest possible moment, following the pause (of roughly December–March) demanded by the Urals–Siberian winter, by which time a planned levy of the entire male population of Siberia of the 1897–1900 age group might have put a million men at his disposal.[26] Unsurprisingly, in the chaotic situation of 1918–19, less than 10 percent of that number actually materialized, to be added to the 50,000 or so fighters already in the field. Moreover, no time was allowed prior to the commencement of active operations in March 1919 to train these raw recruits effectively, still less to inculcate in them any notion of the aims of the White movement, while the uniforms and weapons supplied for them by the Allies were too often delayed en route along the congested, single-tracked railway line from Vladivostok to the unfeasibly isolated Urals front, or disappeared into the black hole of Siberia's booming black market. General Knox, head of Britmis and notional *Chef d'Arrière* of White forces in Siberia, was apoplectic at this combination of carelessness and corruption. After several months of argument, he did at least prevail upon Kolchak's commanders to begin building and training five reserve divisions in the rear, but the orders for this would only be issued after the offensive had begun.[27]

Clearly, Kolchak's planned offensive was also going to get underway before any simultaneous and combined attack from Denikin's forces in South Russia could be arranged: having been repulsed one more time from Tsaritsyn in January 1919, the Don Army had retreated to its home territory, while the Volunteers were fully engaged in consolidating their hold on the North Caucasus. This lack of coordination has generally been deemed to have been fatal to the White cause, as it allowed their opponents to re-deploy their forces, from east to south, along internal lines of communications, to face successive rather than joint offensives. What caused such disjunction, however, is a matter of debate. Poor communications are often cited, usually with a reference to the fate of General A.N. Grishin–Almazov—ambushed by a Red flotilla on the Caspian, as he attempted to ferry documents from Ekaterinodar to Omsk—adduced as proof.[28] But this is not a convincing argument as, although the Reds' unbroken hold on the entire length of the Volga down to Astrakhan separated Kolchak from Denikin, the two White leaders and their staffs were fully able to communicate by telegraph and frequently did so (to arrange a joint political offensive against the Prinkipo Proposal in February 1919, for example). Similarly, analyses that suggest that Kolchak refused to wait for Denikin because of some alleged desire to win the "race to Moscow" take no account of the admiral's selfless character, or of evidence in the discussions and orders of the White command in Siberia that make it entirely clear that the Russian Army decided not to wait for Denikin simply because its leaders entirely failed to appreciate that it might be necessary to do so. In coming to that decision, the aforementioned Colonel Lebedev, Kolchak's parvenu chief of staff, seems to have been most culpable, but he did not act alone.[29] Baron A.P. von Budberg, a senior army bureaucrat attached to Omsk's *stavka*, wrote a diary of his experiences of this time that alternately seethes with anger and gawps in disbelief at the manner in which Kolchak was enchanted by a starry-eyed carapace of youthful advisors who would repeatedly reassure him that the "gang of criminals and adventurers" currently squatting in the Kremlin would soon be ousted, that the Red Army consisted of nothing but "the dregs of society" and would soon be swept away to allow him to "enter Moscow to the accompaniment of church bells."[30]

A further repercussion of all this was that if it was deemed unnecessary to unite with Denikin, other options opened up for the strategic weight and direction of Kolchak's advance. Clearly, it would not be toward the south if combination with Denikin was not required. But nor would it be toward the north—the direction favored by an unlikely alliance of General Knox (who envisaged a move from Perm′ through Kotlas to Vologda, where a union with Allied forces in North Russia might be effected), General Gajda (who envisaged further laurels for his Siberian Army if the bias was toward an advance from his trophy city of Perm′), and the newly elevated General Lebedev. Indeed, according to one wry observer of the Omsk scene, the main reason for Kolchak's *stavka* favoring the northern direction "was the possibility of avoiding union with Denikin, because the infants who occupy senior posts [at Omsk] are terrified that they would be replaced by more senior and experienced specialists" should Kolchak's forces unite with those of Denikin.[31] Personal factors may have played a part here too, as the blunt Knox, who felt he knew more about the Russian army than most Russians (and, after almost a decade in the country, he might well have done) and the pushy Gajda (who had entered the world war as a *Feldscher* in the Austrian army), both clearly irritated Kolchak. But most important again, was that some sort of victory was urgently required, in the very shortest possible time, in order to impress the Allies. Thus when Kolchak's offensive came, it would be a general one, along the entire front, with such bias as there was favoring the center and a push back through Ufa toward the middle Volga and the most direct route to Moscow.[32]

The order of battle of Kolchak's forces in early March 1919 consisted of, from north to south: Gajda's Siberian Army of around 45,000 men (supported by the Siberian Flotilla on the upper Kama river), with its headquarters at Ekaterinburg; General M.V. Khanzhin's 42,000-strong Western Army, based at Cheliabinsk, which was to be reinforced by a new corps under Colonel V.O. Kappel′ as the offensive progressed; and the Southern Army Group of Ataman Dutov (from May 1919 the Southern Army, of some 25,000 men, under General G.A. Belov). South of the Dutov–Belov group were stretched troops of the Orenburg and Urals Cossacks, numbering another 20,000 fighters, who were held up before the Red occupation of Orenburg but whose extreme left flank bulged forwards almost to the banks of the lower Volga. Facing them along the Reds' Eastern Front (again from north to south) were around 120,000 men of the 3rd, 2nd, 5th, 1st, and 4th Red Armies, who were numerically weaker but had many more artillery pieces, were reinforced by the Volga–Kama Military Flotilla, could summon many more reserves from the Soviet center, and had an ally in the forces of the Turkestan ASSR (concentrated on the Aktiubinsk Front and pushing northwards along the railway towards Orenburg). It might have been of significance too that of Kolchak's chief commanders during the advance, only Khanzhin was a full general of anything but the most recent vintage in March 1919: Gajda had the rank of lieutenant-general (since January 1919), but a mere eighteen months earlier could only boast of the rank of captain in the army of Montenegro, which he had been awarded in 1915; Dutov had the rank of major-general, but had commanded only a regiment in 1917 (albeit with some distinction); Belov had gained the rank of major-general only as recently as 15 August 1918; and the hapless Lebedev had been made major-general by Kolchak only in January 1919. Of course, the introduction of new blood into the commanding staff was not necessarily a bad thing and some of these men were of proven talent—Gajda, for example, had greatly distinguished himself in the Battle of Zborov (1–2 July 1917) against the Austrians, and, as commander of the Eastern Group of the Czechoslovak Legion, had performed miracles in clearing the Bolsheviks from Omsk, Novonikolaevsk, and Irkutsk in May–July 1918, before going on to secure the vital circum-Baikal tunnels of the Trans-Siberian Railroad—but time would tell that they were not necessarily the best new blood the Siberian forces had to offer and that commanders overlooked by Kolchak because of their previous associations with Komuch (notably Colonel V.O. Kappel') might have been wiser choices to lead the advance.

From 4 March 1919 onwards, with skis and sledges employed to make progress through the deep snow still lying in the Urals passes, the offensive commenced along the entire front and was, initially, successful beyond even the predictions of Omsk's optimists during its first month: the Western Army took Ufa from the 5th Red Army by 16 March, then Sterlitamak (6 April 1919), Belebei (7 April 1919), and Bugul'ma (10 April 1919), bringing Khanzhin within striking distance of the Volga crossings at Samara and Simbirsk. Meanwhile to the south, Dutov's Cossacks captured Orsk (9 April 1919) and pushed on toward Orenburg and in the north the Siberian Army captured Sarapul (10 April 1919) and closed on Glazov. At this point, however, impetuosity and hot-headedness took hold: instead of digging in on the river Ik and sitting out the worst of the spring thaw, when snowmelt transformed roads into rivers, the Western Army pushed on (taking Buguruslan on 15 April 1919), as Kolchak, on 12 April 1919, ordered that all Red forces east of the Volga were to be eliminated. By this point 180,000 square miles of territory (populated by some five to seven million souls souls) had been engulfed by the Siberian Whites, together with at least 20,000 prisoners and many guns and armored trains.[33] It seemed impressive but not everybody was fooled: "Don't think that our successful advances are a result of military prowess," an officer warned the Kadet Lev Krol', "for it is all much simpler than that—when they run away we advance; when we run away they will advance."[34] Moreover, Khanzhin's vanguard had lost touch with its supply trains and commissaries and—forced to live off the land like occupiers, not liberators—were the living, breathing, and all-consuming contradiction of the crudely reproduced leaflets they distributed among the villages promising the hungry Urals that "Bread is Coming!" from Siberia.

It would soon be time, as Krol' had been warned, for the Siberian Whites to run away. The Red Eastern Front, erroneously set up by its commander Colonel S.S. Kamenev to absorb a strong push from the Siberian Army (and in general deprived of manpower and other resources, as the Red command prioritized the Western Front and Ukraine over the winter of 1918–19), had been forced to fall back before Khanzhin's initially rampant Western Army (which had a 4:1 local advantage in men and artillery over the opposing 5th Red Army around Ufa). But in April 1919, new reserves (many of them from central Russian Bolshevik and trade union organizations) were poured into that sector, swelling a Maneuvering Group under the hugely talented Red commander M.V. Frunze which, as the spring floods receded in May, would push northwards from Buzuluk to bite into the side of the White salient formed by Khanzhin's over-extended advance: Belebei was duly recaptured on 15 May, and on 7 June the charismatic *Komdiv* V.I. Chapaev led the 25th Rifle Division in an audacious storming of the Belaia river to break into Ufa on 9 June 1919, where they found huge supplies of oil and grain. To the north, Gajda's Northern Army was still advancing at this point, capturing Glazov in early June, but, with its left flank now exposed by the sudden disintegration of the Western Army, was forced to turn and flee, abandoning Glazov on 13 June, reaching Perm' (their point of departure in March) by the end of June and surrendering the key Urals city of Ekaterinburg on 15 July 1919 to the vanguard of the 2nd Red Army that had advanced 200 miles in less than four weeks.[35] At this point Trotsky and Glavkom Vācietis argued for calling a halt, but were overruled by Lenin and, at the instigation of Eastern Front commander S.S. Kamenev, the pursuit of the Whites beyond the Urals was continued.[36] Soon thereafter, in July 1919, Kamenev replaced Vācietis as *glavkom* and the latter was given three months in prison to reconsider his strategy.[37]

Over the coming months, Kolchak made several attempts to staunch the wounds inflicted upon the Russian Army, but to no avail. First Kappel''s Volga Corps was thrown into the fray, followed by General Knox's still skeletal reserve formations from the rear; but, utterly unprepared, both forces melted away overnight, as thousands of White conscripts deserted to the oncoming Reds, many of them sporting their newly issued British uniforms and holding their newly acquired Remington rifles from the United States.[38] Others went over to the partisan forces that by the summer of 1919 had made much of the Siberian rear a no-go area for the Kolchak authorities beyond the narrow and fragile ribbon of the Trans-Siberian Railroad (which was still policed by Czech and other Allied troops, though they were more motivated to protect it as their own escape route to the east than by any will to maintain Kolchak's lifeline from the Pacific Coast).

Next, having on 23 May 1919 added the portfolio of minister of war to his résumé, Colonel Lebedev oversaw a complete restructuring of the remaining forces of Kolchak's Russian Army into a White Eastern Front in June–July.[39] Then, at Cheliabinsk in July, he attempted to set a trap for the Reds, but the pincers of his uncoordinated counter-attack failed to meet and the helter-skelter retreat was resumed.[40] After this debacle—which was doubly embarrassing as it coincided with the Omsk Diplomatic Conference, at which Allied representatives gathered at Kolchak's capital to consider how their governments might best aid the admiral—Lebedev was sacked in August, but this could not alter the verdict of the Allied delegates that Kolchak was now a lost cause. (For several of them, it was their first venture from Vladivostok into darkest White Siberia.) To confirm that conclusion, another effort to check the Red advance between the rivers Ishim and Tobol', masterminded by Kolchak's new commander-in-chief General Diterikhs, was similarly botched in early September 1919, as key army groups (notably the Siberian Cossacks Corps of Ataman P.P. Ivanov-Rinov) failed to move on the field of battle quite as smoothly as they did on paper.[41] Diterikhs's services were then also briskly dispensed with, but Kolchak's capital, Omsk, could not be saved by his pugnacious successor, General K.V. Sakharov, despite the latter's fashioning of the optimistically monikered "Moscow Army Group" from the remnants of the White Eastern Front: depleted forces of the Reds' 27th Rifle Division, who had advanced 150 miles in two days, entered and captured the city early on 14 November 1918, before half the defending garrison was even awake—or, rather, half of those garrison units that remained in Omsk, for by that point "Devil Take the Hindmost" had replaced "All for the Army" as the Whites' slogan of the hour. Fleeing officers were particularly anxious to remove tell-tale signs of their status in case they were apprehended by the Reds, with the result that Omsk's streets "were so thickly littered with epaulettes as to suggest the idea of fallen leaves in autumn," according to a British witness.[42]

Sakharov was then arrested by the exasperated General A.N. Pepeliaev on 9 December 1919, and replaced as commander by General Kappel', but by then the remains of Pepeliaev's own 1st Army had mutinied around Tomsk, while their former commander, General Gajda—who had been sacked in early July 1919 for having criticized Lebedev's direction of the Spring Offensive and refused to recognize the authority of General Diterikhs, and for allegedly harboring SRs in his army[43]—had placed himself at the head of a mutiny against Kolchak at Vladivostok (the Gajda putsch) that had been organized by local SRs and encouraged by British diplomats. Likewise, General B.M. Zinevich, suddenly elevated to the post of commandant of the region's largest industrial city, Krasnoiarsk, when his predecessor (General Markovs-kii) fled, also led its garrison in revolt in support of a nebulous SR–Menshevik organization, the Political Center, which was emerging from the underground in towns all along the Trans-Siberian Railroad. Meanwhile, the remnants of the Southern Army and its Urals and Orenburg Cossack auxiliaries were by now cut off from the main White force: some fled south towards the Caspian (and ultimately Persia), while others followed Dutov toward Semirech'e (and ultimately Chinese Turkestan).[44]

Over the summer and autumn of 1919, extensive government reshuffles removed from office the members of Kolchak's cabinet most despised for their scheming (Mikhailov, jointly Minister of Finance and Minister of Trade and Industry), corruption (N.S. Zefirov, Minister of Food), and inertia (General N.A. Stepanov, Minister of War). Prime Minister P.G. Vologodskii, Minister of Justice G.G. Tel'berg, Foreign Minister I.I. Sukin, and Minister of Marine Rear Admiral M.I. Smirnov were also removed, "as men too unpopular and too closely connected to the very acme of tyranny, the Supreme Ruler," noted Kolchak's secretary.[45] But reshuffling such a depleted deck was ultimately unimpressive to either domestic or foreign observers (and certainly no further rumor of recognition was reported from Paris): the new government named itself the "Cabinet of Solidarity," but looked more like a cabinet of mediocrity, to which the addition of a few figures of reputed "national standing" who had arrived from South Russia added little luster.[46] Meanwhile, an array of popular assemblies—a State Economic Conference and a Zemskii Sobor' ("Assembly of the Lands") among them—summoned by the admiral to broaden the support of his regime and to demonstrate its democratic credentials, either were stillborn or became centers of opposition to the regime.[47] The Omsk government itself then hurriedly retreated to Irkutsk, where, in a neat and vengeful reversal of Omsk's own mistreatment of the Ufa Directory in October–November 1918, it found itself first snubbed by the revivified local socialist organizations that it courted and was then forcibly removed from power by an uprising of the Political Center across the New Year of 1919–20.[48] White Siberia, clearly, was descending into chaos, as the Supreme Ruler and his forces set out eastwards from Omsk in an operation, the Great Siberian (Ice) March, that was flattered with onomastic echoes of the Volunteers' heroic campaign across the Kuban of two years earlier, but was actually a humiliating and unremitting Via Dolorosa for the Siberian Whites and engraved memories only of horror, not glory, in the consciousness of those who survived it to drag themselves into Transbaikal in early 1920.[49]

There, at Chita, the unedifying prospect of being incorporated into the Far Eastern (White) Army of Ataman Semenov, whose murderous and tyrannical warlord regime at Chita had done so much to besmirch the White banner over the previous year, proved too much for some White leaders (Generals Diterikhs, Khanzhin, and Voitsekhovskii among them), who swiftly moved on toward the Maritime Province or Manchuria. Those who remained would receive their campaign medal for the Siberian Ice March, but their award's outward resemblance to that representation of a sword on crown of thorns sported by the *pervopokhodniki* struck a false note at heart. Among the posthumous recipients of the Order of the Great Siberian (Ice) March were some of the latest fallen heroes of the White movement in the east, including General Kappel', lost to frostbite in the east Siberian taiga, as his force was obliged to forge a route around the Red uprising at Krasnoiarsk in January 1920. His followers, in another echo of the branding of the "colorful regiments" of the Volunteer Army, now dubbed themselves the *"kappel'evtsy."*[50] But—emblematically of the chaos now descending upon White Siberia—when he found out that Semenov was welcoming the *kappel'evtsy* into his army, General Sakharov refused to serve alongside them, regarding the division as the bearers of the "democratic spirit" of the ranks of Komuch's People's Army, in which their units had been born. Sakharov found even more repugnant that Semenov had named another unit after General Pepeliaev, the very man who had arrested him in December 1919, and moved promptly into emigration. There, Sakharov would fire off a series of histories of the civil war in the east, excoriating the Allies, the Czechs, the SRs, and Pepeliaev for the fate of White Siberia—even as Pepeliaev remained in the field, engaged in partisan warfare against the Reds in the frozen taiga of Iakutia until June 1923. This was a fitting testimony for the fissile history of the Whites in the east.[51]

* * *

In sharp contrast to the sniping of the Whites—and despite the earlier tussle over strategy and command involving Trotsky, Vācietis, and S.S. Kamenev—following a July 1919 overhaul of the RVSR, which introduced more order into its proceedings by trimming its membership and formalized a closer supervision of its staff, the Red Army's command became increasingly harmonious, effective, and efficient. As priority shifted over the summer of 1919, to meet the growing threat from the Whites in the south (necessitating the creation of a new South East Front in September 1919), and weight was given too to the Turkestan Front (including the transfer to it of the 1st and 4th Red Armies in August 1919), Red commanders of the Eastern Front had every right to complain of shortages of men and supplies. Yet they still bettered their opponents. Indeed, the advance on the Eastern Front in the second half of 1919 exemplified the strengths of the Red Army's soldiering—and particularly its ability to mix precocious but untutored talent with experience. At *komandarm* level, the 26-year-old future marshal of the Soviet Union M.N. Tukhachevskii (5th Red Army), who had a 1914 rank of sub-lieutenant and little experience of fighting in the Great War (having spent most of it as a POW in Bavaria's Ingolstadt fortress, alongside none other than Charles de Gaulle), and the Bolshevik ensign G.D. Gai (1st Red Army) vied in heroics with the seasoned *genshtabisty* F.M. Afanas'ev (2nd Red Army), M.I. Alafuzo (3rd Red Army), and V.S. Lazarevich (4th Red Army). At the level of front commander, the inexperienced but brilliant Mikhail Frunze kept up the momentum of the counter-offensive against Kolchak before being transferred to the command of the Turkestan Front. Illustrating the Reds' flexibility, Frunze was replaced on the Eastern Front (on 15 August 1919) by his polar opposite, General V.A. Ol'derogge (a veteran of service with the imperial army in the Russo-Japanese War), who would push eastwards to Krasnoiarsk before the front was disbanded on 15 January 1920—the day on which a train carrying a very special passenger steamed into Irkutsk station.

* * *

Admiral Aleksandr Kolchak was to be among those Siberian Whites who did not reach Transbaikal. On 4 January 1920, in an obscure railway siding at Nizhneudinsk in Eastern Siberia that must have evoked memories of the one near Pskov that had witnessed the abdication of Nicholas II in March 1917, Kolchak had stood down as supreme ruler, passing authority in South Russia to General Denikin and command of the Far East to Ataman Semenov. But although vouchsafed passage to the Far East by the Allies—the former Supreme Ruler's train henceforth sported the flags of the Allied powers and was guarded by a Czech battalion—on arrival at Irkutsk both Kolchak and the remainder of the Imperial Russian Gold Reserve that was aboard his echelon were traded like so much war booty to the Political Center, the new SR–Menshevik insurgent authority around Baikal, by the Czechoslovak Legion. The nominal commander of the Legion, General Maurice Janin, shamefully refrained from interfering in this business (and, in truth, could probably not have persuaded the otherwise stranded and vulnerable Czechs to act otherwise). In return, the Legionnaires received guarantees of their own safe passage to the east, which they further buttressed by securing a truce with pursuing Red forces at Kuitun on 15 February 1920. Following a brief interrogation by the Political Center and the Bolshevik *revkom* that soon succeeded SR–Menshevik rule at Irkutsk,[52] Kolchak was executed by Cheka firing squad on the morning of 7 February 1920 to dissuade White units approaching from the west from attempting to rescue him, and his body submerged beneath the ice of the river Ushakovka outside Irkutsk prison. Such was the tawdry and ignoble end of the White movement in Siberia, although a lengthy coda remained to be played out in the Far East.[53]

Denikin's Moscow Offensive

The chief reason for the inability of General Denikin to move his forces toward a union with Kolchak's Russian Army in the spring of 1919 was that he was still engaged in a general restructuring of the White armies in South Russia (to incorporate their Cossack allies) and had also fully to secure their rear and their base territory in the North Caucasus.[54] Regarding the latter, the 11th and 12th Red Armies (constituting the Caspian–Caucasus Front, from 8 December 1918) had been mortally weakened by the Volunteers' second Kuban campaign and were (with Tsaritsyn under siege) almost completely isolated from Moscow, but, despite the ice in the northern Caspian rendering temporarily useless the Astrakhan–Caspian Military Flotilla, Red forces in the region could be resupplied to some extent by camel train from the Bolshevik stronghold of Astrakhan (where successive pro-White rebellions involving the Astrakhan Cossack Host were suppressed by Soviet forces in January–February and August 1918 and March 1919). This Red threat to the White rear was only nullified by a new campaign in early 1919 that sent White forces under General Wrangel and Generals A.G. Shkuro and V.L. Pokrovskii (both of whom were noted for their utter ruthlessness in dealing with the enemy) down the railway line parallel to the northern slopes of the Caucasus range to capture Kislovodsk, Piatigorsk (both 20 January 1919), Grozny (5 February 1919), and—after a brief siege—the capital of the Terek Cossack Host, Vladikavkaz (10 February 1919). In this campaign, the Whites had sometimes uncertain allies among the so-called Mountain Peoples of the North Caucasus, but Soviet forces, which were already disorganized and poorly disciplined, faced a temporarily more devastating foe in the typhus epidemic that decimated the 11th Red Army (although as a sign of its indiscriminate fickleness, the typhus then infected and almost killed Wrangel).[55] An early Soviet account estimated that in its 250-mile retreat from Kizliar to the Red haven of Astrakhan, the 11th Red Army suffered 25,000 casualties.[56]

Wrangel's glittering success in the south-east, against what had once been a 150,000-strong Red force (albeit now reduced to a vagrant and diseased rabble), was not repeated to Denikin's north. A Don Cossack offensive did reach Liski (just 80 miles south of Voronezh) in November 1918, and Tsaritsyn remained under siege until January 1919, but Moscow was now throwing men and supplies at the Southern Front (which reached a strength of 120,000 men with almost 500 guns and 2,000 machine-guns by February 1919) and had salved the command irritations enflamed by *voenspets*–commissar friction during the Tsaritsyn affair both by recalling Stalin and other troublesome commissars and replacing the *voenspets* at the center of the dispute, General P.P. Sytin, in November 1918. Sytin's immediate successor as front commander, Colonel P.A. Slaven, might have caused a disaster when he deserted to the Whites, but his successor (from 24 January 1919), the exceptionally able Colonel V.M. Gittis, organized a successful offensive from January 1919 against the Don Army. By April 1919, forces of the Southern Front (chiefly the 8th, 9th, 13th Red Armies and the 2nd Ukrainian Soviet Army) had recaptured Rostov-on-Don, and forced the rivers San and Manych, and were advancing on Bataisk and Tikhoretsk in the northern Kuban. The Cossacks' plight, though, at least had the advantage of forcing a unified command upon anti-Bolshevik forces in the south: with the Germans evacuating and their

Ukrainian puppet Hetman ensconced in a sleeper berth on the express train to Berlin, the Don Cossacks had no choice but to switch their *orientatsiia* toward the pro-Allied Volunteers, even if this compromised their urge for autonomy.[57] Consequently, at a meeting at Torgovaia *stanitsa* (Sal'sk, 100 miles south-east of Rostov) on 8 January 1919, the Don Army's leadership agreed to its forces' subordination to the Volunteers' command. General Krasnov, now an awkward reminder of the Cossacks' recent past as the Kaiser's ally (or "whore," as, according to Krasnov, Denikin preferred bluntly to phrase it)[58] did the honorable thing and resigned as Host *ataman* on 19 February 1919, to be replaced by the pro-Volunteer *pervopokhodnik* General A.P. Bogaevskii.[59] Similar arrangements were then made with the host governments of the Kuban and Terek Cossacks; and thus were created the Armed Forces of South Russia, with General Denikin as main commander-in-chief.

This organizational success was augmented by other developments that, by the summer of 1919, had swung the fortunes of war in the anti-Bolsheviks' favor in the south. One important factor was the arrival at Novorossiisk of the first consignments of Allied aid—contingents of weapons that would eventually amount to almost 200,000 rifles and 500 million rounds of ammunition, over 1,000 heavy guns and 6,200 machine-guns, as well as around sixty tanks and 168 aircraft (together with vital training crews and engineers and spare parts, those associated with armory located at the Taganrog "Tankadrome").[60]

Another bonus for the Whites was that even as Red forces moved south, in January–April 1919—far from their Moscow central command (where the RVSR had to deal simultaneously with the advance of Kolchak and the Red Army's efforts to push into the Baltic and Ukraine), away from their bases and into the very hostile Cossack lands—the local Bolsheviks again engaged in ultra-radical policies that turned the populace against them. This time, added to the usual ultra-Bolshevik agenda of forced requisitions and Cheka expeditions, was a round of "de-Cossackization" that had resulted in the mass execution of at least 8,000 Don Cossacks within a few weeks of an order from the Bolshevik Central Committee of 24 January 1919 that called for "merciless mass terror" against the Don Host and implied the extermination of its military and political elite.[61] A new uprising of the Don Cossacks began immediately across the northern Don territory (centered on Veshenskaia *stanitsa*, under Coronet P. Kundinov), in the rear of the Southern Front. There, from 11 March 1919 onwards, an estimated 30,000 insurgents created havoc in the rear of the 9th Red Army, while receiving supplies dropped by air from Denikin's British planes, and tied down a similar number of Red troops in a hastily assembled counter-insurgency force that took several weeks to crush the

"Veshensk Rebellion." Meanwhile, the Don Army of General P.Kh. Popov extended is sphere of operations further and further northward.[62]

Also a factor here was that the Whites were relieved of any meaningful pressure on their left flank, in south-eastern Ukraine. There, the disorder engendered to the west by the Hryhroriiv uprising had been echoed with a turn against Moscow among the Bolsheviks' other main Ukrainian ally, Nestor Makhno's Revolutionary Insurgent Army. Makhno and his anarchists—although, contrary to legend, no strangers to military hierarchy—chafed under the discipline demanded of them as a constituent force of the 14th Red Army by the commander of the Southern Front, Colonel Gittis, and resisted the extension of formal Soviet power into their own home region (the so-called "Free Territory") around Guliai-Pole (the birthplace, in Ekaterinoslav *guberniia*, of Nestor Makhno, Petr Gavrilenko, Semen Karetnikov, Fedor Shchus', G.S. Vasilevskii, B.V. Veretel'nikov, and several other senior Makhnovist commanders). Consequently, in May–June 1919, White forces commanded by the energetic and unpredictable General Shkuro were able to burst through the Makhnovist lines.[63] Trotsky immediately declared Makhno to be an outlaw and there ensued another of the series of Soviet–Makhno conflicts that dotted the calendar of the civil war in this region.[64]

Despite these factors favoring the Whites, the Reds retained a numerical advantage over their opponents on the Don of something like 2:1 (*c*.90,000:*c*.45,000 troops) in June 1919, and enjoyed very tangible advantages in artillery and machine-guns, but what they still lacked in this very mobile war were large and effective cavalry formations. At this point, the cavalry was still distained by the Bolsheviks, as both an allegedly obsolete form of military organization in the age of the airplane and the tank and, as the most elitist corps of the former imperial army, the most likely breeding ground of counter-revolutionaries. The Whites, by contrast—and perhaps by deliberation—idolized the cavalry and one of their most effective and experienced horse commanders, General V.Z. Mai-Maevskii, as commander of the Azov and then the Don Group of the AFSR and then (from 10 May 1919) commander of the Volunteer Army itself, utilized comparatively small forces of them (in combination with the dense network of railways in the Don region and concentrated aerial surveillance) in a series of brilliantly executed coups to scatter Red forces across the Don in May–June 1919.[65]

In comparison to Lieutenant-General Mai-Maevskii, who had commanded the 1st Guards Army Corps in 1917, Red *komandarmy* on the Southern Front at this juncture were severely lacking in experience. Some had huge promise, especially the Red commanders Tukhachevskii (8th Red Army, 24 January–15 March 1919) and A.I. Egorov (10th Red Army, 26 December 1918–25 May 1919), but most others—A.E. Skachko (2nd Ukrainian Soviet Army, 7 April–7 June 1919), T.S. Khvesin (8th Red Army, 15 March–18 May 1919), V.V. Liubimov (8th Red Army, 3 April–8 May 1919), P.E. Kniagnitskii (9th Red Army, 23 November 1918–6 June 1919), and I.S. Kozhevnikov (13th Red Army, 6 March–16 April 1919)—were of mettle to match only their less than elevated status as junior officers and NCOs in the tsarist army. They tended, rightly, to be removed from their army commands during or soon after the reversals suffered on the Southern Front in the summer of 1919 and none of them would ever rise again to such an exalted post. Moreover, any good work the Red *komandarmy* of the Southern Front may have done in the first half of 1919 was probably undone, as the second half of that year dawned, by the desertion to the Whites of another of their number, Colonel N.D. Vsevolodov. Vsevolodov only commanded the 9th Red Army for ten days (6–16 June 1919) before his flight, but he had been its chief of staff for six months prior to that (29 October 1918–20 April 1919) and had probably been relaying information across the lines before his sudden disappearance.[66]

With the Red Army's Southern Front in disarray and much of its immediate rear in flames, Denikin's forces finally struck in June 1919 (just as Kolchak's Russian Army was abandoning the Urals). In the west, White cavalry overran much of Southern Ukraine, as far as the lower Dnepr and the city of Ekaterinoslav (which fell to General Shkuro's merciless "White Wolves" on 29–30 June 1919), while General N.N. Shilling's 3rd Army Corps (the former Crimean–Azov Volunteer Army) cleared the Reds from the Crimea and moved across the Perekop isthmus into northern Tauride. In the center of the AFSR front, meanwhile, Mai-Maevskii's Volunteer Army smashed the Reds' hurriedly improvised Khar'kov Fortified Region and, on 27 June 1919, occupied Khar'kov itself—the major industrial city of eastern Ukraine, a key railway junction and capital of the (chiefly phantom) Ukrainian SSR—while the Don Army (under General V.I. Sidorin) united with the Cossack rebels at Veshenskaia to expel Soviet forces from the entire Host territory by the end of June. Further east, after a series of initially repulsed northward advances from the Manych, the Kuban Cossacks of the Caucasian Army (commanded by the inspirational General Wrangel) finally, with the aid of British aircraft and tanks, broke through the barbed-wire-ringed defenses of Tsaritsyn, and occupied the long-besieged "Red Verdun" on 30 June 1919, snaring 40,000 prisoners and more than 2,000 railway wagons of stores and munitions in the process.[67] Trotsky's imprecation in May 1919 that "This spring and this summer we must finish with the Southern Front for good and all" had been spectacularly ineffective.[68]

* * *

On 3 July 1919, having attended a victory parade of Wrangel's forces outside the Kazan' Cathedral in central Tsaritsyn, General Denikin then delivered one of the most fateful orders of the entire civil war. According to the main commander's Order No. 08878, better known as the "Moscow Directive," the AFSR was instructed to move on to a general advance, along the network of railway lines converging on the ancient capital—a strategic offensive aimed at "the occupation of the heart of Russia, Moscow." To that end, the Volunteer Army was to progress on a line through Kursk, Orel, and Tula to Moscow; the Don Army was to pass through Voronezh and Riazan' to Moscow; and the Caucasian Army was to move in a loop from Tsaritsyn through Saratov, Nizhnii Novgorod, and Vladimir to Moscow.[69] Posters and banners urging forces "To Moscow" suddenly sprang up across the White territory. To some, including Wrangel, this smacked of recklessness, but Denikin was probably right to gamble on a repeat of the sort of impulsive victory the Volunteers had already pulled off—by sheer force of will, time and time again, and against numerically superior forces—before the Red Army's rich and populous base territory could produce numbers of recruits and weapons that no amount of appeals to the "White idea" could out-gun.

Interestingly, Denikin's order made no mention of operations west of the River Dnepr, which he clearly intended to act as a defensive barrier on the left flank of the AFSR (and perhaps as a cordon against the Ukrainian anarchy that seemed to infect all who came in contact with it), but it was in the nature of the civil-war chaos that it was beyond the Dnepr, in right-bank Ukraine, where many initial AFSR successes actually came. As the Red Ukrainian Front shattered and the 14th Red Army disintegrated, White forces captured Poltava (29 July 1919), Kherson, and Nikolaev (18 August 1919). On 23 August 1919, assisted by marines landed by the Black Sea Fleet, White forces also captured the key port of Odessa and on the same day entered the Ukrainian capital, Kiev.[70]

A second impressive White operation launched in these weeks was also absent from the Moscow Directive (which might suggest that Denikin's control of the AFSR was less complete than he might have wished): on 10 August

1919, taking advantage of a gap in the Southern Front at Novokhopersk, between the 8th and 9th Red Armies, General K.K. Mamontov launched an immensely damaging excursion of Cossack forces (the 4th Don Cavalry Corps) into the rear of the Red lines (the "Mamontov Raid"), capturing Tambov (18 August 1919, almost netting Trotsky himself in the process), wrecking lines of communication to the Reds' Southern Front and forcing the Soviet authorities to declare a state of siege across a broad region encompassing Riazan', Tula, Orel', Voronezh, Tambov, and Penza *gubernii*. For one day (11–12 September 1919), Mamontov even occupied the city of Voronezh, where his larcenous troops made merry and looted everything they could carry, as they had throughout the operation.[71]

Meanwhile, further east, Wrangel's Caucasian Army (manned chiefly by Kuban Cossacks) pushed north from Tsaritsyn, up the Volga through Kamyshin (captured by forces commanded by General V.L. Pokrovskii on 28 July 1919) to a point just 60 miles short of Saratov in the first days of August. But, hampered by the absence of a railway line along the Volga, the Caucasian Army, which was in dire need of supplies and reinforcements, could get no further in a sector that was also being rapidly reinforced by the Reds with units switched from the Eastern Front (notably, most of the complement of the former 2nd Red Army). The Caucasian Army was also in desperate need of reserves and re-provisioning, but got scant help from the Kuban—despite a series of urgent appeals from Wrangel to Ataman V.G. Naumenko and even a personal emergency begging mission to Ekaterinodar by Wrangel that it must have pained the haughty baron terribly to undertake.[72] Consequently, by the end of August, Wrangel's forces were back in Tsaritsyn. Faced thereafter with a special "Striking Group" of Red Forces commanded by the *voenspets* Colonel V.I. Shorin (reconstituted as a new South Eastern Front from 27 September 1919), the Caucasian Army might have lost Tsaritsyn too had Shorin not been obliged to divert troops westward to deal with the Mamontov Raid, and would never again make significant northward progress (although it would not surrender Tsaritsyn until 2 January 1920). Wrangel's force's intermittent contacts on the left bank of the Volga with outliers of Kolchak's fugitive Urals Army only sharpened a bitter sense of what might have been had the southern and Siberian White armies been able to combine effectively.

With its left flank fanning out across Ukraine and its right flank stalled on the Volga, the AFSR's double-pronged spearhead was now formed by the Volunteer Army and the Don Army. Their departure north was delayed by a series of Red counter-attacks in August–September and, as the juncture between them was levered open in August, by a 100-mile thrust to Kupansk (captured on 25 August 1919) launched in mid-August by a Red strike force consisting of the 8th Red Army and parts of the 13th Red Army under Lieutenant-General V.I. Selivachev, former commander of the imperial Russian 7th Army in 1917. But Selivachev's group of forces progressed no further than Kupansk and the entire Red front seemed in disarray at this point, as Trotsky, Lenin, S.S. Kamenev, the RVSR and its Field Staff, and the Bolshevik Party leadership all proposed conflicting schemes and choices of commander to deal with the AFSR.[73] So, in late September, Denikin's great Moscow offensive got underway, with its spine along the Khar'kov–Kursk–Orel–Tula–Moscow railway and its mailed fist consisting of the crack divisions of the Volunteer Army—notably its "colorful units" (the *Drozdovtsy, Kornilovtsy,* and *Markovtsy*), named for the fallen heroes of 1918.[74] Kursk was captured on 20 September 1919, with Red units deserting en masse to Mai-Maevskii's forces, and on 14 October 1919, the city of Orel fell to the *Kornilovtsy*, placing the White vanguard just over 200 miles from Moscow, primed to advance further and anticipating the opportunity to rearm en route, as their forces passed through the city of Tula, home of the arsenal founded by Peter the Great 200 years earlier. On the Volunteers' right flank, meanwhile, General Shkuro captured Voronezh on 30 September 1919 and welcomed the Don Army into the city a few days later.

The North West Army, the Landeswehr War, and the Siege of Petrograd

Denikin's now converging thrusts toward Moscow seemed all the more inexorable and irresistible because they coincided with another White advance, by the North West Army on Petrograd—precisely the sort of combined and synchronous operations that had eluded the AFSR and Kolchak's Russian Army six months earlier. The North West Army (which until 1 July 1919 was called the Northern Army Corps) was created on 19 June 1919, in Estonia, on the basis of the former Pskov Volunteer Corps (numbering perhaps 6,000 men in total) and other White units operating in the Baltic region, many of which had initially been sponsored, armed, and uniformed by the local German forces.[75]

The Pskov Volunteer Corps had been created at its namesake city, from September 1918 onwards, by Captains V.G. von Rozenberg and A.K. Gershel'man (local representatives of an underground officer organization in Petrograd) and was then commanded by General A.E. Vandam (from October 1918), Colonel A.F. Dzerozhinskii (January–May 1919), and Major-General

A.P. Rodzianko (from 1 June 1919). By late November 1918, with the encouragement and assistance of local German forces, it had registered some 4,500 volunteers—about half of them officers of the imperial Russian Army (some of them repatriated from German POW camps), the rest consisting of students and other elements—but was nevertheless forced out of the city by the Red Army, as the Germans withdrew after the armistice. Most of the Corps then moved on to Estonian territory. Although the Pskov Corps was now formally subordinated to the Estonian Army, as the Russian Whites found themselves in the uncomfortable position of fighting the Bolsheviks on the nationalists' side during the Estonian War of Independence, the Estonian authorities regarded them with suspicion bordering on hostility (and rightly so, as most of the White officers of the Pskov Corps were firmly opposed to Estonian independence). Consequently, the Estonians insisted, on 4 December 1918, that the Corps' complement should not exceed 3,500 men, although by the time of its offensive in May 1919 it probably numbered some 4,500 once again. Its chief components were the 1st Pskov Volunteer Rifle Regiment, the 2nd Ostrovskii Volunteer Rifle regiment, the 3rd Rezhitsk Volunteer Rifle Corps, and the Independent Detachment of S.N. Bułak-Bałachowicz (which had deserted from the Red Army near Luga in November 1918), each of which mustered some 800 men. On 1 June 1919, the Pskov Rifle Corps was named as an Independent Corps of the Northern Army. On 19 June 1919 the Corps left the Estonian Army, and from 1 July 1919 it formed the kernel of the new White North West Army.[76]

Command of the North West Army was then taken by General N.N. Iudenich, one of Russia's most successful commanders of the world war, whose tenure as commander of the Caucasus Army had witnessed the notable victory over the Turks at the Battle of Sarıkamış (December 1914–January 1915). On 5 June 1919, Iudenich (who had previously been working underground against the Bolsheviks in Petrograd before fleeing to Finland, in October 1918, to found the anti-Bolshevik Russian Committee in Helsinki) had been named by Admiral Kolchak as main commander of forces on the North West Front.[77] An initial move against Petrograd, in May–June 1919, however, achieved little success, despite the arrival of Iudenich during its prosecution: the Northern Corps undertook an offensive from 13 May 1919, capturing Gdov (15 May 1919), Iamburg (17 May 1919), and, once more, Pskov (25 May 1919), but were then driven back from Luga and Gatchina in early June and finally evacuated Pskov on 28 August 1919. Apart from the superior strength of local Red forces, this failure was caused chiefly by the grave distractions being created in the rear of the North West Front by White units that were nominally subordinate to its command. The very weakly developed White political authorities in the region (the North West Government, chaired by the oil baron S.G. Lianozov, who also served also as Minister of Foreign Affairs and Minister of Finance in that cabinet, bearing witness, perhaps, to the dearth of political talent available to Iudenich) proved also to be entirely incapable of motivating the local population to support the anti-Bolshevik drive.[78] That, however, did not prevent the ever-optimistic Whites from fashioning a very short-lived (and Kadet-dominated) Petrograd Government in October 1919, ready to assume control of the city once the Bolsheviks had fled.

In theory, the North West Front included also the rogue Western Volunteer Army that had been created by the unpredictable General P.R. Bermondt-Avalov, who, in the course of the civil wars, was a cuckoo in several other forces' nests. In the spring and summer of 1919, certainly, Bermondt-Avalov seemed more interested in allying with German formations in the Baltic theater, loosely united as the Baltische Landeswehr, notably those of General Rüdiger von der Goltz (the Iron Division), who arrived from his previous service in Finland to drive the Latvian national government of Kārlis Ulmanis out of Riga on 22–23 May 1919, establishing there the short-lived pro-German puppet regime of Pastor Andrievs Niedra, before turning north to attack Estonia—all part of the so-called Landeswehr War. Soon, though, outnumbered by the 8,000-strong Estonian 3rd Division (incorporating the Latvian Northern Brigade of Jorģis Zemitāns), commanded by General Ernst Põdder, which could also deploy armored trains captured from the Red Army and the battle-hardened partisan unit founded by Julius Kuperjanov, the Bermondtians were put to the sword. After a major battle on 23 June 1919, the Estonians also recaptured Cēsis (Wenden) from von der Goltz and the Germans hastily began to retreat towards Riga. On 3 July 1919, with Estonian and Latvian forces at the gates of Riga, a ceasefire was hastily imposed by the Allies and German forces were ordered to leave Latvia—although many surreptitiously joined the Bermondtians, who remained in the field and even captured part of Riga again in November 1919, before being forced to disperse by the Allies.[79]

While this distraction was being played out in his rear, Iudenich set about expanding and restructuring the other, marginally more controllable, forces at his command. Thus, from 24 August 1919, the North West Army consisted of the 1st and 2nd Army (Rifle) Corps (commanded by General A.P. von der Pahlen and General E.K. Arsen'ev respectively) and the 1st

(Independent) Infantry Division. By October 1919, this had expanded to two rifle corps, five infantry divisions, and other smaller units (totaling some 18,500 men in the active army and 50,000 in all), supported by four armored trains, six tanks, two armored cars, and six aircraft. The North West Army also had operational command of some small sections of the White Fleet (flotillas on the River Narva and Lake Chud, for example). One in ten of the complement of the army were officers, including fifty-three generals.

Despite the failure of its May–June 1919 offensive, Iudenich's force had at that point moved beyond the Estonian border to occupy a strip of chiefly Russian-populated territory east of the River Narva and Lake Chud. It had the advantage that the Red Army was facing revolts within its own forces and had to deal also with the troublesome presence of the Royal Navy in the Baltic and even in the Gulf of Finland.[80] The North West Army also had at its back the Estonian Army of General Johan Laidoner. The Estonian forces remained generally inactive on the anti-Bolshevik front, but were, at least—in comparison to Denikin's struggles with the Georgians around Sochi and the Mountaineers in the North Caucasus—not overtly hostile (and, indeed, were only too glad to help usher the Russian Whites as far as possible off Estonian territory). Iudenich was thus able to launch a strategic offensive on 12 October 1919, capturing Luga (16 October 1919), thereby cutting Red communications to Pskov (which Estonian forces, now commanded by the talented General Jānis Balodis, entered on 20 October), and even investing the Petrograd palace suburbs of Gatchina (16 October 1919) and Tsarskoe Selo (20 October 1919), which were only 25 and 12 miles respectively from Nevskii Prospekt and the beckoning Winter Palace itself. The commanders of the armies of both Kolchak and Denikin had imagined at various points that they could hear the tolling of the Kremlin bells in Moscow, but Iudenich's men really could see the autumn sun glinting off the great golden dome of St Isaac's Cathedral in central Petrograd, whose defenses had been depleted by the dispatch to other fronts of many of its Bolshevized workers and sailors.[81]

With the arrival of Trotsky's train in the revolutionary citadel of Petrograd on 17 October 1919, however, the Whites' fortunes changed forever. In energetic collaboration with Colonel V.M. Gittis (now commander of the Western Front) and *komandarm* Colonel S.D. Kharlamov and General N.D. Nadezhnyi—all of them the sort of tough and experienced *voenspetsy* that Trotsky had long favored—a hurriedly reinforced 7th Red Army (with a strength of 40,000 men, 453 field guns, 708 machine-guns, six armored trains, and twenty-three aircraft) was able to halt the advance of General D.R. Vetrenko's 3rd Division of the North West Army before it severed the vital artery of the Moscow–Petrograd railway. Soviet forces then initiated an immediate counter-offensive, on 21 October 1919, that rapidly overwhelmed their opponents, who were inferior in numbers and arms. As Iudenich's shattered forces limped back across the Estonian border, they were disarmed and interned by their unwelcoming hosts.[82] This final development coincided with the arrangement of a Soviet–Estonian ceasefire (5 December 1919) and a formal armistice on 31 December 1919 (there had actually been no fighting to speak of between the two sides for six months), which led swiftly to the subsequent Treaty of Tartu (2 February 1920), bringing an end to the civil-war hostilities between the two countries and sealing the independence of Estonia. That settlement was, in turn, succeeded by the equally quite uncontentious treaties of the RSFSR with Lithuania (Treaty of Moscow, 12 July 1920), Latvia (Treaty of Riga, 11 August 1920), and Finland (Treaty of Tartu, 14 October 1920) that brought to a close the civil wars and wars of independence in the north-west.[83]

* * *

Here we might briefly pause to consider the role that Leon Trotsky, the architect of the Red Army, had played in all this. The dramatic arrival of his train at Petrograd during the days of Iudenich's offensive might have been the war commissar's finest hour as an inspirer and organizer of the Red Army. A contemporary testament, from his friend Karl Radek, does a good job of conveying the awe in which Trotsky was subsequently held by some elements of the party (and suggests the origins of more jealous functionaries' subsequent resentment of such a star). Radek—who, of course, should not be mistaken for a typical Bolshevik, but was nevertheless (despite his cultured individualism) representative of one strand of Bolshevism—in a work devoted to "The Organizer of Victory," proposed that "L.D. [Lev Davidovich] Personified the Revolution." In 1923, he wrote:

> It was only a man who works like Trotsky, a man who spares himself as little at Trotsky, who can speak to the soldiers as only Trotsky can—it was only such a man who could be the standard bearer of the armed working people. He has been everything in one person. He has thought out the strategic advice given by experts and has combined it with a correct estimate of the proportions of social forces; he knew how to unite in one movement the impulses of fourteen fronts, of the ten thousand communists who informed headquarters as to what the real army is and how it is possible to operate with it; he understood how to combine all this in one strategic plan and one scheme of organization, And in all this splendid work he understood better than anyone else how to apply the knowledge of the significance of the moral factor in war.[84]

The emphasis of "the moral factor," here, was an interesting aspect of Radek's analysis. We will return to that. In general, though, Trotsky's transformation from a propagandist, with a few months' experience as a war correspondent in the Balkans in 1912,[85] to the organizer of a multi-million-strong army was remarkable. He was not immune from strategic mistakes: his baiting of the Germans at Brest-Litovsk in February 1918 bought little time, angered the German military, and might have led to their deciding to topple the Soviet regime rather than treat with it; and in June–July 1919, had he been allowed to curtail the Red Army's advance across the Urals, Kolchak's forces might have been able to regroup and join forces with Denikin during the latter's Moscow offensive. But Trotsky's ability to inspire loyalty, his ability to choose wise advisors, and, perhaps above all, his willingness to modify his principles (in particular with regard to the creation of a traditional army staffed by tsarist officers) more than compensated for that. As the *voenkom* himself put it:

> Without constant changes and improvisations the war would have been utterly impossible for us ... I do not want to say that we always succeeded in this. But as the civil war has demonstrated, we did achieve the principal thing—victory.[86]

Also in his arsenal Trotsky had the mobile command and propaganda center to which he and others simply referred as "the train" (formally known as the Train of the Chairman of the Revvoensovet of the Republic). This remarkable institution was formed in Moscow on 7 August 1918, during the great crisis on the Volga. It initially consisted of two armored engines and twelve wagons and was immediately dispatched for Sviiazhsk, on the Volga Front, with a unit of Latvian Riflemen on board. In the course of the civil wars, the train made thirty-six such visits to the various Red fronts and traveled at least 75,000 miles. The train, recalled Trotsky, initiated changes at the front, regulated them, and tied the front to the rear: "The train earned the hatred of its enemies and was proud of it."[87] As the insightful and cultured A.V. Lunacharskii put it, in his collection of candid pen-portraits of his comrades, this was something that Lenin simply could not have done. Although he was soon back at work after the assassination attempt of August 1918, Lenin was never again fully fit and:

> could never have coped with the titanic mission, which Trotsky took upon his shoulders with those lightening moves from place to place, those astounding speeches, those fanfares of on-the-spot orders, the role of being the unceasing electrifier of a weakening army, now at one spot, now at another. There is not a man on earth who could have replaced Trotsky in that respect.[88]

The train, from which Trotsky and his reputation became inseparable, was in action against White forces on thirteen occasions during the civil wars, suffered fifteen casualties (and fifteen more "missing"), and was awarded the Order of the Red Banner for its part in deflecting the North West Army's advance on Petrograd of October 1919. However, its role was not chiefly to fight. Rather, the train provided a secure and mobile base for the central army command and was an inspirational symbol of Bolshevik authority. As Trotsky put it in his memoirs: "The strongest cement in the new army was the ideas of the October Revolution, and the train supplied the front with this cement."[89]

North Russia

Iudenich's efforts might have borne richer fruit had Petrograd been seriously and simultaneously threatened from the north in 1919. But, although Allied forces and their Russian and Karelian allies were advancing down the Murmansk–Petrograd railway to Medvezhia Gora (Medvezh'egorsk), on the northern shores of Lake Onega, and then on toward Petrozavodsk by late May 1919, although a Finnish unit had at the same time crossed the border and was closing on the same city by June, and although (also in May–June) British marines (with a small fleet of well-armed monitors and gunboats) undertook offensives up the rivers Vaga and Northern Dvina toward Kotlas, as other interventionist forces (including US detachments) sortied down the railway from Arkhangel'sk towards Vologda, none of this seriously threatened Petrograd or offered succor to Iudenich.[90] Indeed, it was not intended to do so. The Finns (in their so-called Aunus Expedition, one of several campaigns known collectively as the Kinship Wars) were seeking to detach southern (Olonets) Karelia from Soviet Russia and knew that such an outcome would hardly be countenanced by the Whites, while the British offensives and the 8,000-strong North Russian Relief force that arrived in May–June 1919 were intended only to push the Bolsheviks back, so as to facilitate the complete withdraw of Allied forces that had been agreed upon in April 1919, got underway in June of that year and was completed with the evacuation of Arkhangel'sk (26–27 September 1919) and Murmansk (12 October 1919). Even the construction by the British of a seaplane and motor-boat facility at Medvezhia Gora seems not to have been intended to facilitate a further White advance on Petrograd, but only to ensure that the collapse of the Russian Whites—although it would certainly come—would not come until at least a decent interval had elapsed since the hurried departure of their erstwhile "allies." The abandoned Russians were hardly fooled: Colonel L.V. Kostandi, chief of operations on General Miller's staff, returned his British service awards to the Allied commander, General Edmund Ironside, while the fighter ace Major A.A. Kazakov, the most notable Russian pilot of the era, in an act of protest deliberately smashed his British plane into the ground on 1 August 1919, killing himself instantly in a suicidal act of protest against the perfidy of the Allies.[91]

The last chapter of the northern saga of the civil wars closed with the evacuations of Arkhangel'sk and Murmansk by their last, desperate White defenders in early 1920, but it had always been the strangest of the theaters of struggle. It boasted by far the greatest concentration of Allied troops of the intervention (if one discounts the peculiar Japanese presence in the Far East) and, in the towering and bluff commander of Allied British forces, General Edmund ("Tiny") Ironside, had a figurehead that no Bolshevik propagandist of anti-imperialism could have better caricatured.[92] White forces in the north were also well served by General Miller: his anti-revolutionary credentials (involving almost being lynched by soldiers in April 1917, for banning those under his command from sporting red ribbons) might have been at least matched by those of Admiral Kolchak (who had thrown his Sword of Honor into Sevastopol' harbor rather than surrender it to Red sailors in July 1917) and was bested by Kornilov (who had deserters illegally hanged in June 1917), but no other White or nationalist soldier was better qualified militarily than Miller, who had commanded the 26th Army Corps of the Russian Army at the peak of his long career. Yet, in this sparsely populated polar wilderness, where many potential peasant conscripts were Karelians and shied away from the Russian incomers (or even sought union with Finland), Miller was all too often the epitome of the general without troops. Although the Whites would claim a complement of more than 50,000 in late 1919 (after the Allies had departed and the situation was rendered entirely hopeless), Miller's Northern Army rarely mustered more than 5–10,000 volunteers, as men were rounded up and pressed into service, received their rations and uniforms, and then routinely disappeared back into the taiga. This necessitated such local innovations as the Slavo-British Legion, which is now chiefly remembered for all the wrong reasons—as the only unit of the civil war in which Russian conscripts mutinied against and then killed four of their British officers.[93]

Miller's counterpart on the other side of the front was the commander of the 6th Red Army A.A. Samoilo, who, being also a veteran *genshtabist* (and chief of staff of the imperial Russian 10th Army in 1917), would have been well known to the White leader. Their subsequent fates evoke the diverse paths available to those who survived the civil wars. Far from settling down to an uncomfortable life as a Paris taxi driver or doorman, Miller devoted himself to the White cause, becoming head of the movement's army-in-exile, ROVS, from May 1930, only to be abducted by Stalin's NKVD in September 1937 and smuggled back to Moscow, where he was subsequently executed. For his part, Samoilo, like most other *voenspetsy*, was retired from his command after the civil war and moved into education work. But unlike most *voenspetsy*, he was not done away with in the OGPU's Operation "Spring" of 1930–31, or in the army purges of the 1937–38, but survived, was made lieutenant-general of aviation of the Soviet Army in 1940, at longlast joined the Communist Party in 1944, and in retirement, during Khrushchev's post-Stalin thaw, was even allowed to write his memoirs.[94]

The Collapse of the AFSR, October 1919–April 1920

What proved to be the turning point for the Reds on the Southern Front against Denikin came when Glavkom Kamenev and Trotsky put together a new striking group, featuring strong contingents of the Red veterans of the Latvian and Estonian Riflemen, which drove into the left flank of the Volunteer Army, almost cutting off the *Kornilovtsy* and facilitating the Reds' reoccupation of Orel on 20 October 1919, thereby denying White forces the opportunity of re-equipping at Tula. At the same time, the Volunteers were hit on the opposite flank by an impressive raid launched by a new Red phenomenon—S.M. Budennyi's 1st Cavalry Corps (from 19 November 1919, the 1st Cavalry Army, or *Konarmiia*), the result made flesh of Trotsky's summons of six weeks earlier, "Proletarians, To Horse!"[95] This unexpected transformation of "Communists into cavalrymen," as Trotsky put it (although, in truth, the cavalrymen themselves were overwhelmingly of Cossack not proletarian origin), forced General Shkuro to surrender the key city of Voronezh to Budennyi on 24 October 1919, effectively severing the Volunteers' communications with the Don Army to their east and with their main fortified rear on the Don. When the *Konarmiia* then pushed on to capture the railway junction at Kastornoe (on the Voronezh–Kursk line), disaster loomed for the Whites—and loomed larger when Khar'kov fell as early as 11 December 1919. Until this point, the Volunteers' 150-mile withdrawal had been relatively orderly, but beyond Khar'kov, with the railway lines crammed with typhus-ridden civilian refugees and military casualties, a further headlong 300-mile flight began that by the first week of 1920 saw the remains of the force that had been, just two months earlier, so close to capturing Moscow streaming across the frozen river Don and once more into the North Caucasus.[96]

In rapid pursuit was the *Konarmiia*, now boasting more than 15,000 horsemen supported by eight armored trains and its own squadron of aircraft. It and other Red forces, now vastly outnumbering and out-gunning their opponents, captured Rostov-on-Don and Novocherkassk on the same day, 7 January 1920, but were then briefly delayed as the ice on the Don began to break up.[97] Meanwhile, the left flank of the AFSR also recoiled from the 12th and 14th Red Armies, as Kiev fell on 16 December 1919 and Odessa on 7 February 1920.[98] The attempted White evacuation of the latter—the third such awful hemorrhage the great port had suffered during the civil wars—was a shambles, with the local commander General Shilling (formally governor-general and commander of the Military Forces of New Russia and Crimea) drawing universal criticism for abandoning tens of thousands of retreating AFSR forces and civilians to the Reds.[99] About 27,000 stranded Whites in right-bank Ukraine, cut off from any hope of escape via the Black Sea ports, then embarked in late January with their commander, General N.E. Bredov, on a painful 300-mile forced march northward along the left (Russian, now Soviet) bank of the Dnestr, having been forbidden to cross to the sanctuary of the formerly Russian (now Romanian) right (Bessarabian) bank by the nervous authorities in Bucharest. As if that was not humiliation enough, the survivors of the "Bredov March" were interned in Poland, when forced across its border by a Red Army that Piłsudski was still, in naked self-interest, refusing to fight.[100] The only saving grace for the AFSR was that General Slashchov's 3rd Corps of the Volunteers had cut through Makhno's insurgents in Northern Tauride to reach and then hold the Perekop isthmus, thereby safeguarding the Crimean peninsula as a haven for the fleeing Whites.

As might be expected, the victors of this very dramatic turnaround won the most enduring laurels of the civil war. And none was more laurelled than Semen Budennyi: the son of a landless peasant from the Don Cossack lands, he became one of the five inaugural Marshals of the Soviet Union in 1935 and (unlike the other four) remained of untarnished reputation in the USSR. Despite a very mixed (some would claim disastrous) record of command early in the Second World War, he was wheeled out on parade to display his ever more extravagant moustaches and rekindle memories of glorious times, almost until the day of his death in 1973. Conversely, the White collapse sowed discord among the White leadership and a sense of disorientation, as participants in the retreat tried to keep track of kaleidoscopic changes in command—and even of where Denikin and his *stavka* were actually located, as headquarters shifted almost weekly (from Taganrog, to Rostov, to Tikhoretskaia, to Ekaterinodar, and finally to Novorossiisk in the first weeks of 1920). One of Denikin's first reactions to the sudden collapse was to replace General Mamontov at the head of the Don Army with General S.G. Ulagai, thus infuriating the Don Cossacks (who were already deserting en masse to the Reds, as the latter approached their home territories). In December 1919, Denikin then transferred General Wrangel to the command of the Volunteer Army (replacing the now permanently drunk Mai-Maevskii, who was retired). This was far too late for Wrangel to effect the sort of concentrated Cossack push against Moscow that he had long favored over Denikin's multi-pronged Moscow Directive, and the baron was quick to remind Denikin of this—in a typically tactless letter he sent to his commander in mid-February 1920. Although a recent biographer of Wrangel has highlighted that the baron subsequently censored the letter for publication in his memoirs, omitting passages that he deemed to have been too personal in their attacks on Denikin—expunging, for example, a description of Denikin as a man "poisoned by ambition and the taste of power, surrounded by dishonest flatterers" and one who was "no longer preoccupied with saving the country, but only with preserving power"[101]—Denikin would, of course, have seen the original version and was consequently enraged. Moreover, and most disloyally, the contents of the letter had been leaked by Wrangel to the press and were published widely. One can sense the rage bubbling beneath the surface of Denikin's outwardly calm reply of 25 February 1920:

Dear Sir, Peter Nikolaevich!

Your letter has come just at the right time—at the most difficult moment, when all my spiritual strength must be concentrated on preventing the collapse of the front. I hope that you are satisfied.

If I still had a vestige of doubt concerning your role in the struggle for power, your letter has eliminated it completely. It does not contain a single word of truth. You know this. It presents monstrous accusations, which you do not believe yourself. They are obviously made for the same purpose for which your preceding pamphlet-reports were reproduced and circulated.

You are doing everything you can to undermine the government and bring on disintegration.

There was a time when, suffering from a grave illness, you said to [your chief of staff] Iuzefovich that this was God's punishment for your inordinate ambitiousness. May He forgive you now for the harm you have done to the Russian cause.

A. Denikin[102]

The extent, beyond talk and denunciations, of Wrangel's "conspiracy" against Denikin remains obscure. Wires were certainly crossed at a very confused and nervous time, and the fact that several key commanders were sending Denikin telegrams at this time urging him to make Wrangel commander of the Crimea need not necessarily have portended any coup. Moreover, Wrangel certainly had nothing to do with a rogue White band of deserters and various malcontents under a Captain Orlov, who at this time were advancing from the central mountains of the Crimea towards Sevastopol' and issuing proclamations in which Wrangel was hailed as "our new leader" and calling upon "officers, Cossacks, soldiers and sailors" to join in the cry of "Long live General Wrangel—the strong man with the mighty soul!"[103] But that could have not failed to confirm further in Denikin's mind that he was under a concerted attack from his (in)subordinates. Consequently, in the midst of all this, Wrangel was removed from his active command (2 January 1920). He was subsequently accused of conspiring against the AFSR leadership and, on 28 February 1920, was obliged to leave Russia for exile in Constantinople.[104]

There was still some time for the playing out of feuds in the Red ranks also, as delays in crossing the Don and the Manych enflamed those anxious for a quick kill and made vulnerable those who, for various reasons, had earned the enmity of the man of the moment, Budennyi. Thus, first Colonel Shorin was dismissed as head of the South East Front, which finally took Tsaritsyn only on 2 January 1920, having been set that task back in August 1919. Then, the charismatic cavalryman B.M. Dumenko, a rival to Budennyi as the "first saber of the republic" and chief inspirer of the liberation of the Don over the previous months, was arrested and shot for involvement in the death of his military commissar.[105]

Moreover, the Reds were not without broader tribulations of their own: by early 1920 the forces in the south-east were very far from their home territories, were occupying generally hostile Cossack lands (and were poised to attack more of the same), and were exhausted after their 450-mile counter-thrust against the Whites. Even Budennyi no longer seemed invincible, as his typhus-ravaged force lost most of its artillery in a disastrous effort to storm the Manych, leading to fulminations from Lenin in Moscow regarding the poor state of the troops on the Caucasus Front and "the flabbiness of the over-all command" and panicky predictions that Rostov, Novocherkassk, and even the Donbass might soon be surrendered to the Whites.[106] Denikin, therefore, ignored murmurings that he should resign and recall Wrangel, while making more changes and concessions to local sentiments in a last-ditch effort to shore up his regime.

It was, thus, the *ataman* of the Don Cossack Host, General A.P. Bogaevskii, who was chosen to replace the disgraced Volunteer General Lukomskii as head of the Government of the Main Commander of the AFSR (itself merely a new version of the Special Council, but with appropriately repositioned deck-chairs), while it was the commander of the Don Army, General V.I. Sidorin, who took command of the front. But this was all to no avail: a general All-Cossack Supreme Krug gathered in January 1920 (with representatives of the Don, Kuban, Terek, Astrakhan, and other hosts) was not in the mood to bar-gain with the AFSR commanders over more promises of land reforms and national assemblies. Indeed, the Supreme Krug looked very much like a revivi-fication of the separatist United Government of the South Eastern Union of Cossack Hosts that the Volunteers had been struggling to keep in abeyance ever since arriving in the south-east two years earlier.[107] It was clear that Denikin's heavy-handed treatment of the Kuban Rada back in November 1919 (when he had arrested ten of its members and forced Ataman A.P. Filimonov to resign) had not expunged from it all thoughts of separatism, while his sudden dismissal of the much-loved (if insubordinate) General Shkuro from command of the Kuban Army at the end of February 1920 won him few friends in Ekaterinodar (even if Shkuro had actually spoken out there quite often against Kuban sepa-ratism). Around this time, as a British officer noted, the Cossack ranks within the AFSR suddenly began to thin out:

> Gradually their forces were drifting away to their villages, disappearing in ones and twos and groups during the night, or simply turning away in front of the despairing eyes of their officers and shuffling off sometimes as a complete squad, company or even regiment, sick of the fighting and the mismanagement and the overwhelming strength of the Reds. There was nothing anyone could do to stop them.[108]

To make matters worse, just as Kolchak's Siberia had sprouted a number of anti-White SR organizations as the Russian Army collapsed in late 1919 (the Political Center, the Committee for the Convocation of a Zemskii Sobor', etc.), in early 1920 an unexpected second blossoming of the democratic counter-revolution overran much of the rear of the AFSR, especially in the wooded hills of the coastal Black Sea region of the North Caucasus, where there lurked thousands of deserters and refugees from all sorts of civil-war armies that were being loosely organized by fugitive SRs (notably V.N. Sama-rin-Fillipovskii and Colonel N.V. Voronovich, the former a long-standing SR and the latter an officer of the tsarist era with SR sympathies) and around the picturesque resort town of Sochi further south. This self-styled "Green" movement was coordinated from November 1919 onwards by a united Black Sea Liberation Committee.[109]

For the White movement in 1920, then, February may have been the cruelest month. On a single day, 7 February 1920, Supreme Ruler Admiral Kolchak was executed at Irkutsk, while the last White toe-hold in Ukraine was lost with the botched evacuation of Odessa. Meanwhile, the internment of Iudenich's forces in Estonia was completed, as was that of the *Bredovtsy* in Poland. On 10 February 1920, Red forces captured Krasnovodsk (today's Türkmenbaşy), on the shores of the eastern Caspian, consolidating Soviet power in Central Asia and forcing onward the withered remnants of the 15,000 Urals Cossacks who had departed southward from Gur'ev on 5 January 1920.[110] Finally, on 19–21 February 1920, 1,000 White soldiers were evacuated from Arkhangel'sk, leaving tens of thousands more to their fate.[111] Denikin did manage a brief resurgence, and Don Cossack forces recaptured Rostov on 20 February 1920, but it was a false dawn and, for the remainder of that bitter and fateful month, his forces retreated toward the Kuban. Harried, however, by a newly reorganized, 160,000-strong Caucasian Front of the Red Army (commanded by the energetic and now near ubiquitous Tukhachevskii)[112] and with the 1st Cavalry Army pressing in along the Tsaritsyn–Ekaterinodar railway on their right flank, there was nothing Denikin's forces could actually do when they got to the Kuban other than abandon its capital, Ekaterinodar, without a fight, on 17 March, and then strike out for the last remaining port in anti-Bolshevik hands, Novorossiisk. Their fading hope was of evacuation by sea, before that city fell either to the Reds advancing on it along the Rostov railway from the north or to the SR-insurgent forces of the Black Sea Liberation Committee approaching it from the south (who had captured Tuapse, 75 miles south of Novorossiisk, on 17 February 1920).

Novorossiisk in February 1920 was inundated by "a sea of wounded, sick and refugees," according to one eyewitness:

> It was freezingly cold ... Bodies lay in all sorts of corners, while the hospitals were besieged by sick, frozen and hungry people for whom nothing could be done, so that those stricken with typhus remained just where they happened to fall. One Russian colonel lay for a fortnight in the cupboard where he had crept when he was taken ill ... The whole foreshore was packed with people, carts and animals—whole families on their knees, praying for help, while the criminals of the underworld came out and in the confusion preyed on the elderly and defenceless ... Young girls—some of high birth—prostituted themselves to earn enough money to pay the passage for themselves and their families to the ruthless and money-grabbing barge captains ... It was a sick, desperate, terrified city ...

If the other [surrendered] towns and cities to the north had been disasters, Novorossiisk was the worst of the lot as the wreckage of a whole nation funneled down to the sea and the only remaining seaport in the area.[113]

About 35,000 White soldiers and casualties did eventually find berths on Russian and Allied vessels by the last days of March, but almost as many again (and untold numbers of civilians) were captured in the port when the Red Army arrived on 26–7 March 1920, in time to begin a desultory shelling of the departing vessels (which included the battleship HMS *Emperor of India*, the destroyer HMS *Stuart*, and the commandeered German transport ships *Hanover* and *Bremerhaven*, the French cruiser *Waldeck-Rousseau* and the USS *Galveston*). Having reached the docks, the Red soldiers could only stand and stare mutely at the bodies of hundreds of dead horses slaughtered there by their heartbroken Cossack masters. In the water floated the already bloated corpses of more dispatched mounts and many human suicides; beneath it were to be found the sunken skeletons of numerous British-supplied tanks, aircraft, and other stores for which the evacuation fleet had no capacity.[114] This was only the beginning: 60,000 more Whites were surrounded and captured at Sochi in April 1920, by which time the SR forces there had also been tamed and purged,[115] while a guerilla war in the Kuban region initiated by White fugitives who adopted the grandiose title of the People's Army for the Regeneration of Russia, commanded by General M.A. Fostikov, achieved little more than providing an excuse for further Red retributions and massacres.[116]

4

1920–21

BATTLES IN THE MARCHLANDS

That around 50,000 seasoned (if temporarily demoralized, disorganized, and disoriented) White forces had been ferried from Novorossiisk and other ports into Crimea, or had slipped into the sanctuary of the peninsula from the north, and would have to be dealt with at some point, could not disguise or diminish the magnitude of the Red victory over the AFSR in early 1920. That victory was probably the key one of all the civil wars. Equally, though, that was not the end of the Red campaigns, for seizing the North Caucasus and routes to it from the Soviet center offered the long-cherished opportunity of carrying the momentum of revolutionary conquest forward, to overwhelm foes more distant: notably, those ensconced beyond the 1,000-mile-long mountain range that formed an intermittently ferocious, but not at all impassable, barrier across the Caucasian land-bridge from Europe into Asia. First stop on such a route would be the independent Transcaucasian republics of Azerbaijan, Armenia, and Georgia, with each of which Moscow had scores to settle that dated back to their declarations of statehood in May 1918, not to mention their subsequent decimation of Bolshevik organizations by nationalist forces in that region (especially at Tiflis and Baku). To coordinate this attack politically, a Caucasian Bureau (Kavbiuro) of the RKP(b) was established (under local Bolshevik luminaries Sergo Ordzhonikidze and S.M. Kirov)—which was sometimes attended by Lenin's once-named "favorite Georgian," Stalin—to work alongside something over 150,000 Red forces on the Caucasian Front, under the successive commands of M.N. Tukhachevskii (4 February–24 April 1920), I.T. Smilga (acting, 24 April–15 May 1920), and V.M. Gittis (15 May 1920–29 May 1921), all of whom were now experienced civil-war commanders and strategists of the highest order.

Transcaucasian Campaigns

Only their distance from Moscow, and the protection accidentally afforded to them by the presence of White forces to the north, and the seas on their flanks had quarantined the three small and mutually disputatious Transcaucasian republics of Georgia, Armenia, and Azerbaijan from Soviet invasion until 1920, as well as the presence in their region of first German and Turkish and then Allied interventionists.[1] But now the Allies had withdrawn (with the exception of the British garrison at Batumi, which would leave in mid-July 1920), and the Whites had been shoved aside, leaving the three republics fatally exposed. Thus although the command of the Red Fleet would not yet venture to advance its military flotillas from the Don and the Sea of Azov into the Black Sea (where Allied vessels still lurked, along with Wrangel's White Fleet), the northern Caspian was in Soviet hands and the Volga–Caspian Military Flotilla (from July 1920 the Caspian Fleet) was extending its operations southward, to offer extensive naval support to the 11th Red Army as it cleared the Terek and then Daghestan of White stragglers. This was most unfortunate for the Azeris, and their port-capital of Baku, which found itself first in line for the Red Army's attentions in Transcaucasia. Unlucky too was the fact that a Red advance into the region could utilize the Rostov–Baku railway, which, having pressed along the steppe north of the main Caucasus range, then ranged south, hugged the Caspian's western coastline, and snaked through Daghestan to Derbent, and then into Azerbaijan itself. But this amorphous—and often despised—Muslim population of the old empire was always going to be a prime target for the Reds, as the Azeris (or "Tatars," as the Russians called them) were not well organized—either politically or militarily—and, worse, were sitting atop of what the elite of imperial Russians cherished most in these former imperial *gubernii* in the far south (apart, in the case of the most privileged, from their palaces and dachas along the sub-tropical Black Sea coast): oil. Indeed, Baku had been the source of more than half the world's oil production (and 95 percent of Russia's output) on the eve of the First World War. Thus, on 22 March 1920, even as Bolshevik spies were reporting that General Denikin was enjoying the anachronous spectacle of a parade of the 2nd Battalion of the

Royal Scots Fusiliers at Novorossiisk, and as anarchy descended upon that port, it is not surprising that Red Army Glavkom Kamenev, with much urgency, issued the order that "the entirety of the former Baku *guberniia*" should immediately be occupied by the 11th Red Army.[2]

It is unlikely that the small Azeri army could ever have mounted effective resistance to this Red thrust—not least because it lacked experienced generals, Muslims generally having been forbidden to obtain rank in the imperial Russian forces. Consequently, as the Soviet forces approached, General Samad Bey Mehmandarov (Makhmandariov), the Azeri Minister of War, stunned the parliament in Baku by admitting that the entire Azeri army could not hope to defeat even a single Red battalion.[3] In addition, the many Turkish advisors to the Azeri army, who were anxious (in order to disturb the post-war settlement as it pertained to Anatolia) to forge closer links between Moscow and the new Kemalist regime in Ankara, were duplicitously advising the Azeris that they had nothing much to fear from the Bolsheviks. Thus, resistance was likely to have been minimal, even had 22 March 1920 not also been a day marked by a renewed and unfortunately diversionary outbreak of hostilities in the Azeri–Armenian War that had been rumbling on since 1918. This time, vicious fighting was erupting in the far west of the country, in the hotly disputed region of Nagorno-Karabakh, culminating on 26 March 1920 with the massacre of Armenian civilians at Shusha by the Azeri army (the "Shusha Massacre").[4] Soon afterwards an uprising of local Bolsheviks, who had been joined by the left wing of the Hummet party (now renamed the Azeri Communist Party), seized parts of Baku, and on 28 April 1920 advance units of the 11th Red Army arrived there to oversee the immediate proclamation of the Azerbaijan Soviet Socialist Republic.

Although hundreds of Azeri officers were immediately imprisoned, and many executed, while Soviet forces incurred immediate and widespread hatred for their extremely violent suppression of a rebellion in northern Elizavetpol' *guberniia* (the "Ganja Uprising," 25–31 May 1920), in which more than 1,000 Muslim rebels were killed, many more Azeri officers and men were soon pressed into the Red ranks. Some of them, it should be recorded, enlisted not too unwillingly, as the 11th Red Army's next moves were to push the Armenians out of Shusha (5 June 1920), and then to reclaim Karabakh for the newly minted Soviet Azerbaijan, and to then join a Turkish assault on Armenian forces occupying Nakhchivan that thus (on 28 July 1920) ejected the Armenian army from another region claimed by Azerbaijan.[5] Subsequently, on 10 August 1920, a Soviet-brokered ceasefire agreement was signed at Yerevan, under which the still—if precariously—independent Armenia (very reluctantly) recognized Azeri control of Karabakh and the temporary independence (under joint Azeri–Soviet–Turkish protection) of Nakhchivan, although fighting sporadically continued.[6]

Meanwhile, from September to November 1920, the Democratic Republic of Armenia was engaged in the last battles of its separate conflict with Turkish forces (the Turkish–Armenian War), over areas of eastern Anatolia that, since the 1915 anti-Turkish revolt of Armenians (the "Van Resistance") and the Russian advances in 1916, had been fashioned into an Administration for Western Armenia. By late November 1920, the fighting had advanced almost to the gates of Yerevan. Although a Turkish–Armenian ceasefire was then brokered, this and other struggles—not to mention an influx of tens of thousands of hungry and diseased refugees—had so dilapidated Armenia that the country was entirely unable to resist a second Soviet–Azeri invasion on 28 November 1920 (prompted by renewed outbreaks of inter-ethnic violence in Sharur and Karabakh that, it was alleged, had been incited by the government in Yerevan).[7] On 4 December 1920, Red forces duly entered Yerevan and prepared for the promulgation of the Armenian Soviet Socialist Republic, thereby also effectively bringing an end to the Armenian–Azerbaijani War (which, proportionally, had been among the bloodiest of the civil-wars era). By the subsequent Treaty of Moscow ("The Treaty of Brotherhood," 16 March 1921), between the RSFSR and the Kemalist Grand National Assembly of Turkey,[8] and the Treaty of Kars (13 October 1921) between the three Transcaucasian republics and Turkey,[9] the disputed region of Alexandropol was returned to Armenia, while Nakhchivan became an autonomous region of Azerbaijan.

All of this was a clear attempt by the Soviet government to appease Kemalist Turkey (to which the Red Army had been ferrying weapons across the Black Sea since the recapture of Odessa in February 1920) and to buttress Ankara's hostility to the Allies. It was also, as (with little exaggeration) Armenian nationalists claim to this day, a punishment inflicted on Armenia as a consequence of the widespread uprising against Soviet power that gripped the country in February 1921, and temporarily drove the Red Army out of Yerevan—an uprising that continued to tie down Soviet forces in the southern region of Zangezur, where an independent Mountainous Republic of Armenia was proclaimed, until July 1921. The Kars and Moscow settlements were bitterly resented by the Armenians, who lost through them not only Nakhchivan (to add to Nagorno-Karabakh) to Azerbaijan, but also, most sorely, their claims to territories in eastern Anatolia that had been promised to them by the Allies under the Treaty of Sèvres (10 August 1920) and which contained two of the most cherished symbols of Armenian identity: Mount Ararat and the ancient Armenian capital of Ani (Abnicum).[10] Over the following decades, Armenia would suffer waves of arrests, imprisonments, and executions of its cultural and political elites—partly as a consequence of Moscow's suspicions of Armenia's ties to its huge diaspora across the Middle East and the wider world. Not that this signaled any real favoritism toward Azerbaijan on Moscow's part: the Soviet leadership regarded with acute alarm Baku's proximity to the large Azeri population in northern Persia (recently swollen by a flood of political refugees from the civil wars in Transcaucasia) and therefore unleashed a series of purges against the Azeri elites over the following years—those of 1924 and 1930 being particularly brutal. Meanwhile, as elsewhere in the new Soviet Union, a campaign against the Islamic religion led to the closure of thousands of mosques and religious schools.[11]

* * *

The four-month pause between the Soviet offensives in Nagorno-Karabakh and Nakhchivan, in June–July 1920, and that against Yerevan in November of the same year can be explained by the outbreak of general Soviet–Polish hostilities in April–May of that year, which soon developed into a full-scale war, as well as by the White threat re-emerging from the Crimea in June–July 1920. Also pertinent here, though, were Soviet concerns not to discomfit their partners in the ongoing, and very delicate, negotiations that would lead to the Anglo-Soviet Trade Agreement (in March 1921) by acting too precipitously in an area in which London—especially that bit of Westminster closed off by a door marked "Curzon"—had a special interest.[12]

These factors too, for a while, reprieved—and allowed to survive, for a while—the Democratic Republic of Georgia. The Menshevik regime in that country endured, despite a number of Soviet probings (in April–May 1920), through the Darial Gorge, into South Ossetia (Tskhinvali) and along the Black Sea littoral towards the chiefly Muslim region of Abkhazia (both of which regions had ambitions to secede from Georgia and both of which alleged cruel treatment in the civil-war years at the hands of the Georgian republic's security police, the People's Guard).[13] It survived, also, a planned Bolshevik coup in Tiflis that was forestalled by Georgian forces. But local Bolsheviks were soon persuaded—in the case of Sergo Ordzhonikidze, who was also probing at eastern Georgia from Azerbaijan, *ordered*, very strictly, by Lenin himself—to desist from such activities, as Sovnarkom went so far as signing a full treaty, the Treaty of Moscow (7 May 1920), with their erstwhile Menshevik rivals. Under the terms of this treaty (Article I), Georgian independence was recognized by the RSFSR (which, perversely, became, therefore, the first state in the world to grant such recognition to the Georgian republic). However, as the Moscow treaty also demanded that Georgia must sever all links with undefined "counter-revolutionary forces," expel foreign missions, and (under Article X) legalize the Bolshevik Party on its territory, as well as declaring the strategic mountain passes through the Caucasus (which had to that point been garrisoned by the Georgians) to be neutral and demilitarized, signing this treaty was the equivalent of the Georgian Mensheviks sawing through the already creaking branch on which they were sitting.[14]

That, however, was for the future. The more immediate and very unfortunate consequence of the treaty was that the most serious uprising of the (ethnically and linguistically Iranian) South Ossetians against Georgia—that of April 1920—could be dealt with by Tiflis with a free hand, as the Bolshevik leadership in Moscow looked (diplomatically) aside. Estimates of those killed in South Ossetia in this period by the Georgian Mensheviks' People's Guard, which also razed dozens of villages and indiscriminately ruined crops across the region, range from 5,000 to 20,000, while it is thought that at least 20,000 and possibly as many as 35,000 South Ossetians fled northwards through the mountain passes to seek refuge with their brethren in the Soviet zone, in what would become the North Ossetian Autonomous *Oblast'* of the RSFSR in 1924.[15]

Nevertheless, a Soviet mission was soon resident in Tiflis, primed to act when the time was ripe.[16] With an armistice signed with Poland in October 1920, with Wrangel's Whites swept from the Crimea into exile during the following month, and with assurances from Soviet representatives in London that the projected trade agreement would be signed no matter what verbal protests the British government might feel constrained to make against further Soviet advances in Transcaucasia, a workers' uprising broke out—exactly on cue, having been prearranged by Sergo Ordzhonikidze[17]—in the Borchalinsk and Akhalkaksk *uezdy* of Georgia on 11 February 1921. Within two weeks, the Georgian capital was under the control of local Bolsheviks and units of the 11th Red Army. The Georgian army, in contrast to that of neighboring Azerbaijan, boasted very many experienced tsarist officers (including the *genshtabisty* Generals Alexander Andronikashvili, Giorgi Kvinitadze, and Ilia Odishelidze); but the Menshevik government had never fully trusted the army, preferring its own paramilitary People's Guard, commanded by the former Bolshevik Vladimir ("Valiko") Jugheli, whose forces, for all their ferocity, were no match for the now battle-hardened 11th Red Army.[18] The Menshevik ministers, therefore, having dug their own graves, fled to Batumi, and then (on 18 March 1921, aboard the French cruiser *Ernest Renan*) went into exile, eventually settling at Leuville-sur-Orge near Paris, where they founded the government-in-exile of the Georgian Democratic Republic. Even prior to embarkation, though, the Menshevik government had been replaced at Tiflis by the new Georgian Soviet Socialist Republic (proclaimed on 25 February 1921). This was the final ingredient that Moscow was already preparing to add to the unemulsive mix of a Transcaucasian Soviet Federative Socialist Republic.[19]

However, partly as a consequence of its international support,[20] partly because of the long-lingering internecine social-democratic bitterness that soured relations between Moscow and Tiflis, partly because of the Georgian clans' warrior traditions, and partly because its mountainous terrain made the country almost uniquely difficult to conquer, the civil war in Georgia was a long way from being won by the Reds in February 1921. Extensive guerrilla resistance to Soviet rule, eventually coordinated by agents of the Paris-based Committee for the Liberation of Georgia (Damkom, an uneasy alliance of the Georgian Mensheviks and their former rivals, the National Democrats) ebbed and flowed continuously and very violently across the region—notably in the Svanetian uprising (September 1921) and the Kakhet–Khevsureti rebellion (of 1921–22). Widespread arrests of Georgian Mensheviks and nationalists by the Cheka in 1923 seemed to have defused the crisis, but then a huge uprising, in August 1924, saw at least 4,000 Georgians killed in the three weeks of fighting, which was especially heavy in the western coastal region of Guria. Between 7,000 and 10,000 prisoners were subsequently executed by the Cheka (arousing murmurs about the use of "excessive force" even in Moscow) and perhaps as many as a further 20,000 were deported.[21]

The Bolsheviks' inability to exert control in this relatively far-flung province was a consequence of the persistence of its deeply felt national spirit, the chronic numerical weakness of local party organizations, and the lingering influence of the Mensheviks, but was eventually managed by the introduction of the New Economic Policy (NEP, see below, pp. 209–10), which addressed at least some of the concerns of the Georgian populace. Also of import was Moscow's cultivation of support among the non-Georgian populations of the region: thus a separate Abkhazian SSR was established as early as 31 March 1921 (although its constitutional status was somewhat ambiguous), while, within the Georgian SSR, were established the Adzharian Autonomous Soviet Socialist Republic (16 July 1921), and the South Ossetian Autonomous Oblast' (20 April 1922).[22] This was an effective policy of divide and rule.

Nevertheless, the extension of Soviet rule into Transcaucasia was thus a far lengthier and more fraught and complex process than the Soviet leadership had probably hoped when Glavkom Kamenev had ordered that first advance into the region in March 1920. Given the distances from Moscow and the need to tread warily around international issues, this was probably inevitable; as it was also inevitable that, in having broader concerns than its new Transcaucasian republics, Moscow would make agreements, in the Soviet–Turkish treaties of Moscow and Kars in 1921, with the traditional Muslim foe of Christian Georgia and Armenia that would appall their peoples—and even some local Bolshevik atheists. Moscow's response to criticisms here was that it was not now dealing with a degenerate Muslim sultan in Constantinople, but with a vigorous, secular, and modernizing force, under Kemal Atatürk in Ankara, whose partnership in disrupting the post-war order was every bit as much anticipated as was the subsequent Soviet–German axis secured at the Treaty of Rapallo (16 April 1922).[23] Thus, as a recent account has it, "In less than two years ... Russia had metamorphosed from the greatest threat to the Ottoman empire to the best hope for Muslim sovereignty in Anatolia."[24]

* * *

Moscow's willingness, in the far south, to manufacture local compromises for the sake of broader geopolitical ends extended also, beyond the Caucasian ridge, into the ultramontane region's south-eastern, Persian marches. There, in and beyond Persian Azerbaijan, encouraged by the 11th Red Army's advance on Baku in April 1920, by the landing of the Red Astrakhan–Caspian Military Flotilla at Enzeli (Anzali) in May 1920 (and by its seizure there of the White's Caspian Flotilla from British custody), and by the Komintern's circulation of invitations to "progressive forces" across Asia (but especially the Middle East) to attend a forthcoming grandiloquently described Congress of the Peoples of the East (to convene in Baku in September 1920), there was proclaimed, just across the border from Soviet Azerbaijan at Resht (Rasht, in north-western Persia), on 5 June 1920, a Soviet Republic of Gīlān. Led by an uneasy alliance of the veteran rebel leader Mirza Kuchuk Khan, of the Persian Constitutional Movement (who had already once before led his forces against the imperial regime in Tehran) and the Marxist revolutionary Kaidar Khan Tariverdev (known as "the Bomb-maker"), this potential ally and (for Moscow, at the very least) useful anti-imperialist tool was initially proffered aid from Soviet Russia. However, the Constitutionalists and their Jangali ("forest people") partisan allies were abruptly dropped by Moscow when the Tehran government agreed terms that led to the mutually advantageous Soviet–Persian Treaty of Friendship (26 February 1921).[25] From that treaty, Moscow gained the valuable extra-territorial right to pursue its White, Musavet, and other enemies across the Azeri border into Persia (while at the same time, of course, startling the interested imperial power, Britain, which had already been so humiliated at Enzeli), if Tehran was unable to suppress them itself. As the price for securing it, though, Kuchak Khan was, almost literally, sacrificed: after he had perished of frostbite, his corpse was butchered by his Persian pursuers who then put his severed head on display at Resht and Tehran to deter a Jangali revival. "Bomb-maker" Haidar Khan, meanwhile, was killed in prison.[26]

* * *

Despite widespread distress among Asian socialists and nationalists at the Bolsheviks' apparent betrayal of Kuchuk Khan, Moscow was nevertheless able to make considerable political capital from Muslim and Asian anti-British agitation at the Congress of the Peoples of the East, which opened at Baku on 2 September 1920 and was attended by some 1,891 delegates (including, according to Soviet sources, 1,273 Communists, although that was surely an exaggeration) of around thirty nationalities. Among them were Turks, Persians, Indians, Chinese, and representatives of the various non-Russian peoples of the Central Asian, North Caucasian, and Transcaucasian regions of the new Soviet state. It helped Moscow's cause no end, of course, that at that precise moment much of the Muslim world was aflame (and thus distracted from events at Gīlān) over the manner in which, at the recent Treaty of Sèvres (10 August 1920), the Allies had dismembered the territory and severely restricted the temporal powers of the Turkish sultan, who was also the nominal caliph (*khalīfah*, spiritual head) of the entire Muslim world. The horrible Amritsar massacre, in British India, would also have been fresh in the minds of many delegates to the Baku congress.

However, there was undoubtedly an element of political theater to the entire affair (exemplified by the stage-managed public hanging of effigies of Lloyd George, President Millerand, and Woodrow Wilson). H.G. Wells, who was in Russia at the time, characterized it as "an excursion, a pageant, a Beano," adding that "As a meeting of Asiatic proletarians it was preposterous" and chortling at the "quite wonderful accumulation of white, black, brown, and yellow people, Asiatic costumes and astonishing weapons," which delegates kept drawing or unsheathing to compare.[27] This seems condescending now, but, at times, the proceedings probably did more resemble a bazaar than a conference: the Bolshevik E.D. Stasova (who, like other atheistic party members, objected to the sessions being so frequently interrupted for prayer meetings) recorded, with obvious disappointment, that prominently in attendance were "a variety of khans and beks, who decided to utilize their journey to Baku to attend to various commercial matters—the selling of carpets, leatherwork and so forth."[28] Other witnesses noted that anti-clerical tirades from the podium received an at best lukewarm reception from the floor of the hall.[29] Also, even when politics managed to take center stage, some profound and unresolved differences arose in the debates (and not all because of the problems of translation in what might have been dubbed the Congress of Babel)— over the eternal quandary of whether or not socialists should offer conditional support to the liberal (and, in the colonial case, national-liberationist) aspirations of their native bourgeoisie, for example. And, most emblematically, despite the promises of the congress chairman, G.E. Zinov'ev, that the meeting would reconvene on an annual basis, the First Congress of the Peoples of the East was also the last. Yet a few major and quite concrete achievements resulted from the Baku congress, including the creation of a standing Council of Action and Propaganda, which would continue its work on a permanent basis, and— perhaps the most lasting and influential of all—a resolution to found, in Moscow, a University of the Peoples of the East, which would go on to train several generations of Asian revolutionaries.[30]

* * *

The sorts of compromises Moscow brokered for the sake of its own security with Ankara, Tehran, and Berlin in 1921–22 have sometimes led commentators to read back into the revolutionary period a pre-Stalinist flowering of the concept of "Socialism in One Country," and to argue that Soviet Russian security had begun to outweigh proletarian internationalism in the minds of leaders in the Kremlin long before Lenin was interred in his mausoleum outside it. As we have seen, concerns about the security of the world's first socialist revolution (the Bolshevik's "healthy baby") had, indeed, guided the Soviet leadership since the seizure of power in 1917, and they were certainly prioritized during the Brest-Litovsk crisis in 1918, as the toddling Soviet state found its feet. Moreover, such tactics were not made ad hoc, but had a rather firm grounding in Lenin's reading of Marx and understanding of history: since the publication of a study of "Socialism and the War" in the Bolshevik journal *Sotsial-demokrat* in July–August 1915, Lenin had been apt to argue that a single, isolated socialist state might successfully battle imperialism alone, providing its economy was properly organized, so as to release the creative premium of the embattled proletariat.[31] Yet, equally, flourishes of pan-European and expansionary revolutionary idealism and optimism were hardly altogether absent from Soviet policy—in, for example, the ultra-Bolshevik policies introduced by local cadres as the Red Army moved first into the Baltic region and then across left-bank Ukraine in early 1919, and were certainly evident in both Antonov-Ovseenko's thrust into right-bank Ukraine (aimed at Romania and Hungary), in April–May 1919, and in Sergo Ordzhonikidze's pugnacious spoiling for a fight with Georgia a year later. All this was reflective of a very deep-rooted strain of Left Bolshevism that both predated, and then co-existed with, Lenin's generally more level-headed piloting of the post-October party—and which would also outlive the first Soviet leader.[32] But this virulent strain was not one to which the "old man" was entirely immune—as events in Poland in 1920 were to demonstrate.

The Ukrainian–Polish, Soviet–Polish, Soviet–Belarussian, and Polish–Lithuanian Wars, and the wars against the Jews

Having been partitioned between Austria, Prussia, and Russia in the late eighteenth century, and having failed in its various strivings toward reunion and revival in the nineteenth century (even as the Polish national idea, defined chiefly in opposition to its perceived Russian mirror-image, flourished), in the twentieth century the entirely unexpected outcome of the First World War in Eastern Europe, in which all three of Poland's dissectors and persecutors were defeated, suddenly presented Poles with the opportunity for unification and liberation in 1918. The abruptness and unexpectedness of this outcome of the world war left many issues unresolved (or even unexplored). Not least among them was the conundrum of where, precisely, the new Second Polish Republic's eastern border might be placed among the kaleidoscope of ethnicities that blurred the edges between it and Russia. This was further complicated, of course, at the close of the world war, by the conflict between US President Woodrow Wilson's pious espousal of self-determination and the European Allies' (not unreasonable) fear that the equally sudden and unexpected revolutionary developments in Russia might all too soon be echoed—on their doorstep—in Berlin, Budapest, and Vienna. In such an unmapped moment, within a pan-European paroxysm of violence, it is not surprising that Polish issues would be resolved by force of arms, not diplomacy—and, of course, if the Allies had their way, in favor of Poland, not Bolshevik Russia.[33]

That might, not right, would prevail in this most pained post-world war theater was made apparent in Poland's first skirmishes over the eastern border question, in the Ukrainian–Polish War, contesting ownership of L'viv/Lwów (Lemberg) and its hinterlands (which the Ukrainians called Western Ukraine and the Poles called Eastern Galicia). Although the Ukrainians were first to act (as Austria–Hungary disintegrated at the end of the world war), proclaiming a Western Ukrainian People's Republic (WUPR) in the 1918 November Uprising at Lemberg that gathered around itself former Ukrainian units of the Austro-Hungarian Army, Polish numerical predominance in the city and reinforcements arriving from the west along the Przemyśl–Lemberg railway rapidly ensured that the governing Rada of the WUPR was almost immediately forced to retreat eastwards to Ternopil' (Ternopol') and then to Stanyslaviv in December 1918.[34] (It was at this point that the WUPR entered a political union with the UNR, under the Act of Zluka of 22 January 1919, although retaining almost full autonomy over its armed forces.) Allied efforts at mediation in this horribly bitter struggle came to little, and by late May 1919, the WUPR's Ukrainian Galician Army (UGA) was penned into a tight corner between the Zbruch and Dnestr rivers. The UGA (which was commanded, from December 1918 to June 1918, by the talented General Mykhailo Omel'ianovych-Pavlenko) had some mettle, not least in a nucleus of three corps of Ukrainian Sich Riflemen (of the former Austrian Army), and a WUPR offensive of May 1919 briefly breached communications between L'viv/Lwów and Poland's Przemysly staging-post, but the WUPR forces were chronically short of arms and, in the long term, stood no chance against the comparatively huge numbers of new forces and supplies Poland could ship to the Galician front. Consequently, on 16–17 July 1919, the Ukrainian Galician Army was forced to retreat across the Zbruch, where it subsequently merged with the Ukrainian Army of the Ukrainian National Republic.[35]

However, under extreme pressure throughout 1919 from both the Bolsheviks and the Whites that, as we have seen, denied the UNR possession of its own capital, Kiev, and then ultimately reduced the Ukrainian Army to a beggarly, partisan war (the first of its subsequently much over-mythologized "Winter Campaigns"), the UNR leadership (dominated by Symon Petliura) eventually abandoned the WUPR and its trans-Zbruch cause.[36] Polish governance of Eastern Galicia was subsequently confirmed in the UNR–Polish Treaty of Warsaw (21–4 April 1920), in exchange for Poland offering the UNR a military alliance against the Red Army (which, of course, had by that time swept the AFSR clear of all Ukraine).[37] By then, the WUPR leadership, under the liberal lawyer Yevhen Petrushevych, was already in exile, in the familiar surroundings, for these former bourgeois citizens of the Dual Monarchy, of Vienna. From the former Habsburg capital, its urbane members would project a steady stream of invective against Petliura and his rude, East Ukrainian, peasant cousins for several years—made all the more bitter by the fact that the Allies had tacitly accepted Poland's display of might and would grant *de jure* recognition to the incorporation of Western Ukraine/Eastern Galicia into Poland in 1923.

* * *

That resurrected Poland's ambitions extended beyond most-coveted Eastern Galicia, to some point far in the east of the 300-mile band of polyglot territory between indisputably ethnic Poland and indubitably ethnic Russia, was long clear from the pronouncements of the new state's president and commander-in-chief, Józef Piłsudski, another (like Petliura) of the socialists on horseback that featured so prominently in European politics in these years. Piłsudski—a striking figure of a man, who sported a Cossack- or (more properly) *haidamak*-style flowing moustache—was a veteran Polish socialist and former terrorist, but, as a native of Zalavas (Zułów), in eastern Lithuania (on the outer reaches of Polish ambitions toward the eastern territories, the *Kresy Wschodnie*, in the civil-war era) had always had a strong admixture of anti-Russianism in his politics. Like many of his countrymen who had been schooled under the Pole-baiting Russian system in Lithuania and eastern Poland, he nurtured an incurable romantic sense of belonging to those territories, and kept close to his heart the opening lines of the epic poem, *Pan Tadeusz* (1834), by Adam Mickiewicz, the Polish national bard:

> Lithuania, my land, you are like health.
> Only he who has lost you, will know of your worth.

By the revolutionary era, having created a Polish Brigade within the Austrian Army during the First World War, Piłsudski's Polish nationalism had morphed into a grand internationalist scheme to forge a federation of all the western and southern border peoples of the Russian Empire, to protect them against their hulking and still predatory neighbor. This putative union he called Międzymorze—"Between the [Black and Baltic] Seas"—sometimes termed the Intermarum.[38]

With what looked like the first building block of Międzymorze in place, in the form of the alliance with the UNR, Piłsudski set about the furthering his plans. The strategic junctions of Dvinsk (in January 1920) and Mozyr (in

March 1920) having already been captured by Polish forces on 24 April 1920, the very day upon which the military terms of the Polish–Ukrainian Treaty of Warsaw were settled, he launched "Operation Kiev," sending around 75,000 men—three Polish armies (the 2nd, 3rd, and 6th Armies) and two Ukrainian divisions—onto Ukrainian territory guarded by the Red Army's Western and South West Fronts (numbering about 120,000 men combined).[39] The Polish uhlans entered Zhitomir on day two of the offensive; Kiev itself was reached by Polish and Ukrainian units on 7 May 1920; a bridgehead on the left bank of the Dnepr was then established; and the railway line north to Polish-held Minsk was threatened, as was Cherkassy (and the route to Odessa) to the south. This caused some consternation in the Red command, with Trotsky wiring E.M. Sklianskii, deputy chair of the Revvoensovet of the Republic, from Gomel', on 10 May 1920:

> We have lost a great deal of time as regards the Western Front. The administrative machinery is weak; the army commanders and commissars are below the average level. Yet we have operating against us for the first time a regular army led by good technicians. The best army commanders must be taken from all fronts and posted here as divisional commanders. Existing divisional commanders must be appointed to be brigade commanders, members of military revolutionary councils to be brigade commissars and so on, after explaining, on behalf of the Military Revolutionary Council of the Republic and of the C.C. of the Party, that this is no reduction in rank but results from the necessity of counter balancing the strength of the enemy with an organization that is vigorous and skilful. The weak place is in the junior commanders, especially in the artillery. Haste is needed in order to make up for lost time.[40]

Yet, for all that almost panicky reshuffling of personnel, a week later a huge Red counter-attack was ordered on the South West Front (commanded by A.I. Egorov), which had been reinforced with Budennyi's 1st Cavalry Army, freed for action elsewhere in the aftermath of the rout of the AFSR in the North Caucasus. In fact, Egorov's front had been poised to launch its own strategic offensive against Poland just as the Poles struck: consequently, the Ukrainian capital was recaptured by Soviet forces on 13 June 1920 (Zhitomir and Berdichev having already fallen to Budennyi's cavalry on 8 June, freeing thousands of Red prisoners to return to the ranks), and the South West Front pressed steadily thereafter westward, toward L'viv.

Further north (on the Western Front), prospects also seemed bright for the Red Army, as Sovnarkom had (on 12 July 1920) concluded an alliance for joint action against the Poles with the Lithuanian government (the Treaty of Moscow). Piłsudski had hoped to attract the Lithuanians, in particular, to his federal schemes, but the belligerent attitude towards Lithuania of the conservative opposition in Poland (especially the National Democrats, led by Roman Dmowski) undermined him. Equally, the liberal Lithuanian government at Kaunas had no truck with the Lithuanian nobility's romantic and, as they saw it, outdated attraction to Poland. Polish–Lithuanian (and Polish–Allied) relations had been particularly soured by the so-called "Sejny Uprising" in the ethnically mixed region of Sejny (Seinai) in August 1919, when Poles rose up against the Lithuanian authorities, who claimed governance of the region. German forces that had occupied the area during the First World War withdrew in July–August 1919, and handed control to the Lithuanians (distrusting the Poles, as allies of the French), but incoming Allied representatives had drawn a demarcation line (the "Foch Line," 27 July 1919) that granted much of the disputed Suwałki (Suvalkai) region to Poland and demanded that the Lithuanian Army withdraw behind it. The Lithuanians, complaining that the Foch Line had been settled upon in talks between the Allies and the Poles in Paris to which no Lithuanian representative had been accredited, only partially complied, refusing to abandon Sejny in particular (where the population was split virtually equally between Poles and Lithuanians, and whose seminary had played a pivotal role in the Lithuanian national revival of the nineteenth century). Then, on 23 August 1919, around 1,000 Polish irregulars (led by Adam Rudnicki and Wacław Zawadzki) initiated the uprising. Although Piłsudski, mindful of the fragility of his Międzymorze project, had advised against the uprising, soon afterwards regular Polish forces of the 41st Infantry Regiment arrived and drove the Lithuanians back beyond the Foch Line. Hence, in large part, Lithuania's treaty with Moscow.[41]

Thus, with any potential threat from Lithuania neutralized, a huge group of forces commanded by Tukhachevskii (comprising the 3rd, 4th, 15th, and 16th Red Armies) prosecuted a lightning offensive that netted Minsk (11 July), Vil'na (14 July), and Grodno (19 July 1920). This had many positive consequences for the Red Army: it opened direct communications with the new Soviet ally, Lithuania; it unblocked the main railway line to Warsaw from Petrograd; it isolated the Polish Army's left flank from potential union with the Latvian Army (thereby inducing the Ulmanis government finally to sign the Soviet–Latvian Treaty of Riga, on 12 August 1920); and, finally, it allowed the Soviet Western Front to push Polish forces back across the river Bug on 1 August 1920, and then press on toward Warsaw and the Vistula, which was reached a mere fortnight later.

All this was a signal of profound revolutionary intent: the Allies had, on 11 July 1920, proposed a Polish–Soviet border (the so-called "Curzon Line") akin to that of the Prussian–Russian border of 1797, but on 17 July 1920 this notion had been resolutely rejected by the Soviet government, which could sense the ongoing turmoil in Berlin (the recent, March 1920, failed right-wing Kapp putsch was interpreted as "Germany's Kornilov Affair"—that is, as the prelude to "Germany's October") and had the eyes of delegates to the Second Congress of the Komintern in Moscow focused expectantly upon it. The excitement in Moscow was intense: "We were all following with pleasure the response of the Red Army to Pilsudski's aggression and Tukhachevsky's bold march on Warsaw was filling us all with hope," recalled the French Communist, Alfred Rosmer, who was then residing in the Soviet capital.[42] At this point, however, with Berlin just 400 miles to the west of the apparently unstoppable Red Army on the Vistula—in fact, elements of G.D. ("Gaia") Gai's 3rd Cavalry Corps were by this point operating west of Warsaw and south of Danzig, just 200 miles from Berlin—and as all Europe held its breath, the fortunes of war began, incredibly, to turn in favor of the Poles.[43]

Contrary to the hopes of those Komintern delegates in Moscow who, like Rosmer, were eagerly shuffling red flags westward toward Berlin across a large map of Europe, Polish workers and peasants rallied to the national cause and resisted the Russian invasion, rather than rushing to sign a fraternal alliance with their Soviet brethren "over the corpse of the Polish bourgeoisie," as Trotsky had predicted back in April.[44] Indeed, as Soviet forces advanced, tens of thousands of patriotic volunteers swelled the Polish Army's ranks to at least 120,000 by mid-August (equal to the combined manpower of the Reds' Western and South West Fronts), while Soviet commanders could use their fingers to count the number of Poles who came forward to join the Bolsheviks.[45] Poland was greatly aided at this juncture by resuscitated Allied involvement (famously including the Polish–American volunteer Kościuszko Squadron and a French military mission under General Maxime Weygand, in which Charles de Gaulle served) that mixed the symbolic with the operationally decisive.[46] Meanwhile, a weighty advantage was bestowed upon the defenders by the waywardness that, again, seized Soviet commanders, military planners, and politicians once the scent of glorious revolution spritzed their nostrils. This time, blame could be (and was) leveled at Egorov and his chief military commissar, Josef Stalin, who kept intently setting Budennyi's cavalry on Lwów, rather than diverting the Red Cossack forces northwards to aid Tukhachevskii, as his army group closed on Warsaw. But Tukhachevskii's forces had also advanced too soon, too far, and too quickly either to maintain adequate communications with their rear or to have allowed the armies of the South West

Front to swing far enough northwards to have been of significant assistance at Warsaw, even if they had rapidly inundated Lwów (which, after all, it had been Glavkom Kamenev's explicit direction, as late as 13 August 1920, that they should do).[47] The consequence was that, although the Reds' impressive 3rd Cavalry Corps (under G.D. Gai) had stormed across the Vistula as early as 10 August 1920, and threatened to reel around to attack Warsaw from the west, the Polish 1st Army (under General Franciszek Latinik) was able to resist the main Soviet assault from the east, blocking Tukhachevskii's forces at Radzymin (on 13 August), while a counter-attack of the Polish 5th Army (under General Władysław Sikorski) halted the 3rd and 15th Red Armies around Nasielsk on 14–15 August 1920.[48]

Additional Polish forces, among them the Reserve Army, then joined the fray, cutting northward through the inviting gap between the two Soviet fronts and threatening to cut off the over-extended head of Tukhachevskii's group. The Poles' thereafter legendary "Miracle on the Vistula" was complete, while the puppet governments that the Bolsheviks had prepared to install in a Soviet Western Ukraine (Galrevkom) and a Soviet Poland (Polrevkom) were left kicking their heels in the rear and were soon disestablished.[49] What remained of Tukhachevskii's forces then poured back eastwards in absolutely chaotic scenes, abandoning all of eastern Poland, Lithuania, and much of western Belorussia, deserting even the line of the river Neman in late September, and surrendering Minsk on 15 October 1920.

* * *

This Red withdrawal presented Belarussian nationalists with the brief mirage of the sort of independent state that was being forged by the Baltic peoples to their north and (unsuccessfully) the Ukrainians to their south. A Belarussian Democratic Republic, under the self-proclaimed social democrat President Jan Serada (a veteran, with the rank of colonel, in the Russian Army), had been proclaimed by members of the Belarussian national movement at Minsk as early as 9 March 1918, while the region was occupied by German forces. The Belarussian Republic's claims to statehood, however, were somewhat dubious: it had no constitution or defined territoriality, no armed force of its own, and was not recognized by any of the major powers. As was the case in Ukraine, moreover, Belarussians were in a distinct minority in the major towns and cities, including Minsk (where they were outnumbered by Jews).[50] When German forces retreated from (and the Red Army advanced into) the region in December 1918, its governing council, the Belarussian Rada, retreated to Hrodno (Grodno) in Lithuania (although Serada chose to remain on Soviet territory).

However, as, in September–October 1920 the Soviet–Polish front moved eastward, and became gradually less active, the town of Slutsk, 65 miles south of Minsk, was left temporarily in a neutral zone. Although Polish and Soviet negotiators of what was to become an armistice seem to have agreed that Slutsk was destined to be assigned as Soviet territory, local supporters of the redubbed Belarussian National Republic (BNR), led by Pavel Zhauryd, summoned a regional congress at Slutsk on 14 November 1920. Its 107 delegates passed votes in favor of the BNR and determined to resist, by the force of such arms as they possessed, any attempt by the Red Army to occupy Sluchyna (the Slutsk district). The latter task was placed in the hands of a seventeen-strong Rada of Sluchyna, chaired by Uladzimyr Prakulevich, who selected Zhauryd as head of the militia. Over the following week around 10,000 men were mobilized, in two regiments, as the Slutsk Brigade. Battles against the approaching Red Army (the "Slutsk Defense") began on 27 November 1920, but by 31 December 1920 the last remnants of the isolated and poorly armed Slutsk Brigade had been driven across the border into Poland by Soviet forces.[51]

Meanwhile, to the south, Budennyi finally abandoned the siege of Lwów on 31 August 1920, and, over the following days, was defeated by Polish cavalry at the Battle of Komarovo (Komarów)—the greatest cavalry battle since the Napoleonic era, and, indeed, the last significant cavalry battle of the twentieth century. The 1st Cavalry Army was, at one point, completely surrounded by the enemy, but managed to break through Polish lines and escape to the east. It was, however, unable to regroup and temporarily ceased to exist as a meaningful unit: Hrubeshiv (Hrubieszów) was surrendered on 5 September and Rovno on 18 September 1920. By the end of that month, Polish forces had reached the Sluzha (Słucza) River, the line held by the Red Army before its Warsaw offensive. Soon afterwards, Budennyi's scattered force, having lost thousands of men and horses, had to be altogether withdrawn from the front, but not before the Red Cossacks of the 1st Cavalry Army had added to their already infamous ledger of atrocities against the civilian population in the frontal zone.[52] Predictably, given Cossack traditions, the chief targets of their predations were the Jews, whose fate in the "Russian" Civil Wars we should pause here to consider. For, as the author of one recent study of the period has properly asserted, "without the Jewish question, there is no history of the Revolution."[53]

* * *

Since the partitions of Poland in the late eighteenth century, and the concomitant westward migration of the borders of the Russian Empire, Jews were prominent along the western marchlands of the former Russian Empire (their enforced, segregated "Pale of Settlement" in tsarist times). Although, according to the 1897 census, Jews constituted only 4.13 percent of the empire's population, in towns like Rovno and Białystok (scene of an infamous pogrom in June 1906 that had helped fix the word itself into the English language), for instance, three out of four residents were Jewish. During the revolution and civil wars, Jews in these regions were subjected to terrible violence, from all sides in the struggles. It was the triple tragedy of the Jews of the Pale that they were despised—as alleged usurers, exploitative traders and merchants and speculators—by the local Ukrainian, Polish, and Belorussian peasant populations, and that this profile mapped surprisingly well on to that of the bourgeois "enemies of socialism" identified in Bolshevik propaganda, while, for the Whites, they were anti-Orthodox aliens and Bolsheviks.[54] As the 1st Cavalry Army toured (and scoured) this territory, the combination of "Red" and "Cossack" in its complement proved, therefore, to be a potentially cruel and bloody cocktail. One does not have to read far into Isaak Babel's account of Budennyi's Polish campaign to find observation such as:

> It so chanced that I was billeted in the house of a red-haired widow who smelt of grief and widowhood ... Right under my window some Cossacks were trying to shoot an old silvery-bearded Jew for spying. The old man was uttering piercing screams and struggling to get away. Then Kudrya of the machine gun section took hold of his head and tucked it under his arm. The Jew stopped screaming and straddled his legs. Kudrya drew out his dagger with his right hand and carefully, without splashing himself, cut the old man's throat ...[55]

Polish forces too, however, as very many witnesses attest, were also all too capable of antisemitic violence. In an early passage of his masterful *Red Cavalry*, Babel is tormented by nightmares of horrific violence in another *shtetl* billet. His hostess wakens him:

> "Good sir", she said, you're calling out in your sleep and you're tossing to and fro. I'll make you a bed in another corner, for you are pushing my father about.

> She raised her thin legs and rounded belly from the floor and removed the blanket from the sleeper. Lying on his back was an old man. His throat had been torn out and his face cleft in two; in his beard blue blood was clotted like a lump of lead.

> "Good sir," said the Jewess, shaking up the feather bed, "the Poles cut his throat, and he begging them: 'Kill me in the yard so that my daughter shan't see me die.' But they did as suited them. He passed away in this room ..."[56]

If anything, the horrors of the campaign were tempered in Babel's published stories. He was less circumspect in his (originally private) diary, noting on 3 June 1920 (the very first surviving entry):

Zhitomir pogrom, organized by the Poles, continued, of course, by the [Red] Cossacks.

When our advance troops appeared the Poles entered the town, stayed for 3 days, there was a pogrom, they cut off beards, that's usual, assembled 45 Jews in the marketplace, led them to the slaughteryard, tortures, cut out tongues, wails heard all over the square. They set fire to 6 houses, I went to look at Koniuchowski's house on Cathedral Street. They machine-gunned those who tried to rescue people. The yardman, into whose arms a mother dropped a child from a burning window, was bayoneted ...[57]

That was in early July 1920, but nothing much changes over the course of the Soviet–Polish War. Almost two months later, at Komarów, Babel recorded the following:

Indescribable terror and despair.

They tell me about it. Privately, indoors, they're afraid the Poles may come back. Captain Yakovlev's Cossacks were here yesterday, a pogrom. The family of David Zys, in people's homes, a naked, barely breathing prophet of an old man, an old woman butchered, a child with fingers chopped off, many people still breathing, stench of blood, everything turned upside down, chaos, a mother sitting over her sabred son, an old woman lying twisted up like a pretzel ... 15 people killed ... The worst of it is—our men nonchalantly walk around looting wherever possible, stripping mangled corpses.

The hatred is the same, the Cossacks just the same, the cruelty the same, it's nonsense to think one army is different than another.[58]

It is the Poles' eventual ally, though, the unruly Ukrainian Army of the UNR and, specifically, its commander ("Supreme Otaman," *Golovnoi otaman*), Symon Petliura, that have most often been singled out for vilification in regard to the slaughter of the Jews in Ukraine. There were around 1,500 pogroms in 1,300 localities across Ukraine and Galicia alone in 1918 and 1919. Estimates as to their outcome vary from around 50,000 killed to around 200,000 killed, with another 200,000 casualties and mutilations, plus unknown numbers of rapes and attacks on private property and synagogues. Most of these pogroms—and certainly the most brutal and extensive— occurred during the rule in those regions of the Directory of the UNR in 1918–19.[59]

Explanations of what caused the slaughter in Ukraine—the most terrible sequence of attacks on Jews prior to the Holocaust[60]—are equally various.

They include: the popular identification of Jews with Bolshevism; Jewish Bolsheviks' own animosity toward devout Jews; long-established, regional economic antagonisms (greatly exacerbated by war and revolution); right-wing, proto-fascist racism; the all-pervading opportunistic, criminal, and bestial desire, during chaotic times, to rob, rape, and plunder, as a consequence of which the weakest suffer most; the dire and all-pervading scarcity of food and material goods of these times; a general sense of betrayal and a consequent search for scapegoats; and Ukrainian revenge against the Jewish community for voting the "wrong" way in elections to the Constituent Assembly, or in the Ukrainian Rada's deliberations on independence for Ukraine. These are just some of the interpretations posited over the years, although clearly none of them provide an all-encompassing (or even entirely logical) explanation of the terrible events. But at the root of the problem, surely, was the deeply (and, on the part of the tsarist authorities, deliberately) inculcated antisemitism of imperial Russian society over previous centuries, which had been acutely intensified for the 15 million mobilized men of 1914–17 by their service in the profoundly and unabashedly antisemitic Russian Army. It is certainly notable, as Oleg Budnitskii has recently discussed, that the "pogroms" in Ukraine of 1918–19 were unusual, in that they were not, as had been traditionally the case with pogroms (and is implied in the very meaning of the word), civilian affairs that started either spontaneously or at the instigation of the local authorities. They were, rather, for the most part, attacks on Jews begun, specifically, by soldiers—soldiers of all contending sides in the civil wars (many and sometimes most of whom would have served previously in the tsarist army).[61] That said, we should of course recognize that Ukraine–Galicia–Poland–Lithuania was an expanse of territory so contested during the "Russian" Civil Wars that soldiers (regular and irregular) represented a most unusually high proportion of the population—more than enough to cancel out, certainly, the efforts towards combating antisemitism within its lands that the UNR authorities undertook (including the creation on 27 May 1919 of a widely empowered "Special Investigatory Commission for the Investigation of Anti-Jewish Pogroms").[62]

As Budnitskii has also reminded us, dwelling upon the Ukrainian pogroms should not lead us to considering Jews only as victims in these years: that Jews played a prominent role in the Bolshevik party (and had their own section, the Evsektsiia, of the Central Committee) and, indeed, in the Cheka and the Red Army is undeniable, even if their influence was greatly exaggerated in White propaganda. As Budnitskii notes of the "Russian" Civil Wars, "in this tragedy,

Jews were among the victims *and* among the executioners."[63] Equally confounding to traditional views of the subject is that that the Whites did not officially proscribe Jewish organs of self-government and did not, as a matter of routine, close Jewish schools and religious establishments. Consequently, many prominent Jews supported the Whites (at least in the early stages of the civil wars).[64] The Bolsheviks, on the other hand, did close down Jewish religious and educational establishments (just as they did Orthodox ones). The difference was that the Soviet government did not discriminate against Jews as individuals and often dealt ruthlessly with perpetrators of pogroms. The Whites (who, confoundingly, had a General Iudenich among their foremost leaders) did discriminate against Jews on a day-to-day basis, despite the protestations of Admiral Kolchak and (especially) General Denikin (who did not want their reputation sullied in London, Paris and Washington); they were responsible for many pogroms; and White perpetrators of such horrors almost always went unpunished—indeed, they were frequently rewarded or lauded in the antisemitic White press—with the consequence that in White-held territory "the life and property of Jews were more vulnerable than at any other time in Russian history."[65] It is probably going too far to proceed from this (as Budnitskii does) to the conclusion that the concomitant moral dissolution experienced within Denikin's forces was "one of the most important factors leading to the defeat of the Whites," but it clearly did not help in the maintenance of civil order and military discipline on the White side.[66] But given the very accelerated rate of assimilation demonstrated by Soviet Jews in the 1920s, it is probably almost true, as Budnitskii concluded, that "The experience of Civil War showed the majority of the Jewish population of the country that it could feel secure only under Soviet power."[67]

They certainly did not feel safe under White rule. As Peter Kenez noted, the Russian officer corps, which was at the heart of the White movement, "had long been anti-Semitic." Officers instinctively identified Jews with the notions of liberalism and socialism that they themselves generally despised and this prognosis of the disease that, in their eyes, had infected Russia in the course of the revolution—and, in general, by their land's "progress" toward modernity—seemed to be forcefully affirmed by their experience of the civil wars:

> They always disliked Jews; now their anti-Semitism reached pathological proportion. This new and passionate anti-Semitism was born out of the need to explain, not so much to others, as to themselves, why the revolution had occurred. In the view of the reactionary officers it was the alien Jews who were primarily responsible. They were the microbes that destroyed the healthy body politic of old Russia. As the officers became even more frustrated by the confusing world around them, their

anti-Semitism became increasingly pathological. They murdered more and more Jews and it was necessary to justify themselves by thinking up sinister Jewish conspiracies. Perhaps paradoxically, participation in pogroms increased anti-Semitism ... It alone enabled them to make sense of a world that to them seemed senseless. In this respect, at least, the White officers were precursors of the Nazis.[68]

As noted above, however, most of the controversy surrounding the perpetration of pogroms in Ukraine centers on the tenure of the Directory of the UNR; and, ever since, arguments have raged regarding the extent to which its leader and main commander, Symon Petliura, was culpable for this tragedy. Generally, Jewish sources have charged that, as head of the UNR, Petliura should shoulder responsibility.[69] Ukrainian émigré historiography, conversely, has sought to establish that Petliura was not culpable for events that were beyond the control of a weak and besieged government in a chaotic land, and to highlight, instead, atrocities committed by the Whites, by Ataman Hryhoriiv's and Makhno's forces and (especially) by the Red Army.[70] Petliura had only a limited time in emigration to defend himself: on 25 May 1926, he was shot dead on the streets of Paris by the Bessarabian Jew Shalom Schwartzbard, who claimed to be exacting revenge for the tens of thousands of Jews (among them fifteen members of his own immediate family) who had been killed in pogroms in Ukraine during the period of Petliura's rule. The case, tried in October 1927 at the Paris Assizes—according to a contemporary commentary in *Time* magazine, "one of the most gruesome, bloodcurdling, impassioned trials ever to be held in that vaulted hall of justice"—became an international *cause célèbre*, as the defense (led by the flamboyant left-wing jurist Henri Torres) attempted to prove Petliura's guilt, while the prosecution alleged that Schwartzbard was a Soviet agent. Schwartzbard hardly sought to deny the murder, telling the court that, having identified his target on the Rue Racine (and armed with a photograph of Petliura in one jacket pocket and a revolver in the other), he accosted the Ukrainian leader and shot him five times:

> When I saw him fall I knew he had received five bullets. Then I emptied my revolver [into the body]. The crowd had scattered. A policeman came up quietly and said: "Is that enough?" I answered: "Yes." He said: "Then give me your revolver." I gave him the revolver, saying: "I have killed a great assassin." When the policeman told me Petlura was dead I could not hide my Joy. I leaped forward and threw my arms about his neck.[71]

Despite thus confessing to having gunned down Petliura, Schwartzbard was acquitted by the French jury, with nugatory damages of one franc apiece being awarded to his victim's wife and brother. The controversy surrounding the *Golovnoi Otaman* seems unlikely to subside even now, as his grave in Paris remains a magnetic shrine for émigré and domestic Ukrainian nationalists, while, in June 2009, the former Kominterna Street in the Ukrainian capital of Kiev was renamed Symon Petliura Street. Meanwhile, at Beersheba in Israel, a street has been named for "The Avenger (Shalom Schwartzbard)."[72] The "Russian" Civil Wars have, thus, literally, taken to the streets.

* * *

Back in the autumn of 1920, even as the fighting continued on the rapidly eastward-moving Soviet–Polish front, armistice negotiations were awkwardly convened at Minsk and subsequently (as the Reds surrendered Minsk to the Poles) Riga, leading to a ceasefire in October 1920, and, ultimately, a full Soviet–Polish peace, the Treaty of Riga (18 March 1921). Under the terms of that agreement, Poland shifted its eastern border about 100 miles east of that accorded to Warsaw by the Allies with the Curzon Line, but recovered, in effect, only those eastern borderlands lost to Russia in the third partition of Poland of 1795, including Grodno, Równo, and Lwów (as well as Wilno/Vilnius, although a certain amount of subterfuge deployed, in the so-called "Żeligowski mutiny" there of October 1920, was required to secure that rather significant and largely artificial victory).[73] Other territories and populations in the east, including those around Kiev and Minsk, had to be recognized by Warsaw as now lying within the new Ukrainian SSR and Belorussian SSR, respectively. Piłsudski's dreams of Międzymorze thus had to be shelved, while Petliura and the émigré UNR government found themselves as stateless as their erstwhile allies of the WUPR and were soon no longer welcome even in Warsaw (after efforts, in November 1920, to again invade Ukraine from Polish territory threatened to derail the uneasy Polish–Soviet détente). For this compromise, the Polish leader sustained some criticism domestically, but the debt that bourgeois Europe owed to Piłsudski's bloodied corps remains incalculable.[74] Lenin might have written of the Riga settlement "We have won. Anyone who examines the map will see that we have won, that we have emerged from this war with more territory than we had before we started it,"[75] but he wrote that through gritted teeth. Berlin, however tenuously, had been, conceivably, within the grasp of the Red Army in August 1920. It would not again be so until April 1945, in very different circumstances.

In this great contest, the Soviet leadership had clearly failed to reckon with the morale of Poles defending their own territory: the coherence, history, and consistency of the national movement in Poland were (respectively) closer, longer, and thicker than had been the case in any of the other border regions yet captured by the Red Army: it was certainly more substantial than the national movements of Estonia, Latvia, and Lithuania, from which Soviet forces had already been expelled. Moreover, the Polish population was larger (comprising around 20 million ethnic Poles in 1920) than other would-be secessionists,[76] and the country was far more industrialized: the textile city of Łódź, for example, was one of the most technically developed in the entire world at this point. Moscow, perhaps giddy with the recent success over the AFSR, had even failed to calculate that a Polish Army of 750,000 men that had had eighteen months to prepare for the contest might prove a rather more formidable opponent than the comparatively ramshackle forces of Denikin's Cossack–Volunteer alliance or Kolchak's uneasy Siberian–Komuch conglomerate, neither of which mustered more than about 120,000 men at their peak. The Whites, of course, were operating from far less secure, less developed, and less populous base territories than those enjoyed by Piłsudski's army (whose territory was also, it is worth repeating, his own). That such a gamble—to advance on Warsaw—might be made by the Soviet leadership surely evinces an enduring commitment to the cause of proletarian internationalism. Such a marriage might be regarded as either inspiring in its purity or distressing in its naivety, or it might be regarded as a cover for Soviet Russian imperialism, but nothing can alter the fact that the gamble was made.[77] What is more, even while miscalculating what, in hindsight, appear to have been impossible odds, the Soviet high command, the Bolshevik Central Committee, Sovnarkom, and the Komintern all knew very well that they were taking a gamble: for, by this point, although victorious on many fronts, the Red Army was spread thinly around them, with a weakening rear. As Glavkom Kamenev put it on 15 July 1920, as the momentous decision to move into Poland was being debated:

> But even if we cross [the Curzon Line] and smash Poland, we will still be in an immensely difficult strategic situation, as the front will have been greatly extended in a situation where there are no reserves and our enemies will need only a small concentration of fresh forces at the right point to shake the whole front, just as we did during the battle against Denikin.[78]

The implications of this were clear. But, in agreeing to treat with Poland at such an early stage (as noted above, the ceasefire negotiations actually opened at Minsk in October 1920, when the city was still in Soviet hands), however, factors other than the temporary advantages enjoyed by the Poles were uppermost in the mind of the political leadership in Moscow and the Soviet high command. The former, as we shall see, was aware that civil-war struggles had brought the Soviet economy to its knees by mid-1920, and that internal security might soon be threatened from quarters that had been regarded as solid.[79] The latter, equally, would have been alive to the fact that its own hands were not entirely free to deal with Poland, as there was still a lot of fighting to be done in Transcaucasia, in Central Asia, in Siberia and the Far East, and, most immediately, once again, in White-held regions of South Russia.

Wrangel and the Crimea

Unfortunately for Moscow, the 35,000 Whites evacuated from Novorossiisk in late March 1920 had not sailed away into the sunset, but merely made the short hop to the Crimean peninsula, to disembark thereafter at the ports and resort towns of Kerch, Feodosiia, Yalta, Sevastopol', and Evpatoriia. Awaiting this army—now billeted, incongruously, on Russia's Riviera—was a new commander, General Baron Petr Nikolaevich Wrangel, selected to succeed Denikin by a conference of AFSR commanders at Yalta on 4 April 1920, and recalled from the exile in Constantinople to which he had earlier been consigned by Denikin.[80] The strikingly tall and extravagantly attired Wrangel, who wore his nobility unabashedly on the sleeve of his Circassian *cherkeska*, could not have provided a more contrasting figure to the rather dumpy and plebeian Denikin. Wrangel vowed too that his regime, which would privilege order, obedience, and justice, would expunge all memories of Denikin's ochlocratic "Grabarmiia." To this end, he ordered the shooting of all looters, retired a number of miscreant generals (including, eventually, the now unhinged General Slashchev), formed a cabinet (the Government of South Russia) that included some notably moderate elements (including the liberal, former Marxist P.B. Struve as Minister of Foreign Affairs), and summoned back from Paris, to be his prime minister, the joint architect of the pre-war Stolypin peasant reforms—the former tsarist Minister of Agriculture A.V. Krivoshein. This government (albeit, as was usual with the White governments, with an eye fixed steadily on the impression they might make on the increasingly uninterested Allies) promulgated a remarkably radical land reform (distributing landlords' properties to the peasantry) and promised a fair hearing to anyone who deserted to the Russian Army from the Reds. Relations with the Crimean Tatars, who made up more than a quarter of the local population, were never easy, but Wrangel was able to capitalize on the fact that the Tatar national party (Milliy Firqa) and political structures (the Crimean-Tatar National Republic) had been decimated by the Bolshevik invasions of 1918 and 1919. Seeking allies wherever he could find them, Wrangel also made conciliatory approaches to the Ukrainians, Georgians, and other nationalities that Denikin had offended. He even sent a delegation offering an alliance to Makhno.[81]

Yet, for all that, Wrangel's focus was on the army. He had already had a meteoric military career, rising to the rank of major-general in the imperial army before his fortieth birthday (despite initially favoring a career as a mining engineer over the army) and was always regarded as a star in the already glittering Guards Cavalry Regiment to which he was assigned. True, he was not without enemies in the southern White camp—where the only guaranteed method of securing acclaim seemed to be to die and to have a regiment named in one's honor—and snipers among the *pervopokhodniki* would target the fact that he had joined the movement late, having spent most of 1917–18 at his dacha in Yalta, rather than braving the horrors of the First Kuban (Ice) March. But he had impressed greatly during the campaign across the Kuban and the Terek in the early months of 1919, and had masterminded the much-feted (and potentially key) capture of Tsaritsyn in June 1919.

No general alive or dead, however, could have faced down the might of the Red Army alone, in 1920, from Wrangel's position. His army, rechristened (echoing Kolchak's earlier such boastful endowment) the Russian Army, amounted to only around 40,000 active men (including 7,000 survivors of the Bredov March, who finally arrived from Poland, via Romania, in August 1920); and his base territory of the half-province of Crimea, although securely nestled in a Bolshevik-free Black Sea, was populated by only about a million souls, compared to more than a million fighters available to Trotsky and a full Red Army roster by mid-1920 of almost 5 million drawn from a territory that encompassed most of what had been the Russian Empire, with a population approaching 100 million. No wonder that, when accepting the post of commander-in-chief of what remained of the Whites in South Russia, Wrangel took, like Kolchak before him, the illustrious and enigmatic title of "ruler" (*pravitel'*) but dropped the admiral's pretense of supremacy. Indeed, Wrangel insisted that all his subordinates accept that his task was to preserve the army, not to achieve victory in the civil wars.

That, nevertheless, did not rule out offensive operations and, in an attempt to extend his base and to reincorporate the Cossack populations into the White Army, Wrangel ordered an ambitious amphibious landing on the Kuban coast in early August, to be commanded by General Ulagai. Ulagai had served, with some distinction, with Wrangel at Tsaritsyn in the summer of 1919, and at the head of the Composite Cossack Cavalry Group of the Volunteer Army during the retreat from Orel in November–December of that year. The Kuban expedition proved to be a failure, however, evoking little response from a Kuban population that by this point must have been sick of the war, and Ulagai's men were lucky to escape encirclement by Soviet forces before being ingloriously transported back to the Crimea three weeks after their disembarkation. They brought back with them the mean prize of an additional 1,500 men and 600 horses, but had entirely failed in their efforts to inspire yet another anti-Soviet Cossack uprising, and had not secured the source of foodstuffs so desperately needed by the hungry, refugee-swollen population of the Crimea, which was sealed off from its normal sources of grain in the northern Tauride, the mainland half-province immediately abutting the peninsula.[82]

Another factor debilitating Wrangel was the waning support for the Whites from the Allies, whose never-secure attentions were now turning elsewhere. France, in keeping with its policy of building a *cordon sanitaire* around Bolshevik Russia,[83] offered some assistance (although Paris's price included an option on the Black Sea Fleet and the promise of monopoly stakes in railways in areas liberated from the Bolsheviks), and, on 23 August 1920, even declared its official recognition of the Wrangel regime, but little of substance was delivered to the Crimea.[84] Where Britain stood was baldly spelled out to Wrangel in a note delivered to him by Rear-Admiral George Hope on 3 June 1920:

Sir!

I beg leave to inform you that I have received a message from the British High Commissioner at Constantinople directing me to inform you that His Majesty's Government are a good deal disquieted by rumours of your intention to take the offensive against the Bolshevik forces. I am also directed to inform you that if you attack, His Majesty's Government's plan for negotiating with the Soviet Government will inevitably fall through and His Majesty's Government will be unable to concern themselves any further with the fate of your army.[85]

That message could not have been clearer (or more hurtful), and was fully understood, but Wrangel's highly developed sense of honor could not allow him to let slip any chance of attacking the Bolsheviks, no matter how hopeless now was the prospect of a total victory. In this regard, the Polish–Ukrainian advance on Kiev in April–May 1920 was simply too good an opportunity to miss. Thus, in the first week of June 1920, Wrangel's 1st (Volunteer) Army Corps (commanded by General A.P. Kutepov), which included what remained of the elite *Kornilovtsy*, *Markovtsy*, and *Drozdovtsy* divisions (the "colorful" units of the AFSR), burst out from behind its defenses on the Perekop isthmus and forced its way into Northern Tauride, reaching the lower Dnepr within a matter of days, pushing north as far as Aleksandrovsk (Zaporozh'e) and threatening even Ekaterinoslav.[86] Meanwhile, to the east, forces commanded by General P.K. Pisarev advanced across the Taganach rail bridge, via Chongar, to the mainland and thence toward Melitopol', as General Slashchev's 2nd Army Corps simultaneously undertook an amphibious attack on the northern shore of the Sea of Azov, catching the 13th Red Army by surprise, encircling its 1st Cavalry Corps, and capturing 3,000 horses, before pushing as far to the east as the industrial town of Mariupol' by 15 September 1920.

With the execution of these maneuvers, the expanse of territory and population within Wrangel's realm had suddenly doubled. The holy grail, however, lay in the west—beyond the Reds' heavily fortified bridgehead at Khakovka, on the left bank of the Dnepr—and the majestic prospect of union with the Poles, somewhere in the vicinity of Cherkassy. This required Wrangel's forces to cross the Dnepr, which Kutepov's Kuban cavalry managed to do at Uchel'ka, where a pontoon bridge was constructed, on 6 October 1920, even briefly capturing Nikopol', while the *Kornilovtsy* forced the river at Khortitsa and pushed southward.[87] However, Red forces remained firmly dug in on the left bank at Khakovka and the *Kornilovtsy* had no time to cut them off from the rear before, on 12 October 1920, the Soviet–Polish ceasefire was signed at Riga and Wrangel's fate was sealed.

* * *

With the Western and South West Fronts secured by the Riga armistice, Glavkom Kamenev finalized the new Southern Front against Wrangel that had been established, based at Khar'kov, on 21 September 1920, and which was to be commanded by M.V. Frunze, diverted from his service on the Turkestan Front. To it were assigned the 6th and 13th Red Armies (joined by the 4th Red Army from 18 October 1920), as well as both the 1st and 2nd Cavalry Armies and the Revolutionary Insurgent Army of Ukraine, Makhno having once again agreed to an alliance with the Bolsheviks. Some of these Red forces—about 8 percent of which were RKP(b) members (an unusually high proportion)—had been transferred from the Polish front (notably, both 1st and 2nd Cavalry Armies); others, including the 51st Rifle Division (commanded by the veteran of the "Urals Army March," V.K. Bliukher), had come all the way from Eastern Siberia. Bliukher's crack division, alongside the ubiquitous Latvian Riflemen, was instrumental in the Red victory in the Battle of Kakhovka in October 1920 on the lower Dnepr, after a prolonged and bloody contest, in which White forces deployed tanks and aircraft in concentrations hitherto not witnessed in the civil wars (but to no effect against the solidly entrenched Soviet bridgehead). All told, Frunze's Southern Front against Wrangel mustered 188,000 infantry, cavalry, and other front-line troops, with 3,000 machine-guns, 600 artillery pieces, and twenty-three armored trains, as well as several hundred *tachanki*, marshalled chiefly by Makhno's forces.[88] Against such a juggernaut, Wrangel's exhausted contingents, which were outnumbered 5:1, stood little chance. Knowing that if he retreated into Crimea his forces would never again summon the will or the strength (and still less the international support) to break out again, Wrangel determined to hang on in the Northern Tauride for as long as he could. But, ultimately, the only possible strategy was to withdraw on to the peninsula, before the Red cavalry could cut off that escape route, and in mid-October the retreat began.

Less than half the White forces that had advanced out of the Crimea in June returned there in October. As they limped back across the Perekop onto the peninsula, frustrating Trotsky's exhortation of the Southern Front of 27 October 1920 to "Don't Let Them Get Away!",[89] all the remaining Whites had at their backs was the Turkish Wall—an 8-mile-long rampart-and-ditch earthwork construction that had been laid across Perekop isthmus by the Crimean khans to protect their lands from marauding Cossacks from the north. That eighteenth-century barrier across the land-bridge into Crimea, newly reinforced and armored with machine-gun and artillery emplacements, and backed up by armored trains, seemed now to be a godsend to the Whites and their Cossack allies. With such defenses in place, "All the forces of Sovdepia cannot frighten the Crimea," proclaimed a White newssheet.[90] But they could not have prepared themselves for what the heavens next bestowed: an unusually early and sharp −20°C October frost, and a bizarre combination of high winds, that cleared the water and firmed up the surface of the Sivash salt flats stretching alongside the Perekop causeway. This fortuitous meteorological oddity—an event that occurs only two or three times each century—allowed Red forces simply to bypass the White garrisons on the Turkish Wall by advancing over the normally impassable Sivash on the night of 7–8 November 1920. As more Reds broke into the peninsula on the eighth, Bliukher's 51st Division having surged over the Turkish Wall, the isolation of the Red advance guard was ended and the gates to the Crimea were thrown wide open.[91]

Accepting the inevitability of defeat, following a meeting of his council on 8 November, Wrangel gave the order on 11 November 1920 to begin preparations for the evacuation of Crimea.[92] Ships of the Whites' Black Sea Fleet and the French navy were readied for the evacuation and by 14–16 November

1920, as Wrangel's flagship, the honorific *General Kornilov* (formerly the Bogatyr-class cruiser, the *Kagul*), steamed out of Feodosiia with the general on board, by Wrangel's own estimation, "On 126 ships, 145,693 people were conveyed toward Tsargrad. All vessels arrived there safely, with the exception of the destroyer *Zhivoi*, which went down in a gale."[93]

Those who were left behind—and despite Wrangel's claim in his memoirs that all who wished to embark were embarked, there were many of them—were not so fortunate: as the Whites departed, a *revkom* under the Hungarian revolutionary Béla Kun (who had escaped to Russia following the failure of the Hungarian Soviet Republic he had led in 1919) and the much-feared Bolshevik military commissar Rozaliia Zemliachka (Zalkind) took up residence in Crimea and unleashed a wave of reprisals, in which it is now thought at least 12,000 people were executed.[94]

Even those who had escaped from the Crimea in November and from Novorossiisk in March 1920 had not obtained lifelong immunity from Red revenge, however. Rather than face a life in exile, thousands chose voluntarily to return—to uncertain and usually unbearable fates. The unstable inter-war years in the new Eastern European and Balkan states that provided precarious refuge for many of the stateless Cossacks and White soldiers then also provided ample opportunities for political assassinations, misadventures, and kidnaps by the Soviet intelligence services.[95] Finally, with the success of Tito's Communist partisans in Yugoslavia and the invasion of much of Eastern Europe by the Red Army in 1944–45, tens of thousands of White émigrés were rounded up in Yugoslavia, Bulgaria, and Czechoslovakia and "repatriated" to the USSR, whether or not they had collaborated with Axis forces (and whether or not, indeed, in the case of the younger generation, they had ever before set foot in Russia or been a citizen of that country)—very frequently with the assistance of British and American forces to which they had attempted to surrender. The majority were sent into the labor camp system, while the most prominent of those snared, including Generals P.N. Krasnov, A.K. Shkuro, and Sultan-girei Klych, were subsequently tried in Moscow and then executed as traitors—a designation that denied them the firing squad and condemned them to an ignominious death by hanging.[96]

5

1917–21

ON THE INTERNAL FRONTS

The economic, political, and military structure of the Soviet zone was established, in all its essentials, by the summer of 1918 and underwent little fundamental change until the spring of 1921 (and, even then, chiefly only in economic matters). That is not to say that, between those dates, as the Red Army battled White, Black (anarchist), Green, Nationalist, and Interventionist foes on its external fronts, the Bolsheviks' control of the territory they held was not contested, on a variety of internal fronts, by either diffuse or organized oppositions (or sometimes both at the same time), or that the governing party itself was united on all issues. It certainly was not. In fact, Lenin's regime faced persistent internal challenges to its governance—armed and unarmed, martial and ideological, as well as economic—in principle and in practice. However, these challenges remained largely isolated from one another; and, importantly, were never so extensive as to replicate the no-go, partisan-infested regions that spread like a typhus rash across the White rear in Ukraine, South Russia, and, especially, Siberia.[1] More importantly, attacks on the internal fronts only reached dangerous proportions for the Soviet government from late 1920 onwards. By that time, as we have seen, west of Irkutsk, the Kolchak regime was dead and buried—or, at least, submerged beneath the ice—although its progeny clung on in the Far East; Wrangel's boats had sailed; and a bargain had been struck with Poland that, together with the 1920 treaties with Finland and the new Baltic states, had delimited and provisionally secured Soviet Russia's western border (albeit at a point further east than Moscow would have desired).

Moreover, although whenever the Hydra of popular resistance or opposition to Soviet rule raised its many heads there were instinctive (and, in the light of what would engulf the USSR in the 1930s, ominous) murmurings in Moscow of espionage, foreign subversion, and a renewed round of intervention, the fact of the matter was that, with the exception of Japanese forces in the Far East, the last contingents of the interventionist armies had left Russia in the first half of 1920 and were in no hurry to return. Furthermore, the Allied economic blockade of the RSFSR had been officially lifted in January 1920, and pens across the globe were poised to sign a series of mutually profitable agreements between Moscow and its former interventionist enemies, of which the Anglo-Soviet Trade Agreement of 16 March 1921 was only the first. The prime mover in all this had been the British premier, David Lloyd George, who (though no lover of socialism in any form, and not averse to cheering on the Whites when they were on the advance) had resisted the imprecations of his war minister, Winston Churchill, that nothing less than the fate of Western civilization demanded that the Bolshevik baby be strangled at birth. Lloyd George had, rather, long insisted that outside interference in Russia was unfeasible and that the one thing certain to invigorate Bolshevism would be an Allied attempt to crush it by force.[2] On 16 April 1919, in a statement to the House of Commons, while making no excuses for having assisted pro-Allied elements in 1918, and continuing to protect them from the Bolsheviks, he had charged "that to attempt [further] military intervention in Russia would be the greatest act of stupidity that any Government could possibly commit," explaining:

> If we conquered Russia—and we could conquer it—you would be surprised at the military advice which is given us as to the number of men who would be required, and I should like to know where they are to come from. But supposing you had them. Supposing you gathered together an overwhelming army, and you conquered Russia. What manner of government are you going to set up there? You must set up a government which the people want; otherwise it would be an outrage of all the principles for which we have fought in this War. Does anyone know for what government they would ask, and if it is a government we do not like, are we to reconquer Russia in order to get a government we do like?[3]

Six weeks earlier, on 4 March 1919, Lloyd George had already obtained the War Cabinet's agreement to the total withdrawal of British troops from North Russia before the end of the summer of 1919, and had at the same time begun the process that would lead to a similar decision regarding the British units still lingering in Transcaucasia.[4]

Of course, even two years later, when these policies bore fruit in the trade agreement, there was no guarantee that the apparent détente evoked by the series of treaties would endure, but for the moment it was there—and on some levels was reinforced by the Soviet government's increasing involvement in multinational conferences, cultural exchanges and the like in the early 1920s[5]—and consequently the attention of the Kremlin's new inhabitants could be focused inward, whenever and wherever that was necessary. Most important here, for our purposes, was that the Bolshevik leadership proved far more adept at dealing with the domestic challenges of economic, political, and military organization than did its opponents.

War Communism: Its Nature and its Consequences

One of the central arguments Lenin had advanced in favor of the Bolsheviks' seizure of power in September–October 1917 was that in Russia, as in all combatant states, the circumstances of the world war had placed so much economic leverage in the hands of governments, as opposed to private individuals, that control of the economy and state power could be seized simultaneously. As Lenin postulated in early October 1917:

> Capitalism has created an accounting *apparatus* in the shape of the banks, syndicates, postal service, consumers' societies, and office employees' unions. *Without big banks socialism would be impossible.*

> The big banks *are* the "state apparatus" which we *need* to bring about socialism, and which we *take ready-made* from capitalism; our task here is merely to lop off what *capitalistically mutilates* [of] this excellent apparatus, to make it *even bigger*, even more democratic, even more comprehensive. Quantity will be transformed into quality. A single State Bank, the biggest of the big, with branches in every rural district, in every factory, will constitute as much as nine-tenths of the *socialist* apparatus. This will be country-wide *book-keeping*, country-wide *accounting* of the production and distribution of goods, this will be, so to speak, some thing [*sic*] in the nature of the *skeleton* of socialist society.[6]

In his book *State and Revolution* (mostly written pre-February 1917, but not finished or published until 1918), Lenin was quite circumspect about precisely when the capitalist state might whither away and when, specifically, the development of modern capitalism might attain such a level as to facilitate the end of "the antithesis between mental and physical labour" that perpetuates it and the dawn of a communistic era, in which "every literate person" was capable of performing the basic procedures of "accounting and control" to which capitalism had been distilled.[7] But, in October 1917, again, he was clearly optimistic that horizon was, at least, in sight:

> We can "lay hold of" and "set in motion" this "state apparatus" (which is not fully a state apparatus under capitalism, but which will be so with us, under socialism) at one stroke, by a single decree, because the actual work of book-keeping, control, registering, accounting and counting is performed by *employees*, the majority of whom themselves lead a proletarian or semi-proletarian existence.
>
> As for the higher officials, of whom there are very few, but who gravitate towards the capitalists, they will have to be dealt with in the same way as the capitalists, i.e., "severely". Like the capitalists, they will offer *resistance*. This resistance will have to be *broken*, and if the immortally naïve Peshekhonov, as early as June 1917, lisped like the infant that he was in state affairs, that "the resistance of the capitalists has been broken", this childish phrase, this childish boast, this childish swagger, *will be converted by the proletariat into reality*.
>
> We can do this, for it is merely a question of breaking the resistance of an insignificant minority of the population, literally a handful of people ... and the Soviets will institute such *supervision* that every Tit Titych will be *surrounded* as the French were at Sedan. We know these Tit Tityches by name: we only have to consult the lists of directors, board members, large shareholders, etc. There are several hundred, at most several thousand of them in the *whole* of Russia, and the proletarian state, with the apparatus of the Soviets, of the employees' unions, etc., will be able to appoint ten or even a hundred supervisers [sic] to each of them, so that instead of "breaking resistance" it may even be possible, by means of *workers' control* (over the capitalists), to make all resistance *impossible*.[8]

Thus, following a Sovnarkom decree of 14 November 1917,[9] a largely improvised system of workers' control was initiated in Soviet Russia over the winter of 1917–18, with authority vested in hastily elected and nebulous factory committees. (In the first few post–October months, the Bolsheviks tended to distrust the trade unions as strongholds of Menshevism, particularly in the light of the Vikzhel affair.) This, at least, proved that the Bolsheviks' advocacy of worker power was not mere cant, intended to win recruits for their seizure of power, although that aspect was not altogether absent.[10] Certainly, though, the experiment with workers' control in 1917–18 was a disaster. Over-zealous Bolshevik workers tended, at best, to scare experienced factory managers away (often deliberately and cruelly) but were unable to manage production themselves, while many workers interpreted the absence of authority in the workplace as a licence to pilfer or, at least, to do as little work as possible. Even a Bolshevik leader of so staunchly a pro-worker mien as the former *metalist* A.G. Shliapnikov (who, having abandoned his lathe, was at this point Acting People's Commissar for Trade and Industry) was shocked by what he saw and quickly began to argue for an immediate return to more centralized direction and one-man management.[11]

Consequently, production plummeted: tellingly, according to one carefully researched account, half of the fall in production of Russia's industry during the period 1913 to 1919 took place in 1918.[12] Unemployment soared (a phenomenon sorely exacerbated by the demobilization of seven million soldiers of the imperial army); and, as peasants concentrated on seizing land rather than producing food (or selling their produce for worthless paper money), bread rations fell to just two ounces a day in many cities, leading to wide-scale worker protests and the election of independent worker councils that attempted to free themselves of interference on the part of trade union officials (who, by the spring of 1918, were usually Bolshevik appointees). Such events—touted as being "spontaneous," but usually involving Mensheviks and SRs hostile to the Bolshevik regime—were very common even in Petrograd.[13] In fact, the capital (and the northern cities in general) suffered disproportionately, as supplies of food and fuel (for both domestic and industrial usage) dwindled with the separation in 1918 from the Soviet zone of the main areas of food and fuel production of the old empire (Ukraine, the North Caucasus, Transcaucasia, the Urals, and Western Siberia), as a consequence of the Brest-Litovsk treaties and the subsequent upsurge of the counter-revolution around the periphery. Although the Soviet leadership might have attempted to conceal this disaster, notably through the closure of the opposition press,[14] its desperation was revealed by a Sovnarkom appeal of 10 May 1918, which frankly admitted that: "Petrograd is experiencing an unprecedented catastrophe. There is no bread ... The Red capital is on the brink of ruin from starvation."[15] All the northern cities were hungry during the world war and the civil wars, but Petrograd faced a particular problem, in that very little intensive agriculture had developed in its immediate environs. This was partly a consequence of the adverse climate and poor soils of the region, but was also a result of local peasants having opted, since the emancipation of 1861, to earn a cash income in the capital's booming industrial economy by entering the urban labor market, rather than, for example, developing a market-gardening sector.[16] St Petersburg—exemplifying the mixed legacy of its founder—was (and, one might say remains) an unnatural city.

The Soviet cities suffered also as a result of the disorientation of their industries, which had been largely devoted to war production. In Petrograd alone, between 1 January and early April 1918, an additional 134,000 workers (46 percent of the city's labor force) joined the already swollen ranks of the unemployed, as 265 factories sat idle.[17] This then had immediate knock-on effects politically, as the Mensheviks enjoyed a sudden electoral revival in polls for local soviets in the spring of 1918: they won the elections held to city soviets in all the major cities of the Central Industrial Region and most of its smaller cities (including Kaluga, Kostroma, Riazan, Vladimir, Tver, Iaroslavl', Rybinsk, etc.) and, sometimes in a bloc with the SRs, did just as well in less industrialized regions of the south and east. This, in turn, induced widespread falsification of the results by the Bolshevik authorities, the effective exclusion of the Mensheviks from future elections, and no little violence on the part of the Soviet government against opposition parties and organizations said to be influenced by them (unions, factory assemblies, etc.).[18]

In response to the economic crisis, from May to June 1918, the Bolsheviks rapidly fell back on a more *dirigiste* economic program, which came to be called "War Communism."[19] This label was only applied *post facto*, by Lenin, in April 1921,[20] and was made at that juncture in order to drive home the political point that the program had been forced upon the Soviet regime by the circumstances of the civil wars and would not otherwise have been inflicted upon the population. However, it actually had as many roots in Bolshevik ideology as did the more anarchistic and libertarian affections for workers' control that characterized the Left of the party.[21] Certainly, influential Bolsheviks such as N.I. Bukharin, L.B. Krasin, and Iu. Larin eulogized the economic structure of the civil-war period as being the process of transformation into socialism, while their comrade L.N. Kritsman nostalgically entitled his 1929 study of it "The Heroic Period of the Great Russian Revolution."[22] For some such "utopian" Bolsheviks, state control of the economy was even envisioned as a civil-war weapon, with which could be destroyed the last vestiges of capitalism: the Soviet government's cancellation of all state debts it had inherited in February 1918 was greeted by such elements as detonating a bomb under capitalism worldwide; meanwhile, domestically, wrote the Bolshevik economist E.A. Preobrazhenskii, by destroying savings and the value of money, the printing presses that were pouring out inflationary Soviet banknotes during the civil wars could be conceived of as "the machine-gun of the Commissariat of Finance, which directs its fire into the rear of the bourgeoisie."[23] Yet, the measures that defined the new economic era were introduced piecemeal and Alec Nove was probably right to talk of "the slide into War Communism,"[24] while R.W. Davies concluded that "The truth seems to be that each major step was undoubtedly a response to emergency," rather than being mainly determined by ideology.[25]

In any case, the assertion by Evan Mawdsley that "'War' Communism was essentially *the* economic policy of victorious Bolshevism"[26] can only be fully accepted if one accepts, with Mawdsley, that the civil wars started after the October Revolution. This author does not, proposing instead, as we have seen, that the October Revolution was but one phase of the (early) civil wars in "Russia." Nevertheless, it is true that the fundamental administrative apparatus of War Communism had, tellingly, been forged during the apparent flowering of workers' control in the immediate aftermath of the October Revolution. A Sovnarkom decree of 14 December 1917 nationalized the banks, while a decree of VtsIK of 5 December 1917 established VSNKh (Vserossiiskii Sovet Narodnogo Khoziastva, the Supreme Council of the National Economy), which came to concern itself chiefly with industrial affairs.[27] But the process accelerated dramatically from the spring of 1918 onward, as the economic emergency triggered by the intensification of the civil wars demanded solutions (and Left Bolshevik radicals, disturbed by the treaty with Germany, demanded pacification and satisfaction in other spheres of the new, revolutionary state's activities). Key here were the declaration by VTsIK of a state "food dictatorship" from 9 May 1918, a decree on means of food procurement of 13 May 1918, and a decree on the nationalization of large industrial enterprises (28 June 1918).[28]

Subsequently, as it came to fruition, the essential characteristics of the Soviet economy under War Communism were: a high degree of central control over the production and distribution of goods; a state monopoly on foreign trade (although there was precious little of that before 1921) and a strict regulation of internal trade (to the extent that all private trade came to be regarded, essentially, as illegal by 1920); the imposition of strict discipline in the factories (including the adoption and lauding of the principals of Taylorism) and a move toward one-man management by "experts";[29] obligatory labor service for members of the bourgeoisie; the requisitioning of grain and other agricultural produce from the peasantry (*prodrazverstka*); the rationing of food and other products and efforts to victual the urban population through communal cafeterias; and a tendency for direct exchange of goods and services to obviate the need for currency. The "system," though, was never generally codified, worked haphazardly—"a partly organized chaos," Alec Nove neatly termed it[30]—and featured some notable false starts.

One failed experiment of the early War Communism period was the introduction of Committees of the Village Poor (Kombedy), following a VTsIK decree of 11 June 1918.[31] The Kombedy were intended to harness the perceived antagonism of allegedly poor peasants toward their allegedly wealthier neighbors: in short, to extend the civil war into the village. However, even if such rural class differentiation had ever existed beyond the pages of Lenin's twenty-year-old (and largely deluded) thesis on the subject (*The Development of Capitalism in Russia*, 1899), it had been obscured by the equalizing tendencies of the villagers' seizure of landlords' property in 1917–18, together with the forced reintegration into the village land pool of those plots that had been fenced off by separators under the pre-war Stolypin land reforms. In fact, as the number of comparatively poor and comparatively rich peasants declined post-October, the countryside experienced a process of "middle-peasantization" (*oseredniachenie*), while the traditional and autonomous structures of peasant self-government (the *mir*, or village commune) had been strengthened by the collapse of other competing agencies in 1917 (landlords, *zemstva*, etc.) and the insubstantiality of new ones (village and district soviets, and the land committees established by the Provisional Government). This rendered the village at once more united and less pervious to outside influences than it ever had been.[32] Unsurprisingly, therefore, when it was perceived by the Soviet government that even where Kombedy had been established they were sometimes institutions populated only by outsiders to the village (migrants, refugees, etc.) or, if they contained locals, were frequently utilized by the peasants to organize *against* Soviet power, the institution was abolished following a vote at the 6th All-Russian Congress of Soviets in November 1918. This was followed by the adoption of a Lenin-penned "Resolution on the Attitude to the Middle Peasants," validated at the 8th Congress of the RKP(b) on 23 March 1919, in which the party vowed to overcome its anti-peasant prejudices, to learn to cooperate with the "ordinary" villager, to tax the middle-peasants (*seredniaki*) "very mildly" and not to confuse them with the exploitative kulaks.[33] The latter had been the chief target of an emergency tax levied in November 1918, but even that experiment with the use of economic cudgels against the kulaks was not repeated.

Moreover, it has been fairly clearly established that, even in respect of many of its other features—ones that endured or were even expanded upon even after the main fronts of the civil wars had been closed—War Communism simply did not work. Gross output of all Russian industries by 1921 had fallen by almost 70 percent compared to 1913 levels (with key heavy industries particularly badly stricken and producing only a minute fraction of the iron and steel, for example, that they had managed before the war).[34] Particularly and most damagingly, the state was unable regularly to supply food to the northern cities, for example: gross agricultural production in 1921 was only 60 percent of what it had been in 1913, while railway tonnage carried (including almost all south-to-north food supplies) fell by 75 percent over the same period and gross industrial production was something close to 20 percent of what it had been prior to the world war, with the cotton (7 percent) and metal (10 percent) industries particularly badly hit.[35] In these conditions, with wages at around 4 percent of their pre-war levels, the employed were hardly better off than the unemployed.[36] Consequently, although the Cheka, for form's sake, occasionally raided private markets (such as Moscow's daily teeming Sukharevka), and while communal dining rooms offered menus listing only a dozen different ways to prepare a potato, urban provisioning was overwhelmingly left to the whim of private traders (usually petty operators) throughout the civil-war period.[37] Even they, however, could not meet the demand and, facing starvation, city-dwellers left the cities in droves: the population of Petrograd, for example, fell by around two-thirds (from 2,500,000 to 750,000) between 1917 and 1920, and Moscow by more than one-third.[38] Victor Serge later recalled his impressions of first setting foot in Petrograd in January 1919, having been deported back to Russia from France:

> We were entering a world frozen to death. The Finland Station, glittering with snow, was deserted. The square where Lenin had addressed a crowd [on his return on 4 April 1917] from the top of an armoured car was no more than a white desert surrounded by dead houses. The broad, straight thoroughfares, the bridges astride the Neva, now a river of snowy ice, seemed to belong to an abandoned city; first a gaunt soldier in a grey greatcoat, then after a long time a woman freezing under her shawls, went past like phantoms in an oblivious silence ... It was the metropolis of Cold, of Hunger, of Hatred, and of Endurance.

One of Serge's first conversations was with the wife of G.E. Zinov'ev, the Bolshevik boss in Petrograd, who informed him that "Hunger riots may start ... Typhus has killed so many people that we can't manage to bury them; luckily, they are frozen ..."[39] Every cloud ...

The author Evgenii Zamiatin, long sympathetic to the Bolsheviks but arrested by the Cheka in 1919 during a clampdown on Left-SRs in Petrograd, left a remarkable fictional portrait of the former capital in that year in the first lines of his short story *Peshchera* ("The Cave," 1922), in which the neo-classical beauty of Peter's now petrified city has been obscured by a reversion to stone-age conditions, in which the city's once proud inhabitants have been replaced by some subterranean species of troglodytes:

Glaciers, mammoths, wastelands; night, black, something like houses in the cliffs, in the cliffs—caves. Who knows who blows at night on the stone pathway between the rocks, sniffing out the path and disturbing the dusty white snow—maybe a mammoth, maybe the wind: maybe—there is wind; maybe—there is ice, and the roar of some sort of huge mammoth. One thing's clear: it's winter. And you must clench your teeth harder to stop them chattering, and you have to chop wood with a stone axe, and every night you carry your fire from cave to cave, always deeper, and you must wrap yourself in more and more shaggy hides.

Between the rocks, where a century ago stood Petersburg, at night wanders the mammoth ...

The starving and freezing intelligentsia couple at the center of Zamiatin's tale worship "a greedy cave god—the cast iron stove," but ultimately perish.[40] Reality was hardly more comforting: in a reversal of the brave new world that Bolshevism had promised, life itself seemed to be approaching a state of suspended animation, as amenorrhoea (failure to menstruate) reached epidemic levels, affecting 50–70 percent of women in many Soviet cities.[41] Even cities and regions that had traditionally been food-rich suffered inordinately: located in the immediate rear of the Eastern Front, the city of Samara, on the Volga, starved as Red forces requisitioned foodstuffs and draft animals. Its weakened citizens consequently fell victim all too easily to disease: deaths from infectious diseases in Samara province rose from 16,000 in 1918 to over 200,000 in both 1919 and 1920.[42]

The more enterprising and healthy denizens of these half-deserted cities became *meshochniki* (so-called "bagmen"), ferrying their portable possessions to the countryside in sacks to be bartered for food. For fuel, meanwhile, furniture, books, fences, and anything else flammable was immolated. During the winter of 1918–19, the sight of entire wooden houses being demolished by freezing scavengers was common. The looting of bourgeois property, which was to some extent encouraged by the authorities—either deliberately or, indirectly, by the Bolsheviks' generic demonization of the *burzhui* (bourgeois) "enemy"—offered some respite for the desperate, though; while the bourgeoisie and wealthier elements of the intelligentsia counted themselves fortunate if the worst indignity they suffered was to surrender rooms in their apartments and houses to proletarian guests, who could count upon the support of their elected "house committee" to sanction their right to burn the stair rods. "Fortunately the town residences of the late bourgeoisie contained quite a lot in the way of carpets, tapestries, linen and plate," remembered Victor Serge:

> From the leather upholstery of sofas one could make passable shoes; from the tapestries, clothing ... I myself burned the collected *Laws of the Empire* as fuel for a neighbouring family, a task which gave me considerable satisfaction.[43]

This process of resettlement (*pereselenie*) began as an elemental upsurge and, by 1919–20, was only gradually brought under any vestige of control by the city authorities.[44]

Nor could the system of War Communism be guaranteed to meet its other basic task of provisioning the Red Army, which instead was very often forced to resort to self-supply (*samoobespechenie*): very often Red units simply requisitioned food, horses, carts, young men (and women), and whatever else they needed, from whatever village or town in which they happened to be billeted. The brilliant Red Army commander Mikhail Tukhachevskii would later posit this as one of the great advantages of the revolutionary army—a living force, at one with the people, which could regenerate and support itself as it moved forward.[45] But it is safe to say that, by and large, that was a fantasy: Russian, Siberian, Ukrainian, and other villagers of the civil-war era did not view their military lodgers, Red or White, so welcomingly. Most accounts agree that billeted Reds treated their hosts with marginally more respect than did the Whites (or the often lawless forces of the Ukrainian Army or the Makhnovists), but this was not always the case—if, for example, the Red commissar was one who had half digested Marx's (perhaps mistranslated) ruminations on "the idiocy of rural life"[46] and wished to make plain what he, a worker, thought of peasants (especially if he sought to distance himself from his own peasant roots); or if the village in which a unit was billeted was Jewish or German.[47] Those few outsiders who journeyed to the Soviet countryside in 1919 were sometimes puzzled by the peasants' affirmation that they "liked the Bolsheviks, but detested these Communists." What the villagers meant was that they were in favor of Lenin's advocacy of land seizure of 1917, but were distinctly less keen on the food requisitioning (*prodrazverstaka*) his renamed party implemented through the deployment of requisitioning detachments of the newly recruited Food Army (Prodarmiia) from May 1918 onwards.[48]

Peasant Hostility to Soviet Rule: The Volga, the Urals, Tambov, and Western Siberia

The consequence of the party's deficit of popularity in the countryside was a series of uprisings that broke out in the villages—particularly (but far from exclusively) those in the immediate rear of a Red front, which were the most likely to be subjected to impromptu and locally organized Red Army requisitions.[49] These disturbances began in the spring of 1918 and were particularly virulent in the rear districts of the newly formed Eastern Front. According to

Donald Raleigh, for example, "Beginning in Saratov Uezd in May 1918, distur-bances spread to Volsk, Khvalynsk, Serdobsk, Kuznetsk, Atarsk, Petrovsk and the German colonies, some fifty volosts in all" across Saratov *guberniia*. Moreo-ver, these uprisings took the form of collective actions of entire villages. They were forcibly suppressed, but violence erupted again in Saratov *uezd* in May, July, September, and November 1918, "as a result of grain seizures, squabbles over compiling inventories of grain and livestock, the activities of the *kombedy*, 'counterrevolutionary' agitation, and discontent with Soviet power."[50]

Another recent study has detailed the prevalence of peasant uprisings from August 1918, further north, in Viatka *guberniia*, particularly in its more pros-perous southern *uezdy*, and has revealed that the most serious rebellions were led by agents of the Commissariat of Food, in Moscow, who had turned ren-egade. Here, the experience of Soviet government had been horrendous for many peasants: the number of cattle and horses in Viatka province declined from over 160,000 in 1916 to just over 100,000 in 1921, and grain output fell catastrophically, from around 28 million to 4 million *pudy*, over the same period.[51] An additional and aggravating factor, it seems, was that Viatka's peas-ants preferred to sell their produce to private traders, who (presumably not being subject to rules and regulations determined in Moscow) could be more responsive to the ebb and flow of supply and demand and could offer margin-ally higher prices than the state agencies.[52]

More worrying still for the Soviet authorities was that, despite the abolition of the *kombedy* in late 1918, as units of Kolchak's Western Army advanced through Ufa *guberniia* in March–April 1919 they were frequently greeted by villagers offering the traditional welcoming gifts of bread and salt, while the wheels of the Whites' progress toward the Volga were undoubtedly greased by the disruption caused to the rear of the Red Eastern Front at this time by another rash of uprisings (under the slogan "For Soviet Power but Against the Bolsheviks") across Simbirsk, Samara, and Kazan' *gubernii*. During what became known as the "Chapan War" (after the local peasants' preference for wearing kaftans, *chapany*), the city of Chistopol' fell to the rebels on 7 March 1919 and Soviet forces from the 4th Red Army had to be diverted from the front to expel them.[53] All told, from January to June 1919 peasant distur-bances occurred in 124 *uezdy* of European Russia.[54]

These events might have been explained by the delay in news arriving of the Soviet government's announcement of its change in attitude toward the mid-dle peasant, or by the villagers' inclination, as a means of self-defense, to offer support to whichever side in the civil wars that, at any given moment, seemed to be winning. Neither of these things held true late the following year, however, when first Ufa, then Tambov provinces (in the Western Urals and in south-east European Russia, respectively), erupted and then, from January 1921 much of Western Siberia (including Tiumen', Omsk, and Akmolinsk *gubernii* and the eastern stretches of Cheliabinsk and Ekaterinburg *gubernii*) were overrun by peasant rebellions.

The uprising in Ufa *guberniia*, the so-called "Pitchfork Rebellion," was contained with relative ease. It stemmed directly from peasant resistance to the food requisitioning detachments (*prodotriady*) of the People's Commissariat for Food Supply in Menselinsk *uezd* on 4 February 1920, the flashpoint being the refusal of local military leaders to release peasants from the village of Yanga Yelan who had been arrested for failing to hand over the requested supplies. Their fellow villagers then attacked and killed members of the *prodotriad* and circulated appeals for an uprising. On 9–10 February 1920, Soviet leaders at Menselinsk and Zaisk were also attacked and killed and the rising spread to the neighboring Belebei and Birsk *uezdy* of Ufa *guberniia* and the Chistopol' *uezd* of Kazan' *guberniia*, uniting Russian peasants with members of the local Bashkir and Tartar populations. (Many of the latter would have been supporters of the Idel-Urals Republic proclaimed by a Muslim Congress at Kazan' on 12 December 1917 and crushed by Red Guards in April 1918.) Some sources have it that as many as 50,000 rebels may have been involved, but they were poorly armed (largely with pitchforks and staves) and were easily crushed by the heavily armored Red Army and Cheka detachments sent to the area in March 1920.[55] As many as 3,000 rebels may have been killed or executed and many villages were razed.[56]

That, however, was not quite the end of the story, as in July–September 1920 rebellion again raised its head across the Urals region in the so-called "Sapozhkov Uprising." A.V. Sapozhkov (who, according to Soviet sources, was a former member of the Party of Left Socialists-Revolutionaries) had been dismissed from his post as head of the 9th Cavalry Division of the Red Army by K.A. Avksent'evskii, commander of the Trans-Volga Military District. Some 4,000 former Red Army soldiers (most of whom had been recruited from the Urals region) rapidly joined Sapozhkov in defying the Red command. On 14 July 1920, his forces, dubbed the "1st Red Army of Justice," captured Buzuluk before moving on Ural'sk and Pugachev (Nikolaevsk), backed by a further 2,000 new recruits. Sapozhikov, as was becoming the pattern in rebellions against Bolshevik rule at this time, promised "Soviets without Communists." Eventually sufficient Red forces were concentrated to crush the rebels, but not before disorder had spread across extensive tracts of the Volga and Urals territory, from Tsaritsyn to Saratov and as far east as Ufa and Orenburg—that is, those same districts in which the Pitchfork Rebellion had flourished earlier in 1920. The last remnants of the Army of Justice were destroyed on 6 September 1920, near Lake Bak-Baul in Astrakhan *guberniia*. Sapozhkov was killed in this battle.[57] Not however, before, rural disturbances had spread to nearby Saratov *guberniia*.[58]

Both the Tambov uprising and the Western Siberian uprising were less easily quashed than those in the Volga–Urals region, as they rapidly assumed a mass character, in which political and military leaderships (sometimes dominated by SRs or former SRs, as in the case of the Tambov leader A.S. Antonov) emerged to organize the peasantry, and led to the construction of real and substantial internal fronts, on which the Red Army battled peasant forces that could be numbered in the tens of thousands and proved themselves capable of capturing and holding large towns. A feature of the Siberian uprising that was especially galling to the Soviet government was the prominence in the ranks of the rebels of former members of anti-Kolchak partisan forces that had merged with the Red Army as it advanced eastwards in 1919–20.[59]

The causes of these rebellions could very often be traced to a single incident. In Tambov, which had the misfortune of being situated at the juncture of two Red fronts (the Eastern and Southern, and subsequently the South Eastern) and was frequently invaded by the Whites (during the Mamontov Raid, notably),[60] it was the second visit, within a very short space of time, of a grain requisitioning detachment to the same village, Kamenka, in the south-east corner of the province, in August 1920. But the tinder of peasant resentment was so dry that the uprising would then spread like wildfire. In a frank report to Lenin of 16 July 1921, Tukhachevskii (installed in April 1921 as commander of Red forces of Tambov province) was remarkably candid about what had inspired the insurgency. He cited "dissatisfaction with the food policy of requisitioning" as a national phenomenon and was particularly critical of "the clumsy and exceptionally harsh enforcement of it by the food requisitioning organs on the spot" in Tambov itself, as well as the powerful hold the PSR had over the region through its Union of Working Peasants.[61] In a very lengthy analysis of the Tambov experience, sent to Lenin on 20 July 1921, V.A. Anotonov-Ovseenko (since February 1921 chairman of the VTsIK Plenipotentiary Commission for Tambov *guberniia*), although deploying the usual Soviet terminology of "kulaks" and "bandit gangs" to describe the hardly gang-like 21,000-strong rebel army that the Red Army had to confront across the province, was even more critical of Soviet policy:

In general the Soviet regime was, in the eyes of the majority of the peasants, identified with flying visits by commissars or plenipotentiaries who were valiant at giving orders to the *volost'* Executive Committees and village Soviets and went around imprisoning the representatives of these local organs of authority for the non-fulfillment of frequently quite absurd requirements. It was also identified with the food requisitioning units, which often acted directly to the detriment of the peasant economy, without in any way profiting the State. The peasantry, in their majority have become accustomed to regarding the Soviet regime as something extraneous in relation to themselves, something that issues only commands, that gives orders most zealously, but quite improvidently.[62]

Most common, Antonov-Ovseenko noted, were peasant complaints against the dictatorship of the proletariat: "What sort of worker-peasant regime is it that we have?" they would ponder—"The regime in fact is that of the workers at the expense of the peasants."[63] Finally, "In summing up the experience of the Tambov gubernija the following needs to be said," he ventured:

> The peasant uprisings develop because of widespread *dissatisfaction on the part of the small property-owners in the countryside with the dictatorship of the proletariat, which directs at them its cutting edge of implacable compulsion, which cares little for the economic peculiarities of the peasantry* and does the countryside no service at all perceptible on either the economic or the educational side.[64]

To remedy matters, in a region that had been particularly adversely affected by the shifting fronts of the civil wars, he suggested the merciless expunging of the rebel leadership, combined with a no less thorough, root-and-branch overhaul of the local Soviet administration and a campaign of re-education. Tellingly, though, as a first step, he had some months earlier suggested the dispatch of two divisions of seasoned Red troops to the province.[65] Soon afterwards, Tukhachevskii had arrived and began a process of pacification of the region through (by his Order No. 130, of 12 May 1921) assigning Red forces to the villages, to guard against renewed flarings-up of rebellion, as the major Antonovite groups were extinguished one by one.[66] One recent account has it that Tambov *guberniia* experienced a gross loss of 240,000 people in the course of the suppression of the Tambov rebellion, most of them while under internment or during subsequent repressions rather than in the actual fighting (although this figure includes questionable estimates of the "unborn").[67]

In the end, of course, there could only be one victor in these unequal struggles, which, although almost simultaneous, remained isolated from one another.[68] That victor would be the force that could deploy tens of thousands of trained and battle-hardened soldiers, supported by armored trains, tanks, aircraft, and (in the case of Tambov, and apparently for the first time in the civil war) poison-gas brigades.[69] That victor was, of course, the Red Army, largely free by the spring of 1921 of other commitments and headed by experienced commanders with whom the rebels could not compete: notably, Tukhachevskii in Tambov and I.N. Smirnov and V.I. Shorin in Western Siberia. But post mortems of the events by the Soviet leadership revealed worrying indications that although isolated incidents like the one at Kamenka might be the trigger for outbreaks of rebellion, the fundamental causes lay far deeper.

The Makhnovshchina

By far the best-known of all the anti-Bolshevik insurgencies of the civil-wars era was centered on south-eastern Ukraine and was named after its leader, the enigmatic and posthumously iconic Nestor Makhno.[70] Batko ("Little Father") Makhno was born, in 1888, of poor peasant stock in Huliai-Pole, Ekaterinoslav *guberniia*, and was converted to anarchism during the 1905 Revolution, as a member of the Union of Poor Farmers. His father died when he was an infant, so he worked as a shepherd from the age of seven and as a metalworker in his teens, attending school only briefly. Following his arrest in 1908, for killing a policeman, in 1910 Makhno was condemned to death by the court of the Odessa Military District; however, the sentence was commuted to life imprisonment because of his youth. Freed in 1917 from Moscow's Butyrka prison, in which he had befriended the anarchist P.A. Arshinov, he returned to Huliai-Pole to chair its soviet and to organize numerous revolutionary communes. Evading capture by forces of the Austro-German intervention that occupied Ukraine in the aftermath of the Treaty of Brest-Litovsk, in June 1918 he visited Moscow and met Lenin, Iakob Sverdlov, and Prince Peter Kropotkin, before establishing a peasant army in south-eastern Ukraine.

Throughout its existence, the territorial heart of the Makhnovshchina (the "Makhno movement") remained the Huliai-Pole district, although what was sometime called the Free Territory expanded and contracted and, amoeba-like, sent out offshoots and tentacles to other parts of Ukraine, the Don, and the North Caucasus. Beginning as a loose-knit guerilla force in resistance to the Austro-German intervention and the Ukrainian State of Hetman Skoropadskii, subsequently, during the course of the civil wars, Makhno's followers, organized into the Revolutionary Insurgent Army of Ukraine (RIAU), found themselves in conflict with forces of the Ukrainian Directory, the White forces of the AFSR, and the Red Army, as well as with other partisan groups (such as that of Ataman Nykyfor Hryhoriiv). The high tide of the Makhnovshchina lasted from November 1918 (when the Central Powers withdrew from Ukraine) to June 1919, in which period the Free Territory extended from Berdiansk through Donetsk, Aleksandrovsk, and Ekaterinoslav.

In areas where the Makhnovists were dominant, the population was urged to abolish capitalism, to expropriate private land and factories, to organize itself through popular assemblies, and to implement the free exchange of goods between town and countryside. Peasants were advised to establish producer communes and to work collectively; workers were informed of the advantages of self-management. Some educational experiments were also introduced, with schools run along the lines advocated by the Catalan anarchist Francesc Ferrer. Political parties were expressly forbidden from operating and a system of "free soviets" was insisted upon: unlike the so-called tyrannical "political soviets" of the Bolsheviks and other socialists, the Makhnovists claimed, "the free Soviets of workers and peasants were to be organs of social-economic self-management. Each soviet was only to carry out the will of the local workers and their organizations." Thus, when the Makhnovists captured an area they put up posters reading, "The freedom of the workers and peasants is their own and is not subject to any restriction. It is for the workers and peasants themselves to act, to organize themselves, to agree among themselves in all aspects of their lives, as they themselves see fit and desire ... The Makhnovists can do no more than give aid and counsel ... In no circumstances can they, nor do they wish to, govern."

Makhno was himself preoccupied with leading the army and the ideological backbone of the movement was therefore supplied chiefly by members of the anarchist federation Nabat (among them Voline and Peter Arshinov), who flocked to the Free Territory. Undoubtedly, the movement was a high-minded and principled one: it may have attracted its share of wayward and even criminal elements, as did all sides in the civil wars, but the Makhnovists were far from the gang of debauched bandits that Red propaganda portrayed them to be. On the other hand, for all Makhno's talk of freedom and hostility to the state, the exigencies of civil wars meant that he had sometimes to resort to conscription and had to run a secret police force of his own (the Kropotkin Guard) to hunt down enemies and infiltrators within the anarchist camp. As Voline later noted, "the constant state of war in the entire region made the creation and functioning of [free soviets] very difficult, and the organization was never carried through to its logical conclusions."

The Makhnovists were twice allied with the Reds in order to jointly oppose the Whites. The first occasion was in the spring and summer of 1919, to fight the White cavalry of General Shkuro of the AFSR, as they pushed through the Donbass into Ukraine. However, fearful of the spread of libertarian ideas into the ranks of the Red Army and angry that the Makhnovists had failed to hold the line against White advances, thereby contributing to the collapse of the Southern Front, Trotsky broke that alliance and, in July 1919, declared Makhno to be an outlaw. As the Reds were expelled from Ukraine and Denikin swept in, the Makhnovists were pushed westwards to Peregonovka by October 1919. There they turned, defeated the Whites (who were preoccupied with the front against the Red Army, which was by then approaching Orel), held off forces of the Ukrainian Army, and turned back east, toward Huliai-Pole, cutting a huge swathe through Denikin's rear, severing AFSR lines of communication with the front, and thus facilitating the Red Army's rapid drive towards the Black Sea, the Sea of Azov, and the North Caucasus over the winter of 1919–20.

In the summer of 1920, a second Red–Black alliance was forged to fight the Russian Army of General P.N. Wrangel when it burst out of the Crimea. The RIAU subsequently played a very significant part in storming the Perekop isthmus and driving Wrangel's forces out of Crimea in October–November 1920, but again the alliance was broken by the Reds and Makhno was again declared to be an outlaw (and several of his commanders were arrested and executed by the Cheka). Thereafter, despite occasional large-scale desertions from the Red Army to the Makhnovists (as, for example, in the case of the Maslakov mutiny),[71] the Free Territory was absorbed into the Soviet state and the Makhnovshchina was extinguished, although embers of anarchist rebellion would occasionally flare up in Southern Ukraine throughout the Soviet period.[72]

Over the following months Makhno waged an itinerant struggle against the Soviet government along the shores of the Sea of Azov and the Don River and in the Volga region. In March 1921, his group (1,500 horsemen and two infantry regiments) then moved towards Chernigov. They managed to escape from Red encirclement on 11 March 1921, but Batko was struck by a bullet that entered his thigh and exited through his stomach, after which he lost consciousness. At dawn on 17 March 1921, near Novospaskovka, they were caught up with again by Red cavalry. In a letter to his mentor, Arshinov, Makhno explained what then ensued:

> After pursuing us for 25 versts (we were completely exhausted and really incapable of fighting), these horsemen threw themselves on us. What were we to do? I was not only incapable of getting into the saddle; I could not even sit up. I was lying in the bottom of the cart, and saw a terrible hand-to-hand battle—an unbelievable

hacking—take place about 100 yards away from me. Our men died only for my sake, only because they would not abandon me.

After months of further flight, further losses (including that of his treasured commander Fedir Shchus') and much regrouping, Makhno continued:

At the beginning of August 1921, it was decided that in view of the severity of my wounds I would leave with some of our commanders to get medical treatment abroad.

About this time our best commanders—Kozhin, Petrenko and Zabud'ko—were seriously wounded.

On August 13, 1921, accompanied by 100 horsemen, I set out towards the Dnieper, and on the morning of the 16th we crossed between Orlik and Kremenchug with the help of 17 peasant fishing boats. On this day I was wounded six times, but not seriously.

Makhno then ran into a Red ambush and was placed on a horse to escape:

We were caught in a trap. But, without losing courage, we attacked and beat the 38th Regiment of the 7th Cavalry Division, and we then rode 110 versts without stopping. Defending ourselves continuously from the furious attacks of all these troops, we finally escaped, but only after having lost 17 of our best comrades.

On August 22, they had to take care of me again; a bullet struck me in the neck and came out of the right cheek. Once again I was lying in the bottom of a cart. On the 26th, we were obliged to fight a new battle with the Reds. We lost our best fighters and comrades: Petrenko-Platonov and Ivanyuk. I was forced to change our route for the last time, and on August 28, 1921, I crossed the Dneister. I am now abroad.[73]

After enduring internment in Romania, Makhno moved to Poland, only to be arrested in October 1922 and charged with an attempt, in league with Soviet diplomats, to incite an anti-Polish rebellion in Eastern Galicia (Western Ukraine). He denied the charge, adding that he personally had saved Poland in 1920 by refusing to join the Soviet offensive on Warsaw. He was acquitted on 27 November 1922, and subsequently moved to Danzig to evade the attentions of the Polish police, but was arrested there too. Eventually, in April 1925, Makhno settled in the Vincennes district of Paris.[74]

Red Terror

Meanwhile, by 1920, the popularity of the Bolsheviks in the cities and towns they held seems, as far as it can be imperfectly measured by circumstantial evidence, to have declined catastrophically also. Since the earlier low point of the crisis in the spring of 1918, some factors generating worker discontent had been ameliorated: many of the closed factories of 1917–18 had been re-opened to meet Red Army demand for war materials (although supplies of anything more sophisticated than a bullet, and even many bullets, were largely derived from inherited imperial stock); food supplies to the cities and factory towns remained meager, but were a little more regular and, when available, were distributed according to rationing systems that were of Byzantine complexity and easily cheated but seemed at least well-intentioned (unless you were an unemployed *burzhui*);[75] the onslaught of the Whites had also focused minds in the Soviet zone on what might be the alternative to the rule of Lenin, if the Kremlin was surrendered to Kolchak; and, it would have been noticed, some elements of other socialist parties—including Mensheviks-Internationalists, the Narod Group of the PSR, and the Party of Revolutionary Communism (a successor to the Left-SRs)[76]—had offered their conditional support to the Bolshevik regime and were (albeit precariously and intermittently) allowed to operate legally on Soviet soil. This fragile compromise hardly amounted to more than buffing the sharpest edges off the Bolshevik dictatorship—and was certainly intended as nothing more—but was better than what had happened earlier.

What had happened earlier, in the autumn of 1918, was horrible: a bloody wave of Red Terror instituted by the Cheka, in the aftermath of the "revelation" (or, mostly, invention) of the Lockhart Plot, all-too-real Allied landings around Russia (from Arkhangel'sk to Vladivostok, via Baku), the assassination of the Petrograd Cheka boss Moisei Uritskii, and the attempted assassination of Lenin at the Mikhelson factory in Moscow on 30 August 1918.[77] The bourgeoisie and its representatives (in Soviet eyes)—including officers and officer cadets, Kadets, priests, teachers and students, as well as several former tsarist ministers—were the primary target of the thousands of arrests and the 8,000–15,000 shootings that, within eight weeks, had followed Sovnarkom's decree "On Red Terror" of 5 September 1918.[78] The principle that guided actions such as these was established by the Chekist Mārtiņš Lācis, who infamously declared that he saw his organization's task as "the extermination of the bourgeoisie as a class", and determined that a suspect's social class, not the evidence against him or her, should be uppermost in the mind of an investigator:

> You need not prove that this or that man acted against the interests of the Soviet power. The first thing you have to ask an arrested person is: to what class does he belong, where does he come from, what kind of education did he have, what is his occupation? These questions are to decide the fate of the accused. That is the quintessence of the Red Terror.[79]

But many workers too had fallen victim for their alleged counter-revolutionary crimes, while many entirely innocent people were also executed.[80] Promises issued by the Soviet government in early 1919 to rein in the Cheka seemed not to amount to very much. A campaign led by L.B. Kamenev entirely to close down the institution, for example, was vetoed by Lenin in favor of abolishing only the lowest tiers of the Cheka (which did tend to be the most lawless) and constraining the powers of others. Yet, almost immediately afterwards, on 22 February 1919, the revamped main Menshevik newspaper *Vsegda Vpered* ("Always Forward") was suddenly repressed and Menshevik party leaders were arbitrarily arrested.[81] Moreover, workers understood that although the Terror had intensified only in the autumn of 1918, its executioner, the Cheka, had been one of the very first institutions founded (on 7 December 1917) by the Soviet state—that it was, in fact, an essential and entirely necessary element of the revolution in the eyes of many Bolsheviks. Moreover, sudden waves of arrests and executions would periodically engulf the big cities of the Soviet zone throughout the ensuing years. In the autumn of 1919, for example, as Denikin's forces closed on Moscow, the Cheka uncovered the machinations of the Tactical Center—a sort of umbrella organization for the remnants of the various anti-Bolshevik underground organizations that had sprung up and been cut down in 1918—and executed dozens of its real and alleged members.[82]

The figure most closely associated with the Terror was the Cheka boss, the Jesuit-educated Catholic turned Bolshevik zealot Feliks Dzierżyński, whose statue in Moscow's Lubianka Square was among the first to be attacked and toppled during the collapse of Communism seventy years later. However, the revolutionary ascetic and fanatical "Iron Feliks" seems only once to have exceeded Lenin's will—when he was suspected of complicity in the Left-SRs' assassination of the German ambassador, Count Mirbach, in July 1918, and was briefly arrested and suspended from office. In general, Lenin was certainly not opposed to the deployment of violence. A few weeks after the October Revolution he wrote, for example, that a range of methods could be used to control the former ruling classes (and others who inhibited the building of socialism):

> Variety is a guarantee of effectiveness here, a pledge of success in achieving the single common aim—to *clean* the land of Russia of all vermin, of fleas—the rogues, of bugs—the rich, and so on and so forth. In one place half a score of rich, a dozen rogues, half a dozen workers who shirk their work ... will be put in prison. In another place they will be put to cleaning latrines. In a third place they will be provided with "yellow tickets" after they have served their time, so that everyone

shall keep an eye on them, as *harmful* persons, until they reform. In a fourth place, one out of every ten idlers will be shot on the spot.[83]

Many Lenin-authored documents urging mass executions have now been published. Among the first was a letter of 11 August 1918 to comrades in Penza, in which Lenin urged that, to staunch a "kulak uprising," they should:

Hang (hang without fail, *so the people see*) *no fewer than one hundred* known kulaks, rich men, blood suckers ... Take from them *all* the grain ... Designate hostages ... Do it in such a way that for hundreds of versts around, the people will see, tremble, know ... Telegraph receipt and *implementation*.

He then rather superfluously post-scripted the instruction to his comrades that, in order to fulfill this order, they should "Find some truly *hard people*."[84]

In these sympathies and imprecations Lenin was loudly echoed by Trotsky. In a rebuttal of criticisms launched against the illegalities and moral outrages that Karl Kautsky and other German socialists alleged had been perpetrated by the Soviet regime, Trotsky thundered in 1920 that without the use of terror the revolution would wither, for:

It is only possible to safeguard the supremacy of the working class by forcing the bourgeoisie, accustomed to rule, to realize that it is too dangerous an undertaking for it to revolt against the dictatorship of the proletariat, to undermine it by conspiracies, sabotage, insurrections, or the calling in of foreign troops. The bourgeoisie, hurled from power, must be forced to obey ... The Russian White Guards ... cannot be convinced or shamed, but only terrorized or crushed.

Thus:

The man who repudiates terrorism in principle—i.e., repudiates measures of suppression and intimidation towards determined and armed counter-revolution, must reject all idea of the political supremacy of the working class and its revolutionary dictatorship. The man who repudiates the dictatorship of the proletariat repudiates the Socialist revolution, and digs the grave of Socialism.

In coming to this conclusion, Trotsky noted that "the priests used to terrify the people with future penalties," but always bolstered their case with "the material fire of the Holy Inquisition."[85] As materialists, the Bolsheviks could wield only their own version of the latter, he charged in his 1920 pamphlet, *Terrorism and Communism*. By that time at least 500,000 alleged enemies of the Soviet state had perished in Cheka dungeons. Few of them would have been dealt with through the bloodless impartiality preached by Dzierżyński; some of them would have fallen victim to the sort of criminal psychopaths drawn to such work under any regime; some, indeed, would have been dealt with by former employees of the tsarist secret police, now employed as "specialists" in interrogation and torture by the Cheka.[86]

The Trade Union Question and the Workers' Opposition

To exacerbate these pre-existing tensions between workers and their putative "workers' state," as the civil wars wound down in 1920 there appeared a raft of new, chiefly ideologically driven Bolshevik initiatives that would re-ignite worker protests and strikes and lead to the opening of new fronts within the Soviet zone: between Lenin's government and the proletariat; between the Bolsheviks and some of their hitherto most fervent supporters; and even within the party itself. The conflict—which was actually an old one, dating back to nineteenth-century disputes among Russian social democrats about the political and cultural immaturity of Russian workers—recrudesced within the RKP(b) in late 1920, during the 8th All-Russian Congress of Soviets, in Moscow. Having no longer to concentrate its energies on day-to-day survival—with Wrangel's forces driven into exile and the Poles, for the moment, inactive—in the late autumn of 1920 the party's thoughts drifted toward the future and, specifically, the issue of what should be the role of the chief workers' organization, the trade unions, in a workers' state (although this debate had been brewing for most of the year before that, as the Bolsheviks contemplated victory in the civil wars). One author's claim that, in terms of its impact on party unity, this squabble matched that over the question of war or peace in 1918 is probably too strong,[87] but it was certainly of profound practical and ideological significance.

Back in 1917, when considering workers' "autonomous organizations," the Bolsheviks had strongly favored factory committees, which (being shop- or factory-based) competed for influence with the Menshevik-dominated (profession-oriented) trade unions. This influence at low level facilitated Bolshevik ascendancy in the October Revolution and was useful in the implementation of workers' control, but as that policy became discredited over the winter of 1917–18, factory committees were ordered to subject themselves to the—now Bolshevik-led—unions at the All-Russian Congress of Trade Unions on 20–27 January 1918. Thereafter, between congresses, the unions (and, through them, the chiefly moribund factory committees) were subordinated to the standing All-Russian Central Council of Trade Unions.[88] That body then became Sovnarkom's main weapon in the battle to persuade workers to forfeit to the state the control of industrial enterprises they had seized and to follow the guidance of the trade unions, in order that local interests should not prevail over the broader demands of the national industrial economy (now governed by VSNKh, which from the spring of 1918 was purged of members loyal to the Left Bolsheviks). Nevertheless, it would be wrong to assume that all agitation for hierarchy, centralization, and order came from the top down: in some regions and in some sectors of the industrial economy, as the civil wars flared, pressure for more centralized direction could come also from below, as panicked workers adjusted to new conditions.[89] Equally, the unions could sometimes act as mediators between workers and bosses, as one-man management returned to the factories under War Communism. But, as time went on, the unions' independence in this regard was eroded and the right to strike was removed. Indeed, it became clear that elements within the Soviet government regarded the trade unions as, ultimately, a branch of the state machinery (specifically, of the People's Commissariat for Labor)—a development that the somewhat inert Bolshevik head of the union organization, M.P. Tomskii, seemed disinclined to resist.

Matters came to a head in December 1920, however, when Trotsky—who by then rivaled Lenin as the face of the party, by virtue of his civil-war heroics (not least, his recent marshaling of the defense of Petrograd against Iudenich in October 1919)—began pushing this process to its logical conclusion. The war commissar advocated nothing less than the "statification" of the unions, through their fusion with the chief organs of governmental industrial administration. Trotsky's argument—which, in the abstract, displayed his usual impeccable logic—was that, in a workers' state, the only concern of trade unions could be with increasing productivity, as all other matters of concern to workers were resolved by the responsible organs of the workers' state, in the interest of the workers. In making such a case, Trotsky drew ammunition from his own relatively successful recent experience (20 March–10 December 1920) as Acting People's Commissar for Ways and Communications and head of Tsektran (the Central Committee of the Union of Workers in Rail and Water Transport), during which he had overseen what amounted to the militarization of the Soviet railroad system.[90]

Trotsky was additionally, in this regard, to point to another innovation for which he could claim some credit (if that is the right word)—the Labor Armies.[91] This was the term applied to units of the Red Army that when decommissioned, as the civil wars wound down (or appeared to wind down) in early 1920, were not disbanded or demobilized but were, instead, switched from military activity to economic tasks (such as logging, mining, and transport duties), yet remained subject to military discipline and command. For Trotsky, again, this all seemed perfectly logical: it was nothing more than the transformation of the duty of universal military service (*Vsevobuch*), which the Soviet government had had no compunction whatsoever about imposing upon its citizens in 1918 to fight the civil wars, into a duty of universal labor service to rebuild the country now that, in 1920, the civil wars were all-but won.[92] After all, that year had also seen the widespread adoption of *subbot-niki*—"volunteer" weekend workdays, which were actually all-but compulsory (and always entirely wage-free), and during which even Lenin was obliged to carry the odd log.[93]

For those with warmer blood, however, the Labor Armies smacked of the era of serfdom—and, specifically, the Military Colonies improvised a century earlier by Alexander I and his despised grand vizier, Count A.A. Arakcheev.[94] Although the militarization of labor had been a creeping feature of Soviet life since April 1918, when key workers in the mining industry had been forbidden to leave their jobs, putting the case as bluntly as Trotsky tended to do aroused opposition from Lenin (supported by G.V. Zinov'ev and others in the so-called "Platform of 10"), who proposed that the trade unions should maintain some independence as "schools for Communism," gradually drawing non-party workers into socially responsible labor and true proletarianism. In a speech of 30 December 1920, Lenin baldly stated that he was "amazed at the number of theoretical mistakes and glaring blunders" Trotsky had made in his recent pamphlet on *The Role and Tasks of the Trade Unions*: "How could anyone starting a big Party discussion on this question produce such a sorry excuse for a care-fully thought[-]out statement?", he pondered. For Lenin:

On the one hand, the trade unions, which take in all industrial workers, are an organisation of the ruling, dominant, governing class, which has now set up a dictatorship and is exercising coercion through the state. But it is not a state organisation; nor is it one designed for coercion, but for education. It is an organisation designed to draw in and to train; it is, in fact, a school: a school of administration, a school of economic management, a school of communism. It is a very unusual type of school, because there are no teachers or pupils; this is an extremely unusual combination of what has necessarily come down to us from capitalism, and what comes from the ranks of the advanced revolutionary detachments, which you might call the revolutionary vanguard of the proletariat. To talk about the role of the trade unions without taking these truths into account is to fall straight into a number of errors ...

But the dictatorship of the proletariat cannot be exercised through an organisation embracing the whole of that class, because in all capitalist countries (and not only over here, in one of the most backward) the proletariat is still so divided, so degraded, and so corrupted in parts (by imperialism in some countries) that an organisation taking in the whole proletariat cannot directly exercise proletarian dictatorship. It can be exercised only by a vanguard that has absorbed the revolutionary energy of the class. The whole is like an arrangement of cogwheels. Such is the basic mechanism of the dictatorship of the proletariat, and of the essentials of transition from capitalism to communism.[95]

We can take that or leave it as a guide to trade unionism, but clearly, despite the wonders he had performed with the Red Army, Trotsky was already and still vulnerable in 1920 to attacks from those more deeply embedded in the Bolshevik hierarchy than he—indelibly an ex-Menshevik—would ever, or could ever, be.[96]

* * *

Trotsky's advocacy of the Labor Armies and the statification of the trade unions was also criticized by members of the Workers' Opposition, a powerful and very widely supported party faction, formed chiefly from trade union leaders and industrial administrators, that had coalesced since the autumn of 1919, when one of its most prominent spokesmen, the Bolshevik metalworker A.G. Shliapnikov, issued a call for trade unions to take control of the higher organs of the state and for them to be granted control of industrial production. Shliapnikov and his supporters (such as S.P. Medvedev) alleged that both the party and the state were becoming stifled by bureaucracy, corruption, and cronyism, as a consequence of the huge influx into the administration of what they regarded as contagious bourgeois and petty-bourgeois elements, and were especially critical of the powers granted under War Communism to industrial "experts" (although they were not opposed to the employment of experts *per se*). As a remedy, the Workers' Opposition advocated political and economic decentralization and the replacing of existing structures with a hierarchy of elected worker assemblies, organized on a sectoral basis (textiles, metalworking, mining, etc.), with an elected "All-Russian Congress of Producers" at its apex. Thirty-eight Bolshevik leaders signed the theses of the Workers' Opposition in December 1920 (although it had many thousands of followers in the factories, particularly in the metalworking sector, and was especially well supported in central Russia and the Urals).

One particularly notable adherent to the cause was the Bolshevik feminist A.M. Kollontai, who authored the pamphlet entitled *The Workers' Opposition* that was widely circulated at the Tenth Congress of the RKP(b) in March

1921, and which provided the fullest exposition of the organization's platform. Among Kollontai's forthrightly stated arguments was the assertion that:

> The Workers' Opposition sprang from the depths of the industrial proletariat of Soviet Russia. It is an outgrowth not only of the unbearable conditions of life and labour in which seven million industrial workers find themselves, but it is also a product of vacillation, inconsistencies, and outright deviations of our Soviet policy from the clearly expressed class-consistent principles of the Communist programme.

She lambasted the amount of influence that specialists had accrued for themselves in the organization and management of the industrial economy, expressing the ingrained enmity of the Bolsheviks' left wing for:

> the petty-bourgeois elements widely scattered through the Soviet institutions, the elements of the middle class, with their hostility towards Communism, and with their predilections towards the immutable customs of the past, with resentments and fears towards revolutionary arts. These are the elements that bring decay into our Soviet institutions, breeding there an atmosphere altogether repugnant to the working class.

Finally, she averred that:

> The working class and its spokesmen, on the contrary, realise that the new Communist aspirations can be obtained only through the collective efforts of the workers themselves. The more the masses are developed in the expression of their collective will and common thought, the quicker and more complete will be the realization of working class aspirations, for it will create a new: homo-geneous, unified, perfectly-arranged Communist Industry. Only those who are directly bound to industry can introduce into it animating innovations ...

> Production, its organization—this is the essence of Communism. To debar the workers from the organization of industry, to deprive them, that is, their individual organizations, of the opportunity to develop their powers in creating new forms of production in industry through their unions, to deny these expressions of the class organization of the proletariat, while placing full reliance on the "skill" of specialists trained and taught to carry on production under a quite different system of production—is to jump off the rails of scientific Marxist thought. That is, however, just the thing that is being done by the leaders of our Party at present.[97]

However, for reasons to be explored below, the party leadership was in no mood to tolerate internal opposition at that moment—least of all an opposition based on a *Weltanschauung* that was so fundamentally at odds with what had thus far been achieved in Soviet Russia—and, at the tenth congress, the Workers' Opposition was effectively banned by resolutions "On the Syndicalist and Anarchist Deviation in the Party" and "On Party Unity" (the so-called "Ban on Factions") passed on 16 March 1921: by the former, the party resolved "to consider propagation of these ideas as incompatible with membership in the Russian Communist Party."[98] Among its other work, the congress also settled the trade union question: the program of the Platform of 10 was adopted, with 336 votes cast in its favor (as opposed to fifty for Trotsky's platform and just eighteen for the Workers' Opposition).[99]

Worker–Sailor Opposition to the Soviet State: Petrograd and Kronshtadt, February–March 1921

The guillotine was effectively brought down on the divisive trade union question and on the Workers' Opposition because, as delegates to the 10th Party Congress gathered in Moscow in March 1921, the Bolshevik Party was facing the most testing of all the challenges to its rule that had been encountered on the internal fronts since the seizure of power in October 1917. As we have seen, Lenin had anticipated civil war when he made the revolution: the army generals and other elites, he knew, would not surrender their positions willingly; non-Russian regions, in which religious authorities or the bourgeoisie were particularly powerful (Poland, for example), could be expected to erect high tariffs against the import of Russian soviets; and no matter what (largely false) hopes were entertained for an alliance between the proletariat and the poor peasantry, it was axiomatic to a Marxist that the village would resist the abolition of private property, which was the ultimate goal of the socialist revolution. Even the protests, strikes, and resistance the Bolsheviks had faced from elements of the industrial proletariat in Petrograd, Moscow, and elsewhere in the Soviet heartland could be explained by the low ("semi-peasant") cultural level of the Russian proletarian, whose links to his ancestral village and the antiquated attitudes that prevailed there were still strong.[100] What the Bolsheviks had not expected was that a challenge would arise that, although limited in geographical scope and in the number of its participants, would strike at the very heart of the revolution and the legitimacy of the Soviet system, for it came from those who had contributed more than any others to the making of the October Revolution and the consolidation of Soviet power over the key winter of 1917–18—those whom, in July 1917 Trotsky had reportedly dubbed "the glory and pride of the revolution"[101]—the sailors of the Baltic Fleet, crowded into their base at Kronshtadt, on Kotlin island, 20 miles out in the Gulf of Finland from the wooden wharves and granite embankments of Petrograd. But it was in Petrograd itself that the sparks of the Kronshtadt revolt were ignited.

* * *

Speaking strongly in favor of regarding War Communism as something more essential to Bolshevism than a series of improvised measures to deal with the military emergency is the fact that the system only attained its highest form in late 1920, after the major battles of the civil wars had been won. Startlingly, for example, a VSNKh decree nationalizing small industrial enterprises (down to five workers if the factory was mechanized, or ten if it was not) was issued on 29 November 1920, twelve days *after* the last of General Wrangel's ships had sailed away from the Crimea.[102] Subsequently, on 28 December 1920, the Eighth All-Russian Congress of Soviets decreed that Sowing Committees would oversee peasant agriculture. The latter has generally been interpreted to be an unprecedented attempt by the Soviet state to direct food production (not just distribution)—almost a herald of the collectivization campaign to be launched by Stalin some eight years later.[103]

Petrograd—the always hungry Soviet citadel that was furthest placed from where most Russian food was grown—was the over-pressurized barometer of reaction to all this.[104] If food supply was going to be a problem anywhere in the Soviet zone, it was likely to be in northerly Petrograd. But the situation was clearly exacerbated by the Bolsheviks' management of the city. The Petrograd party boss, G.E. Zinov'ev, has gained a reputation for spinelessness—chiefly as a consequence of the savaging he endured as the focus of Trotsky's ire in his *Lesson of October* of 1924, in which Zinov'ev was excoriated for his timidity: first, in October 1917 (when he had opposed the seizure of power); and secondly, as chair of the Komintern, for failing properly to support the German party in its own October, in 1923. Tasteless and unconfirmed tales abound also of Zinov'ev begging Stalin's executioners for mercy, as he was dragged from his cell to be shot in August 1936, following his confession of treachery and Trotskyism at the first great purge trial in Moscow. Whatever the accuracy of such legends, however, Zinov'ev was certainly not weak in his handling of affairs in Petrograd in 1920–21. Quite the opposite: he was a bully.[105] As noted earlier, prominent among the improvised means for survival developed by Russian urbanites during the hunger years of the civil wars had been food-gathering trips to the countryside. But in Petrograd, under Zinov'ev, as the screws of War Communism tightened, this concession to private trade was withdrawn. As the American anarchist Emma Goldman recalled of her time in Petrograd in 1920:

> Apropos of the opportunities of bringing something from the country, a whole book could be written on that alone. With the prohibition of trading came the "Zagraditelny otryad," the detachment of soldiers–Chekists at every station to

confiscate everything brought by private persons to the city. The wretched people, after untold difficulties of obtaining a pass for travel, after days and weeks of exposure at the stations, or on the [train] roofs and platforms, would bring a pood of flour or potatoes, only to have it snatched from them by the otryad.

In most cases the confiscated stuff was divided by the defenders of the Communist State among themselves. The victims were fortunate if they escaped further trouble. After they were robbed of their precious pack, they were often thrown into gaol for "speculation."

Even more galling, Goldman continued, was that "The number of real speculators apprehended was insignificant in comparison with the mass of unfortunate humanity that filled the prisons of Russia for trying to keep from starving to death."[106] Voices too were raised, as bread rations fell toward zero, against what was coming to be perceived as the unequal system of apportionment, which meant that some categories of workers received far more than others, while reports circulated of the extravagant living of party bosses and their wives and mistresses. It mattered not whether such reports were true, if they were believed.[107] And all this coming to a head, of course, after the defeat of Wrangel and after the securing of a not unfavorable armistice with Poland in October–November 1920.

In response to these deprivations, confiscations, and aberrations, and as sixty of the largest of the Petrograd factories were forced to close for lack of fuel, over the winter of 1920–21 spontaneous meetings and strikes took place across those of the dying city's factories that remained open: among them, the Patronnyi munitions works, the Trubochnyi and Baltiiskii mills, and the Laferme factory.[108] The workers demanded that the government see reason, but Zinov'ev's natural inclination was not to negotiate but to declare war: he created and led a Petrograd Committee of Defense to organize the stifling of further protests and, on 24 February 1921, sent troops into the Vasilevskii Ostrov workers' district to enforce his will. The dispersed workers merely moved to the city center, however, and encouraged dockers and Admiralty workers to join them. As the confrontation escalated, leaflets began to appear on the streets, proclaiming "Down with the hated Communists! Down with the Soviet government! Long Live the Constituent Assembly!" and Emma Goldman's companion, the anarchist Alexander Berkman, also then resident in Petrograd, was recording in his diary that:

Many arrests are taking place. Groups of strikers surrounded by Tchekists, on their way to prison, are a common sight. Much indignation in the city. I hear that several unions have been liquidated and their active members turned over to the Tcheka.[109]

On 26 February 1921, the Petrograd Soviet duly ordered that the Trubochnyi and Laferme works be closed, while disturbances were reported at the Putilov factory (where 6,000 labored in shops that had once housed 30,000 proletarians) and SR and Menshevik-authored leaflets began appearing on the streets.[110] This all seemed ominously reminiscent of February 1917, but, by the following day, the disturbances were beginning to be controlled. Large numbers of police and *kursanty* (Red officer cadets) were deployed and arrests of known or suspected Mensheviks were made.[111] At the same time, emergency rations were distributed and Zinov'ev ended the ban on private trade, stood down the *zagraditel'nyi otriady*, and even promised to lay on additional trains to take foraging workers to the countryside. By the first days of March, most of the recently closed factories in Petrograd were again open.[112]

* * *

By that time, however, unrest had spread across the water (or, rather, in the northern winter, ice) to Kronshtadt and the damage had been done—damage that would scar the face of Soviet communism throughout its life. On 26 February 1921, a delegation of sailors from the base had visited Petrograd to investigate the causes of the strikes and returned with a report that painted Zinov'ev's regime in very black colors. Two days later, on 28 February 1921, a meeting of the crews of the two battleships docked at Kronshtadt, the *Petropavlovsk* and the *Sevastopol'*, convened an emergency meeting that approved a fifteen-point resolution ("The *Petropavlovsk* Resolution"). This called for, *inter alia*: new elections to the soviets, by secret ballot and on the basis of "an equal franchise" (as opposed to the current arrangement, whereby workers' votes were weighted heavier than those of other classes); freedom of speech for all proponents of anarchism and left-socialism and the liberation of all prisoners who professed these creeds; freedom of assembly and of trade union organizations; the abolition of the requisitioning detachments and of Cheka guard detachments in factories; and the equalization of rations for all workers.[113] A few days later a document authored by the Kronshtadters, and entitled "What We Are Fighting For," added:

> In carrying out the October Revolution, the working class was hoping to throw off the yoke of oppression. Yet that revolution resulted in an even greater enslavement of the human person.

> The power of the police–gendarme monarchism fell into the hands of the conquering Communists, who instead of freedom gave the working people the constant fear of ending up in a Cheka dungeon, the horrors of which have surpassed those of a tsarist gendarme prison by many degrees ...

But what is more vile and criminal than all else is the moral servitude created by the Communists: they have violated even the interior life of the working people, forcing them to think only in the Communist way.

They chained workers to their machines with the help of official trade unions, transforming their labor from a joy into a new slavery. The peasants, whose protests manifested themselves in spontaneous rebellions, and the workers, who were forced by the circumstances of their lives to go on strike, met with mass executions and the sort of bloodthirstiness for which the tsar's generals were famous ...

[But] the long patience of the working people has reached its end. Here in Kronshtadt, the first stone of the third revolution has been laid—a revolution that will break the last chains hobbling the working masses and that will open a new path for socialist creativity ... The current takeover gives the working people an opportunity to finally have their own freely elected soviets, working without any coercive party pressure, and to revamp the official trade unions into voluntary associations of workers, peasants and the laboring intelligentsia. At last, the police club of the Communist autocracy has been smashed.[114]

That "current takeover" began, on 1 March 1921, when a general meeting of the sailors of the Baltic Fleet, held on Anchor Square in Kronshtadt, approved the *Petropavlovsk* Resolution and shouted down the representatives of the Soviet government, premier M.I. Kalinin and N.N. Kuz′min (chief commissar of the Baltic Fleet). Kalinin and Kuz′min (along with some 200 other Bolsheviks) were subsequently arrested by the rebels, who elected a Provisional Revolutionary Committee (of six civilians and nine sailors), chaired by S.M. Petrichenko, on 2 March 1921.[115] The Soviet government responded with a series of ultimata, demanding the release of its delegates and an end to the revolt, which it tendentiously described as "SR-Black Hundred" in spirit and "undoubtedly prepared by French counter-intelligence," while claiming that at the head of the "mutiny" was "the White general [V.N.] Kozlovskii," one of the military specialists Trotsky had placed in charge of artillery on the island. However, being patently and patiently firm in their commitment to Soviet power (albeit "without Communists") and never once referencing the Constituent Assembly,[116] the Kronshtadters demands were certainly not "counter-revolutionary" in that sense and seem less inspired by populist (SR) or social-democratic (Menshevik) ideas than by anarchism and libertarian-communism, although the subsequent (and internet-ongoing) efforts of anarchists and libertarian-communists to claim the Kronshtadters exclusively as their own has rather muddied the waters in this regard.[117] Some sailors too seem to have been inspired by sympathies for the plight of the peasantry in Tambov, Ukraine, and elsewhere, with whom many had family connections. Among them was Petrichenko himself, who was reported by the *New York Times* on 31 March 1921 as saying, "For years, the things happening at home while we were at the front or at sea were concealed by the Bolshevik censorship. When we returned home our parents asked us why we fought for the oppressors. That set us thinking."[118] In addition, there were certainly very local crises relating to the personnel, administration, and morale of the Baltic Fleet: these were particular to the fleet, which had been almost entirely confined to port, under strict tsarist and then Soviet discipline (for the running of a large ship requires discipline, order, and hierarchy under any political system) and served to amplify the sailors' reaction to the general situation across Soviet Russia.[119]

When the rebels refused to comply with the government's demands (although Kalinin and Kuz'min were allowed to leave the island), the 7th Red Army, commanded by M.N. Tukhachevskii (again brought in especially to deal with a sudden emergency), launched an assault against Kotlin on 7–8 March 1921.[120] However, this attack had been hastily prepared—fear that the ice surrounding the island would soon melt, rendering it virtually impregnable, had injected a special urgency into the situation[121]—and approximately 10,000 Soviet combatants (with eighty-five field guns and ninety-six machine-guns) were repulsed by the rebels (who controlled 280 field guns and thirty machine-guns). The Kronshtadters were also able to utilize the weaponry of the two Dreadnoughts in the Kronshtadt harbor, each armed with twelve 304-mm (12-inch), sixteen 120-mm, and eight 75-mm guns, although only about half of these weapons could be used in the fighting, due to the orientation at which the immobile, iced-in ships were anchored. Also, despite the presence of Cheka forces and blocking detachments to force them on to the ice, some Red units had mutinied and expressed sympathy for the Kronshtadters—declaring, even, that they wanted to be Kronshtadters! Prominent among the mutineers were men of three regiments of the supposedly crack 27th Omsk Rifle Division (formerly a unit of the 5th Red Army, named for its role in the defeat of Kolchak and its capturing of his capital) that had once been commanded by the then revered (if later ridiculed) Red martyr V.I. Chapaev. This was shocking to the Red command, as the 27th had been Tukhachevskii's first choice as a spearhead for the attack on the island. Dozens of these mutineers were executed.[122]

Then, in line with an order issued by Tukhachevskii at 4.50 a.m. on 17 March 1921, a second attack on the island was launched, following a lengthy artillery barrage, with some 25–30,000 Red soldiers moving out onto the ice—or, rather, terrifyingly, into a foot or so of water with melting ice moving around beneath it. In those circumstances, as the dark waters rose, it is unclear what advantage the white robes in which many were "camouflaged" might have bestowed. They were supplemented by a mass of artillery on the northern and southern shores of the gulf (including many heavy guns brought north, like Tukhachevskii himself, from the now inactive fronts against Poland) and by an influx of around 300 senior Bolsheviks who had rushed to the scene from the 10th Party Congress in Moscow.[123] Again, though, it remains unrecorded what military impact most of these untrained delegates had; and it has been suggested that the Red artillery (and the few bomber aircraft deployed) did more damage to their own forces (by breaking up the ice) than to the "enemy." But nevertheless, by 17–18 March 1921, the rebellion had been crushed and Kronshtadt town and fortress and all the island of Kotlin were back in Soviet hands. Tukhachevskii, having not set foot on the island, two days later passed on his command to A.I. Sediakin and returned south to Smolensk to oversee the reorganization of the Western Front, now that the Treaty of Riga (18 March 1921) had sealed the peace with Poland. The plans he had laid for using poison gas to clear the battleships at Kronshtadt harbor had not had to be implemented because sailors on board the battleships *Petropavlovsk* and *Sevastopol'*, upon learning of plans by the rebel leaders to scupper the vessels, overthrew them, took control, and surrendered. Yet another civil war within a civil war.

The number of dead and wounded on both sides of this geographically confined but immensely significant civil-war front remains a matter of dispute. Official Soviet sources claimed at the time that some 1,000 rebels were killed, 2,000 wounded, and 6,528 captured during the fighting, while the Red Army suffered 527 fatalities and 3,285 wounded, but this is likely to be a gross distortion of the true number of casualties: recently published Soviet documents indicate that at least twice as many rebels were killed in the fighting, while up to 2,000 Red soldiers may have lost their lives. Moreover, it has been estimated that more than 2,000 Kronshtadters were subsequently executed by the Cheka and that as many again were dispatched to prison camps in the White Sea (on the Solovetskii islands) and elsewhere, most of them with five-year sentences. In contrast, none of the Bolshevik officials held by the rebels had been killed or injured. Several thousand sailors (perhaps as many as 8,000 and among them Petrichenko) escaped across the ice to Finland.[124] When the ice on the gulf soon thereafter melted, hundreds of corpses were also washed up on Finnish shores, prompting an official complaint to Moscow from Helsinki about health risks.[125]

A mystery also surrounds the appearance in the French newspaper *Le Matin*, two weeks prior to the rebellion, of reports about a revolt alleged to be in process at Kronshtadt. This may have been linked to a "Memorandum on the Question of Organizing an Uprising at Kronshtadt" that was probably drafted by émigré Kadets and other members of the National Center.[126] That document (which seems to have been written in January 1921) contained very detailed and precise information about how the resources, personnel, and arms at Kronshtadt might be used for a rebellion in March 1921; but why exiled anti-Bolsheviks should contemplate organizing a rebellion in a town that was at that point still renowned as a bastion of Bolshevism remains to be explained. As Paul Avrich concluded, although these reports foreshadowed quite accurately the coming events on Kotlin, "False rumors of this type—stimulated by wishful thinking and by the general ferment inside Russia—were by no means rare at the time."[127] One might even allow that they would have been more unusual had one or two of them not turned out to be so perspicacious.

Greater controversy in the historical literature surrounds the composition of the crews of the Baltic Fleet at Kronshtadt in 1921. Later, in exile, in response to criticism from Emma Goldman, Victor Serge, and other anarchists that he had betrayed the revolution in crushing Kronshtadt, Trotsky and his supporters claimed that most of the proletarian Kronshtadters of 1917—those whom the former Commissar for War had once lauded as "the glory and pride of the revolution"—were no longer present at the naval base by 1921 (having been dispatched to the various fronts of the civil wars during the preceding three years), and that those who remained had had their revolutionary zeal diluted by a new influx of petit-bourgeois, peasant elements.[128] The historian Israel Getzler, however, published data in 1983 indicating that at least 75 percent of the sailors of the Baltic Fleet in 1921 had been drafted into service prior to 1918 and that on the *Petropavlovsk* and the *Sevastopol'* no less than 93.9 percent of the crews were pre-1918 recruits. What had changed, Getzler discovered, was the decline of seasoned and experienced Bolsheviks among them: only 12 percent of Kronshtadt Bolsheviks in 1921 had joined the party before January 1919.[129]

Also on 18 March 1921, and apparently without irony, the Bolsheviks held celebrations in memory of the Paris Commune, founded that day, exactly half a century earlier, in 1871: "The victors are celebrating the anniversary of the Commune of 1871," Alexander Berkman confided bitterly to his diary. "Trotsky and Zinoviev denounce Thiers and Gallifret for the slaughter of the Paris rebels ..."[130] This horrible coincidence—as suggested by Berkman's eloquent ellipsis—was too much for many anarchist allies of the regime, who thereafter washed their hands of the Bolsheviks. As Emma Goldman recorded:

> Kronstadt broke the last thread that held me to the Bolsheviki. The wanton slaughter they had instigated spoke more eloquently against them than aught else. Whatever their pretences in the past, the Bolsheviki now proved themselves the most pernicious enemies of the Revolution. I could have nothing further to do with them.[131]

For Berkman:

> Grey are the passing days. One by one the embers of hope have died out. Terror and despotism have crushed the life born in October. The slogans of the Revolution are forsworn, its ideas stifled in the blood of the people. The breath of yesterday is dooming millions to death; the shadow of today hangs like a black pall over the country. Dictatorship is trampling the masses under foot. The Revolution is dead; its spirit cries in the wilderness ...
>
> I have decided to leave Russia.[132]

Goldman and Berkman were at least at liberty and were able to leave Russia later in the year.[133] Other anarchists were not so lucky, having suffered disproportionately in the Red Terror. Indeed, their sufferings had begun, on 11–12 April 1918, five months earlier than the main bout of Terror, when, in a Cheka raid on the House of Anarchy on Moscow's Malaia Dmitrovka *ulitsa*, the headquarters of the Federation of Anarchist Organizations, about forty anarchists were killed and some 500 arrested.[134] Nevertheless, during Iudenich's advance on Petrograd in October 1919, some anarchists had been released from prison to assist in the defense of the city, although they had subsequently been re-incarcerated.[135] More recently, on 13 February 1921, anarchists (including some released from prison on license) had been allowed to organize a large ceremony to mark the burial in Moscow's Novodevich'e cemetery of Prince P.A. Kropotkin. However, as "Kropotkin lay there like a sleeping wizard" and "a packed and passionate multitude thronged around the bier," one witness recalled, "the shadow of the Cheka fell everywhere."[136] Soon, predictably, the anarchists were hit again, as mass arrests of professors of their creed were instituted across Bolshevik Russia in the wake of the Kronshtadt events. Back in prison, they suffered frequent beatings and torture. Executions followed: the poet Lev Chernyi, former head of the Moscow Federation of Anarchists, and the former Wobblie Fania Baron (who had stood guard over Kropotkin's body as it lay in state at the House of Trade Unions' Hall of Columns in February) were both shot by the Cheka in September 1921, for example. Finally, on 5 January 1922, ten other prominent anarchists (including Voline, Gregory Maximoff, and Efim Iarchuk) were expelled from the country after a prolonged hunger strike.[137]

The New Economic Policy

Lenin subsequently wrote that the events at Kronshtadt "lit up reality like a flash," causing some observers to infer that the Soviet government's subsequent abandonment of War Communism and the gradual introduction of a new economic policy (subsequently sanctified and capitalized as the New Economic Policy), the essence of which entailed the replacement of force with incentive in the state's economic dealings with the peasantry (and a necessarily consequential downgrading of the interests of workers), was introduced as a consequence of the rebellion; but, in fact, plans for NEP's introduction predated the sailors' rebellion by many weeks and the origins of those plans had an even lengthier gestation.

A recent biographer's dismissal of Trotsky's claim to have "invented" the NEP in a memorandum entitled "Basic Questions of our Food and Agrarian Policy" that he had presented to the Bolshevik Central Committee on 20 March 1920 is in line with entire libraries of Stalinist works on the subject, but is not uncontested.[138] Indeed, the first point of Trotsky's 1920 memorandum spoke of the possibility of replacing "confiscation of surpluses with a certain percentage deduction (a kind of progressive income tax), calculated so that it would still be advantageous to increase cultivation," which is a pretty accurate précis of the resolution "On the Replacement of the Requisition with a Tax in Kind" that was passed, almost unanimously, by the Tenth Party Congress on 15 March 1921. According to that resolution, which was the foundation stone of NEP, *prodrazverstka* (requisitioning) was to be replaced by a regulated tax in kind (*prodnalog*), initially set at 10 percent of any surplus a village might produce. The remainder of the surplus could be sold (at a profit) to state agencies or private traders (NEPmen)—as private trade, at a low level, was also gradually legalized.[139] The aim was said to be to cement the union (*smychka*) between the workers and the peasantry, although NEP might better be interpreted, in the light of the upsurge of peasant uprisings in 1920–21 noted above, as an attempt to appease the peasantry and to maximize production. Indeed, the assertion of one authority that "the peasants won on the internal front" cannot lightly be dismissed.[140]

In supplementary measures, introduced across 1921 and early 1922, most medium- and small-sized industrial enterprises were leased back to private owners or to co-operatives and were expected to operate on established capitalist methods of accounting (*khosraschet*). Only 8.5 percent of industrial enterprises, the "commanding heights" of the economy (coal, iron, steel, etc.) were eventually retained in state hands (coordinated by VSNKh), although these (usually) large factories still employed around 80 percent of industrial workers and produced more than 90 percent of total industrial output even at the peak of NEP in 1925–26. Banks, railroads, and foreign trade also remained a state monopoly. Retail prices, though, were determined by the free market (although some effort was made, albeit ineffectively, to fix the price of essential goods such as matches, kerosene, salt, and tobacco, over which state trusts maintained a monopoly). This is not the place to engage in an analysis of the rights or wrongs, or successes or failures of NEP. It will suffice to note that those 1918 heralds of War Communism, such as E.A. Preobrazhenskii, were (to say the least) dismayed: as petty traders prospered and workers faced unemployment, in this deregulated economy, as prostitutes plied their trade in newly opened nightclubs around Petrograd and decadent poets of Soviet Russia's version of the Jazz Age posted their verses in magazines that featured—would you believe it!—advertisements, and as champions of NEP (such as the convert from Left Bolshevism, Bukharin) called upon the peasantry to "Enrich yourselves!", by the mid-1920s many on the Left of the party interpreted those initials as representing a "New Exploitation of the Proletariat" and were more than ready to swing behind the new attack on the peasantry and "advance toward socialism" inaugurated by Stalin's collectivization campaign in 1928. This was the case even if that meant disavowing their former hero, Trotsky, who by that date had been first sacked, then isolated, and then exiled by the man he had crossed in the Tsaritsyn affair of 1918.[141]

The Demise of the Mensheviks and the PSR

Yet, to recap, back in 1921, NEP had been adopted all but *nem. con.* That near unanimity, however, tells its own story, for further back again, in March 1920, Trotsky's afore-cited resolution on economic reform had been decisively rejected by the Bolshevik Central Committee, by eleven votes to four, and the War Commissar had apparently been "accused of being a free-trader" by none other than Lenin.[142] Perhaps his comrades felt that Trotsky's suggestion smacked of his former Menshevism. It certainly resembled the program for economic recovery suggested in the Menshevik pamphlet *Chto delat'?* ("What Is To Be Done?") that had been published in July 1919. In fact, so close was the resemblance of the latter to what Lenin began to propose in 1921 that, as André Liebich noted, the Mensheviks "had good reason to see NEP as an expropriation of their own ideas."[143] Yet, that notwithstanding, surely Sergei Lavrov was correct to assert that, ultimately, the question of "Who said it first?" has little traction here, as this affinity of viewpoints "was not so much the result of ideological interplay as of an appreciation of obvious economic facts."[144]

That it might have been the Mensheviks who "said it first," however—and many of them were only too eager to claim credit—did have a significance in a subtly different and subsequent manner. In his speech opening the Eleventh Congress of the RKP(b) on 27 March 1922, shortly before the first of three strokes that would lead, inexorably, to his death in January 1924,[145] Lenin—at that point still at the height of his oratorical powers—explained why, in a passage worth quoting at length:

> The other day I read an article by Comrade Rakosi in No. 20 of *The Communist International* on a new book by Otto Bauer, from whom at one time we all learned, but who, like Kautsky, became a miserable petty bourgeois after the war.[146] Bauer now writes: "There, they are now retreating to capitalism! We have always said that it was a bourgeois revolution."
>
> And the Mensheviks and Socialist-Revolutionaries, all of whom preach this sort of thing, are astonished when we declare that we shall shoot people for such things. They are amazed; but surely it is clear. When an army is in retreat a hundred times more discipline is required than when it is advancing, because during an advance everybody presses forward. If everybody started rushing back now, it would spell immediate and inevitable disaster.
>
> The most important thing at such a moment is to retreat in good order, to fix the precise limits of the retreat, and not to give way to panic. And when a Menshevik says, "You are now retreating; I have been advocating retreat all the time, I agree with you, I am your man, let us retreat together," we say in reply, "For the public manifestations of Menshevism our revolutionary courts must pass the death sentence, otherwise they are not our courts, but God knows what."
>
> They cannot understand this and exclaim: "What dictatorial manners these people have!" They still think we are persecuting the Mensheviks because they fought us in Geneva [i.e. before the February revolution]. But had we done that we should have been unable to hold power even for two months. Indeed, the sermons which Otto Bauer, ... the Mensheviks and Socialist-Revolutionaries preach express their true nature—"The revolution has gone too far. What you are saying now we have been saying all the time, permit us to say it again." But we say in reply: "Permit us to put you before a firing squad for saying that. Either you refrain from expressing your views, or, if you insist on expressing your political views publicly in the present circumstances, when our position is far more difficult than it was when the white-guards were directly attacking us, then you will have only yourselves to blame if we

treat you as the worst and most pernicious whiteguard elements." We must never forget this.[147]

The message was clear: the NEP concessions to the peasantry and the relaxation of other economic state controls did not equate to an end to the civil wars. It was time, in fact, to put an end to another internal front that flared up and died down on a number of occasions over the previous years: thus, on 8 June 1922, prominent members of the PSR appeared on trial in Moscow, accused of various crimes, including the organization of terrorist attacks against Soviet leaders (Lenin, Volodarskii, Uritskii, etc.). Despite repeated appeals by the leadership abroad of the PSR "To Socialist Parties of the Entire World" and to the Komintern, on 7 August 1922 twelve of the defendants (including nine PSR Central Committee members) were subsequently sentenced to death. This sentence was, on the direct order of the Bolshevik Central Committee (which feared world and popular revulsion), immediately suspended, and in January 1924 the sentences were commuted to terms of imprisonment and exile, which were, however, endlessly extended.[148] Perhaps because the Bolshevik leadership felt the SR trial to have been a political failure and something of an embarrassment before the world—although a few more minor characters cooperated with the prosecution, the key defendants not only refused to plead guilty but (with the aid of a delegation of foreign socialists) defended themselves and were to some extent encouraged to do so—this experiment in show trials was not repeated in a hurry.[149]

The Mensheviks, who, unlike many SRs, had never fought against the Soviet government, were not quite so roughly treated, although hundreds of them, including the entire Central Committee, were arrested in 1921 and around a dozen of their leaders (including Fedor Dan) were forced into exile abroad in 1922.[150] Most of them settled in Berlin, where Iulii Martov published astute commentaries on developments in Soviet Russia in his *Sotsialisticheskii Vestnik* ("The Socialist Herald"). Many of those who remained in Russia accommodated themselves to one degree or another to the Soviet government, often working (with all the enthusiasm and dedication one might expect of devotees of state intervention and socialist planning) in the economic apparatus of the new state. Their lives, however, would rarely be comfortable ones,[151] and even the most loyal (including V.G. Groman and N.N. Sukhanov) found themselves arraigned as traitors and wreckers in Stalin's "Menshevik Trial" of 1931, following which (despite the prosecution's demands for the death penalty) seven were imprisoned for ten years, four for eight years, and three for five years—terms that almost none of them would survive.[152]

On the Anti-Religious Front

Finally, the year 1922 witnessed also the Soviet government's first concentrated attack on the Orthodox Church as, in the words of one commentator, "the last bastion of organized resistance to the new regime."[153] Formally, the Orthodox Church had remained neutral in the civil wars. Patriarch Tikhon, elected to that restored office by a grand Church Council (*Sobor'*) in November 1917, appealed often for an end to the bloodshed and, apparently for fear of reprisals, refused to offer a public blessing to the White forces (even when they were within striking distance of Moscow and Petrograd in October 1919).[154] But, on 19 January 1918, he had nevertheless anathematized the Bolsheviks, for their use of terror, and had urged the clergy to defend their parishes against the revolutionary regime by prayer and peaceful resistance.[155] A low-level campaign had ever since then been waged by the Bolsheviks against the Church, with hostilities opened by the Sovnarkom decree "On the Separation of the Church from the State" of 5 February 1918, which deprived the Russian Orthodox Church of its legal person status and all its property (including Church buildings) and forbade the teaching of religion in all schools, state and private. When attempts at actual confiscation of Church properties subsequently aroused demonstrations of protest by workers and peasants, these were fired upon by Cheka units and arrests and executions of clergy and lay activists mounted. The Church itself claimed that, in the period 1918 to 1920, twenty-eight bishops and thousands of parish clergy were shot, often having been accused of offering funds and blessings to White forces. There is no doubt that many did: in White-held areas volunteer religious units of the Orthodox were sometimes formed (for example, the Holy Cross *druzhina* in Siberia) and autonomous Church councils were founded that disobeyed Tikhon and openly supported the White cause. The most important of the latter was the Provisional Higher Church Administration of South Russia, members of which, in emigration in 1921, formed the Higher Russian Church Administration Abroad (renamed the Bishops' Synod of the Russian Orthodox Church Abroad in 1922), based at Sremski Karlovci in Serbia (the headquarters of General Wrangel). This claimed, falsely, to be a free representative of Tikhon and, in his name, called for an anti-Bolshevik crusade and renewed military intervention in Russia.

Despite Tikhon's efforts to disassociate himself from the "Karlovcians," in repeated encyclicals (of 5 May 1922 and 1 July 1923), this was seized upon by the Soviet government to renew its attack on the Orthodox Church within Russia. That offensive surged during the great famine along the mid-Volga in

1921–22, when Sovnarkom ordered that all Church valuables were to be confiscated and thereafter either sold or melted down to be sold as bullion, in order to provide funds for relief efforts.[156] The Church, having already surrendered its property, agreed to hand over all its valuables except for the consecrated vessels used in the Eucharist, but the state demanded those as well, leading to many violent clashes and more arrests, exiles, and executions.[157] Tikhon himself was imprisoned for more than a year (May 1922–June 1923), eliciting worldwide condemnation of the Soviet government from religious leaders.[158] Before he died (in April 1925, possibly as a consequence of poisoning by the Cheka) Tikhon was declared deposed by the Living Church. That, however, did not protect members of the latter from the mass execution of Orthodox clergymen and religious leaders of all sorts that would accompany the collectivization campaign of 1928–32 and the subsequent Terror of the 1930s.

The Famine of 1921–22

The campaign against the Church of 1922 was a desperately cynical and underhand affair, in which the human suffering of millions of starving peasants along the Volga, as well as in the Urals region and Ukraine, was exploited by the Soviet government in order to provide cover for its renewed attacks on Christian believers. It is possible too that some Bolsheviks saw the famine as a golden opportunity to strengthen Soviet power in the countryside, as hunger sapped the peasants' will to resist.[159] The Bolsheviks' handling of the famine crisis, as it began to develop, was also hopelessly incompetent: Moscow seems to have ignored the portents of widespread starvation in 1920 and 1921—and research now suggests that "the famine actually began in 1920 and in some regions as early as 1919"[160]—fearing that to acknowledge it, and to seek aid from abroad, might at worst facilitate renewed intervention and at best be regarded as an admission of the failure of the October Revolution and the entire Soviet project. Even when foreign aid was countenanced, it was accepted almost by accident and was set about with all sorts of limitations upon what the aid organizations involved (chiefly the American Relief Administration) could and could not do, and was damagingly encumbered by any number of administrative interferences that undoubtedly cost many lives.[161]

It is true also that the Soviet leadership terminated foreign famine relief in mid-1923, rather earlier than it was advisable to do so—and at the risk of precipitating another tragedy—in order to justify renewed grain exports to Europe that were required for general economic development.[162] It would be mistaken, however, to attribute the 1921 famine to any deliberate moves on the part of the Bolsheviks to somehow starve out their enemies. This was not a man-made famine, although the general man-made mayhem of the previous decade, for which many actors other than the Bolsheviks were responsible, certainly made a contribution: the famine, in fact, had numerous complex causes and, in some respects, the efforts made by Soviet Moscow at fighting the crisis were impressive.[163]

Nevertheless, the events along the mid-Volga in 1921–22 were unspeakably horrific and costly in lives. Estimates of the number of human deaths (nobody counted the animals) caused by the great hunger vary: although 5 million (or about half as many who had died in the previous four years of civil war) is the figure most often quoted, a carefully researched Russian account published in 2000 concludes that "by May 1922, around 1 million peasants had died of hunger and illness."[164] Most of these deaths resulted, however, not directly from starvation but from the increased likelihood of the starving and malnourished succumbing to the already existing epidemics of typhus, cholera, dysentery, and other water-borne diseases, as well as, especially, vector-borne maladies such as smallpox (which was being widely and rapidly spread by refugees fleeing the famine regions).[165] In the light of this, it could be argued that the Soviet government's decision in 1923 to resume grain exports in an attempt to revive the entire economy of the area it controlled was not as heartless as it has sometimes been portrayed. At the same time, though, we should concede that believers could be forgiven for arguing that this new plague, replete with evidence of cannibalism and other horrors, was God's vengeance against a people that had succumbed to revolution and to Bolshevism.

6

1921–26

THE ENDS OF THE "RUSSIAN" CIVIL WARS

The date at which the "Russian" Civil Wars can properly be said to have ended is perhaps not quite as controversial a topic as the date of their various outbreaks, but is nevertheless worth considering—not least because many authors and commentators have clearly got it wrong. It is certain that the usual dates of termination of studies of the fighting, in either November 1920 (the Red Army's defeat of Wrangel) or March 1921 (the formal end of War Communism, the introduction of the New Economic Policy, and the peace with Poland), are too early. After all, the political struggle against the PSR, the Mensheviks, and anarchists went on for many months after that, as did the campaign against the Church and the struggle in the countryside against peasant rebels from Western Siberia, through Tambov to Ukraine.[1] Also, although NEP was proclaimed in March 1921, conditions of hyperinflation, zero growth, and famine pertained for many more months and, as a recent account has it, "recovery was marked only in the following year";[2] so those who regard the inauguration of NEP as a caesura are in difficulties. Those who take a more extended geographical view of the wars sometimes choose October 1922 as their termination date—the point of the White evacuation of Vladivostok, in the Far East.[3] But even that is neither accurate nor sensible, as White partisans' resistance to the Red Army in Iakutia extended the fighting in Eastern Siberia to at least June 1923. In the early 1920s, moreover, guerilla warfare against Soviet rule in Georgia was also ceaseless, reaching a peak only in the general

August uprising of 1924. And, if we extend our view from there, across the Caspian into Central Asia, a good case can be made for considering June 1926 as the end date.[4] That will be the date favored herein for the termination of the "Russian" Civil Wars, although it can be accepted that other conceptions of what constituted the conflicts might suggest even later dates. For example, one influential work on the period regards the Bolsheviks' struggles with the peasantry of the revolutionary era and the Stalin era as a "single great conflict in two acts, 1918–1922 and 1928–1933," merely interrupted by the "breathing space" (*peredyshka*) of NEP, a sort of "peasant Brest-Litovsk"—a truce that Moscow was always going to break once it had recovered from its poundings in the first rounds of the contest.[5] This is an intriguing concept, but should not lead us into the false dichotomy of concluding that because Stalin launched a war on the peasants in 1928 Lenin was dissembling when he wrote of the NEP, in 1921, that N. Ossinskii was correct in deducing that the policy should be taken "seriously and for a long time." As Lenin explained, "I think he is quite right":

> The policy is a long-term one and is being adopted in earnest. We must get this well into our heads and remember it, because, owing to the gossip habit, rumours are being spread that we are indulging in a policy of expedients, that is to say, political trickery, and that what is being done is only for the present day. That is not true. We are taking class relationships into account and have our eyes on what the proletariat must do to lead the peasantry in the direction of communism in spite of everything. Of course, we have to retreat; but we must take it very seriously and look at it from the standpoint of class forces. To regard it as a trick is to imitate the philistines, the petty bourgeoisie, who are alive and kicking not only outside the Communist Party.[6]

There was no doubt that at some stage, quite distant in the future, Lenin had it in mind to go back on the offensive against the peasantry—or what we might call, in the light of what he followed this up with, the fortress of the village—but this does not necessarily mean he intended to do so in the sense of an all-out, frontal assault. Rather, he told a gathering of Moscow Bolsheviks in October 1921:

> I would like to take for the purpose of analogy an episode from the Russo-Japanese War ... The episode I have in mind is the capture of Port Arthur by the Japanese General Nogi. The main thing that interests me in this episode is that the capture of Port Arthur was accomplished in two entirely different stages. The first stage was that of furious assaults; which ended in failure and cost the celebrated Japanese commander extraordinarily heavy losses. The second stage was the extremely arduous, extremely difficult and slow method of siege, according to all the rules of the art. Eventually, it was by this method that the problem of capturing the fortress was

solved. When we examine these facts we naturally ask in what way was the Japanese general's first mode of operation against the fortress of Port Arthur mistaken? Were the direct assaults on the fortress a mistake?

... At first sight, of course, the answer to this question would seem to be a simple one. If a series of assaults on Port Arthur proved to be ineffective—and that was the case—if the losses sustained by the assailants were extremely heavy—and that, too, was undeniably the case—it is evident that the tactics of immediate and direct assault upon the fortress of Port Arthur were mistaken, and this requires no further proof. On the other hand, however, it is easy to understand that in solving a problem in which there are very many unknown factors, it is difficult without the necessary practical experience to determine with absolute certainty the mode of operation to be adopted against the enemy fortress, or even to make a fair approximation of it. It was impossible to determine this without ascertaining in practice the strength of the fortress, the strength of its fortifications, the state of its garrison, etc. Without this it was impossible for even the best of commanders, such as General Nogi undoubtedly was, to decide what tactics to adopt to capture the fortress. On the other hand, the successful conclusion of the war called for the speediest possible solution of the problem. Furthermore, it was highly probable that even very heavy losses, if they were inevitable in the process of capturing the fortress by direct assault, would have been more than compensated for by the result; for it would have released the Japanese army for operations in other theatres of war, and would have achieved one of the major objects of the war before the enemy (the Russian army) could have dispatched large forces to this distant theatre of war, improved their training and perhaps gained immense superiority.

If we examine the course of the military operations as a whole and the conditions under which the Japanese army operated, we must come to the conclusion that these assaults on Port Arthur were not only a display of supreme heroism on the part of the army which proved capable of enduring such huge losses, but that they were the only possible tactics that could have been adopted under the conditions then prevailing, i.e., at the opening of hostilities. Hence, these tactics were necessary and useful; for without a test of strength by the practical attempt to carry the fortress by assault, without testing the enemy's power of resistance, there would have been no grounds for adopting the more prolonged and arduous method of struggle, which, by the very fact that it was prolonged, harboured a number of other dangers. Taking the operations as a whole, we cannot but regard the first stage, consisting of direct assaults and attacks, as having been a necessary and useful stage, because, I repeat, without this experience the Japanese army could not have learnt sufficiently the concrete conditions of the struggle ... [But] since the previous tactics had proved mistaken, they had to be abandoned, and all that was connected with them had to be regarded as a hindrance to the operations and dropped. Direct assaults had to cease; siege tactics had to be adopted; the disposition of the troops had to be changed, stores and munitions redistributed, and, of course, certain methods and operations had to be changed. What had been done before had to be resolutely, definitely and clearly regarded as a mistake in order to remove all obstacles to the development of the new strategy and tactics, to the development of operations which were now to be conducted on entirely new lines. As we know, the new strategy and tactics ended in complete victory, although it took much longer to achieve than was anticipated.

I think this analogy can serve to illustrate the position in which our revolution finds itself in solving its socialist problems of economic development. Two periods stand out very distinctly in this connection. The first, the period from approximately the beginning of 1918 to the spring of 1921; and the other, the period from the spring of 1921 to the present.[7]

In this long, drawn-out, second stage of siege, the Bolsheviks' tactics, Lenin subsequently came to argue—albeit somewhat cautiously—should rest on the principal and practice of cooperation: the entire peasant class, he argued, should be organized into co-operative societies as a means of gradually inculcating socialism in the villages. This was now feasible, as the means of production were in the hands of the workers' state and Bolshevik co-operatives would not fall into the muddled mire of idealism, cronyism, and capitalism that had compromised the old, SR-dominated co-operative networks in Russia. That, however, was for the long-term future ("At best we can achieve this in one or two decades," he predicted) and, in any case, written (or, rather dictated) in early January 1923, the piece "On Co-Operation" was one of the very last articles that Lenin would complete before his illnesses completely paralyzed him and the piece was quickly forgotten in Soviet Russia.[8]

Moreover, in 1921, the pressing tasks for the immediate future were the containment of internal political opposition (dealt with above) and the winding-up of the last military fronts of the civil wars that are the subject of this chapter.

Far Eastern Dying Embers

By the time the forces of Wrangel were being pressed back into Crimea in October–November 1920, the Red Army commanded sufficient men and resources to deal simultaneously, and with little undue effort, with one of his former subordinates, Ataman Semenov, at the other end of the country, in Transbaikalia. Earlier in the year, in February 1920, with the AFSR not yet eliminated and the Poles clearly girding themselves to advance, "Not a Step Further East" had been adopted as the Red Army's order of the day in Siberia, as it reached Irkutsk, as all available forces were required in the west. Thus, on 2 February 1920, the Politburo had announced itself to be "unconditionally opposed to committing military and other forces beyond Irkutsk" and had deemed it the "unconditional duty" of I.N. Smirnov, chief military commissar of the 5th Red Army, "to strain every nerve to deliver to [European Russia] as rapidly as possible the maximum number of Siberian troops, locomotives and railway coaches."[9] Moreover, the Soviet government feared clashing with the still sizable Japanese forces that were deployed along the Trans-Siberian and Chinese Eastern Railroads. Consequently, the Eastern Front had been disestablished on 15 January 1920 and, after entering Irkutsk in early March 1920, Red forces had not proceeded beyond Lake Baikal. Meanwhile, to act as a buffer between the new Soviet border east of Irkutsk and the interventionists, there was proclaimed, at a "Congress of Toilers" at Blagoveshchensk on 6 April 1920, a nominally independent Far Eastern Republic (FER). This had a coalition government, included SRs and Mensheviks in its administration, and had its own armed forces, the People's-Revolutionary Army, but its self-government was a chimera: the FER was always and entirely controlled by Moscow through the Bolsheviks' Far Eastern Bureau (Dal'biuro), led by A.M. Krasnoshchekov (who was also the first prime minister of the FER); as was its army, into which were incorporated forces from the Red Army's disestablished Eastern Front, and which was initially commanded by G.Kh. Eikhe, former commander of the 5th Red Army.[10] Still, the "independence" of the FER was a useful fiction that suited the climate of the times, as the Allies also sought to wash their hands of their former—but now embarrassing (for they had failed)—White protégés, and were coming, albeit uneasily, to normalize relations with this strange new regime in Moscow. Even the Japanese, albeit after lengthy negotiations, signed a peace treaty with the FER (the Gongota Agreement, 15 July 1920), although at that point Tokyo refused to acknowledge the FER's claim to sovereignty over the Maritime Province and its chief city, Vladivostok. Also, the FER never achieved international recognition. Yet, it traded with the outside world and sent a reputation-boosting (albeit unaccredited) delegation to the Washington Conference in November 1921, which sought to clear up Pacific and naval affairs that the Paris Peace Conference had not finalized (and in which the United States was especially interested).[11]

From its inception, the FER's People's-Revolutionary Army, which initially mustered around 20,000 men—quite a number in that sparsely populated region—was given the strategic task of clearing the territory claimed by the FER (essentially, all those parts of the former Russian Empire east of Lake Baikal) of forces of the Japanese intervention and the post-Kolchak, White formations that still lingered thereabouts. The Japanese would still have to be dealt with using kid gloves, as, although they had retreated from Transbaikalia and most of the Amur, their grip on the Pacific Coast had actually been tightened since other Allied contingents, including the Americans, had evacuated the region.[12] Having lost the support of his Japanese sponsors, on the other hand, Ataman Semenov's Far Eastern (White) Army, based at Chita, was now extremely vulnerable. After all, few of the local population, who had endured two years of Semenov's barbarous rule, were likely to spring to that monster's defense.[13] Yet, although Verkhneudinsk had been captured in March 1920, thereby clearing Semenov's forces from western Transbaikalia, two further P-RA efforts to expel him from the east of the region, in the early summer of 1920, ended in failure. But, following the Gongota Agreement, and the subsequent Japanese withdrawal from the vast Amur region, the Ataman's forces were easily driven from Chita on 22 October 1920. They then fled across the border into Manchuria and, thence, along the CER to the Maritime Province and back under Japanese cover.[14] At the same time—and just as, in the far south of European Russia, Wrangel was retreating toward the Crimean ports, prior to their evacuation—the Japanese withdrew from Khabarovsk, allowing the P-RA to capture that very important town, the headquarters of the Ussurii Cossack Host, which had been the center of a notoriously brutal White warlordship under Ataman I.M. Kalmykov in earlier years.[15]

Then, in May–August 1921, the P-RA, in an action coordinated with the 5th Red Army and pro-Soviet Mongolian forces (the Mongolian People's Partisans) of Damdin Sükhbaatar, engaged with the grandly named but hopelessly weak East Asian Cavalry Division of Semenov's former associate, the remarkable (but clearly unhinged) Baron R.F. Ungern von Sternberg, which was attempting to invade the FER from its base in Mongolia. The 5th Red Army eventually drove the Whites from the Mongolian capital, Urga (Ulan Bator), on 6 July 1921, thereby facilitating the subsequent establishment of the Mongolian People's Republic (proclaimed on 26 November 1924, following the demise of the dissolute Bogdo Khan, Mongolia's first and last Buddhist emperor).[16]

As Moscow had earlier abandoned the Soviet Republic of Gīlān in 1920 and had been unable to send aid to maintain Béla Kun's Hungarian Soviet Republic in 1919, this desolate, landlocked outpost of Communism, sandwiched between the most remote regions of Eastern Siberia and Northern China, remained the Bolsheviks' only successful attempt to export their revolution in the civil-war era. The relationship between the two very different states was sealed by the Soviet–Mongolian Treaty of Friendship, signed at Moscow on 5 November 1921—or, by the Mongol reckoning, "on the 6th day of the 10th moon of the 11th year of the 'Exalted by the Many' (the 11th year of the reign of the Bogdo Khan)"—which assorted oddly with the Bolsheviks' reform of the Russian calendar to conform with European norms. Under its terms, each contracting party agreed to suppress organizations hostile to the other that was operating on its territory, to facilitate trade and the exchange of ambassadors and consuls, and so forth. The RSFSR, in addition, "responding to the wise measures of the People's Government of Mongolia in the matter of organizing telegraphic communications not dependent on the rapacious tendencies of world imperialism," was contracted to transfer to Mongolian ownership all Russian telegraphic installations on Mongolian territory.[17]

As for Ungern, on either 19 or 22 August 1921 (sources differ), he and some thirty Mongol troops of his dwindling and fractious command were waylaid and captured, in the open steppe, by the Red troopers of P.E. Shchet-inkin (former chief of staff of the anti-Kolchak Taseevo Partisan Republic, who had recently returned to the east after playing a prominent part in the defeat of Wrangel). According to some accounts Ungern's men had bound him and forced him to surrender, yet what is certain is that he was then taken to Soviet Siberia. Some sources have it that his transfer was slowed, as he was exhibited in a cage to curious locals at railroad stations along the way, but his progress could not have been gravely interrupted by such carnivalesque dis-plays, as the following month, on 15 September 1921, after a brief trial before the Supreme Extraordinary Revolutionary Tribunal at Novonikolaevsk—where, dressed in the yellow kaftan of a Mongolian lama, he was accused and found guilty of the mass murder of Siberian and Mongolian workers and peasants, banditry, the instigation of pogroms, plotting to restore the Romanov dynasty, and collaborating with the Japanese to overthrow Soviet power and divide Russia—the "Bloody Baron" was summarily executed by firing squad.[18]

* * *

Meanwhile, on the Pacific Coast, in a coup of 27 May 1921, White forces (which included the remnants of the *kappel'evtsy*), led by the former com-mander of Semenov's Far Eastern (White) Army, G.A. Verzhbitskii, over-threw the Leftist local government at Vladivostok (the Provisional Government of the Maritime Region Zemstvo Board), which had succeeded Kolchak's military governors in the port and had subsequently recognized the authority of the FER. The Whites established a more right-wing authority, the Maritime Zemstvo Government. This was headed by two local businessmen, the brothers N.D. and S.D. Merkulov. The Merkulov regime mustered its forces behind an effective Japanese cordon around Vladivostok—indeed, it was in essence a Japanese puppet—before deploying its White Insurgent Army (commanded by another veteran of Semenov's 1920 army, General V.M. Molchanov) northward over the autumn of 1921. Its fiercely executed campaign forced the P-RA to abandon Khabarovsk on 22 December of that year, allowing Molchanov's units to advance west along the Amur branch of the Trans-Siberian Railroad as far as Volochaevka station.[19] A P-RA counter-offensive in the New Year, however, masterminded by the now campaign-seasoned Soviet commander M.K. Bliukher, who had returned east, with his laurels, from his great feats against Wrangel's Russian Army in Tauride, drove the Whites back and out of Khabarovsk on 22 February 1921.

The following autumn, in what amounted to the last major military (but not civil) operation of the "Russian" Civil Wars, the P-RA undertook a campaign southward through the Maritime Province, forcing back the dregs of White forces in the region, which since June 1922 had been reorganized once more under Kolchak's former commander, General Diterikhs (who had recently deposed the Merkulovs). In a final, desperate throw of the dice, Diterikhs staked all on unabashed reaction and an appeal to Great Russian traditions that seemed all the more anachronous in this Pacific outlier of the empire, where Chinese and Korean immigrants and native tribes mixed not only with Russians but with the descendants of other nationalities (chiefly Poles and Ukrainians) who had been exiled there by the tsars or had migrated eastwards to escape tsarist oppression.[20] In July 1922, a regional Zemskii Sobor ("Assembly of the Lands") was summoned by Diterikhs at Vladivostok, with Patriarch Tikhon, the head of the Russian Orthodox Church, named as its honorary chairman.[21] Its opening session, on 23 July 1922, took place beneath proudly displayed imperial flags. Among the first acts of this tragic-comic assembly was its recognition, by a landslide vote on 3 August 1922, of the Grand Duke Nikolai Nikolaevich Romanov as rightful tsar of Russia, thereby (in theory) resurrecting tsarist rule over the last foothold of the Whites on Russian territory. Such was Diterikhs' devotion to Holy Russia that he decreed that local government in his domains (and the future resurrected empire) was to be based on the parish and only those of the Orthodox confession would be regarded as full citizens. At the same time, Diterikhs began to style himself as *Voevoda* ("military governor") of the Far East and rechristened his armed forces in equally archaic terms as the Zemskaia Rat' ("Zemstvo Host").[22] Despite this debilitating nomenclature, elements of the Host enjoyed some success in early September 1922, advancing back along the Ussurii Railroad toward Khabarovsk once more, but grandiloquent onomastics and florid uniforms counted for little against the overwhelming forces the Reds were now at liberty to bring to bear on the situation. The Zemstvo Host was soon driven back by the P-RA, which was operating in loose coordination with at least 5,000 Red partisans at large in the Maritime Province. When, following an agreement with the Red command, the remaining 20,000 Japanese forces in the area were evacuated from Vladivostok that October, as the P-RA captured the important coal-mining town of Spassk (8–9 October 1922), which had long been a center of Red partisan activities, and closed rapidly on Vladivostok, Diterikhs's regime disintegrated.[23] Soon afterwards, he and 10,000 White military and civilian refugees were evacuated from nearby Pos'et Bay to Korea, by the White Siberian Flotilla commanded by Admiral G.K. Stark. With no further need to preserve the fiction of the FER's independence from Moscow, on 14 November 1922, the People's Convention at Chita voted for formal union with the RSFSR. That union was, predictably, granted on the following day by a decree of VTsIK, thereby extending the Soviet dominion to the Pacific Coast.

* * *

Although almost so, the evacuation of the Siberian Flotilla (which moved despondently from Korea to Shanghai and thence to the Philippines before many of its passengers found their way to California)[24] was not quite the end of the White movement in the Far East, as just before FER forces had closed on Vladivostok in October 1922, a 750-strong Siberian Volunteer *Druzhina*, led by General A.N. Pepeliaev, had set out, via the Sea of Japan and the Sea of Okhotsk, to join with remnants of Kolchak's forces calling themselves the Iakutsk People's Army—a 1,500-strong insurgent force, commanded by Coronet M.Ia. Korobeinikov—that had, in March 1922, rebelled against Soviet power in central Iakutia, 1,500 miles north-east of Lake Baikal. Pepeliaev (who was, it will be recalled, the brother of Kolchak's last prime minister), having landed on the Okhotsk coast, eventually forged contact with Korobeinikov, deep in the eastern Siberian taiga, but not before the latter's forces had been driven out of the town of Iakutsk itself. A renewed Red Army offensive from Iakutsk, of February to March 1923, led by I.Ia. Strod, then ousted the Whites from Sasyl-Sasyg and Amga, while on 24 April 1923 additional Red forces (commanded by V.S. Vostretsov) arrived in the region, having been also transported from Vladivostok, on board the steamers *Stavropol'* and

Indigirka, to this most extraneous of all battlefields of the civil wars in Russia. Further defeats for what was now the last remaining White force on Russian soil predictably ensued: near Okhotsk on 6 June 1923; and, near Aian, on 16 June 1923. After this, Pepeliaev surrendered. He, 103 of his officers, and 230 White soldiers were then transported to Vladivostok for trial.[25]

Those pathetic numbers of White partisans captured in Iakutia speak toward a conclusion of civil-war matters. And, at this point, quite understandably, Soviet leaders really did consider the civil wars to have been won in the Far East. Yet, at the same time, they were all too conscious both that Japanese ambitions might again be revived in the region—as they indeed were, with the establishment of the puppet state of Manchukuo in Manchuria from 1932—and that ready to hand to apply pressure against the Soviet border (or to act as a recruitment pool for a fifth column inside it) were the tens of thousands of White émigrés crowding the railway center of Harbin, on the Chinese Eastern Railroad, and other Russian enclaves in Northern China. Among them were many former members of the Kolchak and other White governments and armies in the east. Some of the latter would subsequently find employ with the Japanese, although others would embrace one of the various intriguing ideologies preaching reconciliation with, and return to, the USSR.[26] Some former Whites would altogether renounce their past allegiances and throw in their lot with the Cheka: prominent among them—and neatly for our chronology—seems to have been none other than the by-then Lieutenant-General P.P. Ivanov-Rinov, who in 1916 had been active in the suppression of the rebellion in Central Asia that sparked the "Russian" Civil Wars and who died (his family believe) at Irkutsk, in 1926, having returned to Soviet territory the previous year. Whether this move was voluntary or forced upon Ivanov-Rinov by the Cheka remains a mystery: his descendants claim the latter, but at the time he was denounced as a traitor by the Siberian Cossack Host, which on 29 November 1925 stripped him of his title of Host Ataman.[27] Either way, shadowy figures such as Ivanov-Rinov and other émigrés would keep the Soviet intelligence service busy throughout the troubled inter-war period in Northern China. Soviet–Japanese military clashes on the Manchurian border in 1939 (the battles of Khalkhin Gol) then ratcheted up the tension, although the Moscow–Tokyo Neutrality Pact of April 1941 and Japan's decision that year to concentrate its expansionist ambitions on Indo-China rather than Eastern Siberia offered respite. The Pact did not, though, prevent the Soviet invasion of Japanese-held Manchuria in August 1945, nor did it prevent the subsequent extradition from that region of some of the most wanted men of the civil-war years: chief among those flown from Manchuria to Moscow in August 1945 were Ataman Semenov and Kolchak's Finance Minister, I.A. Mikhailov, both of whom were subsequently executed.

Civil Wars and Jihad in Central Asia

White émigré accounts of the "Russian" Civil Wars have often regarded the events at Vladivostok in 1922 as marking the end of the conflict. Historians in Europe and the United States, by contrast, as we have seen, have usually either explicitly or implicitly opted for November 1920 or March 1921. But neither such approach is any more justified or sustainable than dating the conflict's outbreak to the summer of 1918, as the wars in the extensive Central Asian reaches of the former Russian Empire continued long after 1922. This was a very particular struggle (or, rather, series of struggles), in which the Red Army faced opponents that usually had little in common with any other of their previous adversaries—least of all the Whites.

In fact, the bedraggled White forces belonging to Kolchak's Eastern Front that had retreated into Central Asia, or had been stationed in that vast expanse of territory, were eliminated or neutralized with relative ease by the Reds, once their communications to and supplies lines from the north (that is, Omsk) had been severed or captured by the advance of V.A. Ol'derogge's Eastern Front through Siberia in the second half of 1919. Chief among these were forces of the Orenburg Cossack Host, under Ataman Dutov, that had formed the Orenburg Army in 1918.[28] Having finally, on 28 November 1918, regained their Host capital, Orenburg, through which ran the rail link from European Russia and Samara to Tashkent, Dutov's Cossacks had struggled to hold it and had been driven out by the 1st Red Army on 31 January 1919. A lengthy Cossack siege of Orenburg again ensued, but, as the White Western Army to its north recoiled and further Red forces were affixed to the new Turkestan Front, the Cossacks gave way: in September 1919, Soviet forces from the north finally broke through along the Orenburg–Tashkent railroad to unite with those of the Turkestan Red Army's Aktiubinsk Front, thereby ending the isolation of the Turkestan ASSR and sending Orenburg Cossack forces (chiefly the 1st Orenburg and 11th Iaits Corps) reeling eastward across the Turgai steppe toward Semipalatinsk. On 6 January 1920, they would be incorporated (as the Orenburg Detachment) into the Semirech'e Army of Ataman B.V. Annenkov, which (based on the Semirech'e Cossack Host) had represented—or, more accurately, in its blatant banditry, misrepresented—White rule across that region since October 1918.

Annenkov was nominally subordinate to Kolchak, but had presided over another zone of White warlordism that was hardly less tyrannous than that of his fellow atamans in the Far East. Like the fiefdoms of Semenov *et al.*, this Cossack-bandit territory was soon cleared by Soviet forces (which from December 1919 were able to utilize the railroad that ran south from Novonikolaevsk, on the Trans-Siberian line, to Semipalatinsk), and in March–May 1920 Annenkov and Dutov led their men across the Kara-sarik Pass (at an altitude of 19,000 feet) and other perilous routes into Chinese Turkestan (Sinkiang/Xinjiang), where they were immediately interned by the local authorities. Some 5,000 Cossacks subsequently returned to Soviet Russia; 8,000 others (commanded by General A.S. Bakich) set off on a forced march across the deserts of Dzungaria to join Ungern in Mongolia—a journey that many of them would not survive. Elements of the remainder of the fugitive Orenburg and Semirech'e horsemen would find employ in the various armies of the Chinese civil wars brewing in that remote region over the following decades. But not Dutov: the man who had orchestrated one of the first uprisings against Soviet power, in October 1917, was killed soon after his arrival in China, in what appears to have been a botched attempt by the Cheka to kidnap him.[29] Annenkov also fell into the Cheka net (in equally uncertain circumstances) in April 1926, and was executed after a brief trial at Semipalatinsk in July–April 1927.[30]

* * *

Some 1,200 miles south-west of Semirech'e, at Tashkent, the Turkestan Soviet Republic, despite its isolation from Bolshevik Russia until September 1919, had for two years prior to that constituted a remarkably resilient citadel of Soviet power. Based upon the concentrated Russian populations of the Central Asian towns and railroad centers, but also drawing support from modernizing elements among the broader Muslim population (the Young Bukharan Party, the Young Khivan Party, etc.), the local soviet had immediately declared in favor of the October Revolution in 1917, pronounced the existence of the first manifestation of the Turkestan ASSR on 30 April 1918, and had thereafter, amid the sparsely populated and starkly contrasting reaches of steppe and mountains that surrounded it, gathered a small and irregular army (the Turkestan Red Army) to defend itself against a variety of anti-Bolshevik forces that were only marginally weaker than it was itself.[31] (No single force in the region numbered more than a few thousand fighters at any point during the civil wars.) Cut off from Moscow by the uprising of the Orenburg Cossacks in late

1917, the Tashkent regime first sought to build a Soviet alternative to the Muslim-led Kokand Autonomy (led by Mustafa Chokaev) to its east and to the Kazakhs' Alash Orda regime at Semey (Semipalatinsk), both of which had been founded in November–December 1917. It had also, from the summer of 1918, to maintain a Semirech'e Front in the north-east, against Annenkov's Cossacks, although the latter seem to have been too preoccupied with relentless rapine in their home territory to pose a serious threat to Tashkent.

The Tashkent Soviet also faced internal subversion, notably from the nebulous Turkestan Military Organization, which counted among its membership Colonel P.G. Kornilov (brother of General L.G. Kornilov) and its own treacherous Commissar for Military Affairs, K.P. Osipov, and which staged a series of uprisings. The most serious of these (the "Osipov Uprising"), was launched on 19 January 1919 by Osipov and other members of the Turkestan Military Organization, with the support of a sizable portion of the local garrison (2,000 men, by some counts, of that 5,000-strong force) and Allied agents in the region, such as Colonel F.M. Bailey.[32] In preceding months, relations within the government, and between it and the Tashkent populace, had become strained due to food shortages, the brutal imposition of Red Terror against perceived enemies, and the perception that Russian Bolsheviks in the regime were too eager to kowtow to Moscow. By 20 January 1919, the rebels had control of most of the city and had captured and executed a number of Bolshevik members of the government of the Turkestan ASSR (the so-called "Fourteen Turkestan Commissars") but had failed to gain control of several key strategic points (notably the railroad station) or any of the local arsenals, allowing Red forces to regroup and drive the Osipovites from Tashkent on 21 January 1919 (although not before they had robbed the State Bank). The rebels subsequently joined the Basmachi fighters loyal to the Emir of Bukhara, Seyyid Mir Mohammed Alim Khan.

The anti-Bolshevik Kokand regime, meanwhile, was effectively dispersed by Red Guards in February 1918, but thereafter resistance in the Ferghana Valley experienced a renaissance under the rebel leader Igrash-bey, whose forces mushroomed from around 4,000 in 1918 to 20,000 (or, by some estimates, 30,000) by the summer of 1919, while pro-Soviet forces of the Young Bukharan Party were expelled from Bukhara by the khan, and their fellow Young Khivans were denied control of their own capital by the support offered to the Khan of Khiva (Sayid Abdullah) by the powerful Muslim warlord Junaïd-khan.

* * *

Yet, apart from the front against the Orenburg Cossacks (the aforementioned Aktiubinsk Front, which was chiefly active in 1919), Tashkent faced its most serious and active civil-war opposition from Ashkhabad (Aşgabat), to the west, which sat astride the second chief route out of the region—the railway line to Krasnovodsk, on the eastern shore of the Caspian Sea—and against which the Tashkent Bolsheviks directed their Transcaspian Front.

Following the successful anti-Bolshevik Ashkhabad uprising of 11–12 July 1918, a Menshevik–SR Transcaspian Provisional Government (under the SR railwayman A.F. Funtikov) had been established at Ashkhabad and had spread its authority all across the former Transcaspian *oblast'* by the end of that month.[33] The regime enjoyed moral, financial, and (limited) military support and guidance from a British military mission (Norperforce), commanded by General Wilfred Malleson at Meshed, across the border in Northern Persia.[34]

The Transcaspian government was routinely (and predictably) vilified in later Soviet histories, as it was regarded as being complicit, under British guidance, in the infamous execution, between the stations of Pereval and Akhcha-Kuyma (on the Transcaspian Railroad), on 20 September 1918, of the "Twenty-Six Commissars." They were the group of Bolsheviks, Dashnaks, and Left-SRs, the former leaders of the Baku Commune, who, following the collapse of that regime on 26 July 1918, had been imprisoned on 14 August 1918 by the succeeding SR-, Menshevik-, and Dashnak-dominated Central Caspian Dictatorship. On 14 September 1918, as the Ottoman Army of Islam stormed Baku, Red Guards led by Anastas Mikoian broke into the Bailovskii prison and freed them. The commissars then fled by sea, on board the ship *Turkmen*, hoping to reach Bolshevik-held Astrakhan, but for reasons that remain obscure the ship's captain instead sailed for Krasnovodsk, on the eastern shore of the Caspian Sea. There, they were detained by troops loyal to the Ashkhabad government. When the commissars' presence at Krasnovodsk became known to General Malleson he asked the British intelligence officer at Ashkhabad, Captain Reginald Teague-Jones, to suggest to the local authorities that the prisoners be taken to India as hostages, in the hope of arranging an exchange for British citizens held in Russia (notably the members of a British military mission recently captured at Vladikavkaz). Teague-Jones attended the meeting of the Transcaspian government at which the commissars' fate was to be decided, but apparently did not communicate Malleson's suggestion and subsequently insisted he had left the meeting before a decision was taken. He discovered the next day (he later testified) that the Transcaspian government had ordered that the men should be executed.

The sentence was carried out at around 6.00 a.m. on 20 September 1918—although, for reasons unclear, only twenty-six of the thirty-five men in captivity were executed.[35] Following the civil wars, the Soviet government placed the blame for the execution of the twenty-six commissars at the doors of the British, even alleging that it had been British agents on board the *Turkmen* that had directed it to Krasnovodsk. They were aided in this by the testimony of F.A. Funtikov, the aforementioned leader of the Ashkhabad regime, who (before he was tried and shot at Baku in 1926) charged that Teague-Jones had personally ordered the executions.[36] For the remainder of the history of the USSR, wherein innumerable monuments to the twenty-six commissars were raised, the issue would sour Anglo-Soviet relations.[37] It would also have a lasting impact on the life of Teague-Jones, who went thereafter, for most of the remainder of the twentieth century, under an assumed name ("Ronald Sinclair"), for fear of being hunted down by the Cheka or its successors, although he remained a British intelligence officer for the rest of his career. Only after the death of "Ronald Sinclair," aged a venerable 100 years, at a Plymouth retirement home in England, in November 1988 was his true identity revealed.[38]

* * *

Nevertheless, the Transcaspian government was far from the counter-revolutionary puppet it was painted as in Soviet propaganda and seems to have been initially popular with Russian and Ukrainian railroad workers along the Ashkhabad–Krasnovodsk line. It became distinctly less popular, however, as it was forced to accept the authority of emissaries of the AFSR, claiming command over the region and its existing and future military formations (loosely reconfigured as a White Turkestan Army) in the name of General Denikin in early 1919. Consequently, with local partisan assistance, on 9 July 1919 Tashkent's Red troops re-entered Ashkhabad. With the rail route to Tashkent from Orenburg opened in September 1919, Red reinforcements then flooded the region and soon pushed the AFSR's makeshift defenses back along the line to Krasnovodsk and thence across the Caspian in February 1920—just in time for them to unite with White forces retreating into the North Caucasus and to compete for a berth on the ships gathering for the chaotic evacuation at Novorossiisk.

With the forces of the democratic counter-revolution and the Whites thereby dealt with in turn, and with stocks of arms, men, and food flowing in along the Orenburg railroad from Soviet Russia in 1920, Tashkent was then able to concentrate its fire upon two other centers of anti-Soviet power in western Turkestan: the Khanate of Khiva and the Emirate of Bukhara—the already enervated and last remnants of the Mongols' Golden Horde, which had been corralled into the Russian Empire in 1873. The respective heads of these former Russian protectorates (Khan Said-Abdulla and Emir Said-mir Moham-med Alim-Khan) were ejected in February and September 1920, in turn, to be replaced by the Khorezm People's Soviet Republic (26 April 1920) and the Bukharan People's Soviet Republic (8 October 1920). In nurturing these experimental administrations, however, Moscow had constantly to struggle against the anti-Muslim and centralizing proclivities of local Russians, who had allied themselves with the Soviet cause for ethnic as much as political reasons, as well as the pronounced chauvinism of local Bolsheviks. To ensure that non-Russians—specifically, progressive Muslim proponents of Jadidism—were both represented and heard, a Turkestan Commission of VTsIK was established on 8 October 1919, as well as, subsequently, a Turkestan Bureau (Turkbiuro) of the RKP(b).

The pan-Islamic, modernizing Jadid movement, which had a great influence among the Turkic population of southern and eastern Russia in the revolution-ary era, was spawned from the efforts to modernize the schooling of Muslims within the Russian Empire of N.I. Ilminskii (1822–91), a Russian professor of theology at Kazan' University. He had introduced the teaching of Russian into the *madrassas* at higher levels, and at lower levels had encouraged instruction in non-Islamic subjects in the native language. Although Ilminskii aimed at socializing the Muslims of the empire, his work provoked a reaction by Tatar intellectuals, who feared it would lead to Russianization. Following the exam-ple of "New Method" (*Usul-Jadid*) schools of the Crimean Tatar Ismail bey Gasprinskii (1851–1914), progressive Muslims set about modernizing their own schools, teaching Ottoman Turkish rather than Arabic and adding secular subjects to the religious curriculum, and began to spread Jadidism to non-Tatar Turks, such as the Kazakhs and Uzbeks. The central thrust of the movement, in the light of Russia's penetration of Central Asia, was to safeguard indige-nous Islamic culture by adapting it to the modern state and modern technol-ogy (notably, the printing press). By the beginning of the twentieth century, however, Jadidism had developed a sharpish political edge and had even, to an extent, embraced the emancipation of women. Hence, it was from Jadid schools that there emerged in Central Asia such liberal, pan-Islamic move-ments as the Young Tatars, the Young Bukharan Party, and the Young Khivans (all taking their name from the Young Turks, who had instituted the constitu-tional era in the Ottoman Empire from 1908), who sought to overthrow both tsarist rule and the rule of the traditional Muslim clerical elite.[39]

The Bolsheviks' Turkestan Commission and the Turkbiuro, consequently, oversaw and promoted the advancement of native Central Asian leaders, such as the Kazakh Turar Ryskulov, to prominence in the Turkestan ASSR. The RVSR, as late as 13 June 1923, was also very keen to resolve that local national units should be recruited in Turkestan over the next eighteen months.[40] Generally, though, in the period 1921–23, Moscow was coming to regard indigenous Muslims in the regions (and, indeed, in Moscow), with suspected pan-Turkic tendencies, as swinging policy too far in the opposite direction from Communist internationalism and atheism, and the Jadids were consequently reined in—both in Tashkent and (relatedly and more famously) in the case of the powerful Volga Tatar Communist, Mirsäyet Soltangäliev, in Moscow.[41] After that, of course, things got worse: it is believed that only one of the prominent Jadids of 1920–21 (Sadriddin Aini) survived the purges of the 1930s.[42] Soltangäliev's fate was equally grizzly.[43]

Reinforcing the re-centralizing tendencies that came to the fore within and around Josef Stalin's Commissariat of Nationalities at this point was that, although Soviet power now seemed to have been firmly established in the cities of Khiva, Bukhara, and Tashkent, across the vast sub-continental expanse of Central Asia—from the mountainous east, around Ferghana, to the Turkmen steppes of the west—it was very far from secure. Hiding out across the region (and sometimes over the borders in Persia and Afghanistan) were relatively small but seemingly inexterminable groups of guerilla fighters, whom the Soviet government termed Basmachi ("Raiders," which has overtones of "bandits").[44] The leaders of these groups usually framed their opposition to the Sovietization of Central Asia in religious terms, but found support not only among the indigenous Muslim population but also among Russian settlers, who found their only recently established claims to land and water in these arid lands under threat from the usual ultra-Bolshevik economic policies assayed by the newly installed Soviet authorities in the border regions.

* * *

The Basmachi—and the Soviet battle with those rebels—although hitherto much neglected, has come under renewed scholarly attention in the West since the USSR's invasion of Afghanistan in 1979 provoked new generations of Muslim guerillas into action, but awaits its definitive history.[45] What is clear, however, is that the Basmachi revolts evolved through a series of relatively distinct chronological phases; and that, although they were played out in one of the most remote of all reaches of the former imperial space, they nevertheless had significant international dimensions.[46] Moreover, one pioneering study of the phenomenon suggested that "In the history of the Turkestan's war of liberation, the Basmachi must be seen not only as a mere uprising but as an armed civil war against Soviet supremacy."[47] In truth, the movement was more disjointed and less unified than that fully allows, but the operations of the Basmachi certainly should be viewed as an integral part of the broader civil wars of the period and were certainly something more than an outbreak of accidentally synchronous insurgencies.[48] Indeed, just as we have seen that the 1916 revolt in Central Asia can be regarded as the opening stage of the "Russian" Civil Wars, the Red Army's battles against the Basmachi can be regarded as their conclusion. During these last battles of the "Russian" Civil Wars, which raged long after 1921 or 1922, it is thought that 574,000 Red soldiers were killed, compared to around 50,000 among the rebels, while famine and disease accounted for several hundred thousand further deaths.[49]

The first phase of the revolts, from early 1918 (although it is clear that the movement's immediate roots lay in the anti-Russian uprisings of 1916), saw the establishment of Basmachi forces numbering up to 30,000 opposing the Soviet overthrow of the Kokand Autonomy, many in the name of (and subsidized by) Said-mir Mohammed Alim-khan, the Bukharan ruler. Among the largest of these was the group commanded by Madamin-bek. By the summer of 1920, these forces, which were initially allied to the anti-Bolshevik (and chiefly Russian) Peasant Army of Ferghana of K.I. Monstrov, had established control over the rich (but traditionally conservative and Islamically deferential) Ferghana Valley, in south-east Turkestan, in opposition to the Tashkent-based Turkestan Red Army and its associated forces of the newly proclaimed Khorezm and Bukharan People's Soviet Republics. Meanwhile, what was essentially the army of the deposed emir of Bukhara, commanded by Muhammad Ibrahim-bek, tied down the Red Army around Bukhara and in the Gissark valley until 1923. From 1920 to 1921, however, Soviet forces regained some ground, by a mixture of concentrated and heavy military offensives (now that their White opponents were on the point of defeat and the rail routes to Tashkent were open from both Orenburg and Krasnovodsk)—one of which killed Madamin-bek—and political, economic, and religious concessions, including the return to the local populace of clerically owned property (the *waqf*) and toleration of religious schools and courts. This, together with the new trading freedoms offered by the NEP (in a region that, as a cotton-growing mono-economy, had suffered grave economic hardships during its isolation from its chief customer, Russia), was sufficient to win over some of the population—or, at least, to guarantee its neutrality in the Red–Basmachi struggle. In this phase, nevertheless, the Soviet government, and still more the local Red Army command, always found it difficult to understand or even properly to define the causes of the uprising against them, but showed some ingenuity in opening a new "front" against their adversaries through exploiting, in their favor, tensions between the genders in the strictly patriarchal Muslim societies of Central Asia.[50] Here, then, it might be possible to speak of a civil war between the sexes.

A second phase of this prolonged coda to the Central Asian civil wars began in November 1921, with the dramatic arrival in Soviet Turkestan of the former Turkish general and war minister Enver Pasha, who—on the run from the Kemalist regime that had retrospectively accused him of precipitating a national catastrophe through pushing Turkey into the First World War on the side of the Central Powers—had made an agreement with Moscow in 1920, but then revolted against the Bolsheviks and joined the Basmachi in the light of the Soviet government's putative partnership (manifested in the Treaties of Moscow and Kars of 1921) with Kemal Atatürk. As an outsider (and as an anti-clerical modernizer), Enver alienated many of the more religious Basmachi groups, but, being married into the Ottoman sultans' family, he managed, loosely, to unite others into a more regular army of at least 16,000 men, under his own general command (although only 2,000 of that number were directly subordinate to him). By early 1922, Enver had overrun much of the nebulous Bukharan People's Soviet Republic and had also attracted to his cause some disillusioned Jadid former collaborators with the Soviet regime.

Such a broad political alliance was, however, difficult to manage or maintain: many of the ultra-conservative Basmachi ("bigots," Enver called them in his private correspondence) regarded the Jadids, not the Bolsheviks, as their main enemy and there were bitter hostilities between groups of different ethnic origins (especially between Turkmens and Uzbeks and Kirghiz and Uzbeks). Moreover, Moscow responded by a new round of concessions and a greater effort to induce the Muslim populace to join Russian Red forces to fight the Basmachi in the name of modernization and the "overthrow of the tyranny of the mullahs." Subsequently, in a series of major battles over the summer of 1922, Red forces (commanded by the *voenspetsy* V.I. Shorin and N.E. Kakurin) enjoyed notable successes against Enver (who was wounded in battle and then died on 4 August 1922 near Baldzhuan).[51] At this point, although some groups held on in remote mountain fastnesses, the Basmachi movement proper on Soviet territory could be said to have been nearing its demise. However, the local Soviet authorities still endured intermittent but very damaging acts of sabotage, ambush, and assassination and scattered raids against military strong-holds across the region.

The final phase of the Muslim rebel movement, and of the "Russian" Civil Wars *in toto*, began in 1923, when Basmachi leaders who had formerly fled into Afghanistan began to launch regular raids across the border into Soviet territory and attempted to internationalize the struggle, so as to involve both Afghanistan and Persia. They were largely unsuccessful, however: partly because of the ambivalent-to-negative attitude toward them of the British imperial authorities in India, Persia, and Mesopotamia (who, unsurprisingly, feared that Muslims in their own realms might be attracted to the guerilla model for throwing off imperial subjugation assayed by the Basmachi) and partly because of Moscow's assiduous cultivation of better relations with its southern neighbors, on the basis of its treaties with Persia and Afghanistan of February 1921.[52]

Nevertheless, this phase of the struggle is properly held to have come to an end only in June 1931, with the Reds' capture and execution of Ibrahim-bek, although further small pockets of resistance held out until at least 1934, and possibly, according to unconfirmed reports, until 1938. From the mid-1920s, though, Soviet forces of the Central Asian Military District had been engaged in only relatively minor security operations; these were skirmishes, police actions, and border-control events, not warfare. Significantly, the last active front of the Red Army that was born in the civil wars to be closed was the Turkestan Front: on 4 June 1926. It was replaced by the peacetime operation and administration of the Central Asian Military District. This can best serve as the terminal date of the "Russian" Civil Wars—albeit in a region that (bely-ing once again the traditional nomenclature) is considerably closer to Mumbai than it is to Moscow.

CONCLUSION

RED VICTORIES, RED DEFEATS

Societies should really know better than to commemorate civil wars, for their outcomes are all too frequently, in the long term, ephemeral. Hubris demands, though, that the immediate victors of such internecine conflicts usually do celebrate, and then commemorate. Thus, having won most of the "Russian" Civil Wars over the fate of the vast tsarist empire, the Bolsheviks duly set about memorializing themselves and their triumphs through naming and renaming buildings, streets, squares, parks, towns, mountains, lakes, and other architectural and geographical features (and even satellites) in honor of their civil-war heroes, as well as constructing elaborate pieces of sculpture and other public art in celebration of their victories in the revolutions and civil wars.[1] Some of these, such as the vigorous re-enactments of the Bolsheviks' semi-mythical "storming" of the Winter Palace in October 1917 (there was actually not much of a fight) and various other public spectacles choreographed during and in the years after the civil wars, were deliberately fleeting, and were not intended to last—some even featured cardboard cut-outs of revolutionary leaders and imperialist enemies, which would naturally have been ephemeral.[2] Many early statues and *bas-reliefs* of Bolshevik icons set up around Soviet cities were also mere plaster casts and, therefore, subject to the rapid erosion inevitably inflicted by the unforgiving Russian weather. But other memorials, clearly, were intended to endure.[3] However, just like the aforementioned 15-ton statue of Dzierżyński ("Iron Feliks"), in Lubianka Square, that was so grievously assaulted by Muscovites in August 1991, these representations of Bolshevik victors and victories of the "Russian" Civil Wars, no matter how hefty, were demolitions waiting to happen, and the "War of Statues" was, with the collapse of the USSR in 1991, then duly launched.[4]

Even the most sacred memorials to the Bolshevik fallen have now been expunged, and are unalterably gone, especially in the non-Russian successor states to the USSR: for example, the monument to the "Fourteen Turkestan Commissars," those unlucky men slain by anti-Bolshevik rebels at Tashkent during the Osipov Rebellion in January 1919, was removed by the city authorities in 1996; and, in 2000, the obelisk at their grave site was demolished and the commissars' remains reburied in an inconspicuous plot in a city cemetery. Likewise, and even more emblematically, the gargantuan Twenty-Six Commissars Memorial at Baku, raised in 1958 above the spot on Sahil Square where the martyrs' remains had been ceremonially reburied in 1920 (and which, in the USSR, was a site ranked second only to the Lenin Mausoleum in Soviet sanctity), had its "eternal" flame extinguished after the declaration of Azeri independence in December 1991. Then, to hardly a murmur of local resistance, in January 2009, the entire monument was demolished and replaced with a rather bland fountain.[5] The knock-on (or knock-down) effect has since crossed the border, into the first socialist satellite of the former USSR, with a large Lenin statue removed from central Ulaanbaatar (Ulan Bator) in the autumn of 2012; subsequently, on 12 January 2013, the Mongolian government resolved (with, one would like to believe, a knowing touch of irony) that its capital's expansive Lenin Museum would soon be transformed into a center to house and display the country's rich heritage of fossilized dinosaurs.[6] Surprisingly, a memorial to a civil-war leader that has endured longer than most is that to Stalin, in his Georgian hometown of Gori, in the shape of the Joseph Stalin Museum, built (from 1951) around the wretched hovel in which he was raised. However, in the aftermath of the 2008 Soviet–Georgian War, on 24 September 2008, Georgia's Minister of Culture, Nikoloz Vacheishvili, announced that the Stalin museum would be transformed into a "Museum of Russian Aggression." The first signs of this re-branding were manifested on 25 June 2010, when a large bust of Lenin's "favorite Georgian" was removed (in the dead of night) from a nearby square and the Tbilisi government announced that it would be replaced by a monument to "the victims of Russian aggression."[7] Meanwhile, in Kyrgyzstan, the first Friday in August has been declared a day of remembrance for the victims of the tsar's repression of the 1916 uprising that began the "Russian" Civil Wars, and dubitable moves are afoot to have the Russian Army's actions recognized as acts of genocide.[8] In Russian cities too, however, and perhaps especially in the capital, the process of de-memorializing the Bolshevik victory is now very well advanced.[9]

Those often crudely fashioned Soviet monuments were, of course, for the most part felled quite easily: as the American humorist P.J. O'Rourke once archly observed, "Commies love concrete," but never quite mastered how to make it.[10] But so too, surely, will degrade some of the repulsive behemoths recently raised in their stead: anti-Commies, it seems, also love concrete (and other equally coarse agglomerates), but how long, for example, will the brutalist statue of Admiral Kolchak that was erected in Irkutsk in 2004 be allowed to insult the beautiful Znamenskii Monastery adjacent to which it incongruously lurks?[11] Certainly, many Russians must hope that a gaudy statue of Prometheus that was unveiled in Tbilisi in November 2007 by the Georgian President Mikheil Saakashvili and the Polish President Lech Kaczyński will not long survive—symbolizing (and potentially resuscitating), as it very pointedly and intentionally does, the inter-war efforts of Georgians and Poles to forge a multinational alliance of secessionist nationalities ("Prometheans") against Moscow.[12] What we can say, with some certainty, is that claims staked for a place in popular culture by the new victors in the struggle over the legacy of the Russian Empire will surely not endure: 2008's Russian blockbuster movie, *Admiral'* (dir. Andrei Kravchuk), about Kolchak, and Poland's 2011 equivalent, *Bitwa warzawska 1920* ("Battle of Warsaw, 1920," dir. Jerzy Hoffman), about the Soviet–Polish War, were among the most costly (and financially successful) films ever produced in their respective countries, but (as is generally the case with movies marked and marketed by indexes of dollars-per-frame) had little artistic merit, had nothing of substance to say about the civil wars, and will certainly soon be forgotten.[13] In Latvia there has appeared the rather less visually impressive *Rigas Sargi* ("Defenders of Riga," dir. Aigars Grauba, 2007), which focuses on the Latvian War of Independence (in particular the nationalists' battles of November 1919 against the Western Volunteer Army of General P.R. Bermondt-Avalov), but few people outside of Latvia noticed.

One must hope that more permanent, presumably, will be the re-interment of the remains of some White heroes in Russia's most holy places that has occurred recently. A few years earlier, it could not have been imagined that, in October 2005, in accordance with the wishes of his daughter (the author Marina Grey), and by the authority of President Vladimir Putin of Russia, General Denikin's remains, having been transported from their resting place at St Vladimir's Cemetery in Jackson, New Jersey, could be reburied, with full military honors, at the Donskoi Monastery in Moscow.[14] Yet more surreally, on 13 January 2007, Denikin was joined at the Donskoi by the remains of Colonel V.O. Kappel'—despised until, and after, his unfortunate end in White Siberia by his superior officers—which had been salvaged from Harbin.[15] But such gravesites attract controversy: Kappel's memorial is reported to have been damaged recently, while General Gajda's grave, in Prague's Olšanské Cemetery, has become a shrine for right-wing and nationalist organizations in the Czech Republic and is, therefore, periodically vandalized by Czech anti-fascist groups. Perhaps these gravesites too, then, will not endure.

* * *

Yet, for as long as the Soviet-era statues fall, and for as long as the new anti-Bolshevik memorials stand, it may seem that the Bolsheviks did not even win the "Russian" Civil Wars. But we did not actually need the collapse of Communism and the disintegration of the USSR to tell us that. Despite the to-be-expected assumptions and trajectories of Soviet histories—and the less predictable, but remarkably similar, conclusions of the most influential Western accounts of the "Russian" Civil Wars—those intractable, Gordian conflicts did not, universally, even at the time, end in a "Red Victory." After all, as we have seen, Finland successfully resisted Soviet rule; in the Estonian War of Independence, the Estonians were victorious; in the Latvian War of Independence, the Latvians triumphed—against the Bolsheviks and the Germans; and in the Lithuanian Wars of Independence, the Lithuanians were largely victorious—certainly in conflicts against the RSFSR—although they lost their own late-1920 war against Poland (and, with it, their putative capital, Vilnius).[16] Quite definitely, the Red Army was defeated in what was perhaps, historically, the most important of the many "Russian" Civil Wars of this era—and one that certainly outgrew Winston Churchill's churlish dismissal of the events in Eastern Europe as the "Pygmy Wars"[17]—the Soviet–Polish War. The Polish victory in that conflict would almost certainly have changed the history of Europe and the world. We will never know whether the Red Army could subsequently have fully occupied Germany in 1920, but the presence of Tukhachevskii and Trotsky in a Soviet Berlin, which was certainly feasible had Warsaw fallen, would undoubtedly have set the continent on a path other than that it took.[18] As it was, the dream of a European revolution to echo "Glorious October" remained a dream: the Red Army did not invest Berlin—just as, a year earlier, it had been unable to push through Ukraine, Bessarabia, and the Bukovina to shore up the Hungarian Soviet Republic. In rather different circumstances, as we have seen, the possibility of a Soviet Persia was shelved in 1920, and the fragile Soviet Republic of Gīlān was allowed to crumble, as the price paid for an agreement with Tehran that was steeped in

Realpolitik. In fact, the only successful export of the Bolshevik revolutionary experiment prior to the Second World War was to Mongolia—a place that could not have been further removed from Karl Marx's conception of a proletarian society.

Of course, in other struggles, the Reds did emerge victorious. The White forces of Admiral Kolchak and Generals Kornilov, Alekseev, Denikin, Iudenich, and Miller were, after all, repulsed in their advances on Moscow and Petrograd from South Russia, Siberia, the North West, and the North. Perhaps the gravest of the Bolsheviks' wars against secessionist nationalities, the Soviet–Ukrainian War, was also, eventually (at the third attempt), won by Moscow in 1920. In Transcaucasia, the briefly independent republics of Azerbaijan, Armenia, and Georgia were toppled, one by one, during 1920 and 1921. The Bolsheviks' socialist rivals, the Mensheviks, the Socialists-Revolutionaries, and the Popular Socialists, were all also defeated or emasculated in the course of the civil wars, as were—often more bloodily—the anarchists. But whether or not all this amounted to a complete and unsullied victory remains a moot point. For, as we have seen, one of the chief end points of the "Red Victory" in European Russia was the merciless quashing of the uprising at Kronshtadt in February–March 1921. As long ago as 1954, in his generally positive assessment of the architect of the Red victories, Leon Trotsky, even Isaac Deutscher was obliged to entitle his chapter on that affair "Defeat in Victory."[19] What Deutscher was suggesting, from the vantage point of his office at the London School of Economics, was that, as the civil wars wound down, the Soviet government, in the terrible violence it exerted against its erstwhile most fervent supporters—albeit for the sake of its own survival— had tragically forfeited its moral right to rule and to represent the prospect of human progress that the Russian Revolution had seemed to offer. At more or less the same time, in the USSR, the novelist and journalist Vasily Grossman was causing one of the most sympathetic characters of his magisterial fictional treatment of the USSR's experience of the Second World War to come to a similar conclusion about the fate of the Russian Revolution in general. Thus, the former commissar, N.G. Krymov, arrested and languishing in the Lubianka after serving at the front during the battle of Stalingrad, "after being interrogated—groaning," reflected that:

> all these things no longer seemed quite so hard to understand. The hide was being flayed off the still living body of the Revolution so that a new age could slip into it; as for the red bloody meat, the steaming innards—they were being thrown onto the scrapheap. The new age needed only the hide of the Revolution—and this was

being flayed off people who were still alive. Those who then slipped into it spoke the language of the Revolution and mimicked its gestures, but their brains, lungs, livers and eyes were utterly different.[20]

"Krymov" was musing on the events of 1943, but the same sentiments could equally apply to the experience of 1916–26, the years of the "Russian" Civil Wars.

Certainly the Bolshevik Party that entered the civil wars in 1917 emerged from them in a very different form. It was much larger, less intellectual, more prone to centralization of authority, more bureaucratic, less tolerant of difference, and, despite Lenin's internationalist efforts, more Russian in its complexion. It even dressed differently: as the Stalin–Trotsky rivalry of the 1920s defined the two opposite poles of Bolshevism, the leaders of both sides limbered up for their bouts in matching military tunics. The party spoke differently and more martially: after the civil wars, every political initiative was a "campaign" (*kampaniia*) or a "struggle" (*bor'ba*), conducted on a front (the "economic front," the "front against illiteracy"), often by a "brigade" (*brigada*) of workers' or party specialists; and, of course, as Stalin famously had it, there was "no citadel that the Bolsheviks cannot storm." The "Russian" Civil Wars were thus, in short, the military mulch in which germinated the seeds of the Stalinist horrors of the following decades—and, of course (and horribly), some of the more depressing terrors of the 1930s would involve the decimation and degradation of the Soviet heroes of the civil wars at the hands of men who had played negligible or nugatory roles in those battles. To deny any of this seems perverse,[21] yet the horrors of the 1930s commenced with attacks on elements of the Soviet state of the civil-war years that Joseph Stalin had found most objectionable: the "Menshevik" trial of 1931 (in which, naturally, no current members of the Menshevik Party were arraigned, the focus being on former Mensheviks of the civil-wars era) and the OGPU's arrest of more than 3,000 former *voenspetsy* in its Operation "Spring" of that same year.[22] Equally, what might be conceived of as the last round of the "Great Purges" came at the end of the Second World War, as the NKVD dealt with those émigré White and Cossack military and political leaders it had finally snared during the Soviet Army's invasions of Eastern Europe in 1944–45 and Manchuria in August 1945.[23] In the middle of all that, on 21 August 1940, Leon Trotsky, Stalin's arch rival from the days of the "Tsaritsyn affair" of 1918 onwards, was assassinated by an NKVD agent at his home in Coyoacán, Mexico, where he had eventually settled after being expelled from the USSR by Stalin in January 1929.[24] The concept of a "Red victory" in all this seems very, very hard to distinguish, while the murder in Latin America of the Jewish founder of the Red Army by a Spanish Communist (Ramón Mercader) explodes again the notion of our subject as a "Russian" civil war.

* * *

Questions remain also, as we have seen, as to whether the Soviet government's inability, during the years of the civil wars, to implement its preferred policies in the countryside, in the face of peasant resistance to socialism, can be conceptualized as "victory." After all, during the years of the civil wars, the peasantry constituted some 85 percent of the population of the contested regions. Can any force that did not conquer and corral them be regarded as victorious? Of course, armed rural resistance to the Soviet government was not tolerated and was brutally crushed in Tambov, the Urals, Western Siberia, and elsewhere, while Makhno was chased out of the country with so much lead in his body that it is a miracle he was able to float across the Dnestr, but for a decade after the Bolshevik Revolution of 1917 (and particularly at the height of the NEP, in 1925–26), it could be argued, the "Soviet peasantry" ploughed furrows that were far more, autonomously, their own than at any time in recent Russian history: the Russian peasants of the 1920s were, actually, in no way "Soviet." Just as the Bolsheviks had been obliged to accept, at Brest-Litovsk in 1918, a humiliating peace treaty with Austro-German imperialists as the price for survival, so too, in 1921, in surrendering "War Communism" in exchange for the NEP, they put their signatures to a "peasant Brest."[25] Whither, then, the Red "victory?" Although one has to concede that the Bolsheviks did manage to mobilize a huge army that became increasingly "peasant" in its social make-up and had more success (or, more accurately, less failure) than its White opponents in keeping peasant recruits from desertion, there surely was no "Red victory" here either, in the broader sense—at least until, from 1928 onwards, the peasantry of the USSR was coerced into collectivization by the Soviet state, under Stalin, in a manner never envisioned by Lenin but, arguably, implicit in Lenin's thinking.[26] This renewed Bolshevik offensive in the countryside, culminating in Stalin's unleashing of a terror-famine against peasants across many regions, but particularly the civil-wars anti-Bolshevik strongholds of Ukraine and the Kuban, certainly looked very much like a war to one of the few Western witnesses able to observe it. In May 1933, Malcolm Muggeridge reported that:

> On a recent visit to the Northern Caucasus and the Ukraine, I saw something of the battle that is going on between the government and the peasants. The battle-

field is as desolate as in any war and stretches wider; stretches over a large part of Russia. On the one side millions of starving peasants, their bodies often swollen from lack of food; on the other, soldier members of the GPU carrying out the orders of the dictatorship of the proletariat. They had gone over the country like a swarm of locusts and taken away everything edible; they had shot or exiled thousands of peasants, sometimes whole villages; they had reduced some of the most fertile land in the world to a melancholy desert.[27]

In this sense, the horrors of collectivization and what Ukrainians call the *Holodomor* ("Hunger Extermination"), in which at least 5 million people died, were not self-contained events: they were the catastrophic codas to the "Russian" Civil Wars.

* * *

That having been said, toward the ends (or, in some cases, the postponements) of the various civil wars in which it was engaged, the Soviet government was in a position to implement, in the shape of the Union of Soviet Socialist Republics, a reconstitution of—or, at least, a reconfiguration of—the Russian Empire (albeit missing much of its western borderlands for the first two decades) that was to endure for the next seventy years.[28] That achievement is deserving of recognition and demands explanation. The Bolshevik Party that had masterminded it had been, at the beginning of 1917, a tiny faction on what most regarded as the lunatic fringe of Russian politics. In February 1917, it had perhaps 10,000 members and even by the end of that year its complement was dwarfed by that of the Party of Socialists-Revolutionaries. So far off the radar of contemporary observers were the members of Lenin's party that, even when the Bolsheviks took power in October 1917, neither the British nor the American press or governments even knew what to call them, usually opting in the early weeks for the confusing term of "Maximalists."[29] How this tiny party—led by what were widely regarded as mouthy but essentially milksop intellectuals, political theorists, and journalists—with a rank-and-file membership of at best semi-literate workers and peasants, fashioned the 5 million-strong Red Army of 1920 and guided it to victory over most of its opponents during the "Russian" Civil Wars remains an intriguing question.

In his enduringly influential study of the period, Evan Mawdsley supplied a generally convincing answer, which focused on the popularity of Bolshevik policies both before and in the months immediately following the October Revolution.[30] After all, whatever may have been the results of the elections to the Constituent Assembly, there is no doubt that Lenin's initial promises of peace, land redistribution, workers' control, and Soviet power were hugely popular and facilitated his party's seizure and rapid consolidation of power across most of the old empire. The Bolshevik leader's critique of the reliability of the election results to the Constituent Assembly also had some substance and there really was a "Triumphal March of Soviet Power." There was resistance—from Kerensky and Krasnov, from the Ukrainian Rada, from Atamans Dutov and Semenov, from the Volunteers, from the Kokand Autonomy, from General Dowbor-Muśnicki, from the Transcaucasian Commissariat, and from the 6,000 officer cadets in Moscow who held the Kremlin and the Alexander Military School for over a week (from 26 October to 2 November 1917), under heavy shelling from Red Guards. But, with the exception of the last of these foci of resistance, opposition to the Bolsheviks was initially scattered, weak, and, above all, peripheral. Although (as the spectacular collapse of its power in Siberia in May–June 1918 would demonstrate) the Soviet government could not dig firm roots in the outlying regions of the old empire in the few months' grace it had before the Treaty of Brest-Litovsk, the ensuing democratic and White counter-revolutions and the landing of Allied forces in North Russia, the Caspian, and the Far East would snatch the periphery away, Moscow was able to consolidate its control over most of European Russia. In August 1918, as the civil-war fronts consolidated and the war became one between the rulers of quite discretely defined territories, within the Soviet zone—what the Whites sometimes termed "Sovdepiia," the land of the Soviets of (workers', peasants', and soldiers') deputies—were to be found all, or part of, no less than thirty provinces of the tsarist empire.[31] Through the ebbings and flowings of the remainder of the civil wars, the Bolsheviks were never to be dislodged from what Mawdsley nicely termed that "Aladdin's cave"—a rich storehouse of the war industries, arsenals, personnel, supplies, and command and communications networks of the old army (tens of thousands of whose officers Trotsky pressganged or persuaded to join the Red Army, along with untold numbers of military doctors, vets, technicians, telegraphists, engineers, cartographers, surveyors, etc.). Moreover, the Red zone, which covered almost a million square miles and had a population of some 60 million souls (more than any other country in Europe at that time), was far more urban, industrialized, and ethnically homogenous than the peripheral lands in which its White opponents were based. As Evan Mawdsley concluded, "Gaining and keeping control of this heartland in 1917–1918 was the decisive achievement [of the Reds] in the civil war."[32]

Not least it meant that, although they were avowed opponents of nationalism and were fiercely internationalist in outlook, the Bolsheviks could afford to move tactically and tactfully on the "national question," always besting the Whites in this regard (even when, as we have seen, local Bolsheviks in the Baltic and Ukraine became overly zealous centralizers). The Soviet government generally bided its time, until circumstances permitted it to enter and sometimes win wars of conquest against non-Russian nationalist opponents. However, in those wars, Bolshevik victory was secured against truly powerful opponents only in Ukraine and, to a lesser extent, Transcaucasia and Central Asia. Usually acting in Moscow's favor in these victories was that Allied support was denied to their opponents—particularly those in Kiev and Tiflis (both tainted by the fateful "German orientation" of 1918) but also the Basmachi, who were regarded with some suspicion by the British, fearful of the spread of radical Islamism to India. Where Allied support was proffered in any significant weight to nationalist forces (as in the case of the emergent Baltic states and Poland), it was usually decisive and "Red Victory" would have to wait until the Second World War. Finland was an odd case, winning its independence with the aid of German intervention.

Of course, all was not scatheless even within Sovdepiia. After it had lost its hold on the very productive periphery of the old empire, Soviet Moscow found itself at the center of a very hungry and often very cold zone, as severed from it had been most of the food-producing regions of the former empire (in Ukraine, the North Caucasus, and Western Siberia), as well as sources of coal in the Donbass and the Urals, vital fuel oils and industrial lubricants from around Groznyi and Baku, and raw cotton from Central Asia. Consequently, as we have seen, the 1917–18 popularity of the Bolsheviks was fleeting and, from the spring of 1918 until the tactical retreat signaled by NEP in 1921, the Soviet government was faced with, at best, a lack of enthusiasm among the workers and peasants of Sovdepiia and, at worst, open rebellions against it, culminating in the Bolshevik–peasant civil wars across much of Soviet Russia in 1920–21, and the tragic rebellion of the Kronshtadt sailors in February–March 1921. Those uprisings were usually more a response to perceived (and actual) Bolshevik tyranny (the "Commissarocracy") and Red Terror than to economic hardship, but tyranny and terror were the means to which the Bolsheviks had had to resort, under "War Communism," to marshal often desperately dwindling resources toward the front. Indeed, the mechanisms the Bolsheviks developed within the Red Army support services and in the shape of the Council of Workers' and Peasants' Defense to direct resources (both material and human) toward the most hard-pressed areas of the many Red fronts were among their most impressive achievements during the civil wars.

The Revvoensovet of the Republic (and its subordinate bodies) was another superbly efficient unifying center of command and control. It never developed a grand strategy for the revolutionary army (which, as we know, was nothing of the sort) and usually just responded to events as they unfolded, but it provided focus and generally allowed room for military commissars to influence the Red Army's life and sense of purpose, particularly after the concessions granted at the 8th Congress of the RKP(b) in March 1919, and the subsequent creation of the Political Administration (PUR) of the Red Army.

Certainly the Whites never developed anything as complex or effective as that. But then, the Whites had far fewer material (especially industrial), intellectual, or human resources to muster. Moreover, even where resources were available, in lands with few or no railroads or useful waterways on which to transport orders, persons, or goods, in comparison to the far more richly endowed Red zone, such supplies could prove stubbornly difficult to direct and distribute. Works on the civil wars routinely reference the Bolsheviks' control of the web of railroads spreading out from Moscow, but European Russia's major rivers, mostly rising in the central zone and then flowing outwards towards the periphery, many linked by canals, were also at their command. A telling contrast here was the relative ease and speed with which the Bolsheviks were able, in June 1918, to transfer, through the Mariinskii Canal System, three torpedo boats from the bases of the Baltic Fleet in north-west Russia to form the nucleus of the powerful Volga Military Flotilla on the Eastern Front, while Kolchak's Minister of Marine, Admiral M.I. Smirnov, struggled to transport along the unreliable, overloaded, and single-tracked Trans-Siberian Railroad, to his Kama Flotilla, a few guns from the Royal Navy's HMS *Suffolk*, which was docked 4,000 miles away from the Urals, at Vladivostok.[33] Internal lines of communication were equally invaluable to the Reds in June–July of 1919, when forces were rapidly transferred from the Eastern Front (as Kolchak retreated) to the Southern Front (as Denikin advanced), and in October 1919, when Trotsky's brilliantly managed reinforcement of Petrograd kept Iudenich out of the Red citadel.

Relatively extensive distribution networks and a concentration of material resources and human capital were also at the heart of an aspect of the Red war effort that has traditionally attracted a lot of attention, not least because that was its very intent: propaganda. A huge amount of effort and resources were poured into broadcasting the Bolsheviks' revolutionary message, eventually (from August 1920) through an Agitprop ("Agitation and Propaganda") section of the Central Committee of the RKP(b) itself, but from early 1918 through an ad hoc yet nevertheless impressive and extensive array of governmental and party agencies. The entire enterprise relied upon the large number of talented painters, illustrators, photographers, authors, poets, typographers, and other artists who were willing—and even eager—to serve the Soviet state: M. Cheremnykh, V.V. Maiakovskii, K.S. Malevich, I.A. Maliutin, D.S. Moor, and A.M. Rodchenko were but the most glittering of these ranks of the Red army of artists. The first agit-train ("agitation-train"), which was named *The V.I. Lenin*, went into service on the Volga Front on 13 August 1918, loaded with posters, leaflets, and agitators (and later with the avuncular Soviet "premier," M.I. Kalinin, aboard, whom Trotsky mischievously dubbed the "All-Union [Village] Elder"); later additions to the propaganda fleet included *The October Revolution* and *The Red East*, *The Red Cossack* and *The Soviet Caucasus*, whose names reflected their fields of operation. There were also several Soviet agit-ships, notable among them *The Red Star* (at one point staffed by Lenin's wife, N.K. Krupskaia), which made summer voyages along the Volga in 1919 and 1920, towing a barge that contained an 800-seat cinema.

The images and methods used in Soviet agitprop of the civil-war era combined a peculiar and uniquely effective mixture of the revolutionary modernism and elements of Russian folk art, which perhaps reached its apogee in the so-called "ROSTA Windows": stenciled and painted propaganda posters that were displayed in the Moscow (and later regional and even foreign) offices of the Russian Telegraph Agency (Rossiiskoe Telegrafnoe Agentsvo), the state news agency that was founded on 7 September 1918, by VTsIK. The style of these creations has been enduringly influential, and coffee-table books of Soviet propaganda abound, usually featuring famous examples of posters from the civil-war years.[34] The Reds also inherited the resources to manufacture propaganda films during the war—although the supplies of raw film stock across Russia were pitifully low, Moscow commanded most of it. These were primitive efforts, but nevertheless impressed one British officer in South Russia, who viewed a few captured reels at Khar'kov in 1919: "In contrast to the Whites' unsophisticated efforts, there was no mistaking the cunning of their preparation or the appeal to the uneducated and morbid minds of the people whose sympathies the Bolsheviks were striving to enlist," recorded Brigadier H.N.H. Williamson, sourly.[35] In truth, however, how much these mighty agitational efforts influenced popular opinion is impossible to judge. And it is clear that the most celebrated examples of the art of the revolution were only deployed from mid-1920 onwards, when the war against the Whites was (more or less) already won, the wars against the Baltic states were (definitely) already lost, and the war against Poland was about to be lost.

Certainly, though, the Bolsheviks' enemies produced nothing to match this avalanche of artful agitation. Partly, this was a consequence of a lack of resources in the chiefly rural and peripheral zones occupied by the various anti-Bolshevik forces: Makhno, for example, had the support of a number of very talented agitators, most of them (like Peter Arshinov and Voline) attached to the Nabat anarchist federation, but they struggled to muster even the most basic tools of the propagandists. Consequently, proclamations of the Revolutionary-Insurgent Army of Ukraine could be found printed (smudged, semi-legibly) on the blank side of everything from pages from an account ledger to wrappings from a candy factory.[36] The Whites in Siberia complained also of a famine of writers, illustrators, artists, paper, ink, printing presses, and other vital ingredients of political agitation that limited any effort to popularize their regime. Indeed, so weak were their efforts in this regard that, on one occasion, on a visit to a village just a few miles from Omsk in August 1919, Kolchak's administrative secretary was unable to find a single peasant who could recognize a photograph of the "supreme ruler," although some offered the opinion that this always closely shaven and dapper man was "probably an Englishman."[37] In the south, where many members of the anti-Bolshevik intelligentsia and artistic communities had fled in 1918, the Whites were somewhat better served, and from September 1918 an Information-Agitation Agency (Osvedomitel'noe-agitatsionnoe Agentsvo), Osvag, was attached to the Special Council of the Main Commander of the Armed Forces of South Russia. But, although one study of the activities of Osvag has concluded that "it was a very effective instrument of information control and manipulation of the press,"[38] most other accounts of the period disagree: Peter Kenez, for example, describes Denikin, when abolishing the Special Council in December 1919, as deliberately deciding not to include a separate propaganda department within his new Government of the Main Commander, so little was the regard in which Osvag's previous achievements was held.[39] What is surely most remarkable, though, is that even without effective propaganda agencies—indeed, even while largely viewing propaganda and politics as tawdry, impure, and ungentlemanly—the Whites were able to come within a whisker of defeating the Bolsheviks, who were addicted to agitation and were able to spread their message so effectively along internal lines across Sovdepiia that the image of Lenin was approaching iconic status long before the ends of the "Russian" Civil Wars.[40]

* * *

In terms of external lines of communication, in contrast, Sovdepiia was at a great disadvantage to its White and most of its nationalist opponents (especially after the end of the world war brought an end to the German blockade of the Baltic and the Turks' closure of the Straits). The consolidation of large and relatively powerful Polish and Romanian states in the last days of the world war and its immediate aftermath also had the effect of throwing up a barrier against Bolshevism from the Baltic to the Black Sea. At the Paris Peace Conference, the Allies were only too keen to bolster this *cordon sanitaire*, even to the extent of condoning (in due course) the rather dubiously rightful occupation of Vilnius by Poland and Bucharest's annexation of Bessarabia.[41] The Red Army's efforts to breach this blockade ended first in disappointment, in May–June 1919 (when the Hungarian Soviet Republic could not be reached and rescued), and then in disaster, in July–August 1920 (when Tukhachevskii's forces were defeated in the Soviet–Polish War and Moscow was forced to concede territory to Poland that added another 100-mile cushion to the anti-Bolshevik buffer). As noted above, had Red forces broken through the cordon to reach the very deprived and disturbed territories of defeated Germany, Austria, and Hungary, at a time when, nearby, even victorious (but disappointed) Italy was in the throes of revolutionary upheaval (with 100,000 workers occupying factories across that country's north), the history of twentieth-century Europe would surely have taken a very different path.[42]

One reason, of course, for the Bolsheviks' reversal, as they sought to export the revolution to Europe, is that their opponents, especially the Poles, had been reinforced by Allied aid. Polish patriots might or might not be correct to insist that undiluted, historical Polish national spirit, not ephemeral Allied military missions in Warsaw, conjured up the "Miracle on the Vistula" in August 1920, but Allied material support was surely vital (and quite possibly decisive). Lloyd George's disillusionment with the intervention meant that his more bellicose war minister, Winston Churchill—who was apt to describe the Bolsheviks as "Swarms of typhus-bearing vermin ... vampires ... troops of ferocious baboons"[43]—was able to donate only fifty aircraft to the Polish cause, but that was the same number that Red forces defending Petrograd in late 1919 had had at their disposal, while the French extended credits of 375 million francs to the Polish Purchasing Agency in Paris, allowed a 50 percent discount on goods transferred from the surplus stores of L'Armée d'Orient in Salonika and Galatea, and facilitated the purchase of 100,000 Austrian Mannlicher rifles in Italy, along with a fleet of Balilla aircraft. The United States, meanwhile granted a credit of 56 million dollars to Poland to buy stocks left behind in France by the American army.[44] These were very sizable contributions.

Apart from this direct intervention to bolster the Polish roadblock on the route to Berlin, we should bear in mind that the huge amounts of aid that the Allies had earlier channeled to the Whites might not have been sufficient to enable Kolchak or Denikin to reach the Kremlin, but, without it, no advances at all would have been possible from the un-industrialized White fastnesses of the North Caucasus and Siberia. Yet, advances there had been—to the approaches to the Volga by Kolchak's Russian Army in April–May 1919 and to within 250 miles of Moscow by Denikin's AFSR in October of that year, while, with British tanks and aircraft in the van, General Iudenich's North West Army had reached the suburbs of Petrograd in October 1919. Even Wrangel's hopeless (but noble) excursion into the Northern Tauride had cost the Red Army many thousands of lives and an incalculable amount of expended ammunition and had also destroyed weaponry that might otherwise have been directed against Warsaw.[45] In other words, direct Allied intervention in the "Russian" Civil Wars may not have prevented a White defeat, but it was possibly the key factor in forestalling the sort of Europe-wide "Red victory" that Lenin had envisioned when urging his comrades to seize power in October 1917, and had re-imagined again a year later.

* * *

Although the European revolution was, therefore, to remain a mirage—Komintern efforts to rekindle it thereafter with uprisings in Germany in 1923 and Estonia in 1924 were, respectively, doomed and damp squibs—the "Russian" Civil Wars were far from over with the retreat from Poland in 1920. However, the question of when they terminated is as interesting, loaded, and, ultimately, unanswerable a line of enquiry as the question of when they began. Certainly most works on the subject bring down the curtain in March 1921, with the Soviet government's transition to the New Economic Policy announced at the 10th Congress of the RKP(b). That has always been an odd choice of date, as works on the civil wars emphasize armies and military men, not statistics and economists, until that point; and, in March 1921, Trotsky, S.S. Kamenev, Tukhachevskii, Frunze, *et al.* did not suddenly obey the stage order "*exeunt*," to be replaced by the lively new party star Bukharin exhorting the peasantry to "enrich yourselves" under NEP.[46] That would not come until the high tide of NEP in 1925. And, to blur matters further, a recent work by probably the most percipient of Lenin scholars has asserted that even the basic building blocks of NEP were not even nearly in place until 1922, which was "the real year of transition."[47] That may be a perhaps more appropriate date for the end of the civil wars (given the winding-down of large-scale operations in the Far East in October–November of that year and the union of the Far Eastern Republic with the RSFSR the following month), but, in turn, could only be entirely correct if one considers NEP to have been a genuine attempt to find a less confrontational means of establishing socialism than civil wars. But Lenin certainly did not think that way, as we have seen. For him, NEP was a tactical retreat *in* the civil wars, and one that allowed for subsequent sallies, often very sanguinary, against political opponents—Mensheviks (including, especially, Georgian ones), SRs, and anarchists—which we must surely allow were essential to the "Russian" Civil Wars. Actually, those wars would only come formally to an end in June 1926, with the transformation of the Red Army's last active front, the Turkestan Front, into the peacetime order of the Turkestan Military District. By that date, also, Leon Trotsky had been relieved of his post as People's Commissar for Military and Naval Affairs (on 26 January 1925) by Stalin's clique; and his successor, the civil-war hero Mikhail Frunze, had died in mysterious circumstances that seemed to be a rehearsal for the macabre dances of death that were to grip the USSR in the 1930s, their brutal climax being marked by the arrest, torture, and execution of Tukhachevskii and many other civil-war veterans in 1937.[48]

Yet, although the last Red front had been deactivated in 1926, "victory," on the Bolsheviks' own terms, had not been achieved. According to Bukharin and E.A. Preobrazhenskii's "ABC of Communism" (*Azbuka kommunizm*) of 1920, victory should have been signaled by the complete disappearance of the Red Army, for, as they asserted at the height of the civil wars, "The Red Army is Provisional": whereas, they argued, under the capitalist system, the bourgeoisie "constructs its instrument of power—the army—on the basis of an understanding that it would rule 'for ever'":

> The proletariat regards its own Red Army in quite another light. The Red Army has been created by the workers for the struggle with the White Army of capital. The Red Army issued out of the civil war; it will disappear when a complete victory has been gained in that war, when class war has been abolished, when the dictatorship of the proletariat has spontaneously lapsed. The bourgeois army is born of bourgeois society, and the bourgeoisie wishes this child to live for ever because it reflects the imperishability of the bourgeois régime. The Red Army, on the other hand, is the child of the working class, and the workers' desire for their child a natural and glorious death. The day when the Red Army can be permanently disbanded will be the day on which will be signalized the final victory of the communist system.

The authors went on to declare that "The Communist Party must make it clear to the soldiers of the Red Army that if that army should gain victory over the White Guards of capital, the victors would be the soldiers of the last army in the world."[49] That final Red victory, needless to say, was never achieved.

* * *

To revisit, in conclusion, an earlier theme, it was a hopeful sign, given the venal and vengeful spirit of those times, that even in the most craven and culturally destructive years of the Russian presidency of Boris El'tsin in the 1990s, no state-sponsored vandalism or other indignities were inflicted upon the Kremlin Wall Necropolis in Moscow, the last resting place of the many Soviet heroes of the "Russian" Civil Wars who were lucky enough to pass away before Stalin took to having such giants shot in cellars and their corpses disposed of in unmarked pits.[50] There was much talk in the El'tsin era (and since) of removing the remains of Lenin—the essential legitimizing symbol of the Soviet state—from his Red Square Mausoleum and burying him elsewhere: specifically, alongside his mother in St Petersburg's Volkovskoe cemetery (as had, it is frequently asserted, been his wish, although there is no written evidence for that), but nothing has come of this. Whether this is because Lenin's remains are still too widely regarded as sacred (not least by the still puissant Communist opposition in the Russian Republic), or because anti-Communists want to keep him on display as a warning (or regard him as unfit for burial in the "sacred soil" of Russia), or because his embalmed corpse is still the most visited tourist attraction in ultra-capitalist contemporary Moscow, remains a point most moot. It is, though, worth noting that 80 percent of state funding of the Lenin Mausoleum and its honor guard were removed by El'tsin on 6 October 1993, less than two years after the collapse of the USSR.[51] The now seemingly waxen remains of what was once Lenin, however, when considered alongside the Moscow re-interment of Denikin, surely signal that the Red-vs-White aspect of the "Russian" Civil Wars is now immutably moribund. Though still a political and commercial plaything, Lenin's corpse is no more vital than the civil-war battle re-enactments now popular in Russia and sometimes involving the local branches of General Wrangel's once proud émigré organization, the All-Russian Military Union (ROVS). In contrast, issues over which were fought the many other "Russian" Civil Wars with which this volume has been concerned—Azeri–Armenian clashes, Armenian–Turkish relations, Russo-Ukrainian tribulations, Russo-Georgian wars, Muslim insurgency in the North Caucasus, and definitions of citizenship in the Baltic states—having been unfrozen by the end of the Cold War and the disintegration of the USSR, are still very much alive.

Photo 1: Men of the 7th Infantry Division of the Armed Forces of South Russia in British uniforms (Russian State Archive of Film and Photography, Krasnogorsk).

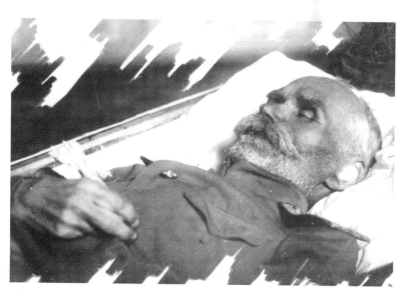

Photo 2: General M.V. Alekseev in his open coffin: Ekaterinodar, October 1918 (Russian State Archive of Film and Photography, Krasnogorsk).

Photo 3: Kalmyk cavalry of the Don Army (Andrei Simonov Collection).

Photo 4: Colonel V.G. Buizin, commander of the Partisan Regiment General Alekseev, with his wife, V.I. Buizina, who served as his adjutant. Note her four wound stripes (Russian State Archive of Film and Photography, Krasnogorsk).

Photo 5: Austro-Hungarian troops hanging Ukrainian dissidents: summer 1918 (Central Museum of the Armed Forces, Moscow).

Photo 6: Czech legionnaires entrenched (Nik Cornish Collection).

Photo 7: General A.I. Denikin (rear seat, left) converses with his chief of staff, General I.P. Romanovskii: Taganrog, 1919 (Russian State Archive of Film and Photography, Krasnogorsk).

Photo 8: General A.I. Denikin (back to camera) having issued the Moscow Directive before Tsaritsyn Cathedral, 3 July 1919. On horse, with sword raised in tribute, is General K.K. Mamontov; on foot, saluting, in black Circassian uniform, is General P.N. Wrangel (Russian State Archive of Film and Photography, Krasnogorsk).

Photo 9: General F.C. Poole arriving at Novocherkassk (23 November 1918) and saluting General A.I. Denikin (Central Museum of the Armed Forces, Moscow).

Photo 10: General E.K. Miller (with sword) converses with General W.E. Ironside: Arkhangel'sk 1919 (Nik Cornish Collection).

Photo 11: M.I. Kalinin (left) and S.M. Budennyi in the rear seat of a staff car: Polish front, August 1920 (Russian State Archive of Film and Photography, Krasnogorsk).

Photo 12: Nestor Makhno. To his right, in sailor's cap, is Fedir Shchus' (Russian State Archive of Film and Photography, Krasnogorsk).

Photo 13: On board a vessel of a Red Military Flotilla (Central Museum of the Armed Forces, Moscow).

Photo 14: Men of Colonel A.P. Liven's Volunteer Detachment in German uniforms: Latvia, 1919 (Nik Cornish Collection).

Photo 15: Red armoured car unit (Central Museum of the Armed Forces, Moscow).

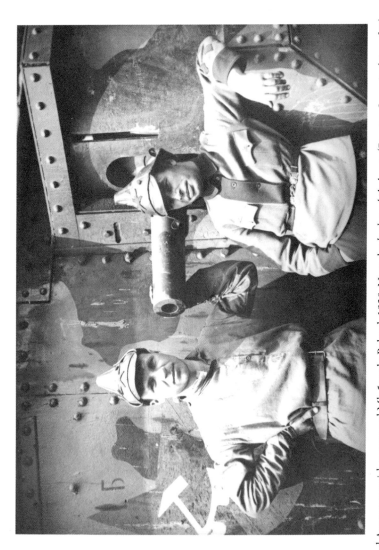

Photo 16: Red Army men with a captured Mk.5 tank: Poland, 1920. Note the *budenovki* helmets (Russian State Archive of Film and Photography, Krasnogorsk).

Photo 17: Red Gunners with a 122mm Krupp Howitzer, built under licence in tsarist Russia (Central Museum of the Armed Forces, Moscow).

Photo 18: Red Army infantry: Eastern Front, 1919 (Central Museum of the Armed Forces, Moscow).

Photo 19: Tachankas of the Red 2nd Cavalry Army, 1920 (Central Museum of the Armed Forces, Moscow).

Photo 20: Makhnovists. Left to right: Efim Taranovskii, Fedir Shchus' and 'Kuzhin' (Russian State Archive of Film and Photography, Krasnogorsk).

Photo 21: L.D. Trotsky and (third from left) Ia.M. Sverdlov present honours to a Red Army unit outside the Bolshoi Theater: Moscow, 1919 (Russian State Archive of Film and Photography, Krasnogorsk).

Photo 22: White armoured cars at Tsaritsyn, August 1919. Left to right: 'The Eagle-eyed', 'The Brave', 'The Mighty'. Note British instructors, in shorts (Russian State Archive of Film and Photography, Krasnogorsk).

Photo 23: The White armoured train 'United Russia' (Russian State Archive of Film and Photography, Krasnogorsk).

Photo 24: R.F. Ungern von Sternberg under guard: Novonikolaevsk, September 1921 (Central Museum of the Armed Forces, Moscow).

Photo 25: General P.N. Wrangel with Circassian bodyguards: Tsaritsyn, 1919 (Russian State Archive of Film and Photography, Krasnogorsk).

NOTES

INTRODUCTION: A WORLD WAR CONDENSED

1. Peter Kenez, "Western Historiography of the Russian Civil War," in Leo Schelbert and Nick Ceh (eds), *Essays in Russian and East European History: Festschrift in Honor of Edward C. Thaden*, Boulder: East European Monographs, 1995, p. 198.

2. Alan Wood, "The Bolsheviks, the Baby and the Bathwater," *European History Quarterly*, vol. 22, no. 4 (1992), pp. 483–94.

3. Alan Wood, *The Romanov Empire, 1613–1917*, London: Hodder Arnold, 2007, p. 343. These sentiments are echoed in Introduction to the most recent study of the period: Abraham Ascher, *The Russian Revolution: A Beginner's Guide*, Cambridge: OneWorld, 2014.

4. The first edition was published in New York in 1919 by Boni & Liveright, Inc. for International Publishers, the publishing house of the American Communist Party (of which Reed was a founding member). That volume contained an Introduction by none other than V.I. Lenin, in which the Bolshevik leader stated: "With the greatest interest and with never slackening attention I read John Reed's book ... Unreservedly do I recommend it to the workers of the world." It has since appeared in hundreds of editions in dozens of languages, just as Lenin wrote that he hoped it would. Whether Lenin would have appreciated its, to be polite, emasculation as the feature film *Reds* (dir. Warren Beatty, 1981) is hardly open to debate.

5. John Reed, *Ten Days that Shook the World*, New York: International Publishers, 1919, p. 112. Another (equally highly charged) account of the events confirms that Petrograd, on 26 Oct. 1917, "did not smell of gunpowder, despite the revolt." See Sergei Mstislavskii, *Five Days which Transformed Russia*, London: Hutchinson, 1988, p. 120. Despite later pretensions and filmic reconstructions, the capture of the Winter Palace was very far from being another storming of the Bastille.

6. David Bullock, *The Russian Civil War, 1918–22*, Oxford: Osprey, 2008, p. 7.

7. V.V. Erlikhman, *Poteri narodonaseleniia v XX veke: spravochnik*, Moscow: Russkaia Panorama, 2004, p. 18; and Iu.A. Poliakov, *Sovetskaia strana posle okonchaniia grazhdanskoi voiny: territoriia i naselenie*, Moscow: Nauka, 1986, p. 104. These sources cite fatalities in action of 950,000 in the Red Army, 650,000 among White and nationalist forces, and 900,000 among partisan forces, with a further two million deaths due to terror (1,200,000 killed by the Reds, 300,000 by the Whites, and 500,000 by partisan forces) and six million due to hunger and disease. (The figure of 900,000 deaths among partisan forces seems high, but that would at

least partly compensate for the fact that these calculations cite fatalities only from the spring of 1918 onwards.) To put the figure of a total of 10,500,000 deaths in perspective, the Russian deaths in the First World War were approximately 3,700,000 by recent estimates (2,000,000 military deaths and 1,700,000 civilian): Erlikhman, *Poteri narodonaseleniia v XX veke*, p. 18. For comparison, it is worth noting that in Europe's other great internecine conflict of the twentieth century, the Spanish Civil War, it is likely that losses amounted to around 530,000, with perhaps 50,000 more fatalities in Franco's prison camps during the immediate post-war period. Given that Spain's population in 1936 was approximately 25 million, while the population of the Russian Empire in 1917 was approximately 160 million, it seems that mortality was around three times greater in the Russian Civil War than in the Spanish Civil War.

8. Frank Lorimer, *The Population of the Soviet Union: History and Prospects*, Geneva: League of Nations, 1946, p. 29. Unsurprisingly, the gathering of data for the 1926 census was not unproblematic, but the greatly esteemed Lorimer insisted that its findings, published in fifty-six volumes, were "one of the most complete accounts ever presented of the population of any country": ibid., p. xiii. A recent, sober Russian analysis, while detailing the problems associated with statistics from this period (and decrying the exaggerated and unscientific estimates of 40 million deaths to be found in the popular press of the late *glasnost'* period, when sensationalism was rife), nevertheless concludes that in 1926 there was a population deficit "in the amplitude of 20–25 million" people in the USSR: Iu.A. Poliakov (ed.), *Naselenie Rossii v XX veke, Tom 1: 1900–1939*, Moscow: ROSSPEN, 2000, pp. 95–6.

9. For an impressive collection of photographs that provide a visceral impression of how the battlefields looked, see Nik Cornish, *The Russian Revolution: World War to Civil War, 1917–1921*, Barnsley: Pen & Sword Books, 2012.

10. As the events of the First World War in the East are quite inseparable from the wars that continued to engulf Russia and its neighbors for many more years, there is a strong case for the inclusion of the massacre of Armenians in Turkey of April 1915 onward, now widely recognized as genocide, as an elementary part of the "Russian Civil War" (although this has not been attempted herein). After all, the Armenians' chief crime, in the eyes of their Turkish oppressors, was that so many of their fellow countrymen were fighting on the side of the Russian Empire, which, although collapsing, had territorial ambitions of its own in eastern Anatolia. The literature on these events is now huge, but a good place to start is: Richard G. Hovannisian (ed.), *The Armenian Genocide in Perspective*, New Brunswick, NJ: Transaction Books, 1986.

11. Michael Kellogg, *The Russian Roots of Nazism: White Émigrés and the Making of National Socialism, 1917–1945*, Cambridge University Press, 2005. However, although it is undeniable that White émigrés such as F.V. Vinberg and Alfred Rosenberg had a profound influence upon the propagation of antisemitic ideas in inter-war Germany, it is surely going too far to suggest, as has Richard Pipes, that attacks on Jews in the immediate aftermath of the Russian Revolution and the widespread White association of Jews with Bolshevism somehow "led to the systematic mass murder of Jews at the hands of the Nazis" and that "the rationale for Nazi extermination of the Jews came from Russian right-wing circles." See Richard Pipes, *Russia Under the Bolshevik Regime, 1919–1924*, New York: A.A. Knopf, 1993, pp. 112, 258. Pipes is here echoing a much earlier argument, made in Walter Laqueur, *Russia and Germany*, London: Weidenfeld and Nicolson, 1965, p. 115.

12. Isaac Babel, *1920 Diary*, New Haven: Yale University Press, 1995, pp. 18, 114.

13. The subject of this quite offensively over-romantic feature, Admiral A.V. Kolchak, deserved better: he would be spinning in his grave, if he had one. As if in response—war by means other than those that Clausewitz could have ever imagined—the most costly ever Polish film produced to date (with the added fire-power of 3D) appeared in 2011: *Bitwa Warzawska 1920* ("Battle of Warsaw, 1920," dir., Jerzy Hoffman), presenting (ironically) a distinctly one-dimensional view of the Soviet–Polish War.

14. Direct comparisons between the two major European civil wars of the first half of the twentieth century are surprisingly rare, although both are sometimes incorporated into the controversial conception of the events of the 1914–45 period as a unitary "European Civil War." See, for example, F.J. Romero Salvadó, "The European Civil War: Reds versus Whites in Russia and Spain, 1917–1939," in Jeremy Black (ed.), *European Warfare, 1815–2000*, Basingstoke: Palgrave, 2002, pp. 104–25.

15. See: W. Bruce Lincoln, *Red Victory: A History of the Russian Civil War*, New York: Simon and Schuster, 1989, p. 11; and Evan Mawdsley, *The Russian Civil War*, Boston: Allen & Unwin, 1987, p. xi. Readers should note that references hereafter to Mawdsley refer to the original edition, but that the 2008 edition (published by the Birlinn press of Edinburgh) is to be preferred for consultation on account of its revised and updated notes on sources and bibliography.

16. Geoffrey Swain, *Russia's Civil War*, Stroud: Tempus, 2000, p. 18.

17. Ronald G. Suny, *The Revenge of the Past: Nationalism, Revolution and the Collapse of the Soviet Union*, Stanford University Press, 1993. This point is made also in the opening words of the author's Introduction to Rex A. Wade, *The Bolshevik Revolution and Russian Civil War*, Westport, CT: Greenwood Press, 2001, p. xix.

18. It was only while making the final preparation of this book for publication that I came across another work that systematically uses this designation: William G. Rosenberg, "Paramilitary Violence in Russia's Civil Wars, 1918–1920," in Robert Gerwath and John Horne (eds), *War in Peace: Paramilitary Violence in Europe after the Great War*, Oxford University Press, 2013, pp. 21–39.

19. It was as a fifteen-year-old "O"-level student that I first encountered the subject, in a section of a *Philips Historical Atlas for Schools*: I can distinctly remember being intrigued by a page in that book containing a map of the "Russian Civil War" that seemed to indicate that Siberia, which seemed an awfully long way from Prague, had been overrun by a Czechoslovak Legion, and that its capital, Omsk—seemingly as distant from the seas as it was possible to get—was the seat of a government led by an admiral.

20. See James D. White, *The Russian Revolution, 1917–1921: A Short History*, London: Edward Arnold, 1994, p. vi. As an indication of the abundance of the harvest of new materials through which historians now have to sift (and a lot of preliminary bibliographical investigations are now devoted to sorting the wheat from the chaff), it will suffice to note that when, in 1996, I published a monograph dealing with the events of the civil war in Siberia, it included a 67-page bibliography of works in many languages that was considered by reviewers to be admirably comprehensive. A book on the same subject published in Moscow in 2007 included a "brief guide" to only Russian-language literature on the same subject that ran to 136 pages. Startlingly, among the approximately 1,700 items it listed was barely a handful referenced in my book. Compare Jonathan D. Smele, *Civil War in Siberia: The Anti-Bolshevik Government of Admiral Kolchak, 1918–20*, Cambridge University Press, 1996, pp. 683–750 and A.V. Kvakin (ed.), *S Kolchakom—protiv Kolchaka*, Moscow: Agraf, 2007, pp. 310–446.

21. For example, on the Red Army: http://www.rkka.ru/index.htm; and on the Red Navy: http://www.rusnavy.ru/ussr.htm. On the Whites: http://www.whiterussia1.narod.ru/index.html; http://ricolor.org/history/bldv/; http://www.dk1868.ru/; and http://www.zaimka.ru/white/.

22. Extensive references to these sources are provided in the Bibliography to this volume, but a good place to start is http://www.hrono.ru/: an invaluable historical encyclopedia with particular focus on Russia. Useful online encyclopedias of Ukraine (http://www.encyclopediaofukraine.com/default.asp), Armenia (http://www.armenian-history.com/index.htm), and Transcaucasia (http://www.eng.kavkaz-uzel.ru/) are also available (all in English).

23. Evan Mawdsley noted that "The crucial point is whether the 'Revolution' and the 'Civil War' were two distinct things" before asserting, categorically, that "They were not" (Mawdsley, *The Russian Civil War*, p. 289). But earlier in his book, as we shall see, he had been at pains to define a precise starting point for the "civil war" on the morrow of the October Revolution.

24. The "Time of Troubles" was the term retrospectively applied to the turbulent period in Russian history of the late sixteenth and early seventeenth centuries (roughly from 1598 to 1613), from the death of the last Rurikid tsar, Feodor I, to the accession of the first Romanov tsar, Mikhail I. This was a plague-time, of pestilence, socio-moral anarchy, anomie, fire, foreign intervention, and religious doubt and apostasy.

25. At the Berlin congress, Russia had been forced by the other Powers to relinquish most of its hard-won advantages gained following the defeat of Turkey in the war of 1877–78, codified at the subsequent (aborted) Treaty of San Stefano (1878)—notably a large Bulgarian state (carved from the sultan's provinces), generally presumed to be a Russian client, that would have stretched to the Aegean and almost to the Adriatic. In 1908, Russia had been humiliated again, as the Austrians absorbed the chiefly Slavic province of Bosnia–Herzegovina, without the Russians receiving the privileges at Constantinople that they had hoped to accrue as compensation.

26. The "Eastern Question" was concerned, essentially, with what would become of the territories ruled by the Turkish sultan should the Ottoman Empire collapse—as, since, at the latest, its defeat in war against Russia in 1768–74, it seemed increasingly likely to do. Russia's prime concern was that, in the event of a division of the empire, it would gain suzerainty of Constantinople and would thereby have control of the strategically and (increasingly) economically important Straits separating the Black Sea from the Mediterranean, while at the same time promoting Russia's role as protector of the Orthodox subjects of the sultan that had been established at the Treaty of Küçük Kaynarca (Kuchuk Kainardzhi) in 1774.

27. The name of the first newspaper of the united Russian Social Democratic Labor Party (founded in 1898), which was to spawn the Bolsheviks, was *Iskra* ("The Spark," published from 1900). This was derived from a response by the Decembrist poet A.I. Odoevskii to Pushkin's own eulogy to the exiled revolutionaries: "From this spark will come a conflagration."

28. The word "intelligentsia" (from Latin, *intelligentia*) was first used in its modern, sociological sense in Russian and Polish in the first half of the nineteenth century.

29. On the history of Russia in the nineteenth century, see: David Saunders, *Russia in the Age of Modernization and Reform, 1801–1881*, London: Longman, 1992; Hans Rogger, *Russia in the Age of Modernization and Revolution, 1881–1917*, London: Longman, 1983; and Peter Waldron, *The End of Imperial Russia, 1855–1917*, Basingstoke: Macmillan, 1997. Also Jonathan D. Smele, *The Russian Revolution: From Tsarism to Bolshevism*, Frederick, MD:

The Modern Scholar/Recorded Books, 2009. Among many older studies of the period, notable for its generous coverage of the non-Russian peoples of the empire, is Edward C. Thaden, *Russia Since 1801: The Making of a New Society*, New York: Wiley-Interscience, 1971. More generally, see Roger Bartlett, *A History of Russia*, London: Palgrave, 2005.

30. Although perhaps more typical were the dreadful events of May 1896, when over 1,000 of the celebrants of Nicholas's ascent to the throne were crushed to death in a stampede on Khodynka field in Moscow and as many again injured. "Nicholas the Unlucky" might really have been a more fitting sobriquet, but that does not excuse the Tsar grossly insulting the victims by attending a ball on the evening of the Khodynka tragedy rather than visiting hospitals or offering prayers. See Helen Baker, "Monarchy Discredited? Reactions to the Khodynka Coronation Catastrophe of 1896," *Revolutionary Russia*, vol. 16, no. 1 (2003), pp. 1–46.

31. On Stolypin and the post-1905 peasant reforms, see: Abraham Ascher, *P.A. Stolypin: The Search for Stability in Late Imperial Russia*, Stanford University Press, 2001; Peter Waldron, *Between Two Revolutions: Stolypin and the Politics of Renewal in Russia*, London: UCL Press, 1998; and A.V. Zenkovsky, *Stolypin: Russia's Last Great Reformer*, Princeton, NJ: Kingston Press, 1986. Stolypin's aim, broadly speaking, was to replace the dominance of the village commune (*mir*) in the Russian countryside through fostering private ownership of land and a new class of conservatively minded peasant proprietors. He called it a "wager on the strong."

32. In 1907, around 212,000 heads of peasant household had applied for title to their lands; this rose to 650,000 in 1909, but then declined precipitously to 120,000 in 1914 and 36,000 in 1915: W.E. Mosse, "Stolypin's Villages," *Slavonic and East European Review*, vol. 43 (1965), p. 263. Many of those "separators" who left the commune were forced by their neighbors to rejoin it in 1917–18: Orlando Figes, "The Russian Peasant Community in the Agrarian Revolution, 1917–1918," in Roger Bartlett (ed.), *Land Commune and Peasant Community in Russia*, London: Macmillan, 1990, pp. 237–53.

33. On Rasputin and the royal couple, see the sometimes melodramatic but generally plausible account in Edvard Radzinsky, *Rasputin: The Last Word*, London: Weidenfeld & Nicolson, 2000.

34. We are enriched by two brilliant popular histories of this phenomenon: Peter Hopkirk, *On Secret Service East of Constantinople: The Plot to Bring Down the British Empire*, Oxford: Oxford University Press, 1995; and Sean McMeekin, *The Berlin–Baghdad Express: The Ottoman Empire and Germany's Bid for World Power, 1898–1918*, London: Allen Lane, 2010.

35. The seminal work here is Leopold H. Haimson, "The Problem of Social Stability in Urban Russia, 1905–1917," *Slavic Review*, vol. 23, no. 4 (1964), pp. 619–42; vol. 24, no. 1 (1965), pp. 1–22, which inspired a generation of historians and generated much commentary. For references, see Smele, *The Russian Revolution and Civil War*, pp. 99–100.

36. On the Duma period, see: Anna Geifman (ed.), *Russia under the Last Tsar: Opposition and Subversion, 1894–1917*, Oxford: Blackwell, 1999; Geoffrey Hosking, *The Russian Constitutional Experiment: Government and Duma, 1907–1914*, Cambridge University Press, 1973; and, especially, Robert B. McKean, *Between the Revolutions: Russia, 1905–1917*, London: The Historical Association, 1998.

37. A position known as "defensism." The exception was the handful of Bolshevik deputies who, to much public acclaim, were promptly tried as traitors and exiled to Siberia. On the impact of the war on socialist parties in Russia and across Europe, see the still invaluable: Merle Fainsod, *International Socialism and the War*, Cambridge, MA: Harvard University Press,

1935; Georges Haupt, *Socialism and the Great War: The Collapse of the Second International*, Oxford: Clarendon Press, 1972; and David Kirby, *War, Peace and Revolution: International Socialism at the Crossroads, 1914–1918*, Aldershot: Gower, 1986.

38. Nicholas and Alexandra and their four daughters and their son (the sickly, hemophiliac Alexei, heir to the throne), after more than a year of confinement and exile, were all executed by local Bolsheviks at Ekaterinburg during the night of 17–18 July 1918. The remains of the seven Romanovs were interred in the Cathedral of Peter and Paul in St Petersburg in 1998 (a group of five) and 2008 (the two others). The best recent account of these much-studied (and, until recently, gruesomely mysterious) events is Helen Rappaport, *Ekaterinburg: The Last Days of the Romanovs*, London: Windmill Books, 2009. See also Helen Slater, *The Many Deaths of Nicholas II: Relics, Remains and the Romanovs*, London: Routledge, 2007. On Nicholas, see Edvard Radzinsky, *The Last Tsar: The Life and Death of Nicholas II*, London: Hodder & Stoughton, 1992; and Dominic Lieven, *Nicholas II: Emperor of All the Russias*, London: Pimlico, 1994.

39. The classic account, in English, of Russia's military performance during the war is N.N. Golovine, *The Russian Army in the World War*, New Haven: Yale University Press, 1931, although it contains many errors and omissions. Very critical views of the subject can be found in Soviet works of the 1920s, though following the rise to power of Stalin such condemnations were tempered by Russian nationalism, especially during and after the Second World War. A thorough and effective historical reassessment of Russia's performance only really began, in the West, with Norman Stone, *The Eastern Front, 1914–17*, London: Hodder and Stoughton, 1975 and was continued in David R. Jones "Imperial Russia's Forces at War," in Allan R. Millett and Williamson Murray (eds), *Military Effectiveness, Vol. 1: The First World War*, Boston: Allen and Unwin, 1988, pp. 249–329, the latter condensed as David R. Jones, "The Imperial Army in World War I," in Frederick W. Kagan and Robin Higham (eds), *The Military History of Tsarist Russia*, London: Palgrave, 2002, pp. 227–48. See also Nik Cornish, *The Russian Army and the First World War*, Stroud: Spellmount, 2006. On issues of supply, see Keith Neilson, *Strategy and Supply: The Anglo-Russian Alliance, 1914–1917*, London: Allen and Unwin, 1984; and on economic mobilization see also Lewis H. Siegelbaum, *The Politics of Industrial Mobilization in Russia, 1914–1917: A Study of the War-Industries Committees*, London: Macmillan, 1983. On Russia's greatest success of the war, see Timothy C. Dowling, *The Brusilov Offensive*, Bloomington: Indiana University Press, 2009. Essential background is also supplied in William C. Fuller Jr, *Civil–Military Conflict in Imperial Russia, 1881–1914*, Princeton, NJ: Princeton University Press, 1985. Post-Soviet Russian historiography has yet to find its feet on this subject, but a sample of its best practitioners can be found in O.R. Airapetov (ed.), *Posledniaia voina imperatorskoi Rossii. Sbornik statei*, Moscow: Tri Kvadrata, 2002 and N.N. Smirnov *et al.* (eds), *Rossiia i pervaia mirovaia voina*, St Petersburg: D. Bulanin, 1999. The Eastern Front is also particularly well served in two recent general surveys in English: Hew Strachan, *The First World War*, New York: Viking, 2004; and Norman Stone, *World War One: A Short History*, London: Allen Lane, 2007.

40. McKean, *Between the Revolutions, passim*.

41. This point was brilliantly expanded upon in Peter Gatrell, *A Whole Empire Walking: Refugees in Russia during World War I*, Bloomington: Indiana University Press, 1999.

42. See Matitiahu Mayzel, *Generals and Revolutionaries: The Russian General Staff during the*

Revolution—A Study in the Transformation of a Military Elite, Osnabrück: Biblio-Verlag, 1979.

43. See also Roger Pethybridge, *The Spread of the Russian Revolution*, London: Macmillan/St Martin's Press, 1972, pp. 1–56 (Chapter One, "The Railways").

44. As one recent commentator has it, "Swords were ploughed into shares": Wood, *The Romanov Empire*, p. 351.

45. It is interesting that Nicholas earned no discernable credit for the Russian Army's very respectable performance in 1916. Not that Nicholas deserved it—his chief of staff, later the civilwar commander of the White forces in South Russia, General M.V. Alekseev, was responsible for all significant strategic decisions—but, as tsar, he might justifiably have expected it. It is worth remembering also, though, that Nicholas's decision to assume the command was not as wrong-headed as has often been assumed. As David Jones noted, if the incumbent commander, Grand Duke Nikolai Nikolaevich (the Tsar's first cousin, once removed), was to be replaced, family protocol dictated that his successor could only be a Romanov of equal or higher standing. The field of candidates there was populated sparsely and the Tsar's sense of duty, for which he deserves some credit, dictated that he put himself forward. See David R. Jones, "Nicholas II and the Supreme Command: An Investigation of Motives," *Study Group on the Russian Revolution: Sbornik*, no. 11 (1985), pp. 47–83. On socio-economic conditions in Russia during the war, see: Peter Gatrell, *Russia's First World War: A Social and Economic History*, London: Longman, 2005; and W. Bruce Lincoln, *Passage through Armageddon: The Russians in War and Revolution*, New York: Simon and Schuster, 1986. The twelve volumes published from 1928 to 1932 in the Yale University Press "Russian Series of the Economic and Social History of the War" are now period pieces, but are seeded with gems. See also R.W. Davies (ed.), *From Tsarism to the New Economic Policy: Continuity and Change in the Economy of the USSR*, London: Macmillan, 1990.

46. The purpose and nature of Miliukov's rabble-rousing and perhaps epoch-changing address is analyzed in Thomas M. Bohn, "'Dumheit oder Verrat'—Gab Miljukow am 1. November 1916 das 'Sturmsignal' zur Oktoberrevolution?" *Jahrbücher für Geschichte Osteuropas*, vol. 41, no. 93 (1993), pp. 361–93. The Kadets (members of the Constitutional Democratic Party) are usually described as "liberals"—not least in the title of the best Western study of them (William G. Rosenberg, *Liberals in the Russian Revolution: The Constitutional Democratic Party, 1917–1921*, Princeton University Press, 1974)—but were more radical than any West European liberal party, having, for example, a commitment to the compulsory purchase by the state of private land (for redistribution to the peasantry) at the heart of their party program. See Ingeborg Fleishchhauer, "The Agrarian Program of the Russian Constitutional Democrats," *Cahiers du Monde Russe et Soviétique*, vol. 20, no. 2 (1920), pp. 173–201. Even the more sensible of Soviet historians routinely characterized them as a counter-revolutionary "bourgeois" party—see N.G. Dumova, *Kadetskaia kontrrevoliutsiia i ee razgrom*, Moscow: Nauka, 1982—which they were not (they drew membership and support chiefly from the professions, especially the Law and academia), although in 1917 they certainly moved toward the Right.

47. Guchkov (who became war minister in the first Provisional Government of 1917) seems to have intended to establish a regency, with the invalid teenage Tsarevich, Aleksei Nikolaevich (born in 1904), as a puppet emperor, perhaps preceded by a provisional military dictatorship. On Guchkov's plans, see: William E. Gleason, *Alexander Guchkov and the End of the Russian Empire*, Philadelphia: The American Philosophical Society, 1983; S.P. Mel'gunov,

Na putiak k dvorstovomu perevorotu. Zagovory pered revoliutsiei 1917 goda, Paris: Knizhnoe delo "Rodnik," 1931; and, especially, Semion Lyandres, *The Fall of Tsarism: Untold Stories of the February 1917 Revolution*, Oxford: Oxford University Press, 2013, pp. 269–90. Also of interest is: James D. White, "Lenin, the Germans and the February Revolution," *Revolutionary Russia*, vol. 5, no. 1 (1992), pp. 1–22.

48. This forms one of the more sensible arguments promoted in the otherwise intriguingly eccentric George Katkov, *Russia, 1917: The February Revolution*, London: Longmans, Green & Co., 1967.

49. See: Sir Peter Bark, "The Last Days of the Russian Monarchy: Nicholas II at Army Headquarters," *Russian Review*, vol. 16, no. 3 (1957), pp. 35–44; Nicolas de Basily, *Diplomat of Imperial Russia, 1903–1917*, Stanford: Hoover Institution Press, 1973; and General G. Danilov, "How the Tsar Abdicated," *The Living Age*, no. 336 (Apr. 1929), pp. 99–104.

50. The best survey of the February Revolution is Tsuyoshi Hasegawa, *The February Revolution: Petrograd 1917*, Seattle: University of Washington Press, 1981. But see also, for contrast, E.N. Burdzhalov, *Russia's Second Revolution: The February 1917 Uprising in Petrograd*, Bloomington: Indiana University Press, 1987. Also recommended, for a sample of late-Soviet and post-Soviet Russian views are: V.S. Diakin, "The Leadership Crisis in Russia on the Eve of the February Revolution," *Soviet Studies in History*, vol. 23, no. 1 (1984–85), pp. 10–38; and O.R. Airapetov, *Generaly, liberaly i predprinimateli. Rabota na front i na revoliutsiiu (1907–1917)*, Moscow: Modest Kolerov, 2003.

1. 1916–18: THE BEGINNINGS OF THE "RUSSIAN" CIVIL WARS

1. Edward D. Sokol, *The Revolt of 1916 in Russian Central Asia*, Baltimore: Johns Hopkins University Press, 1954, p. 13.

2. To reinforce the foregrounding of imperial concerns in the civil wars, it might be worth recalling here that, according to one credible version, the "Whites" of the civil-war era took their name from Skobelev, a national hero who was known as the "White General" on account of the white dress uniform he insisted on wearing into battle, while mounted on a white charger.

3. Andreas Kappeler, *The Russian Empire: A Multi-Ethnic History*, Harlow: Pearson, 2001, pp. 190–200.

4. Daniel Brower, *Turkestan and the Fate of the Russian Empire*, London: Routledge Curzon, 2002, p. 152.

5. "Ukaz rossiiskogo imperatora Nikolaia II 'O privlechenii muzhskogo inorodcheskogo naseleniia imperii dlia robot po ustroistvu oboronitel'nykh sooruzhenii i voennykh soobshchenii v raione deistvuiushchei armii, a ravno dlia vsiakikh inykh neobkhodimkh dlia gosudarstvennoi oborony rabot'," in A.R. Sadykov and A. Bermakhanov (eds), *Groznyi 1916-i god: Sbornik dokumentov i materialov*, Almaty: Qazaqstan, 1998, vol. 1, p. 13; "Vosstanie v 1916 g. v Srednei Azii," *Krasnyi arkhiv*, vol. 3 (1929), p. 48.

6. Kuropatkin was named at the same time as Ataman of the Semirech'e Cossack Host.

7. Kappeler, *The Russian Empire*, p. 352.

8. "Dzhizakskoe vosstanie v 1916 g.," *Krasnyi arkhiv*, vol. 5 (1933), p. 63.

9. "Vosstanie v 1916 g. v Srednei Azii," p. 90.

10. Kh.T. Tursunov, *Vosstanie 1916 goda v Srednei Azii i Kazakhstane*, Tashkent: Gos. izd-vo Uzbekskoi SSR, 1962, pp. 320–21; Sokol, *The Revolt of 1916 in Russian Central Asia*, p. 159.

See also A.V. Ganin, "Posledniaia poludennaia ekspeditsiia Imperarorskoi Rossii: Russkaia armiia na podavlenii turkestanskogo miatezha, 1916–1917 gg.," in O.R. Airapetov *et al.* (eds), *Russkii sbornik: Issledovaniia po istorii Rossii XIX–XX vv.*, Moscow: Modest Kolerov, 2008, pp. 152–214.

11. Paul Nazaroff, *Hunted through Central Asia*, Edinburgh: Blackwood, 1932, pp. 166–7.

12. For a brief summary, see Abraham Ascher, "Introduction," in Jonathan D. Smele and Anthony Heywood (eds), *The Russian Revolution of 1905: Centenary Perspectives*, London: Routledge, 2005, pp. 2–3.

13. See: David Longley, "Iakovlev's Question, Or the Historiography of the Problem of Spontaneity and Leadership in the Russian Revolution of 1917," in Edith Rogovin Frankel, Jonathan Frankel, and Baruch Knei-Paz (eds), *Revolution in Russia: Reassessments of 1917*, Cambridge: Cambridge University Press, 1992, pp. 365–87; Michael Melancon, "Rethinking Russia's February Revolution: Anonymous Spontaneity or Socialist Agency?" (Carl Beck Papers in Russian and East European Studies, no. 1,408), Pittsburgh: Center for Russian and East European Studies, University of Pittsburgh, 2000. Also Boris Elkin, "The Doom of the Russian Monarchy," *Slavonic and East European Review*, vol. 47 (1969), pp. 514–24.

14. This conception of February as the first stage of the civil wars is in line with the argument presented in Iu.A. Poliakov, "Grazhdanskaia voina v Rossii: vozniknovenie i eskalatsiia," *Otechestvennaia istoriia*, no. 6 (1992), pp. 33–5. Poliakov notes that V.I. Lenin too held this belief.

15. It might be pertinent, while waxing theatrical, to note here that the most resonant images of 1917 that have been retained in the popular mind, of armored-car-borne Bolsheviks storming the Winter Palace in October, were not derived from documentary films or photographs of real events (which took place in the dark, with no cameras present), but from staged reconstructions of later years, most of them drawn from Sergei Eisenstein's stunning film *Oktiabr'* (1927). On the other hand, perhaps the second-most familiar image, of corpses and injured people strewn across the streets of Petrograd (specifically, the crossroads of Nevskii Prospekt and Sadovaia Ulitsa), as other crouching figures scatter, is a photographic record of a real event. However, it was taken (by Viktor Bulla) not during the October Revolution that it is routinely displayed to illustrate—in TV documentaries and in books—but at 2.00 p.m. on 4 July 1917, during the July Days: David King, *Red Star over Russia: A Visual History of the Soviet Union from 1917 to the Death of Stalin*, London: Tate Publishing, 2009, pp. 32–3. The importance of symbolism in 1917 and the theatricality of February have been extensively explored by the Russian historian Boris Kolonitskii. See, especially: Orlando Figes and Boris Kolonitskii, *Interpreting the Russian Revolution: The Language and Symbols of 1917*, New Haven: Yale University Press, 1999; Boris Kolonitskii, "Fevral'skaia revolutsiia kak simbolicheskii perevorot: Otrazenie v russkoi onomastike," *Russian Studies: Ezhekvartal'nik Russkoi Filologii i Kultury*, vol. 3, no. 3 (2000), pp. 92–101; and B.I. Kolonitskii, *Simboly vlasti i bor'ba za vlast': k izucheniiu polititicheskoi kultura rossiiskoi revoliutsii 1917 goda*, St Petersburg: Liki Rossii, 2012.

16. It would be inappropriate here to provide full references to the many acres of printed sources available on the events of 1917. For that, the reader is directed to Jonathan D. Smele (comp., ed., annot.), *The Russian Revolution and Civil War, 1917–1921: An Annotated Bibliography*, London: Continuum, 2003, and to two indispensable works of reference on the period: Edward Acton, Vladimir Iu. Chernaiev, and William G. Rosenberg (eds), *Critical Companion to the Russian Revolution, 1914–1921*, London: Edward Arnold, 1997; and Harold

Shukman, *The Blackwell Encyclopedia of the Russian Revolution*, Oxford: Blackwell, 1988. Excellent bibliographical and historiographical guides are also offered by the contributors to Robert Service (ed.), *Society and Politics in the Russian Revolution*, London: Macmillan, 1992. Regarding surveys of the period, although the first volume of William H. Chamberlin, *The Russian Revolution, 1917–1921*, London: Macmillan, 1935 is the fullest, and remains valuable, it has unavoidably dated. The best recent contributions are: Christopher Read, *From Tsar to Soviets: The Russian People and their Revolution, 1917–1921*, London: Routledge, 1996; and Rex A. Wade, *The Russian Revolution, 1917*, Cambridge: Cambridge University Press, 2000. A stimulating introduction to the historiography of 1917 is provided in Edward Acton, *Rethinking the Russian Revolution*, London: Edward Arnold, 1990, although regarding Soviet works this needs to be supplemented with the richly stimulating observations in: James D. White, *The Russian Revolution, 1917–1921: A Short History*, London: Edward Arnold, 1994; and James D. White "Early Soviet Historical Interpretations of the Russian Revolution, 1918–24," *Soviet Studies*, vol. 37, no. 3 (1985), pp. 330–52. For those interested in exploring the historiographical debates on 1917 that were inspired by the rise of a "revisionist" (generally radical) school, countered by a "triumphalist" (generally conservative) school, the following are key: John E. Marot, "Class Conflict, Political Competition and Social Transformation: Critical Perspectives on the Social History of the Russian Revolution," *Revolutionary Russia*, vol. 7, no. 2 (1994), pp. 111–63; John E. Marot, "A 'Postmodern' Approach to the Russian Revolution: A Comment on Suny," *Russian Review*, vol. 54, no. 2 (1995), pp. 260–64. Steve Smith; "Writing the History of the Russian Revolution after the Fall of Communism," *Europe–Asia Studies*, vol. 46, no. 4 (1994), pp. 563–78; Ronald G. Suny, "Toward a Social History of the October Revolution," *American Historical Review*, vol. 88, no. 1 (1983), pp. 31–52; and Ronald G. Suny, "Revision and Retreat in the Historiography of 1917: Social History and its Critics," *Russian Review*, vol. 53, no. 2 (1994), pp. 165–82. The chief target of the revisionists, Harvard professor and member of Ronald Reagan's National Security Council, Richard Pipes, did not deign to respond directly to them in his *magnum opus* on the period: Richard Pipes, *The Russian Revolution, 1899–1919*, London: Collins Harvill, 1990. But see Richard Pipes, "1917 and the Revisionists," *The National Interest*, no. 31 (Spring 1993), pp. 68–79; and Richard Pipes, *VIXI: Memoirs of a Non-Believer*, New Haven: Yale University Press, 2003 (especially pp. 107–12, 212–16, and 234–41). The most recent extended analysis is Rex A. Wade, "The Revolution at Ninety-(One): Anglo-American Historiography of the Russian Revolution of 1917," *Journal of Modern Russian History and Historiography*, vol. 1 (2008), pp. 1–42.

17. Devastated by this development, both Miliukov, the Kadet leader, and Guchkov, leader of the Octobrists, were immediately moved to resign from their posts as (respectively) foreign minister and war minister in the Provisional Government, but were persuaded to think again.

18. See Lionel Kochan, "Kadet Policy in 1917 and the Constituent Assembly," *Slavonic and East European Review*, vol. 45 (1967), pp. 183–93; and Thomas Riha, "1917—A Year of Illusions," *Soviet Studies*, vol. 19, no. 1 (1967), pp. 115–22.

19. Victor Chernov, *The Great Russian Revolution*, New York: Russell & Russell, 1966, pp. 233–64.

20. On the three parties of the coalition see: William G. Rosenberg, *Liberals in the Russian Revolution: The Constitutional Democratic Party, 1917–1921*, Princeton: Princeton University Press, 1974; John D. Basil, *The Mensheviks in the Revolution of 1917*, Columbus, OH: Slavica Publishers, 1984; and Oliver H. Radkey, *The Agrarian Foes of Bolshevism: Promise and Default*

of the Russian Socialist-Revolutionaries, February–October 1917, New York: Columbia University Press, 1958.

21. Louise E. Heenan, *Russian Democracy's Fatal Blunder: The Summer Offensive of 1917*, New York: Praeger, 1987.

22. Robert P. Browder and Alexander F. Kerensky (eds), *The Russian Provisional Government, 1917: Documents*, Stanford: Stanford University Press, 1961, vol. 3, pp. 1,735–42. Otherwise, Verkhovskii warned quite perceptively, the Bolsheviks would seize power within five days.

23. The Kadets knew that talk of peace among the soldiery, no matter how much it was buttressed by mentions of "revolutionary defensism," would sap morale and engender instead insipient defeatism. The latter was non-partisan, but was encouraged by the Bolsheviks (following Lenin's advocacy, since September 1914, of transforming the world war into an "international civil war") and as such was termed "trench Bolshevism" by the foremost historian of the Russian rank and file: Allan K. Wildman, *The End of the Russian Imperial Army*, 2 vols, Princeton: Princeton University Press, 1980/7.

24. On foreign policy issues in 1917, see Rex A. Wade, *The Russian Search for Peace, February–October 1917*, Stanford: Stanford University Press, 1969; and Rex A. Wade, "Argonauts of Peace: The Soviet Delegation to Western Europe in the Summer of 1917," *Slavic Review*, vol. 26, no. 3 (1967), pp. 453–67.

25. On the various right-wing conspiratorial groups' auditioning of candidate dictators in 1917, see James D. White, "The Kornilov Affair—A Study in Counter-Revolution," *Soviet Studies*, vol. 20, no. 2 (1968), pp. 187–205.

26. P.N. Miliukov, *The Russian Revolution*, vol. 1, Gulf Breeze, FL: Academic International Press, 1978, p. 202.

27. See Semion Lyandres, *The Bolsheviks' "German Gold" Revisited: An Inquiry into the 1917 Accusations*, Pittsburgh: University of Pittsburgh Press, 1995. Documents of the Provisional Government's investigations into the affair are now available as O.K. Ivantsova (ed.), *Sledstvennoe delo bol'shevikov: Materialy Predvaritel'nogo sledstviia o vooruzhenom vystuplenii 3–5 iiulia 1917 g. v g. Petrograde protiv gosudarstvennoe vlasti. Iiul'–oktiabr 1917g. Sbornik dokumentov v 2 knigakh*, Moscow: ROSSPEN, 2012.

28. For a balanced assessment of the issues and a good bibliography see Jorgen L. Munck, *The Kornilov Revolt: A Critical Examination of the Sources*, Aarhus: Aarhus University Press, 1987.

29. The most assured analysis of the background to the civil wars opens with a chapter on the August events entitled "The Failed White Counter-Revolution": see Geoffrey Swain, *The Origins of the Russian Civil War*, London: Longman, 1996, pp. 14–40.

30. Richard Abraham, *Alexander Kerensky: The First Love of the Revolution*, London: Sidgwick and Jackson, 1987.

31. Indeed, in 1918 the pejorative term "Kerenskyism" (*kerenshchina*) would come to denote the politics of indecisiveness and phrase mongering that the civil-war Right identified as the curse of 1917 and which they feared was—Hydra-like—raising its head again in the course of the so-called democratic counter-revolution, as SR-dominated authorities sought to establish themselves along the Volga, in Siberia, and in North Russia. On Kerensky's post-1917 travails, see Jonathan D. Smele, "'*Mania Grandiosa*' and 'The Turning Point in World History': Kerensky in London in 1918," *Revolutionary Russia*, vol. 20, no. 1 (2007), pp. 1–34.

32. A.F. Kerensky, *The Prelude to Bolshevism: The Kornilov Rebellion*, London: T. Fisher Unwin, 1919.

33. Although the breadth of the differences between Bolsheviks and Mensheviks has been long exaggerated in both Soviet and Western historiography, fed by the latter absorbing myths propagated by the former and by a misreading of much of Lenin's seminal work on party organization. On that matter, see Lars T. Lih, *Lenin Rediscovered: "What is to be Done?" in Context*, Boston: Brill, 2005.

34. "April Theses," in V.I. Lenin, *Collected Works* (hereafter Lenin, *CW*), vol. 24, Moscow: Progress Publishers, 1960–78, pp. 19–26.

35. N.N. Sukhanov, *The Russian Revolution, 1917: A Personal Record*, London: Oxford University Press, 1955, pp. 281–5.

36. Given the number of professional army officers who, from late 1917, would offer or grant their services to the Red Army, either as committed Bolsheviks or, more commonly, as "military specialists" (see below, pp. 80–3), it is doubtful they ever were. Equally, most Mensheviks, during the later fighting, would display a benevolent neutrality toward the Soviet government, although some would join the anti-Bolsheviks. To further blur the lines, it might be pointed out that very notable among the latter was Ivan Maiskii, who before and during the Second World War would nevertheless serve as ambassador to London of the USSR.

37. See, especially, Robert Service, *The Bolshevik Party in Revolution: A Study in Organizational Change, 1917–1923*, London: Macmillan, 1979, pp. 37–62. The *vox populi*, for English-speaking readers, is best heard through Mark D. Steinberg (ed.), *Voices of Revolution, 1917*, New Haven: Yale University Press, 2001.

38. See Alexander Rabinowitch, *Prelude to Revolution: The Petrograd Bolsheviks and the July 1917 Uprising*, Bloomington: Indiana University Press, 1968.

39. See "On Slogans," in Lenin, *CW*, vol. 25, pp. 185–92.

40. It is not generally understood that soviets (literally "councils") had originally been conceived of in Russia, during the 1905 Revolution, as strike committees—something a long way from revolutionary staffs and even further from instruments of government. See Oskar Anweiler, *The Soviets: The Russian Workers, Peasants and Soldiers Councils, 1905–1921*, New York: Pantheon Books, 1974. Lenin's reconfiguration of their purpose in 1917 was one of his greatest achievements, but that reconfiguration could not be completed for as long as "compromisers" (SRs and Mensheviks) dominated the soviets.

41. See "The Bolsheviks Must Assume Power" and "Marxism and Insurrection," in Lenin, *CW*, vol. 26, pp. 19–21, 22–7 (emphasis in original).

42. See Central Committee minutes of 10 and 16 Oct. 1917 in *The Bolsheviks and the October Revolution: Central Committee Minutes of the Russian Social-Democratic Labour Party (Bolsheviks), August 1917–February 1918*, London: Pluto Press, 1974, pp. 85–95 and 95–110; and "Letter to Central Committee Members," in Lenin, *CW*, vol. 26, pp. 234–5.

43. Since the Bolshevik–Menshevik schism, Trotsky had sought to encourage a reunion of the factions, most recently as a leader of the Inter-District Group of the RSDLP (the Mezhraionka), but in July–August 1917, chiefly as a consequence of despairing of the Mensheviks' attitude to the war, had joined the Bolsheviks (along with most of the other members of the Mezhraionka). Such was the number of leading members of the Mezhraionka that were prominent in subsequent events (including V.A. Antonov-Ovseenko, A.A. Ioffe, L.M. Karakhan, A.V. Lunacharskii, and Moisei Uritskii) that it might almost be conjec-

tured—as it was by White, *Lenin*, p. 148—that the October Revolution might better be regarded as a triumph of the Inter-District Group more than of the Bolsheviks, but the most thorough examination of the organization's history to date refutes this. See Ian D. Thatcher, "The St Petersburg/Petrograd Mezhraionka, 1913–1917: The Rise and Fall of a Russian Social Democratic Workers' Party Unity Faction," *Slavonic and East European Review*, vol. 87, no. 2 (2009), pp. 319–20.

44. The classic discussion of the October Revolution in English remains Alexander Rabinowitch, *The Bolsheviks Come to Power: The Revolution of 1917 in Petrograd*, New York: W.W. Norton, 1976. See also James D. White, "Lenin, Trotsky and the Art of Insurrection: The Congress of Soviets of the Northern Region, 11–13 October 1917," *Slavonic and East European Review*, vol. 77, no. 1 (1999), pp. 117–39.

45. Swain, *Origins of the Russian Civil War*, p. 69. It has led another commentator to go further and portray Lenin's actions as the opening salvos of a civil war launched by the Bolshevik leader within the international socialist movement, in order to secure Bolshevik dominance of it, ahead of the majority German social democrats and their defensist allies: see Piero Melograni, *Lenin and the Myth of World Revolution: Ideology and Reasons of State*, Atlantic Highlands: Humanities Press International, 1989.

46. Swain, *Origins of the Russian Civil War*, pp. 63, 69. See also Geoffrey Swain, "Before the Fighting Started: A Discussion of 'The Third Way'," *Revolutionary Russia*, vol. 4, no. 2 (1991), pp. 210–34.

47. See Jonathan Daly and Leonid Trofimov (eds), *Russia in War and Revolution, 1914–1922: A Documentary History*, Indianapolis: Hackett, 2009, p. xix.

48. "War After the War: Conflicts, 1919–23," in John Horne (ed.), *A Companion to World War I*, Oxford: Wiley-Blackwell, 2010, p. 560.

49. Rex A. Wade, "The October Revolution, the Constituent Assembly, and the End of the Russian Revolution," in Ian D. Thatcher (ed.), *Reinterpreting Revolutionary Russia: Essays in Honour of James D. White*, Basingstoke: Palgrave, 2006, pp. 72–85.

50. The Bolsheviks also alleged (with some reason) that the elections to the Assembly were undemocratic, as party lists had been drawn up before the Party of Left Socialists-Revolutionaries had split from the SR mainstream, thereby denying voters a choice between candidates in favor of Soviet power (the Left-SRs) and those who opposed it (the PSR). See "Theses on the Constituent Assembly," and "Declaration of the Rights of Working and Exploited People," in Lenin, *CW*, vol. 26, pp. 379–83, 423–25; and *Dekrety Sovetskoi vlasti, Tom I: 25 Oktiabria 1917 g.—16 mart 1918 g.*, Moscow: Gosizdat, 1957, pp. 329–37.

51. Wade, "The October Revolution," p. 74.

52. Ibid., pp. 82–4.

53. Or that Bolshevik authoritarianism evolved over 1917–18 in an accidental and ad hoc manner, as a consequence of the civil-war emergency, which is the thrust of Alexander Rabinowitch, *The Bolsheviks in Power: The First Year of Soviet Rule in Petrograd*, Bloomington: Indiana University Press, 2007.

54. But see below, pp. 58–60, 151–7, 164–6.

55. Although the outbreak of the Soviet–Ukrainian War might be dated to the attempted Bolshevik coup at Kiev on 29 Nov. 1917 and serious fighting between the two sides continued throughout Dec. of that year, it was only in its Fourth Universal, of 9 Jan. 1918, that the Ukrainian Central Rada declared independence from Russia. In its Third Universal, of 20 Nov. 1917, the Rada had continued to aspire to a federation. For all four Universals of

the Rada, see: Taras Hunczak (ed.), *The Ukraine, 1917–1921: A Study in Revolution*, Cambridge, MA: Harvard University Press, 1977, pp. 382–95.

56. On 26 Mar. 1918, at Tiflis, the Transcaucasian Commissariat (a heritage of the pre-October days) ceded power to the Transcaucasian Sejm, which on 9 Apr. 1918 would proclaim the independent Transcaucasian Democratic Federative Republic. This all post-dated the dispersal of the Constituent Assembly. But it post-dated that event by several weeks and could be argued to be more directly a consequence of the Treaty of Brest-Litovsk and the impending seizure of most of Transcaucasia by the Turks.

57. See "On the History of the Question of the Unfortunate Peace (Theses on the Question of the Conclusion of a Separate and Annexationist Peace)," in Lenin, *CW*, vol. 26, pp. 442–50. Lenin's twenty-one theses were written on 7 Jan. 1918 (a twenty-second being added on 21 Jan. 1918).

58. Members of the Constituent Assembly who wrote important and very influential histories of the Russian Revolution, while subsequently in emigration, included V.M. Chernov (who was its chairman), A.F. Kerensky, and P.N. Miliukov.

59. Aleksandr Blok, "Twelve," in a new translation by Maria Carlson: http://russiasgreatwar. org/docs/twelve_notes.pdf

60. It was originally the influential novelist, poet, and historian N.M. Karamzin (1766–1826) who had thus labelled St Petersburg (a neo-classical European city built on a Russian swamp), but the city's exceptional nature became a constant trope in the long nineteenth century of Russian literature, from Pushkin's *Bronze Horseman* (1833) to Andrei Bely's *Petersburg* (1916).

61. Oliver Radkey, *Russia Goes to the Polls: The Election to the All-Russian Constituent Assembly, 1917*, Ithaca, NY: Cornell University Press, 1989, pp. 148–51. On the Petrograd and other rear garrisons, see Mikhail Frenkin, *Zakhvat vlasti Bol'shevikami v Rossii i rol' tylovykh garizonov armii: podgotovka i provedenie oktiabr'skogo miatezha 1917–1918 gg.*, Jerusalem: Stav, 1982.

62. Orlando Figes, *A People's Tragedy: The Russian Revolution 1891–1924*, London: Pimlico, 1997, pp. 518–19. A recent study has concluded that even in areas where peasants voted en masse (indeed, en bloc) for the PSR and expressed deep trust in what they routinely referred to as "the *muzhiks'* party," they had no substantial interest in party policy. See Sarah Badcock, "'We're for the *Muzhiks'* Party!' Peasant Support for the Socialist Revolutionary Party during 1917," *Europe–Asia Studies*, vol. 53, no. 1 (2001), pp. 133–49.

63. Even when the Assembly delegates went "to the peasants," attempting to plant a Committee of Members of the Constituent Assembly in the SR heartland of Samara in June 1918, the harvest was feeble, particularly with regard to persuading peasants to join their anti-Bolshevik People's Army. See below. Also Scott Smith, "The Socialists-Revolutionaries and the Dilemma of Civil War," in Vladimir N. Brovkin (ed.), *The Bolsheviks in Russian Society: The Revolution and Civil Wars*, New Haven: Yale University Press, 1997, pp. 83–104.

64. That the Cossacks then fled south to attend to local concerns on the Don does, however, prefigure the various Cossacks hosts' prioritizing of local concerns over national ones that in 1918 would lead them into partnership with the Germans and in 1919 was to bedevil the efforts of their White allies to reconstruct a "Russia, One and Indivisible." Perhaps, in retrospect, the most revealing aspect of the Kerensky–Krasnov affair was the manner in which some officers' detestation for the fallen premier was so profound that they were even prepared to assist the Red Guards in defending Petrograd against Krasnov's Cossacks. See David

R. Jones, "The Officers and the October Revolution," *Soviet Studies*, vol. 28, no. 2 (1976), pp. 207–23. Observing the actions of one Colonel Walden in this regard, Trotsky noted that "he harbored such a strong hatred for Kerensky that this inspired in him a temporary sympathy for us": L.D. Trotskii, *Sochinenii*, Moscow: Gosizdat, 1925–27, vol. 2, p. 100.

65. Perhaps the most reviled of the anti-Bolshevik leaders of the Russian Civil Wars and the epitome of the *atamanshchina* (warlordism) that plagued the White cause, G.M. Semenov was born at the Transbaikal Cossack settlement of Duruguevskaia *stanitsa* to a Cossack father and a Russian mother. After graduation from the Orenburg Military School (1911), he served with the 1st Nerchinsk Regiment of the Transbaikal Cossacks in the First World War, under the command of P.N. Wrangel (1914–16). In 1917, after sending a personal appeal to A.F. Kerensky, he led a mission to raise volunteer units for the Russian Army from the Buriat and Cossack population of Transbaikalia. The October Revolution found Semenov still in Transbaikalia, at Berezovka stanitsa, where he formed a Buriat-Mongol–Cossack partisan detachment to challenge Red Guards in the area, thereby initiating the civil war in the Russian Far East. After suffering defeat, on 2 Dec. 1917 he retreated with his men into Manchuria, where he reformed and re-equipped his forces, now termed the Special Manchurian Detachment, for a new raid into Transbaikalia, launched on 29 Jan. 1918. After initial success, and the capture of Dauria, he was again repulsed by the Red forces of S.G. Lazo and forced back into Manchuria, setting up camp at Manzhouli (Manchuria) Station. Another advance on Chita was repulsed in Apr.–May 1918. Following the collapse of Soviet power east of Lake Baikal, Semenov's detachment (by now having received financial aid from Britain and France) re-entered Russian territory, capturing Verkhneudinsk (20 Aug. 1918) and Chita (26 Aug. 1918). He made the latter his base and established a personal fiefdom in Transbaikalia, benefiting from his stranglehold on the Trans-Siberian and Chinese Eastern Railroads and the covert support of the Japanese interventionist forces in the region, who were keen to sow seeds of disunity among the Whites. In June 1919, he was elected Host Ataman of the Transbaikal Cossacks, his enemies said illegally.

66. *Dekrety Sovetskoi vlasti, Tom I*, pp. 154–6.

67. Evan Mawdsley, *The Russian Civil War*, Boston: Allen & Unwin, 1987, p. 4.

68. The arrest and experience of Kornilov and the twenty-one other military leaders detained at Mogilev and subsequently incarcerated at Bykhov is captured in the memoirs of the secretary of the Officers' Union, who was among them: S.N. Riasianskii, "Bykhovskie uzniki," in G.N. Sevost'ianov *et al.* (eds), *Delo L.G. Kornilova: materialy Chrezvychainoi komissii po rassledovaniiu dela o byvshem Verkhovnom glavnokomanduiushchem generale L.G. Kornilove i ego souchastnikakh. Avgust 1917 g.—iiun 1918 g.*, Moscow: Demokratiia, 2003, vol. 1, pp. 406–32. See also A.S. Lukomskii, *Vospominaniia*, Berlin: Otto Kirkhner, 1922, vol. 1, pp. 258–73.

69. Peter Kenez, *Civil War in South Russia, 1918: The First Year of the Volunteer Army*, Berkeley: University of California Press, 1971, pp. 55–8. John Bradley (*Civil War in Russia, 1917–1920*, London: B.T. Batsford, 1975, p. 39) concurs with Wade that "Only after all the conventional methods of disputing power with the Bolsheviks had failed them did their opponents have recourse to the ultimate means, civil war," but in the same paragraph describes the Alekseev Organization as indicating that the generals had earlier "decided on civil war."

70. "The Russian Revolution and Civil War," in Lenin, *CW*, vol. 26, p. 29. As is all too often the case with Lenin, conclusions drawn here have to be tempered with the fact that, in his report to the Third All-Russian Congress of Soviets in January 1918, the Bolshevik leader later took

credit for the *Bolsheviks* having "started" the civil war: "[O]ur reply to all these charges of instigating civil war is: yes, we have openly proclaimed what no other government has been able to proclaim. The first government in the world that can speak openly of civil war is the government of the workers, peasants and soldiers. Yes, we have started and we are waging civil war against the exploiters." See Lenin, *CW*, vol. 26, pp. 461–2. Still, irrespective of "who started it," it is incontrovertible that, in the words of Israel Getzler, "Civil war is what Lenin wanted and civil war is what he got." See Israel Getzler, "Lenin's Conception of Revolution as Civil War," *Slavonic and East European Review*, vol. 74, no. 3 (1996), p. 465.

71. David R. Stone, "The Russian Civil Wars," in Robin Higham and Frederick W. Kagan (eds), *The Military History of the Soviet Union*, Basingstoke: Palgrave, 2002, pp. 13–33.

72. Vladimir N. Brovkin (ed.), *The Bolsheviks in Russian Society: The Revolution and the Civil Wars*, New Haven: Yale University Press, 1997.

73. Rex A. Wade, *The Bolshevik Revolution and Russian Civil War*, Westport, CT: Greenwood Press, 2001.

74. Following the Russo-Swedish (Finnish) War of Feb.–Sep. 1809, the Finnish lands were constituted as a grand principality, with its own parliament and constitution, ruled by the Russian tsar (as grand prince of Finland) but separate from the Russian Empire. This situation survived the creeping Russification of the late nineteenth century. After the Napoleonic Wars, Congress Poland (the Kingdom of Poland) was created at the Congress of Vienna, with similar guarantees of autonomy and a liberal constitution and was ruled by the Russian tsar as king of Poland. However, Polish autonomy was forcefully eroded by the Russians in the nineteenth century and Russification was intense. Finally, in 1867, after a series of earlier encroachments, Polish autonomy was altogether abrogated and even the name was wiped from the map, as Congress Poland was formally integrated into the Russian Empire as the Vistula Region (Privislinskii Krai). Nevertheless, Russian rule was resisted, passively and actively, by the Poles. Moreover, from 1915 to 1916 Poland was occupied by the Central Powers (chiefly Germany), who planned to establish a new (Regency) Kingdom of Poland under their protection, while in March 1917 the new Provisional Government of Russia recognized Polish independence, as did the Allies later that year.

75. For a consideration of the city's mixed heritage see John Czaplicka, "Lviv, Lemberg, Leopolis, Lwów, Lvov: A City in the Crosscurrents of European Culture," *Harvard Ukrainian Studies*, vol. 24 (2000), pp. 13–45. Also Frank Golczewski, "Polen, Ukrainer und Juden in Lemberg, 1918," *Slavica Gandensia*, vol. 20 (1993), pp. 177–92.

76. As early as 20 Nov. 1917, the new Soviet government, Sovnarkom, issued an "Appeal to the Laboring Muslims of Russia and the East." See Rex A. Wade (ed.), *Documents of Soviet History*, vol. 1., Gulf Breeze, FL: Academic International Press, 1991, pp. 50–51. On Bolshevik policy regarding the Muslim world see: Peter Hopkirk, *Setting the East Ablaze: Lenin's Dream of an Empire in Asia*, Oxford: Oxford University Press, 1986; Alexander G. Park, *Bolshevism in Turkestan, 1917–1927*, New York: Columbia University Press, 1857; Ivar Spector, *The Soviet Union and the Muslim World, 1917–1958*, Seattle: University of Washington Press, 1959, and R. Vaidyanath, *The Formation of the Soviet Central Asian Republics: A Study in Soviet Nationalities Policy, 1917–1936*, New Delhi: People's Publishing House, 1967.

77. See below, pp. 213–14.

78. Adam Zamoyski, *Warsaw, 1920: Lenin's Failed Conquest of Europe*, London: HarperCollins, 2008, p. 74. Earlier, for their part, as the Poles advanced on Kiev in April 1920, the Bol-

shevik Central Committee—using language laced with references to historical invasions of the Fatherland, including the Poles' capture of Moscow and Smolensk in 1610–11 and the wars of 1812 and 1914, in which, as all Russians knew, Polish legions had joined the French and then the German–Austrian enemy—addressed an appeal "not just to the working class to defend the Soviet Republic, but to 'all workers, peasants and honorable citizens of *Rossiya*', that vast, vague mystical empire which the revolution was supposed to have destroyed": Norman Davies, *White Eagle, Red Star: The Soviet–Polish War, 1919–20*, London: Orbis Books, 1983, p. 115.

79. On this phenomenon, see: Harun Yilmaz, "An Unexpected Peace: Azerbaijani–Georgian Relations, 1918–20," *Revolutionary Russia*, vol. 22, no. 1 (2009), pp. 37–67.

80. This famous force, the praetorian guard of the Soviet state in 1918, was derived from the 130,000 Latvians mobilized by the imperial Russian authorities in 1915–17 to defend their country against the advancing Germans: Andrew Parrott, "The Baltic States from 1914 to 1923: The First World War and the Wars of Independence," *Baltic Defence Review*, vol. 2, no. 8 (2002), p. 147. Less well known is the contribution to the anti-Bolsheviks of the Polish Legion in Russia. This force had its origins with the formation at Samara of a Polish volunteer unit (formally, the 5th Polish Rifle Division) from 1 July 1918 under Walerian Czuma (1890–1962), a veteran of the Polish Legions (formed by Józef Piłsudski in Austrian Galicia from 1914 to fight against imperial Russia). Most of its original complement were POWs of the Austrian army, but as the Polish Legion retreated into Siberia in 1918–19, it gathered recruits from local Polish communities that were descended from exiles and emigrants in the Russian Empire and came to number 16,000 men. In 1919 they did guard duty on the Trans-Siberian Railroad, but as the anti-Bolshevik movement in Siberia collapsed in late 1919, the Legion disintegrated: some 1,000 men forced their way eastwards (eventually reaching Vladivostok and being shipped back to Poland by the Allies, arriving there in June 1920); some mutinied and joined the Reds; and others (some 5,000) formally surrendered to the Soviet authorities at Krasnoiarsk on 8 January 1920. Those of the latter group who survived a typhus epidemic were eventually repatriated to Poland under Article IX of the Treaty of Riga (18 Mar. 1921). Many of those Russian- or Siberian-born Poles shipped home by the Allies and those repatriated by the Soviet authorities had never before set foot on Polish soil. Those shipped home, under Colonel Kazimierz Rumsza, became the core of the Siberian Brigade of the 5th Polish Army (formed on 12 July 1920) and joined the defense of the Modlin Fortress from 13 Aug. 1920, at the height of the Soviet–Polish War, and participated also in the Polish–Lithuanian War of September–October 1920, combating Lithuanian forces around Suwałki.

81. *Grazhdanskaia voina i voennaia interventsiia v SSSR: Entsiklopediia*, Moscow: Sovetskaia Entsiklopediia, 1987, p. 236.

82. The role of Internationalists in the Red Army is still one of the most difficult aspects of the "Russian" Civil Wars to evaluate, as both Soviet historians and émigrés tended (for very different reasons) to exaggerate their importance: for the former, the Internationalists—the subject of no less than 600 books published in Soviet Russia to the mid-1980s according to A.Ia. Manusevich (*Internatsionalisty: uchastie trudiashchikhsia stran Tsentralnoi Iugo-Vostochnoi Evropy v bor' be za vlast' Sovetov v Rossii, 1917–1920 gg.*, Moscow: Nauka, 1987, p. 7)—symbolized the international proletarian revolution; for the latter, although their observations tended to appear more often in the form of pejorative asides than heavy tomes of documents and memoirs, they symbolized the illegitimacy and alien nature of Bolshevik rule in Russia.

83. A.Ia. Manusevich, *Internatsionalisty:* p. 7.

84. In describing the Red Army, in everything from propaganda leaflets and press releases to official orders and private letters, White officers would habitually characterize their enemy as "the agonizing yoke of Latvians, Jews, Magyars and Chinamen": Jonathan D. Smele, *Civil War in Siberia: The Anti-Bolshevik Government of Admiral Kolchak, 1918–20*, Cambridge: Cambridge University Press, 1996, p. 219. This tendency later extended to their memoirs of the civil wars.

85. John Erickson, "Red Internationalists on the March: The Military Dimension, 1918–1922," in Cathryn Brennan and Murray Frame (eds), *Russia and the Wider World: Essays for Paul Dukes*, Basingstoke: Macmillan, 2000, pp. 126–52. On the Latvians as Internationalists, see: Marc Jansen, "International Class Solidarity or Foreign Intervention? Internationalists and Latvian Rifles in the Russian Revolution and Civil War," *International Review of Social History*, vol. 31, no. 1 (1986), pp. 68–79.

86. G.V. Shumeiko (ed.), *Boevoe sotruzhestvo trudiashchiiksia zarubeznykh stran s narodami Sovetskoi Rossii (1917–1922)*, Moscow: Sovetskaia Rossiia, 1957, pp. 178–9.

87. Although it is worth noting that the Internationalist experiment of this period also provided the model (and some of the personnel) of the International Brigades during the Spanish Civil War. For example, one of the most celebrated Soviet military advisors to the brigades (and commander of the 11th Brigade), "General Emilio Kléber," was actually Manfred Stern (b. 1896, as a Jew in Austrian Bukovina), who began his career in the Red Army (and later the Soviet intelligence services) as an Internationalist in 1918, having been released from a POW camp at Krasnoiarsk. After being recalled to Moscow from Spain in 1937, Stern was arrested in 1938, found guilty of counter-revolutionary activities, and sent to the camps for fifteen years. He died in the Gulag in 1954. Likewise, the commander of the 12th International Brigade in Spain, Pavol Lukács (Máté Zalka, real name Béla Frankl), had fought with a detachment of Hungarian Internationalists around Khabarovsk in 1918–19. The commander of the 15th Brigade, János Gálicz ("General Gal") also fought with the Reds in 1918–20. Gal was executed in Moscow in 1939. Karol Wacław Świerczewski, who (under the name "General Walter") commanded the 14th International Brigade in Spain, also fought with the Red Army from 1918 to 1921. He died in March 1947 from wounds incurred during an ambush organized by the nationalist Ukrainian Insurgent Army near Baligród in south-eastern Poland. Jānis Bērziņš, one of the most fearsome early Chekists, was also active in Spain before being recalled, arrested, and shot in 1938. On these and other Soviet advisors in Spain, see R. Dan Richardson, "The Defense of Madrid: Mysterious Generals, Red Front Fighters, and the International Brigades," *Military Affairs*, vol. 43, no. 4 (1979), pp. 178–85.

88. The case of Russian Jews in England is explored (by one whose father was affected) in Harold Shukman, *War or Revolution? Russian Jews and Conscription in Britain, 1917*, London: Vallentine Mitchell, 2006; and in Sascha Aurerbach, "Negotiating Nationalism: Jewish Conscription and Russian Repatriation in London's East End, 1916–1918," *Journal of British Studies*, vol. 46, no. 3 (2007), pp. 594–620. The fate of the Lithuanians in Scotland is discussed in Murdoch Rodgers, "The Anglo-Russian Military Convention and the Lithuanian Community of Lanarkshire, Scotland, 1914–1920," *Immigrants and Minorities*, vol. 1, no. 1 (1982), pp. 60–88; James D. White, "Scottish Lithuanians and the Russian Revolution," *Journal of Baltic Studies*, vol. 6, no. 1 (1975), pp. 1–8; and James D. White, "Vincas Kapsukas and the Scottish Lithuanians," *Revolutionary Russia*, vol. 17, no. 2 (2004), pp. 67–89.

Into this category could be added the rather better known American anarchists Alexander Berkman and Emma Goldman, as well as Victor Serge, who was deported to Russia from France.

89. The Turco-Tatar group included Volga Tatars, Crimean Tatars, and what were later called Azeris.

90. Richard Pipes, *The Formation of the Soviet Union, 1917–1923*, Cambridge, MA: Harvard University Press, 1954, pp. 289–90. On problems associated with the 1897 census, see Juliette Cadiot, "Searching for Nationality: Statistics and National Categories at the End of the Russian Empire (1897–1917)," *Russian Review*, vol. 64, no. 3 (2005), pp. 440–55. One complicating factor was that when asked what language they spoke, many villagers were apt to reply "peasant" or something equally unhelpful to the census-takers. When traveling around Galicia during the First World War, for example, Arthur Ransome found that: "The peasants working on the land were very unwilling to identify themselves as belonging to any of the warring nations. Again and again, on asking a peasant to what nationality he belonged, Russian, Little-Russian [Ukrainian] or Polish, I heard the reply, 'Orthodox', and when the men were pressed to say to what actual race he belonged I heard him answer safely 'We are local'": Rupert Hart-Davis (ed.), *The Autobiography of Arthur Ransome*, London: Jonathan Cape, 1976, p. 191. A later commentator's assertion that Ransome's bamboozlement was a consequence of genuine uncertainty on the part of the region's inhabitants, "rather than the result of proverbial peasant guile," seems sensible: Z.A.B. Zeman, *Pursued by a Bear: The Making of Eastern Europe*, London: Chatto & Windus, 1989, p. 21. On the history of the Russian Empire, *qua* empire, see: Andreas Kappeler, *The Russian Empire: A Multi-Ethnic History*, Harlow: Pearson, 2001; and Geoffrey Hosking, *Russia: People and Empire, 1552–1917*, London: Fontana, 1997.

91. For example, the very prominent place given to Latvians in Swain, *Origins of the Russian Civil War*, Swain, *Russia's Civil War*, Stroud: Tempus, 2000, and James D. White, *The Russian Revolution, 1917–1921: A Short History*, London: Edward Arnold, 1994.

92. In nineteenth-century Russia this distinction was not always (or even often) sustained: see Theodore R. Weeks, "Russification: Word and Practice, 1863–1914," *Proceedings of the American Philosophical Society*, vol. 148 (2004), pp. 471–2. It became more so after 1917, but even then was not always adhered to in Russian: as much for stylistic reasons as anything other (or more sinister) that one suspects, the words *Grazhdanskaia voina v Rossii* ("The Civil War in Russia") have been used in the Soviet and post-Soviet period as synonymous with *Grazhdanskaia voina v SSSR* ("The Civil War in the USSR").

93. In this regard, it is instructive (and typical of one of the more perspicacious White commentators on the civil war) that General A.I. Denikin entitled his memoirs of the period "Notes on the Russian Time of Troubles": *Ocherki russkoi smuty*, 5 vols, Paris and Berlin: Povolzky, 1921–26. It is typical too that this was emphasized in the best Western monograph on the subject: Mawdsley, *The Russian Civil War*, p. 280. But Denikin was not alone and the term crops up in memoirs of the civil-war period authored by many others who lived through it. For example, the account of a Jewish child: Abraham Gootnik, *Oh Say, Can You See: Chaos and Dreams of Peace*, Lanham, MD: University Press of America, 1987, pp. 74–5. It has been adopted also by the author of one recent and particularly insightful survey of the period: V.P. Buldakov, *Krasnaia smuta: Priroda i posledstviia revolutsionnogo nasiliia*, Moscow: ROSSPEN, 1997. The horrific and chaotic features of the struggle are made especially prom-

inent in W. Bruce Lincoln, *Red Victory: A History of the Russian Civil War*, New York: Simon and Schuster, 1989.

94. Although political violence in Europe had, of course, roots that predated the First World War. See: A.J. Mayer, *The Furies: Violence and Terror in the French and Russian Revolutions*, Princeton: Princeton University Press, 2000; and W.J. Mommsen and G. Hirschfeld (eds), *Social Protest, Violence and Terror in Nineteenth- and Twentieth-century Europe*, London: Macmillan/Berg, 1982. It is also a phenomenon now widely held to have been related to the European experience of imperialism. See David Thomson's musings on "The Era of Violence: A 'Concatenation of Crises,'" in *The New Cambridge Modern History*, vol. 12, Cambridge: Cambridge University Press, 1960, Chapter 20. For a recent survey of the subject in its "Russian" context, which concludes that "the syndrome of violence characterizing Russia's civil wars was ... unparalleled in form or content anywhere in Europe after 1918, at least until the Nazis formally came to power," see William G. Rosenberg, "Paramilitary Violence in Russia's Civil Wars, 1918–1920," in Robert Gerwath and John Horne (eds), *War in Peace: Paramilitary Violence in Europe after the Great War*, Oxford: Oxford University Press, 2013, pp. 21–39 (here p. 39).

95. See Peter Holquist, *Making War, Forging Revolution: Russia's Continuum of Crisis, 1914–1921*, Cambridge, MA: Harvard University Press, 2002. Another key early work in establishing the "continuum" paradigm, and one of key importance to students of the period, was Joshua A. Sanborn's *Drafting the Russian Nation: Military Conscription, Total War and Mass Politics, 1905–1925*, DeKalb: Northern Illinois University Press, 2003. For a discussion of aspects of this approach, see Don K. Rowney, "Narrating the Russian Revolution: Institutionalism and Continuity across Regime Change," *Comparative Studies in History and Society*, vol. 47, no. 1 (2005), pp. 79–105. The tendency among Western scholars toward downplaying the significance of 1917 as a point of rupture—even of sometimes regarding the October Revolution as an interesting but essentially diversionary *entr'acte*—continues to this day, with varying degrees of success. Perhaps the most ambitious and rewarding recent example has been Aaron B. Retish, *Russia's Peasants in Revolution and Civil War: Citizenship, Identity and the Creation of the Soviet State, 1914–1922*, Cambridge: Cambridge University Press, 2008. Of especial note also is the international collaborative project to mark the centenary of Russia's participation in the First World War, the revolutions of 1917, and the civil wars (coordinated by Anthony J. Heywood, John W. Steinberg, and David McDonald), entitled "Russia's Great War and Revolution, 1914–1922: The Centennial Reappraisal," which will see the publication of numerous edited volumes from 2013. The project's website can be accessed at http://russiasgreatwar.org/index.php

96. A key work here, on the impact of the world war on everyday mores, is Peter Gatrell, *A Whole Empire Walking: Refugees in Russia during World War I*, Bloomington: Indiana University Press, 1999. On culture and the arts—for the civil wars also saw the modernist and the abstract challenge the traditionalist and figurative, in a struggle in which the Bolsheviks were not always clear as to which side they favored—good introductions are supplied by: Abbott Gleason, Peter Kenez, and Richard Stites (eds), *Bolshevik Culture: Experiment and Order in the Russian Revolution*, Bloomington: Indiana University Press, 1985; Nils Å. Nilsson (ed.), *Art, Society, Revolution: Russia, 1917–21*, Stockholm: Almqvist & Wiksell International, 1979; William G. Rosenberg (ed.), *Bolshevik Visions: The First Phase of the Cultural Revolution in Soviet Russia*, Ann Arbor: Ardis Publishers, 1984; and Richard Stites, *Revolutionary Dreams: Utopian Vision and Experimental Life in the Russian Revolution*, London:

Oxford University Press, 1989. A particularly stimulating brief discussion is Robert Russell, "The Arts and the Russian Civil War," *Journal of European Studies*, vol. 20, no. 79 (1990), pp. 219–40, but this subject has inspired a wealth of literature, as evinced in Smele, *The Russian Revolution and Civil War*, Chapter 24.

97. Geoff Eley, "Remapping the Nation: War, Revolutionary Upheaval and State Formation in Eastern Europe, 1914–1923," in Peter J. Potichnj and Howard Aster (eds), *Ukrainian–Jewish Relations in Historical Perspective*, Edmonton: Canadian Institute of Ukrainian Studies, 1988, pp. 205–46. New light on this subject has been cast by Mark von Hagen, *War in a European Borderland: Occupation and Occupation Plans in Galicia and Ukraine, 1914–1918*, Seattle: Herbert J. Ellison Center for Russian, East European, and Central Asian Studies, University of Washington, 2007; and Peter Gatrell, "War, Population Displacement and State Formation in the Russian Borderlands, 1914–1924," in Nick Baron and Peter Gatrell (eds), *Homelands: War, Population and Statehood in Eastern Europe and Russia, 1918–1924*, London: Anthem Press, 2004, pp. 10–34. See also Vejas Gabriel Liulevicius, *War Land on the Eastern Front: Culture, National Identity and German Occupation in World War I*, Cambridge: Cambridge University Press, 2000.

98. Although recent attempts to bring events on the Eastern Front to a wider, popular audience have embraced chronologies that suggest such links. See Michael S. Neiberg and David Jordan, *The Eastern Front, 1914–1920: From Tannenberg to the Russo-Polish War*, London: Amber, 2008; and Jonathan D. Smele, "War and Revolution in Russia: The Eastern Front, 1914–1921," http://www.bbc.co.uk/history/worldwars/wwone/eastern_front_01.shtml. An intermediate position, regarding the civil wars as being inextricably fused with the October Revolution, is adopted by Mawdsley (*Russian Civil War*) and finds an echo in Roi Medvedev, *Russkaia revoliutsiia 1917 goda: Pobeda i porazhenie bol'shevikov (k 80-letiu Russkoi revoliutsii 1917 goda)*, Moscow: Izd-vo "Prava Cheloveka," 1997.

99. One might add that the world-war-to-civil-wars linkage was reinforced by the fact that, as neither the Bolsheviks nor their opponents were able to manufacture much in the way of uniforms, weapons, or other matériel (and still less in terms of trains, tanks, aircraft, ships, etc.), all sides in the civil wars had to rely upon stockpiles from the world war (either from Russian stores and arsenals or from Allied surpluses). Even the emblematic apparel of Soviet Chekists (or "leatherjackets," as they were popularly known) of the civil-war era was filched from a wartime consignment of clothing sent to the Russian Army from Britain.

100. Indeed, in so far as, even as late as Dec. 1984, upon first meeting the British Prime Minister Margaret Thatcher Mikhail Gorbachev (then merely a member of the Soviet Politburo) felt obliged to remind her that British forces had once invaded Soviet Russia, this toxic aspect of the "Russian" Civil Wars had a half-life as long as any other consequence of the conflicts.

101. See, for example, some of the best-known posters of the civil-war era reproduced in Stephen White, *The Bolshevik Poster*, New Haven: Yale University Press, 1988. Bolshevik propagandists found caricaturing the French to be more problematic: Marianne, with her Phrygian "cap of liberty," would have struck a discordant note, so a plump bourgeois resembling Clemenceau was usually cast in her stead.

102. Mawdsley, *The Russian Civil War*, p. 283. The nadir of Soviet simplification and distortion of the civil war is available in English as Maksim Gor'kii *et al.* (eds), *History of the Civil War in the USSR*, 2 vols, London: Lawrence & Wishart, 1937–47.

103. One of Admiral Kolchak's most senior officers, later his commander-in-chief, General

K.V. Sakharov, claimed in July 1919 that "The Bolsheviks are still entirely a German organization": Smele, *Civil War in Siberia*, pp. 219–24. On White propaganda efforts and their perceptions of the Bolsheviks, see also Christopher Lazarski, "White Propaganda Efforts in the South during the Russian Civil War, 1918–1919 (the Alekseev–Denikin Period)," *Slavonic and East European Review*, vol. 70, no. 4 (1992), pp. 688–707.

104. The *ne plus ultra* of this approach is to be found in the scabrid memoirs and monographs of the aforementioned General Sakharov: K.V. Sakharov, *Belaia Sibir'. Vnutrennaia voina 1918–1920gg.*, Munich: [H. Graf?], 1923; and K.W. Sakharow, *Die tschechischen Legionen in Sibirien*, Berlin and Charlottenburg: Heinrich Wilhelm Hendrick Verlag, 1930. For a recent echo of this approach, hardly more temperate, see Ilya Slonim, *Stillborn Crusade: The Tragic Failure of Western Intervention in the Russian Civil War, 1918–1920*, New Brunswick, NJ: Transaction Publishers, 1996.

105. Again, it is worth noting that this issue had arisen long before October 1917 and had, in fact, had been alive even before the First World War, as many experienced Russian politicians believed that autocratic Russia's association with the Western democracies (the Triple Entente) might be fatal and preferred a realignment with the country's monarchical and conservative friends in Berlin and Vienna that dated back to the Holy Alliance of 1814. Among such critics of Russian policy was the influential former finance minister and prime minister Sergei Witte.

106. Again, the outstanding Western monograph on the subject reminds us of this: see Mawdsley, *The Russian Civil War*, p. 39. However, the extent to which, in Western historiography, the Allied intervention in Russia displaced the "German" (meaning Austro-German and Turkish, with a scattering of White Finns) is evinced by the contrasting lengths of the chapters covering those subjects and the number of published items they discuss in Smele, *The Russian Revolution and Civil War*: Chapter 15 ("The Invasion and Intervention of the Central Powers," pp. 250–65) discusses 170 items; Chapter 16 ("The Allied Intervention," pp. 266–318) discusses 519 items.

107. See Wolfditer Bihl, "Österreich-Ungarn und der 'Bund zur Befreiung der Ukraina," in *Österreich und Europa: Festschrift für Hugo Hantsch zum 70 Geburtstag*, Graz: Styria, 1965, pp. 505–26; Oleh S. Fedyshyn, "The Germans and the Union for the Liberation of Ukraine, 1914–1917," in Taras Hunczak (ed.), *The Ukraine, 1917–1921: A Study in Revolution*, Cambridge, MA: Harvard University Press, 1977, pp. 305–22; and Helga Grebing, "Österreich-Ungarn und die 'Ukrainische Aktion' 1914–1918. Zur Österreichisch-Ungarischen Ukraine-Politik im ersten Weltkrieg," *Jahrbücher für Geschichte Osteuropas*, vol. 7 (1959), pp. 270–96.

108. Actually, matters were not so clear cut as that, as the Kuban Host was formed of two distinct and quite hostile groups: the *lineitsy* (line) Cossacks, who dwelt on the upper Kuban River, were of Russian heritage and generally were pro-Volunteer; and the coastal Black Sea Cossacks, who were of Ukrainian descent and had a strained relationship with the Volunteers. In the spring of 1918, the Black Sea Cossacks even sent delegates to negotiate a putative alliance with the pro-German Ukrainian State of Hetman P.P. Skoropadskii.

109. In part, the Lithuanians' motive was to seek German support against potential incursions and territorial claims from Poland (recognized as independent by the Russian Provisional Government in April 1917 and subsequently by the Allies). Given their own territorial disputes with Berlin, in Silesia and elsewhere, the Poles could not look to Germany for assistance, but some were (opportunistically) pro-Austrian, as Vienna had allowed anti-Russian

Polish forces (under the future Polish head of state Józef Piłsudski) to organize on its territory during the world war. Equally, Estonian and Latvian proponents of independence refused to accommodate themselves to German occupation in 1918, being all too well aware that Berlin would always favor their rivals, the Baltic German nobility of Estland, Lifland, and Courland provinces, who were seeking to establish a United Baltic Duchy, in union with the Kingdom of Prussia. On German policy in the occupied region and local reactions to it, see Liulevicius, *War Land on the Eastern Front*.

110. See Timothy Snyder, *The Red Prince: The Fall of a Dynasty and the Rise of Modern Europe*, London: The Bodley Head, 2008. Wilhelm's father, Charles Sefan, who had deliberately wed his daughters to Polish princes of the Czartoryski and Radziwiłł lines, was one of the contenders for the throne of the Kingdom of Poland proposed but never realized by the Central Powers during the First World War. Given Polish and Ukrainian counter-claims to Eastern Galicia, this extended the "Russian" Civil Wars into the heart of the house of Habsburg.

111. Ronald G. Suny, *The Making of the Georgian Nation*, London: I.B. Tauris, 1989, p. 193.

112. Although to a large extent the Armenians had brought this on themselves, having provoked the Turks and disgusted their allies by committing innumerable atrocities against Muslim villages during their retreat from Anatolia. They in turn, of course, would argue that this was a justifiable revenge for previous Turkish atrocities against Armenians (notably the attempted genocide of 1915).

113. Although the decision in favor of maintaining the Bolsheviks in power was a hotly contested one in German governmental and military circles. See Holger H. Herwig, "German Policy in the Eastern Baltic Sea in 1918: Expansion or Anti-Bolshevik Crusade?" *Slavic Review*, vol. 32, no. 2 (1973), pp. 339–57.

114. The flames of this controversy were famously ignited by Fritz Fischer, *Griff nach der Weltmacht. Der Kriegszielpolitik des kaiserlichen Deutschland, 1914/18*, Düsseldorf: Droste Verlag, 1961 and A.J.P. Taylor, *The Origins of the Second World War*, London: Hamish Hamilton, 1961. Its heat was most intense for those Ukrainian, Russian, and Cossack émigrés who, during the Second World War, once again chose the "German orientation" and collaborated with the Nazis in the hope of toppling Stalin and "liberating" their homelands.

115. On the Left-SRs, see Lutz Häfner, *Die Partei der linken Sozialrevolutionäre in der Russischen Revolution von 1917–1918*, Cologne: Böhlau, 1994; and V.V. Shelokhaev *et al.* (eds), *Partiia Levykh sotsialistov-revolutsionerov: dokumenty i materialy, 1917–1925*, 3 vols, Moscow: ROSSPEN: 2000–. A good summary of the party's activities is E. Cinella, "The Tragedy and Triumph of the Russian Revolution: Promise and Default of the Left Socialist Revolutionaries in 1918," *Cahiers du Monde Russe et Soviétique*, vol. 38, nos 1–2 (1997), pp. 45–82.

116. Lenin's analogy was made in a speech to the Bolshevik Central Committee on 11 Jan. 1918. See *The Bolsheviks and the October Revolution*, p. 174. On the Left Bolsheviks, see Ronald I. Kowalski, *The Bolshevik Party in Conflict: The Left Communist Opposition of 1918*, London: Macmillan, 1991.

117. The fullest account of the negotiations remains John W. Wheeler-Bennett, *The Forgotten Peace: Brest-Litovsk, March 1918*, London: Macmillan, 1938. The treaty detached all of Russia's territorial gains in Eastern Europe dating back to the seventeenth century (including Finland, the Baltic provinces, Belorussia, Poland, and Ukraine), as well as more recent

gains (in 1878 and since 1914) in Eastern Anatolia—including Kars, Ardahan, and Batumi (known to the Turks as Elviye-i Selâse, the "three provinces")—and forced demobilization on the Soviet government, as well as demanding that all Russian naval vessels be confined to port. More than one-third of the old empire's population (56 million people), one-third of its rail network, half its industry, three-quarters of its supplies of iron ore, and nine-tenths of its coal were thereby immediately transferred to the control of Germany and her allies, while all Russian claims to privileges within Persia and Afghanistan were also forfeited. The fullest version of the treaty (and its variants and supplements) is available online at Yale Law School's Avalon Project: http://avalon.law.yale.edu/20th_century/bl34. asp#treatytext. Symbolically, in our portrait of the convoluted fealties of the times, the chief Soviet signatory of the treaty was the aristocrat and former Menshevik and tsarist diplomat G.V. Chicherin, Commissar for Foreign Affairs, Trotsky having refused to so debase himself.

118. *The Bolsheviks and the October Revolution*, pp. 217–23.

119. Consequently, notes Alexander Rabinowitch (*The Bolsheviks in Power*, p. 204), the proceedings of the congress "were, predictably, perfunctory." On Sverdlov's maneuverings see Charles Duval, "Yakov M. Sverdlov and the All-Russian Central Executive Committee of Soviets (VTsIK)," *Soviet Studies*, vol. 31, no. 1 (1979), pp. 3–22.

120. Richard K. Debo, *Revolution and Survival: The Foreign Policy of Soviet Russia, 1917–18*, Liverpool: Liverpool University Press, 1979, p. 161. Often forgotten is that, on the Soviet side, the apparent arch "peace-monger," Lenin, endorsed this and, in fact, having secured the vote for peace in the Bolshevik CC meeting of 23 Feb. 1918, then hastened to join his comrades in a unanimous vote in favor of "immediate preparations for a revolutionary war": *The Bolsheviks and the October Revolution*, p. 223.

121. For a brilliantly colorful and detailed account of the Turkish invasion of Transcaucasia in 1918, see W.E.D Allen and Paul Muratoff, *Caucasian Battlefields: A History of the Wars on the Turco-Caucasian Border, 1828–1921*, Nashville: The Battery Press, 1999, pp. 457–96. See also: Michael A. Reynolds, *Shattering Empires: The Clash and Collapse of the Ottoman and Russian Empires, 1908–1918*, Cambridge: Cambridge University Press, 2011, pp. 219–38. Reynolds emphasizes that the Turks' determination to seize Baku was strengthened by rumors and then hard news of an agreement in Aug. 1918 under which Moscow agreed to supply a large portion of the region's oil to the Sultan's ally in Berlin.

122. On the creation of the Red Army, see below. On the attempted scuppering of the Black Sea Fleet, see: F.F. Raskolnikov, *Tales of Sub-Lieutenant Ilyin*, London: New Park Publications, 1982, pp. 21–53. On Left Bolshevik and Left-SR breaches of the treaty see: Ronald I. Kowalski, *The Bolshevik Party in Conflict*, pp. 180–81; and Häfner, *Die Partei der linken Sozialrevolutionäre*. As late as 30 June 1918, on the eve of the gathering of the Fifth All-Russian Congress of Soviets, the Left SRs were able to organize meetings all over Moscow on the theme of "Aid to the Ukrainian Insurgents." See Shelokhaev *et al.* (eds), *Partiia Levykh sotsialistov-revolutsionerov*, vol. 2, pp. 406–7.

123. *The Bolsheviks and the October Revolution*, pp. 213–15.

124. On Lockhart's relations with Trotsky see R.H. Bruce Lockhart, *Memoirs of a British Agent*, London: Putnam, 1932, pp. 195–307. In his autobiography, Trotsky makes no mention whatsoever of his contacts with Lockhart and other Allied representatives in Petrograd and Moscow. Indeed, the sole reference to Lockhart is as an "instigator" of the anti-Bolshevik

Iaroslavl' uprising of July 1918. See L.D. Trotsky, *My Life: An Attempt at an Autobiography*, Harmondsworth: Penguin, 1975, p. 411.

125. Lockhart, *Memoirs*, p. 271.

126. National Archives (Kew, London), FO 371/3285/89219: Lockhart to FO, 20 May 1918. Lockhart immediately turned his attention to offering moral and financial support to underground anti-Bolshevik organizations in Moscow with which he was in contact, notably the Union for the Regeneration of Russia and B.V. Savinkov's Union for the Defense of the Fatherland and Freedom, informing Whitehall on 29 May 1918 that it was now inconceivable that the Germans would overthrow the Bolsheviks. Rather: "They will play with them in order to maintain a free hand in [the] South East and in [the] Caucasus ... As this change in German policy renders the chances of Bolshevik consent to intervention very remote we must look to other parties for support ... Certain other parties are ready to support us provided we act quickly ... certainly not later than June 20th" (FO 371/3285/95628: Lockhart to FO, 29 May 1918). He also at this point arranged for the smuggling out of Russia of the former prime minister, Kerensky, who was on a mission to London and Paris to curry Allied support for the anti-Bolshevik movement in Russia: see Smele, "Mania Grandiosa." On Lockhart and Allied–Soviet relations in this period see also Swain, *Origins*, pp. 138–44. Little has been published in English on the anti-Bolshevik underground of 1918, with the exception of the disappointing Christopher Lazarski, *Lost Opportunity: Attempts at Unification of the Anti-Bolsheviks, 1917–1919—Moscow, Kiev, Jassy, Odessa*, Lanham: University Press of America, 2008. Far superior (but unpublished) is Benjamin Wells, "The Union of Regeneration: The Anti-Bolshevik Underground in Revolutionary Russia, 1917–1919," Queen Mary, University of London PhD thesis, 2004. See also, Swain, *Origins*, pp. 160–67, 172–5; and G.Z. Ioffe, *Krakh rossiiskoi monarkhicheskoi kontrrevoliutsii*, Moscow: Nauka, 1977, pp. 100–15.

127. Lockhart did not arrive in Russia until the last days of January 1918. Prior to his arrival, however, efforts to keep Bolshevik Russia in the war on the Allied side had been consistently and vigorously pursued by the correspondent of the *Daily News*, Arthur Ransome. The irrepressible Ransome—who was no socialist, but simply a firm believer that the Bolsheviks were the most reliable anti-German force in the East—knew both Lenin and Trotsky (he would later marry Trotsky's secretary), was a personal friend of Karl Radek (head of the press department of the People's Commissariat of Foreign Affairs), and was consulted with regularly by the British ambassador to Russia, Sir George Buchanan. Not all British officials in Petrograd were so keen on his views or activities, though. Ransome recorded in his diary that during one of his interviews with Buchanan "Col. Knox, our military attaché and a rabid interventionist, came into the room and broke into the conversation, addressing me, and saying 'You ought to be shot!'" See Hugh Brogan, *The Life of Arthur Ransome*, London: Hamish Hamilton, 1984, p. 162. Also Roland Chambers, *The Last Englishman: The Double Life of Arthur Ransome*, London: Faber and Faber, 2009, p. 185. The imaginative lives of several generations of British children would have been greatly impoverished had the colonel's wish been granted and the future author of the *Swallows and Amazons* series been executed. For his part, General Alfred Knox would serve as head of the British military mission to Siberia in 1918–19, championed the White cause in the civil wars, and took a hand in the rise of Admiral Kolchak to the role of supreme ruler at Omsk. On Knox, see John Long, "General Sir Alfred Knox and the Russian Civil War: A

brief Commentary," *Sbornik of the Study Group on the Russian Revolution*, no. 9 (1983), pp. 54–64.

128. Permission for the local soviet to deal with the Allies had been granted during a panic on 1 March, when, due to some crossed wires, it appeared that the Germans at Brest-Litovsk were not going to sign a peace after all. See Debo, *Revolution and Survival*, pp. 153–4. Nevertheless, Moscow's willingness immediately to turn to the Allies reveals that the impulse to work with either group of "imperialists" remained strong.

129. See Debo, *Revolution and Survival*, pp. 266–7. Also Richard H. Ullman, *Anglo-Soviet Relations, 1917–1921: Vol. 1, Intervention and the War*, Princeton: Princeton University Press, 1961, pp. 114–19.

130. Clifford Kinvig, *Churchill's Crusade: The British Invasion of Russia, 1918–1920*, London and New York: Hambledon Continuum, 2006, pp. 17–18; Michael Wilson, *For Them the War Was Not Over: The Royal Navy in Russia, 1918–1920*, Stroud: The History Press, 2010, pp. 27–9; and Mirko Harjula, *Venäjän Karjala ja Muurmanni 1914–1922*, Helsinki: Suomalaisen Kirjallisuuden Seura, 2007, pp. 76–85.

131. George Hill, *Go Spy the Land*, London: Cassell and Company, 1932, pp. 177, 190ff. This collaboration adds a twist to the intriguing possibility that British intelligence services, having waylaid Trotsky in Canada during his attempt to return to Russia from the United States in 1917 (for fear that he was a German agent), had allowed him to proceed to Petrograd in the hope that, whether wittingly pro-British or not, he might act as an anti-German "agent of influence" in revolutionary Russia. See: Richard B. Spence, "Interrupted Journey: British Intelligence and the Arrest of Leon Trotskii, April 1917," *Revolutionary Russia*, vol. 13, no. 1 (2000), pp. 1–28; A.D. Harvey, "Trotsky at Halifax, April 1917," *Archives*, vol. 22, no. 97 (1997), pp. 170–74; and David R. Jones, "Documents on British Relations with Russia, 1917–1918," *Canadian–American Slavonic Studies*, vol. 9, no. 3 (1975), pp. 361–70. As a mark of the confusion of the times, Trotsky himself had believed that many Bolsheviks and Mensheviks had wanted him to be detained in Canada for as long as possible to keep him away from Russia: Angelica Balabanoff, *My Life as a Rebel*, London: Hamish Hamilton, 1938, pp. 176–7.

132. Lockhart, *Memoirs*, pp. 242, 274.

133. Roy Bainton, *Honoured by Strangers: The Life of Captain Francis Cromie CB, DSO, RN, 1882–1918*, Shrewsbury: Airlife Publications, 2002, pp. 220–24. See also Cromie's correspondence and other important materials reproduced in David R. Jones, "Documents on British Relations with Russia, 1917–1918," *Canadian–American Slavonic Studies*, vol. 7, no. 2 (1973), pp. 219–37; no. 3, pp. 350–75; no. 4, pp. 498–510; and vol. 8, no. 4 (1974), pp. 544–62.

134. Lt-Colonel F.M. Bailey, *Mission to Tashkent*, London: Jonathan Cape, 1946 (Chapter 18).

2. 1918–19: THE TRIUMPHAL MARCH OF REACTION

1. I.A. Chemeriskii, "Eserovskaia gruppa 'Narod' i ee raspad," in I.I. Mints (ed.), *Bankrotstvo melkoburzhuaznykh partii Rossii, 1917–1922gg.*, Moscow: Nauka, 1977, pp. 77–86. On the SR trial, see below, p. 212.

2. Rex A. Wade (ed.), *Documents of Soviet History*, vol. 1, Gulf Breeze: Academic International Press, 1991, pp. 343–4.

3. Stephen Blank, "The Struggle for Soviet Bashkiria, 1917–1923," *Nationalities Papers*, vol. 11,

no. 1 (1983), pp. 1–26; Richard Pipes, "The First Experiment in Soviet National Policy: The Bashkir Republic, 1917–1920," *Russian Review*, vol. 9, no. 4 (1950), pp. 303–19; and Serge A. Zenkovsky, "The Tataro-Bashkir Feud of 1917–1920," *Indiana Slavic Studies*, vol. 2 (1958), pp. 37–62.

4. Yamauchi Masayuki, *The Green Crescent under the Red Flag: Enver Pasha in Soviet Russia, 1919–1922*, Tokyo: Institute for the Study of Languages and Cultures of Asia and Africa, 1991.

5. Naturally, this did not prevent Zin'kovskii from being executed as a terrorist in 1937.

6. See below, p. 212.

7. The exemplary case here was that of General Radola Gajda, who in Nov. 1918 organized an attempted coup at Vladivostok against the White regime that he had previously served (and of which he had, at one stage, been considered as a candidate for leadership). But in terms of aiding the Red victory in Siberia, of more immediate utility was the case of Colonel B.M. Zinevich, who, as commander of its garrison, led the revolt at Krasnoiarsk against White rule in December 1919 and handed the city over to the 5th Red Army. Zinevich's reward was a bullet from a Cheka Mauser. See Jonathan D. Smele, *Civil War in Siberia: The Anti-Bolshevik Government of Admiral Kolchak, 1918–20*, Cambridge University Press, 1996, pp. 552–70, 590–92.

8. Likewise, the influential Kuban Cossack politician A.I. Kulabukov was arrested and publicly hanged by the White leader General Denikin in Nov. 1919, when he returned from the Paris Peace Conference, where he had signed an agreement with the Mountain Republic of the Peoples of the North Caucasus that spoke of "the full political independence of the Kuban." Kulabukov's "treachery" to the White cause was but one feature of a campaign of anti-Russianism that had swept through the Kuban since 13 June 1919, when an unknown assailant, presumed to be a White officer, had assassinated the president of the Kuban Rada, N.S. Riabovol, at Rostov: Peter Kenez, *Civil War in South Russia, 1919–1920*, Berkeley: University of California Press, 1977, p. 119.

9. See below, p. 212.

10. See William S. Graves, *America's Siberian Adventure, 1918–1920*, New York: Jonathan Cape and Harrison Smith, 1931, *passim*.

11. See Nick Baron, *The King of Karelia: Col P.J. Woods and the British Intervention in North Russia, 1918–1919*, London: Francis Boutle, 2007. In the first stages of this struggle the White Finns, therefore, found themselves at war with the population of a region that their nationalist ideology identified as the crucible of all things truly "Finnish"—Karelia being at the heart of the epic *Kalevala* (1835 and 1849), compiled from Finnish and Karelian folklore and mythology by the botanist and philologist Elias Lönnrot.

12. See Bülent Gökay, "Turkish Settlement and the Caucasus," *Middle Eastern Studies*, vol. 32, no. 2 (1996), pp. 45–76. Most members of the Armenian Revolutionary Federation (Haigagan Heghapokhakan Dashnaksutiun), the Dashnaks, adhered to a temporary suspension of their struggle for independence from tsarist Russia during the course of the world war.

13. See: Vasyl Kuchabsky, *Western Ukraine in Conflict with Poland and Bolshevism, 1918–1923*, Edmonton and Toronto: Canadian Institute of Ukrainian Studies Press, 2011; and Matthew Stachiw and Jaroslaw Sztendera, *Western Ukraine at the Turning Point of Europe's History, 1918–1923*, 2 vols, New York: Shevchenko Scientific Society, 1969–71. As one source has it, dividing the Ukrainian cause was the fact that the leaders of the UNR and the WUPR "liked each other's enemies": Serhy Yekelchyk, *Ukraine: Birth of a Modern Nation*, Oxford

University Press, 2007, p. 78. On Ukraine's leaders in the revolutionary period, see Olga Andriewsky, "The Making of the Generation of 1917: Towards a Collective Biography," *Journal of Ukrainian Studies*, vol. 29, nos 1–2 (2004), pp. 19–37.

14. Vytautas Lesčius, *Lietuvos kariuomenė nepriklausomybės kovose 1918–1920*, Vilnius: Generolo Jono Žemaičio Lietuvos Karo Akademija, 2004; Piotr Łossowski, *Stosunki polsko-litewskie w latach 1918–1920*, Warsaw: Książka i Wiedza, 1966.

15. Henry K. Norton, *The Far Eastern Republic of Siberia*, London: Allen & Unwin, 1923. On the Japanese intervention, see: Paul E. Dunscomb, *Japan's Siberian Intervention, 1918–1922: "A Great Disobedience Against the People"*, Lanham: Lexington Books, 2011. See also below, pp. 220–3.

16. On ROVS, see Paul Robinson, *The White Russian Army in Exile, 1920–1941*, Oxford: Clarendon, 2002.

17. See: Richard Spence, *Boris Savinkov: Renegade on the Left*, Boulder: East European Monographs, 1991; and Edward van der Rhoer, *Master Spy: A True Story of Allied Espionage in Bolshevik Russia*, New York: Charles Scribner's Sons, 1981. When, despite his admission of organizing armed opposition to the Soviet government in his trial of 1924, Savinkov was sentenced not to death but to ten years' imprisonment, which he began serving in a carpeted apartment with a car on call, rumors circulated that perhaps he had been in the pay of the Cheka all along. He nevertheless committed suicide on 7 May 1925 by throwing himself from a window in the Lubianka (although there have been many suggestions, notably by Alexander Solzhenitsyn, that he was pushed).

18. Mikhail Agursky, "Defeat as Victory and the Living Death: The Case of Ustrialov," *History of European Ideas*, vol. 5, no. 2 (1984), pp. 165–80; Hilda Hardeman, *Coming to Terms with the Soviet Regime: The "Changing Signposts" Movement among Russian Émigrés in the Early 1920s*, Dekalb: Northern Illinois University Press, 1994; E. Oberländer. "Nationalbolschewistische Tendenzen in der russischen Intelligenz. Die "Smena Vech"-Diskussion, 1921–22," *Jahrbücher für Geschichte Osteuropas*, vol. 16, no. 2 (1968), pp. 194–211.

19. For an exceptionally detailed and useful investigation of the fate of the civil-war commanders, see O.F. Survenirov, *Tragediia RKKA, 1937–1938*, Moscow: Terra, 1998.

20. On Slashchev, see: L.I. Petrusheva, "'Groza tyla i liubimets fronta': General Ia.S. Slashchov v 1919–1921 gg.," in S.V. Karpenko (ed.), *Novyi istoricheskii vestnik: izbranooe 2000–2004*, Moscow: Izdatel'stvo Ippolitova, 2004, pp. 245–66; and A.S. Krupchinin, "P.N. Vrangel' i Ia.S. Slashchov: konflikt lichnostei ili konflikt strategii?" in S.M. Iskhakov (ed.), *Krym. Vrangel'. 1920 god*, Moscow: Izd. "Sotsial'no-politicheskaia MYSL'," 2006, pp. 39–55.

21. Anthony Kröner, *The White Knight of the Black Sea: The Life of Peter Wrangel*, The Hague: Leuxenhoff, 2010, p. 329. On Burtsev, see Robert Henderson, "Vladimir Burtsev and the Russian Revolutionary Emigration: Surveillance of Foreign Political Refugees in London, 1891–1905," Queen Mary, University of London PhD thesis, 2008.

22. The UNR had declared the independence of Ukraine in its Fourth Universal of 9 Jan. 1918, having (despite the October Revolution) asserted only autonomy in its Third Universal of 7 Nov. 1917. Certainly a more correct translation of this polity's name (Ukrainska Narodnia Respublika) would be the "Ukrainian People's Republic," but the designation of "people's republic" became problematic after the Second World War, as such entities were associated with the Soviet satellites in Eastern Europe. Consequently, Ukrainian émigré and Western authors preferred "National" to "People's" in their works. I have chosen to echo them.

23. For the Soviet government's ultimatum to the Rada of 17 Dec. 1917, in which these charges

are laid, see James Bunyan and H.H. Fisher (eds), *The Bolshevik Revolution, 1917–1918: Documents and Materials*, Stanford: Stanford University Press, 1934, pp. 439–40. See also Roman Szporluk, "Lenin, 'Great Russia,' and Ukraine," *Harvard Ukrainian Studies*, vol. 28, nos 1–4 (2006), pp. 611–26. On the foundation of the Ukrainian Army, see Viktor Holubko, *Armiia Ukrainskoi Narodnoi Respubliky, 1917–1918: Utvorennia ta borot'ba za derzhavu*, Lviv: Kal'variia, 1997.

24. Serhy Yekelchyk, "Bands of Nation Builders? Insurgency and Ideology in the Ukrainian Civil War," in Robert Gerwath and John Horne (eds), *War in Peace: Paramilitary Violence in Europe after the Great War*, Oxford: Oxford University Press, 2013, pp. 114–18.

25. John S. Reshetar, *The Ukrainian Revolution, 1917–1920: A Study in Nationalism*, Princeton: Princeton University Press, 1952, pp. 89–114. A pro-Ukrainian chronicle of these events is offered in Wolodymyr Kosyk, "Première aggression de la Russie soviétique contre l'Ukraine (1917–1918)," *L'Est Européen*, no. 230 (Apr.–June 1993), pp. 59–62; no. 231 (Oct.–Dec. 1993), pp. 37–45; and no. 233 (Jan.–Mar. 1994), pp. 56–8. The meaning and nature of the revolutionary events in Ukraine are discussed in a special issue of the *Journal of Ukrainian Studies*, vol. 24, no. 1 (1999), which includes: Vladyslav Verstiuk, "Conceptual Issues in Studying the History of the Ukrainian Revolution," pp. 5–20; and Marko Bojcun, "Approaches to the Study of the Ukrainian Revolution," pp. 21–38.

26. Reshetar, *The Ukrainian Revolution*, p. 114.

27. Bunyan and Fisher (eds), *The Bolshevik Revolution*, pp. 449–51.

28. V.A. Smolii (ed.), *Istoriia Ukrainy*, Kiev: Al'ternatyvy, 1997, p. 230.

29. H. Lapchynsky, "Borotba za Kyiv. Svichen 1918 r.," *Litopys revoliutsii*, no. 2 (1928), p. 212, quoted in Yekelchyk, "Bands of Nation Builders?" p. 117.

30. Mikhail Bulgakov, *Belaia gvardiia* ("The White Guard," 1926). The brutal events in Kiev—specifically, the Bolshevik uprising at the city's Arsenal on 28–9 Jan. 1918 and Ukrainian forces' suppression of it a week later—also provided the subject matter for an early masterpiece of Soviet cinema, *Arsenal* (1928), by the esteemed Ukrainian director A.P. Dovchenko.

31. Forces loyal to Rumcherod (the Central Executive Committee of the Soviets of the Romanian Front, the Black Sea and Odessa Military District) and its successor (from 18 Jan. 1918), the Odessa Soviet Republic, were easily dispersed by the Romanians. A Bolshevik Bessarabian government in exile, the Bessarabian Soviet Republic, was later proclaimed (on 5 May 1919) at Odessa, and shortly afterwards moved its nominal "capital" to Tiraspol', in Kherson *guberniia*. However, although units of the 2nd Ukrainian Soviet Army and the 3rd Ukrainian Soviet Army managed to establish bridgeheads on the right bank of the Dnestr over the following weeks, the Bessarabian Soviet Republic failed to exert control over any part of historical Bessarabia, which on 9 Apr. 1919 formally united with Romania.

32. On the First Kuban (Ice) March, see Peter Kenez, *Civil War in South Russia, 1918: The First Year of the Volunteer Army*, Berkeley: University of California Press, 1971, pp. 96–132. Numerous memoirs by participants are collected as: *Lednoi pokhod* (*Beloe delo*, vol. 2), Moscow: Golos, 1993; *Pervyi Kubanskii "Lednoi" Pokhod*, Moscow: Tsentrpoligraf, 2001; and *Pervye boi Dobrovol'cheskoi armii*, Moscow: Tsentrpoligraf, 2001, pp. 238–418. The last of these volumes also includes (pp. 419–516) a collection of memoirs relating to General Drozdovskii's campaign, on which see also M.G. Drozdovskii, *Dnevnik*, Berlin: Knigoizdatel'stvo Otto Kirchner, 1923. An unusual view of the battles for Rostov, Taganrog, and Novocherkassk in Dec. 1917 and Jan. 1918 can be found in Diane Koenker and Steve Smith (eds), *Eduard M. Dune, Notes of a Red Guard*, Urbana: University of Illinois

Press, 1993, pp. 93–114. Those battles are covered also from the Volunteers' point of view in *Pervye boi Dobrovol'cheskoi armii*, pp. 9–237.

33. The Latvian National Council (Tautas Padome) waited until then, declaring independence on 18 Nov. 1918. Despite these declarations, however, the lingering presence of German forces in the Baltic, endorsed—indeed, required—by the Allies under the terms of the armistice of 11 Nov. 1918, as a buffer against Bolshevik incursions, would lead to complications during the following year, as *Freikorps* elements, together with Baltic German politicians, sought to salvage some gains for Berlin, notably in the Landeswehr War (see below, p. 128).

34. The following is chiefly based upon C. Jay Smith, *Finland and the Russian Revolution, 1917–1922*, Athens: University of Georgia Press, 1958; and, especially, Anthony F. Upton, *The Finnish Revolution, 1917–1918*, Minneapolis: University of Minnesota Press, 1980. See also: Pala Suomen Historia (http://www.palasuomenhistoriaa.net/en/?Turning_points_in_Finnish_history:The_1918_Civil_war_and_the_birth_of_the_Finnish_Army); and Heikki Ylikangas, *Der Weg nach Tampere. Die Niederlage der Roten im finnischen Bürgerkrieg 1918*, Berlin: Berliner Wissenschafts-Verlag, 2002. In Finland, following the White victory, the conflict was not officially referred to as a civil war, but rather as the suppression of a "mutiny" or "revolt," or—to emphasize (or, rather, to exaggerate) the Red Russian role in it—as a "War of Liberation."

35. See David G. Kirby, "Revolutionary Ferment in Finland and the Origins of the Civil War, 1917–1918," *Scandinavian Economic History Review*, vol. 26, no. 1 (1978), pp. 15–35.

36. On the ethnic aspect of the war, which was as complex in Finland as anywhere else in Russia, see Pekka Kalevi Hamalainen, *In Time of Storm: Revolution, Civil War and the Ethnolinguistic Issue in Finland*, Albany: State University of New York Press, 1979.

37. And the Finnish Social Democratic Party owed far more to its German equivalent than to the Bolsheviks.

38. A. Harding Ganz, "The German Expedition to Finland, 1918," *Military Affairs*, vol. 44, no. 2 (1980), pp. 84–9.

39. http://vesta.narc.fi/cgi-bin/db2www/sotasurmaetusivu/stat2. See also Pertti Haapala and Marko Tikka, "Revolution, Civil War, and Terror in Finland in 1918," in Gerwarth and Horne (eds), *War in Peace*, pp. 72–84.

40. Mandy Lehto-Hoogendorn, "The Persistence of a Painful Past: The Finnish Civil War of 1918," *The Masaryk Journal*, vol. 3, no. 1 (2000), pp. 83–94.

41. For a very insightful review of Finnish research into the subject, see Ohto Manninen, "Red, White and Blue in Finland, 1918: A Survey of Interpretations of the Civil War," *Scandinavian Journal of History*, vol. 3, no. 3 (1978), pp. 229–49.

42. Formally, under Article VII of the treaty of 9 Feb. (27 Jan.) 1918, Ukraine's grain was to be exchanged in return for a loan, but the terms of the subsequent commercial treaty effectively established Austro-German control over the Ukrainian economy. See *Texts of the Ukrainian Peace*, Cleveland: John T. Zubal Publishers, 1981; and http://ia700307.us.archive.org/27/items/treatyofpeacesig00ukraiala/treatyofpeacesig00ukraiala.pdf. For a discussion of the treaty, see Stephan M. Horak, *The First Treaty of the First World War: Ukraine's Treaty with the Central Powers of February 9, 1918*, Boulder: East European Monographs, 1988.

43. The illustrations provided of uniforms in the "Men-at Arms" series of the Osprey Press often seem rather over-imaginative, but those of the elaborate confections favored under the Hetmanate, provided in P. Abbot and E. Pinak in *Ukrainian Armies, 1914–55*, Oxford: Osprey, 2004, would be fantastical if only half accurate. One resident of Kiev in 1918, the author

Konstantin Paustovskii, commented that, "It was difficult to tell whether anything consequential was happening or if the city was merely acting out a play, with characters dressed
like old-time Ukrainian peasant rebels": K.G. Paustovskii, *Povest o zhizni*, Moscow: Sovetskaia Rossiia, 1966, vol. 1, p. 783. Another noted that although the economy was in chaos,
one booming sector seemed to be sign painting, as everyone scrambled to change Russian
signs into Ukrainian ones: A.A. Gol'denveizer, "Iz kievskikh vospominanii (1917–1921
gg.)," *Arkhiv Russkoi Revoliutsii*, vol. 6 (1922), pp. 231–2. Another interesting and not
unsympathetic first-hand account is: Jean Pellisier, *La tragédie ukrainienne*, Paris: Bibliothèque Ukrainienne Symon Petlura, 1988. The Cossack myth was partly generated by certain romantic tropes within nineteenth-century Ukrainian literature: George G. Grabowicz,
"Three Perspectives on the Cossack Past: Gogol', Ševčenko, Kuliš," *Harvard Ukrainian Studies*, vol. 5 (1981), pp. 135–70. In general, on the Skoropadskii coup, see Oleh S. Fedyshyn,
Germany's Drive to the East and the Ukrainian Revolution, New Brunswick, NJ: Rutgers
University Press, 1971, pp. 133–58.

44. Fedyshyn, *Germany's Drive to the East*, pp. 190–91.

45. Skoropadskii's reign remains, nevertheless, somewhat enigmatic. On the one hand, most
analyses of the Hetmanate were penned by or drew upon the writings of those who fought
against him, or utilized German or Austrian sources, and therefore have their limitations:
see, for example, Taras Hunczak, "The Ukraine under Hetman Pavlo Skoropadskyi," in Taras
Hunczak (ed.), *The Ukraine, 1917–1921: A Study in Revolution*, Cambridge, MA: Harvard
University Press, 1977, pp. 61–81. The only exception, until recently, has been: Jaroslaw Pelenski, "Hetman Pavlo Skropadsky and Germany (1917–1918) as Reflected in His Memoirs," in Hans-Joachim Torke and John-Paul Himka (eds), *German–Ukrainian Relations in
Historical Perspective*, Edmonton: Canadian Institute of Ukrainian Studies Press, 1994,
pp. 69–83. That work portrayed the Ukrainian State as something rather more substantial
than a German satellite, but to make that case drew chiefly upon Skoropadskii's memoirs,
subsequently published as: Pavel/Pavlo Skoropadsky/Skoropads'skyi, *Spohady: kinets'
1917—hruden' 1918*, ed. Jaroslaw Pelenski, Kiev/Philadelphia: National Academy of Sciences of Ukraine, M.S. Hrushevs'kyi Institute of Ukrainian Archaeology and Fontology,
V.K. Lypinsky East European Research Institute, 1995. According to the foremost American expert on the subject, despite their obvious bias and limitations, these memoirs nevertheless offer some convincing counterweight to the traditional view and demonstrate that
the Hetman himself was sincere in his espousal of Ukraine's right to an equal place alongside Russia in the struggle against Bolshevism and in a future federation: Mark von Hagen,
"I Love Russia but Want Ukraine: How a Russian Imperial General Became Hetman Pavlo
Skoropadsky of the Ukrainian State," in Frank Sysyn and Serhii Plokhii (eds), *Synopsis: A
Collection of Essays in Honor of Zenon E. Kohut*, Edmonton: Canadian Institute of Ukrainian Studies Press, 2005, pp. 115–48.

46. Konovalets would find greater renown as head of the anti-Soviet, émigré Organization of
Ukrainian Nationalists in inter-war Europe. He was assassinated by the NKVD in Rotter-
dam in 1938—killed by a bomb hidden inside a box of chocolates: *Murdered by Moscow:
Petlura, Konovalets, Bandera*, London: Ukrainian Publishers, 1958.

47. The National Archives, CAB 23/127, 14 Nov. 1918.

48. The National Archives, CAB 23/511, 29 Nov. 1918.

49. Geoffrey Bennett, *Cowan's War: The Story of British Naval Operations in the Baltic, 1918–
1920*, London: Collins, 1964, pp. 34–7.

50. Among those who left office were the nowadays much-revered founding fathers of independent Ukraine: the social democrat Volodymyr Vynnychenko and Mykhailo Hrushevsky of the Ukrainian PSR.

51. Not that such subtleties had been altogether lost upon Ukrainian Catholic Uniates, as they regarded the Russian Orthodox to their north and east. On events in Transcaucasia from Feb. 1917 to May 1918, which saw the collapse of the Transcaucasian Federation and the (somewhat reluctant) establishment of the three republics (most of whose leaders would have preferred to have remained in a federation with a democratic Russia) see: Firuz Kazemzadeh, *The Struggle for Transcaucasia, 1917–1921*, New York: Philosophical Library, 1951, pp. 32–127; Michael A. Reynolds, *Shattering Empires: The Clash and Collapse of the Ottoman and Russian Empires, 1908–1918*, Cambridge: Cambridge University Press, 2011 (especially Chapter 7, "Forced to be Free"); and Werner Zürrer, *Kaukasien, 1918–1921. Der Kampf der Grossmächte um die Landbrücke zwischen Schwarzem und Kaspischem Meer*, Düsseldorf: Droste Verlag, 1978.

52. This was an echo of the earlier invitation of the Murmansk Soviet to British forces. The Bolsheviks' political opponents were greatly encouraged in their efforts by the British consul at Baku, but, interestingly, only after he had narrowly failed in his intense efforts to have the Bolshevik Shaumian invite in Dunsterforce. See Ranald MacDonell, *"... And Nothing Long"*, London: Edward Arnold, 1938. The British commander's own memoirs also offer important insights into relations with Bolshevik and anti-Bolshevik forces in the region: Major-General Lionel Charles Dunsterville, *The Adventures of Dunsterforce*, London: Edward Arnold, 1920. For an insightful account of how Dunsterville and other British generals attached to such missions tended to re-orient British policy from an anti-German to an anti-Bolshevik direction, see Brock Millman, "The Problem with Generals: Military Observers and the Origins of the Intervention in Russia and Persia, 1917–1918," *Journal of Contemporary History*, vol. 33, no. 2 (1988), pp. 291–320.

53. See Ronald G. Suny, *The Baku Commune, 1917–1918*, Princeton University Press, 1972; and Bülent Gökay, "The Battle for Baku (May–September 1918): A Peculiar Episode in the History of the Caucasus," *Middle Eastern Studies*, vol. 34, no. 1 (1998), pp. 30–50. Most of the Bolshevik leaders of the Commune were subsequently arrested and would find fame in death as the twenty-six commissars executed by anti-Bolshevik authorities in Transcaspia in September 1918. See below, Chapter Four, n. 122.

54. As noted above, in Transcaucasia, in contrast to the pattern in the western theater, those who had most resisted the incursion of the Central Powers (chiefly the Armenians) were not rewarded with unconditional Allied support (although nor were their chief rivals, the Azeris, who had welcomed the Turks). On the other hand, the Georgians, who had accepted German protection, were rather ill-used by the Allies, although complicating factors here were the Georgian regime's avowed socialism—Tiflis made no attempt to ditch its equivalents of Vynnychenko and Hrushevsky to appease London and Paris—and its determination to hold on to the region of Sochi that was claimed by the Allies' White friends.

55. On the inter-ethnic violence in Transcaucasia and its origins, see: Michael G. Smith, "Anatomy of Rumor: Murder Scandal, the Musavet Party and the Narrative of the Russian Revolution in Baku, 1917–1920," *Journal of Contemporary History*, vol. 36, no. 2 (2001), pp. 211–40; and Uğur Ümit Üngör, "Paramilitary Violence in the Collapsing Ottoman Empire," in Gerwarth and Horne (eds), *War in Peace*, pp. 175–80.

56. Sorokin, following a distinguished career in early Red formations in the region, was named

as temporary commander of the Red Army of the North Caucasus on 3 Aug. 1918, and from 3 Oct. 1918 was commander of the 11th Red Army. In that capacity, he unleashed a regime of terror in the area under his control—according to Soviet historians, as a deliberate ploy to disorganize the Soviet regime in the North Caucasus. On 21 Oct. 1918, he suddenly ordered the execution of a group of members of the Bolshevik Kuban Committee and members of the Central Executive Committee of the North Caucasus Republic, as well as I.I. Matveev (the commander of the Taman Red Army). He was also responsible for the execution, on 19 Oct. 1918, of a number of captured tsarist officers (including Generals R.D. Radko-Dmitriev and N.V. Ruzskii), but on 28 Oct. 1918 a Second Extraordinary Congress of Soviets of the North Caucasus declared Sorokin to be an outlaw and removed him from his military posts. On 30 Oct. 1918, he was arrested near Stavropol', and he was subsequently killed in prison there by a Red commander before he could be brought to trial. See N.D. Karpov, *Miatezh glavkoma Sorokina: pravda i vymysli*, Moscow: Russkaia Panorama, 2006.

57. Although, as mentioned, German forces were obliged by the terms of the Compiègne (Rethondes) armistice of 11 Nov. 1918 to remain on guard against Bolshevism in the Baltic theater, no such provision was made for Ukraine, from which they were required to withdraw. See John M. Thompson, *Russia, Bolshevism and the Versailles Peace*, Princeton: Princeton University Press, 1966, pp. 25–7.

58. On the 1918 Don rebellion, see Arthur E. Janke, "The Don Cossacks on the Road to Independence," *Canadian Slavonic Papers*, vol. 12, no. 3 (1970), pp. 273–94. Also Rudolf Karmann, *Der Freiheitskampf der Kosaken. Die Weiße Armee in der russischen Revolution 1917–1920*, Puchheim: IDEA, 1985, pp. 149–76.

59. The Cossacks' near success at Tsaritsyn was at least partly a consequence of disputes in the hierarchy of the Southern Group of Red forces centered on the Volga city, as J.V. Stalin and his supporters sought to diminish the authority of military specialists. This was the so-called Tsaritsyn affair.

60. Except where stated otherwise, the following account of the revolt of the Legion is drawn from: Gustav Becvar, *The Lost Legion: A Czechoslovak Epic*, London: Stanley Paul & Co., 1939; J.F.N. Bradley, *The Czechoslovak Legion in Russia, 1914–1920*, Boulder: East European Monographs, 1991; Margarete Klante, *Von der Wolga zum Amur. Die tschechische Legion und der russische Bürgerkrieg*, Berlin: Ost-Europa Verlag, 1931; and Gerburg Thunig-Nittner, *Die Tschechoslowakische Legion in Russland. Ihre Geschichte und Bedeutung bei der Entstehung der 1. Tschechoslowakischen Republik*, Wiesbaden: Breyer, 1970.

61. Victor M. Fic, *The Bolsheviks and the Czechoslovak Legion: The Origin of their Armed Conflict, March–May 1918*, New Delhi: Abhinav Publications, 1978, pp. 40–60.

62. See: Rhodri Jeffreys-Jones, "W. Somerset Maugham: Anglo-American Agent in Revolutionary Russia," *American Quarterly*, vol. 28, no. 1 (1976), pp. 90–106; and Geoffrey Swain, "Maugham, Masaryk and the 'Mensheviks,'" *Revolutionary Russia*, vol. 7, no. 1 (1994), pp. 78–97.

63. As had been the case with the above-mentioned January 1918 revolt, around Minsk, of General Józef Dowbor-Muśnicki's 1st Polish Corps, which was almost as numerous as the Czechoslovak Legion, and which withdrew behind German lines into Poland in February 1918. However, when, in mid-February 1918, the Germans resumed their advance into Russia, in the aftermath of the rupture of peace negotiations at Brest-Litovsk, the Corps was incorporated into the German forces as an auxiliary unit and played a leading role in the capture of Minsk (18 Feb. 1918)—an event of enormous significance in persuading a majority of the

Bolshevik Central Committee finally to vote in favor of signing the Treaty of Brest-Litovsk. The Polish Corps then remained in Belorussia for some months, performing police duties under the German authorities, before being disbanded over the period May–July 1918, when its usefulness to the Germans had diminished. The majority of its complement was then allowed passage into Poland, where they later regrouped as the 1st Polish Army Corps, again under Dowbor-Muśnicki. The Corps, in fact, became the nucleus of the new Polish Army and played major roles in various actions over the coming years, including the Soviet–Polish War. See Józef Dowbor-Muśnicki, *Moje wospomnienia*, Warsaw: F. Wyszyński i S-ka, 1935.

64.   Oliver Radkey, *Russia Goes to the Polls: The Election to the All-Russian Constituent Assembly, 1917*, Ithaca: Cornell University Press, 1989, pp. 148–50.

65.   On these events see Smele, *Civil War in Siberia*, pp. 13–33. The history of the Provisional Siberian Government is now fully traceable in: V.I. Shishkin (ed.), *Vremennoe Sibirskoe Pravitel'stvo, 26 maia—3 noiabria 1918 g.: sbornik dokumentov i materialy*, Novosibirsk: Sova, 2007. For the proclamation of the Urals government, see: S. Piontkovskii (ed.), *Grazhdanskaia voina v Rossii (1918–1921 gg.): khrestomatiia*, Moscow: Kommunisticheskii Universitet, 1925, p. 248.

66.   The PGAS had initially tried its luck at Harbin, headquarters of the Russian enclave of the Chinese Eastern Railroad (CER) in Manchuria, but was ejected from there by a rival claimant, the director of the CER, General D.L. Khorvat, who headed his own Far Eastern Committee with pretensions to all-Russian power. Indeed, Khorvat would soon follow the PGAS onto Russian territory proper and proclaim himself supreme ruler of Russia at Grodekovo, in the Maritime Province, on 4 Aug. 1918, before subordinating himself to the PSG (as its high plenipotentiary for the Far East) on 31 Aug. 1918. See Smele, *Civil War in Siberia*, pp. 37–9. On the PGAS see V.V. Maksakov (ed.), "Vremennoe pravitel'stvo avtomnoi Sibiri," *Krasnyi Arkhiv* (1928), no. 4, pp. 86–138; (1929), no. 4, pp. 37–106; (1929), no. 5, pp. 31–60. On the often uncivil war of words between the SR leader of the PGAS, P.Ia. Derber, and the arch reactionary Horvath, see A.P. von Budberg, "Dnevnik," *Arkhiv russkoi revoliutsii*, vol. 13 (1923), pp. 150–205.

67.   On this phenomenon, see Anthony P. Allison, "Siberian Regionalism in the Revolution and Civil War, 1917–1920," *Siberica*, vol. 1, no. 1 (1990), pp. 78–97. The best study on Siberian *oblastnichestvo* was never published: Stephen D. Watrous, "Russia's 'Land of the Future': Regionalism and the Awakening of Siberia, 1819–1894," University of Washington PhD Thesis, 1970. That monumental dissertation was partly summarized in Stephen D. Watrous, "The Regionalist Conception of Siberia, 1860–1920," in Galya Diment and Yuri Slezkine, *Between Heaven and Hell: The Myth of Siberia in Russian Culture*, New York: St Martin's Press, 1993, pp. 113–32. See also Norman G.O. Pereira, "Regional Consciousness in Siberia before and after October 1917," *Canadian Slavonic Papers*, vol. 30, no. 1 (1988), pp. 2–21.

68.   There was a conundrum here: as mentioned above, the PSR won huge majorities in the 1917 elections to the Constituent Assembly. The party did especially well east of the Urals (or "beyond the rock," as the saying went): of 494,525 votes cast in Tobol'sk *guberniia*, for example, 388,328 (78.6 percent) went to the SRs and a mere 12,061 (2.4 percent) to the Bolsheviks (Radkey, *Russia Goes to the Polls*, p. 150). Yet at the heart of the PSR's program and its entire ethos was a commitment to a redistribution of the lands of private landowners on the basis of peasant communal practices that had no resonance at all in Siberia, where, with the exception of a few estates in Western Siberia, there were no large landowners and where the commune was almost unknown. See John Channon, "Regional Variation in the Commune:

The Case of Siberia," in Roger Bartlett (ed.), *Land Commune and Peasant Community: Communal Forms in Imperial and Early Soviet Society*, Basingstoke: Macmillan, 1990, pp. 66–85.

69. There was some substance to this. Admiral Kolchak, when asked why he kept Vologodskii as premier—he remained as such, despite ill health, until 22 Nov. 1919—responded: "Remember, he is needed here as *le vieux drapeau*." K.V. Sakharov, *Belaia Sibir'. Vnutrennaia voina 1918–1920gg.*, Munich: [H. Graf?], 1923, p. 89.

70. See Smele, *Civil War in Siberia*, pp. 56–62. Of course, agents of the National Center and its ilk had also headed south to assist and advise the Volunteers. Indeed, geography ensured that communications between anti-Bolshevik centers in Ukraine, South Russia, and the North Caucasus and their headquarters in Moscow were stronger (albeit hardly uncomplicated) than was the case for Siberia and the East. (Some Kadets even traveled quite regularly back and forth between Moscow and the North Caucasus in 1918.) Like Pepeliaev (who was to mastermind the coup that would bring Kolchak to power at Omsk in November 1918), these personnel were not without influence on events in 1918, shaping the political program of the Volunteers: P.B. Struve, for example, was instrumental in drafting the founding document of a Political Council to advise General Kornilov in January 1918, and V.V. Shul'gin was the main author of the "The Statute on the Special Council attached to the Supreme Ruler of the Volunteer Army" of August 1918. However, as, throughout 1918, the Volunteers were fighting for their lives, politics remained very much a secondary concern for the Whites in the South. Moreover, the political battle was more clear-cut: you were either for the Soviet regime or against it. There was no middle ground, no regionalist diversions, and no "democratic counter-revolution." That stage was skipped in South Russia—although, as we have seen, Cossack separatism was an always-present complicating factor.

71. The Siberian Cossack Host was established only in 1808, but had received regular injections of "new blood" through the recruitment of more recent Russian and Ukrainian peasant settlers from the 1890s onwards. In contrast, the Don Cossack Host had its roots in the sixteenth century and viewed Russian settlers on its lands (*inogorodnye*) with deep suspicion, particularly as the incomers' numbers swelled in the late nineteenth century. The Terek Host had been established as long ago as 1577, while the Kuban Host's Ukrainian origins—Catherine II had in the 1790s exiled the unruly Zaporozhian Host from the lower Dnepr—helped it to inure itself against the Russians. It will suffice to note that the Siberian and other Cossack hosts east of the Urals (the Semirech'e, Transbaikal, Amur, and Ussuri Hosts) barely feature in general histories of the Cossacks: see, for example, Robert H. McNeal, *Tsar and Cossack, 1855–1914*, London: Macmillan, 1987. Notable too is that in 1900 the number of male Cossacks under arms among the Don Host was 70,000, among the Kuban Host it was 53,000, and among the Siberian Host it was a measly 9,800: A. Zaitsov, *1918 god: ocherki po istorii russkoi grazhdanskoi voiny*, Paris: n.p., 1934, p. 137.

72. Smele, *Civil War in Siberia*, pp. 40–4. Volkov was subsequently instrumental in the Kolchak coup: ibid., pp. 102, 111–12.

73. On the issue of the chronological parameters of the democratic counter-revolution, see: Jonathan D. Smele, "Introduction," in David N. Collins and Jonathan D. Smele (eds), *Kolchak i Sibir': dokumenty i issledovaniia, 1919–1926*, vol. 1, White Plains, NY: Kraus International, pp. xii–xiii; and L.A. Shikanov, "K voprosu o kronologicheskikh ramkakh 'demokraticheskoi' kontrrevoliutsii v Sibiri," in Iu.V. Korablev and V.I. Shishkin (eds), *Iz istorii interventsii i grazhdanskaia interventsiia na Sovetskom Dal'nem Vostoke, 1917–1922 gg.*, Novosibirsk: Nauka, 1985, pp. 65–7.

74. C.H. Ellis, *The Transcaspian Episode, 1918–1919*, London: Hutchinson, 1963; and Lt Col. D.E. Knollys, "Military Operations in Transcaspia, 1918–1919," *Journal of the Central Asian Society*, vol. 13, no. 2 (1926), pp. 88–110.

75. On events in North Russia, see: V.I. Goldin, *Kontrrevoliutsiia na severe Rossii i ee krushenie, 1918–1920 gg.*, Vologda: Vologodskii ped. inst., 1989; V.I. Goldin (ed.), *Belyi sever, 1918–1920 gg.: memuary i dokumenty*, 2 vols, Arkhangel'sk: Pravda Severa, 1993; Liudmila G. Novikova, "A Province of a Non-Existent State: The White Government in the Russian North and Political Power in the Russian Civil War, 1918–20," *Revolutionary Russia*, vol. 18, no. 2 (2005), pp. 121–44; and Liudmila G. Novikova, *Provintsial'naia "kontrrevoliutsiia": Beloe dvizhenie i Grazhdanskaia voina na russkom Severe, 1917–1920*, Moscow: Novoe Literaturnoe Obozrenie, 2011.

76. The corpses and scattered remains of the victims of political violence at Omsk were almost invariably discovered along the banks of its main river, the Irtysh.

77. Allied forces had first landed at Vladivostok in April 1918, but arrived in large numbers only from July to August 1918 onwards—once President Woodrow Wilson had agreed to dispatch US troops to join the Japanese, British, French, and other contingents in the venture—although few of them would ever leave the Maritime Province. Vologodskii's sojourn in the Far East is recounted in his memoirs, which are an excellent (if hardly unbiased) source on the politics of the civil war in Siberia: Semion Lyandres and Dietmar Wulff, *A Chronicle of the Civil War in Siberia and Exile in China: The Diaries of Petr Vasil' evich Vologodskii, 1918–1925*, Stanford: Hoover Institution Press, 2002, vol. 1, pp. 124–59.

78. On the politics of Komuch, see Stephen M. Berk, "The Democratic Counter-Revolution: Komuch and the Civil War on the Volga," *Canadian Slavic Studies*, vol. 7 (1973), pp. 443–59. This article was drawn from the author's superb but regrettably unpublished dissertation: Stephen M. Berk, "The Coup d'État of Admiral Kolchak and the Counter-Revolution in Siberia and East Russia, 1917–1918," Columbia University PhD Thesis, 1971. Komuch's chief policy documents and other materials are available in: Piontkovskii (ed.), *Grazhdanskaia voina v Rossii (1918–1921 gg.)*, pp. 211–46. A fuller record of its meetings and proclamations is B.F. Dodonov (ed.), *Zhurnaly zasedanii, prikazy i materialy Komiteta chlenov Vserossiiskogo Uchreditel'nogo sobraniia (Iiun'—Oktiabr' 1918 goda)*, Moscow: ROSSPEN, 2011.

79. Only three of the eight members of the SR Central Committee present at the State Conference voted in favor of the Ufa agreement (although, once it had been agreed, most of them reluctantly accepted it, as did a Siberian conference of SRs in late September). See Scott Smith, *Captives of Revolution: The Socialist Revolutionaries and the Bolshevik Dictatorship, 1918–23*, Pittsburgh: University of Pittsburgh Press, 2011, pp. 146, 153.

80. See A.F. Iziumov (ed.), "Ufimskoe gosudarstvennoe soveshchanie," *Russkii istoricheskii arkhiv*, no. 1 (1929), pp. 274–5.

81. L.A. Krol', *Za tri goda: Vospominaniia, vpechatleniia i vstrechi*, Vladivostok: Tip. T-va izd. "Svobodnaia Rossiia," 1921, p. 140.

82. On the Omsk coup, see Smele, *Civil War in Siberia*, pp. 50–107.

83. The title of "supreme ruler" was adopted over the more blunt "dictator," according to one of Kolchak's closest confidants, I.I. Sukin, so as "to maintain the decorum of the civic spirit": Smele, *Civil War In Siberia*, p. 109 (n. 6). Also V.V. Zhuralev, "'Prisoiv takovomu litsu naimenovanie verkhovnogo pravitelia': K voprosu o titule, priniatom admiralom A.V. Kolchakom 18 noiabria 1918 g.," *Antropologicheskii forum*, no. 8 (2008), pp. 353–86.

84. In Aug. 1917, Kolchak, whom (as one of Russia's few successful commanders of the First World War) many had favored for the role of military dictator that was subsequently assigned to Kornilov, had been dispatched on a pointless mission to the United States by Kerensky to get him out of the country. He returned to the Far East in Oct. 1917 and offered his services to the British, who sent him to assist General Khorvath's efforts in Manchuria. However, despairing of reining in Ataman Semenov and of bringing any semblance of order to the anarchic anti-Bolshevik formations in the region, Kolchak subsequently retired to Japan. There he met General Alfred Knox of Britimis, who promptly ferried what he called "the best Russian for our purposes in the Far East" (WO 33 962/186, Knox to the Director of Military Intelligence, 31 Aug. 1918) to Omsk. There, on 4 Nov. 1918, he became Minister of War and Marine in the government of the Directory (which had co-opted, en bloc, the cabinet of the PSG).

85. On the consolidation of the Kolchak regime in late 1918, see Smele, *Civil War in Siberia*, pp. 108–23, 188–99.

86. V.V. Zhuravlev (ed.), *Privetstvennye poslaniia Verkhovnomu Praviteliu i Verkhovnomu Glavnokomanduiushchemu admiralu A.V. Kolchaku. Noiabr' 1918—noiabr' 1919 g.: sb. dokumentov*, St Petersburg: Izdatel'stvo Evropeiskogo universiteta v Sankt-Peterburge, 2012, pp. 18–19, 181.

87. The British War Cabinet had decided, in principle, on 14 Nov. 1918, to recognize the Directory as the all-Russian government. See Michael Kettle, *Russia and the Allies, 1917–1920: Churchill and the Archangel Fiasco*, London: Routledge, 1992, pp. 8–13.

88. Smele, *Civil War in Siberia*, pp. 181–82.

89. On the fate of the reserve, which initially amounted to just over 650 million gold roubles, see Jonathan D. Smele, "White Gold: The Imperial Russian Gold Reserve in the Anti-Bolshevik East, 1918–? (An Unconcluded Chapter in the History of the Russian Civil War)," *Europe–Asia Studies*, vol. 46, no. 8 (1994), pp. 1317–47; and Oleg Budnitskii, *Den'gi russkoi emigratsii: kolchakovskoe zoloto, 1918–1957*, Moscow: Novoe Literaturnoe Obozrenie, 2008.

90. L.D. Trotsky, *My Life: An Attempt at an Autobiography*, Harmondsworth: Penguin, 1975, pp. 396–400; Jan M. Meijer (ed.), *The Trotsky Papers, 1917–1922*, The Hague: Mouton, 1964, vol. 1, pp. 69–71; L.D. Trotsky, *How the Revolution Armed, Vol. 1: 1918*, London: New Park Publications, 1979, p. 313. Also, Geoffrey Swain, "Trotsky and the Russian Civil War," in Ian D. Thatcher (ed.), *Reinterpreting Revolutionary Russia: Essays in Honour of James D. White*, Basingstoke: Palgrave, 2006, pp. 86–7. For a colorful first-hand account of the fighting at this crucial juncture, see Larissa Reissner, "Sviajsk," *Cahiers Léon Trotsky*, vol. 12 (1982), pp. 51–64.

91. On Murav'ev: Geoffrey Swain, "Russia's Garibaldi: The Revolutionary Life of Mikhail Artemevich Muraviev," *Revolutionary Russia*, vol. 11, no. 2 (1998), pp. 54–81; and V.A. Savchenko, "Glavnokommanduiushchii Murav'ev: '... Nash lozung—byt' besposhchadnymi'," in V.A. Savchenko, *Avantiuristy grazhdanskoi voiny: istoricheskoe issledovanie*, Khar'kov: Folio, 2000, pp. 44–64.

92. Geoffrey Swain, "The Disillusioning of the Revolution's Praetorian Guard: The Latvian Riflemen, Summer–Autumn 1918," *Europe–Asia Studies*, vol. 51, no. 4 (1999), pp. 667–86.

93. On Savinkov, see: Spence, *Boris Savinkov*, pp. 209–16; and Karol Wedziagolski, *Boris Savinkov: Portrait of a Terrorist*, Clifton, NJ: The Kingston Press, 1988, pp. 53–65. The genesis

and course of the Iaroslavl' revolt is adumbrated in E.A. Ermolin and V.N. Kozliakov (eds), *Iaroslavskoe vosstanie, 1918*, Moscow: Mezhdunarodnoe Fond "Demokratiia," 2007.

94. On the Red Terror, see below, pp. 191–5. On the Lockhart Plot, which may have been a Cheka-staged sting (although, as ever, it is difficult to pin down anything involving Sidney Reilly), see Gordon Brook-Shepherd, *The Iron Maze: The Western Secret Services and the Bolsheviks*, London: Macmillan, 1998, pp. 81–118; Richard K. Debo, "Lockhart Plot or Dzerzhinskii Plot?" *Journal of Modern History*, vol. 43, no. 3 (1971), pp. 413–39; John W. Long, "Searching for Sydney Reilly: The Lockhart Plot in Revolutionary Russia, 1918," *Europe–Asia Studies*, vol. 47, no. 7 (1995), pp. 1,225–43; Robert Service, *Spies and Commissars: Bolshevik Russia and the West*, London: Macmillan, 2011, pp. 155–65; and Geoffrey R. Swain, "'An Interesting and Plausible Proposal': Bruce Lockhart, Sidney Reilly and the Latvian Riflemen, Russia, 1918," *Intelligence and National Security*, vol. 14, no. 3 (1999), pp. 81–102.

95. On the end of the old army, see M. Frenkin, *Russkaia armiia i revoliutsiia, 1917–1918*, Munich: Logos, 1978, Chapter 7. On the early days of the Red Army, see: John Erickson, "The Origins of the Red Army," in Richard Pipes (ed.), *Revolutionary Russia*, Cambridge, MA: Harvard University Press, 1968, pp. 224–56; and David Footman, "The Beginnings of the Red Army," in David Footman, *Civil War in Russia*, London: Faber & Faber, 1961, pp. 135–66. For two very insightful first-hand accounts, see: M.D. Bonch-Bruevich, *From Tsarist General to Red Army Commander*, Moscow: Progress Publishers, 1966; and A.F. Ilyin-Zhenevsky, *The Bolsheviks in Power: Reminiscences of the Year 1918*, London: New Park Publications, 1984.

96. This mirage not only affected the party Left. In April 1917, in his "April Theses," Lenin had called for "Abolition of the police, the army, the bureaucracy," adding a note of clarification that this meant "The standing army to be replaced by the arming of the whole people": Lenin, "The Tasks of the Proletariat in the Present Revolution," *CW*, vol. 24, p. 23. And, as recently as September 1917, Lenin had written that "The substitution of a people's militia for the police is a reform that follows from the entire course of the revolution … There is only one way to *prevent* the restoration of the police, and that is to create a people's militia and to fuse it with the army (the standing army to be replaced by the arming of the entire people). Service in this militia should extend to all citizens of both sexes between the ages of fifteen and sixty-five without exception": Lenin, "The Tasks of the Proletariat in Our Revolution," *CW*, vol. 24, p. 70.

97. Ilyin Zhenevsky, *The Bolsheviks in Power*, p. 33. The author of this work—later a world-class chess player, who beat the famous Capablanca at a Moscow tournament in 1925—was the younger brother of the "Red Admiral," F.F. Raskol'nikov.

98. Quoted in Ilyin-Zhenevsky, *The Bolsheviks in Power*, pp. 29–30 (emphasis in original).

99. N.N. Movchin, *Komplektovanie Krasnoi armii*, Moscow: Gosizdat, 1926, p. 36.

100. Indeed, partisans of what became known as *partizanshchina* would point out that the few glimpses of steel in the panicky response of Soviet forces to the German advance in late February 1918 involved the brief recapture of Pskov by the 1st Partisan Brigade and operations in the rear of enemy lines by Red volunteer units near Minsk. See Swain, *Origins of the Russian Civil War*, p. 134. Also, some of the most remarkable (and subsequently much fêted) achievements of Red forces over the summer of 1918 involved independent, essentially partisan formations: the marches of the Taman (Red) Army and the Urals Army March, for example. In addition (although it would have been heresy for any Soviet leader

to make such an analogy) the tremendously successful Revolutionary-Insurgent Army of Ukraine, commanded by the anarchist Nestor Makhno, exhibited the acme of the volunteer/partisan principle during its civil-war operations of 1918 to 1920. In the light of all this, Ronnie Kowalski's conclusion that the Left Bolsheviks' hopes for revolutionary war were entirely unrealistic might be a little pessimistic: Ronald I. Kowalski, *The Bolshevik Party in Conflict: The Left Communist Opposition of 1918*, London: Macmillan, 1991, pp. 76–8.

101. These aspects of Trotsky's character are foregrounded in the portrait offered in Geoffrey Swain, *Trotsky*, Harlow: Pearson, 2006.

102. Trotsky, *How the Revolution Armed, Vol. 1: 1918*, pp. 19–23 (emphasis in original).

103. N. Bukharin and E. Preobrazhensky, *The ABC of Communism*, Harmondsworth: Penguin, 1969, pp. 255–7.

104. Ibid., pp. 257–8.

105. Ibid., p. 259.

106. Trotsky, *How the Revolution Armed, Vol. 1: 1918*, pp. 43, 47. In point of fact, a decree formally delineating "The Procedure for Appointment to Posts in the Workers' and Peasants' Red Army" was not issued by VTsIK until 22 Apr. 1918, but instructions from the War Commissariat on 21 Mar. 1918 had already established the principle that the election of officers should cease and, as early as 27 Dec. 1917, had determined that officers should only be dismissed if it could be demonstrated that there were suitably qualified personnel available to replace them.

107. On the Supreme Military Council, see below, p. 84.

108. On the service of the officers of the Academy of the General Staff (*genshtabisty*) in Red forces, see: A.V.Ganin, "O roli ofitserov General'nogo shtaba v grazhdanskoi voine," *Voprosy istorii*, no. 6 (2004), pp. 98–111; V.V. Kaminskii, "Vypuskniki Akademii gereral'nogo shtaba na sluzhbe v Krasnoi Armii," *Voenno-istoricheskii zhurnal*, no. 8 (2002), pp. 54–61; V.V. Kaminskii, "Russkie genshtabisty v 1917–1920: Itogi izucheniia," *Voprosy istorii*, no. 12 (2002), pp. 40–51; V.V. Kaminskii, "Brat protiv brat: ofitsery-genshtabisty v 1917–1920gg.," *Voprosy istorii*, no. 11 (2003), pp. 115–26; and Steven J. Main, "Pragmatism in the Face of Adversity: The Bolsheviks and the Academy of the General Staff of the Red Army during the Russian Civil War, 1918–1921," *Journal of Slavic Military Studies*, vol. 8, no. 2 (1995), pp. 333–55. The background of the *genshtabisty*'s willingness to serve in the Red Army is expertly traced in Matitiahu Mayzel, *Generals and Revolutionaries: The Russian General Staff during the Revolution—A Study in the Transformation of a Military Elite*, Osnabruck: Biblio-Verlag, 1979.

109. See S.M. Kliatskin, *Na zashchite Oktiabria: Organizatsiia reguliarnoi army i militsionnoe stroitel'stvo v Sovetskoi respublike, 1917–1920*, Moscow: Nauka, 1965, pp. 160–1.

110. *Dekrety Sovetskoi vlasti*, vol. 1, pp. 356–7; cf. Erich Wollenberg, *The Red Army: A Study of the Growth of Soviet Imperialism*, Westport, CT: Hyperion Press, 1973, p. 365 (Appendix 1: "The Scheme for a Socialist Army").

111. The oppositionists' ire that Sovnarkom seemed intent on reducing commissars to the status of functionaries, despite their rapidly expanding command experience—most eloquently distilled in a speech to the Eighth Congress of 20 Mar. 1919 by V.M. Smirnov (*8-oi S″ezd*, pp. 153–9)—was salved by the replacement, on 18 Apr. 1919, of the somewhat haphazardly functioning All-Russian Bureau of Military Commissars (Vsebiurvoenkom, created by the People's Commissariat for War on 8 Apr. 1918) with the more robust and active

Political Administration of the Revvoensovet of the Republic (Politicheskoe upravlenie RVS Respubliki). The latter, generally known as PUR, was chaired by the Leftist I.T. Smilga. See: Francesco Benvenuti, *I bolscevichi e l'armata rossa, 1918–1922*, Naples: Bibliopolis, 1982, pp. 135–82; and Francesco Benvenuti, "La 'Questione militare' al'VIII Congresso della RKP(b)," *Studi Storici*, vol. 35, no. 4 (1994), pp. 1,095–121. Also, for the stenographic records, "Deiatel'nost Tsentral'nogo Komiteta partii v dokumentakh (sobytiia i fakty): Mart 1919g. VIII s″ezd RKP(b): Stenogramma zasedenii voennoi sektsii s″ezda 20 i 21 marta 1919 goda i zakrytogo zasedenii s″ezda 21 marta 1919 goda," *Izvestiia TsK KPSS*, vol. 1 (1989), much of which is summarized in V.P. Bokarev, *VIII s″ezd RKP(b)*, Moscow: Politizdat, 1990, pp. 53–77. On Smilga and PUR, see: Mark von Hagen, *Soldiers in the Proletarian Dictatorship: The Red Army and the Soviet Socialist State, 1917–1930*, Ithaca, NY: Cornell University Press, 1990, pp. 67–181; and, especially, Steven J. Main, "The Creation, Organization and Work of the Red Army's Political Apparatus during the Civil War, 1918–20," University of Edinburgh PhD Thesis, 1990.

112. Bukharin and Probrazhensky, *The ABC of Communism*, pp. 265–6.

113. *How the Revolution Armed, Vol. 1: 1918*, pp. 199–210.

114. A.V. Ganin, "Workers and Peasants Red Army 'General Staff Personalities' Defecting to the Enemy Side in 1918–1921," *Journal of Slavic Military Studies*, vol. 26, no. 2 (2013), pp. 259–309. In this article, Ganin also offers numerous interesting suggestions as to why some officers deserted and some did not.

115. L.D. Trotsky, "Voennye spetsialisty i Krasnaia armiia," *Voennoe delo*, no. 2 (21 Jan. 1919), quoted in ibid., p. 309. Despite slurs against them to the contrary, even members of the Military Opposition recognized that the military specialists were a necessary evil. They were appeased, moreover, as the proportion of *voenspetsy* among the Red command declined as the civil wars progressed and more Red commanders were trained: in 1918, at least 75 percent of the command staff of the Red Army was made up of military specialists; in 1919, that figure fell to 53 percent; in 1920, it fell again to 42 percent; and in 1921, it fell again to 34 percent. But, throughout the struggle, at least until 1921, almost all commanders of Red fronts and individual Red armies were *voenspetsy*, as were the successive commanders-in-chief, Colonels Jukums Vācietis and S.S. Kamenev. On the *voenspetsy*, see also A.G. Kavtaradze, *Voennye spetsialisty na sluzhbe Respubliki Sovetov 1917–1920 gg.*, Moscow: Nauka, 1998.

116. In a typically perverse Stalinist twist, the city that was the site of this snub was renamed Stalingrad in 1925. On the Tsaritsyn affair see: Richard Argenbright, "Red Tsaritsyn: Precursor of Stalinist Terror," *Revolutionary Russia*, vol. 4, no. 2 (1991), pp. 157–83; and Robert C. Tucker, *Stalin as Revolutionary*, New York: Norton, 1974, pp. 100–7. In a report to Lenin of 11 Jan. 1919, Trotsky wrote: "I consider the protection given by Stalin to the Caricyn [Tsaritsyn] trend the most dangerous sort of ulcer, worse than any act of perfidy or treachery on the part of the military specialists": Meijer (ed.), *The Trotsky Papers*, vol. 1, p. 251.

117. See, for example, the report on "The Position of Officers in the Red Army" provided by General D.V. Filat'ev to Denikin's Special Council on 7 May 1919: A.V. Kvakin (ed.), *V zhernovakh revoliutsii. Russkaia intelligentsia mezhdu belymi i krasnymi v porevoliutsionnye gody: sbornik dokumentov i materialov*, Moscow: "Russkaia Panorama," 2008, cited at: http://www.hrono.info/dokum/191_dok/19190507filat.html

118. *How the Revolution Armed, Vol. 1: 1918*, pp. 557–8.

119. It no doubt helped that Mikhail Dmitrievich Bonch-Bruevich's elder brother, Vladimir, was a respected Old Bolshevik and scholar, who, from Nov. 1917 to Oct. 1920, served as chief secretary to Sovnarkom. On the decision to move the Soviet capital to Moscow, see Ewa Béard, "Pourquoi les bolcheviks ont-ils quitté Petrograd?" *Cahiers du Monde Russe et Soviétique*, vol. 34, no. 4 (1993), pp. 407–28.

120. For an appreciation of this inheritance, see N.E. Kakurin, *Kak srazhalas' revoliutsiia, 1917–21*, vol. 1, Moscow: Gosizdat, 1925, p. 135.

121. *Dekrety Sovetskoi vlasti*, Moscow: Gospolizdat, 1957–2009, vol. 3, p. 268.

122. See: A.P. Nenarkov (ed.), *Revvoensovet Respubliki (6 sent. 1918 g.—28 avg. 1923 g.)*, Moscow: Politizdat, 1991; and M.M. Slavin, *Revvoensovety v 1918–1919 gg: Istoriko-iuridicheskii ocherk*, Moscow: Nauka, 1974.

123. Movchin, *Komplektovanie Krasnoi armii*, pp. 52–3.

124. For the decree "On the Formation of the Council of Defense," see *Dekrety Sovetskoi vlasti*, vol. 4, pp. 92–4.

125. Thomas H. Rigby, *Lenin's Government: Sovnarkom, 1917–1922*, Cambridge: Cambridge University Press, 1979, pp. 76, 84.

126. Evan Mawdsley, *The Russian Civil War*, Boston: Allen & Unwin, 1987, p. 61.

127. For a brilliant discussion of all this, based on a broad array of officer memoirs, see David R. Jones, "The Officers and the October Revolution," *Soviet Studies*, vol. 28, no. 2 (1976), pp. 207–23. Also Ganin, "Workers and Peasants Red Army."

128. Later again, more carrots would be offered, with the barrage of propaganda to the effect that the Red Army was the defender of the Soviet "Motherland" against all foreign interventions. This proved particularly effective during the Soviet–Polish War of 1920 and would attract to the Soviet side theretofore hostile or neutral tsarist officers, prominent among them the former commander-in-chief of the Russian Army General A.A. Brusilov. The latter issued appeals to his fellow officers to join the Red Army in *Pravda* (7 and 28 May 1920). Brusilov might, by conviction, have been a natural "White," but he harbored hostility towards Denikin's forces for having in 1919 executed his son, Aleksei, who was serving in the Red Army.

129. Ilyin-Zhenevsky, *The Bolsheviks in Power*, p. 39.

130. *Dekrety Sovetskoi vlasti*, vol 2, pp. 155–6.

131. Meijer (ed.), *The Trotsky Papers*, vol. 1, p. 69.

132. Jukums Vācietis (1873–1938), the son of an impoverished Latvian farm laborer, entered military service as a volunteer in 1891, graduated from the Academy of the General Staff in 1909, and by August 1917 had risen to the command of the 2nd Latvian Rifle Brigade of the Russian Army, having served with distinction in the First World War. Krylenko made him chief of the Operational Department of the Revolutionary Field Staff—and in that capacity, in Krylenko's absence, he was, in effect, the last commander of the imperial army—before assuming command of the Latvian Riflemen on 13 Apr. 1918. He was politically sympathetic to the Left-SRs, but opposed their determination to continue hostilities against Germany and oversaw the crushing of their uprising in Moscow in July 1918 before being sent to command the Eastern Front. He was then named as main commander of the Red Army on 2 Sep. 1918. He was dismissed on 8 July 1919 (see below) but, after a brief period of imprisonment, remained in service in administrative and teaching roles. Vācietis was arrested on 29 Nov. 1937, and on 26 July 1938 was found guilty of espionage (for Germany since 1918 and for Latvia since 1921) and of membership of a "terrorist organiza-

tion" by the Military Collegium of the Supreme Court of the USSR and was sentenced to death. He was shot two days later at Kommunarka in Moscow *oblast'*, and was buried there. During his interrogation, under torture, he denounced twenty others as co-members of a "Latvian fascist organization," all of whom were subsequently arrested and most of whom were also shot. Vācietis was posthumously rehabilitated by the Supreme Court of the USSR on 28 Mar. 1957. His pre-civil war career is detailed in Uldis Gērmanis, *Oberst Vācietis und die lettischen Schützen im Weltkrieg und in der Oktoberrevolution*, Stockholm: Almqvist & Wiksell, 1974. See also: Jukums Vācietis, "Moia zhizn' i moi vospominaniia," *Daugava*, nos 3–5 (1980).

133. The People's Army might have been able to have offered more resistance had it been able to summon reinforcements from its ally, the Orenburg Cossack Host, but the Orenburg Cossacks, under Ataman A.I. Dutov, were pressed sorely from the rear, along the Orenburg–Tashkent railway (where 12,000 Red forces from the Turkestan Group were to reach Aktiubinsk in Nov. 1918), and were also engaged in their own battles around the host capital with local Red forces (many of which escaped from the Cossacks' grip in July 1918 and, under the command of V.K. Bliuker, undertook the epic Urals Army March that saw them unite with the 4th Red Army at Kungur on 21 Sep. 1918).

134. Bonch-Bruevich was engaged thereafter in scientific and teaching work for the Red Army. Although he was briefly detained during a general sweep of the former *voenspetsy* by the Cheka in 1931 ("Operation 'Spring'"), he was released and returned to work and was even promoted to the rank of lieutenant-general in 1944. He died, at the age of eighty-six, in 1956.

135. In Russian usage of the civil-war era the term "front" denoted not a location but the highest operational–strategic grouping of armed forces (usually a number of separate armies) and could be translated as "army group." Initially, from June 1918, these were created on an ad hoc basis, but from September 1918 Red fronts were organized according to directives of the RVSR. The first Red fronts (the Northern–Urals–Siberian Front, the Eastern Front, the Northern Front, the Southern Front, and the Ukrainian Front) were usually established simultaneously with the formation of the armies that were their constituent parts. Later fronts (the Caspian–Caucasian Front, the Western Front, the Turkestan Front, the South East Front, the South West Front, the Caucasian Front, and the second Southern Front, against Wrangel) were created from the redeployment of pre-existing armies. Red fronts would generally consist of two to six field armies, other independent forces, reserve forces, and specialist units (such as armored trains and air forces), occasionally supplemented by military flotillas (the Volga Military Flotilla, the Astrakhan–Caspian Military Flotilla, etc.) and (from mid-1919 onwards) cavalry armies (the 1st Cavalry Army and the 2nd Cavalry Army). In isolated areas, local Bolsheviks also created independent local fronts, usually in the rear of White forces (the Semirech'e Front, the Ferghana Front, the Aktiubinsk Front, etc.).

136. If any reminder was needed of how perilous the situation was becoming, it was provided in these months by the fate of F.F. Raskol'nikov, who was effectively commander of the Red Navy: on 27 Dec. 1918, Raskol'nikov's flagship, the *Spartak*, was run aground off Revel while being pursued by vessels of the Royal Navy (chiefly the destroyer HMS *Wakeful*). Raskol'nikov was taken into custody by the British and the *Spartak* was gifted to the Estonians, who promptly executed most of its crew. See Jonathan D. Smele, "A Bolshevik in Brixton Prison: Fedor Raskol'nikov and the Origins of Anglo-Soviet Relations," in Thatcher

(ed.), *Reinterpreting Revolutionary Russia*, pp. 110–11; and Geoffrey Bennett, *Cowan's War*, pp. 29–46. More generally, see Edgar Anderson, "British Policy Toward the Baltic States, 1918–1920," *Journal of Central European Affairs*, vol. 19, no. 3 (1959), pp. 276–89; and Edgar Anderson, "An Undeclared War: The British–Soviet Naval Struggle in the Baltic, 1918–1920," *Journal of Central European Affairs*, vol. 22, no. 1 (1962), pp. 43–78.

137. The Izhevsk-Votkinsk uprising was fairly disastrous for the Reds, as Izhevsk produced 25 percent of Russia's infantry rifles and was the sole producer of rifle and revolver barrels, while Votkinsk produced armor for naval needs (transformed in the civil wars to plating for armored trains also). See P.N. Dmitriev and K.I. Kulikov, *Miatezh v Izhevsk-Votkinskom raione*, Izhevsk: Udmurtiia, 1992, pp. 7–8. On the revolt, see Aaron B. Retish, Russia's *Peasants in Revolution and Civil War: Citizenship, Identity and the Creation of the Soviet State, 1914–1922*, Cambridge: Cambridge University Press, 2008, pp. 179–88. On the fate of the participants in the rising, in Siberia and the Far East, see A.G. Efimov, *Izhevtsy i Votkintsy, 1918–1920*, Moscow: Airis Press, 2008 (originally published privately by Efimov in San Francisco in 1975).

138. There is some evidence to suggest that the withdrawal of forces of the People's Army towards Ufa was altogether more orderly than has generally been allowed (certainly in Soviet histories). See, for example, the account in Serge P. Petroff, *Remembering a Forgotten War: Civil War in Eastern European Russia and Siberia, 1918–1920*, Boulder: Eastern European Monographs, 2000, pp. 106–8; and P.P. Petrov, *Rokovye gody*, California, 1965, pp. 119–25. This has led one historian of the period to suggest that, had the Omsk coup of 18 Nov. 1918 not thrown confusion to their ranks, the former forces of Komuch might have rallied before Ufa in late November 1918 and resumed a full offensive, as Red units (notably the Latvian Riflemen) lost their nerve. See Geoffrey Swain, "The Democratic Counter-Revolution Reconsidered" (forthcoming).

139. G.I. Klerzhe, *Revoliutsiia i Grazhdanskaia voina: lichnye vospominaniia (chast' pervaia)*, Mukden: Tip. Gazety "Mukden," 1932, pp. 113–14.

140. William A. Brown, *The Groping Giant: Revolutionary Russia as Seen by an American Democrat*, New Haven: Yale University Press, 1920, p. 176. Lebedev (b. 1882), who had graduated from the Academy of the General Staff in 1911, had served on various army staffs and had taught at the Academy before and during the First World War, but his major qualifications for such an exalted post in Kolchak's army seem to have been that he had helped found the Officers' Union in 1917 and, as an instigator of the Kornilov affair, had been imprisoned with the Bykhov generals. In White Siberia, where conspiracy was king, this sort of thing mattered. Moreover, he therefore carried with him a whiff of the Volunteers (although some sources have it that he only made his way to Siberia in Feb. 1918 because General Kornilov had dismissed him as a disruptive element among his staff).

141. M.A. Molodtsygin, *Krasnaia Armiia: rozhdenie i stanovlenie, 1917–1920 gg.*, Moscow: RAN, 1997, p. 134.

142. Erik C. Landis, "Who were the 'Greens'? Rumor and Collective Identity in the Russian Civil War," *Russian Review*, vol. 69, no. 1 (2010), p. 31.

143. Orlando Figes, "The Red Army and Mass Mobilization during the Russian Civil War, 1918–1920," *Past and Present*, no. 129 (1990), pp. 168–211.

144. *Dekrety Sovetskoi vlasti*, vol. 2, pp. 541–4. See Joshua A. Sanborn, *Drafting the Russian Nation: Military Conscription, Total War and Mass Politics, 1905–1925*, DeKalb: Northern Illinois University Press, 2003, p. 45

145. Very important here was the creation by VTsIK, in late December 1918, of a Central Anti-Desertion Commission: M.A. Molodtsygin, *Raboche-krest'ianskii soiuz, 1918–1920*, Moscow: Nauka, 1987, p. 138.

146. Sanborn, *Drafting the Russian Nation*, p. 50

147. Meijer (ed.), *The Trotsky Papers*, vol. 1, pp. 70–71.

148. S.P. Olikov, *Dezertirstvo v Krasnoi armii i bor'ba s nim*, Moscow: Izdanie Voennoi tipografii Upravleniia delami Narkomvoenmor i RVS SSSR, 1926, p. 39. "Women, Throw Out the Deserter!" urged Bolshevik propaganda posters of the time: David King, *Russian Revolutionary Posters*, London: Tate, 2013, p. 35.

149. Sanborn, *Drafting the Russian Nation*, pp. 51–2.

150. Ibid., p. 54. Sanborn's approach and findings are expanded upon in a recent study of a front-line locality: Alistair S. Wright, "'Stemming the Flow': The Red Army Anti-Desertion Campaign in Soviet Karelia (1919)," *Revolutionary Russia*, vol. 25, no. 2 (2012), pp. 141–62.

151. Movchin, *Komplektovanie Krasnoi armii*, pp. 100–1.

152. Although the Legion would continue to perform a vital task for the Whites in policing the essential supply line of the Trans-Siberian Railway from Omsk to Lake Baikal in 1919, and in 1920 would intervene again to, conversely, seal the fate of the Whites' Supreme Ruler by handing Admiral Kolchak over to revolutionary authorities at Irkutsk as the price of their unhindered passage to Vladivostok and eventual repatriation.

153. Lenin, *CW*, vol. 28, pp. 149–50.

154. *Direktivy komandovaniia frontov Krasnoi Armii (1917–1922 gg.): Sbornik dokumentov*, Moscow: Voenizdat, 1971–8, vol. 1, pp. 468–9.

155. A.P. Gritskevich, *Zapadnyi Front RSFSR, 1918–1920: Bor'ba mezhdu Rossiei i Pol'shei za Belorossiiu*, Minsk: Kharvest, 2010, pp. 99–150; and James D. White, "The Revolution in Lithuania, 1918–1919," *Soviet Studies*, vol. 23, no. 2 (1971–72), pp. 186–200. Soviet Russia was here able to take advantage of the fact that although the Polish head of state, Józef Piłsudski, was intent on building a Baltic–Black Sea confederation (Międzymorze), tying Poland to Lithuania, Belarussia, and Ukraine, in early 1918 he was far from having even the basic means at hand to achieve such complex ends and was content, for a while, to tolerate the efforts of his more pacifist Prime Minister, Ignacy Paderewski, to reach a tactical accommodation with Moscow. On the Międzymorze project, see below, pp. 153–4.

156. Jaan Anvelt and other members of the Commune would subsequently participate in the failed Communist coup in Tallinn of 1 Dec. 1924. Anvelt was killed during the purges in 1937.

157. See Endel Krepp, *The Estonian War of Independence, 1918–1920*, Stockholm: Estonian Information Bureau, 1980; and Eric A. Sibul, "Logistical Aspects of the Estonian War of Independence, 1918–1920," *Baltic Security and Defence Review*, vol. 12, no. 2 (2010), pp. 108–33.

158. On 16 Nov. 1918, Latvian units on the Eastern Front had been ordered to withdraw and reassemble on the Latvian border.

159. George Popoff, *The City of the Red Plague: Soviet Rule in a Baltic Town*, London: George Allen & Unwin, 1932, p. 87.

160. Ibid., pp. 117–31.

161. Ibid., pp. 153–5.

162. See James D. White, "National Communism and World Revolution: The Political Consequences of German Military Withdrawal from the Baltic Area, 1918–19," *Europe–Asia Studies*, vol. 46, no. 8 (1994), pp. 1,362–3 and *passim*.

163. Before they departed from Riga, the Bolsheviks executed dozens of prisoners in the city jail and many local pastors and priests. See Popoff, *City of the Red Plague*, pp. 210–21.

164. Stanley Page, *The Formation of the Baltic States*, Cambridge, MA: Harvard University Press, 1959, pp. 135–41; Georg von Rauch, *The Baltic States: The Years of Independence, 1917–1940*, London: Hurst, 1974, pp. 56–8; David Footman, "The Civil War and the Baltic States, Part 1: Von der Goltz and Bermondt-Avalov" (St Antony's Papers on Soviet Affairs, Oct. 1959). The (Red) Army of Soviet Latvia had been disestablished as early as 7 June 1919, with its forces reconfigured as the 15th Red Army.

165. The author of a recent (and excellent) history of the civil war in Ukraine tellingly entitled the section in which he discusses the Hetmanate "The Nation against the Regime." See B.F. Sodatenko, *Grazhdanskaia voina v Ukraine (1917–1920 gg.)*, Moscow: Novyi Khronograf, 2012, pp. 200–12.

166. The resignation of most socialists from the governing Directory of UNR was not entirely amicable: the usual anti-Bolshevik divisions had already become apparent between those (chiefly members of the Ukrainian PSR and Ukrainian SDLP) who advocated an immediate radical program of land reform to nurture popular support and those (chiefly the UNR's head of military affairs, Symon Petliura, and his coterie) who courted bourgeois and Allied support. Many Leftist members of the UPSR and USDLP would subsequently support Soviet power in Ukraine, uniting in Aug. 1919 as the Ukrainian Social Democratic Labor Party (Independents), which subsequently became the Ukrainian Communist Party (Borotbists): Iwan Majstrenko, *Borot'bism: A Chapter in the History of Ukrainian Communism*, New York: Praeger, 1954.

167. On the repercussions of this particular conundrum for Allied leaders who were bound, in principle, to the notion of self-determination, see Laurance J. Orzell, "A 'Hotly Disputed' Issue: Eastern Galicia at the Paris Peace Conference, 1919," *Polish Review*, vol. 25, no. 1 (1980), pp. 49–68. Also Matvy Stachiw and Jaroslaw Szetandera, *Western Ukraine at the Turning Point of Europe's History, 1918–1923*, 2 vols, New York: Shevchenko Scientific Society, 1969–71. On Allied attitudes to the issue of Ukrainian independence in general in this period, see: Emmanuel Evain, *Le problème de l'indépendance de l'Ukraine et la France*, Paris: F. Alcan, 1931; Taras Hunchak, "Sir Lewis Namier and the Struggle for Eastern Galicia, 1918–1920," *Harvard Ukrainian Studies*, vol. 1, no. 2 (1977), pp. 198–210; David Saunders, "Britain and the Ukrainian Question, 1912–20," *English Historical Review*, vol. 103, no. 406 (1988), pp. 40–68; Leonid C. Sonevytsky, "The Ukrainian Question in R.H. Lord's Writings on the Paris Peace Conference of 1919," *Annals of the Ukrainian Academy of Arts and Sciences in the United States*, vol. 10, no. 1 (29) (1962–63), pp. 65–84; and Constantine Warvariv, "America and the Ukrainian National Cause, 1917–1920," in Hunczak, *The Ukraine*, pp. 352–81.

168. See Kubchasky, *Western Ukraine in Conflict with Poland and Bolshevism, passim*.

169. J. Okhotnikov and N. Batchinsky, *La Bessarabie et la Paix européenne*, Paris: Association des Émigrés Bessarabiens, 1927; and N.V. Berzniakov *et al.* (eds), *Khotinskoe vosstanie: dokumenty i materialy*, Kishinev: Shtiintsa, 1976.

170. What constituted "Ukraine," which had never—unlike Finland, or even Georgia, for example—had a clearly defined spatial identity, was a problem in itself for the advocates of Ukrai-

nian independence. For Russians, the vagueness of Ukraine's ambitions was compounded by onomastics: in Russian, "Ukraine" means something as vague as "On the Outlying Lands."

171. On this issue, see: Mark Baker, "Beyond the National: Peasants, Power, and Revolution in Ukraine," *Journal of Ukrainian Studies*, vol. 24, no. 1 (1999), pp. 39–67; Steven L. Guthier, "The Popular Base of Ukrainian Nationalism in 1917," *Slavic Review*, vol. 38, no. 1 (1979), pp. 30–47; Mark von Hagen, "The Dilemmas of Ukrainian Independence and Statehood, 1917–1921," *The Harriman Institute Forum*, vol. 7 (1994), pp. 7–11; Evan Ostryzniuk, "The Ukrainian Countryside during the Russian Revolution, 1917–1919: The Limits of Peasant Mobilization," *Ukrainian Review*, vol. 44, no. 1 (1997), pp. 54–63; and Arthur Takach, "In Search of Ukrainian National Identity, 1840–1921," *Ethnic and Racial Studies*, vol. 19, no. 3 (1996), pp. 640–59.

172. Ukrainians were even scarcer in peripheral, riverain, and littoral eastern, south-eastern, and southern cities such as Khar'kov, Rostov, and Odessa. See: Steven L. Guthier, "Ukrainian Cities during the Revolution and Interwar Era," in Ivan L. Rudnytsky (ed.), *Rethinking Ukrainian History*, Edmonton: Canadian Institute of Ukrainian Studies, 1981, pp. 156–79; Bohdan Krawchenko, "The Social Structure of the Ukraine at the Turn of the Twentieth Century," *East European Quarterly*, vol. 16, no. 2 (1982), pp. 171–81; and Bohdan Krawchenko, "The Social Structure of Ukraine in 1917," *Harvard Ukrainian Studies*, vol. 14, nos 1–2 (1990), pp. 97–112.

173. Yekelchyk, *Ukraine*, p. 70.

174. Mawdsley, *The Russian Civil War*, p. 252.

175. Makhno promptly shot him dead (or had him shot—versions differ), which put a lot of people out of their misery—especially Jews, who seemed to be Hyhroriiv's only consistent enemy. See: W. Bruce Lincoln, *Red Victory: A History of the Russian Civil War*, New York: Simon and Schuster, 1989, pp. 314–16; and Arthur E. Adams, *Bolsheviks in the Ukraine: The Second Campaign, 1918–1920*, New Haven: Yale University Press, 1963, pp. 147–57, 402–4. Also: Iu.O. Fedorovskii, "O vziamootnosheniiakh atamana Grigor'eva i bat'ki Makhno v 1919 godu," *Voprosy istorii*, no. 9 (1998), pp. 169–71; and V.A. Savchenko, "'Pogromnyi ataman Grigor'ev," in V.A. Savchenko, *Avantiuristy grazhdanskoi voiny: istorischeskoe issledovanie*, Khar'kov: Folio, 2000, pp. 87–128.

176. This applied to Bolsheviks as much as it did to their White opponents, although the aversion to Ukrainian independence of the Soviet government chimed well with the latter's statist predilections and favoring of economies of scale when it came to questions of nation building. Thus, at the height of the Red Army's crisis beyond the Dnepr in May 1919, Trotsky would declare that "This is not just a Ukrainian question, for the Ukraine is part of the Federative Soviet Republic. The Soviet land as a whole is very greatly interested ..." *How the Revolution Armed, Vol. 2: 1919*, p. 265 ("Lessons from the Ukraine," 11 May 1919). A few weeks later, he added that "The heavy ears of wheat in the fields of the Ukraine show the economic might that all the workers and peasants of Russia will be able to develop if they pursue their cause to the end": *How the Revolution Armed, Vol. 2: 1919*, p. 343 ("The Harvest and the War," 19 July 1919).

177. The speech is reproduced in Denikin, *Ocherki russkoi smuty*, vol. 5, pp. 142–4.

178. See below.

179. The term "Kievan Rus'" had only been coined as recently as the nineteenth century, as Rus-

sian nationalists began to explore their history, and so had a special and still fresh resonance in the revolutionary era.

180. For a still unequalled general analysis, see: Reshetar, *The Ukrainian Revolution*.

181. See: Michael J. Carley, *Revolution and Intervention: The French Government and the Russian Civil War, 1917–1919*, Kingston: McGill University Press, 1983, pp. 105–81; George A. Brinkley, *The Volunteer Army and Allied Intervention in South Russia, 1917–1921: A Study in the Politics and Diplomacy of the Russian Civil War*, Notre Dame: University of Notre Dame Press, 1966, pp. 113–46; George A. Brinkley, "Allied Policy and French Intervention in the Ukraine, 1917–1920," in Hunzak, *The Ukraine*, pp. 323–51; Colonel Jean Chabanier, "L'Intervention alliée en Russie méridionale, décembre 1918—mars 1919," *Revue Historique de l'Armée*, vol. 16, no. 4 (1960), pp. 74–92; and J. Kim Munholland, "The French Army and Intervention in Ukraine," in Peter Pastor (ed.), *Revolutions and Interventions in Hungary and its Neighbor States, 1918–1919*, Boulder: East European Monographs, 1988, pp. 335–56. For a well-informed and critical eye-witness account by a French journalist who knew Odessa well, see: Jean Xydias, *L'Intervention française en Russie, 1918–1919. Souvenirs d'un témoin*, Paris: Éditions de France, 1927. A small portion of the Allied forces was based also at Sevastopol'.

182. On the Jassy Conference, see: George A. Brinkley, pp. 79–88; Christopher Lazarski, *Lost Opportunity*, Lanham: University Press of America, 2008, pp. 101–16; Robert H. McNeal, "The Conference of Jassy: An Early Fiasco of the Anti-Bolshevik Movement," in John S. Curtiss (ed.), *Essays in Russian and Soviet History*, New York: Columbia University Press, 1963, pp. 221–36; and, especially, Benjamin Wells, "The Union of Regeneration: The Anti-Bolshevik Underground in Revolutionary Russia, 1917–1919," Queen Mary, University of London PhD Thesis, 2004, Chapter Four.

183. The Galician Army of the WUPR benefited from a long tradition of Ukrainian national organization in the former Austrian territories, which contrasted starkly with the suppression of the national movement in the Russian Empire, as well as by its employment of a large number of German and Austrian majors and colonels (although it lacked experienced generals).

184. Adams, *Bolsheviks in the Ukraine*, pp. 31–90, 278–320, 350–71. See also Volodymyr Horak, *Povstantsi Otamana Hryhor'ieva (serpen' 1918—serpen' 1919 rr.) Istorychne doslidzhennia*, Fastiv: Polifast, 1998.

185. Carley, *Revolution and Intervention*, pp. 159–81.

186. This was made evident in an order from Lenin to Antonov-Ovseenko in late Apr. 1919, insisting that the fate of the revolution in Hungary had now moved down the agenda and that Antonov-Ovseenko should concentrate on containing the domestic counter-revolution (specifically the uprising of the Don Cossacks of the spring of 1919, on which see below): Lenin, *CW*, vol. 44, p. 215. Similarly, while insisting in a note to Vācietis of 22 Apr. 1919 that "firm contact by railway be established with Soviet Hungary," Lenin made clear that no occupation of Galicia and Bukovina should be attempted for fear of distracting Soviet forces in Ukraine from their priorities on the Don: Meijer (ed.), *The Trotsky Papers*, vol. 1, p. 375.

187. The Estonian Constituent Assembly (Asutav Kogu) was elected on 5–7 Apr. 1919; that of Latvia (Satversmes Sapulce) on 17–18 Apr. 1920; and that of Lithuania (Steigiamasis Seimas) on 14–15 Apr. 1920. In all three, liberal parties outnumbered socialists and conservatives, although in Estonia and Latvia the social democrats were the largest single parties.

188. The career of the historian Mikhail Hrushevsky is instructive here: he was welcomed home from exile as a national hero in Ukraine in 1917 (and was elected, *in absentia*, to the chair of the Ukrainian Central Rada before he had even reached Kiev) and has been treated with no less reverence in post-Soviet Ukraine, where his name and face are ubiquitous (adorning, for example, the street on which is currently situated the Ukrainian parliament), yet he fell into dispute with the UNR in 1918–19 and returned to exile in 1919 before spending the last decade of his life seeking to accommodate himself to a Soviet Ukraine. A sympathetic but not hagiographic biography is Thomas M. Prymak, *Mykhailo Hrushevsky: The Politics of National Culture*, Toronto: University of Toronto Press, 1987. The other Ukrainian hero of 1917, Volodymyr Vynnychenko, did not return permanently to Soviet Ukraine but came very close to doing so: Christopher Gilley, "Volodymyr Vynnychenko's Mission to Moscow and Kharkov," *Slavonic and East European Review*, vol. 84, no. 3 (2006), pp. 508–37.

3. 1919–20: WHITE THRUSTS, RED RIPOSTES

1. And, after all, Kolchak was "supreme ruler," a position recognized by Denikin's Order No. 145 of 30 May 1919: Denikin, *Ocherki russkoi smuty*, vol. 5, pp. 97–8; N.I. Astrov, "Priznanie gen. Denikinym adm. Kolchaka: prikaz 30 maia 1919g.—No. 145", *Golos minuvshago na chuzhoi storone*, vol. 14, no. 1 (1926), pp. 210–21. The White leaders General Miller in North Russia and General Iudenich in the north-west did likewise.

2. The best work on the subject—Rosenberg, *Liberals in the Russian Revolution*—demonstrates that, in general, the political parties of the Right having disintegrated in 1917, the once radical Kadets shifted their center of gravity to the right in the course of the civil wars and became the "leadership corps" of the White regimes in Siberia and South Russia. The most considered Soviet work on the subject goes so far as to conclude that their rightward progress was so extreme that the Kadets, in fact, forfeited all their liberal credentials and fully embraced the cause of counter-revolution and reaction: Dumova, *Kadetskaia kontrrevoliutsiia i ee razgrom*. Members of the party were certainly deeply involved in bringing Kolchak to power in 1918 and in sustaining the Supreme Ruler in 1919. On 5 Feb. 1920, it was more than symbolic that the most senior Kadet in Siberia, V.N. Pepeliaev, was executed alongside Admiral Kolchak at Irkutsk. The Kadets' role in Kolchak's information services can be traced in E.V. Lukov and D.N. Shevlev, *Osvedomitel'nyi apparat beloi Sibiri: struktura, funktsii, deiatel'nost' (iiun' 1918—ianvar' 1920 g.)*, Tomsk: Izdatel'stvo Tomskogo Universiteta, 2007.

3. Smele, *Civil War in Siberia*, p. 256.

4. United States, Department of State, *Documents Relating to the Foreign Policy of the United States: 1919 (Peace Conference Papers)*, Washington, DC: Government Printing Office, 1939–40, vol. 5, pp. 497–8, 528–30; vol. 6 pp. 73–5. Although, tellingly, these considerations were also in large part prompted by the success on the field of battle that Kolchak's forces were enjoying in April–May 1919: Smele, *Civil War in Siberia*, pp. 211–13.

5. It is worth recalling here that Kolchak and Denikin hailed from relatively lowly backgrounds, as had Alekseev and Kornilov before them: none of them were of noble birth—indeed, Denikin's father had been born a serf—none of them had a vested interest in property, and all owed their military positions to the relatively meritocratic ethos of the late-Imperial Russian Army and Navy.

6. H.N.H. Williamson, *Farewell to the Don*, London: Collins, 1970, pp. 63–7. Precisely parallel

scenes were witnessed by British officers in Siberia in Oct. 1918, where the scandals usually involved Ataman I.N. Krasil'nikov of the Siberian Cossack Host (one of those subsequently responsible for the arrest of the Directory and the elevation of Kolchak): Smele, *Civil War in Siberia*, p. 82.

7. This was admitted by Denikin's closest advisors: compare the terms of Denikin's decrees on land and labor policy (available in English in Chamberlin, *The Russian Revolution*, vol. 2, pp. 482–4) to the reports of their implementation recorded in Lukomsky, *Vospominaniia*, vol. 2, pp. 185–92. For a fuller discussion of how Denikin's policies were frustrated by his subordinates, see Kenez, *Civil War in South Russia, 1919–1920*, pp. 86–109. A prize example here was that Denikin would introduce a law on the eight-hour day only on 12 Dec. 1919, as his forces were in full flight from the industrial centers of Ukraine and Russia—and even then including in the small print a provision allowing factory owners annually to impose on their workers 400 hours per man of compulsory overtime, thereby rendering the entire exercise meaningless. In towns seized by the Volunteers the ritual of public floggings of union "trouble-makers" became the norm.

8. Smele, *Civil War in Siberia*, pp. 274–89. Also, Stolypin's Minister of Agriculture, A.V. Krivoshein, was influential among the Whites in South Russia in 1919. See A.K. Krivoshein, *Aleksandr Vasil'evich Krivoshein: Sud'ba rossiiskogo reformatora*, Moscow: Moskovskii Rabochii, 1993.

9. Jonathan D. Smele, "'What Kolchak Wants!' Military Versus Polity in White Siberia, 1918–1920," *Revolutionary Russia*, vol. 4, no. 1 (1991), pp. 52–110. It should also be mentioned here that the impressively successful manifestation of the democratic spirit that pertained among Siberia's peasantry, the almost universally engaged cooperative movement, was treated with self-defeating and shabby hostility by Kolchak's government. See Smele, *Civil War in Siberia*, pp. 424–49.

10. Ibid., pp. 289–96. It is now possible to trace in precise detail the political discussions within the White camps and their legislative outcomes through: E.V. Lukov and D.N. Shevelev (eds), *Zakonodatel'naia deiatel'nost Rossiiskogo pravitel'stva admirala A.V. Kolchaka: noiabr' 1918 g.—ianvar' 1920 g.*, 2 vols, Tomsk: Izd-vo Tomskogo Universiteta, 2002–3; and *Zhurnaly zasedanii Osobogo soveshchaniia pri Glavnokomanduiushchem Vooruzhennymi Silami na Iuge Rossii A.I.Denikine. Sentiabr 1918-go—dekabr 1919 goda*, Moscow: ROSSPEN, 2008. See also O.A. Kudinov, *Konstituttsionnye proekty Belogo dvizheniia i konstitutstionno-pravovye teoriu rossisskoi beloemigratsii (1918–1940 gg.), ili Za chto ikh rasstrelivali i deportirovali (dlia tekh, kto khochet poniat' smysl prava). Monografiia*, Moscow: Os'-89, 2006, pp. 12–25.

11. It is nowadays almost impossible to find new works published in Russia that are anything but worshipful of Kornilov, Kolchak, Denikin, and the other White leaders. One notable exception is P.A. Golub, *V zastenkakh Kolchaka: pravda o Belom admirale*, Moscow: Izdatel'stvo Patriot, 2010. Golub took his title from a pamphlet published in 1920 by the SR central committee member D.F. Rakov, who was arrested and imprisoned during the Kolchak coup of Nov. 1918.

12. Peter Kenez, "The Relations between the Volunteer Army and Georgia, 1918–1920: A Case Study in Disunity," *Slavonic and East European Review*, vol. 48 (1970), pp. 403–24.

13. See: Anna Procyk, *Russian Nationalism and Ukraine: The Nationality Policy of the Volunteer Army during the Civil War*, Edmonton: Canadian Institute of Ukrainian Studies, 1995.

14. Peter S. Wandycz, "Secret Soviet–Polish Peace Talks in 1919," *Slavic Review*, vol. 24, no. 3

(1965), pp. 425–49. Denikin was well aware of what his principles had cost him: in his *Kto spas' Sovetskuiu vlast' ot gibeli?* Paris: Maison de la Presse, 1937, he asked "Who saved Soviet power from death?" and gave the unequivocal answer that it was Piłsudski.

15. Alex Marshall, *The Caucasus under Soviet Rule*, London: Routledge, 2010, pp. 51–128. Moreover, the direct corollary of this was to cement (on 16 June 1919) a full military alliance against the AFSR between the Azeri and Georgian republics, which felt themselves to be next in line: Yilmaz, "An Unexpected Peace." Only the presence of the British in the region prevented these allies from attacking Denikin's forces in Daghestan, but they were sorely provoked: at one stage Denikin insisted that all trade on the Caspian had to be carried on Russian vessels and that the Azeri merchant fleet should be confined to port. This instruction, Baku was informed, was based on Article VIII of the 1828 Russo-Persian Treaty of Turkmanchai (http://www.hist.msu.ru/ER/Etext/FOREIGN/turkman.htm). Interestingly, Moscow agreed that the relevant terms of that agreement (which had brought to an end the Russo-Persian War of 1826–28) should be annulled in the Soviet–Persian Treaty of 26 February 1921 (http://www.worldlii.org/int/other/LNTSer/1922/69.html). Denikin enjoyed rather better, but far from harmonious, relations with Armenia, which was involved in extensive territorial disputes with both Georgia and, especially, Azerbaijan: Artin H. Arslanian and Robert L. Nichols, "Nationalism and the Russian Civil War: The Case of Volunteer Army–Armenian Relations, 1918–1920," *Soviet Studies*, vol. 31, no. 4 (1979), pp. 559–73. On the Terek Republic, see Alex Marshall, "The Terek People's Republic, 1918: Coalition Government in the Russian Revolution," *Revolutionary Russia*, vol. 22, no. 2 (2009), pp. 203–21.

16. Smele, *Civil War in Siberia*, pp. 296–301.

17. G.K. Gins, *Sibir' soiuzniki i Kolchak: povorotnyi moment russkoi istorii, 1918–1920gg. (Vpechatleniia i mysli chlena Omskogo pravitel'stva)*, Peking: Izd. "Obshchestva Vozrozhdeniia Rossii v g. Kharbine," 1921, vol. 2, p. 375.

18. On the *Weltanschauung* of the Whites and its origins in the pre-revolutionary military caste see: Peter Kenez, "The Russian Officer Corps before the Revolution: The Military Mind," *Russian Review*, vol. 31, no. 3 (1972), pp. 226–37; Peter Kenez, "A Profile of the Pre-Revolutionary Officer Corps," *Californian Slavic Studies*, vol. 7 (1973), pp. 128–45; Peter Kenez, "The Ideology of the White Movement," *Soviet Studies*, vol. 32, no. 1 (1980), pp. 58–83; and Leonid Heretz, "The Psychology of the White Movement," in Brovkin (ed.), *The Bolsheviks in Russian Society*, pp. 105–21. Also illuminating in this regard is Paul Robinson, "'Always with Honour': The Code of the White Russian Officers," *Canadian Slavonic Papers*, vol. 41, no. 2 (1999), pp. 121–41.

19. N.A. Andrushkevich, "Poslednaia Rossiia," *Beloe delo*, no. 4 (1928), p. 109; Gins, *Sibir', soiuzniki i Kolchak*, vol. 2, pp. 61–2; D.B. Filat'ev, *Katastrofa belogo dvizheniia v Sibiri, 1918–1922gg. (Vpechatleniia ochevidsta)*, Paris: YMCA-Press, 1985, p. 116.

20. K.S. Burevoi, *Kolchakovshchina*, Moscow: Gosizdat, 1919, pp. 20–21.

21. This incensed White supporters around Europe. See *The Case for Bessarabia* (preface by P.N. Miliukov), London: The Russian Liberation Committee, 1919; and *The Roumanian Occupation in Bessarabia*, Paris: Lahure, 1920. For a more balanced view, see Sherman D. Spector, *Rumania at the Paris Peace Conference: A Study of the Diplomacy of Ioan C. Bratianu*, New York: Bookman Associates, 1962.

22. Gins, *Sibir', soiuzniki i Kolchak*, vol. 2, p. 88. Although the Supreme Ruler would have taken

some comfort from the fact that Prinkipo was chosen as a venue for the mooted conference because Clemenceau refused even to contemplate inviting a Bolshevik delegation to Paris.

23. On the Bullitt Mission, see *The Bullitt Mission to Russia: Testimony before the Committee on Foreign Relations, United States Senate*, New York: W.B. Heubsch, 1919.

24. Gins, *Sibir', soiuzniki i Kolchak*, vol. 2, pp. 294–5.

25. *How the Revolution Armed*, vol. 2, p. 493. On the Nansen scheme, see Herbert Hoover, *The Memoirs of Herbert Hoover*, vol. 1, London: Macmillan, 1952, pp. 411–20.

26. Although the moderately more clement conditions further south allowed for campaigning in January 1919, during which month the 4th and 1st Red Armies captured the Cossack capitals of Orenburg and Ural'sk.

27. Smele, *Civil War in Siberia*, pp. 225–9.

28. See, for example, Bradley, *Civil War in Russia*, p. 166.

29. Smele, *Civil War in Siberia*, pp. 238–48.

30. Von Budberg, "Dnevnik," *passim* (here especially vol. 14, pp. 225–38).

31. Ibid., vol. 14, pp. 242–3.

32. Smele, *Civil War in Siberia*, pp. 229–38.

33. Ibid. pp. 308–12.

34. Krol', *Za tri gody*, p. 172.

35. The best treatments of these events were penned by a Red commander of the time: G.Kh. Eikhe, *Ufimskaia avantiura Kolchaka (mart–aprel' 1919g.): pochemu Kolchak ne udalas' prorvat'sia k Volge na soedinenie s Denikinym*, Moscow: Voenizdat, 1960; and G.Kh. Eikhe, *Oprokinutyi tyl.* Moscow: Voenizdat, 1966. A generally reliable account too is L.M. Spirin, *Razgrom armii Kolchaka*, Moscow: Voenizdat, 1957.

36. Smele, *Civil War in Siberia*, pp. 315–17.

37. On Vācietis's fate, see above (Chapter Two, n. 132)

38. General Knox received a sarcastic telegram from the Red command, thanking the British for this unexpected contribution to the defense of the Soviet republic. See L.H. Grondijs, *La Guerre en Russie et en Sibérie*, Paris: Éditions Bossard, 1922, p. 528.

39. The chief constituents of this Eastern Front were: the 1st Army (created from the northern group of forces of the former Siberian Army), commanded by General A.N. Pepeliaev (the younger brother of Kolchak's last prime minister); the 2nd Army (created from the southern group of forces of the former Siberian Army), commanded by Lieutenant-General N.A. Lokhvitskii (to 1 Sep. 1919) and then Major-General S.N. Voitsekhovskii; the 3rd Army (from the Volga, Urals and Ufa groups of forces of the former Western Army), commanded by General K.V. Sakharov; and the Independent Southern Army (called the Orenburg Army after Sep. 1919), commanded by Major-General G.A. Belov and (from Sep. 1919) Ataman A.I. Dutov. For more details, see: "Vostochnyi front Admirala A.V. Kolchaka," http://east-front.narod.ru/index.htm; and E.V. Volkov, N.D. Egorov, and I.V. Kuptsov, *Belye generaly Vostochnogo fronta Grazhdanskoi voiny: biograficheskii spravochnik*, Moscow: Russkii Put', 2003.

40. Smele, *Civil War in Siberia*, pp. 481–4.

41. A general problem for Kolchak, which manifested itself in the failed Ishim–Tobol' operation, was that he could not draw upon the phalanxes of Cossack cavalry that were available to Denikin in South Russia. In the world war, the Don Cossack Host had mobilized 100,000 fighters, the Kuban Host 89,000, and the Terek Host 18,000. By contrast, the Siberian Cossack Host had mobilized only 11,500 men. The Orenburg Host and Urals Host had mobi-

lized more (30,000 and 13,000 men, respectively), but remained isolated from Omsk throughout 1919 and were only loosely incorporated into the Russian Army and the White Eastern Front. (Indeed, so distant were they from Kolchak's capital that the Urals Army passed into the operational control of General Denikin from June 1919.)

42. Smele, *Civil War in Siberia*, p. 597.

43. For Gajda's critique of the offensive—specifically, the "anti-democratic" spirit of the White officers—see Ronald I. Kowalski, *The Russian Revolution, 1917–1921*, London: Routledge, 1997, pp. 119–21. See also [N.S. Kalashnikov], "Itogi vesennogo nastuplenie," *Sibirskii arkhiv*, vol. 2 (1929), pp. 81–7.

44. Smele, *Civil War in Siberia*, pp. 521–70. See below, pp. 227–8.

45. Gins, *Sibir', soiuzniki i Kolchak*, vol. 2, pp. 448–50.

46. Among the new arrivals, drawn from Denikin's surfeit of political advisors, were P.A. Buryshkin (a leading figure in the former right-liberal Progressist Party), the Kadet A.A. Cherven-Vodali, and S.N. Tret'iakov (formerly head of the Moscow Stock Exchange).

47. Smele, *Civil War in Siberia*, pp. 504–20.

48. Ibid., pp. 570–80, 608–26; and G.A. Vendrykh, *Dekabr'sko-ianvarskii boi 1919–1920 gg. v Irkutske*, Irkutsk: Gosizdat, 1957. Many of the leading figures of the Kolchak government were subsequently captured by advancing Soviet forces. They were tried at Novonikolaevsk in May 1920 and several of them were subsequently executed. See V.I. Shishkin (ed.), *Protsess nad kolchakovskimi ministrami: mai 1920*, Moscow: Mezhdunarodnyi Fond "Demokratiia," 2003.

49. A collection of memoirs of this episode is available in *Velikii Sibirskii lednoi pokhod*, Moscow: Tsentropoligraf, 2004. An impressive semi-fictionalized memoir is: Olga Ilyin, *White Road: A Russian Odyssey, 1919–1923*, New York: Holt, 1984.

50. S.S. Balmasov *et al.* (eds), *Kappel' i kappel'evtsy*, Moscow: Posev, 2003.

51. As too was the fact that when the commander of the American Expeditionary Force in Siberia, General William S. Graves, wrote a book that was overtly critical of Kolchak's forces (*America's Siberian Adventure*, New York: Jonathan Cape and Harrison Smith, 1931), Sakharov immediately challenged him to a duel!

52. The record of Kolchak's interrogation was preserved and subsequently published in English (with extensive and very useful annotations) as Edna Varneck and H.H. Fisher (eds), *The Testimony of Kolchak and Other Siberian Materials*, Stanford: Stanford University Press, 1935. Unfortunately, Kolchak was executed before the interrogation could be completed and only that portion of his life prior to the Omsk coup of November 1918 was properly investigated.

53. Smele, *Civil War in Siberia*, pp. 551–667. The Czechs certainly acted dishonestly in this affair, but their lack of regard for Kolchak is understandable, given the constant abuse of them as "half-Bolsheviks" that he had voiced over the previous year.

54. The following is drawn chiefly from: Mawdsley, *The Russian Civil War*, pp. 161–77; Kenez, *Civil War in South Russia, 1919–1920*, pp. 27–44; and M.A. Kritskii, "Krasnaia armiia na iuzhnom fronte v 1918–1920 gg," *Arkhiv Russkoi revoliutsii*, vol. 18 (1926), pp. 254–300.

55. Anthony Kröner, *The White Knight of the Black Sea: The Life of General Peter Wrangel*, The Hague: Leuxenhoff Publishing, 2010, pp. 125–34; P.N. Vrangl', *Vospominaniia*, Frankfurt: Posev, 1969, vol. 1, pp. 69–123. See also Alex Marshall, *The Caucasus under Soviet Rule*, pp. 111–18.

56. N.L. Ianchevskii, *Grazhdanskaia bor'ba na Severnom Kavkaze*, Rostov-on-Don: Sevkavkniga, 1927, vol. 2, p. 69

57. For an examination of the Don Host's aims and self-perceptions in this period, see Peter Kenez, "The Ideology of the Don Cossacks in the Civil War," in R. Carter Elwood (ed.), *Russian and East European History: Selected Papers from the Second World Congress of Soviet and East European Studies*, Berkeley Slavic Specialists, 1984, pp. 160–84.

58. P.N. Krasnov, "Vsevelikoe Voisko Donskoe," *Arkhiv Russkoi revoliutsii*, vol. 5 (1922), pp. 204–5.

59. A Don Cossack Host *krug* (council) had already dismissed or forced the resignation of a number of Krasnov's pro-German and unabashedly autonomist advisors (among them the popular commander of the Don Army, General S.V. Denisov).

60. The memoirs of Brigadier Williamson, whose role was to oversee the distribution of British supplies to the AFSR, are full of asides regarding how recklessly and inefficiently the Russians used the matériel they were given, however. Not all of this can be accounted for by prejudice. See: Williamson, *Farewell to the Don, passim.*

61. V.L. Genis, "Raskazachivanie v Sovetskoi Rossii," *Voprosy istorii*, vol. 1 (1994), pp. 42–55; Peter Holquist, "'Conduct Merciless Mass Terror': Decossackization on the Don in 1919," *Cahiers du Monde Russe*, vol. 38, nos 1–2 (1997), pp. 127–62; and Holquist, *Making War, Forging Revolution*, pp. 166–205. That the Don Cossacks had been among the first to rise in arms against Soviet power in October 1917 was a lesson not forgotten and frequently cited by the Soviet leadership. Any commander who forgot this could expect the sort of treatment meted out to the Red Cossack F.K. Mironov, who, having already been temporarily exiled to the Western Front in the spring, was lucky to escape execution for criticizing Soviet policy towards the Cossacks in August-September 1919 (although this did not save him from execution in 1921). Swain, *Russia's Civil War*, pp. 93–96, 110–13. On Mironov, see also Sergei Starikov and Roy Medvedev, *Philip Moronov and the Russian Civil War*, New York: Knopf, 1978; and V. Danilov and T. Shanin (eds), *Filipp Mironov: Tikhyi Don, 1917–1921 gg.*, Moscow: Mezhdunarodnaia Fond "Demokratiia," 1997.

62. Brian Murphy, "The Don Rebellion, March–June 1919," *Revolutionary Russia*, vol. 6, no. 2 (1993), pp. 315–50; and A.V. Venkov, *Veshenskoe vosstanie*, Moscow: Veche, 2012. The events of the "Veshensk Rebellion" form a particularly dramatic section of the narrative of M.A. Sholokhov's epic novel *The Quiet Don* (1926–40).

63. On Shkuro, see: Vitalii Baradym, *Zhizn' Generala Shkuro*, Krasnodar: Sov. Kuban, 1998; and his memoirs, A.G. Shkuro, *Zapiski belogo partizana*, Buenos Aires: Seiatel', 1961.

64. See Trotsky, *How the Revolution Armed, Vol. 2: 1919*, pp. 277–81 and 294–6 ("An End to Makhnovism"); and Peter Arshinov, *History of the Makhnovist Movement, 1918–1921*, London: Freedom Press, 1921, pp. 120–32. On Makhno, see below, pp. 188–91.

65. Mai-Maievskii's performance only narrowly outshone that of Wrangel, who organized a brilliant cavalry thrust across the river Manych on 17–18 May 1919, capturing 15,000 prisoners and forcing the retirement of the 10th Red Army toward Tsaritsyn.

66. Very embarrassing to Trotsky was that a week before Vsevolodov's spectacular departure he had boasted that "For every traitor we have now hundreds of former officers who have bound their fate with the Red Army and are working honourably and successfully. Our recruitment of military specialists has been completely justified": "Denikin's Offensive", *How the Revolution Armed, Vol. 2: 1919*, p. 325.

67. Allied contributions to the Tsaritsyn campaign are captured in Marion Aten and Arthur

Orrmont, *The Last Train over Rostov Bridge*, New York: Julian Messner, 1961, and feature briefly in H.A. Jones, *Over the Balkans and South Russia, Being the History of No. 47 Squadron, Royal Air Force*, London: Edward Arnold, 1923. On the vital contribution of tanks and aircraft to Wrangel's victory, see also T.G. Ageeva, *Kavkazskaia armiia P.N. Vrangelia v Tsaritsyne*, Volgograd: Volgogradskoe Nauchnoe Izdatel'stvo, 2009, pp. 86–132.

68. "Our Southern Front" (11 May 1919), *How the Revolution Armed, Vol. 2: 1919*, p. 253.

69. Vrangel', *Vospominaniia*, vol. 1, pp. 160–62.

70. Forces of the Ukrainian Army had actually moved into Kiev a day before the Whites arrived, but immediately withdrew. Aware that a Denikin victory would be fatal to the cause of Ukrainian independence, in these same days Petliura's mission in Warsaw was arranging an armistice with Poland.

71. On the "Mamontov Raid," see Erik Landis, *A Civil War Episode: General Mamontov in Tambov, August 1919*, Pittsburgh: Center for Russian and East European Studies/University Center for International Studies, University of Pittsburgh, 2002. It was at this point that peasants began to refer to the southern Whites as the *Grabarmiia* (from *Grabovaia armiia*, the "Pillaging Army")—a play on the proper abbreviated name of the *Drobrovol'naia armiia* (Volunteer Army), the *Dobrarmiia*. See Kröner, *The White Knight of the Black Sea*, pp. 171–2.

72. Ibid., pp. 163–4. With Denikin having moved his staff and government from Ekaterinodar to Taganrog, the pro-Ukrainian separatists in the Kuban Rada (chiefly Cossacks of the Black Sea section of the Host, the descendants of the deported Zaporozhians of the 1790s), were gaining the upper hand, obliging Naumenko to resign, in impotent protest, on 14 Sep. 1919. On the genesis of separatism among the Kuban Cossacks, see Ja-Jeong Koo, "Universalising Cossack Particularism: 'The Cossack Revolution' in Early Twentieth Century Kuban," *Revolutionary Russia*, vol. 25, no. 1 (2012), pp. 1–29.

73. Mawdsley, *The Russian Civil War*, pp. 176–7; Swain, "Trotsky and the Russian Civil War," pp. 99–103; and Swain, *Trotsky*, pp. 113–15. *Voenspets* Selivachev seems to have paid with his life for his failure, although official records stated that he died of typhus on 17 Sep. 1919.

74. R.G. Gagkuev (ed.), *Drozdovskii i Drozdovtsy*, Moscow: Posev, 2006; R.G. Gagkuev *et al.* (eds), *Markov i Markovtsy*, Moscow: Posev, 2001; and E.E. Messner, *Kornilovtsy: 1917—10 iuniia 1967*, Paris: Izd. Ob"edineniia chinov Kornilovskogo Udarnogo Polka, 1967.

75. Prominent among the latter was the volunteer detachment of Russian officers (the Libau Volunteer Detachment) organized by the eminent Baltic German nobleman Colonel Prince A.P. Liven.

76. On the early history of White formations in the north-west, see "Antibolshevistkaia Rossiia: Istoriia Severo-zapadnoi armii (1918–1920 gg.)," http://www.antibr.ru/studies/ao_szarm_k.html. On this theater of the war in general see the encyclopaedic Reigo Rozental', *Severno-zapadnoi armiia: khronika pobed i porazhenii*, Tallinn: Argo, 2012, from which much of what follows here was drawn.

77. On Iudenich's career, see: A.F. Medvetskii, *General ot infanterii General N.N. Iudenich v gody obshchenatsional'nogo krizisa v Rossii (1914–1920 gg.): monograficheskoe issledovanie*, Samara: PGATI, 2005; N. Rutych, "Iudenich Nikolai Nikolaevich: General ot infanterii," in N. Rutych, *Belyi front general Iudenicha: Biografii chinov Severno-Zapadnoi armii*, Moscow: Russkii Put', 2002, pp. 18–118; and A.V. Shishov, *Iudenich: general suvorovskoi sholy*, Moscow: Veche, 2004.

78. In truth, the government had only been created to appease Allied missions in the region.

On the North West Government, see Piontkovskii (ed.), *Grazhdanskaia voina v Rossii (1918–1921 gg.)*, pp. 605–28. Also Vasilii Gorn, *Grazhdanskaia voina na Severozapade Rossii*, Berlin: Gamaiun, 1923.

79. Bermondt-Avalov retired to Germany, where he became an active figure on the extreme right of émigré politics, notably as a member of the pro-Nazi Russian National Liberation Movement, before moving on, via Italy, to Belgrade in 1936. Apparently (and rather characteristically), he had fallen out with the German Nazis and been deported by Hitler's government. Following the 1941 coup in Yugoslavia that was led by the anti-Axis Dušan Simović, Bermondt-Avalov then emigrated to the United States. On the Landeswehr War, the colonel's own memoirs are highly partial, but still useful: Pavel Bermondt-Avalov, *Im Kampf gegen den Bolschewismus. Erinnerungen von General Fürst Awaloff, Oberbefehlshaber der Deutsch-Russischen Westarmee im Baltikum*, Glückstadt, Hamburg: Verlag J.J. Augustin, 1925.

80. Red defenses in the region had been softened up by a serious revolt of the garrison at the fortress of Krasnaia Gorka, on the southern shore of the Gulf of Finland, in June 1918, and by the Royal Navy's successful coastal motor boat raids against the Baltic Fleet in June and August 1919, featuring the Victoria Cross-winning exploits of Captain Augustus Agar. See Augustus Agar, *Baltic Episode: A Classic of Secret Service in Russian Waters*, London: Hodder & Stoughton, 1963; and Harry Ferguson, *Operation Kronstadt*, London: Hutchinson, 2008. The Allied presence in the region is usefully discussed in a range of chapters collected as: V.A. Shishkin (ed.), *Interventsiia na Severo-Zapade Rossii v 1917–1920 gg.*, St Petersburg: Nauka, 1995.

81. If the Whites had actually been able to hear the Kremlin bells, they would have been enraged: in 1918 those in the Spasskaia tower, which had formerly pealed "God Save the Tsar", had been re-set to play the "Internationale."

82. Karsten Brüggermann, *Die Gründung der Republik Estland und das Ende des "Einem und unteilbaren Rußland": Die Petrograder Front des Russischen Bürgerkrieges, 1918–1920*, Wiesbaden: Otto Harrassowitz Verlag, 2004; N.A. Kornatovskii, *Bor'ba za Krasnyi Petrograd, 1919*, Leningrad: Izd-vo "Krasnoi Gazety," 1929; and A.V. Smolin, *Beloe dvizhenie na severo-zapade rossii, 1918–1920 gg.*, St Petersburg: Dmitrii Bulanin, 1999. White views critical of Iudenich's generalship include the memoirs of the man he ousted as commander of the North West Army: A.P. Rodziainko, *Vospominaniia o Severo-Zapadnoi Armii*, Berlin: Presse, 1920; and Hilja Kukk, "The Failure of Iudenich's North-Western Army in 1919: A Dissenting White Russian View," *Journal of Baltic Studies*, vol. 12, no. 4 (1981), pp. 362–83. The latter cites the debilitating internecine rivalries that bedeviled a force top-heavy with tsarist generals, but crucial to the North West Army's failure were local variants of the *atamanshchina* that more famously damaged White efforts elsewhere: Colonel Bermondt-Avalov, as we have seen, crowned a long career of insubordination by refusing to divert his Germanophile Western Volunteer Army from its efforts to conquer Latvia to join the advance on Petrograd; while, as the advance collapsed, the equally ungovernable General S.N. Bułak-Bałachowicz attempted a coup against Iudenich at Tallinn. On Bułak-Bałachowicz see Richard B. Spence, "Useful Brigand: 'Ataman' S.N. Bulak-Balakhovich, 1917–1921," *Revolutionary Russia*, vol. 11, no. 1 (1998), pp. 17–36. See also Gleb Drujina, "The History of the North-West Army of General Iudenich," Stanford University PhD Thesis, 1950. An additional factor was that the Finns remained neutral. Had General Mannerheim not been defeated by Kaarlo Juho Ståhlberg in independent Finland's first presidential election in July 1919, this might not have been the case.

83. The Bolshevik Central Committee had agreed as early as 11 Sep. 1919 that formal peace terms should be proposed to Finland, Latvia, and Lithuania. See Alfred E. Senn, "The Bolsheviks' Acceptance of Baltic Independence, 1919," *Journal of Baltic Studies*, vol. 26, no. 2 (1995), pp. 145–50.

84. Karl Radek, "The Organizer of Victory," in Leon Trotsky, *Military Writings*, London: Pathfinder Press, 1971, p. 17. On Trotsky as an inspirer, see Neil M. Heyman, "Leon Trotsky: Propagandist to the Red Army," *Studies in Comparative Communism*", vol. 10, nos 1–2 (1977), pp. 34–43.

85. Neil M. Heyman, "Leon Trotsky's Military Education: From the Russo-Japanese War to 1917, *Journal of Modern History*, vol. 45, no. 2 (1973) (microfiche supplement), pp. 71–98.

86. Trotsky, *My Life*, p. 433.

87. Ibid., pp. 433, 437.

88. A.V. Lunacharsky, *Revolutionary Silhouettes*, London: Penguin, 1967, p. 68.

89. Trotsky, *My Life*, pp. 427–39. By late 1919, the configuration of Trotsky's train had developed to embrace two separate echelons that included several armored wagons (with turrets and embrasures for machine-guns and cannon), flatbed trucks to transport armored cars and other vehicles (including Trotsky's own command car, a Rolls-Royce that had been commandeered from the tsar's garage), a telegraph station, a radio station, an electricity-generating wagon, a printing house (with presses), a library, a secretariat wagon, a kitchen, a bath wagon, and even a special wagon for transporting a small aircraft. Also on board were a special guard unit of some 100 elite troops (mostly Latvians), who dressed in a special red uniform and hat of Red Army style, as well as cooks and other staff, mechanics, technicians, political agitators, and secretaries. By 21 January 1921 there were 407 people attached to the institution of "the train," doing eighty different jobs. On the impact of Trotsky's train upon the theaters of war in which it appeared, and upon its general operation, see: Robert T. Argenbright, "Honour Among Communists: 'The Glorious Name of Trotsky's Train,'" *Revolutionary Russia*, vol. 11, no. 1 (1998), pp. 45–66; and N.S. Tarkhova, "Trotsky's Train: An Unknown Page in the History of the Civil War," in Terry Brotherstone and Paul Dukes (eds), *The Trotsky Reappraisal*, Edinburgh University Press, 1992, pp. 27–40.

90. Equally, that on 21 Mar. 1919 a North Russian patrol under Captain Alashev encountered units affiliated to Admiral Kolchak's Northern Army at the unfeasibly remote village of Ust'-kozhva, near Pechora (about 750 miles north of Ekaterinburg) did not presage the union between the Whites in Siberia and those in the North of which General Knox and others had long had dreamed.

91. British forces were withdrawn at the same time from Transcaucasia (19–20 Oct. 1919), leaving only a token contingent at Batumi. A month later, on 29 Nov. 1919, the Soviet diplomat M.M. Litvinov met the British representative James O'Grady in Denmark, initiating the discussions (buttressed by an agreement on 20 Jan. 1920 by the Allied powers to lift their economic blockade of Soviet Russia) that would lead, through an agreement on the exchange of prisoners of war (the Copenhagen Agreement, 12 Feb. 1920) to the Anglo-Soviet Trade Agreement of 16 Mar. 1921 and, in due course, London's full recognition of the Soviet government on 1 Feb. 1924.

92. Ironside had seen action in the South African War of 1899–1902, as an intelligence officer, subsequently operated underground, disguised as a Boer, in German South West Africa (work that, it has been suggested, inspired the character of Richard Hannay in the novels of John Buchan, notably *The Thirty-Nine Steps*), and during the First World War rose to the

command of the 99th Infantry Brigade on the Western Front (Sep. 1918). Ironside was raised to the peerage in 1941, choosing the title Baron Ironside of Archangel.

93. They killed four Russian officers too. See Christopher Dobson and John Miller, *The Day We Almost Bombed Moscow: The Allied War in Russia, 1918–1920*, London: Hodder and Stoughton, 1986, pp. 210–12.

94. A.A. Samoilo, *Dve zhizni*, Moscow: Voenizdat, 1958; and A.A. Samoilo and M.I. Sboichakov, *Pouchitel'nyi urok: Boevye deistviia Krasnoi Armii protiv interventov i belogvardeitsev v Severe Rossii v 1918–1920 gg.*, Moscow: Voenizdat, 1962. Miller had earlier left his own brief version of events: E.K. Miller, "Bor'ba za Rossiiu na Severe, 1918–1920 gg.," *Belo delo*, vol. 4 (1928), pp. 5–11. See also V.I. Goldin and John W. Long, "Resistance and Retribution: The Life and Fate of General E.K. Miller," *Revolutionary Russia*, vol. 12, no. 2 (1999), pp. 19–40. The best English-language treatment of the civil war in this theater remains unpublished: John W. Long, "Civil War and Intervention in North Russia, 1918–1920," Columbia University PhD thesis, 1972. Excellent introductions, though, are: David Footman, "Murmansk and Archangel," in David Footman, *Civil War in Russia*, London: Faber & Faber, 1961, pp. 167–210; Liudmila G. Novikova, "A Province of a Non-Existent State: The White Government in the Russian North and Political Power in the Russian Civil War, 1918–20," *Revolutionary Russia*, vol. 18, no. 2 (2005), pp. 121–44; and Liudmila G. Novikova, "Northerners into Whites: Popular Participation in the Counter-Revolution in Arkhangel'sk Province, Summer–Autumn 1918," *Europe–Asia Studies*, vol. 60, no. 2 (2008), pp. 277–93. In Russian: V.I. Goldin, *Interventsiia i antibol'shevistckoe dvizhenie na Russkom Severe, 1918–1920*, Moscow: Izd-vo Moskovskogo Universiteta, 1993; and Liudmila Novikova, *Provintsial'naia "kontrrevoliutsiia": Beloe dvizhenie i Grazhdanskaia voina na russkom Severe, 1917–1920*, Moscow: Novoe Literaturnoe Obozrenie, 2011.

95. "Proletarians, To Horse!" (11 Sep. 1919), *How the Revolution Armed, Vol. 2: 1919*, pp. 412–14, which seems to have resulted from a report Trotsky had received presenting a very critical review of how the Reds' lack of cavalry had handed success to the Whites in the Mamontov Raid: see V.P. Butt *et al.* (eds), *The Russian Civil War: Documents from the Soviet Archives*, London: Macmillan, 1996, p. 63. Trotsky's words provided, in turn, the inspiration for Aleksandr Apsit's lithograph "*Na konia, proletarii!*" which Stephen White deemed to be "among the finest examples of heroic-revolutionary poster work of the whole civil war period" (although he misdated it to "early 1919"): White, *The Bolshevik Poster*, pp. 29, 31.

96. With Trotsky preoccupied in Petrograd and Glavkom Kamenev sometimes sidelined by the Soviet leadership, much of the initial impetus for this can be credited to Stalin, as chairman of the Revvoensovet of the Southern Front, and to front commander A.I. Egorov. (See Mawdsley, *Russian Civil War*, pp. 203–4.) Neither's civil-war reputation has been much gilded by non-Stalinist historians, but it is worth remembering that this was a partnership that lasted as long as Stalin's soliciting of Egorov's complicity (which the latter was happy to grant) in the framing of his fellow marshal of the Soviet Union, M.N. Tukhachevskii, in May–June 1937. After that, though, Stalin appears to have tired of sharing the monopoly of glory he was demanding as "architect of the civil-war victory": Egorov was arrested as a spy in March 1938 and subsequently executed.

97. This was a surprise, as just a few days earlier the ice had been thick enough for 6-inch howitzers to be dragged across it, guided by a trail of bonfires: Williamson, *Farewell to the Don*, pp. 239–40.

98. Following this third Soviet invasion of Ukraine, the Ukrainian SSR was resurrected, under

the Ukrainian Bolshevik G.I. Petrovskii. Having learned some of the lessons of previous failures to Sovietize the country, Petrovskii's regime sought coalition with individual *Borotbisty*, although their party was forced to disband and their efforts to forge a truly independent existence for the party they formed together with local Bolsheviks, the Ukrainian Communist Party (Borotbists), was stymied by the Komintern's rejection of its application to join it. Nevertheless, the Ukrainization of local life made great strides in the 1920s. See Jurij Borys, *The Sovietization of Ukraine, 1917–1923: The Communist Doctrine and Practice of National Self-Determination*, Edmonton: Canadian Institute of Ukrainian Studies, 1980.

99. See F. Shteinman, "Otstuplenie ot Odessa," *Beloe delo*, vol. 10. Moscow: Rossiiskii Gos. Gumanitarnyi un-t, 2003, pp. 313–29.

100. See the account by General B.A. Shteifon: B.A. Shteifon, "Bredovskii pokhod," *Beloe delo*, vol. 10. Moscow: Rossiiskii Gos. Gumanitarnyi un-t, 2003, pp. 1–298.

101. Vrangel', *Vospominaniia*, vol. 1, pp. 296–302.

102. Ibid., vol. 1, p. 302.

103. Alexis Wrangel, *General Wrangel, 1878–1929: Russia's White Crusader*, London: Leo Cooper, 1987, p. 144.

104. Together with Wrangel were dismissed and exiled his alleged co-conspirators Generals A.S. Lukomskii and P.N. Shatilov and the commander of the Black Sea Fleet, Admiral D.V. Neniukov, and his chief of staff, Admiral A.D. Bubnov.

105. On the Dumenko affair, which remains to be fully explained, see V.D. Polikarpov, "Tragediia komkora Dumenko," *Don*, no. 11 (1988), pp. 142–8. Also V.V. Karpenko, *Komkor Dumenko*, Saratov: Privolzhckoe Knizhnoe Izd.-Vo, 1976.

106. Meijer (ed.) *The Trotsky Papers*, vol. 2, pp. 39, 61.

107. Although, formally, the Supreme Krug abolished the dormant United Government, there was the implicit suggestion that it, the Supreme Krug, had replaced it.

108. Williamson, *Farewell to the Don*, p. 249.

109. See: Landis, "Who were the 'Greens'?" pp. 43–6; Karmann, *Der Freiheitskampf der Kosaken*, pp. 549–52; and Swain, *Russia's Civil War*, pp. 128–32.

110. At most, 215 Urals Cossacks made it as far south as the Persian border by 20 May 1920, although others give a figure of 162. On this extraordinary campaign see the account of their Ataman: V.S. Tolstov, *Ot krasnykh lap v neizvestnuiu pal' (pokhod ural'tsev)*, Constantinople: Tip. izd. Tv.-a "Pressa," 1921. Also L.L. Masianov, *Gibel' Ural'skogo kazach'ego voiska*, New York: Vseslavianskoe Izd.-vo, 1963.

111. Among the latter was the aforementioned Colonel Kostandi, who chose not to board General Miller's ship during the evacuation but to remain at Arkhangel'sk to negotiate a peaceful transfer of the city into Bolshevik hands, as the 6th Red Army approached. This he did, but his fate was to suffer immediate imprisonment and then execution a year later at the hands of the Cheka in Moscow.

112. On Tukhachevskii, see Neil Harvey Croll, "Mikhail Tukhachevsky in the Russian Civil War," University of Glasgow PhD Thesis, 2002. Also B.N. Sokolov, *Mikhail Tukhachevskii: zhizn' i smert' 'Krasnogo marshala'*, Smolensk: Rusich, 1999.

113. Williamson, *Farewell to the Don*, pp. 276–81.

114. Émigré eye-witness accounts of the bedlam on the docks of Novorossiisk—for example N.S. Karinskii, "Epizody iz evakuatsii Novorossiiska," *Arkhiv Russkoi revoliutsii*, vol. 12 (1923)—are barely reflected in the most famous Soviet-era painting of the scene, I.A. Vlad-

imirov's *Flight of the Bourgeoisie from Novorossiisk (1920)*, in which slightly flustered officers and gentlemen carrying samovars and trombones patiently endure the sort of mildly disorderly queue found daily at Russian tram-stops. They were poorly reflected too in British War Office accounts of the events of 26–7 March 1920, which even the fusty official *History of the Royal Scots Fusiliers, 1919–1959*, Glasgow University Press, 1963, describes as "matter of fact."

115. Colonel Voronovich escaped abroad, initially settling in Prague. He subsequently published a collection of materials on the Black Sea insurgency: N. Voronovich (ed.), *Sbornik dokumentov i materialov. Zelenaia kniga: Istoriia krest'ianskogo dvizheniia v Chernomorskoi guberniia*, Prague: Izd. Chernomorskoi Krest'ianski Delegatsii, 1921.

116. E. Zhulikova, "Povstancheskoe dvizhenie na Severnom Kavkaze v 1920–25 godakh (dokumental'nye publikatsii noveishaia otchestvennaia istoriografiia," *Otchestvennaia istoriia*, no. 2 (2004), pp. 159–69. See also Alex Marshall, *The Caucasus under Soviet Rule*, pp. 157–60.

4. 1920–21: BATTLES IN THE MARCHLANDS

1. Although British involvement in Allied intervention in Transcaucasia has received very full coverage (see the works listed in Jonathan D. Smele (ed.), *The Russian Revolution and Civil War, 1917–1921: An Annotated Bibliography*, New York: Continuum, 2003, pp. 284–9), little has been written on the contribution of their junior partners. But see Marta Petricioli, "L'occupazione italiana del Caucaso: 'nun ingrato servizio' da rendere a Londra," *Il Politico*, vol. 37 (1972), pp. 99–141.

2. *Direktivy Glavnogo komanovaniia Krasnoi armii*, pp. 736–7. Baku *guberniia* occupied the eastern (coastal) reaches of Azerbaijan, the (inland) west being chiefly included in Elizavetpol' *guberniia*. It is interesting that, in these operations, command of the spearhead force (the 11th Red Army) was given, successively, to the Red commanders M.I. Vasilenko (19 Dec. 1919–28 Mar. 1920 and 26 July–12 Sep. 1920) and M.K. Levandovskii (29 Mar.–12 July 1920), signaling perhaps that the days of the *voenspetsy* were now numbered. Their successor, A.I. Gekker, occupied an intermediate position: he had been a staff captain in the imperial army and had briefly attended the Academy of the General Staff in 1917, but that same year had joined the Bolsheviks.

3. A. Baikov, "Vospominaniia o revoliutsii v Zakavkazii," *Arkhiv Russkoi revoliutsii*, vol. 9 (1923), p. 174. Mehmandarov was one of the very few Azeris to have reached high rank in the Russian Army, having been made general of artillery in March 1915 (after a career that stretched back to the Russo-Turkish War of 1877–78). Another was his deputy minister, General Ali-Agha Shikhlinskii, the so-called "God of Artillery," a veteran of the Russo-Japanese War, who had achieved the rank of lieutenant-general in the Russian Army in Apr. 1917, and was promoted to general of artillery in the Armenian Army in June 1919. Despite the fact that, after the collapse of the Azeri republic, both of these generals collaborated with the Soviet regime, they remain widely revered in contemporary Azerbaijan, where streets, parks, and ships were named in their honor. Shikhlinskii was also the subject of the rather partial documentary film, *Schitalsia bogom artillerii* ("He was thought of as the God of Artillery," dir. Z. Shikhlinskii, 1996).

4. This meant that, as the 11th Red Army approached, only 3,000 men of the Azeri army were left to protect the Derbent–Baku line, with another 2,000 in the garrison at Baku.

5. The Azeri–Armenian conflict in Nakhchivan, where a clear majority of the population were Armenian, had flared up in late 1918, as local Muslims declared an independent Aras (sometimes Araks or Araxi) Republic there, in late 1918, in the wake of the Turkish withdrawal. In late June 1919, Armenian forces, supported by a British mission, then occupied Nakhchivan and liquidated the Aras Republic in the so-called Aras War.

6. The standard work on Azerbaijan in this period is Tadeusz Swietochowski, *Russian Azerbaijan, 1905–1920: The Shaping of National Identity in a Muslim Community*, Cambridge: Cambridge University Press, 1985 (here, pp. 165–90). The proclamation of the Azeri SSR was not quite the end of the matter, as occasional outbreaks of resistance to Sovietization erupted over the following years, until at least 1924. One of the most serious of these occurred in the southern region of Lenkoran in November-December 1920: A.V. Kadishev, *Interventsiia i Grazhdanskaia voina v Zakavkaz'e*, Moscow: Voenizdat, 1960, pp. 350–54.

7. Although (unlike Azerbaijan) it boasted some very experienced former generals of the imperial army (such as Kritopor Araratov, Movses Silikyan, and Tovmas Nazarbekian), Armenia was swamped with hundreds of thousands of refugees fleeing from Turkish oppression in the Armenian lands they occupied to the south and had been cruelly prostrated by famine, disease, and economic collapse. The standard work on the sorry history of Armenia in this period is Richard G. Hovannisian, *The Republic of Armenia*, 4 vols, Berkeley: University of California Press, 1971–96.

8. *Dokumenty vneshnei politiki SSSR*, vol. 3, pp. 597–604.

9. The full text, with useful maps, is available at the website of the Georgian Association of Modern Scientific Investigation: http://www.amsi.ge/istoria/sab/yarsi.html

10. On this period across Transcaucasia see: Serge Afanasyan, *L'Arménie, l'Azerbaidjan et la Géorgie: de l'indépendance à l'instauration du pouvoir soviétique, 1917–1923*, Paris: Éditions l'Harmattan, 1981; Firuz Kazemzadeh, *The Struggle for Transcaucasia, 1917–1921*, New York: Philosophical Library, 1951; and Werner Zürrer, *Kaukasien, 1918–1921. Der Kampf der Grossmächte um die Landbrücke zwischen Schwarzem und Kaspischem Meer*, Düsseldorf: Droste Verlag, 1978. See also Richard G. Hovannisian, "Armenia and the Caucasus in the Genesis of the Soviet–Turkish Entente," *International Journal of Middle East Studies*, vol. 4, no. 2 (1973), pp. 129–47.

11. An anti-religious campaign across the North Caucasus in 1925, for example, saw the forced closure of mosques and schools there, the execution of many of the Muslim clergy, and the banning of the use of Arabic. See Alex Marshall, *The Caucasus under Soviet Rule*, London: Routledge, 2010, pp. 175–95.

12. L.B. Krasin, People's Commissar for Foreign Trade, arrived in London for the first round of talks in May 1920; the last contingent of British forces in the region left Batumi on 7–9 July 1920. On the trade talks, see M.V. Glenny, "The Anglo-Soviet Trade Agreement, March 1921," *Journal of Contemporary History*, vol. 5, no. 2 (1970), pp. 63–82. On Curzon and the great importance he ascribed to the Batumi mission, see: John Fisher, "'On the Glacis of India': Lord Curzon and British Policy in the Caucasus, 1919," *Diplomacy and Statecraft*, vol. 8, no. 2 (1997), pp. 50–82; and John D. Rose, "Batum as Domino, 1919–1920: The Defence of India in Transcaucasia," *International History Review*, vol. 2, no. 2 (1980), pp. 266–87.

13. The Georgians, in turn, accused both regions of harboring pro-Soviet sympathies. And it has to be said that most Westerners who visited independent Georgia returned with glowing reports of that "Menshevik Democracy," although a cynic might note that one could probably only expect as much from the likes of socialist leaders such as Ramsay MacDon-

ald and Karl Kautsky who predominated among Western tourists in the world's first social-democratic republic. Certainly one independent and usually well-informed journalist saw things differently, in what he called "a classic example of an imperialist 'small nation.'" Carl Bechhofer recorded that "Both in territory-snatching outside and bureaucratic tyranny inside, [Georgia's] chauvinism was beyond all bounds": Carl E. Bechhofer, *In Denikin's Russia and the Caucasus, 1919–1920*, London: Collins, 1921, p. 14.

14. For the terms of the treaty, see Walter Russell Batsell, *Soviet Rule in Russia*, New York: Macmillan, 1929, pp. 247–54.

15. There were three distinct waves of violent uprisings in South Ossetia against Georgian rule during the "Russian" Civil Wars: in March 1918, October 1920. and April 1920. The last of these, as noted here, was the most extensive and blood-drenched. See: Julian Birch, "The Georgian/South Ossetian Territorial and Boundary Dispute," in John F.R. Wright, Suzanne Goldenberg, and Richard Schofield (eds), *Transcaucasian Boundaries*, London: UCL Press, 1996, p. 157; Avtandil Menteshashvili, "An Assessment of the 1920 Uprising in South Ossetia," *Political History of Russia*, vol. 5, no. 1 (1995), pp. 47–56; and Arsene Saparov, "From Conflict to Autonomy: The Making of the South Ossetian Autonomous Region, 1918–1922," *Europe–Asia Studies*, vol. 62, no. 1 (2010), pp. 99–123.

16. This was led by Sergei Kirov, whose long residence in and links with Vladikavkaz, just over the Caucasus Mountains to the north, would have been both useful and symbolic. See John Biggart, "Kirov before the Revolution," *Soviet Studies*, vol. 23, no. 3 (1972), pp. 345–72.

17. A.V. Kvashonkin, "Sovetizatsiia Zakavkaz'ia v perepiske bol'shevistskogo rukovodstva 1920–22gg.," *Cahiers du Monde Russe*, vol. 38, nos 1–2 (1997), pp. 187–9.

18. Tellingly, tensions between the army leadership and the Menshevik government had induced the commander-in-chief of Georgia's forces, General Giorgi Kvintadze, to tender his resignation on no less than four separate occasions between May 1918 and February 1921: G.I. Kvintadze, *Moi vospominanii v gody nezavisimosti Gruzii, 1917–1921*, Paris: YMCA-Press, 1985.

19. This federation of the Armenian, Azeri, and Georgian SSRs, established on 12 March 1922, was broadly resented by each of its constituents—and even by many local Bolsheviks—and, in the case of Tiflis, gave rise, in the shape of the so-called "Georgian Affair" of 1921–22, to a virtual civil war within the Bolshevik Party, as Moscow Bolsheviks (particularly Georgians in Moscow, such as Stalin and Sergo Ordzhonikidze), sought to corral the more independently minded Georgian Bolsheviks in Tiflis. On these events, see Jeremy Smith, "The Georgian Affair of 1922—Policy Failure, Personality Clash or Power Struggle?" *Europe–Asia Studies*, vol. 50, no. 3 (1998), pp. 519–44.

20. The Georgian regime had been refused entry into the League of Nations in November 1920 (largely because its 1918 alliance with Germany still rankled with Britain and France, who led the campaign against the admission of Georgia), but it did achieve *de jure* recognition by the Allies on 27 Jan. 1921 and subsequently two League of Nations resolutions (of 1922 and 1924) recognized the sovereignty of Georgia. See Zourab Avalishvili, *The Independence of Georgia in International Politics, 1918–1921*, London: Headley, 1940, pp. 216–26, 281–6.

21. Raymond Duguet, *Moscou et la Géorgie martyre. Préface de C. B. Stokes*, Paris: Tallandier, 1927; David M. Lang, *A Modern History of Georgia*, London: Weidenfeld & Nicolson, 1962, pp. 243–4; Ronald G. Suny, *The Making of the Georgian Nation*, London: I.B. Tauris, 1989, pp. 223–34; and Markus Wehner, "Le soulèvement géorgien de 1924 et la réaction des bol-

cheviks," *Communisme*, nos 42–4 (1995), pp. 155–70. Again evincing the umbilical link between the civil war and later periods of Soviet and European history, influential in the suppression of these uprisings, as head of the Special Operations section of the Georgian Cheka, was Lavrenti Beria. See Amy Knight, *Beria: Stalin's First Lieutenant*, Princeton: Princeton University Press, 1993, pp. 32–4. Knight alleges (as have others) that Beria and his superior, E.A. Kvantaliani, even surreptitiously encouraged the August uprising, in order to provide an excuse to destroy what remained of the nationalist and Menshevik opposition in Georgia. This also, she adds ominously, "served as Beria's final induction into the business of mass killing." All those imprisoned and executed as a consequence of "the national-liberation struggle" in Georgia from 1921 to 1924 were rehabilitated by a decree of the Georgian State Council of 25 May 1992: http://www.memo.ru/rehabilitate/laws/resp/gruz.htm

22. Stephen Jones, "The Establishment of Soviet Power in Transcaucasia: The Case of Georgia, 1921–1928," *Soviet Studies*, vol. 40, no. 4 (1988), pp. 616–39. The Abkhazian SSR was downgraded to an autonomous republic within the Georgian SSR in Feb. 1931.

23. A full discussion of Soviet foreign policy in this era is beyond the scope of the present study, but see, in general: Richard K. Debo, *Survival and Consolidation: The Foreign Policy of Soviet Russia, 1918–1921*, Montreal and Kingston: McGill–Queen's University Press, 1992; Timothy E. O'Connor, *Diplomacy and Revolution: G.V. Chicherin and Soviet Foreign Affairs, 1918–1930*, Ames: Iowa State University Press, 1988; and Teddy J. Uldricks, *Diplomacy and Ideology: The Origins of Soviet Foreign Relations, 1917–1930*, London: Sage, 1979. On Soviet–German relations: Gerald Freund, *Unholy Alliance: Russo-German Relations from the Treaty of Brest-Litovsk to the Treaty of Berlin*, London: Chatto & Windus, 1957. On Soviet–Turkish relations: Paul Dumont, "L'Axe Moscou–Ankara: Les relations turco-soviétique de 1919 à 1922," *Cahiers du Monde Russe et Soviétique*, vol. 18, no. 3 (1977), pp. 165–93; and Bulent Gokay, *A Clash of Empires: Turkey between Russian Bolshevism and British Imperialism, 1918–1923*, London: I.B. Tauris, 1996. On Soviet–Iranian relations: Stephen Blank, "Soviet Politics and the Iranian Revolution of 1919–1921," *Cahiers du Monde Russe et Soviétique*, vol. 21, no. 2 (1980), pp. 173–94, and Mikhail Volodarsky, *The Soviet Union and its Southern Neighbours: Iran and Afghanistan, 1917–1933*, London: Frank Cass, 1994.

24. Michael A. Reynolds, *Shattering Empires: The Clash and Collapse of the Ottoman and Russian Empires, 1908–1918*, Cambridge: Cambridge University Press, 2011, p. 255.

25. The text of the treaty is available at: http://www.worldlii.org/int/other/LNTSer/1922/69.html. For a brief but illuminating description of the treaty, see: J. Tapp, "The Soviet–Persian Treaty of 1921," *International Law Quarterly*, vol. 4 (1951), pp. 511–14. On Soviet policy in general in this sphere, see Stephen White, "Soviet Russia and the Asian Revolution, 1917–1924," *Review of International Studies*, vol. 10, no. 3 (1984), pp. 219–32.

26. A complicating factor here was that, for all his adoptions of the proper, Soviet-style nomenclature (his Gīlān Soviet Republic had a Sovnarkom and a Red Army), the politically moderate Kuchak Khan was actually in deep dispute with the Iranian Communist Party, which was based in Baku and had some influence in the Kavbiuro and even in Moscow. On this affair, see: Cosroe Chaqueri, *The Soviet Socialist Republic of Iran, 1920–1921: Birth of the Trauma*, Pittsburgh: University of Pittsburgh Press, 1995; V.L. Genis, "Les bolcheviks au Guilan. La chute du gouvernement de Koutchek Khan (juin–juillet 1920)," *Cahiers du Monde Russe*, vol. 40, no. 3 (1999), pp. 459–96; and Homayoun Katouzian, "Nationalist Trends in Iran, 1921–1926," *International Journal of Middle Eastern Studies*, vol. 10, no. 4 (1979), pp. 533–6. A fascinating first-hand account is: Edith Ybert-Chabrier, "Gilan, 1917–

1920: The Jengelist Movement according to the Memoirs of Ihsan Allah Khan," *Central Asian Survey*, vol. 2, no. 1 (1983), pp. 37–61.

27. H.G. Wells, *Russia in the Shadows*, London: Hodder and Stoughton, 1920, pp. 79–82.

28. E.D. Stasova, *Stranitsy zhizni i bor'by*, Moscow: Gospolizdat, 1957, pp. 109–10.

29. See Ivar Spector, *The Soviet Union and the Muslim World, 1917–1958*, Seattle: University of Washington Press, 1959, pp. 56–7.

30. Among them, Deng Xiaoping and Hồ Chí Minh. The university had branches in many cities in Soviet Asia, including one in Tashkent, originally run by M.N. Roy, that specialized in schooling Indian Communists. See: K.H. Ansari, "Pan-Islam and the Making of the Early Indian Muslim Socialists," *Modern Asian Studies*, vol. 20, no. 3 (1986), p. 528. On the Baku Congress, see Edith Ybert-Chabrier, "Les Délégués au Premier Congrès des Peuples d'Orient (Bakou, 1-er–8 septembre 1920)" *Cahiers du Monde Russe et Soviétique*, vol. 26, no. 1 (1985), pp. 21–42; Cosroe Chaqueri, "The Baku Congress," *Central Asian Survey*, vol. 2, no. 2 (1983), pp. 89–107; and, especially, Stephen White, "Communism and the East: The Baku Congress, 1920," *Slavic Review*, vol. 33, no. 3 (1974), pp. 492–514. The stenographic record of the Congress is available as Brian Pearce (ed.), *Baku, September 1920: Congress of the Peoples of the East—Stenographic Record*, London: New Park Publications, 1977. It seems to have been while attending the congress that John Reed contracted the typhus that would kill him a month later: Tamara Hovey, *John Reed: Witness to Revolution*, Los Angeles: George Sand Books, 1975, pp. 212–16.

31. Lenin, *CW*, vol. 21, pp. 295–338. On this publication and its implications, see Erik van Ree, "Lenin's Conception of Socialism in One Country, 1915–17," *Revolutionary Russia*, vol. 23, no. 2 (2010), pp. 159–81.

32. But, in the USSR, would be castrated by the second. On the flowering and then suffering of left-wing communism in Russia, see: Donald W. Treadgold, *Lenin and his Rivals: The Struggle for Russia's Future, 1898–1906*, London: Methuen, 1955; Robert C. Williams, *The Other Bolsheviks: Lenin and his Critics, 1904–1914*, Bloomington: Indiana University Press, 1986; and Robert V. Daniels, *The Conscience of the Revolution: Communist Opposition in Soviet Russia*, Cambridge, MA: Harvard University Press, 1960. Lenin's injured rebuttal of this strand of thought was captured in "Left Wing Communism: An Infantile Disorder," in V.I. Lenin, *Selected Works*, Moscow: Foreign Languages Publishing House, 1952, vol. 2, Part 2.

33. Especially as no clear ethnic demarcation line could possibly separate the confounding mix of nationalities—Lithuanians, Belorussians, Rusyns, Ukrainians, Jews, and others—who occupied the lands betwixt Russia and Poland. On the Polish question, see: Kay Lundgreen-Nielsen, *The Polish Problem at the Paris Peace Conference: A Study in the Policies of the Great Powers and the Poles, 1918–1919*, Odense: Odense University Press, 1979; Mieczysław B. Biskupski, "War and the Diplomacy of Polish Independence, 1914–1918," *Polish Review*, vol. 35, no. 1 (1990), pp. 5–17; Piotr Wandycz, "Poland on the Map of Europe in 1918," *Polish Review*, vol. 35, no. 1 (1990), pp. 19–25; and Paul Latawski (ed.), *The Reconstruction of Poland, 1914–23*, London: Macmillan, 1992.

34. On this period, see Oleksandr Pavliuk, "Ukrainian–Polish Relations in Galicia, 1918–1919," *Journal of Ukrainian Studies*, vol. 23 (1998), pp. 1–23.

35. A key factor here was that although Poland was at the same time involved in contests to maximize its territories in Silesia and East Prussia, the Second Republic faced no serious disruptions in its rear comparable to those endured by the WUPR (which was, of course, also fighting the Red Army). The Poles were even able to reinforce their army with units return-

ing from service in France, notably the 70,000-strong Blue Army of General Józef Haller de Hallenburg. Haller was a former commander with the Polish Legion of the Austrian Army that had fought in Galicia during the First World War, but had led his men into Russia in March 1918, as he interpreted the Treaty of Brest-Litovsk as stifling hopes for an independent Poland. In Russia, he briefly commanded the 5th Siberian Rifle Division (the nucleus of the Polish Legion) before transferring to the command of Polish forces on the Western Front.

36. The "Winter Campaigns" were the Ukrainian forces' equivalent of the Whites' emblematic "Ice Marches." The first Winter Campaign lasted from 6 Dec. 1919 to 6 May 1920, after the Ukrainian Directory had decided that defense of the UNR by conventional military means was no longer possible. In this campaign Ukrainian forces (mostly consisting of what remained of the Ukrainian Sich Riflemen and the Zaporozhian Corps) were commanded by General Mykhailo Omel'ianovych-Pavlenko. Initially, the Ukrainian forces operated in the Elizavetgrad region, between the Red Army and the Whites, but when the Reds forced General Denikin's armies southward, the Ukrainian group penetrated eastwards, into the rear of the Reds. In February 1920, they crossed the Dnepr river into Zolonosha. Then, in April 1919, they fought their way back towards Iampil, which they reached on 6 May 1920. In this campaign, some 3,000 to 6,000 men (estimates vary) traversed at least 1,750 miles. The second of the Winter Campaigns took place in late 1921, a year after the government of the UNR and the Ukrainian Army had been forced across the River Zbruch onto Polish territory (following the armistice that ended the Soviet–Polish War) and were there disarmed and interned. Some 1,200 volunteers from among the internees, commanded by General Tiutiunnyk and his chief of staff Colonel Iurii Otmarshtian, set off from Poland into the territory of the Ukrainian SSR in October 1921. All of these forces were poorly armed, clothed, and shod. The Podilian group set out on 25 Oct. 1920, and thrust through Podilia to reach the village of Vakhnivka (40 miles north of Kiev), before being forced westwards through Volhynia, crossing the Polish border on 29 Nov. 1921. The Volhynia group advanced on 4 Nov. 1920 and captured Korosten on 7 Nov. 1920, but could not hold it. The group then moved as far east as the village of Leontivka but, having failed to establish a junction with the Podilian group, turned back west. As it retreated, the Volhynia group was encircled by Red cavalry commanded by Hryhorii Kotovski near Bazar, in the Zhitomir region. A large number of its men were killed in battle at Mali Mynky on 17 Nov. 1921, but the majority (443) were captured. It was reported that 359 of them were then executed at Bazar on 23 Nov. 1921. Only around 120 men and the staff of the group breached the encirclement and fought their way back to the Polish border, which they crossed on 20 Nov. 1921. This was the last meaningful act of the Soviet–Ukrainian War.

37. For the story of this relationship see: Michael Palij, *The Ukrainian–Polish Defensive Alliance, 1919–1921: An Aspect of the Ukrainian Revolution*, Edmonton and Toronto: Canadian Institute of Ukrainian Studies Press, 1995.

38. For a sympathetic but not uncritical analysis of Piłsudski's plans, see Marian K. Dziewanowski, *Joseph Pilsudski: A European Federalist, 1918–1922*, Stanford: Stanford University Press, 1969; also, more generally, Stefan Troebst, "'Intermarium' and 'Wedding to the Sea': The Politics of History and Mental Mapping in East Central Europe," *European Review of History*, vol. 10, no. 2 (2003), pp. 293–321. In the inter-war years, this project was expanded by Piłsudski's followers to include all the non-Russian peoples of the former empire, a notion termed Prometheism, which proved particularly attractive to the Georgian emigration in

Poland and elsewhere. (The veteran Menshevik and former prime minister of the Democratic Republic of Georgia, Noe Ramishvili, for example, was a proponent—an affiliation that earned him assassination at the hands of the Cheka in Paris in 1930.) On the Promethean movement, see: Richard Woytak, "The Promethean Movement in Interwar Poland," *East European Quarterly*, vol. 18, no. 3 (1984), pp. 273–8; and T.M. Simonova, "Strategicheskie zamysly nachal'nika pol'skogo gosudarstva Iuzefa Pilsudskogo: Prometeizm vo vneshnei politiki Pol'shi v 1919–1923gg.," *Voenno-istoricheskii zhurnal*, no. 11 (2008), pp. 42–8. Also of interest is Andriy Rukkas, "Georgian Servicemen in the Polish Armed Forces (1922–39)," *The Journal of Slavic Military Studies*, vol. 14, no. 3 (2001), pp. 93–106.

39. The Ukrainian forces were augmented from the 2nd and 3rd Brigades of the Red Ukrainian Galician Army. This force had been constructed by the Red command from those units of the former Ukrainian Galician Army of the WUPR that were absorbed into the Red Army in February 1920, at the close of the Soviet–Ukrainian War. By the end of 1919, the UGA, hemmed into a corner of eastern Podilia and ravaged by typhus, had been reduced to a complement of around 5,000 men. On 12 Feb. 1920, elements of the force (led by the Revolutionary Committee of the UGA) entered negotiations with the Soviet government and it was agreed that the remains of the UGA would become an autonomous part of the Red Army, in order to continue its struggle against Poland over the future of Western Ukraine (Eastern Galicia). The force's commander, General Osyp Mykytka (together with his chief of staff, General Gustav Ziritz), refused to accept this deal; both were taken to Moscow and subsequently executed. Thereafter, V.P. Zatonskii organized the Red Ukrainian Galician Army into three brigades and assigned each to a separate Red Army division. This move, together with continued Soviet interference in the purportedly autonomous force, swiftly led to a breakdown in the agreement, hence the desertion of the 2nd and 3rd Brigades. The 1st Brigade continued to fight, but was defeated and interned by the Poles at Makhniva.

40. Meijer (ed.), *The Trotsky Papers*, vol. 2, p. 204.

41. See: Alfred E. Senn, *The Emergence of Modern Lithuania*, New York: Columbia University Press, 1959, pp. 104–30; and Vytautas Lesčius, *Lietuvos kariuomenė nepriklausomybės kovose 1918–1920*, Vilnius: Generolo Jono Žemaičio Lietuvos Karo Akademija, 2004, pp. 271–8. Skirmishes continued, over the following months, culminating in the Polish–Lithuanian War of 1 Sep. to 7 Oct. 1920, during which Sejny changed hands several times. Eventually, Polish sovereignty over the region was formalized in the Suwałki Agreement of 7 Oct. 1920, which reinstated the Foch Line: Piotr Łossowski, *Konflikt polsko-litewski 1918–1920*, Warsaw: Książka i Wiedza, 1995, pp. 166–75.

42. Alfred Rosmer, *Lenin's Moscow*, London: Pluto Press, 1971, p. 66. Interestingly, among those who advised Lenin against placing too many hopes on the revolutionary potential of the Polish proletariat were those who knew Polish conditions rather better than most Bolsheviks, including Julian Marchlewski and Karl Radek, but Lenin dismissed their doubts: see Clara Zetkin, *Reminiscences of Lenin*, London: Modern Books, 1929, p. 20. Moscow feared also that the price to be paid for such a settlement would include recognition of the White government in Crimea. See: Debo, *Survival and Consolidation*, pp. 218–22.

43. Hence the title of the account of what ensued by the senior British military representative in Poland at the time: Viscount E.V. d'Abernon, *The Eighteenth Decisive Battle of the World: Warsaw, 1920*, London: Hodder & Stoughton, 1931.

44. "Death to the Polish Bourgeoisie," 29 Apr. 1920, *How the Revolution Armed, Vol. 3: 1920*, pp. 127–8.

45. Piotr Wandycz, *Soviet–Polish Relations, 1917–1921*, Cambridge, MA: Harvard University Press, 1969, pp. 230–31; Norman Davies, *White Eagle, Red Star: The Soviet–Polish War, 1919–20*, London: Orbis Books, 1983, pp. 192–4.

46. French policy remained ambivalent: a loan was granted to Warsaw, but one only sufficient to keep Polish forces in the field for two weeks. However, those were a very crucial two weeks. With negotiations for the Anglo-Soviet Trade Agreement already underway, British policy at the time seems to have rested on the hope that the British mission, headed by the Polonophobe Sir Maurice Hankey, might engineer the replacement of Piłsudski by someone who might be induced to do business with the Bolsheviks, rather than continually poking a stick into their kennel. Indeed, Lloyd George's view was that the Poles had "gone rather mad" and were "a menace to the peace of Europe": *Lord Riddell's Intimate Diary of the Peace Conference and After, 1918–1923*, London: Gollancz, 1933, pp. 191–9. Nevertheless, the earlier dispatch of aircraft and other stores to Warsaw was significant. For an interesting view, see Norman Davies, "Lloyd George and Poland, 1919–1920," *Journal of Contemporary History*, vol. 6, no. 3 (1971), pp. 132–54. Polonophile sentiments in the War Office and Foreign Office were being vigorously opposed by a public "Hands off Russia" campaign. On the latter, see L.J. Macfarlane, "Hands off Russia: British Labour and the Russo-Polish War, 1920," *Past and Present*, no. 38 (1967), pp. 126–52. On the Kościuszko Squadron (the 7th Squadron of the Air Force of Poland): [Merian C. Cooper], *Faunt-le-Roy i jego eskradra w Polsce: dzieje eskradry Kościuszki: napisał zastepca dowódcy eskadry*, Chicago: Faunt-le-Roy, Harrison & Co., 1932; Robert F. Karolevitz and Ross S. Fenn, *Flight of the Eagles: The Story of the American Kościuszko Squadron in the Polish–Russian War, 1919–1920*, Sioux Falls: Brevet Press, 1974; and Kenneth A. Murray, *Wings over Poland: The 7th (Kosciusko) of the Polish Air Service, 1919, 1920, 1921*, New York: Appleton, 1932. At the time of writing, a campaign is under way to find sponsors for a feature film to relate "The Greatest Story Never Told"—the history of the Kościuszko Squadron (and especially the story of the moving spirit behind its foundation, Merian C. Cooper): http://www.illuminateamericasheroes.com. On Weygand's mission: Zdzisław Musialik, *General Weygand and the Battle of the Vistula, 1920*, London: J. Pilsudski Institute of Research, 1987.

47. See Evan Mawdsley, *The Russian Civil War*, Boston: Allen & Unwin, 1987, p. 258.

48. General Władysław Sikorski, *La Campagne polono-russe de 1920*, Paris: Payot, 1928.

49. On these organizations, see Kirsteen Davina Croll, "Soviet–Polish Relations, 1919–1921," University of Glasgow PhD Thesis, 2009, pp. 134–67.

50. Aviel Roshwald, *Ethnic Nationalism and the Fall of Empires: Central Europe, Russia and the Middle East, 1914–1923*, London: Routledge, 2001, p. 94. See also Nicholas P. Vakar, *Belorussia, the Making of a Nation: A Case Study*, Cambridge, MA: Harvard University Press, 1956, Chapter 7.

51. Efforts in contemporary Belarus to have 27 November declared a public holiday have been scorned by the regime of Aliaksandr Lukashenka. Both Zhauryd and Prakulevich, after brief periods in emigration, returned to the Belorussian SSR and found work in the 1920s, but both were arrested as "bourgeois nationalists" in the early 1930s. Prakulevich was executed by the NKVD in 1938; Zhauryd died in a labor camp in the Mari region the following year. Their fates were shared by many who had participated in the Slutsk Defense. The Belarussian Rada, meanwhile, was driven into emigration in Czechoslovakia, where its governing Council was led by the historian Vacłaǔ Łastoǔski. At a conference in Berlin in 1925, the Council declared the formal dissolution of the Belarussian Rada, although it subsequently reconvened

and exists in exile to this day: "The Sorrows of Belarus: A Government in Exile, a Country in a Mess," *The Economist* (16 Nov. 2006); "Heart of Darkness: A Ray of Hope from Belarussian Exiles," *The Economist* (13 Mar. 2008); and http://www.radabnr.org/ (official website of the Belarussian Rada). Jan Serada remained in what was to become the Belorussian SSR, working as a teacher in agricultural schools, but suffered endless persecution. In 1941, he was sentenced to ten years in prison. Serada was apparently freed from the Kraslag camp near Krasnoiarsk on 19 Nov. 1943, but his subsequent fate is unknown. Unbiased sources on this period of Belarussian history are almost impossible to find, probably the most reliable being a work originally published in Moscow in 1921: Fiodar Turuk, *Belorusskoe dvizhenie: ocherk istorii natsional'nogo i revoliutsionnogo dvizheniia belorussa*, Minsk: Otpechatana na Minskoi Kartograficheskoi Fabrike Belgeodezii, 1994. But see also Vitaut Kipel and Zora Kipel (eds), *Byelorussian Statehood*, New York: Byelorussian Institute of Arts and Science, 1988. For further bibliographic guidance, see Alexander Nadson, "Selected Bibliography of Works on the Struggle for Belarusian Independence 1900–1921 in the Francis Skaryna Belarusian Library in London," http://www.radabnr.org/en/bibliographyen.htm

52. Budennyi's brutal progress into and retreat from Poland were captured in the justly celebrated collection of short stories by Isaak Babel known in English as *Red Cavalry*. See also Isaac Babel, *Diary 1920*, New Haven: Yale University Press, 1995. The course of the campaigns is discussed in Józef Piłsudski, *Year 1920 and its Climax*, London: Pilsudski Institute of London, 1972, which also includes a translation of Tukhachevskii's "March beyond the Vistula." On the campaigns of the Soviet–Polish War, see also: Davies, *White Eagle, Red Star*, pp. 105–263; A.P. Gritskevich, *Zapadnyi Front RSFSR, 1918–1920: Bor'ba mezhdu Rossiei i Pol'shei za Belorossiiu*, Minsk: Kharvest, 2010, pp. 180–346; and Adam Zamoyski, *Warsaw, 1920: Lenin's Failed Conquest of Europe*, London: Harper Collins, 2008, pp. 32–130. Views from Moscow are dissected in James M. McCann, "Beyond the Bug: Soviet Historiography of the Soviet–Polish War of 1920," *Soviet Studies*, vol. 36, no. 4 (1984), pp. 475–93.

53. S.A. Pavliuchenkov, *Voennyi kommunizm v Rossii: vlast' i massy*, Moscow: RKT-Istoriia, 1997, p. 251.

54. In fact, as Vladimir Buldakov has noted (*Krasnaia smuta*, p. 33), the average income of a Jewish artisan in the early years of the twentieth century was some one-and-a-half to two times lower than that of a local Russian/Ukrainian/Belorussian peasant (150–300 and 400–500 roubles respectively), while 19 percent of Jews "found themselves in the position of paupers, owing their existence to the charity of their fellow Jews." For a documentary survey of the pogroms across the Pale, see L.B. Miliakova *et al.* (eds), *Kniga pogromov: pogromy na Ukraine, v Belorossii i evropeiskoi chasti Rossii v periode grazhdanskoi voiny, 1918–1922 gg. Sbornik dokumentov*, Moscow: ROSSPEN, 2007.

55. Isaac Babel, *The Collected Stories*, London: Methuen and Co., 1957, p. 119. See also V.L. Genis, "Pervaia Konnaia armiia: za kulisami slavy," *Voprosy istorii*, no. 12 (1994), pp. 64–77. Babel felt sufficiently nervous for his own safety to conceal his own Jewishness from the Cossacks behind the Russian pseudonym Kiril Vasil'evich Liutov: Efraim Sicher, "The Jewish Cossack: Isaac Babel in the First Red Cavalry," *Studies in Contemporary Jewry*, vol. 4 (1988), pp. 113–34.

56. Babel, *The Collected Stories*, pp. 42–3. Another character in Babel's tales, a peasant, hearing the cries of Jews being murdered by Poles, muses that "There'll be mighty few of them left after the war": ibid., p. 170.

57. Babel, *1920 Diary*, p. 4. Babel himself wrote a piece entitled "The Killers Must Be Finished Off" for the newspaper *Krasnyi kavalerist* ("Red Cavalryman," 17 Sep. 1920), after hearing of a later pogrom committed by Polish forces at Brody: ibid., pp. 105–6.

58. Ibid., p. 84.

59. Peter Kenez, usually an astute historian of the civil wars, was certainly wrong to assert that "the Volunteer Army succeeded in murdering as many Jews as all other armies put together": Peter Kenez, "Pogroms and White Ideology in the Russian Civil War," in John D. Klier and Shlomo Lambroza (eds), *Pogroms: Anti-Jewish Violence in Modern Russian History*, Cambridge: Cambridge University Press, 1992, p. 302. At most, the Volunteers were responsible for around 20 percent of the number of pogroms (during which, though, the death rate was definitely rather higher than during the less coordinated outrages committed by less-organized Ukrainian and other forces): Oleg Budnitskii, "Jews, Pogroms and the White Movement: A Historiographical Critique," *Kritika*, vol. 2, no. 4 (2001), p. 770. Serhy Yekelchyk ("Insurgency and Ideology," p. 122) attributes 40 percent of the deaths to the Petliurites.

60. With the possible exception of the murky period 1648–54 (and the uprising of the Zaporozhian Cossacks led by Hetman Bohdan Khmel'nytskyi), during which "tens of thousands of Jews—given the lack of reliable data, it is impossible to establish more accurate figures—were killed by the rebels": Orest Subtelny, *Ukraine: A History*, Toronto: University of Toronto Press, 1994, pp. 127–8.

61. Oleg Budnitskii, "Shot in the Back: On the Origins of the Anti-Jewish Pogroms of 1918–1921," in Eugene M. Avrutin and Harriet Murav (eds), *Jews in the East European Borderlands: Essays in Honor of John D. Klier*, Boston: Academic Studies Press, 2012, pp. 187–90. See also: Eric Lohr, "The Russian Army and the Jews: Mass Deportation, Hostages and Violence during World War I," *Russian Review*, vol. 60, no. 3 (2001), pp. 404–19; Terry Martin, "The Origins of Soviet Ethnic Cleansing," *Journal of Modern History*, vol. 70, no. 4 (1998), pp. 813–61; Alexander V. Prusin, *Nationalizing a Borderland: War, Ethnicity and Anti-Jewish Violence in East Galicia, 1914–1920*, Tuscaloosa: University of Alabama Press, 2005. A fascinating first-hand account is S. Ansky, *The Enemy at His Pleasure: A Journey Through the Jewish Pale of Settlement during World War I*, New York: Metropolitan Books, 2002. On the broader picture, see: Robert Gerwarth and John Horne, "Vectors of Violence: Paramilitarism in Europe after the Great War," *Journal of Modern History*, vol. 83, no. 3 (2011), pp. 489–512; Robert Gerwarth and John Horne (eds), *War in Peace: Paramilitary Violence in Europe after the Great War*, Oxford: Oxford University Press, 2013. Here, then, is a further example of continuities between the world war and the civil wars in the collapsing Russian Empire, as emphasized in: Joshua A. Sanborn, "Unsettling the Empire: Violent Migrations and Social Disaster in Russia during World War I," *Journal of Modern History*, vol. 77, no. 2 (2005), pp. 290–324; and Joshua Sanborn, "The Genesis of Russian Warlordism: Violence and Governance in the First World War and the Civil War," *Contemporary European History*, vol. 19 (2010), pp. 195–13.

62. Miroslav Popovich and Viktor Mironenko (eds), *Glavnyi ataman: v plenu nesbytochnykh nadezhd. Simon Petliura*, Moscow: Letnii Sad, 2008, pp. 240–43. It tells all that the commission was established in the wake of a series of bloody pogroms committed, across Kiev *guberniia*, by the forces of the anarchic Otaman Hryhoriiv, as they approached the Ukrainian capital: as many as 1,200 Jews were slaughtered by Hryhoriiv's forces at Uman on 12–14 May 1919, for example. See Nicolas Werth, "Crimes and Mass Violence of the Rus-

sian Civil Wars (1918–1921)," Online Encyclopedia of Mass Violence: http://www.mass-violence.org/Crimes-and-mass-violence-of-the-Russian-civil-wars-1918.

63. Oleg Budnitskii, *Rossiiskie evrei mezhdu krasnymi i belymi, 1917–1920*, Moscow: ROSSPEN, 2005, p. 8.

64. One notable example was the leading Kadet Max Vinaver (1862/3–1926), who journeyed to Ekaterinodar to offer his services to General Alekseev in 1918, before becoming foreign minister of the Crimean Regional Government of Soloman Krym from November 1918 to April 1919. General B.A. Shteifon (1881–1945) of the Volunteer Army (he was chief of staff in General N.E. Bredov's Poltava Detachment during the "Bredov March" of January-February 1920) also had Jewish ancestry, although his father had converted to Orthodoxy.

65. Ibid., p. 495.

66. Ibid., p. 497. Even if he takes his claim too far, Budnitskii is surely right to challenge the assertion of Evan Mawdsley that "the pogroms had no effect on the outcome of the civil war": Mawdsley, *The Russian Civil War*, p. 210. As he points out elsewhere, awareness of the debilitating impact upon army discipline of pogroms could lead even one of the most renowned White antisemites, General A.M. Dragomirov, to issue orders forbidding attacks on Jews: Budnitskii, "Jews, Pogroms and the White Movement," p. 758. (Intriguingly, Dragomirov's first name was Abram.)

67. Budnitskii, *Rossiiskie evrei mezhdu krasnymi i belymi*, p. 500. This statement would be even truer if we could delete that "only."

68. Peter Kenez, *Civil War in South Russia, 1919–20: The Defeat of the Whites*, Berkeley: University of California Press, 1977, pp. 176–7; and Kenez, "Pogroms and White Ideology," pp. 310–11. It would be as well here to restate the obvious: Jews never invaded Russia; Russia, in the eighteenth-century Partitions of Poland grabbed the territories in which Jews had lived for many centuries; and at least two million Jews had removed themselves from the tsar's lands in the half century prior to the revolution of 1917.

69. For example: Elisas Haifetz, *The Slaughter of the Jews in Ukraine*, New York: Thomas Seltzer, 1921; J.B. Schechtman, E. Tcherikower, and N. Tsatskis, *Les Pogroms en Ukraine sous des gouvernements ukrainiens (1917–1919). Aperçu historique et documents*, Paris: Comité des Délégations Juives, 1927; and Saul S. Friedman, *Pogromchik: The Assassination of Simon Petliura*, New York: Hart, 1976. Unfortunately, the most essential work on the period, based upon the personal archive of materials that its author took from Kiev to Germany in 1920, has not been translated into English: Elias Tcherikover, *Di Ukrayner pogromen in yor 1919*, New York: Yidisher Visnshaftekher Institut, 1965. But see the description and analysis of it in Elias Schulman, "The Pogroms in the Ukraine in 1919," *Jewish Quarterly Review*, vol. 57, no. 2 (1966), pp. 159–66.

70. For example: J. Batinsky *et al.* (eds), *The Jewish Pogroms in Ukraine: Authoritative Statements on the Question of Responsibility for Recent Outbreaks against Jews in Ukraine*, Washington, DC: The Friends of Ukraine, 1919; Comité Commémoratif Simon Petlura, *Documents sur les pogroms en Ukraine en 1919 et l'assassinat de Simon Petlura à Paris (1917–1921–1926)*, Paris: Librairie du Trident, 1927; and Taras Hunczak, *Symon Petlura et les Juifs*, Paris: Bibliothèque Ukrainienne Symon Petlura, 1987. The last of these, despite its provenance, is more sober than most such treatments. The tone of the debate can be adduced from an extended review of the work of Friedman (*Pogromchik*), in which it was alleged that "almost every page of Prof. Friedman's book feels the impact of its author's ignorance": Lew

Shankowsky, "Ukraine-Hating as a Synthesis," *Ukrainian Quarterly*, vol. 43, nos 1–2 (1987), pp. 64–99.

71. "France: Petlura Trial," *Time* (7 Nov. 1927).

72. A recent attempt to fashion a new historiographical synthesis that might meld Jewish and Ukrainian versions of the pogroms in Ukraine—Henry Abramson, *A Prayer for the Government: Ukrainians and Jews in Revolutionary Times, 1917–1920*, Cambridge, MA: Ukrainian Research Center for Jewish Studies, Harvard University, 1999—did not meet with universal acclaim. See: Lars Fischer, "The 'Pogromshchina' and the Directory: A New Historiographical Synthesis?" *Revolutionary Russia*, vol. 16, no. 2 (2003), pp. 47–93; and Henry Abramson, "Well—Yes, a New Historiographical Synthesis. A Response to Lars Fischer," *Revolutionary Russia*, vol. 16, no. 2 (2003), pp. 94–100. Also Lars Fischer, "Whither *Pogromshchina*—Historical Synthesis or Deconstruction?" *East European Jewish Affairs*, vol. 38, no. 3 (2008), pp. 303–20, and: Henry Abramson, "Historiography on the Jews and the Ukrainian Revolution," *Journal of Ukrainian Studies*, vol. 15, no. 2 (1990), pp. 33–46.

73. Although Lithuania's possession of Vilnius seemed—but only "seemed," as the city was not mentioned by name—to be confirmed by the Allied-brokered Polish–Lithuanian Suwałki Agreement (7 Oct. 1920), Piłsudski was determined that Wilno should be controlled by Poland. He therefore instructed General Lucjan Żeligowski, who was a native of Lithuania, to lead his forces (the 14,000-strong 1st Lithuanian–Belarussian Infantry Division) in a "mutiny": they were to "desert" from the Polish Army (which was piously observing the Allied pronouncements) and "independently" seize the city, enabling Warsaw to deny all involvement. Żeligowski made his move on 8 Oct. 1920, and on the following day the outnumbered Lithuanian garrison abandoned Vilnius/Wilno. On 12 Oct. 1920, the independence of an "independent" Central Lithuanian Republic was then proclaimed. Following a general election of 8 Jan. 1922, which Lithuania regarded as fixed (and which most Lithuanians and Jews and many Belorussians in Wilno/Vilnius boycotted), the state parliament of the Central Lithuanian Republic, dominated by Polish parties, voted for incorporation into Poland. This request was duly accepted by the Polish Sejm on 22 Mar. 1922, and two days later the Republic of Central Lithuania ceased to exist, its territories being incorporated into Poland's new Wilno voivodship. The union was subsequently endorsed by the Allied Conference of Ambassadors in Paris, but conflict over Wilno/Vilnius soured Polish–Lithuanian relations throughout the inter-war years. See: Łossowski, *Konflikt polsko-litewski 1918–1920*, pp. 112–218.

74. For a rueful and bitter but useful factual account of the negotiating process by which Poland failed to regain two-thirds of the territories it had possessed prior to the First Partition in 1772, see: Stanisław Dabrowski, "The Peace Treaty of Riga," *Polish Review*, vol. 5, no. 1 (1960), pp. 3–34.

75. "Speech Delivered at a Conference of Chairmen of Uyezd, Volost and Village Executive Committees of Moscow Gubernia, October 15 1920," Lenin, *CW*, vol. 31, p. 321.

76. It compared in the civil-war years to around 1 million Estonians, 1.5 million Latvians, 2 million Lithuanians, and 3 million Azeris. More comparable to Poland in population was Ukraine, but, as we know, it was far less united and its national movement and national identity were far less advanced and concrete than were those of Poland.

77. But, for a contrary view, see Thomas C. Fiddick, *Russia's Retreat from Poland, 1920: From Permanent Revolution to Peaceful Coexistence*, London: Macmillan, 1990. Also of interest is Norman Davies, "The Missing Revolutionary War: The Polish Campaigns and the Retreat

from Revolution in Soviet Russia, 1919–1921," *Soviet Studies*, vol. 27, no. 2 (1975), pp. 178–95.

78. *Direktivy Glavnogo kommandovaniia Krasnoi Armii (1917–1920): sbornik dokumentov*, Moscow: Voenizdat, 1969, pp. 610–12. See also Mawdsley, *The Russian Civil War*, pp. 259–61 on these points.

79. As well as those that never had been: in November 1920, 5,000 men loyal to Boris Savinkov's People's Union for the Defense of Russia and Freedom, under Ataman Stanisław Bułak-Bałachowicz, formed the Russian People's Volunteer Army and marched into the Mozyr region of Belorussia. Savinkov was initially very optimistic, writing to his friend, the poet Zinaida Gippius, that "I am convinced we shall reach Moscow. The peasants know we are going to fight for Russia but not for a Tsarist, aristocratic Russia ... In the neighboring villages three thousand of them have signed up as volunteers": Temira Pachmuss (ed.), *Between Paris and St Petersburg: Selected Diaries of Zinaida Gippius*, Urbana: University of Illinois Press, 1975, p. 202. In the aftermath of the Soviet–Polish peace, Savinkov's invaders were forced back into Poland, where they were disarmed. Savinkov and his supporters were expelled from Poland, with just 24 hours' notice, in October 1921: Karol Wedziagolski, *Boris Savinkov: Portrait of a Terrorist*, Clifton, NJ: The Kingston Press, 1988, pp. 155–215.

80. That, following his bitter breach with Wrangel in January-February 1920, Denikin could accept such an appointment, sign the order (No. 2,899) himself, and then retire quietly to Constantinople speaks of his essential humility. That he was thereafter left generally in peace to write his memoirs attests to the respect in which he was held even by those who deposed him. Others were not as fortunate: General I.P. Romanovskii, chief of staff of first the Volunteer Army and then the AFSR, and a trusted confidant of both Kornilov and Denikin, was shot dead in the billiard room of the Russian embassy at Constantinople on 17 April 1920 (Vrangl', *Vospominaniia*, vol. 2, pp. 27–8). The assassin evaded capture and identification, but is believed to have been Lieutenant M.A. Khoruzin, a member of a monarchist organization (and a former employee of the White intelligence service, Azbuka), who, like many others on the Right, considered Romanovskii to be a "liberal," a freemason, and the chief architect of all the failures of the White cause.

81. That was a bad idea. The Insurgent Army's staff immediately had the unfortunate bearer of this "vile offer" executed (Peter Arshinov, *History of the Makhnovist Movement, 1918–1921*, London: Freedom Press, 1921, pp. 173–5), thereby countering reports in the European and Soviet press that a formal "White–Black" military alliance had already been signed: Trotsky, "Makhno and Wrangel," 14 Oct. 1920, *How the Revolution Armed, Vol. 3: 1920*, p. 291. On the politics of the Wrangel regime, see: Anthony Kröner, *The White Knight of the Black Sea: The Life of Peter Wrangel*. The Hague: Leuxenhoff, 2010, pp. 246–60; Nikolai Ross, *Vrangel' v Krymu*, Frankfurt am Main: Posev, 1982; and Donald W. Treadgold, "The Ideology of the White Movement: Wrangel's 'Leftist Policy from Rightist Hands'," *Harvard Slavic Studies*, vol. 4 (1957), pp. 481–97. There is also a variety of very informative articles in S.M. Iskhakov (ed.), *Krym. Vrangel'. 1920 god*. On civil-war Crimea pre-Wrangel, see: Raymond Pearson, "*Nashe Pravitel'stvo*? The Crimean Regional Government of 1918–1919," *Revolutionary Russia*, vol. 2, no. 2 (1989), pp. 14–30; and M.M. Vinaver, *Nashe pravitel'stvo. Krymskiia vospominaniia 1918–1919gg.*, Paris: Imprimerie d'art Voltaire, 1928.

82. Vrangel', *Vospominaniia*, vol. 2, pp. 137–77. See also N.A. Korsakova, "Otnoshenie P.N. Vrangelia k Kubanskomu kazachestvu (po materialam dnevnikov B.G. Naumenko)," in Iskhakov (ed.), *Krym. Vrangel'. 1920 god*, pp. 56–62. General Naumenko, the former

Kuban ataman who participated in the landings, blamed the failure of the expedition on blunders by Ulagai and poor preparation caused by the White leadership's inability to trust the Kuban Cossacks, whom they saw as tainted by separatism. Soviet versions of the episode include: A.V. Golubev, *Vrangelevskie desanty na Kuban, avgust–sentiabr' 1920 goda*, Moscow–Leningrad: Gosizdat, 1920; and A.A. Kondakov, *Razgrom desantov Vrangelia na Kubani*, Krasnodar: Krasnodarnoe Knizhnoe Izd.-vo, 1960.

83. Kalervo Hovi, *Cordon Sanitaire or Barrière de l'Est? The Emergence of the New French Eastern European Policy, 1917–1919*, Turku: Turun Yliopisto, 1975; and Kalervo Hovi, *Alliance de Revers: The Stabilization of France's Alliance Policies in East Central Europe, 1919–1921*, Turku: Turun Yliopisto, 1984.

84. Vrangel', *Vospominaniia*, vol. 2, p. 145; Anne Hogenhuis-Seliverstoff, *Les relations franco-soviétiques, 1917–1924*, Paris: Institut d'Histoire des Relations Internationales Contemporaines, 1981, p. 181; George A. Brinkley, *The Volunteer Army and Allied Intervention in South Russia, 1917–1921: A Study in the Politics and Diplomacy of the Russian Civil War*, Notre Dame: University of Notre Dame Press, 1966, p. 264. After Wrangel's defeat, the French, nevertheless, insisted on asserting their ownership of the remnants of the Black Sea Fleet (redubbed the Russian Squadron) that were steered to Bizerte in Tunisia. When the French government recognized the USSR in 1924, ownership of the squadron reverted to Moscow. In December that year, however, a visiting Soviet technical commission found the vessels to be beyond repair and they were scrapped locally. See: G.L. Iazykov, "Evakuatsiia Chenomorskogo flota iz Kryma v Bizertu v 1920 godu," *Novyi chasovoi*, no. 4 (1996), pp. 160–66; V.E. Kolupaev, "Russkii flot v Afrike," *Voenno-istoricheskii arkhiv*, no. 8 (2002), pp. 3–36; and A.A. Shirinskaia, *Bizerta: Posledniaia stoianka*, St Petersburg: Otechestvo, 2003.

85. Vrangel', *Vospominaniia*, vol. 2, pp. 86–7.

86. On Kutepov, see R.G. Gagkuev and V.Zh. Tsetkov, *General Kutepov*, Moscow: Posev, 2009.

87. Tom Hillman, *The Trans-Dnepr Operation: Wrangel's Last Operation in the Russian Civil War*, n.p.: Gauntlet International, 2004.

88. A.S. Bubnov, S.S. Kamenev, and R.P. Eidman (eds), *Grazhdanskaia voina, 1918–1921*, Moscow: Voennyi Vestnik, 1928, vol. 3, p. 513. The *tachanka* was a sprung carriage, with a lightweight body, which was designed to be pulled by two horses (and sometimes four) and was usually manned by three men. This vehicle became widely adopted during the civil war by cavalry forces, as a high-speed mobile platform for a Maxim gun or other weaponry. An impressive monument to it (*The Legendary Tachanka*, by E.M. Poltoratskii, 1967) stands near Kakhovka and a preserved Makhnovist *tachanka* has pride of place in the Historical Museum at Guliai-Pole. Isaac Babel also hymned it, with characteristic scabrity, in the *Red Cavalry* aside "Discourse on the Tachanka": Babel, *The Collected Stories*, pp. 83–6. "A tachanka! Upon that word had been erected a triangle epitomizing our ways: massacre, tachanka, blood."

89. *How the Revolution Armed, Vol. 3: 1920*, pp. 302–3.

90. *Vremia* ("The Times," 4 Nov. 1920), in A.A. Valentinov, "Krymskaia epopeia (po dnevnikam uchastnikiv i po dokumentam)," *Arkhiv Russkoi revoliutsii*, vol. 5 (1922), p. 82.

91. The element of surprise that favored the Reds here is difficult to fathom, given that upon arrival in Sevastopol' Frunze discovered, from the manager of Wrangel's radio stations, that "absolutely all our ciphers are being deciphered by the enemy in consequence of their sim-

plicity. Our entire radio communication system has been the most splendid source of guidance to the enemy": Meijer (ed.), *The Trotsky Papers*, vol. 2, p. 369.

92. Vrangel', *Vospominaniia*, vol. 2, pp. 230–35.

93. Ibid., vol. 2, p. 342. As his voyage commenced toward "Tsargrad"—the name Russians since Catherine the Great's era had anticipated bestowing upon a Russian Constantinople—the indomitable Wrangel sent a message to the Allied military authorities proposing that his exiled army take over garrisoning duties in the former Turkish capital, which was currently occupied by British and French forces. He was ignored. See Kröner, *The White Knight of the Black Sea*, p. 318. On the evacuation, see the numerous White memoirs assembled in *Iskhod Russkii armii generala Vrangelia iz Kryma*, Moscow: Tsentropoligraf, 2003, pp. 501–628. Wrangel's army, although (largely thanks to the efforts of General M.N. Skalon) extricated from Crimea with more order than Denikin's had been from Novorossiisk, would spend the next two horribly distressing years in camps around the Sea of Marmara and the Aegean, before being dispersed across Europe. Wrangel's All-Russian Military Union (ROVS) would then preserve a degree of unity and battle-readiness among his scattered forces, but even that would eventually wither. See Paul Robinson, *The White Russian Army in Exile, 1920–1941*, Oxford: Clarendon, 2002, *passim*. The general himself died in Brussels in 1927, possibly at the hands of the Soviet intelligence services, although his latest biographer doubts this. See Kröner, *The White Knight of the Black Sea*, pp. 405–7.

94. V.A. Zolotarev *et al.* (eds), *Russkaia voennaia emigratsiia 20-kh—40-kh godov: dokumenty i materialy*, Moscow: Geia, 1998, vol. 1, pp. 23–4. Bullock's figure of 50,000 executions in this period (*The Russian Civil War*, p. 122) is certainly exaggerated. The local population of Crimean Tatars was initially treated with moderation by the Soviet authorities. From 1921 onwards, however, repression, along with forced collectivization and the confiscation of food supplies, reaped havoc. It is thought that as many as 150,000 Crimean Tatars—around half their population—had been killed or deported or had fled abroad by 1933. This was a proportionally greater loss of population than any other suffered by the indigenous peoples of the USSR, but even worse was to come at the end of the Second World War: in May 1944 the entire Crimean Tatar population was deported to Uzbekistan, as alleged collaborators with the Nazis.

95. Such, for example, seems to have been the fate of General V.L. Pokrovskii, Wrangel's successor as commander of the Caucasian Army in December 1919, who was killed at Kiustendil in Bulgaria in very suspicious circumstances in 1922.

96. The sorry story of these events was widely publicized in Nicholas Bethell, *The Last Secret: Forcible Repatriation to Russia, 1944–47*, London: Deutsch, 1974; and Nikolai Tolstoy, *Victims of Yalta*, London: Hodder and Stoughton, 1977. Sultan-girei Klych had been commander, from 21 Dec. 1918, of the "Savage Division" (formally the Cherkess Cavalry Division), formerly General Kornilov's bodyguard. Between the wars he was a prominent figure among anti-Soviet Caucasian émigrés, as a member of the Central Committee of the People's Party of Mountaineers of the North Caucasus, which sought to detach the region from the USSR. During the Second World War, Klych formed a Caucasian Division and joined the Cossack forces of General P.N. Krasnov in collaborating with the Nazis. His unit was interned by the British at Oberdrauburg in May 1945 and (despite his French citizenship) Klych was among 125 Caucasian officers who were subsequently handed over to the NKVD for transfer to Moscow, where he met his fate.

5. 1917–21: ON THE INTERNAL FRONTS

1. The allusion to typhus was made by General A.P. von Budberg, reflecting on the appearance of a map on a wall at the Omsk *stavka*, on which instances of partisan activity had been marked with a red dot: Budberg, "Dnevnik," *Arkhiv Russkoi revoliutsii*, vol. 15 (1924), p. 327. The most extensive and highly organized of the partisan regions was the Taseevo Partisan Republic of southern Eniseisk *guberniia*. On the phenomenon, see: *Partizanskoe dvizhenie v Sibiri. Tom 1: Prieniseiskii krai*, Moscow: Gosizdat, 1925; and V. El'tsin, "Krest'ianskoe dvizhenie v Sibiri v periode Kolchaka," *Proletarskaia revoliutsiia*, no. 49 (1926), pp. 5–48; no. 50 (1926), pp. 51–82. Nestor Makhno was, of course, hugely influential in disrupting the rear of the AFSR during its advance through Ukraine during the autumn of 1919—see Peter Arshinov, *History of the Makhnovist Movement, 1918–1921*, London: Freedom Press, 1921, pp. 145–52—but as a mobile guerila leader rather than as head of a stable partisan zone: the Ukrainian anarchists' so-called Free Territory of the Makhnovshchina, centered around Guliai-Pole in Ekaterinoslav *guberniia*, had been overrun by the Whites and Makhno's army had been driven as far to the west as Peregonovka (100 miles west of Elizavetgrad), in right-bank Ukraine, by 25 Sep. 1919, before overcoming its pursuers and turning back toward the east.

2. On the evolution of Lloyd George's thinking, see Jonathan D. Smele, "A Bolshevik in Brixton Prison: Fedor Raskol'nikov and the Origins of Anglo-Soviet Relations," in Ian D. Thatcher (ed.), *Reinterpreting Revolutionary Russia: Essays in Honour of James D. White*, Basingstoke: Palgrave, 2006, pp. 105–29. Also: Chris Wrigley, *Lloyd George*, Oxford: Blackwell, 1992; and Kenneth O. Morgan, *Consensus and Disunity: The Lloyd George Coalition Cabinet, 1918–1922*, Oxford: Clarendon, 1979 (especially pp. 135–8).

3. "House of Commons Debates," 16 Apr. 1919, vol. 114 cc, 2941–2 (http://hansard.millbanksystems.com/commons/1919/apr/16/military-intervention-greatest-act-of).

4. CAB 23/541, Meeting of 6 Mar. 1919.

5. See, for example, Stephen White, *The Origins of Détente: The Genoa Conference and Soviet Western Relations, 1921–22*, Cambridge: Cambridge University Press, 1985. The normalizing of Soviet–Western relations was further promoted by the placing of the suave former tsarist diplomat G.V. Chicherin (a pub'ished expert on Mozart) in the role of Commissar for Foreign Affairs (30 May 1918–21 Ju 730) and the naming of the sophisticated technocrat L.B. Krasin as People Commissa   ign Trade (11 June 1920–18 Nov. 1925). On the other hand, it should   called tha even while attending the Genoa conference, Chicherin found time to slip along th coast to Rapallo to sign a treaty with Weimar Germany, on 16 Apr. 1922, that angered the Allied powers (even though they did not at that stage know of its secret annexes, arranging for German forces to develop weapons in Soviet Russia that had been banned under the Treaty of Versailles, and for German experts, in return, to train the Red Army).

6. V.I. Lenin, "Can the Bolsheviks Retain State Power?" *CW*, vol. 26, pp. 106–7 (emphasis in original). For an expert and insightful analysis of how Lenin arrived at this conclusion, see George Garvy, "The Origins of Lenin's Views on the Role of Banks in the Socialist Transformation of Society," *History of Political Economy*, vol. 4, no. 1 (1972), pp. 252–63.

7. V.I. Lenin, "The State and Revolution," *CW*, vol. 25, pp. 473–4, 478.

8. Lenin, "Can the Bolsheviks Retain State Power?" *CW*, vol. 26, p. 107. At Sedan, on 2 Sep. 1870, some 100,000 French soldiers of the Army of Châlons, along with Emperor Napoleon III, were captured by the Prussians. A.V. Peshekhonov, one of the founders of the

Party of Popular Socialists, was Minister of Supply in the Provisional Government from 5 May to 31 Aug. 1917.

9. Rex A. Wade (ed.), *Documents of Soviet History*, vol. 1, Gulf Breeze: Academic International Press, 1991, pp. 47–9.

10. On this phase of Soviet economic policy, see: Paul H. Avrich, "The Bolsheviks and Workers' Control in Russian Industry," *Slavic Review*, vol. 22, no. 1 (1963), pp. 47–63; and R.D. Rucker, "Workers' Control of Production in the October Revolution and Civil War," *Science and Society*, vol. 43, no. 2 (1979), pp. 158–85. For a sustained and convincing argument that we should take Lenin's utopian views seriously, see Neil Harding, *Lenin's Political Thought, Vol. 2: Theory and Practice in the Socialist Revolution*, London: Macmillan, 1981 (especially pp. 41–141).

11. See Shliapnikov's report to VTsIk of 20 Mar. 1918, in James Bunyan (ed.), *The Origin of Forced Labor in the Soviet State, 1917–1921: Documents and Materials*, Baltimore: Johns Hopkins University Press, 1967, pp. 20–21. Also Roger Pethybridge, "The Bolsheviks and Technical Disorder, 1917–1918," *Slavonic and East European Review*, vol. 49 (1971), pp. 410–24.

12. Andrei Markevich and Mark Harrison, "Great War, Civil War, and Recovery: Russia's National Income 1913 to 1928," *Journal of Economic History*, vol. 71, no. 3 (2011), p. 687.

13. See D.B. Pavlov (ed.), *Rabochee oppozitsionnoe dvizhenie v bol'shevistskoi Rossii, 1918 g. Sobraniia upolnomochennykh fabrik i zavodov. Dokumenty i materialy*, Moscow: ROSSPEN, 2006. Also William G. Rosenberg, "Russian Labor and Bolshevik Power after October," *Slavic Review*, vol. 44, no. 2 (1985), pp. 212–38. The extent and acuity of these protests was one of the best-kept secrets of Soviet histories of the revolution. Consequently, the publication of a document that detailed a workers' meeting in the Narva Gate district of Petrograd— "Extraordinary Meeting of Delegates of Factories and Plants in the City of Petrograd," *Kontinent*, vol. 2 (1977), pp. 212–41—was met with some incredulity in the West. Much more is now known: Alexander Rabinowitch, "Early Disenchantment with Bolshevik Rule: New Data from the Archives of the Extraordinary Assembly of Delegates from Petrograd Factories," in Kevin Mcdermott and John Morison (eds), *Politics and Society under the Bolsheviks*, London: Macmillan, 1999, pp. 37–46; and Alexander Rabinowitch, *The Bolsheviks in Power: The First Year of Soviet Rule in Petrograd*, Bloomington: Indiana University Press, 2007, pp. 223–31.

14. "The Soviet regime has again throttled several newspapers hostile to it," observed Maxim Gorky on 14 May 1918: Maxim Gorky, *Untimely Thoughts: Essays on Revolution, Culture and the Bolsheviks, 1917–1918*, London: Garnstone Press, 1968, p. 182. Among the newspapers closed between 10 and 14 May 1918 were the Kadets' *Nash vek* ("Our Age") and *Sovremennoe slovo* ("The Modern Word"), the PSR's *Zemlia i volia* ("Land and Freedom"), and the Mensheviks' *Novy luch* ("The New Ray"). In Petrograd, the only evening newspaper to survive this onslaught was the Bolsheviks' own *Verchernaia pravda* ("Evening *Pravda*").

15. James Bunyan (ed.), *Intervention, Civil War and Communism in Russia, April–December 1918: Documents and Materials*, Baltimore: Johns Hopkins University Press, 1936, p. 463.

16. James H. Bater, *St Petersburg: Industrialisation and Change*, London: Edward Arnold, 1976, pp. 387–8.

17. Rabinowitch, *The Bolsheviks in Power*, p. 224. Worker protests were also recorded, though, in more peripheral cities, where, as we have seen in the case of the Urals, they could have more immediate impact upon events at the front. See Stephen M. Berk, "The Class Tragedy

of Izhevsk: Working-Class Opposition to Bolshevism in 1918," *Russian History*, vol. 2, no. 2 (1975), pp. 176–90; and M.S. Bernshtam (ed.), *Narodnoe soprotivlenie v Rossii. Ural i Prikam'e, noiabr' 1917—ianvar' 1919: dokumenty i materialy*, Paris: YMCA, 1982.

18. Vladimir Brovkin, "The Mensheviks' Political Comeback: Elections to the Provincial City Soviets in the Spring of 1918," *Russian Review*, vol. 42, no. 1 (1983), pp. 1–50; and Vladimir Brovkin, "The Mensheviks under Attack: The Transformation of Soviet Politics, June–September 1918," *Jahrbücher für Geschichte Osteuropas*, vol. 32, no. 3 (1984), pp. 378–91.

19. The fullest discussion of this is Silvana Malle, *The Economic Organization of War Communism, 1918–1921*, Cambridge: Cambridge University Press, 1985. The standard Soviet account is E.G. Gimpel'son, *Voennyi kommunizm: politika, praktika, ideologiia*, Moscow: Mysl', 1973. See also S.A. Pavliuchenkov, *Voennyi kommunizm: vlast' i massy*, Moscow: RKT-istoriia, 1997. The journal *Russian Studies in History*, vol. 33, no. 1 (1994), also featured several important and accessible discussions of the subject. A good, brief exposition of the central features of War Communism, as "a specific functional model of the socialist economy," is László Szamuely, "Major Features of the Economy and Ideology of War Communism," *Acta Oeconomica*, vol. 7, no. 2 (1971), pp. 143–60.

20. In his pamphlet on *The Tax in Kind* (Apr. 1921)—or, more specifically, in the notes he wrote in preparation for it—in which he used the term to differentiate the immediately foregoing period from that about to be initiated under the mixed economy of the NEP. Specifically, he wrote of "that peculiar War Communism, which was forced on us by extreme want, ruin and war." See Lenin, *CW*, vol. 32, pp. 320, 342. The coiner of the term "War Communism" may, however, have been Lenin's old rival within the Bolshevik party, A.A. Bogdanov, who had used it as early as 1917: P.A. Pliutto, "Aleksandr Bogdanov on the Period of War Communism," *Revolutionary Russia*, vol. 5, no. 1 (1992), pp. 46–52.

21. It had roots too in the tsarist government's interventionist economic policies during the war, notably the fixed price on grain introduced in 1916, which had been maintained by the Provisional Government in 1917—another fact arguing for the emphasizing of continuities from the world war into the civil wars. See: Jacques Sapir, "La guerre civile et l'économie de guerre: origines du système soviétique," *Cahiers du Monde Russe et Soviétique*, vol. 38, nos 1–2 (1997), pp. 9–28; and Eric Lohr, "War and Revolution, 1914–1917," in Dominic Lieven (ed.), *The Cambridge History of Russia, Volume 2: Imperial Russia, 1689–1917*, Cambridge: Cambridge University Press, 2006, pp. 655–69.

22. By implication, more recent developments were somewhat less than "heroic": L.N. Kritsmann, *Die heroische Periode der Grossen Russischen Revolution. Ein Versuch der Analyse des sogenannten "Kriegskommunismus"*, Vienna and Berlin: Verlag für Literatur und Politik, 1929. For a translation, by Ronald I. Kowalski, of the Foreword, Introduction, and Chapter One of Kritsmann's work, see *Revolutionary Russia*, vol. 2, no. 2 (1989), pp. v–xvii, 1–13. See also: Stephen F. Cohen, "In Praise of War Communism: Bukharin's 'Economics of the Transition Period,'" in Alexander Rabinowitch, Janet Rabinowitch, and Ladis K.D. Kristof (eds), *Revolution and Politics in Russia: Essays in Memory of B.I. Nicolaevsky*, Bloomington: Indiana University Press, 1972, pp. 192–203; Bernard M. Patenaude, "Peasants into Russians: The Utopian Essence of War Communism," *Russian Review*, vol. 54, no. 4 (1995), pp. 552–70; and Paul C. Roberts, "War Communism: A Re-Examination," *Slavic Review*, vol. 29, no. 2 (1970), pp. 238–62.

23. E.A. Preobrazhenskii, *Bumazhnye den'gi v epokhu proletarskoi diktatury*, Moscow: Gosizdat, 1920. By 1 January 1921 there were 1,168,597 million roubles in circulation in Soviet

Russia, compared to 1,530 million on 1 July 1914, but the purchasing power of it had declined to a mere 70 million pre-war roubles. See R.W. Davies, "Changing Economic Systems: An Overview," in R.W. Davies, Mark Harrison, and S.G. Wheatcroft (eds), *The Economic Transformation of the Soviet Union, 1913–1945*, Cambridge: Cambridge University Press, 1994, p. 6.

24. Alec Nove, *An Economic History of the USSR, 1917–1991*, London: Penguin, 1992, p. 47.

25. Davies, "Changing Economic Systems," p. 7.

26. Evan Mawdsley, *The Russian Civil War*, Boston: Allen & Unwin, 1987, p. 74 (emphasis in original).

27. Samuel A. Oppenheim, "The Supreme Economic Council, 1917–1921," *Soviet Studies*, vol. 25, no. 1 (1973), pp. 3–27. For a very detailed study of VSNKh's evolution in northern Russia see Falk Döring, *Organisationsprobleme der russischen Wirktschaft in Revolution und Bürgerkrieg (1918–1920)*, Hanover: Verlag für Literatur und Zeitgeschehen, 1970.

28. See: Bunyan (ed.), *Intervention, Civil War and Communism in Russia*, pp. 460–62; and Wade (ed.), *Documents on Soviet History*, vol. 1, pp. 153–5, 172–4.

29. "Taylorism" (named after the American engineer Frederick W. Taylor), sometimes known as "Scientific Management," involved the analysis of and rationalization of work flows (particularly through the adoption of production lines) in order to maximize industrial efficiency. It sought also to encourage the work ethic, often through the introduction of piecework—hitherto anathema to socialists. Lenin himself had condemned the system as exploitative in a 1914 article: "The Taylor System—Man's Enslavement by the Machine," Lenin, *CW*, vol. 20, pp. 152–4. See: Kendall E. Bailes, "Alexei Gastev and the Soviet Controversy over Taylorism, 1918–1924," *Soviet Studies*, vol. 29, no. 3 (1977), pp. 373–94; and Rainer Traub, "Lenin and Taylor: The Fate of 'Scientific Management' in the (Early) Soviet Union," *Telos*, vol. 37 (1978), pp. 82–92.

30. Nove, *An Economic History of the USSR*, p. 68.

31. *Dekrety Sovetskoi vlasti*, vol. 2, pp. 412–20.

32. See Orlando Figes, "The Russian Peasant Community in the Agrarian Revolution, 1917–1918," in Roger Bartlett (ed.), *Land Commune and Peasant Community in Russia*, London: Macmillan, 1990, pp. 237–53; and Orlando Figes, *Peasant Russia, Civil War: The Volga Countryside in Revolution, 1917–1921*, Oxford: Clarendon, 1989.

33. Lenin, "On the Attitude to the Middle Peasants," *CW*, vol. 29, pp. 217–20.

34. In 1913, 4,200,000 tons of pig iron was produced; in 1921, 100,000 tons (2.38 percent). In 1913, 4,300,000 tons of steel had been produced; in 1921, 200,000 tons (4.65 percent). See Nove, *An Economic History of the USSR*, p. 62.

35. Nove, *loc. cit.*

36. Markevich and Harrison, "Great War, Civil War, and Recovery," p. 687.

37. Arup Banjeri, "Commissars and Bagmen: Russia during the Civil War, 1918–1921," *Studies in History*, vol. 3, no. 2 (1987), pp. 233–74; Mauricio Borrero, *Hungry Moscow: Scarcity and Urban Society in the Russian Civil War, 1917–1921*, New York: Peter Lang, 2003. Also L.N. Suvorova, "Behind the Façade of 'War Communism': Political Power and the Market Economy," *Russian Studies in History*, vol. 33, no. 1 (1994), pp. 72–88.

38. See: Daniel R. Brower, "'The City in Danger': The Civil War and the Russian Urban Population," in Diane Koenker, William G. Rosenberg, and Ronald G. Suny (eds), *Party, State and Society in the Russian Civil War: Explorations in Social History*, Bloomington: Indiana University Press, 1990, pp. 58–80; and Diane Koenker, "Urbanization and Deurbanization

in the Russian Revolution and Civil War," *Journal of Modern History*, vol. 57, no. 3 (1985), pp. 424–50. The day-to-day struggle for food and warmth of the civil-war era urbanite is nowhere more eloquently or lugubriously captured than in Terence Emmons (ed.), *Time of Troubles: The Diary of Iurii Vladimirovich Got'e, Moscow, July 8th 1917 to July 23rd 1922*, London: I.B. Tauris, 1988.

39. Victor Serge, *Memoirs of a Revolutionary, 1901–1941*, London: Oxford University Press, 1963, pp. 70–71. Serge (born Viktor Kabal'chich), the Brussels-born son of exiled Russian populists, was an anarchist activist, author, and literary critic. He was imprisoned in France during the First World War and was arrested again in 1917 as he journeyed from Spain to Russia. In October 1918, he was among a group of Russian anarchists and socialists exchanged for Allied personnel held in Soviet Russia. He joined the RKP(b) in Feb. 1919, but was expelled in 1928 as a member of the Left Opposition. After a spell in exile in Central Asia, he was allowed to leave the USSR in 1936 and settled in Mexico.

40. Evgenii Zamiatin, *Peshchera*: Biblioteka Maksima Moshkova, http://az.lib.ru/z/ zamjatin_e_i/text_0110.shtml (my translation). As one critic commented, "This is a story of the degradation and poverty of people, clinging to a single idea—to get food and fuel. It is a crystalized nightmare, slightly reminiscent of Poe, with the difference that Zamyatin's nightmare is extraordinarily truthful": cited in "The Encyclopedia of Soviet Writers," http:// az.lib.ru/z/zamjatin_e_i/text_0110.shtml. Zamiatin's masterpiece, the dystopian novel *My* ("We," 1924) inspired both Aldous Huxley's *Brave New World* (1932) and George Orwell's *Nineteen Eighty-Four* (1949). The book, which was completed in 1921, earned the dubious honor of being the first work to be banned by Glavlit, the Main Administration for Literary and Publishing Affairs of the RSFSR (founded in 1922), and was smuggled abroad for publication. Zamiatin was effectively gagged thereafter by the Soviet authorities, until being permitted to emigrate in 1931.

41. *Bol'shaia sovetskaia entsiklopediia*, Moscow: Sovetskaia Entsiklopediia, 1929, vol. 2, p. 398.

42. Donald R. Raleigh, *Experiencing Russia's Civil War: Politics, Society and Revolutionary Culture in Saratov, 1917–1922*, Princeton: Princeton University Press, 2002, pp. 199–200.

43. Serge, *Memoirs of a Revolutionary*, p. 116.

44. See Huburtus F. Jahn, "The Housing Revolution in Petrograd, 1917–1920," *Jahrbücher für Geschichte Osteuropas*, vol. 38, no. 2 (1990), pp. 212–27. The housing committee and proletarian squatters' relations with their bourgeois hosts became a favorite subject of satirists in Soviet Russia during the relatively tolerant 1920s, reaching its brilliant acme in Mikhail Bulgakov's *Sobach'e sertse* ("The Heart of a Dog," 1925). The civil-war flight from the city eased pressure on housing and fuel supplies, of course, but it has to be remembered that prior to 1914 St Petersburg had been the most overcrowded (and unhealthy) city in all Europe and that conditions had worsened on every front there during the First World War. See Michael F. Hamm, "The Breakdown of Urban Modernization: A Prelude to the Revolution of 1917," in Michael F. Hamm (ed.), *The City in Russian History*, Lexington: Kentucky University Press, 1976, pp. 182–210.

45. M.N. Tukhachevskii, *Budushchaia voina*, Moscow: Klub Realisty, 1928.

46. According to Hal Draper, Marx's phrase should have been translated as "the isolation of rural life," as at the time Marx was writing the German word "Idiotismus" retained its Greek meaning, derived from "idiotes"—"a private person, withdrawn from public concerns." See Hal Draper, *The Adventures of the Communist Manifesto*, Berkeley: Center for Socialist History, 1998.

47. On the Jews, who have received detailed coverage, see above, pp. 159–64. The travails of German settler villages that dotted some of the most fought-over regions of the civil war (Ukraine, Crimea, the Kuban, the Middle Volga), and whose populations had already suffered years of discrimination as alleged fifth columnists of the Kaiser before and during the First World War, are less well appreciated. For good introductions to the subject, see: Peter Letkemann, "Mennonite Victims of Revolution, Anarchy, Civil War, Disease and Famine, 1917–1923," *Mennonite Historian*, vol. 24, no. 2 (1998), pp. 1–9; Peter Scheibert, "Deutsche Kolonien an der Wolga in den Jahren der Revolution, 1918–1921," *Forschungen zur Osteuropäischen Geschichte*, vol. 25 (1978), pp. 308–18; and John B. Toews, "No Songs were Sung at the Graveside: The Blumenort (Russia) Massacre (10–12 November 1919)," *Journal of Mennonite Studies*, vol. 13 (1995), pp. 51–70. On the self-defense units formed by the normally pacifistic Mennonite settlers, see John B. Toews, "The Origins and Activities of the Mennonite *Selbstschutz* in the Ukraine (1918–1919)," *Mennonite Quarterly Review*, vol. 46 (1972), pp. 5–40.

48. The Russian Social Democratic Labor Party (Bolsheviks) had been formally rechristened as the Russian Communist Party (Bolsheviks) in March 1918, as Lenin sought to draw a line under his group's previous association with the Mensheviks. Peasants, though, were frequently able to deflect or ignore the impositions of the new Soviet authorities: see [A.M. Bol'shakov], "Extracts from *The Soviet Countryside, 1917–1924: Its Economics and Life*," in Robert E.F. Smith (ed.), *The Russian Peasant: 1920 and 1984*, London: Frank Cass, 1977, pp. 29–108. Equally, the regularized food procurement agencies sometimes provided opportunities for peasant communities to engage with the state, through challenging demands for grain and articulating the needs of the village: Erik C. Landis, "Between Village and Kremlin: Confronting State Food Procurement in Civil War Tambov, 1919–20," *Russian Review*, vol. 63, no. 1 (2004), pp. 70–88.

49. For an incomplete and overly provocative—but still useful—survey of what the author labels (from the point of view of Soviet historians) "the unsightly history" of the phenomenon, see Taisa Osipova, "Peasant Rebellions: Origin, Scope, Dynamics and Consequences," in Vladimir N. Brovkin (ed.), *The Bolsheviks in Russian Society: The Revolution and Civil Wars*, New Haven: Yale University Press, 1997, pp. 154–70. An equally skewed and equally useful typology of the risings is attempted in V.N. Brovkin, "On the Internal Front: The Bolsheviks and the Greens," *Jahrbücher für Geschichte Osteuropas*, vol. 37, no. 4 (1989), pp. 541–68. See also: Mikhail Frenkin, *Tragediia krest'ianskikh vosstanii v Rossii, 1918–1921 gg.*, Jerusalem: Leksikon, 1987; T.A. Osipova, "Krest'ianstvo v grazhdanskoi voiny: bor'ba na dva fronta," in I.N. Afanasev (ed.), *Sud'by rosssiiskogo krest'ianstva*, Moscow: Rosskii Gos. gumanitarnyi Universitet, 1996, pp. 90–161; and T.A. Osipova, *Rossiiskoe krest'ianstvo v revoliutsii i grazhdanskoi voine*, Moscow: Izd.-vo Strelets, 2001.

50. Raleigh, *Experiencing Russia's Civil War*, pp. 337–8.

51. Aaron B. Retish, *Russia's Peasants in Revolution and Civil War: Citizenship, Identity and the Creation of the Soviet State, 1914–1922*, Cambridge: Cambridge University Press, 2008, p. 243.

52. Ibid., pp. 170–79. Interestingly, though, Retish also proposes that the Reds' hold on this province improved when top-level Bolsheviks (in this case, A.G. Shlikter) arrived to ensure that *prodrazverstka* was applied uniformly (and therefore, from the peasants' point of view, more fairly). This can be compared to popular attitudes to Red recruitment policies: see above, pp. 89–91.

53. Figes, *Peasant Russia, Civil War*, pp. 205, 324–34. The course of these and other rebellions in the Volga region can be traced in V. Danilov and Teodor Shanin (eds), *Krest'ianskoe dvizhenie v Povolzh'e, 1919–1922: Dokumenty i materialy*, Moscow: ROSSPEN, 2002. See also: V.V. Kondrashin, *Krest'ianskoe dvizhenie v Povolzh'e, 1918–1922*, Moscow: Izd-vo Ianus-k, 2001; and V.K. Vorobev, *Chapannaia voina v Simbirskoi gubernii: mify i realnost'. Zametki kraeveda*, n.p.: Vector-C, 2008. Further north, in Viatka *guberniia*, peasants seem not to have been greeting the arrival of the Whites with open arms, but their regard for the Reds was measured by the fact that a Red Army levy in the Viatka district in May 1919 raised just seventy-eight men; in July, a further 132 were enticed into the Red ranks: Retish, *Russia's Peasants*, p. 183.

54. Osipova, "Peasant Rebellions," p. 163.

55. The Cheka detachments, formally known as the Forces of Internal Security of the Republic, or Voisko VOKHR (*Voisko vnutrennei okhrany respubliki*), were created in accordance with a decree of the Council of Labor and Defense of 28 May 1919, and were allotted the tasks of maintaining internal security, fighting counter-revolution, collecting grain supplies, etc. Voisko VOKR was also considered to be a reserve force of the Red Army.

56. Stéphane Courtois *et al.*, *The Black Book of Communism: Crimes, Terror, Repression*, Cambridge, MA: Harvard University Press, 1999, p. 97.

57. On these events, see Nick Heath, "1920: The Sapozhkov Uprising and the Army of Truth," http://libcom.org/history/1920-sapozhkov-uprising-army-truth. See also Nick Heath, "The Kolesnikov Uprising," http://www.katesharpleylibrary.net/z08n3x

58. See Donald J. Raleigh, "A Provincial Kronstadt: Popular Unrest in Saratov at the End of the Civil War," in Donald J. Raleigh (ed.), *Provincial Landscapes: Local Dimensions of Soviet Power, 1917–1953*, Pittsburgh: University of Pittsburgh Press, 2001, pp. 82–104.

59. A lot more has long been known in the West about the events in Tambov than about those in Siberia or the Urals. A pioneering work was Oliver H. Radkey, *The Unknown Civil War in Russia: A Study of the Green Movement in the Tambov Region, 1920–1921*, Stanford: Stanford University Press, 1976. This expanded upon Seth Singleton, "The Tambov Revolt (1920–1921)," *Slavic Review*, vol. 25, no. 3 (1966), pp. 497–512, which was itself supplemented by Delano DuGarm, "Peasant Wars in Tambov Province," in Brovkin (ed.), *The Bolsheviks in Russian Society*, pp. 177–98. These works have now been superseded by Erik C. Landis, *Bandits and Partisans: The Antonov Movement in the Russian Civil War*, Pittsburgh: University of Pittsburgh Press, 2008. Judiciously selected documents are also available in V.P. Danilov and Teodor Shanin (eds), *Krest'ianskoe vosstanie v Tambovskoi gubernii v 1919–1921 gg., "Antonovshchina": dokumenty i materialy*, Tambov: "Redaktsionno-izdatel'skii otdel," 1994 and in L.G. Protasov (ed.), *Antonovshchina: krest'ianskoe vosstanie v Tambovskoi gubernii: dokumenty*, Tambov: Upravlenie Kul'tury i Arkhivnogo dela Tambovskoi Oblasti, 2007. On the events in Western Siberia, see V.I. Shishkin (ed.), *Za sovety bez kommunistov: Krest'ianskoe vosstanie v Tiumenskoi gubernii 1921 g.*, Novosibirsk: Sibirskii Khronograf, 2000; and V.I. Shishkin (ed.), *Sibirskaia Vandeia*, 2 vols, Moscow: Demokratiia, 2000–1. On another region beset with peasant rebellions throughout the civil war, see S.V. Iarov, *Krest'ianin kak politik. Krest'ianstvo Severo-Zapada Rossii v 1918–1919gg: politicheskoe myshlenie i massovyi protest*, St Petersburg: Dmitrii Bulanin, 1999.

60. On the impact of the Mamontov Raid upon Tambov, see B.V. Sennikov, *Tambovskoe vosstanie 1918–1919 gg. i raskrest'ianivanie Rossii 1929–1933 gg.*, Moscow: Posev, 2004, pp. 52–64.

61. Meijer (ed.), *The Trotsky Papers*, vol. 2, pp. 481–5. The precise nature of the Union of Working Peasants is likely to remain a mystery. The name was attached to the organizational forces behind peasant rebellions across Soviet Russia in 1920 and 1921, both by the rebels themselves and by the Bolsheviks, but it seems to have been a label rather than a meaningful organization in many, if not most, areas.

62. Ibid., vol. 2, p. 495.

63. Ibid., vol. 2, p. 519.

64. Ibid., vol. 2, p. 553 (emphasis in original).

65. Landis, *Bandits and Partisans*, p. 209.

66. Ibid., pp. 214–26. Antonov himself evaded capture and went underground, taking to the forests of his native region, but he was eventually ambushed in June 1922 in the village of Nizhnii Shibriai, having been betrayed to the authorities by a former SR pharmacist from whom he had attempted to procure quinine. He died, alongside his brother Dmitrii, in a shootout with a Cheka detachment and was buried beneath the walls of Kazan' Monastery, in Tambov: Landis, *Bandits and Partisans*, pp. 1–3, 276–80. Unlike Nestor Makhno, who fled across the border into Romania in August 1922 (see Voline, *The Unknown Revolution*, Chicago: Black & Red, 1974, pp. 680–6) and subsequently settled into an unhappy exile in Paris, Antonov was never widely adopted or mythologized thereafter as an anti-Soviet rebel-hero, although a small monument now stands near his grave.

67. Sennikov, *Tambovskoe vosstanie 1918–1919 gg.*, pp. 161–4.

68. According to his later recollections (Arshinov, *History of the Makhnovist Movement*, p. 205), Makhno had attempted to forge a united front against the Bolsheviks by dispatching a unit of "Siberians" to Siberia in the summer of 1921, but they seem to have got no further than Samara. Meanwhile, the Siberian rebels were aware of the Antonov movement, but there appears to have been no direct contact: V.V. Moskovskii, "Vosstanie krest'ian v Zapadnoi Sibiri v 1921 godu," *Voprosy istorii*, no. 6 (1998), pp. 46–63.

69. Sennikov, *Tambovskoe vosstanie*, pp. 86–8.

70. For a well-informed survey of the historiography of the Makhno movement, see Serge Cipko "Nestor Makhno: A Mini-Historiography of the Anarchist Revolution in Ukraine, 1917–1921," *The Raven*, vol. 4, no. 1 (13) (1991), pp. 57–75. Although partisan, also extremely useful (and extensive) is The Nestor Makhno Archive: http://www.nestormakhno.info/. Relevant documents are now usefully collected in V.P. Danilov *et al.* (eds), *Nestor Makhno: krest'ianskoe dvizhenie na Ukraine, 1918–1921: dokumenty i materialy*, Moscow: ROSSPEN, 2006.

71. On Maslakov, see below p. 341 (n. 122).

72. On the Makhnovshchina, see: Arshinov, *History of the Makhnovist Movement*; Michael Malet, *Nestor Makhno in the Russian Civil War*, London: Macmillan, 1982; Michael Palij, *The Anarchism of Nestor Makhno, 1917–1921: An Aspect of the Ukrainian Revolution*, Seattle: University of Washington Press, 1976; Victor Peters, *Nestor Makhno: The Life of an Anarchist*, Winnipeg: Echo Books, 1970; Alexandre Skirda, *Nestor Makhno, Anarchy's Cossack: The Struggle for Free Soviets in Ukraine, 1917–1921*, Edinburgh: AK Press, 2004; A. Shubin, *Anarkhii-mat' poriadka: Mezhdu krasnymi i belymi. Nestor Makhno kak zerkalo Russkoi revoliutsii*, Moscow: Eksmo "Iauza," 2005; and Voline, *The Unknown Revolution*.

73. Arshinov, *History of the Makhnovist Movement*, pp. 200–7.

74. There he was sometimes employed as a carpenter and as a stagehand at the Opera and in various film studios, as well as working at the Renault factory. Thereafter, Makhno devoted him-

self to writing his memoirs, three volumes of which were published from 1929 to 1937. In 1934, in poverty and isolation, he died of the tuberculosis he had originally contracted in tsarist prisons, but his name and achievements remain revered among anarchists the world over. His ashes were interred near the Wall of the Communards in the Père Lachaise Cemetery in Paris.

75. On the ever-changing calculation of rations in the Soviet zone, see Borrero, *Hungry Moscow*, pp. 115–38.

76. On the PRC, see Donald J. Raleigh, "Co-Operation amid Repression: The Revolutionary Communists in Saratov Province, 1918–20," *Cahiers du Monde Russe*, vol. 40, no. 4 (1999), pp. 625–56. The PRC was founded at a conference in Moscow on 25–7 Sep. 1918, attended by former Left-SRs who had opposed their party's uprising of earlier in the year. The party pledged support for Soviet power, disavowed the use of force to overturn the Treaty of Brest-Litovsk (3 Mar. 1918), and favored cooperation with the RKP(b) in order to defend the revolution (at least during the crisis of the civil war). Following instructions from the Komintern, it merged with the RKP(b) in Oct. 1920.

77. It was alleged in the Soviet press (and in later Soviet histories) that one Fania Kaplan fired three shots at Lenin, as he left a factory meeting. He was certainly hit twice, in the shoulder and jaw, but whether the clearly unhinged Kaplan did it, whether she knew what she was doing, and whether she had acted on behalf of the PSR (as the Soviet regime alleged) remain uncertain, as she was almost immediately executed, without trial. See Semion Lyandres, "The 1918 Attempt on the Life of Lenin: A New Look at the Evidence," *Slavic Review*, vol. 48, no. 3 (1989), pp. 432–48. The prominent Bolshevik V. Volodarskii had also, some weeks earlier (on 20 June 1918), been assassinated in Petrograd by an SR terrorist, G.I. Semenov.

78. *Dekrety Sovetsoi vlasti*, vol. 3, pp. 291–2.

79. Fedor Stepun, *Byvshee i nesbyvsheesia*, London: Overseas Publications Interchange, 1990, vol. 2, p. 221. Lācis was the author of a still chilling popular survey of the early years of the Cheka: Martin Latsis, *Dva goda bor' by na vnutrennem fronte. Populiarnyi ozbor dvukhgodichnoi deiatel' nosti ChK*, Moscow: Gosizdat, 1920.

80. According to one prisoner, who was a sixteen-year-old schoolboy at the time, on 2 Sep. 1918, into an already overcrowded but barn-like cell in the courtyard of the Lubianka were marched 100 new prisoners, no less than twenty-seven of whom were called Borisov. It was concluded, with much amusement (even the Borisovs were laughing), that the Cheka had been searching for a certain Borisov but, unsure of his details, and to be on the safe side, had arrested all those Borisovs they could find in the Moscow telephone directory. "I think only Russians in such a situation would find this funny," recalled the witness, before adding the icy coda that "Later, they were all shot": N.V. Volkov-Muromtsev, *Iunost' ot Viaz' my do Feodosii*, Paris: YMCA Press, 1983, p. 159. The Cheka might, of course, have responded that ownership of a private telephone was a pretty accurate marker of a *burzhui*.

81. Vladimir N. Brovkin, *Behind the Front Lines of the Civil War: Political Parties and Social Movements in Russia, 1918–1922*, Princeton: Princeton University Press, 1994, pp. 45–56. Western accounts of the Red Terror, as well as post-Soviet Russian ones, have suffered from a surfeit of polemics, but see: Lennard D. Gerson, *The Secret Police in Lenin's Russia*, Philadelphia: Temple University Press, 1976; and George Leggett, *The Cheka: Lenin's Political Police*, Oxford: Clarendon, 1981. An early émigré account, which is still of interest, is: S.P. Melgounov, *The Red Terror in Russia*, London: J.M. Dent & Sons, 1925. See also: I.S. Rat'kovskii, *Krasnyi terror i deiatel' nost' VChK v 1918 gody*, St Petersburg: izd-vo S.-

Peterburgskogo Univ., 2006; and Iu.G. Fel'shtinskii (ed.), *Krasnyi terror v gody Grazhdans-koi voiny, po materialy Osoboi komissii po rassledovaniiu zlodeianii bol'shevikov*, London: Overseas Publications Interchange, 1992, which collects documents produced by the commission of investigation into the Red Terror appointed by General Denikin at Ekaterinodar on 4 Apr. 1919.

82. On 23 Sep. 1919, alone, it was reported that the prominent Kadet N.N. Shchepkin and sixty-seven other "counter-revolutionaries" had been executed in Moscow in relation to this affair. They were buried in a mass grave in the Kalitnikov cemetery. See O.V. Volobuev (ed.), *Takticheskii tsentr: dokumenty i materialy*, Moscow: ROSSPEN, 2012.

83. Lenin, "How to Organize Competition" (24–7 Dec. 1917), *CW*, vol. 26, pp. 404–15 (emphasis in original).

84. Richard Pipes (ed.), *The Unknown Lenin: From the Secret Archive*, New Haven: Yale University Press, 1996, p. 50 (emphasis in original). Pipes devoted a good part of his career to demolishing "the widely believed distinction between the 'good' Lenin and the 'bad' Stalin": Richard Pipes, *VIXI*, p. 236. This was a distinction, it is almost needless to say, that few other serious historians of the revolution and civil wars had ever recognized. For a more nuanced argument that terror was an essential element of Leninism, see James Ryan, *Lenin's Terror: The Ideological Origins of Early Soviet State Violence*, London: Routledge, 2012. Also Nicolas Werth, "Crimes and Mass Violence of the Russian Civil Wars (1918–1921)," Online Encyclopedia of Mass Violence: http://www.massviolence.org/Crimes-and-mass-violence-of-the-Russian-civil-wars-1918

85. Leon Trotsky, *Terrorism and Communism*, London: New Park Publications, 1975, p. 175.

86. Gerson, *The Secret Police in Lenin's Russia*; and Leggett, *The Cheka*. See also: G.P. Maximoff, *The Guillotine at Work, Vol. 1: The Leninist Counter-Revolution*, Orkney: Cienfuegos Press, 1979.

87. Yoshimasa Tsuji, "The Debate on Trade Unions, 1920–21," *Revolutionary Russia*, vol. 2, no. 1 (1989), pp. 31–100. This article nevertheless remains the most accessible and accurate summary of the debate.

88. The sorry fate of the factory committees provides a mainstay of libertarian critiques of the Bolshevik revolution. See, for example:, Maurice Brinton, *The Bolsheviks and Workers' Control: The State and Counter-Revolution*, London: Solidarity, 1970.

89. See William B. Husband, "Workers' Control and Centralization in the Russian Revolution: The Textile Industry of the Central Industrial Region, 1917–1920," Carl Beck Papers in Russian and East European Studies, no. 403, Pittsburgh: University of Pittsburgh Press, 1985.

90. Geoffrey Swain, *Trotsky*, Harlow: Pearson, 2006, pp. 128–30; Ian D. Thatcher, *Trotsky*, London: Routledge, 2003, pp. 106–8.

91. The initial idea seems to have come from the command of the 3rd Red Army in Siberia, but Trotsky took it up enthusiastically. See V.P. Butt *et al.* (eds), *The Russian Civil War: Documents from the Soviet Archives*, London: Macmillan, 1996, pp. 124–75.

92. Swain, *Trotsky*, pp. 122–6. Thatcher, *Trotsky*, pp. 104–6. Universal obligatory labor, for those aged sixteen to fifty, had actually been decreed as Paragraph 1 of Article I of the Soviet government's 1919 Labor Code: Jonathan Daly and Leonid Trofimov (eds), *Russia in War and Revolution, 1914–1922: A Documentary History*, Indianapolis: Hackett, 2009, p. 317. The first such shock force, the 1st (Urals) Revolutionary Army of Labor, under the command of M.S. Matiiasevich, was created from elements of the 3rd Red Army in the Urals on

15 Jan. 1920. This was followed by the creation of the Ukrainian Labor Army from forces on the South West Front (on 21 Jan. 1920, although, with the onset of the Soviet–Polish War in April 1920, this force was re assigned to military work), the Caucasian Labor Army (also known as the Labor Army of South East Russia) created from the 8th Red Army (23 Jan. 1920), the Reserve Army of the Republic formed from the 2nd Red Army (23 Jan. 1920) that worked to reconstruct the Moscow–Ekaterinburg railroad, the Petrograd Labor Army formed from the 7th Red Army (10 Feb. 1920), the 2nd Special Railroad Labor Army (also known as the Labor Railroad Army of the Caucasian Front) formed from the 2nd Red Army (27 Feb. 1920), and the 2nd (Turkestan) Revolutionary Army of Labor formed from the 4th Red Army (Apr. 1920). In December 1920, the Donetsk Labor Army was added to the list, followed on 15 Jan. 1921 by the Siberian Labor Army. According to Soviet sources, between 15 April and 1 July 1920 2,500,000 Red soldiers were engaged in economic work. On the Labor Armies, see: Bunyan (ed.), *Origin of Forced Labor*, pp. 140–52.

93. In a famous painting by V.G. Krikhatskii, *Lenin at the First Subbotnik*, the Soviet leader is portrayed shifting debris from the Kremlin grounds on 1 May 1920 (although, in a manner that would never have been countenanced by Stalin, the two workers assisting Lenin seem to be taking most of the load). "We have shifted a mountain," Lenin wrote (allegorically), the day following that feat: "From the First Subbotnik on the Moscow–Kazan Railway to the All-Russian May Day Subbotnik," *CW*, vol. 31, pp. 123–5. On the coercive intent of the Subbotniki, see Frederick I. Kaplan, "The Origins and Function of the Subbotniks and Voskreniks," *Jahrbücher für Geschichte Osteuropas*, vol. 13, no. 1 (1965), pp. 30–39.

94. In the Military Colonies, along the provinces of Russia's western borders, entire peasant populations (of state peasants) were pronounced mobilized and were subject to military discipline and command. Objections to the harsh conditions of life for the serf-soldier in the Military Colonies were among the factors motivating the Decembrist conspirators, who were claimed by the Bolsheviks as their spiritual forefathers when they attempted (in December 1825) to force a constitution upon Alexander's successor, Nicholas I. Starting as he meant to go on, Richard Pipes took an unconventionally sympathetic and positive line on this generally vilified institution: Richard E. Pipes, "The Russian Military Colonies, 1810–1831," *Journal of Modern History*, vol. 12, no. 3 (1950), pp. 205–19.

95. Lenin, "The Trade Unions, The Present Situation and Trotsky's Mistakes," *CW*, vol. 32, pp. 19–20.

96. The Labor Armies were formally demobilized on 31 Dec. 1921, by an order of the Council of Labor and Defense, which had been responsible for administering the system.

97. Alexandra Kollontai, "The Workers' Opposition": http://www.marxists.org/archive/kollonta/1921/workers-opposition/index.htm. See also: Barbara E. Clements, "Kollontai's Contribution to the Workers' Opposition," *Russian History*, vol. 2, no. 2 (1975), pp. 191–206.

98. "On Party Unity": *Desiatyi s"ezd RKP(b)*, pp. 571–3; "On the Syndicalist and Anarchist Deviation in the Party": *Desiatyi s"ezd RKP(b)*, pp. 574–6. Nevertheless, Lenin argued that the Oppositionists should not be excluded, and Shliapnikov was even elected to the Central Committee of the RKP(b) at the Tenth Congress. Subsequently, though, a campaign to stifle the independence of trade unions soon took off. Members of the Workers' Opposition did manage to publish a declaration ("The Letter of the 22") in February 1922, addressed to the Komintern, in which the harassment of its adherents was criticized. But subsequently, at the 11th Congress of the RKP(b) (27 Mar.–2 Apr. 1922), they narrowly escaped expulsion from the party. They were then subjected to further restraints. By 1926, almost all

leaders of the group had recanted their errors, although this did not save them (or members of the similar Workers' Group of G.I. Miasnikov) from the predations of Stalin's purges in the 1930s. On the Workers' Opposition, see Barbara Allen, "Alexander Shliapnikov and the Origins of the Workers' Opposition, March 1919–April 1920," *Jahrbücher für Geschichte Osteuropas*, vol. 53, no. 1 (2005), pp. 1–24; and Larry Holmes, "For the Revolution Redeemed: The Workers' Opposition in the Bolshevik Party, 1919–1921," Carl Beck Papers in Russian and East European Studies, no. 802, Pittsburgh: University of Pittsburgh Press, 1990. On the oppositionists' road to Calvary during the 1920s, see Barbara C. Allen, "Friendship in Times of Factionalism and Terror: Aleksandr Shliapnikov and Sergei Medvedev," *Revolutionary Russia*, vol. 20, no. 1 (2007), pp. 75–93. After years of imprisonment and exile, Shliapnikov was executed as a counter-revolutionary on 2 Sep. 1937. Exceptionally, Kollontai survived the purges, serving as Soviet ambassador to Sweden from 1930 to 1945 before enjoying a peaceful retirement in Moscow until her death, at the age of eighty, in March 1952. By then, she had outlived all other members of the Bolshevik Central Committee of 1917 except Stalin, who had been responsible for the murder of most of her colleagues.

99. *Desiatyi s"ezd RKP(b): stenograficheskii otchet*, Moscow: Gospolizdat, 1963, pp. 578–94, 663–74, 685–91.

100. Russian workers often lived with people from their home villages or districts and were united in unions of their fellows called "*zemliachestva*."

101. Precisely where and when Trotsky made that remark has remained somewhat mysterious: Israel Getzler (*Kronstadt, 1917–1921: The Fate of a Soviet Democracy*, Cambridge: Cambridge University Press, 1983) used the phrase as a chapter title, but did not reference it; Paul Avrich (*Kronstadt, 1921*, Princeton: Princeton University Press, 1970) quotes it (p. 3), but again provided no reference; Emma Goldman (*My Disillusionment in Russia*, London: C.W. Daniel, 1925) quoted it (p. 196) as originating in a speech the war commissar made in late 1919, praising the Baltic sailors for their role in the defeat of Iudenich. I am grateful to Ian D. Thatcher for exhuming the actual source: Sukhanov, *The Russian Revolution*, p. 446.

102. The decree is reproduced in translation in William H. Chamberlin, *The Russian Revolution, 1917–1921*, vol. 2, London: Macmillan, 1935, pp. 494–5.

103. "On Measures to Strengthen and Develop Peasant Agriculture": *Dokumenty Sovetskoi vlasti*, vol. 12, pp. 73–88. One historian has argued rather convincingly, however, that the sowing committees are better viewed as an effort by the Soviet government to collaborate with the more productive peasants: Lars T. Lih, "The Bolshevik Sowing Committees of 1920: Apotheosis of War Communism?" Carl Beck Papers in Russian and East European Studies, no. 803, Pittsburgh: University of Pittsburgh Press, 1990. In fact, Lih argues, "War Communism" is entirely a misnomer and best avoided: Lars T. Lih, "The Bolsheviks, Razverstka and War Communism," *Slavic Review*, vol. 45, no. 4 (1986), pp. 673–88.

104. See Roger Pethybridge, *The Spread of the Russian Revolution: Essays on 1917*, London: Macmillan, 1972, pp. 1–56. Before the world war, it is worth noting, the city had drawn fuel (especially coal) from as far afield as Britain, so distant was it from the main "Russian" sources in Ukraine and Poland.

105. On Zinov'ev, see N.A. Vasetskii, "Zinov'ev: strannitsy zhizni i politicheskoi deiate'nost'," *Novaia i noveishaia istorii*, no. 4 (1989), pp. 111–39; and A.P. Smirnov, "'Peterburgskii mif' Grigoriia Zinov'ev," *Istoriia Peterburga*, no. 4 (2006), pp. 9–12.

106. Emma Goldman, *The Crushing of the Russian Revolution*, London: Freedom Press, 1922, p. 13.

107. A particular target of popular opprobrium in this regard was the commander of the Baltic Fleet, F.F. Raskol'nikov, whose glamorous consort, the poet and journalist Larissa Reisner (the "Paris Athena of the Russian Revolution"), apparently had a typically Russian liking for luxuriant furs. On Raskol'nikov, see Smele, "A Bolshevik in Brixton Prison."

108. A similar pattern of events was meanwhile developing in Moscow, albeit with a less pronounced Menshevik coloring: Simon Pirani, "The Moscow Workers' Movement in 1921 and the Role of Non-Partyism," *Europe–Asia Studies*, vol. 56, no. 1 (2004), pp. 143–60.

109. Alexander Berkman, *The Bolshevik Myth (Diary, 1920–1922)*, London: Hutchinson and Co., 1925, pp. 292–3; also Alexander Berkman, "The Kronstadt Rebellion," in Alexander Berkman, *The Russian Tragedy*, London: Phoenix Press, 1986, pp. 61–3. On the strike movement, see also Avrich, *Kronstadt, 1921*, pp. 35–51.

110. Avrich, *Kronstadt, 1921*, pp. 42–5.

111. All told, as many as 5,000 people may have been arrested across Soviet Russia in the first quarter of 1921, including 2,000 Mensheviks (among them all members of the party Central Committee): Leonard Schapiro, *The Origins of the Communist Autocracy: Political Opposition in the Soviet State—The First Phase, 1917–1922*, London: Macmillan, 1955, p. 205. The Mensheviks' leader, Julius Martov, had been allowed to go abroad for health reasons some months earlier, in late September 1920, thereby freeing Lenin from the dilemma of having to sanction the arrest of a once dear friend.

112. At the same time, Raskol'nikov was quietly retired as fleet commander in the Baltic. Within a few months, he (accompanied by Reisner) would be sent abroad, as Soviet ambassador to Afghanistan. In Raskol'nikov's defense—not that a man driven to near insanity and then probably murdered by the NKVD in 1938–39, following his public denunciation of Stalin as the "gravedigger of the revolution," needs much defending—in January 1921 the fleet commander had warned Moscow that conditions at Kronshtadt were so bad (including endemic scurvy among the malnourished sailors) that his men would soon mutiny and turn their guns on Petrograd. See Avrich, *Kronshtadt, 1921*, p. 68.

113. The resolution was reproduced in issue no. 1 of the Kronshtadt *Izvestiia* (3 Mar. 1921): *Izvestia de Kronstadt. Mars 1921*, Paris: Editions Anda Jaleo, 1987, pp. 17–19.

114. *Pravda o Kronshtadte*, Prague: Volia Rossii, 1921, p. 82.

115. Petrichenko (b. 1892), a metal worker before he was mobilized in 1913, had in December 1917 been one of the chief organizers, in opposition to the Estonian national council (the Maapäev), of the short-lived, so-called Socialist Republic of Nargen (the Soviet Republic of Soldiers and Fortress-Builders) on the island of Nargen (now Naissaar), off Revel. He was evacuated from the island to Kronshtadt during the Ice March of the Baltic Fleet.

116. Except negatively, as in the aforementioned proclamation of 3 March, which asserted that "The workers and peasants steadfastly march forward, *leaving behind them the Constituent Assembly*, with its bourgeois regime, and the dictatorship of the Communist party": *Pravda o Kronshtadt*, p. 84, which seems fairly decisive. This stands in sharp contrast to many of the resolutions distributed during the February strikes in Petrograd, evidently by SR or Menshevik sympathizers, which had threatened the Soviet government with the Constituent Assembly: "We know who is afraid of the Constituent Assembly," chided a proclamation of the "Socialist Workers of the Nevskii District," "It is they who will no longer be able to rob the people. Instead they will have to answer before the representatives of the people

for their deceit, their robberies, and all their crimes." See Berkman, "The Kronstadt Rebellion," p. 63.

117. This is not meant as a criticism of the myriad anarchist websites that provide valuable materials on Kronshtadt, Makhno, and anarchism in general during the civil war—least of all the marvelous (and aforementioned) "Nestor Makhno Archive" and the indispensable "Rossiiskie sotsialisty i anarkhisty posle Okiabria 1917 goda" (http://socialist.memo.ru/index.htm). Classic anarchist treatments include Alexander Berkman, *The Kronstadt Rebellion*, Berlin: Der Syndicalist, 1922; Ante Ciliga, *The Kronstadt Revolt*, London: The Freedom Press, 1942; Ida Mett, *La commune de Cronstadt: crépuscule sanglant des Soviets*, Paris: Spartakus, 1938; and (especially) Alexandre Skirda (ed.), *Kronstadt 1921. Prolétariat contre bolchévisme*, Paris: Editions de la Tête de Feuilles, 1972. A selection of documents appears in Paul Avrich (ed.), *The Anarchists in the Russian Revolution*, London: Thames and Hudson, 1973, pp. 50–69. Regarding the PSR's influence on events, it would have been extraordinary had there not been members of what had once been Russia's biggest party on Kotlin in 1921. Nevertheless, it is notable that the sailors' committee provisionally refused the offer of aid from SR leader Viktor Chernov, then in Revel: Avrich, *Kronstadt, 1921*, pp. 124–5.

118. Quoted in Avrich, *Kronstadt, 1921*, p. 67. The veracity of the content of this oft-cited newspaper report is impossible to confirm. It is notable, as Soviet sources emphasized, that the number of names of Ukrainian origin among the Kronshtadt rebel leaders seems high for a fleet based in northern waters, but that does not make the bearers of those names, *ipso facto*, Makhnovists, Hryhvoryvites, Petliurists, or the acolytes of Hetman Skoropadskii. Moreover, there were certainly also many soldiers with Ukrainian names among the Volhynskii regiment that instigated the mutiny of the Petrograd Garrison on 27 Feb. 1917, which was so lauded in Soviet historiography.

119. Evan Mawdsley, "The Baltic Fleet and the Kronstadt Mutiny," *Soviet Studies*, vol. 24, no. 4 (1972–3), pp. 506–21.

120. The following account of the assaults on Kronshtadt and the crushing of the revolt is drawn, unless stated otherwise, from Neil Croll, "The Role of M.N. Tukhachevskii in the Suppression of the Kronstadt Rebellion," *Revolutionary Russia*, vol. 17, no. 2 (2004), pp. 1–48.

121. Secondary accounts and even some contemporary witness accounts of the events in Petrograd and Kronshtadt of February-March 1921 often refer vaguely to an "especially cold" winter, or state that it was "an exceptionally hard one" (see, for example Goldman, *My Disillusionment in Russia*, p. 193) and cite this as a reason for the workers and sailors' disquiet. In fact, meteorological evidence from Baltic weather stations reveals that the opposite was the case: the winter of 1920–21 was unusually mild for the region and the ice-melt could be predicted to happen earlier than usual. See J. Neumann, "A Note on the Winter of the Kronstadt Sailors' Uprising in 1921," *Soviet Studies*, vol. 44, no. 1 (1992), pp. 153–4.

122. Other previously loyal units of the Red Army were also mutinous by this point. During the winter of 1920–21, conditions in the Reds' 1st Cavalry Army were becoming unstable, as food and forage were short in the areas of south-eastern Ukraine in which it was deployed against the Makhno's Revolutionary-Insurgent Army of Ukraine. In January 1921, elements of the army's 4th Division, commanded by the Don Cossack G.S. Maslakov, refused to attack the Makhnovists, describing them as fellow revolutionaries. Subsequently, on 8 Feb. 1921, Maslakov issued a proclamation calling for the overthrow of Bolshevik rule and the election of "free soviets" and declared himself to be a supporter of Makhno, and Masla-

kov's group then united with the Makhnovist detachment of Mikhail Brova near Pavlograd. On 11 Feb. 1921, Maslakov was declared to be a traitor by the Revvoensovet of the 1st Cavalry Army. The following month, he led his men through the Don territory into the Kalmyk steppe, executing any Bolshevik officials that crossed his path, breaking into state grain stores and distributing their contents among the peasants. There, on 23 Mar. 1921, they were surrounded by Red forces at Roguli and virtually annihilated. The few that escaped, with Maslakov among them, then joined with a Kalmyk force to capture Elista, where they shot around 100 Soviet officials. After several failed attempts to rejoin the main body of the Makhnovists (and apparently having failed also in an effort to link up with the rebel forces of A.S. Antonov in Tambov *guberniia*), Maslakov's men eventually broke through Red lines in the Don region and, on 26 July 1921, were reunited with the Makhnovists in Eastern Ukraine. Soon afterwards, however, Maslakov and his rebel followers were smashed by the Reds, although there are contradictory versions of precisely how, when, and where. One version has it that he was betrayed and killed by his own men in the mountains of Ossetia in Sep. 1921. Another, that he met his end in the Tsaritsyn region. Maslakov appears as the "incorrigible partisan" in Isaak Babel's story "Afonkina Bida," part of the *Red Cavalry* collection. On the "Maslakov Mutiny" see Peter Holquist, *Making War, Forging Revolution: Russia's Continuum of Crisis, 1914–1921*, Cambridge, MA: Harvard University Press, 2002, p. 276. Maslakov ("Uncle Maslak") is also commemorated on anarchist websites: Viacheslav Iashchenko, "Srazu Maslaov," http://www.nestormakhno.info/russian/maslakov.htm; Nick Heath, "1921: The Maslakov Mutiny and the Makhnovists on the Don," http://libcom.org/history/maslakov-mutiny-makhnovists-don

123. Poignantly—another civil war within a civil war—among the volunteer shock troops dispatched from Moscow to Petrograd were members of the Workers' Opposition, wishing to demonstrate their loyalty to the party.

124. Petrichenko's subsequent biography is a curious one. At some point in the 1920s (either 1922 or 1927, sources differ), he approached the Soviet ambassador in Riga, was recruited as an agent of the GPU, and returned to Finland via the USSR. Thereafter, he supplied military intelligence to Moscow, although not always reliably or regularly. Nevertheless, in 1941 he was arrested as a spy by the Finnish authorities. In 1945 he was released and returned to the USSR but was soon arrested by the Soviet counter-intelligence services. On 17 Nov. 1945, a special court of the People's Commissariat for Internal Affairs of the USSR found Petrichenko guilty of "participation in a counter-revolutionary terrorist organization and working for the Finnish security services" and sentenced him to ten years in the Gulag, where he soon perished (while traveling from the Solikamsk camp to Aleksandrovsk prison). In 2011, a Russian newspaper published allegations that Petrichenko had actually been working for the Petrograd Cheka in 1921 and that the entire Kronshtadt uprising was a provocation organized by the Soviet security services as an excuse for crushing their enemies: *Vlast'*, no. 5 (7 Feb. 2011).

125. Inspiring also jibes about how the virus of Kronshtadt would continue to spread across the twentieth century. Communists were especially vulnerable to it, as the symptoms involved a disavowal of Communism. Almost yearly, but especially in August 1939, October 1956, and August 1968, there would be an outbreak. (Those dates, of course, refer to the signing of the Nazi–Soviet Pact, the crushing of the Hungarian Revolution, and the Warsaw Pact's invasion of Czechoslovakia.)

126. The Memorandum is reproduced in translation in Avrich, *Kronstadt, 1921*, pp. 235–40.

127. Ibid., p. 97.

128. The debate—much of it featuring in the American Trotskyist journal *New International* in 1938–39—can be followed in Barbara Mutnick (ed.), *Kronstadt, by V.I. Lenin and Leon Trotsky*, London: Monad Press, 1979, pp. 124–41.

129. Israel Getzler, *Kronstadt, 1917–1921*, pp. 210–11. Getzler's findings were largely supported by materials from the Soviet archives that were published after the fall of Communism: V.P. Naumov and A.A. Kos (eds), *Kronshtadt, 1921: dokumenty o sobytiakh v Kronshtadte vesnoi 1921 g.*, Moscow: Mezhdunarodnyi Fond "Demokratiia," 1997; and V.P. Kozlov *et al.* (eds), *Kronshtadtskaia tragediia 1921 goda: dokumenty v dvukh knigakh*, Moscow: ROSSPEN, 1999. See also Israel Getzler, "The Communist Leaders' Role in the Kronstadt Tragedy of 1921 in the Light of Recently Published Archival Documents," *Revolutionary Russia*, vol. 15, no. 1 (2002), pp. 24–44.

130. Berkman, *The Bolshevik Myth*, p. 303.

131. Goldman, *My Disillusionment in Russia*, last lines of Chapter 27.

132. Berkman, *The Bolshevik Myth*, pp. 318–19.

133. They were followed abroad in 1922 by Victor Serge, who accepted a Komintern assignment. Serge had spent much of 1919 defending from attacks by his fellow anarchists the necessity of Bolshevik dictatorship and Red Terror in Soviet Russia, as the price to be paid for victory in the civil wars: see Victor Serge, *Revolution in Danger: Writings from Russia, 1919–1921*, London: Redwords, 1919. But he too could not stomach the slaughter at Kronshtadt, although at the time, as the events of March 1921 had unfolded, "with unutterable anguish" he had declared himself on the side of the Bolsheviks, rather than the rebels. As he later reasoned, "Kronstadt had right on its side" and was "the beginning of a fresh, liberating revolution for popular democracy," but "We were not reasoning in the abstract ... If the Bolshevik dictatorship fell, it was only a short step through chaos to a peasant rising, the massacre of the Communists, the return of the *émigrés*, and in the end, another dictatorship, this time anti-proletarian." Victor Serge, *Memoirs of a Revolutionary*, pp. 128–9.

134. See Paul Avrich, *The Russian Anarchists*, Princeton: Princeton University Press, 1967, pp. 184–5. Nevertheless, anarchist accounts of the Terror often seem the most sober: for example, Maximoff, *The Guillotine at Work*; and Jacques Baynac, Alexandre Skirda, and Charles Urjewicz (eds), *Le Terreur sous Lénine (1917–1924)*, Paris: Le Sagittaire, 1975.

135. Serge, *Memoirs of a Revolutionary*, pp. 93–4. Serge recounts here, though, that some kindly Bolsheviks encouraged and allowed anarchists to escape their re-arrest.

136. Ibid., p. 124.

137. Grigorii Petrovich Maksimov, *A Grand Cause: The Hunger Strike and the Deportation of Anarchists from Soviet Russia*, London: Kate Sharpley Library, 2008; and Avrich, *The Russian Anarchists*, pp. 228–33.

138. Compare Robert Service, *Trotsky: A Biography*, London: Macmillan, 2000, p. 281 with Sergei V. Iarov, "The Tenth Congress of the Communist Party and the Transition to NEP," in Edward Acton, Vladimir Iu. Cherniaev, and William G. Rosenberg (eds), *Critical Companion to the Russian Revolution, 1914–1921*, Bloomington: Indiana University Press, 1997, p. 123.

139. *Desiatyi s"ezd RKP(b)*, pp. 608–9.

140. Osipova, "Peasant Rebellions," p. 173.

141. On the NEP, see: Sheila Fitzpatrick, Alexander Rabinowitch, and Richards Stites (eds),

Russia in the Age of NEP: Explorations in Soviet Society and Culture, Bloomington: Indiana University Press, 1991; Nove, *Economic History of the USSR*, pp. 46–82; and Lewis H. Siegelbaum, *Soviet State and Society between Revolutions, 1918–1929*, Cambridge: Cambridge University Press, 1992. More recent scholarship can be traced via the *NEP-Era Journal*: http://www.d.umn.edu/cla/NEPera/main/index.php. The apostasy of Trotsky's former allies is bitterly recounted in his own testimony to the Dewey Commission—the April 1937 investigation, held at Trotsky's home in Coyoacan, Mexico City, into the charges against the former war commissar that had arisen from the first two purge trials in Moscow. See: *The Case of Leon Trotsky*, London: Pathfinder, 2006.

142. L.D. Trotsky, *My Life: An Attempt at an Autobiography*, Harmondsworth: Penguin, 1975, pp. 481–3. Minutes of the meeting are not extant.

143. André Liebich, *From the Other Shore: Russian Social Democracy after 1921*, Cambridge, MA: Harvard University Press, 1997, p. 107. A translation of the pamphlet appears in Abraham Ascher (ed.), *The Mensheviks in the Russian Revolution*, London: Thames and Hudson, 1976, pp. 111–17. (Ascher, p. 32, states unequivocally that "Ironically, the Mensheviks' economic programme, reviled by the Leninists in 1918 and 1919, was to be adopted by the [Soviet] government in 1921.") The title, echoing the Bolshevik leader's 1902 work on party organization, was undoubtedly a dig at Lenin (who had himself borrowed the title from his boyhood hero, the Populist writer and martyr, N.G. Chernyshevskii, who had published a novel of that name in 1862 that might now most generously be best described as a period piece).

144. Iarov, "The Tenth Congress," p. 123.

145. Although claims have resurfaced in recent years that Lenin actually succumbed to syphilis, probably contracted from a Parisian prostitute around 1903. See: V. Lerner, Y. Finkelstein, and E. Witzturn, "The Enigma of Lenin's Malady," *European Journal of Neurology*, vol. 11, no. 6 (2004), pp. 371–6; and "Vladimir Lenin Died from Syphilis New Research Claims," *The Telegraph*, 22 Oct. 2009.

146. Lenin is referring to an article by the Hungarian Communist Mátyás Rákosi, entitled "The New Economic Policy in Soviet Russia," in which he analyzed a pamphlet called *"Der neue Kurs" in Sowjetrussland* ("'The New Policy' in Soviet Russia") by the Austrian social democrat Otto Bauer that had been published in Vienna in 1921. Rákosi's piece appeared, on 22 Mar. 1922, in issue 20 of *Communist International*, the mouthpiece of the Komintern. Karl Kautsky, leader of the anti-war wing of the German social democrats (and known as "the Pope of Marxism"), had been fiercely critical of the Bolshevik regime.

147. Lenin, *CW*, vol. 33, pp. 282–3.

148. Or, at least, they were for the eleven defendants still alive: Sergei Morozov had by then already committed suicide in prison. Those exiled were subsequently shot or died in the camps: only one, Arkady Al'tovskii, survived, returning from twenty years in the Kolyma camps in 1955 and eventually dying peacefully in Moscow in 1975. On the trial see: Scott B. Smith, *Captives of Revolution: The Socialist Revolutionaries and the Bolshevik Dictatorship, 1918–23*, Pittsburgh: University of Pittsburgh Press, 2011, pp. 240–60; and O.V. Volobuev *et al.* (eds), *Partiia sotsialistov-revolutsionerov: dokumenty i materialy*, Moscow: ROSSPEN, 1996–2000, vol. 3, pp. 813–41, 851–948.

149. See the analysis of Bolshevik reactions to the trial in Marc Jansen, *A Show Trial under Lenin: The Trial of the Socialist Revolutionaries, Moscow, 1922*, The Hague: M. Nijhoff, 1982, pp. 194–5.

150. Leonard Schapiro summed up Lenin's position, as NEP was launched, neatly: "To have left [the Mensheviks] at liberty, even with such restricted political freedom as they had enjoyed in 1919 and 1920, would have invited the obvious question of why the party whose policy had failed should not yield power to the party whose policy was now being adopted": Schapiro, *The Origins of the Communist Autocracy*, p. 204. Alongside the Menshevik leaders, in 1922–23, were exiled, on the so-called "Philosophers' Ships," over 200 prominent Russian scholars, philosophers, cooperators, and other intellectuals. Archly, Trotsky explained to a Western journalist (in *Pravda*, 30 Aug. 1922) that this was an act of "far-sighted humaneness," for, if the civil wars re-ignited, the Cheka would be obliged to shoot such critics of the regime. See Lesley Chamberlain, *The Philosophy Steamer: Lenin and the Exile of the Intelligentsia*, London: Atlantic Books, 2006.

151. A notable exception was the Menshevik jurist A.Ia. Vyshinskii, who, incredibly, later acted as state prosecutor in the great Show Trials of the 1930s and ended his career as foreign minister of the USSR—although, with a record that included his signature on an order to arrest Lenin in July 1917, perhaps his life under Stalin was not that comfortable. See Arkady Vaksberg, *Stalin's Prosecutor: The Life of Andrei Vyshinsky*, New York: Grove Weidenfeld, 1990, p. 25.

152. Groman died in the camps in March 1940; Sukhanov was executed three months later. See Liebich, *From the Other Shore*, pp. 199–214; and Israel Getzler, *Nikolai Sukhanov: Chronicler of the Russian Revolution*, London Palgrave, 2002, pp. 143–87. Also the chapters detailing the Mensheviks' experience of "Prisons, Camps, Exile" and "A Chronicle of Persecution and Resistance," in Vera Broido, *Lenin and the Mensheviks: The Persecution of the Bolsheviks under Bolshevism*, Aldershot: Gower, 1987, pp. 87–158. Extensive documentation of the 1931 trial is available in: A.L. Litvin (ed.), *Men'shevistskii Protsess 1931 Goda*, 2 vols, Moscow: ROSSPEN, 1999.

153. Jonathan W. Daly, "'Storming the Last Citadel': The Bolshevik Assault on the Church, 1922," in Brovkin (ed.), *The Bolsheviks in Russian Society*, p. 235.

154. In January 1919, though he had, sent (by secret courier) a miniature ikon and a warm message of greetings to Admiral Kolchak, blessing him and wishing him success in his "struggle with the atheistic temporal authorities over the suffering Russian people" and in his "Christian struggle for the salvation of the Orthodox Church and Russia": A.V. Klaving (ed.), *Okrest Kolchaka: dokumenty i materialy*, Moscow: AGRAF, 2007, pp. 127–8. For a sympathetic portrait of Tikhon, see: Jane Swan, *A Biography of Patriarch Tikhon*, Jordanville, NY: Holy Trinity Monastery, 1964.

155. Wade (ed.), *Documents of Soviet History*, vol. 1, pp. 94–6.

156. Huge amounts of Russian gold were subsequently sold abroad in the 1920s to finance all sorts of imports of raw materials, machinery, expertise, chemicals, etc. required by the Soviet state's mission to transform Russia into an industrial state. See Jonathan D. Smele, "The Imperial Russian Gold Reserve in the Anti-Bolshevik East, 1918–? (An Unconcluded Chapter in the History of the Russian Civil War)," *Europe–Asia Studies*, vol. 46, no. 8 (1994), pp. 1317–18, and *Russian Gold: A Collection of Articles and Newspaper Editorials Regarding the Russian Gold Reserve and Shipments of Soviet Gold*, New York: Amtorg, 1928.

157. Daly, "Storming the Last Citadel," *passim* and Richard Pipes, *Russia under the Bolshevik Regime*, New York: Knopf, 1994, pp. 337–68. The campaign was notably vicious in Ukraine: Wasyl Veryha, "Looting the Churches in Ukraine in 1922," *Ukrainian Quarterly*, vol. 46, no. 3 (1990), pp. 233–45. The most thorough general studies of Soviet attacks on the

Church remain William B. Husband, *"Godless Communists": Atheism and Society in Soviet Russia, 1917–1932*, DeKalb: Northern Illinois University Press, 2000; and Arto Luukanen, *The Party of Unbelief: The Religious Policy of the Bolshevik Party, 1917–1929*, Helsinki: Suomen Historiallinen Seura, 1994. Useful documents are collected in: Boleslaw Szczesniak (ed.), *The Russian Revolution and Religion: A Collection of Documents Concerning the Suppression of Religion by the Communists, 1917–1925*, Notre Dame: University of Notre Dame Press, 1959.

158. See, for example, the letter of protest addressed to Lenin, signed by, among others, the Archbishop of Canterbury (Randall Davidson), in *The Times* of 1 June 1922, reproduced in Meijer (ed.), *The Trotsky Papers*, vol. 2, pp. 741–3.

159. That certainly is the view (based on extensive archival investigations) expressed in Markus Wehner, "Golod 1921–1922 gg. v Samarskoi gubernii i reaktsiia Sovetskogo pravitel'stva," *Cahiers du Monde Russe*, vol. 38, nos 1–2 (1997), pp. 223–42.

160. Markevich and Harrison, "Great War, Civil War, and Recovery," p. 688, citing Serguei Adamets, *Guerre civile et famine en Russie: Le pouvoir bolchévique et la population face à la catastrophe démographique de 1917–1923*, Paris: Institut d'études Slaves, 2003. See also: A.G. Vishnevskii (ed.), *Demograficheskaia modernizatsiia Rossii, 1900–2000*, Moscow: Novoe Izdatel'stvo, 2006.

161. Charles M. Edmondson, "The Politics of Hunger: The Soviet Response to Famine, 1921," *Soviet Studies*, vol. 29, no. 4 (1977), pp. 506–18. See also: H.H. Fisher, *The Famine in Soviet Russia, 1919–1923: The Operation of the American Relief Administration*, New York: Macmillan & Co., 1927; and Bernard M. Patenaude, *The Big Show in Bololand: The American Relief Expedition to Soviet Russia in the Famine of 1921*, Stanford: Stanford University Press, 2002.

162. Charles M. Edmondson, "An Enquiry into the Termination of Soviet Famine Relief Programmes and the Renewal of Grain Exports, 1922–1923," *Soviet Studies*, vol. 33, no. 3 (1981), pp. 370–85. Also: Wasyl Veryha, "Famine in Ukraine in 1921–1923 and the Soviet Government's Counter Measures," *Nationalities Papers*, vol. 12, no. 2 (1984), pp. 265–86.

163. Christopher Williams, "The 1921 Famine and Periphery Responses," *Revolutionary Russia*, vol. 6, no. 1 (1993), pp. 277–314.

164. Poliakov (ed.), *Naselenie Rossii v XX veke*, vol. 1, p. 133.

165. Stephen Wheatcroft, "Famine and Epidemic Crises in Russia, 1918–1922: The Case of Saratov," *Annales de Démographie Historique* (1983), pp. 329–51. The rise in typhus cases from 1918 in Russia has been called "the greatest typhus epidemic in history": K. David Patterson, "Typhus and its Control in Russia," *Medical History*, vol. 37, no. 4 (1993), pp. 361–81. Nevertheless, smallpox, which was more mortiferous, may have been the bigger killer.

6. 1921–26: THE ENDS OF THE "RUSSIAN" CIVIL WARS

1. Although one must concede that with 3,700,000 Red Army soldiers demobilized in the year following the 10th Congress of the RKP(b) in March 1921, the civil wars adopted a different, less general character: Iu.I. Korablev and M.S. Loginov (eds), *KPSS i stroitel'stvo vooruzhenykh sil, 1918—iiun' 1941*, Moscow: Voenizdat, 1959, p. 190.

2. Andrei Markevich and Mark Harrison, "Great War, Civil War, and Recovery: Russia's National

Income 1913 to 1928," *Journal of Economic History*, vol. 71, no. 3 (2011), pp. 672–703(here p. 688).

3. Such, for example, was the case recently with David Bullock, *The Russian Civil War, 1918–22*, Oxford: Osprey, 2008. These events are mentioned also in the most recent English-language survey of the Russian Revolution, although the author gives more emphasis, in a chapter on "The End of the Revolution?" to the Treaty on the Formation of the USSR of 30 Dec. 1922, which united the RSFSR, the Belorussian SSR, the Ukrainian SSR, and the Transcaucasian SFSR, and to any semblance of popularity of the Soviet government: "From 1920 to 1922 … the process of the revolution—at least the sense of the active participation of the popular movement motivated by the popular programme of peace, bread and land and all power to the soviets—came to an end." See Christopher Read, *War and Revolution in Russia, 1914–22*, Basingstoke: Palgrave, 2013, pp. 195–217.

4. The propagandistic purposes behind Trotsky seeming to have forgotten all this, when he wrote in his memoirs that "The Crimean campaign [against Wrangel] was actually the last campaign of the civil war" (*My Life: An Attempt at an Autobiography*, Harmondsworth: Penguin, 1975, p. 439), are transparent: he wished to downplay the degree of armed hostility to Soviet rule that persisted for the best part of the next decade. The cause or purpose of later historians' myopia is less obvious.

5. Andrea Graziosi, *The Great Soviet Peasant War: Bolsheviks and Peasants, 1917–1933*, Cambridge, MA: Harvard University Ukrainian Research Institute, 1996. A similar conception is evident in Sheila Fitzpatrick, *The Russian Revolution 1917–1932*, Oxford: Oxford University Press, 1982.

6. Lenin, "Summing-up Speech on the Tax in Kind" at the 10th All-Russian Conference of the RKP(b), 27 May 1921, *CW*, vol. 32, p. 429.

7. Lenin, "Report on the New Economic Policy" to the Seventh Moscow Guberniia Conference of the RKP(b), 29 Oct. 1921, *CW*, vol. 33, pp. 84–7.

8. Lenin, "On Co-Operation," 4–6 January, 1923, *CW*, vol. 33, pp. 467–75. Marxists had always evinced suspicion toward an institution in which, as Marx himself put it, workers are "their own capitalists": Karl Marx, *Capital*, Harmondsworth: Penguin Books, 1981, vol. 3, p. 571. See Bruno Jossa, "Marx, Marxism and the Co-Operative Movement," *Cambridge Journal of Economics*, vol. 29, no. 1 (2005), pp. 3–18.

9. Meijer (ed.), *The Trotsky Papers*, vol. 2, p. 41.

10. Eikhe was recalled in April 1921 to oversee the campaign against forces of the bandit-commander Stanisław Bułak-Bałachowicz (whom Trotsky had dubbed the "highwayman general," in Belorussia). See Richard B. Spence, "Useful Brigand: 'Ataman' S.N. Bulak-Balakhovich, 1917–1921," *Revolutionary Russia*, vol. 11, no. 1 (1998), pp. 17–36. His successors included the Bolshevik commanders V.K. Bliuker (June 1921–July 1922), who would subsequently command the Red Banner Far Eastern Army from 1929 until his death in NKVD custody in 1938, and I.P. Uborovich (Aug.–Nov. 1922), who also served as minister of war of the FER, who was executed as a traitor in June 1937. Eikhe somehow survived the purges, wrote some important books on the civil wars in retirement, and died in 1968, at the age of seventy-four.

11. V.V. Sonin, *Stanovlenie Dal'nevostochnoi respubliki (1920–1922)*, Vladivostok: Izd-vo Dal'nevostochnogo Universiteta, 1990; *Iz istorii Dal'nevostochnoi respubliki. Sbornik nauchnykkh trudov*, Vladivostok: Izd-vo Dal'nevostochnogo Universiteta, 1992. The only English-language monograph on the FER is now badly dated: Henry K. Norton, *The Far*

Eastern Republic of Siberia, London: Allen & Unwin, 1923. On the FER at the Washington Conference, see Iu.N. Tsipkin and T.A. Ornatskaia, *Vneshnaia politika Dalnevostochnoi respubliki (1920–1922 gg.)*, Khabarovsk: Otdel nauchnykh izdanii Khabarovskogo kraevogo muzeiia im. N.I. Grodedova, 2008; and Paul Dukes, *The USA in the Making of the USSR: The Washington Conference, 1921–1922 and "Uninvited Russia"*, London: Routledge, 2004.

12. Utilizing the massacre of Japanese forces at the mouth of the Amur perpetrated by the renegade Red partisan Ia.I. Triapitsyn in Mar. 1920 (the "Nikolaevsk Incident") as an excuse, new contingents of Japanese marines were landed at Vladivostok on 4 April 1920, and fanned out across the province, while Tokyo's grip on Northern Sakhalin was also tightened by an influx of new forces. Among those who were killed during and after the offensive was the local Bolshevik leader S.G. Lazo—reportedly burned alive in a locomotive boiler. The last US transports had departed on 1 April 1920, just three days prior to the Japanese moves, but the atmosphere in the port was so poisonous that the second largest Allied contingent, the Canadian Expeditionary Force, had been withdrawn from Vladivostok in June 1919, just a few months after its arrival: Benjamin Issit, *From Victoria to Vladivostok: Canada's Siberian Expedition, 1917–19*, Vancouver: University of British Columbia Press, 2010. On the Nikolaevsk Incident: A.Ia. Gutman, *The Destruction of Nikolaevsk-on-Amur*, Kingston, Ontario: Limestone Press, 1993. On Far Eastern developments in general, the masterful Canfield F. Smith, *Vladivostok under Red and White Rule: Revolution and Counter-Revolution in the Russian Far East, 1920–1922*, Seattle: University of Washington Press, 1975.

13. According to one witness to "the inhuman cruelty, the devilish sadism" of the Ataman, Semenov liked to boast that he could not sleep peacefully at night unless he had killed someone that day: Dmitri Alioshi, *Asian Odyssey*, London: Cassell & Co., 1941, p. 48. He must have usually slept easily, for his victims certainly ran into the thousands.

14. B.M. Shereshevskii, *Razgrom semenovshchiny, aprel' –noiabr' 1920 g.: o roli Dal'nevostochnoi respubliki v bor' be za likvidatsiiu "chitinskoi probki" i ob" edinenie Dal' nego Vostoka*, Novosibirsk: Nauka, 1966.

15. Canfield F. Smith, "Atamanshchina in the Russian Far East," *Russian History*, vol. 6 (1979), pp. 57–67; V.D. Ivanov and O.I. Sergeev, *Ussuriiskoe Kazachestvo v revoliutsiakh 1917 goda i v grazhdanskoi voine na Dal'nem Vostoke*, Vladivostok: DVO RAN, 1999. Also, and especially, Jamie Bisher, *White Terror: Cossack Warlords of the Trans-Siberian*, London: Frank Cass, 2005. Kalmykov's men fled across the Amur into Manchuria, where they were interned by the Chinese authorities. The Ataman was subsequently executed, in October 1920, for his crimes against Chinese citizens.

16. On Mongolian developments, see T.E. Ewing, "Russia, China and the Origins of the Mongolian People's Republic, 1918–1921: A Reappraisal," *Slavonic and East European Review*, vol. 58, no. 3 (1980), pp. 399–421; and F. Isono, "Soviet Russia and the Mongolian Revolution of 1921," *Past and Present*, no. 83 (1979), pp. 116–40.

17. *Dokumenty vneshnei politiki SSSR*, Moscow: Gosizdat, 1957, vol. 1, pp. 476–80.

18. Some sources have it that, after his death, Soviet doctors performed an autopsy on Ungern's head (which, portraits reveal, was remarkably small in comparison to the rest of his body) and found that the right lobe of his brain was almost completely atrophied. Others claim that, after his death, the thirteenth Dalai Lama declared Ungern to have been an incarnation of the Black Mahakala, a six-armed demon prone to manifest itself in a necklace of human skulls. In 1998, his descendants petitioned the Russian authorities for his posthu-

mous rehabilitation, but the application was refused. On Ungern, see Canfield F. Smith, "The Ungernovshchina: How and Why," *Jahrbücher für Geschichte Osteuropas*, vol. 28 (1980), pp. 590–95; James Palmer, *The Bloody White Baron*, London: Faber and Faber, 2008; and, especially, Paul du Quenoy, "Warlordism *à la russe*: Baron von Ungern Sternberg's Anti-Bolshevik Crusade, 1912–1921," *Revolutionary Russia*, vol. 16, no. 2 (2003), pp. 1–27.

19. On Molchanov, see L.Iu. Tremsina (ed.), *V.M. Molchanov: poslednyi Belyi general*, Moscow: Airis-Press, 2009.

20. For example, a sizable Ukrainian community existed in the Maritime Province (constituting about 15 percent of the population 1897), concentrated in the northern reaches of the territory. Calling itself Green Ukraine, during the revolutionary era this community sought autonomy, or even union with the distant Ukrainian National Republic. Its acknowledged leader, Iurii Hlushko ("Mova"), would die of starvation in Nazi-occupied Kiev in 1941.

21. The Zemskii Sobor was the irregular (and largely theatrical) feudal parliament, assembling Russian lords, first summoned by Ivan the Terrible in 1649 and last seen in Moscow in 1684. In July 1922, Patriarch Tikhon was being held under arrest by the Soviet authorities in the Donskoi Cathedral, in Moscow. He died suddenly in April 1925, possibly having been poisoned by the Soviet security services.

22. On these events, see V.Zh. Tsvetkov, *General Diterikhs*, Moscow: Posev, 2004; A.Iu. Khvalin, *Vosstanovlenie monarkhii v Rossii: Priamurskii Zemskii sobor 1922 goda (materialy i dokumenty)*, Moscow: Pravoslavnoe Bratstvo, 1993; and Smith, *Vladivostok under Red and White Rule*, pp. 151–5. Diterikhs's credentials for his role were established in 1919, when at Omsk he had published a pamphlet entitled *Bei zhidov* ("Away with the Yids"). This was exceptional: as Oleg Budnitskii has stated, White leaders, "former generals of the tsarist army, rarely made openly anti-Semitic declarations": Oleg Budnitskii, "Jews, Pogroms and the White Movement: A Historiographical Critique," *Kritika*, vol. 2, no. 4 (2001), pp. 751–72, p. 771.

23. Earlier Soviet efforts to negotiate an agreement with the Japanese had stumbled at a conference at Changchun, south of Harbin, on 4–28 September 1922, at which the RSFSR was represented by A.A. Ioffe, a close associate of Trotsky. Ioffe had balked at Japan's insistence on being granted extensive economic concessions in the Far East and its determination not to evacuate Northern Sakhalin until after the problem of the "Nikolaevsk Incident" had been settled. Consequently, Northern Sakhalin would only be evacuated by Japanese forces after Tokyo's recognition of the USSR on 20 Jan. 1925. See: Paul Dukes, "The Changchun Conference: 4–28 September 1922," in A.L. Litvin (ed.), *Rossiiskaia istoricheska mozaika: sbornik nauchnykh statei*, Kazan': Izdatel'stvo Kazanskogo Matematicheskogo Obshchestva, 2003, pp. 228–51; and George A. Lensen, *Japanese Recognition of the USSR: Soviet–Japanese Relations, 1921–1930*, Tokyo: Sophia University, 1979, pp. 49–84. This left Japan in control of Southern Sakhalin (Karafuto Prefecture), south of the 50th Parallel, which she had annexed following the Treaty of Portsmouth in September 1905 (at the end of the Russo-Japanese War) and would retain until August 1945. During that same month Soviet forces occupied the Kuril Islands, which had been granted to Japan under the terms of the Treaty of St Petersburg (1875), in return for Tokyo's recognition of Russian control of Sakhalin. Sovereignty over the islands remains disputed between Japan and the Russian Federation.

24. Michael Shimkin and Mary Shimkin, "From Golden Horn to Golden Gate: The Flight of the Siberian Russian Flotilla," *Californian History*, vol. 64, no. 4 (1985), pp. 290–94. *Voevoda* Diterikhs did not travel with them. After some months in a refugee camp in Manchuria,

having failed to persuade the Chinese authorities to allow his troops to retain their arms—see V.P. Butt *et al.* (eds), *The Russian Civil War: Documents from the Soviet Archives*, London: Macmillan, 1996, pp. 175–206—in May 1923 he moved to Shanghai, where he settled into émigré life as chief cashier at the local branch of the Franco-Chinese Bank and as an active member of ROVS, chairing its 9th (Far Eastern) Section from 1930 until his death from tuberculosis in 1937. Diterikhs was buried in Shanghai's Liu-Kavzi cemetery (which was demolished and built over during the "Cultural Revolution").

25. On the Iakutsk revolt, see Ivan Ia. Strod, *Civil War in the Taiga: A Story of Guerrilla Warfare in the Forests of Eastern Siberia*, London: Modern Books, 1933. Pepeliav's fate is instructive. He was taken to Vladivostok and imprisoned, before being sentenced to death, in January 1924, at Chita by a military tribunal. This was commuted to ten years' imprisonment by VTsIK (probably because Pepeliaev had agreed to order his men to surrender their arms without resistance at Aian, although it may also have been taken into account that in June 1923, when a fire had broken out on board the ship that was carrying him and his captured *druzhina* from Aian to Vladivostok, it was only through Pepeliaev's taking command of the situation that the vessel was saved). Pepeliaev then, in fact, served thirteen years in the Iaroslavl' Isolation Prison and, latterly, the infamous Butyrki Prison in Moscow, being released on 6 July 1936. He then found employment as a carpenter in a factory at Voronezh, but was again arrested on 20 Aug. 1937. He was sent to Novosibirsk and implicated in the ongoing investigations into an (entirely fictional) anti-Soviet "Kadet-monarchist partisan organization," allegedly connected to White émigrés. On 7 Dec. 1937, a *troika* of the local NKVD ordered that he should be executed and the sentence was carried out a few weeks later. Pepeliaev was posthumously rehabilitated by the Supreme Court of the USSR on 16 Jan. 1989.

26. Among the latter were the influential Kadet who had headed the official Press Bureau at Omsk in 1919, N.V. Ustrialov, who became a leading advocate of *Smenovekhstvo* (the "Change of Pathways" movement), and Kolchak's disgraced Minister of Food and Supply, N.S. Zefirov. Another former Kolchak minister, the Kadet Iu.V. Kliuchnikov (who had served as Minister of Foreign Affairs at Omsk from July 1918 to Jan. 1919), was very active in the same movement in Europe.

27. I have had correspondence to the effect asserted above from the great-granddaughter of Ivanov-Rinov (Jessica Millar Ivanov-Rinov). Jessica's ancestor had been removed from the command of the Siberian Army on 23 Dec. 1918, having featured prominently in the previous days' bloodletting (the "Omsk massacre") in which numerous prominent socialists (including several members of the Constituent Assembly) had been abducted and murdered by White officers and Cossacks. He was subsequently sent to the Far East and, on 22 Jan. 1919, was named as commander of the Maritime Province Military District. In that role, he was distinguished by his pro-Japanese stance and had considerable success in raising troops and in smoothing relations between Admiral Kolchak and Ataman Semenov. Recalled to Omsk on 20 May 1919, from July to Sep. 1919 he commanded the Independent Siberian Cossack Corps and on 5 Nov. 1919 was made assistant commander of the Eastern Front. As Kolchak's forces collapsed and the White capital, Omsk, was abandoned, on 9 Dec. 1919 (together with General Sakharov) Ivanov-Rinov was arrested ("for treachery") at Taishet by General A.N. Pepeliaev, but was soon released. He then spent some months in hiding at Krasnoiarsk, before, in March 1920, making his way to Chita, where he entered the service of the forces of Ataman Semenov (as chief of staff and then chief of the rear in the Maritime

Province). When Semenov's forces were driven into Manchuria, Ivanov-Rinov moved on to Vladivostok and from September 1921 served under General Diterikhs, as commander of the rear districts of the Zemstvo Host. On 26 Oct. 1922, as Soviet forces captured the port, he slipped across the border into Korea. From 1924, he lived in the Italian concession at Tientsin in China and later, at Tsingao, working in the fur trade. In 1925, he began to collaborate with the Soviet agent General Gushchin in recruiting White émigrés to serve in the anti-Kuomintang forces of the Chinese "Red General" Fen Yu-sian, an ally of Moscow. Having been, according to some reports, injured in both legs during a botched police raid on the Soviet consulate, in the autumn of 1925 he returned to Soviet Russia.

28. This was mostly reconstituted as the Southern Army (commanded by General G.A. Belov) on Kolchak's refashioned front in May 1919. When that force divided before the Red advance, with its northern components retreating towards Omsk, its southern ranks were again reconfigured (under Dutov's command) as the Orenburg Army in September 1919.

29. For the arrangements relating to the return of 5,000 Orenburg Cossacks to Russia, see the telegram of I.M. Smirnov to Lenin of 26 Mar. 1921 in Meijer (ed.), *The Trotsky Papers*, vol. 2, p. 433. On General Bakich, see A.V. Ganin, *Chernogorets v russkoi sluzhbe: General Bakich*, Moscow: Russkii Put', 2004. On Dutov and the Orenburg Cossack Host: A.V. Ganin, *Ataman A.I. Dutov*, Moscow: Tsentropoligraf, 2006; and I. Elovskii, *Golodnyi pokhod Orenburgskoi armii: iz vospominanii uchastnika pokhoda*, Peking: Tip. Uspenskago Monastyria pri Russkoi Dukhovnoi Missii, 1921. Dutov was buried at Sai-dun but, according to some accounts, his corpse was soon afterwards disinterred and decapitated (presumably to provide proof of his death). The cemetery was destroyed during the Chinese "Cultural Revolution" of the 1960s. Dutov's defeat in and flight from Semirech'e and his mysterious death were the subject of the interesting Soviet feature film *Konets atamana* ("End of an Ataman," dir. Shaken Aimanov, 1970).

30. On Annenkov, see P.I. Pavlovskii (ed.), *Annenkovshchina (po materialam sudebnogo protsessa v Semipalatinsk 25.vii.1927—12.viii.1927*, Moscow: Gosizdat, 1928. Also B. Urevich, "The End of Ataman Annenkov," *Far Eastern Affairs*, vol. 6 (1990), pp. 92–103. On the leeching into China of the Russian conflict, see: Michael Share, "The Russian Civil War in Chinese Turkestan (Xinjiang), 1918–1921: A Little Known and Explored Front," *Europe–Asia Studies*, vol. 62, no. 3 (2010), pp. 389–420; and Andrew Forbes, *Warlords and Muslims in Chinese Central Asia: A Political History of Republican Sinkiang, 1911–1949*, Cambridge: Cambridge University Press, 1986.

31. The Turkestan Red Army was interesting, however, as it had a higher proportion than any other Soviet force of Internationalists, drawn from the 200,000 or so prisoners of war who had been held across Central Asia since 1914. On this phenomenon, see A.M. Matveyev, "Foreign Prisoners of War in Turkestan, 1917–1918," *Central Asian Review*, vol. 9, no. 3 (1961), pp. 240–50; and Arnold Krammer, "Soviet Propaganda among German and Austro-Hungarian Prisoners of War in Russia, 1917–1921," in Samuel R. Richardson and Peter Pastor (eds), *Essays on World War I: Origins and Prisoners of War*, New York: Brooklyn College Press, 1983, pp. 249–64.

32. Lt-Col. F.M. Bailey, *Mission to Tashkent*, London: Jonathan Cape, 1946, pp. 92–103. See also Paul Nazaroff, *Hunted through Central Asia*, Edinburgh: Blackwood, 1932, pp. 19–48; and S. Piontkovskii (ed.), *Grazhdanskaia voina v Rossii (1918–1921 gg.): khrestomatiia*, Moscow: Kommunisticheskii universitet, 1925, pp. 643ff.

33. On the Transcaspian Government, see: Piontkovskii (ed.), *Grazhdanskaia voina v Rossii (1918–1921 gg.)*, pp. 644–8.

34. On British intervention in this region, see Sir Wilfred Malleson, "The British Military Mission to Turkestan, 1918–1920," *Journal of the Royal Central Asian Society*, vol. 9, no. 2 (1922), pp. 96–110; and T.R. Sareen, *British Intervention in Central Asia and Trans-Caucasia*, New Delhi: Anmol Publications, 1989.

35. Among those who survived was the aforementioned Mikoian (head of state of the USSR from 1964 to 1965), whom Stalin would habitually—and with a characteristic compounding of humor, mockery, cruelty, and threat—dub "the twenty-seventh Commissar."

36. It is notable that in I.I. Brodskii's famous 1925 painting "The Execution of the 26 Baku Commissars," two British officers (with countenances close to those of Malleson and Teague-Jones) are visible in the left foreground as the shootings take place. British officers are also featured prominently in Nikolai Shengalaia's 1932 film *Dvatsat' shest' kommisarov* ("The 26 Commissars"), on which see Michael G. Smith, "Cinema for the 'Soviet East': National Fact and Revolutionary Fiction in Early Azerbaijani Film," *Slavic Review*, vol. 56, no. 4 (1997), pp. 645–78.

37. The official Soviet line on the affair is presented in L.V. Mitrovkin, *Failure of Three Missions: British Diplomacy and Intelligence Efforts to Overthrow the Soviet Government in Central Asia*, Moscow: Progress Publishers, 1987. The sizable holes in the case presented by Moscow are explored in: Brian Pearce, "The 26 Commissars," *Sbornik of the Study Group on the Russian Revolution*, nos 6–7 (1981), pp. 54–66; Brian Pearce, "On the Fate of the 26 Commissars," *Sbornik of the Study Group on the Russian Revolution*, nos 6–7 (1981), pp. 83–95; Brian Pearce, "More about the 26 Commissars," *Sbornik of the Study Group on the Russian Revolution*, no. 9 (1983), pp. 83–5; and Brian Pearce, "A Falsifier of History," *Revolutionary Russia*, vol. 1, no. 1 (1988), pp. 20–23. The most recent study of these events also concludes, convincingly, that Teague-Jones was not at all culpable for the fate of the twenty-six commissars: Taline Ter Minassian, *Reginald Teague-Jones: Au service secret de l'Empire britannique*, Paris: Bernard Grasset, 2012.

38. Reginald Teague-Jones, *The Spy Who Disappeared: Diary of a Secret Mission to Central Asia in 1918*, London: Victor Gollancz, 1988.

39. On Jadidism see: Adeeb Khalid, *The Politics of Muslim Cultural Reform: Jadidism in Central Asia*, Berkeley: University of California Press, 1998; and Adeeb Khalid, "Nationalizing the Revolution in Central Asia: The Transformation of Jadidism, 1917–1920," in Ronald Grigor Suny and Terry Martin (eds), *A State of Nations: Empire and Nation-Making in the Age of Lenin and Stalin*, New York: Oxford University Press, 2001, pp. 145–64. The movement had a counterpart, albeit less effective (and far less well known), in the Union of Allied Mountaineers in the North Caucasus, but circumstances dictated that the UAM follow a more anti-Bolshevik line. See Michael A. Reynolds, "Native Sons: Post-Imperial Politics, Islam, and Identity in the North Caucasus, 1917–1918," *Jahrbücher für Geschichte Osteuropas*, vol. 56, no. 2 (2008), pp. 221–47.

40. V.M. Mikhaleva (ed.), *Revvoensovet Respubliki: protokoly, 1920–1923: sbornik dokumentov*, Moscow: Editorial, 2000, p. 339.

41. Most of the indigenous peoples of the Russian Empire's Central Asian colonies were Turkic-speaking, including the Kazakhs, Uzbeks, Kirgiz, and Turkmens; the chief exception was the Persian-speaking Tadzhiks. On Soltangäliev, see: Alexandre Bennigsen, "Sultan Galiev: The USSR and the Colonial Revolution," in Walter Z. Laqueur (ed.), *The Middle East in*

Transition, New York: Praeger, 1958, pp. 398–414; Stephen Blank, *The Sorcerer as Apprentice: Stalin as Commissar for Nationalities*, Westport: Greenwood Press, 1994, pp. 143–227; Sh.F. Mukhamedyarov and B.F. Sultanbekov, "Mirsaid Sultan-Galiev: His Character and Fate," *Central Asian Survey*, vol. 9, no. 2 (1990), pp. 109–17; and, especially, Jeremy Smith, *The Bolsheviks and the National Question*, Basingstoke: Macmillan, 1999, pp. 103–210. See also B.F. Sultanbekov and D.R. Sharafutdinov (eds), *Neizvestnyi Sultan-Galiev: rassekrechennye dokumenty i materialy*, Kazan': Tatarskoe Knizhnoe Izdatel'stvo, 2002.

42. The case of Turar Ryskulov, one of the most prominent Kazakh figures of the civil-war era, is instructive. Having founded the Revolutionary Union of Kirghiz Youth at Merke in 1917, in September of that year he joined the Bolsheviks and during the civil wars was chairman of the Muslim Bureau of the Central Committee of the Communist Party (Bolshevik) of Turkestan (March 1919–18 July 1920) and chairman of the Central Executive Committee of the Turkestan ASSR (January–18 July 1920). He then moved to Moscow to become Deputy People's Commissar For Nationalities (1921–22), served again as chairman of the Turkestan ASSR (1922–26), and was later deputy chairman of the Sovnarkom of the RSFSR (28 May 1926–May 1937). In that exalted capacity, he performed numerous roles in economic administration, notably overseeing one of the great construction projects of the era—the TurkSib Railroad. He was arrested on 21 May 1937, while on holiday at Kislovodsk, and subsequently executed as a "counter-revolutionary" and "national Communist." See V.M. Ustinov, *Turar Ryskulov: ocherki politicheskoi biografii*, Almaty: Kazakhstan, 1996.

43. In April 1923 Soltangäliev was arrested, accused of treason, pan-Turkism, and conspiracy with the Basmachi. He was expelled from the RKP(b) and imprisoned but later released. In 1928, he was arrested again and, alongside seventy-six others, was charged with membership of a fictional "Soltangälievist counter-revolutionary organization" and of being a proponent of pan-Turkism. He was found guilty and, a death sentence having been commuted in 1931, was imprisoned on the Solovetskii Islands in the White Sea. Although he was released in 1934, and permitted to move to Saratov, he was re-arrested in early 1937. On 8 Dec. 1939 he was sentenced to death, and he was subsequently shot at Lefortovo prison in Moscow. Soltangäliev was posthumously rehabilitated on 30 Apr. 1990.

44. The rebels preferred their own less derogatory designation as *kurbashi* ("Fighters"), but Basmachi has become the accepted term.

45. In the Soviet Union, though, the events had always been kept very much alive in the public imagination through the medium of enduringly popular adventure films—"Easterns," perhaps the equivalent of Hollywood "Westerns"—wherein heroic and sweaty *krasnoarmeitsy* battled (and always bested) exotic natives, just like cowboys clashed with "Indians" on LA studio lots. Prime examples of the genre include: *Ognennie vyorsti* ("Miles of Fire"/"The Burning Miles," dir. S.I. Samsonov, 1957), *Beloe solntse pustyni* ("White Sun of the Desert," dir. V.Ia. Motyl, 1969), *Vstrecha u staroi mecheti* ("Meeting at the Old Mosque," dir. Sukhbat Khamidov, 1969), *Sed'maia pulia* ("The Seventh Bullet," dir. Ali Khramaev, 1972), *Telokhranitel'* ("The Bodyguard," dir. Ali Khramaev, 1979), and *Svoi sredi chuzhiikh, chuzhoi sredi svoikh* ("At Home among Strangers," dir. N.S. Mikhailov, 1974). All these drew upon the classic *Trinatsat'* ("The Thirteen," dir. M.I. Romm, 1936), and seldom involved any more subtlety in their portrayal of the Muslim rebels than had Romm's work.

46. The following, unless signaled as otherwise, is based upon: [Anon.], "Dzunaid-khan, 'King of the Karakum Desert,'" *Central Asian Survey*, vol. 13 (1965), pp. 216–26; Marie B. Broxup, "The Basmachi," *Central Asian Survey*, vol. 2, no. 1 (1983), pp. 57–81; Joseph Castagné,

Les Basmatchis. Le mouvement national des indigènes d'Asie Centrale depuis la Révolution d'octobre 1917 jusqu'en 1924, Paris: Ernest Leroux, 1925; Glenda Fraser, "Basmachi," *Central Asian Survey*, vol. 6 (1987), no. 1, pp. 1–71; no. 2, pp. 7–42; Baymirza Hayit, *Basmatschi. Nationaler Kampf Turkestans in den Jahren 1917 bis 1934*, Cologne: Dreisam-Verlag, 1993; Richard Lorenz, "Economic Bases of the Basmachi Movement in the Ferghana Valley," in Andreas Kappeler, Gerhard Simon, and Edward Allworth (eds), *Muslim Communities Reemerge: Historical Perspectives on Nationality, Politics, and Opposition in the Former Soviet Union and Yugoslavia*, Durham, NC: Duke University Press, 1994, pp. 277–303; Fazal-ur-Rahim Khan Marwat, *The Basmachi Movement in Soviet Central Asia: A Study in Political Development*, Peshawar: Emjay Books International, 1985; Martha B. Olcott, "The Basmachi or Freemen's Revolt in Turkestan, 1918–1924," *Soviet Studies*, vol. 33, no. 3 (1981), pp. 352–69; Alexander G. Park, *Bolshevism in Turkestan, 1917–1927*, New York: Columbia University Press, 1957; William S. Ritter, "The Final Phase in the Liquidation of Anti-Soviet Resistance in Tadzhikistan: Ibrahim Bek and the *Basmachi*, 1924–1931," *Soviet Studies*, vol. 37, no. 4 (1985), pp. 484–93; and S.A. Shumov and A.R. Andreev, *Basmachestvo*, Moscow: Algoritm, 2005.

47. Baymirza Hayit, *Turkestan im XX. Jahrhundert*, Darmstadt: Leske, 1956, p. 173.

48. On the tendency of historical accounts to overstate the unity of purpose and organization among the Basmachi, see William Myer, *Islam and Colonialism: Western Perspectives on Soviet Asia*, London: RoutledgeCurzon, 2002, pp. 79–83.

49. Elikhman, *Poteri narodonaseleniia v XX veke*, p. 19; and G.F. Krivosheeva (ed.), *Grif sekretnosti sniat: Poteri vooruzhennykh sil SSSR v voinakh, boevykh deistviiakh i voennykh konfliktakh*, Moscow: Voenizdat, 1993, p. 62.

50. Helene A. de Lageard, "The Revolt of the Basmachi according to Red Army Journals (1920–1922)," *Central Asian Survey*, vol. 6, no. 3 (1987), pp. 1–35; Gregory J. Massell, *The Surrogate Proletariat: Moslem Women and Revolutionary Strategy in Soviet Central Asia, 1919–1929*, Princeton: Princeton University Press, 1974.

51. Glenda Fraser, "Enver Pasha's Bid for Turkestan, 1920–1922," *Canadian Journal of History*, vol. 22, no. 2 (1988), pp. 197–211; Salahi R. Sonyel, "Enver Pasha and the Basmaji Movement in Central Asia," *Middle Eastern Studies*, vol. 26 (1990), pp. 52–64; Masayuki Yamauchi, *The Green Crescent under the Red Star: Enver Pasha in Soviet Russia*, Tokyo: Institute for the Study of Languages and Cultures of Asia and Africa, 1991; and Şuhnaz Yilmaz, "An Ottoman Warrior Abroad: Enver Paşa as an Expatriate," *Middle Eastern Studies*, vol. 35, no. 4 (1999), pp. 40–69.

52. On the Soviet–Persian treaty, see above. Under the terms of Articles VII and VIII of the treaty with Afghanistan, of 28 Feb. 1921, both contracting parties agreed to respect "the freedom of Eastern nations," including the former khanates of Bokhara and Khiva. Another reason, then, for Moscow's promotion of the Bukharan and Khivan People's Republics. See Jane Degras (ed.), *Soviet Documents on Foreign Policy: Vol. 1, 1917–1924*, London: Oxford University Press, 1951, pp. 233–7.

CONCLUSION: RED VICTORIES, RED DEFEATS

1. The foundation stone of all this, so to speak, was a Sovnarkom decree drafted by Lenin of 12 April 1918, "On the Removal of Monuments Erected in Honor of the Tsars and their Officials and the Setting Up of Designs for Monuments of the Russian Socialist Revolution":

Wade (ed.), *Documents of Soviet History*, Vol. 1, p. 126. See also: John E. Bowlt, "Russian Sculpture in Lenin's Plan of Monumental Propaganda," in Henry A. Millon and Linda Nochin (eds), *Art and Architecture in the Service of Politics*. Cambridge: MIT Press, 1978, pp. 182–93; Christina Lodder, "Lenin's Plan for Monumental Propaganda", in Matthew C. Bown and Brandon Taylor (eds), *Art of the Soviets: Painting, Sculpture and Architecture in a One-party State, 1917–1992*, Manchester: Manchester University Press, 1993, pp. 16–32. The first instance of the practice of renaming—actually long before victory was certain—was the renaming, by a Sovnarkom decree of 14 August 1918, in response to a petition of the MRC of the Kazan' sector of the Eastern Front of 12 August, of the station of Krasnaia Gorka, near Kazan', as "Iudino": see Meijer (ed.), *The Trotsky Papers*, Vol. 1, p. 77. This was to honor the Latvian rifleman Jānis Judeņš, an otherwise much unsung Red hero, who had been killed there in fighting against the Czechoslovak Legion two days earlier. The practice later spread to the naming of such things as military schools (for example, the general staff academy became the Frunze Military Academy in 1926), battleships (for example, the Kirov-class cruiser, built from 1935, which was succeeded by the Chapaev class, from 1939), and tanks (for example, the Stalin-class, from 1943). Budennyi, fittingly, gave his name to a breed of horse (from 1949).

2. On public spectacles see: František Deák, "Russian Mass Spectacles," *Drama Review*, vol. 19, no. 2 (1975), pp. 7–22; James von Geldern, *Bolshevik Festivals, 1917–1920*, Berkeley: University of California Press, 1993; and, especially, Vladimir Tolstoy, Irina Bibikova, and Catherine Cooke (eds), *Street Art of the Revolution: Festivities and Celebrations in Russia, 1918–1933*, London: Thames and Hudson, 1990.

3. One of the first "permanent" structures completed was the brick-built "Monument to the Soviet Constitution" (by D. Osipov and N.A. Andreev), an obelisk with attached statue of liberty. This was erected in Moscow in 1918–19, in place of the destroyed "Monument to General M.D. Skobelev," tsarist hero of the Russo-Turkish War of 1877–78 and the empire's conquest of Central Asia, at Soviet Square (formerly Skobelev Square, and today Tverskaia Square). Skobelev was known by his men as the "White General", as we have seen, which probably influenced the Reds' decision to have his statue demolished. The monument to the constitution (that of July 1918) was itself demolished in 1941, presumably because it tended to remind people that there had once been a constitution other than the "Stalin Constitution" of 1936. In keeping with the nationalistic bent of late Stalinism, in 1954 the monument was replaced with the still-standing statue of Iurii Dolgoruki (1099–1157), usually credited as the founder of Moscow.

4. Actually, it had begun earlier in the so-called People's Republics: thus the statue of Dzierżyński in Dzierżyński Square in Warsaw was removed in 1989 and the name of the place was changed back to Bank Square. Conversely (not to say provocatively), a bronze statue of Dzierżyński— an exact replica of that removed from Moscow in 1991—was raised in the grounds of the military academy in Minsk, Belarus, in May 2006: "Belarus: Monument to Founder of Soviet Secret Police Unveiled in Minsk," http://english.pravda.ru/news/world/26–05–2006/81129-belarus-0/

5. On 26 Jan. 2009, the twenty-six commissars' remains (or, rather, the remains of twenty-three of them, which were all that was recovered) were reburied at Baku's Hovsan Cemetery: "V Azerbaidzhane protiv demontazha memoriala 26 Bakinskikh komissarov protestuiut tol'ka levye," *Kavkazkii uzel* (16 Jan. 2009): http://www.kavkaz-uzel.ru/articles/148040. In fact, the memorializing of the twenty-six commissars had been contested since the first Bolshevik

efforts in March 1919, which coincided with the first anniversary of the widespread attacks on Muslims at Baku (known as the "March Days") that many Azeris blamed on Shaumian and his colleagues. See Michael G. Smith, "The Russian Revolution as a National Revolution: Tragic Deaths and Rituals of Remembrance in Muslim Azerbaijan (1907–1920)," *Jahrbücher für Geschichte Osteuropas*, vol. 49, no. 3 (2001), pp. 379–80.

6. "V.I. Lenin Museum will be Converted into a Central Dinosaur Museum of Mongolia," http://www.infomongolia.com/ct/ci/5483

7. *Civil Georgia* (25 June 2010): http://www.civil.ge/eng/article.php?id=22453. As of the spring of 2013, though, the Stalin museum remained operational.

8. "Tribute Paid to the Memory of the Victims of 1916 Uprising in Kyrgystan," *Central Asia Online* (12 Aug. 2009): http://centralasiaonline.com/en_GB/articles/caii/features/2009/08/12/feature-03

9. See: Benjamin Forest and Juliet Johnson, "Unravelling the Threads of History: Soviet-era Monuments and Post-Soviet National Identity in Moscow," *Annals of the Association of American Geographers*, vol. 92, no. 3 (2002), pp. 48–72; Graham Gill, "Changing Symbols: The Renovation of Moscow Place Names," *Russian Review*, vol. 64, no. 3 (2005), pp. 480–503; and Nurit Schleifman, "Moscow as Victory Park: A Monumental Change," *History and Memory*, vol. 13, no. 2 (2001), pp. 5–34. Even the October Revolution itself is nowadays celebrated by only a few, hardy Communist souls, its place taken by a public holiday celebrating "The Day of National Unity," although only 16 percent of Russians quizzed on the subject in 2009 knew that: "Great October Revolution Day Falls into Oblivion," *Pravda* (4 Nov. 2010): http://english.pravda.ru/russia/politics/04-11-2010/115659-october_revolution_day-0/. In early 1995, though, the right-wing Liberal Democratic Party failed in an attempt to have the Russian parliament pass a law "On Recognizing as Illegal the Coup d'État in Russia of 7 November (25 October) 1917": Frederick C. Corney, "Rethinking a Great Event: The October Revolution as Memory Project," *Social Science History*, vol. 22, no. 4 (1998), p. 390.

10. P.J. O'Rourke, "What Do They Do For Fun In Warsaw?" in P.J. O'Rourke, *Holidays in Hell*, London: Picador, 1989, p. 83.

11. And they may come under attack from those who regard the collapse of the Soviet state as illegitimate and the veneration of its predecessors or opponents as wrong. For example, a new statue of Nicholas II at Taininskoe, near Moscow, was blown up in April 1997 (and one of Peter the Great narrowly escaped the same fate): *Nezavisimaia gazeta*, 8 July 1997. The perpetrators were protesting at plans to bury Lenin, on which see below. See also Wendy Slater, *The Many Deaths of Nicholas II: Relics, Remains and the Romanovs*, London: Routledge, 2007, pp. 116–17.

12. "Tblisi Municipal Portal": http://www.tbilisi.gov.ge/index.php?lang_id=ENG&sec_id=344&info_id=3846

13. Presumably, though, efforts to have Kolchak himself formally rehabilitated by the Russian courts will not cease until proponents of that cause achieve their aim, although petitions to that effect so far have been unsuccessful: "Prokuatora: Kolchaka reabilitirovat' ne budet," *Grani.Ru* (6 Dec. 2004), http://grani.ru/Society/History/m.80895.html. For a thoughtful review of *Admiral'*, see: Denise J. Youngblood, "The Admiral," *Revolutionary Russia*, vol. 25, no. 2 (2012), pp. 219–20.

14. Denikin had spent the years in emigration in France perfecting the art of the memoirist and

studiously avoiding involvement in émigré politics. He moved to the United States after the Second World War, passing through Ellis Island with nine dollars in his pocket, and died of a heart attack at Ann Arbor in 1947. At the 2005 reburial ceremony in Moscow, which was attended by 2,500 people, Patriarch Aleksei II said that "Today's event proves that we are concluding the process of restoring the unity of our people, who were divided by the tragic history of the last century": *The Moscow Times* (4 Oct. 2005). To confound such notions of "unity", if—albeit—for understandable reasons, the descendants of Denikin's *bête noir*, General Wrangel, have adamantly resisted calls to have his remains sent to join Denikin from their resting place in Belgrade's Russian Cathedral (the Church of the Holy Trinity), close to those of General Alekseev.

15. "Posledniaia taina generala Kappelia": http://rusk.ru/st.php?idar=176048. No such reburial can be arranged for General Kornilov. After his death, during the Volunteers' siege of Ekaterinodar on 13 Apr. 1918, he was buried at Gnachbau, a nearby village of German colonists, but on 15 Apr. 1918 his grave was desecrated by Red troops, who exhumed his corpse and later burnt it on a local rubbish dump, after parading it through the streets. However, statues to Kornilov now stand in Krasnodar (Ekaterinodar) and Sevastopol'.

16. Consequently, the new Lithuanian republic existed for twenty years in the bizarre situation of having its constitutionally proclaimed capital, Vilnius, in which Lithuanians constituted about 10 percent of the population, located in another country—a situation underwritten by the international community, through the League of Nations' recognition, on 15 Mar. 1923, of Poland's sovereignty over what the Poles called Wilno. See Alfred E. Senn, *The Great Powers, Lithuania and the Vilna Question, 1920–1928*, Leiden: E.J. Brill, 1966. To add insult to injury, in September 1939, when the USSR invaded Poland, Vilnius initially was incorporated into the Belorussian SSR. In August 1940, though, it was named as the capital of the new Lithuanian SSR.

17. On Armistice night, 11 Nov. 1918, Churchill is supposed to have remarked, "The war of giants has ended, the wars of the pygmies begin." See Winston S. Churchill, *Collected Works, Vol. 27: The Second World War, Vol. 6: Triumph and Tragedy. Epilogue*, London: Library of Imperial History, 1976, Chapter 25.

18. That said, the widespread violence against Jewish communities during the civil wars in these "Bloodlands" (Timothy Snyder, *Bloodlands: Europe between Hitler and Stalin*, London: The Bodley Head, 2010) certainly was a horrific presentiment of what was to come. "In some ways," as Abraham Greenbaum rightly noted of the civil-war pogroms in borderlands of Poland, Lithuania, Belorussia, and Ukraine, "especially since killings were sometimes carried out as a kind of 'national duty' without the usual robbery—they bear comparison with the Holocaust some twenty years later": Abraham Greenbaum, "Bibliographical Essay," in John D. Klier and Shlomo Lambroza (eds), *Pogroms: Anti-Jewish Violence in Modern Russian History*, Cambridge: Cambridge University Press, 1992, p. 380. Yet, it is surely impossible to concur with the assertion of Richard Pipes that "in every respect except for the absence of a central organization to direct the slaughter, the pogroms of 1919 were a prelude to and rehearsal for the Holocaust": Richard Pipes, *Russia under the Bolshevik Regime*, New York: A.A. Knopf, 1993, p. 112. After all, what surely marks the Holocaust as unique was the very presence of that very "central organization." Also, pogroms were not at all limited to Snyder's "Bloodlands" in the civil-war period: witness the slaughter of Jews by the Whites at Elets during the "Mamontov Raid" of August-September 1919. On Ukraine as a

theater of violence, see also Felix Schnell, *Räume des Schreckens. Gewalt und Gruppenmilitanz in der Ukraine 1905–1933*, Hamburg: Hamburger Edition, 2012.

19. Isaac Deutscher, *The Prophet Armed: Trotsky, 1879–1921*, London: Oxford University Press, 1954, Chapter Fourteen.

20. Vasily Grossman, *Life and Fate*, London: Vintage Books, 2006, p. 825. The manuscript of Grossman's novel was confiscated ("arrested," the author preferred to say) by the NKVD in 1960, and was not published in the USSR until 1988.

21. This has not prevented one otherwise esteemed scholar of Stalinism from so doing, repeatedly: Sheila Fitzpatrick, "Civil War as Formative Experience," in Albert Gleason, Peter Kenez, and Richard Stites (eds), *Bolshevik Culture: Experiment and Order in the Russian Revolution*, Bloomington: Indiana University Press, 1985, pp. 57–76; Sheila Fitzpatrick, "The Legacy of the Civil War," in Diane Koenker, William G. Rosenberg, and Ronald G. Suny (eds), *Party, State and Society in the Russian Civil War: Explorations in Social History*, Bloomington: Indiana University Press, 1990, pp. 385–9; and Sheila Fitzpatrick, "Origins of Stalinism: How Important was the Civil War?" *Acta Slavica Iaponica*, vol. 2 (1984), pp. 105–16.

22. Among those immediately executed in this purge was General V.A. Ol'derogge (commander of the Eastern Front, 15 Aug. 1919–15 Jan. 1920, and architect of the defeat of Kolchak). Among those arrested and imprisoned for various lengths of time were Generals S.D. Kharlamov (commander of the 7th Red Army, 26 Sep.–17 Oct. 1919, during its successful defense of Petrograd against the advance of Iudenich's forces), M.S. Matiiasevich (commander of the 3rd Red Army, 7 Oct. 1919–15 Jan. 1920, during its capture of Kolchak's capital, Omsk), D.N. Nadezhnyi (Kharlamov's successor as commander of the 7th Red Army, 17 Oct.–17 Nov. 1919, and later chief inspector of infantry of the Red Army), A.V. Novikov (commander, 14 June–22 July 1919, of the 16th Red Army, during the early stages of the Soviet–Polish War), F.F. Novitskii (assistant commander of the Turkestan Front, Nov. 1919–Oct. 1920), S.A. Pugachev (chief of staff of the Caucasian Front, Mar. 1920–May 1921, during the invasion of Transcaucasia), N.I. Rattel' (chief of the Field Staff of the Revvoensovet of the Republic, 6 Sep.–21 Oct. 1918, and then head of Vseroglavshtab, 22 Oct. 1918–10 Feb. 1921), A.E. Snesarev (commander of the Lithuanian–Belorussian Red Army, 15 Nov. 1918–31 May 1919), and A.A. Svechin (Rattel''s predecessor as chief of Vseroglavshtab, Aug. 1918–11 Oct. 1918). Most of those arrested, even if they survived imprisonment, interrogation, and torture, were soon thereafter re-arrested and executed during the Terror.

23. Among them Ataman Semenov, I.A. Mikhailov, Ataman Krasnov, and General Shkuro.

24. See Bernard M. Patenaude, *Stalin's Nemesis: The Exile and Murder of Leon Trotsky*, London: Faber & Faber, 2009. Trotsky was attacked at his desk, by the ice-pick-wielding assassin. His blood then stained the manuscript of the biography of Stalin on which he was currently working.

25. S.A. Pavliuchenkov, *Krest'ianskaia Brest: ili predistoriia bol'shevistkogo NEPa*, Moscow: Russkoe Knigoizdatel'skoe Tovarishchestvo, 1996.

26. See Andrea Graziosi, *The Great Soviet Peasant War: Bolsheviks and Peasants, 1917–1933*, Cambridge, MA: Harvard University Ukrainian Research Institute, 1996.

27. Malcolm Muggeridge, "The Soviet's War on the Peasants," *Fortnightly Review*, vol. 39 (May 1933), p. 564.

28. The Treaty on the Creation of the USSR was signed by the representatives of the Belorussian SSR, the RSFSR, the Transcaucasian SFSR, and the Ukrainian SSR on 30 Dec. 1922. It united the separate Soviet republics as purportedly equal partners in the Union of Soviet

Socialist Republics (although the RSFSR was by far the largest constituent republic). Subsequent amendments to the treaty admitted newly created Soviet republics to the union, the first instance, falling within our period, being the Uzbek SSR and the Turkmen SSR that were formed in Oct. 1924 from the former Turkestan ASSR (previously part of the RSFSR). The Bukharan and Khorezm People's Republics (also nominally autonomous) were abolished at the same time. The union treaty was terminated on 25 Dec. 1991.

29. This was confusing because of the existence of a Leftist (bordering on anarchist) faction of the PSR called the Maximalists, founded in 1906, which was reconstituted in 1917, with strong support in Petrograd and Kronshtadt. For use of the term to describe the Bolsheviks, see, for example *The New York Times* (7 Nov. 1917) and *The Times* (9 Nov. 1917).

30. Evan Mawdsley, *The Russian Civil War*, Boston: Allen & Unwin, 1987, pp. 272–90.

31. These *gubernii* were: Novgorod, Olonets, Petrograd, Pskov, Vologda (in the Northern Region); Iaroslavl', Kostroma, Moscow, Nizhni Novgorod, Tver, and Vladimir (in the Central Industrial Region); Kaluga, Kursk, Orel, Penza, Riazan, Tambov, Tula, Voronezh (in the Central Agricultural Region); Perm' and Viatka (in the Urals Region); Astrakhan, Kazan', Samara, Saratov, and Simbirsk (in the Volga Region); Chernigov (in Ukraine); and Mogilev, Smolensk, and Vitebsk (in the Western Region). See: *Istoriia Kommunisticheskoi partii Sovetskogo soiuza: atlas*, Moscow: Institut Marksizma-leninizma pri TsK KPSS, 1977, p. 53. Populous and economically rich Red enclaves existed also in the North Caucasus (the North Caucasus Soviet Republic) until late 1918 and around Tashkent (the Turkestan Socialist Federative Republic, later the Turkestan ASSR) throughout the civil wars.

32. Mawdsley, *The Russian Civil War*, p. 274. In comparison, both Britain and France had populations of around about 40 million in 1918. The population of Kolchak's realm in Siberia, the Far East, and the Urals was around 15 million; Denikin's North Caucasus base territory had around 10 million inhabitants, although more than three times that number came briefly and loosely under his control during the autumn offensive of the AFSR in 1919.

33. On the travails of the Trans-Siberian Railroad, "the sick man of Siberia," see Jonathan D. Smele, *Civil War in Siberia: The Anti-Bolshevik Government of Admiral Kolchak, 1918–20*, Cambridge University Press, 1996, pp. 449–65. A particular problem here was that the Trans-Siberian Railroad was designed to ferry Russian goods from European Russia to the Far East, so all its coaling and switching systems had to be thrown, grindingly, into reverse to serve the White war effort—an obstacle that even an engineer as accomplished as John F. Stevens (chief engineer of the Great Northern Railway from 1895 and chief engineer on the Panama Canal from 1905 to 1907) proved incapable of surmounting. Stevens was placed in control of the line by the Inter-Allied Railway Committee established at Harbin by the Allies in Jan. 1919. On Stevens, see Raymond Estep, "John F. Stevens and the Far Eastern Railways, 1917–1923," *Explorer's Journal*, vol. 48, no. 1 (1970), pp. 13–24. Also: Odin A. Baugh, *John Frank Stevens: American Trailblazer*, Spokane, WA: Arthur H. Clark Co., 2005; and Clifford Foust, *John Frank Stevens: Civil Engineer*, Bloomington: Indiana University Press, 2013. The "Russian civil wars" lingered on in North America with the railwaymen's 55-year legal battle with the US government to win pension rights they were due as members of the US Army: Joe M. Feist, "Theirs Not to Reason Why: The Case of the Russian Railway Service Corps," *Military Affairs*, vol. 42, no. 1 (1978), pp. 1–6.

34. Stephen White, *The Bolshevik Poster*, New Haven: Yale University Press, 1988, is the most focused and historical in its approach, but other even more richly illustrated examples include: Viktor N. Duvakin, *Rosta-Fenster: Majakowski aus Dichter und bildender Künstler*, Dres-

den: Verlag der Kunst, 1975; Georg Piltz (ed.), *Russland wird Rot. Satirische Plakate 1918–1922*, Berlin: Eulenspiegel, 1977; and David King, *Russian Revolutionary Posters: From Civil War to Socialist Realism, from Bolshevism to the End of Stalinism*, London: Tate Publishing, 2012. On Bolshevik propaganda in general, see Peter Kenez, *The Birth of the Propaganda State: Soviet Methods of Mass Mobilization, 1917–1929*, Cambridge University Press, 1985. On the agit-trains and agit-barges: Richard Argenbright, "The Soviet Agitational Vehicle: State Power and the Social Frontier," *Political Geography*, vol. 17, no. 3 (1998), pp. 253–72. For some fine examples of early Soviet propaganda: http://eng.plakaty.ru/

35. John Harris (ed.), *Farewell to the Don: The Journal of Brigadier H.N.H. Williamson*, London: Collins, 1970, p. 105.

36. Peter Arshinov, *History of the Makhnovist Movement, 1918–1921*, London: Freedom Press, 1921, p. 265.

37. Smele, *Civil War in Siberia*, p. 359.

38. Christopher Lazarski, "White Propaganda Efforts in the South during the Russian Civil War, 1918–1919 (the Alekseev–Denikin Period)," *Slavonic and East European Review*, vol. 70, no. 4 (1992), pp. 688–707.

39. Peter Kenez, *Civil War in South Russia, 1919–20: The Defeat of the Whites*, Berkeley: University of California Press, 1977, pp. 225–26. What is certain is that Osvag's output was often laced with overt antisemitism, the *éminence grise* behind much of its work being the notorious right-wing Jew-baiter V.V. Shul'gin.

40. See: Nina Tumarkin, "The Myth of Lenin during the Civil War Years," in Gleason, Kenez, and Stites (eds), *Bolshevik Culture*, pp. 77–92; and Nina Tumarkin, *Lenin Lives! The Lenin Cult in Soviet Russia*, Cambridge, MA: Harvard University Press, 1997, pp. 64–111.

41. The French historian André Fontaine contends that the first use of the term *cordon sanitaire* in its diplomatic sense, to mean containment of a dangerous ideological strain, was by the French Prime Minister George Clemenceau in a speech relating to the Allies' policy towards Russia in March 1919. Fontaine regards this as marking the real commencement of the Cold War. See: André Fontaine, *Histoire de la Guerre froide, Vol. 1: De la révolution d'octobre à la guerre de Corée*, Paris: Fayard, 1965.

42. On the post-war revolutionary potentialities in Central and Southern Europe, see: Charles L. Bertrand (ed.), *Revolutionary Situations in Europe, 1917–1922: Germany, Italy, Austria–Hungary*, Montreal: Concordia University and the University of Quebec, 1977; Victor Fay (ed.), *La Révolution d'octobre et le mouvement ouvrier européen*, Paris: Études et Documentation Internationales, 1967; and Albert S. Lindemann, *The "Red Years": European Socialism versus Communism, 1919–1921*, Berkeley: University of California Press, 1974.

43. David Carlton, *Churchill and the Soviet Union*, Manchester: Manchester University Press, 2000, p. 20. For a compendium of Churchill's most unhinged comments on the Soviet government, see Clive Ponting, *Churchill*, London: Sinclair-Stevenson, 1994, pp. 229–30.

44. Norman Davies, *White Eagle, Red Star: The Soviet–Polish War, 1919–20*, London: Orbis Books, 1983, pp. 84–5. On the role of the Allied missions, particularly that of General Maxime Weygand, see: P. S. Wandycz, "General Weygand and the Battle of Warsaw of 1920," *Journal of Central European Affairs*, vol. 19, no. 4 (1959), pp. 357–65, which treats Weygand's input as negligible; and F. Russell Bryant, "Lord D'Abernon, the Anglo-French Mission, and the Battle of Warsaw, 1920," *Jahrbücher für Geschichte Osteuropas*, vol. 38 (1990), pp. 526–47, which, on the basis of documents unavailable to earlier authors, portrays the Allied mission's contribution as essential.

45. That said, huge amounts of Allied arms and uniforms that had been donated first to the imperial army and later to the Whites fell wholesale into Bolshevik hands, including dozens of aircraft and Renault FT-17 tanks abandoned by French forces in Odessa in April 1919. (Some of the latter were dismantled and carefully copied to boost Soviet production.) When the 5th Red Army entered Omsk in November 1919, it bagged 200 Colt machine-guns and 1,000 French *mitrailleuses*, all unassembled in storehouses: G.Kh. Eikhe, *Oprokinutyi tyl*, Moscow: Voenizdat, 1966, pp. 126–27. All these were then turned upon the Reds' enemies.

46. N.I. Bukharin, *Izbrannye proizvedeniia*, Moscow: Izdatel'stvo Politicheskoi Literatury, 1988, pp. 195–6.

47. Lars T. Lih, *Lenin*, London: Reaktion Books, 2011, p. 159.

48. Frunze died on 31 Oct. 1925, during an operation to treat stomach ulcers. As the party Central Committee (and, particularly, its general secretary, Stalin) had insisted that he should submit to treatment, despite the fact that his heart was too weak to permit him to be anaesthetized, speculation immediately arose that his death was a "medical murder"—not least because, in 1926, the author Boris Pil'niak somehow managed to publish a story, *Povest' nepogashennoi luny* ("The Tale of the Unextinguished Moon"), making precisely such an allegation in the leading literary journal of the day, *Novyi mir* ("New World"), although the issue was hurriedly withdrawn. Also, all four surgeons who had operated on Frunze died suddenly in 1934. Tukhachevskii was executed alongside seven other senior Red generals, among them the prominent civil-war commanders: R.P. Eideman (commander of the 13th Red Army, 5 June–10 July 1920); I.E. Iakir; A.I. Kork (commander of both the 15th Red Army, 31 July–15 Oct. 1919 and 22 Oct. 1919–16 Oct. 1920 and the 6th Red Army, 26 Oct. 1920–13 May 1921); V.M. Primakov; and I.P. Uborovich (commander of the 14th Red Army, 6 Oct. 1919–24 Feb. 1920, 17 Apr.–7 July 1920 and 15 Nov.–15 Dec. 1920, the 13th Red Army, 10 July–11 Nov. 1920, and the 5th Red Army, 27 Aug. 1921–14 Aug. 1922). The tribunal that condemned them was chaired by V.V. Ulrikh and included among its members P.E. Dybenko (commander of the Crimean Soviet Army, May–July 1919); S.M. Budennyi (commander of the 1st Cavalry Army, 17 Nov. 1919–Oct. 1923); I.P. Belov (commander of the Turkestan Red Army (8 Apr.–18 Oct. 1919); and V.K. Bliukher (commander of the People's-Revolutionary Army of the Far Eastern Republic, 26 June 1921–14 July 1922). This could, then, be regarded as the culmination of a civil war within the Red Army.

49. N. Bukharin and E. Preobrazhensky, *The ABC of Communism*, Harmondsworth: Penguin, 1969, pp. 267–68.

50. On the El'tsin era in this regard, see Kathleen E. Smith, *Mythmaking in the New Russia: Politics and Memory during the Yeltsin Era*, Ithaca: Cornell University Press, 2002.

51. That generational change might yet provide a solution to the conundrum of "What is to be Done?" with Lenin's remains was recently signaled when the Levada Center, an independent Russian polling organization, found that only 25 percent of those citizens asked believed that Lenin should remain in his mausoleum—the lowest such response since the organization first began posing questions about preferences regarding the fate of the corpse in 1997. The most popular response was that Lenin should be buried alongside his mother, while 19 percent wanted to see him buried in the Kremlin Wall Mausoleum. See "Lenin's Embalmed Corpse Edges Nearer the Exit of his Red Square Mausoleum," *The Guardian* (16 Jan. 2013), http://www.guardian.co.uk/world/2013/jan/16/lenin-body-poll-moving-mausoleum. However, just four days earlier, on a trip to the United States, President Vladimir Putin stated unequivocally that Lenin's remains should stay put: "Lenin's Tomb Should Stay in Red

Square, Putin Says," *The Washington Post* (12 Jan. 2013): http://articles.washingtonpost.com/2013–01–12/world/36312433_1_tomb-soviet-symbolism-levada-center. The caretakers of Lenin's corpse might be sorry to let it go, but could console themselves with the income they have received for private embalming since forming a private company, "Ritual Service," in 1994—just in time to cash in on the booming market in dead Russian gangsters, whose families desired their often gaudy preservation: Ilya Zbarsky and Samuel Hutchinson, *Lenin's Embalmers*, London: The Harvill Press, 1998, pp. 191–207. On the issue, see also: Graham Gill, "'Lenin Lives': Or Does He? Symbols and the Transition from Socialism," *Europe–Asia Studies*, vol. 60, no. 3 (2008), pp. 173–96; and Petra Rethmann, "The Discreet Charm of Lenin," *Journal of Historical Sociology*, vol. 26, no. 4 (2013), pp. 576–94.

BIBLIOGRAPHY

Reference works

Acton, Edward, Vladimir Iu. Cherniaev, and William G. Rosenberg (eds), *Critical Companion to the Russian Revolution, 1914–1921*, Bloomington: Indiana University Press, 1997.

Bol'shaia sovetskaia entsiklopediia, 1st edn, Moscow: Sovetskaia Entsiklopediia, 1929–47. Available online (in Russian) at: http://gatchina3000.ru/great-soviet-encyclopedia/

Deiateli SSSR i revoliutsionnogo dvizheniia Rossii. Entsiklopedicheskii slovar' Granat, Moscow: Sovetskaia Entsiklopediia, 1989.

Gorkin, A.P. *et al.* (eds), *Voennyi entsiklopedicheskii slovar'*, Moscow: Ripol Klassik, 2002.

Grazhdanskaia voina i voennaia interventsiia v SSSR: entsiklopediia, Moscow: Sovetskaia Entsiklopediia, 1987.

Istoriia Kommunisticheskoi partii Sovetskogo soiuza: atlas, Moscow: Institut Marksizma-leninizma pri TsK KPSS, 1977.

Jackson, George and Robert Devlin, *Dictionary of the Russian Revolution*, London: Greenwood Press, 1989.

Jones, David R., *The Military-Naval Encyclopedia of Russia and the Soviet Union*, Gulf Breeze: Academic International Press, 1978– (continued as *The Military Encyclopedia of Russia and Eurasia*, from 2011 edited by William Reger).

Kasatonov, I.V. (ed.), *Morskoi biograficheskii slovar'*, St Petersburg: Logos, 1995.

Kipel, Vitaut and Zora Kipel (eds), *Byelorussian Statehood*, New York: Byelorussian Institute of Arts and Science, 1988.

Kvakin, A.V. (ed.), *S Kolchakom—protiv Kolchaka*, Moscow: Agraf, 2007.

Minahan, James, *The Former Soviet Union's Diverse Peoples: A Reference Sourcebook*, Santa Barbara, CA: ABC-CLIO, 2004.

Mowbray, Stephen A. de, *Key Facts in Soviet History, Vol. 1: 1917–1941*, London: Pinter, 1990.

Nezabytye mogily: Rossiiskoe zarubezh'e. Nekrologi, 1917–1997, 6 vols, Moscow: RGB, 1999–2006.

Politicheskie partii Rossii: konets XIX—pervaia tret' XX veka. Entsiklopediia, Moscow: ROSSPEN, 1996.

Protasov, L.G. (ed.), *Liudi Uchreditel'nogo sobraniia: portret v inter'ere epokhi*, Moscow: ROSSPEN, 2008.

Radkey, Oliver, *Russia Goes to the Polls: The Election to the All-Russian Constituent Assembly, 1917*, Ithaca: Cornell University Press, 1989.

Revoliutsiia i grazhdanskaia voina v Rossii, 1917–1923: Entsiklopediia, 4 vols, Moscow: Terra, 2008.

Russkaia voennaia emigratsiia 20-kh–40-kh godov: dokumenty i materialy, 5 vols, Moscow: Geia/Triada-Kh/RGGU, 1998–2010.

Russkoe zarubezh'e: Zolotaia kniga emigratsii. Pervaia tret' XX veka. Entsiklopedicheskii biograficheskii slovar', Moscow: ROSSPEN, 1997.

Shmaglit, R.G., *Beloe dvizhenie. 900 biografii krupneishikh predstavitelei russkogo voennogo zarubezhia*, Moscow: Zebra, 2006.

Shukman, Harold (ed.), *The Blackwell Encyclopedia of the Russian Revolution*, Oxford: Blackwell, 1988.

Smele, Jonathan D. (ed.), *Historical Dictionary of the "Russian" Civil Wars, 1916–1926*, 2 vols, Lanham: Rowman & Littlefield, 2015.

Velikaia Oktiabr'skaia Sotsialisticheskaia Revoliutsiia: entsiklopediia, Moscow: Sovetskaia Entsiklopediia, 1987.

Voennaia entsiklopediia, Moscow: Voennoe Izdatel'stvo, 1997–.

Volkov, E.V., N.D. Egorov, and I.V. Kuptsov, *Belye generaly Vostochnogo fronta Grazhdanskoi voiny: biograficheskii spravochnik*, Moscow: Russkii Put', 2003.

Volodikhin, D.M., and S.V. Volkov (eds), *Grazhdanskaia voina v Rossii. Entsiklopediia katastrofy*, Moscow: Sibirskii tsiriul'nik, 2010.

Wieczynski, Joseph L. *et al.* (eds), *The Modern Encyclopedia of Russian and Soviet History*, 59 vols + supplements, Gulf Breeze: Academic International Press, 1976–96 (volumes from 1993 entitled *The Modern Encyclopedia of Russian, Soviet and Eurasian History*).

Zaleskii, K.A., *Imperiia Stalina. Biograficheskii entsiklopedicheskii slovar'*, Moscow: Veche, 2000.

Bibliographies

Arans, David (ed.), *How We Lost the Civil War: Bibliography of Russian Émigré Memoirs of the Russian Revolution, 1917–1921*, Newtonville, MA: Oriental Research Partners, 1988.

Ganin, A.V., *Korpus ofitserov General'nogo shtaba v gody Grazhdanskoi voiny, 1917–1922: spravochnye materialy*, Moscow: Russkii Put', 2009.

Grierson, Philip, *Books on Soviet Russia, 1917–1942: A Bibliography and Guide to Reading*, London: Methuen, 1943.

Mehnert, Klaus, *Die Sovet-Union 1917–32. Systematische, mit Kommentaren versehne Bibliographie*, Königsberg: Ost-Europa-Verl., 1933.

Smele, Jonathan D. (ed.), *The Russian Revolution and Civil War, 1917–1921: An Annotated Bibliography*, New York: Continuum, 2003.

Tartakovskii, A.G., Terence Emmons, and O.V. Budnitskii (eds), *Rossiia i rossiiskaia emigratsiia v vospominaniiakh i dnevnikakh: annotirovannyi ukazatel' knig, zhurnal'nykh i gazetnykh publikatsii, izdannykh za rubezhom v 1917–1991 gg.*, 4 vols, Moscow: ROSSPEN, 2003–6.

Victoroff-Toproff, V.V., *Russica et Sovietica. Bibliographie des ouvrages parus en français de 1917 à 1930 inclus relatifs à la Russie et à l'U.R.S.S.*, Saint-Cloud: Éditions Documentaires et Bibliographiques, 1931.

Historiographical Works

Abramson, Henry, "Historiography on the Jews and the Ukrainian Revolution," *Journal of Ukrainian Studies*, vol. 15, no. 2 (1990), pp. 33–46.

BIBLIOGRAPHY

Azovtsev, N.N. and V.P. Naumov, "Study of the History of the Military Intervention and Civil War in the USSR," *Soviet Studies in History*, vol. 10, no. 4 (1971–72), pp. 327–60.

Bojcun, Marko, "Approaches to the Study of the Ukrainian Revolution," *Journal of Ukrainian Studies*, vol. 24, no. 1 (1999), pp. 21–38.

Bordiugov, G.A., A.I. Ushakov, and V. Iu. Churakov, *Beloe delo: ideologiia osnovy rezhimy vlasti*, Moscow: Russkii Mir, 1998.

Budnitskii, Oleg, "Jews, Pogroms and the White Movement: A Historiographical Critique," *Kritika*, vol. 2, no. 4 (2001), pp. 751–72.

Cipko, Serge, "Nestor Makhno: A Mini-Historiography of the Anarchist Revolution in Ukraine, 1917–1921," *The Raven*, vol. 4, no. 1 (13) (1991), pp. 57–75.

Davies, R.W., "Lenin, the Civil War and After," in R.W. Davies, *Soviet History in the Gorbachev Revolution*, London: Macmillan, 1989, pp. 115–26.

Fitzpatrick, Sheila, "New Perspectives on the Civil War," in Diane Koenker, William G. Rosenberg, and Ronald G. Suny (eds), *Party, State and Society in the Russian Civil War: Explorations in Social History*, Bloomington: Indiana University Press, 1990, pp. 3–23.

Goldin, V.N., *Rossiia v grazhdanskoi voine: Ocherki noveishei istoriografii (vtoraia polivina 1980-x—nachalo 90-x gg)*, Arkhangel'sk: Borges, 2000.

Greenbaum, Abraham, "Bibliographical Essay," in John D. Klier and Shlomo Lambroza (eds), *Pogroms: Anti-Jewish Violence in Modern Russian History*, Cambridge: Cambridge University Press, 1992.

Keep, John, "Social Aspects of the Russian Revolutionary Era (1917–1923) in Recent English-Language Historiography," *East European Quarterly*, vol. 24, no. 2 (1990), pp. 159–84.

Kenez, Peter, "Western Historiography of the Russian Civil War," in Leo Schelbert and Nick Ceh (eds), *Essays in Russian and East European History: Festschrift in Honor of Edward C. Thaden*, Boulder: East European Monographs, 1995, pp. 197–215.

Longley, David, "Iakovlev's Question, Or the Historiography of the Problem of Spontaneity and Leadership in the Russian Revolution of 1917," in Edith Rogovin Frankel, Jonathan Frankel, and Baruch Knei-Paz (eds), *Revolution in Russia: Reassessments of 1917*, Cambridge: Cambridge University Press, 1992, pp. 365–87.

Munck, Jorgen L., *The Kornilov Revolt: A Critical Examination of the Sources*, Aarhus: Aarhus University Press, 1987.

Pipes, Richard, "1917 and the Revisionists," *The National Interest*, no. 31 (Spring 1993), pp. 68–79.

Shankowsky, Lew, "Ukraine-Hating as a Synthesis," *Ukrainian Quarterly*, vol. 43, nos 1–2 (1987), pp. 64–99.

Smele, Jonathan D., "Russia: Civil War, 1917–1920," in Charles Messenger (ed.), *Reader's Guide to Military History*, London: Fitzroy Dearborn, 2001, pp. 510–15.

Smith, Steve, "Writing the History of the Russian Revolution after the Fall of Communism," *Europe–Asia Studies*, vol. 46, no. 4 (1994), pp. 563–78.

Suny, Ronald G., "Revision and Retreat in the Historiography of 1917: Social History and its Critics," *Russian Review*, vol. 53, no. 2 (1994), pp. 165–82.

——— "Toward a Social History of the October Revolution," *American Historical Review*, vol. 88, no. 1 (1983), pp. 31–52.

Ushakov, A.I., *Istoriia grazhdanskoi voiny v literature russkogo zarubezh'ia: opyt izucheniia*, Moscow: Rossiia Molodaia, 1993.

Wade, Rex A., "The Revolution at Ninety-(One): Anglo-American Historiography of the

BIBLIOGRAPHY

Russian Revolution of 1917," *Journal of Modern Russian History and Historiography*, vol. 1 (2008), pp. 1–42.

White, James D., "Early Soviet Historical Interpretations of the Russian Revolution, 1918–24," *Soviet Studies*, vol. 37, no. 3 (1985), pp. 330–52.

Wood, Alan, "The Bolsheviks, the Baby and the Bathwater," *European History Quarterly*, vol. 22, no. 4 (1992), pp. 483–94.

Published Documents

Ascher, Abraham (ed.), *The Mensheviks in the Russian Revolution*, London: Thames and Hudson, 1976.

Avrich, Paul (ed.), *The Anarchists in the Russian Revolution*, London: Thames and Hudson, 1973.

Batinsky, J. *et al.* (eds), *The Jewish Pogroms in Ukraine: Authoritative Statements on the Question of Responsibility for Recent Outbreaks against Jews in Ukraine*, Washington, DC: The Friends of Ukraine, 1919.

Baynac, Jacques, Alexandre Skirda, and Charles Urjewicz (eds), *Le Terreur sous Lénine (1917–1924)*, Paris: Le Sagittaire, 1975.

Bernshtam, M.S. (ed.), *Narodnoe soprotivlenie v Rossii. Ural i Prikam'e, noiabr' 1917—ianvar' 1919: dokumenty i materialy*, Paris: YMCA, 1982.

Berzniakov, N.V. *et al.* (eds), *Khotinskoe vosstanie: dokumenty i materialy*, Kishinev: Shtiintsa, 1976.

The Bolsheviks and the October Revolution: Central Committee Minutes of the Russian Social-Democratic Labour Party (bolsheviks), August 1917—February 1918, London: Pluto Press, 1974.

Browder, Robert P. and Alexander F. Kerensky (eds), *The Russian Provisional Government, 1917: Documents*, 3 vols, Stanford: Stanford University Press, 1961.

Bukharin, N.I., *Izbrannye proizvedeniia*, Moscow: Izdatel'stvo Politicheskoi Literatury, 1988.

Bukharin, N. and E. Preobrazhensky, *The ABC of Communism*, Harmondsworth: Penguin, 1969.

The Bullitt Mission to Russia: Testimony before the Committee on Foreign Relations, United States Senate, New York: W.B. Heubsch, 1919.

Bunyan, James (ed.), *Intervention, Civil War and Communism in Russia, April–December 1918: Documents and Materials*, Baltimore: The Johns Hopkins University Press, 1936.

——— *The Origin of Forced Labor in the Soviet State, 1917–1921: Documents and Materials*, Baltimore: The Johns Hopkins University Press, 1967.

Bunyan, James and H.H. Fisher (eds), *The Bolshevik Revolution, 1917–1918: Documents and Materials*, Stanford: Stanford University Press, 1934.

Butt, V.P. *et al.* (eds), *The Russian Civil War: Documents from the Soviet Archives*, London: Macmillan, 1996.

The Case of Leon Trotsky, London: Pathfinder, 2006.

Collins, David N. and Jonathan D. Smele (eds), *Kolchak i Sibir': dokumenty i issledovaniia, 1919–1926*, 2 vols, White Plains, NY: Kraus International, 1988.

Comité Commémoratif Simon Petlura, *Documents sur les pogroms en Ukraine en 1919 et l'assassinat de Simon Petlura à Paris (1917–1921–1926)*, Paris: Librairie du Trident, 1927.

Daines, V.O. and T.F. Kariaeva (eds), *Revvoensovet respubliki: Protokoly, 1918–1919: Sbornik dokumentov*, Moscow: Informatsionno-izdatel'skoe Agentstvo "Russkii Mir," 1997.

BIBLIOGRAPHY

Daly, Jonathan and Leonid Trofimov (eds), *Russia in War and Revolution, 1914–1922: A Documentary History*, Indianapolis: Hackett, 2009.

Danilov, V.P. *et al.* (eds), *Nestor Makhno: krest'ianskoe dvizhenie na Ukraine, 1918–1921: dokumenty i materialy*, Moscow: ROSSPEN, 2006.

Danilov, V.P. and Teodor Shanin (eds), *Krest'ianskoe vosstanie v Tambovskoi gubernii v 1919–1921 gg., "Antonovshchina": dokumenty i materialy*, Tambov: "Redaktsionno-izdatel'skii Otdel," 1994.

———— *Krest'ianskoe dvizhenie v Povolzh'e, 1919–1922: Dokumenty i materialy*, Moscow: ROSSPEN, 2002.

Degras, Jane (ed.), *Soviet Documents on Foreign Policy: Vol. 1, 1917–1924*, London: Oxford University Press, 1951.

Dekrety Sovetskoi vlasti, 17 vols, Moscow: Gosizdat, 1957–2009.

Direktivy Glavnogo kommandovaniia Krasnoi armii (1917–1920): sbornik dokumentov, 3 vols, Moscow: Voenizdat, 1969.

Direktivy komandovaniia frontov Krasnoi armii (1917–1922 gg.): Sbornik dokumentov, Moscow: Voenizdat, 1971–8.

Dodonov, B.F. (ed.), *Zhurnaly zasedanii, prikazy i materialy Komiteta chlenov Vserossiiskogo Uchreditel'nogo sobraniia (Iiun'Oktiabr' 1918 goda)*, Moscow: ROSSPEN, 2011.

Dokumenty vneshnei politiki SSSR, 23 vols, Moscow: Gosizdat, 1957.

"Dzhizakskoe vosstanie v 1916 g.," *Krasnyi Arkhiv*, vol. 5 (1933), pp. 60–91.

Ermolin, E.A. and V.N. Kozliakov (eds), *Iaroslavskoe vosstanie, 1918*, Moscow: Mezhdunarodnoe Fond "Demokratiia," 2007.

"Extraordinary Meeting of Delegates of Factories and Plants in the City of Petrograd," *Kontinent*, vol. 2 (1977), pp. 212–41.

Fel'shtinskii, Iu.G. (ed.), *Krasnyi terror v gody Grazhdanskoi voiny, po materialy Osoboi komissii po rassledovaniiu zlodeianii bol'shevikov*, London: Overseas Publications Interchange, 1992.

Goldin, V.I. (ed.), *Belyi sever, 1918–1920 gg.: memuary i dokumenty*, 2 vols, Arkhangel'sk: Pravda Severa, 1993.

Gorky, Maxim, *Untimely Thoughts: Essays on Revolution, Culture and the Bolsheviks, 1917–1918*, London: Garnstone Press, 1968.

Haifetz, Elisas, *The Slaughter of the Jews in Ukraine*, New York: Thomas Seltzer, 1921.

Ivantsova, O.K. (ed.), *Sledstvennoe delo bol'shevikov: Materialy Predvaritel'nogo sledstviia o vooru-zhenom vystuplenii 3–5 iiulia 1917 g. v g. Petrograde protiv gosudarstvennoe vlasti. Iiul'–oktiabr 1917g. Sbornik dokumentov v 2 knigakh*, Moscow: ROSSPEN, 2012.

Iziumov, A.F. (ed.), "Ufimskoe gosudarstvennoe soveshchanie," *Russkii istoricheskii arkhiv*, no. 1 (1929).

Izvestia de Kronstadt. Mars 1921, Paris: Editions Anda Jaleo, 1987.

Jones, David R., "Documents on British Relations with Russia, 1917–1918," *Canadian-American Slavonic Studies*, vol. 7 (1973), no. 2, pp. 219–37; no. 3, pp. 350–75; no. 4, pp. 498–510; vol. 8 (1974), no. 4, pp. 544–62; vol. 9 (1975), no. 3, pp. 361–70; vol. 13 (1979), no. 3, pp. 310–31.

[N.S. Kalashnikov], "Itogi vesennogo nastuplenie," *Sibirskii arkhiv*, vol. 2 (1929), pp. 81–7.

Kerensky, A.F., *The Prelude to Bolshevism: The Kornilov Rebellion*, London: T. Fisher Unwin, 1919.

Khvalin, A.Iu., *Vosstanovlenie monarkhii v Rossii: Priamurskii Zemskii sobor 1922 goda (materi-aly i dokumenty)*, Moscow: Pravoslavnoe Bratstvo, 1993.

BIBLIOGRAPHY

Klaving, A.V. (ed.), *Okrest Kolchaka: dokumenty i materialy*, Moscow: AGRAF, 2007.

Kowalski, Ronald I., *The Russian Revolution, 1917–1921*, London: Routledge, 1997.

Kozlov, V.P. *et al.* (eds), *Kronshtadtskaia tragediia 1921 goda: dokumenty v dvukh knigakh*, Moscow: ROSSPEN, 1999.

Kvakin, A.V. (ed.), *V zhernovakh revoliutsii. Russkaia intelligentsia mezhdu belymi v krasnymi v porevoliutsionnye gody: sbornik dokumentov i materialov*, Moscow: "Russkaia Panorama," 2008.

Lenin, V.I., *Collected Works*, 4th edn, Moscow: Progress Publishers, 1960–78.

Litvin, A.L., *Men'shevistskii protsess 1931 goda. Sbornik dokumentov*, 2 vols, Moscow: ROSSPEN, 1999.

Lukov, E.V. and D.N. Shevelev (eds), *Zakonodatel'naia deiatel'nost Rossiiskogo pravitel'stva admirala A.V. Kolchaka: noiabr' 1918 g.—ianvar' 1920 g.*, 2 vols, Tomsk: Izd-vo Tomskogo Universiteta, 2002–3.

Lyandres, Semion, *The Fall of Tsarism: Untold Stories of the February 1917 Revolution*, Oxford: Oxford University Press, 2013.

McCauley, Martin (ed.), *The Russian Revolution and the Soviet State, 1917–1921: Documents*, London: Macmillan, 1975.

Maksakov, V.V. (ed.), "Vremennoe pravitel'stvo avtomnoi Sibiri," *Krasnyi arkhiv* (1928), no. 4, pp. 86–138; (1929), no. 4, pp. 37–106; (1929), no. 5, pp. 31–60.

Meijer, Jan M. (ed.), *The Trotsky Papers, 1917–1922*, 2 vols, The Hague: Mouton, 1964–71.

Mikhaleva, V.M. *et al.* (eds), *Revvoensovet Respubliki: protokoly 1920–1923. Sbornik dokumentov*, Moscow: Editorial, 2000.

Miliakova, L.B. *et al.* (eds), *Kniga pogromov: pogromy na Ukraine, v Belorossii i evropeiskoi chasti Rossii v periode grazhdanskoi voiny, 1918–1922 gg. Sbornik dokumentov*, Moscow: ROSSPEN, 2007.

Mutnick, Barbara (ed.), *Kronstadt, by V.I. Lenin and Leon Trotsky*, London: Monad Press, 1979.

Naumov, V.P. and A.A. Koskovskii (eds), *Kronshtadt, 1921: dokumenty o sobytiakh v Kronshtadte vesnoi 1921 g.*, Moscow: Mezhdunarodnyi Fond "Demokratiia," 1997.

Pavlov, D.B. (ed.), *Rabochee oppozitsionnoe dvizhenie v bol'shevistskoi Rossii, 1918 g. Sobraniia upolnomochennykh fabrik i zavodov. Dokumenty i materialy*, Moscow: ROSSPEN, 2006.

Partizanskoe dvizhenie v Sibiri. Tom 1: Prieniseiskii krai, Moscow: Gosizdat, 1925.

Pearce, Brian (ed.), *Baku, September 1920: Congress of the Peoples of the East: Stenographic Record*, London: New Park Publications, 1977.

Piontkovskii, S. (ed.), *Grazhdanskaia voina v Rossii (1918–1921 gg.): khrestomatiia*, Moscow: Kommunisticheskii Universitet, 1925.

Preobrazhenskii, E.A., *Bumazhnye den'gi v epokhu proletarskoi diktatury*, Moscow: Gosizdat, 1920.

Pavlovskii, P.I. (ed.), *Annenkovshchina (po materialam sudebnogo protsessa v Semipalatinsk 25. vii.1927—12.viii.1927)*, Moscow: Gosizdat, 1928.

Pipes, Richard (ed.), *The Unknown Lenin: From the Secret Archive*, New Haven: Yale University Press, 1996.

Popovich, Miroslav and Viktor Mironenko (eds), *Glavnyi ataman: v plenu nesbytochnykh nadezhd. Simon Petliura*, Moscow: Letnii Sad, 2008.

Pravda o Kronshtadte, Prague: Volia Rossii, 1921.

Protasov, L.G. (ed.), *Antonovshchina: krest'ianskoe vosstanie v Tambovskoi gubernii: dokumenty*, Tambov: Upravlenie Kul'tury i Arkhivnogo dela Tambovskoi Oblasti, 2007.

Sadykov, A.R. and A. Bermakhanov (eds), *Groznyi 1916-i god: Sbornik dokumentov i materialov,* 2 vols, Almaty: Qazaqstan, 1998.

Schechtman, J.B., E. Tcherikower, and N. Tsatskis, *Les Pogroms en Ukraine sous des gouvernements ukrainiens (1917–1919). Aperçu historique et documents,* Paris: Comité des Délégations Juives, 1927.

Shelokhaev, V.V. *et al.* (eds), *Partiia Levykh sotsialistov-revolutsionerov: dokumenty i materialy, 1917–1925,* 3 vols, Moscow: ROSSPEN: 2000–.

Shishkin, V.I. (ed.), *Protsess nad kolchakovskimi ministrami: mai 1920,* Moscow: Mezhdunarodnyi Fond "Demokratiia," 2003.

———— *Sibirskaia Vandeia,* 2 vols, Moscow: Mezhdunarodnyi Fond "Demokratiia," 2000–1.

———— *Vremennoe sibirskoe pravitel'stvo, 26 maia—3 noiabria 1918 g.: sbornik dokumentov i materialy,* Novosibirsk: Sova, 2007.

———— *Za sovety bez kommunistov: Krest'ianskoe vosstanie v Tiumenskoi gubernii 1921 g.,* Novosibirsk: Sibirskii Khronograf, 2000.

Shumeiko, G.V. (ed.), *Boevoe sotruzhestvo trudiashchiiksia zarubeznykh stran s narodami Sovetskoi Rossii (1917–1922),* Moscow: Sovetskaia Rossiia, 1957.

Skirda, Alexandre (ed.), *Kronstadt 1921. Prolétariat contre bolchévisme,* Paris: Editions de la Tête de Feuilles, 1972.

Sultanbekov, B.F. and D.R. Sharafutdinov (eds), *Neizvestnyi Sultan-Galiev: rassekrechennye dokumenty i materialy,* Kazan': Tatarskoe Knizhnoe Izdatel'stvo, 2002.

Szczesniak, Boleslaw (ed.), *The Russian Revolution and Religion: A Collection of Documents Concerning the Suppression of Religion by the Communists, 1917–1925,* Notre Dame: University of Notre Dame Press, 1959.

Texts of the Ukrainian Peace, Cleveland: John T. Zubal Publishers, 1981.

Trotskii, L.D., *How the Revolution Armed,* 5 vols, London: New Park Publications, 1979–81.

———— *Military Writings,* London: Pathfinder Press, 1971.

———— *Sochinenii,* 2 vols, Moscow: Gosizdat, 1925–27.

———— *Terrorism and Communism,* London: New Park Publications, 1975.

Tukhachevskii, M.N., *Budushchaia voina,* Moscow: Klub realisty, 1928.

United States, Department of State, *Documents Relating to the Foreign Policy of the United States: 1919 (Peace Conference Papers),* 6 vols, Washington, DC: Government Printing Office, 1939–40.

Valentinov, A.A., "Krymskaia epopeia (po dnevnikam uchastnikiv i po dokumentam)," *Arkhiv russkoi revoliutsii,* vol. 5 (1922), pp. 5–100.

Varneck, Edna and H.H. Fisher (eds), *The Testimony of Kolchak and Other Siberian Materials,* Stanford: Stanford University Press, 1935.

Volobuev, O.V. (ed.), *Takticheskii tsentr: dokumenty i materialy,* Moscow: ROSSPEN, 2012.

Volobuev, O.V. *et al.* (eds), *Partiia sotsialistov-revolutsionerov: dokumenty i materialy,* Moscow: ROSSPEN, 1996–2000.

Voronovich, N. (ed.), *Sbornik dokumentov i materialov. Zelenaia kniga: Istoriia krest'ianskogo dvizheniia v Chernomorskoi guberniia,* Prague: Izd. Chernomorskoi Krest'ianskoi Delegatsii, 1921.

"Vosstanie v 1916 g. v Srednei Azii," *Krasnyi arkhiv,* vol. 3 (1929), pp. 39–94.

Wade, Rex A. (ed.), *Documents of Soviet History,* vols 1–3, Gulf Breeze: Academic International Press, 1991–95.

Zhuravlev, V.V. (ed.), *Privetstvennye poslaniia Verkhovnomu Praviteliu i Verkhovnomu*

BIBLIOGRAPHY

Glavnokomanduiushchemu admiralu A.V. Kolchaku. Noiabr' 1918—noiabr' 1919 g.: sb. doku-mentov, St Petersburg: Izdatel'stvo Evropeiskogo Universiteta v Sankt-Peterburge, 2012.

Zhurnaly zasedanii Osobogo soveshchaniia pri Glavnokomanduiushchem Vooruzhennymi Silami na Iuge Rossii A.I. Denikine. Sentiabr 1918-go—dekiabr 1919 goda, Moscow: ROSSPEN, 2008.

Zolotarev, V.A. *et al.* (eds), *Russkaia voennaia emigratsiia 20-kh—40-kh godov: dokumenty i materialy,* Moscow: Geia, 1998.

Memoirs, Diaries and other First-hand Accounts

Agar, Augustus, *Baltic Episode: A Classic of Secret Service in Russian Waters,* London: Hodder & Stoughton, 1963.

Alioshi, Dmitri, *Asian Odyssey,* London: Cassell & Co., 1941.

Andrushkevich, N.A., "Poslednaia Rossiia," *Beloe delo,* no. 4 (1928), pp. 108–46.

Ansky, S., *The Enemy at His Pleasure: A Journey Through the Jewish Pale of Settlement during World War I,* New York: Metropolitan Books, 2002.

Astrov, N.I., "Priznanie gen. Denikinym adm. Kolchaka: prikaz 30 maia 1919g.—No. 145," *Golos minuvshago na chuzhoi storone,* vol. 14, no. 1 (1926), pp. 210–21.

Aten, Marion and Arthur Orrmont, *The Last Train over Rostov Bridge,* New York: Julian Messner, 1961.

Babel, Isaac, *Diary 1920,* New Haven: Yale University Press, 1995.

Baikov, A., "Vospominaniia o revoliutsii v Zakavkazii," *Arkhiv russkoi revoliutsii,* vol. 9 (1923), pp. 91–194.

Bailey, Lt-Colonel F.M., *Mission to Tashkent,* London: Jonathan Cape, 1946.

Balabanoff, Angelica, *My Life as a Rebel,* London: Hamish Hamilton, 1938.

Balmasov, S.S. *et al.* (eds), *Kappel' i kappel'evtsy,* Moscow: Posev, 2003.

Bechhofer, Carl E., *In Denikin's Russia and the Caucasus, 1919–1920,* London: Collins, 1921.

Becvar, Gustav, *The Lost Legion: A Czechoslovak Epic,* London: Stanley Paul & Co., 1939.

Berkman, Alexander, *The Bolshevik Myth (Diary, 1920–1922),* London: Hutchinson and Co., 1925.

——— "The Kronstadt Rebellion," in Alexander Berkman, *The Russian Tragedy,* London: Phoenix Press, 1986, pp. 61–91.

Bermondt-Avalov, Pavel, *Im Kampf gegen den Bolschewismus. Erinnerungen von General Fürst Awaloff, Oberbefehlshaber der Deutsch-Russischen Westarmee im Baltikum,* Glückstadt/Hamburg: Verlag J.J. Augustin, 1925.

Bonch-Bruevich, M.D., *From Tsarist General to Red Army Commander,* Moscow: Progress Publishers, 1966.

Brown, William A., *The Groping Giant: Revolutionary Russia as Seen by an American Democrat,* New Haven: Yale University Press, 1920.

Budberg, A.P. von, "Dnevnik," *Arkhiv russkoi revoliutsii,* vol. 12 (1923), pp. 197–290; vol. 13 (1924), pp. 197–312; vol. 14 (1924), pp. 225–341; vol. 15 (1924), pp. 254–345.

[Merian C. Cooper], *Faunt-le-Roy i jego eskradra w Polsce: dzieje eskradry Kościuszki: napisał zastepca dowódcy eskadry,* Chicago: Faunt-le-Roy, Harrison & Co., 1932.

Denikin, A.I., *Kto spas' Sovetskuiu vlast' ot gibeli?* Paris: Maison de la Presse, 1937.

——— *Ocherki russkoi smuty,* 5 vols, Paris/Berlin: Povolzky, 1921–26.

Drozdovskii, M.G., *Dnevnik,* Berlin: Knigoizdateltvo Otto Kirchner, 1923.

Dunsterville, Major-General Lionel Charles, *The Adventures of Dunsterforce*, London: Edward Arnold, 1920.

Elovskii, I., *Golodnyi pokhod Orenburgskoi armii: iz vospominanii uchastnika pokhoda*, Peking: Tip. Uspenskago Monastyria pri Russkoi Dukhovnoi Missii, 1921.

Emmons, Terrence (ed.), *Time of Troubles: The Diary of Iurii Vladimirovich Got'e, Moscow, July 8th 1917 to July 23rd 1922*, London: I.B. Tauris, 1988.

Filat'ev, D.B., *Katastrofa belogo dvizheniia v Sibiri, 1918–1922gg. (Vpechatleniia ochevidsta)*, Paris: YMCA-Press, 1985.

Gagkuev, R.G. *et al.* (eds), *Drozdovskii i Drozdovtsy*, Moscow: Posev, 2006.

——— *Markov i Markovtsy*, Moscow: Posev, 2001.

Gins, G.K., *Sibir' soiuzniki i Kolchak: povorotnyi moment russkoi istorii, 1918–1920gg. (Vpechatleniia i mysli chlena Omskogo pravitel'stva)*, 2 vols, Peking: Izd. "Obshchestva Vozrozhdeniia Rossii v g. Kharbine," 1921.

Gol'denveizer, A.A., "Iz kievskikh vospominanii (1917–1921 gg.)," *Arkhiv russkoi revoliutsii*, vol. 6 (1922).

Goldman, Emma, *The Crushing of the Russian Revolution*, London: Freedom Press, 1922.

——— *My Disillusionment in Russia*, London: C.W. Daniel, 1925.

Gootnik, Abraham, *Oh Say, Can You See: Chaos and Dreams of Peace*, Lanham, MD: University Press of America, 1987.

Gorn, Vasilii, *Grazhdanskaia voina na Severozapade Rossii*, Berlin: Gamaiun, 1923.

Graves, William S., *America's Siberian Adventure, 1918–1920*, New York: Jonathan Cape and Harrison Smith, 1931.

Grondijs, L.H., *La Guerre en Russie et en Sibérie*, Paris: Éditions Bossard, 1922.

Hart-Davis, Rupert (ed.), *The Autobiography of Arthur Ransome*, London: Jonathan Cape, 1976.

Hill, George, *Go Spy the Land*, London: Cassell and Company, 1932.

Ilyin, Olga, *White Road: A Russian Odyssey, 1919–1923*, New York: Holt, 1984.

Hoover, Herbert, *The Memoirs of Herbert Hoover*, 2 vols, London: Macmillan, 1952.

Ilyin-Zhenevsky, A.F., *The Bolsheviks in Power: Reminiscences of the Year 1918*, London: New Park Publications, 1984.

Iskhod Russkii armii generala Vrangelia iz Kryma, Moscow: Tsentropoligraf, 2003.

Jones, H.A., *Over the Balkans and South Russia, Being the History of No. 47 Squadron, Royal Air Force*, London: Edward Arnold, 1923.

Karinskii, N.S., "Epizody iz evakuatsii Novorossiiska," *Arkhiv russkoi revoliutsii*, vol. 12 (1923), pp. 149–56.

Klerzhe, G.I., *Revoliutsiia i Grazhdanskaia voina: lichnye vospominaniia (chast' pervaia)*, Mukden: Tip. Gazety "Mukden," 1932.

Koenker, Diane and Steve Smith (eds), *Eduard M. Dune, Notes of a Red Guard*, Urbana: University of Illinois Press, 1993.

Krasnov, P.N., "Vsevelikoe Voisko Donskoe," *Arkhiv russkoi revoliutsii*, vol. 5 (1922), pp. 191–321.

Krol', L.A., *Za tri goda: Vospominaniia, vpechatleniia i vstrechi*, Vladivostok: Tip. T-va izd. "Svobodnaia Rossiia," 1921.

Kritskii, M.A., "Krasnaia armiia na iuzhnom fronte v 1918–1920 gg," *Arkhiv russkoi revoliutsii*, vol. 18 (1926), pp. 254–300.

Kukk, Hilja, "The Failure of Iudenich's North-Western Army in 1919: A Dissenting White Russian View," *Journal of Baltic Studies*, vol. 12, no. 4 (1981), pp. 362–83.

BIBLIOGRAPHY

Kvintadze, G.I., *Moi vospominanii v gody nezavisimosti Gruzii, 1917–1921*, Paris: YMCA-Press, 1985.

Lednoi pokhod (*Beloe delo*, vol. 2), Moscow: Golos, 1993.

Lockhart, Robert H. Bruce, *Memoirs of a British Agent*, London: Putnam, 1932.

Lukomskii, A.S., *Vospominaniia*, 2 vols, Berlin: Otto Kirkhner, 1922.

Lyandres, Semion and Dietmar Wulff, *A Chronicle of the Civil War in Siberia and Exile in China: The Diaries of Petr Vasil'evich Vologodskii, 1918–1925*, 2 vols, Stanford, CA: Hoover Institution Press, 2002.

MacDonell, Ranald *"...And Nothing Long"*, London: Edward Arnold, 1938.

Messner, E.E., *Kornilovtsy: 1917—10 iuniia 1967*, Paris: Izd. Ob"edineniia Chinov Kornilovskogo Udarnogo polka, 1967.

Maksimov, Grigorii Petrovich, *A Grand Cause: The Hunger Strike and the Deportation of Anarchists from Soviet Russia*, London: Kate Sharpley Library, 2008.

Malleson, Sir William, "The British Military Mission to Turkestan, 1918–1920," *Journal of the Royal Central Asian Society*, vol. 9, no. 2 (1922), pp. 96–110.

Miller, E.K., "Bor'ba za Rossiiu na Severe, 1918–1920 gg.," *Belo delo*, vol. 4 (1928), pp. 5–11.

Mstislavskii, Sergei, *Five Days which Transformed Russia*, London: Hutchinson, 1988.

Nazaroff, Paul, *Hunted through Central Asia*, Edinburgh: Blackwood, 1932.

Pachmuss, Temira (ed.), *Between Paris and St Petersburg: Selected Diaries of Zinaida Gippius*, Urbana: University of Illinois Press, 1975.

Paustovskii, K.G., *Povest o zhizni*, Moscow: Sovetskaia Rossiia, 1966.

Pellisier, Jean, *La tragédie ukrainienne*, Paris: Bibliothèque Ukrainienne Symon Petlura, 1988.

Pervye boi Dobrovol'cheskoi armii, Moscow: Tsentropoligraf, 2001.

Pervyi Kubanskii "Lednoi" Pokhod, Moscow: Tsentropoligraf, 2001.

Petrov, P.P., *Rokovye gody*, California, 1965.

Piłsudski, Józef, *Year 1920 and its Climax*, London: Pilsudski Institute of London, 1972.

Pipes, Richard, *VIXI: Memoirs of a Non-Believer*, New Haven: Yale University Press, 2003.

Popoff, George, *The City of the Red Plague: Soviet Rule in a Baltic Town*, London: George Allen & Unwin, 1932.

Raskolnikov, F.F., *Tales of Sub-Lieutenant Ilyin*, London: New Park Publications, 1982.

Reissner, Larissa, "Sviajsk," *Cahiers Lèon Trotsky*, vol. 12 (1982), pp. 51–64.

Riasianskii, S.N., "Bykhovskie uzniki," in G.N. Sevost'ianov *et al.* (eds), *Delo L.G. Kornilova: materialy Chrezvychainoi komissii po rassledovaniiu dela o byvshem Verkhovnom glavnokoman-duiushchem generale L.G. Kornilove i ego souchastnikakh. Avgust 1917 g.—iiun 1918 g.*, Moscow: Demokratiia, 2003, vol. 1, pp. 406–32.

Riddell, George Allardice, *Lord Riddell's Intimate Diary of the Peace Conference and After, 1918–1923*, London: Gollancz, 1933.

Rodzianko, A.P., *Vospominaniia o Severo-Zapadnoi Armii*, Berlin: Presse, 1920.

Rosmer, Alfred, *Lenin's Moscow*, London: Pluto Press, 1971.

Sakharov, K.V., *Belaia Sibir'. Vnutrennaia voina 1918–1920gg.*, Munich: [H. Graf?], 1923.

——— *Die tschechischen Legionen in Sibirien*, Berlin/Charlottenburg: Heinrich Wilhelm Hendrick Verlag, 1930.

Samoilo, A.A., *Dve zhizni*, Moscow: Voenizdat, 1958.

Semenov, G., *O sebe: vospominaniia, mysli i vyvody*, Izdatel'stvo AST, 1999.

Serge, Victor, *Memoirs of a Revolutionary, 1901–1941*, London: Oxford University Press, 1963.

——— *Revolution in Danger: Writings from Russia, 1919–1921*, London: Redwords, 1919.

BIBLIOGRAPHY

Shirinskaia, A.A., *Bizerta: Posledniaia stoianka*, St Petersburg: Otechestvo, 2003.

Shkuro, A.G., *Zapiski belogo partizana*, Buenos Aries: Seiatel', 1961.

Shteifon, B.A., "Bredovskii pokhod," *Beloe delo*, vol. 10, Moscow: Rossiiskii gos. gumanitarnyi un-t, 2003, pp. 1–298.

Shteinman, F., "Otstuplenie ot Odessa," *Beloe delo*, vol. 10, Moscow: Rossiiskii Gos. Gumanitarnyi un-t, 2003, pp. 313–29.

Sikorski, Władysław, *La Campagne polono-russe de 1920*, Paris: Payot, 1928.

Skoropadsky/Skoropads'skyi, Pavel/Pavlo, *Spohady: kinets' 1917—hruden' 1918*, ed. Jaroslaw Pelenski, Kyiv/Philadelphia: National Academy of Sciences of Ukraine, M.S. Hrushevs'kyi Institute of Ukrainian Archaeology and Fontology, V.K. Lypinsky East European Research Institute, 1995.

Stasova, E.D., *Stranitsy zhizni i bor'by*, Moscow: Gospolizdat, 1957.

Steinberg, Mark D. (ed.), *Voices of Revolution, 1917*, New Haven: Yale University Press, 2001.

Strod, Ivan, *Civil War in the Taiga: A Story of Guerrilla Warfare in the Forests of Eastern Siberia*, London: Modern Books, 1933.

Sukhanov, N.N., *The Russian Revolution, 1917: A Personal Record*, London: Oxford University Press, 1955.

Teague-Jones, Reginald, *The Spy Who Disappeared: Diary of a Secret Mission to Central Asia in 1918*, London: Victor Gollancz, 1988.

Tolstov, V.S., *Ot krasnykh lap v neizvestnuiu pal' (pokhod ural'tsev)*, Constantinople: Tip. izd. Tv.-a "Pressa," 1921.

Tremsina, L.Iu. (ed.), *V.M. Molchanov: poslednyi Belyi general*, Moscow: Airis-Press, 2009.

Trotsky, L.D., *My Life: An Attempt at an Autobiography*, Harmondsworth: Penguin, 1975.

Vācietis, Jukums, "Moia zhizn' i moi vospominaniia," *Daugava*, nos 3–5 (1980).

Valentinov, A.A., "Krymskaia epopeia (po dnevnikam uchastnikiv i po dokumentam)," *Arkhiv russkoi revoliutsii*, vol. 5 (1922), pp. 5–100.

Velikii Sibirskii lednoi pokhod, Moscow: Tsentropoligraf, 2004.

Vinaver, M.M., *Nashe pravitel'stvo. Krymskiia vospominaniia 1918–1919gg.*, Paris: Imprimerie d'art Voltaire, 1928.

Volkov-Muromtsev, N.V., *Iunost' ot Viaz'my do Feodosii*, Paris: YMCA Press, 1983.

Vrangl', P.N., *Vospominaniia*, 2 vols (in one), Frankfurt: Posev, 1969.

Wells, H.G., *Russia in the Shadows*, London: Hodder & Stoughton, 1920.

Ybert-Chabrier, Edith, "Gilan, 1917–1920: The Jengelist Movement according to the Memoirs of Ihsan Allah Khan," *Central Asian Survey*, vol. 2, no. 1 (1983), pp. 37–61.

Zetkin, Clara, *Reminiscences of Lenin*, London: Modern Books, 1929.

Published Secondary Works

D'Abernon, Viscount E.V., *The Eighteenth Decisive Battle of the World: Warsaw, 1920*, London: Hodder & Stoughton, 1931.

Abraham, Richard, *Alexander Kerensky: The First Love of the Revolution*, London: Sidgwick and Jackson, 1987.

Abramson, Henry, *A Prayer for the Government: Ukrainians and Jews in Revolutionary Times, 1917–1920*, Cambridge, MA: Ukrainian Research Center for Jewish Studies, Harvard University, 1999.

BIBLIOGRAPHY

——— "Well—Yes, a New Historiographical Synthesis: A Response to Lars Fischer," *Revolutionary Russia*, vol. 16, no. 2 (2003), pp. 94–100.

Acton, Edward, *Rethinking the Russian Revolution*, London: Edward Arnold, 1990.

Adamets, Serguei, *Guerre civile et famine en Russie: Le pouvoir bolchévique et la population face à la catastrophe démographique de 1917–1923*, Paris: Institut D'études Slaves, 2003.

Adams, Arthur E., *Bolsheviks in the Ukraine: The Second Campaign, 1918–1920*, New Haven: Yale University Press, 1963.

Afanasyan, Serge, *L'Arménie, l'Azerbaidjan et la Géorgie: de l'indépendance à l'instauration du pouvoir soviétique, 1917–1923*, Paris: Éditions l'Harmattan, 1981.

Ageeva, T.G., *Kavkazskaia armiia P.N. Vrangelia v Tsaritsyne*, Volgograd: Volgogradskoe nauchnoe izdatel'stvo, 2009.

Agursky, Mikhail, "Defeat as Victory and the Living Death: The Case of Ustrialov," *History of European Ideas*, vol. 5, no. 2 (1984), pp. 165–80.

Airapetov, O.R. (ed.), *Generaly, liberaly i predprinimateli. Rabota na front i na revoliutsiiu (1907–1917)*, Moscow: Modest Kolerov and Tri khvadrata, 2003.

——— *Posledniaia voina imperatorskoi Rossii. Sbornik statei*, Moscow: Tri kvadrata, 2002.

Allen, Barbara, "Alexander Shliapnikov and the Origins of the Workers' Opposition, March 1919–April 1920," *Jahrbücher für Geschichte Osteuropas*, vol. 53, no. 1 (2005), pp. 1–24.

Allen, W.E.D. and Paul Muratoff, *Caucasian Battlefields: A History of the Wars on the Turco-Caucasian Border, 1828–1921*, Nashville: The Battery Press, 1999.

Anderson, Edgar, "British Policy toward the Baltic States, 1918–1920," *Journal of Central European Affairs*, vol. 19, no. 3 (1959), pp. 276–89.

——— "An Undeclared War: The British–Soviet Naval Struggle in the Baltic, 1918–1920," *Journal of Central European Affairs*, vol. 22, no. 1 (1962), pp. 43–78.

Andriewsky, Olga, "The Making of the Generation of 1917: Towards a Collective Biography," *Journal of Ukrainian Studies*, vol. 29, nos 1–2 (2004), pp. 19–37.

Ansari, K.H., "Pan-Islam and the Making of the Early Indian Muslim Socialists," *Modern Asian Studies*, vol. 20, no. 3 (1986), pp. 509–37.

Anweiler, Oskar, *The Soviets: The Russian Workers, Peasants and Soldiers Councils, 1905–1921*, New York: Pantheon Books, 1974.

Argenbright, Richard, "Honour Among Communists: 'The Glorious Name of Trotsky's Train,'" *Revolutionary Russia*, vol. 11, no. 1 (1998), pp. 45–66.

——— "Red Tsaritsyn: Precursor of Stalinist Terror," *Revolutionary Russia*, vol. 4, no. 2 (1991), pp. 157–83.

——— "The Soviet Agitational Vehicle: State Power and the Social Frontier," *Political Geography*, vol. 17, no. 3 (1998), pp. 253–72.

Arshinov, Peter, *History of the Makhnovist Movement, 1918–1921*, London: Freedom Press, 1921.

Arslanian, Artin H. and Robert L. Nichols, "Nationalism and the Russian Civil War: The Case of Volunteer Army–Armenian Relations, 1918–1920," *Soviet Studies*, vol. 31, no. 4 (1979), pp. 559–73.

Ascher, Abraham, "Introduction," in Jonathan D. Smele and Anthony Heywood (eds), *The Russian Revolution of 1905: Centenary Perspectives*, Oxford: Routledge, 2005, pp. 1–12.

——— *P.A. Stolypin: The Search for Stability in Late Imperial Russia*, Stanford: Stanford University Press, 2001.

——— *The Russian Revolution: A Beginner's Guide*, Cambridge: OneWorld, 2014.

BIBLIOGRAPHY

Aurerbach, Sascha, "Negotiating Nationalism: Jewish Conscription and Russian Repatriation in London's East End, 1916–1918," *Journal of British Studies*, vol. 46, no. 3 (2007), pp. 594–620.

Avalishvili, Zourab, *The Independence of Georgia in International Politics, 1918–1921*, London: Headley, 1940.

Avrich, Paul H., "The Bolsheviks and Workers' Control in Russian Industry," *Slavic Review*, vol. 22, no. 1 (1963), pp. 47–63.

——— *Kronstadt, 1921*, Princeton: Princeton University Press, 1970.

——— *The Russian Anarchists*, Princeton: Princeton University Press, 1967.

Badcock, Sarah, "'We're for the *Muzhiks'* Party!' Peasant Support for the Socialist Revolutionary Party during 1917," *Europe–Asia Studies*, vol. 53, no. 1 (2001), pp. 133–49.

Bailes, Kendall E., "Alexei Gastev and the Soviet Controversy over Taylorism, 1918–1924," *Soviet Studies*, vol. 29, no. 3 (1977), pp. 373–94.

Bainton, Roy, *Honoured by Strangers: The Life of Captain Francis Cromie CB, DSO, RN, 1882–1918*, Shrewsbury: Airlife Publications, 2002.

Baker, Helen, "Monarchy Discredited? Reactions to the Khodynka Coronation Catastrophe of 1896," *Revolutionary Russia*, vol. 16, no. 1 (2003), pp. 1–46.

Baker, Mark, "Beyond the National: Peasants, Power, and Revolution in Ukraine," *Journal of Ukrainian Studies*, vol. 24, no. 1 (1999), pp. 39–67.

Banjeri, Arup, "Commissars and Bagmen: Russia during the Civil War, 1918–1921," *Studies in History*, vol. 3, no. 2 (1987), pp. 233–74.

Baradym, Vitalii, *Zhizn' Generala Shkuro*, Krasnodar: Sov. Kuban, 1998.

Baron, Nick, *The King of Karelia: Col P.J. Woods and the British Intervention in North Russia, 1918–1919*, London: Francis Boutle, 2007.

Bartlett, Roger, *A History of Russia*, London: Palgrave, 2005.

Basil, John D., *The Mensheviks in the Revolution of 1917*, Columbus, OH: Slavica Publishers, 1984.

Bater, James H., *St Petersburg: Industrialisation and Change*, London: Edward Arnold, 1976.

Batsell, Walter Russell, *Soviet Rule in Russia*, New York: Macmillan, 1929.

Baugh, Odin A., *John Frank Stevens: American Trailblazer*, Spokane: Arthur H. Clark Co., 2005.

Béard, Ewa, "Pourquoi les bolcheviks ont-ils quitté Petrograd?" *Cahiers du Monde Russe et Soviétique*, vol. 34, no. 4 (1993), pp. 407–28.

Bennett, Geoffrey, *Cowan's War: The Story of British Naval Operations in the Baltic, 1918–1920*, London: Collins, 1964.

Bennigsen, Alexandre, "Sultan Galiev: The USSR and the Colonial Revolution," in Walter Z. Laqueur (ed.), *The Middle East in Transition*, New York: Praeger, 1958, pp. 398–414.

Benvenuti, Francesco, *I bolscevichi e l'armata rossa, 1918–1922*, Naples: Bibliopolis, 1982.

Berk, Stephen M., "The Class Tragedy of Izhevsk: Working-Class Opposition to Bolshevism in 1918," *Russian History*, vol. 2, no. 2 (1975), pp. 176–90.

——— "The Democratic Counter-Revolution: Komuch and the Civil War on the Volga," *Canadian Slavic Studies*, vol. 7 (1973), pp. 443–59.

Bertrand, Charles L. (ed.), *Revolutionary Situations in Europe, 1917–1922: Germany, Italy, Austria–Hungary*, Montreal: Concordia University and University of Quebec, 1977.

Bethell, Nicholas, *The Last Secret: Forcible Repatriation to Russia, 1944–47*, London: Deutsch, 1974.

Biggart, John, "Kirov before the Revolution," *Soviet Studies*, vol. 23, no. 3 (1972), pp. 345–72.

Bihl, Wolfditer, "Österreich–Ungarn und der 'Bund zur Befreiung der Ukraina'," in *Österreich und Europa: Festschrift für Hugo Hantsch zum 70. Geburtstag*, Graz: Styria, 1965, pp. 505–26.

Birch, Julian, "The Georgian/South Ossetian Territorial and Boundary Dispute," in John F.R. Wright, Suzanne Goldenberg, and Richard Schofield (eds), *Transcaucasian Boundaries*, London: UCL Press, 1996, pp. 151–89.

Bisher, Jamie, *White Terror: Cossack Warlords of the Trans-Siberian*, London: Frank Cass, 2005.

Biskupski, Mieczysław B., "War and the Diplomacy of Polish Independence, 1914–1918," *Polish Review*, vol. 35, no. 1 (1990), pp. 5–17.

Blank, Stephen, *The Sorcerer as Apprentice: Stalin as Commissar for Nationalities*, Westport: Greenwood Press, 1994.

——— "Soviet Politics and the Iranian Revolution of 1919–1921," *Cahiers du Monde Russe et Soviétique*, vol. 21, no. 2 (1980), pp. 173–94.

——— "The Struggle for Soviet Bashkiria, 1917–1923," *Nationalities Papers*, vol. 11, no. 1 (1983), pp. 1–26.

Bokarev, V.P., *VIII s"ezd RKP(b)*, Moscow: Politizdat, 1990.

[Bol'shakov, A.M.], "Extracts from *The Soviet Countryside, 1917–1924: Its Economics and Life*," in Robert E.F. Smith (ed.), *The Russian Peasant: 1920 and 1984*, London: Frank Cass, 1977, pp. 29–108.

Borrero, Mauricio, *Hungry Moscow: Scarcity and Urban Society in the Russian Civil War, 1917–1921*, New York: Peter Lang, 2003.

Borys, Jurij, *The Sovietization of Ukraine, 1917–1923: The Communist Doctrine and Practice of National Self-Determination*, Edmonton: Canadian Institute of Ukrainian Studies, 1980.

Bowlt, John E., "Russian Sculpture in Lenin's Plan of Monumental Propaganda," in Henry A. Millon and Linda Nochin (eds), *Art and Architecture in the Service of Politics*, Cambridge, MA: MIT Press, 1978, pp. 182–93.

Bradley, John, *Civil War in Russia, 1917–1920*, London: B.T. Batsford, 1975.

——— *The Czechoslovak Legion in Russia, 1914–1920*, Boulder: East European Monographs, 1991.

Brinkley, George A., "Allied Policy and French Intervention in the Ukraine, 1917–1920," in Taras Hunczak (ed.), *The Ukraine, 1917–1921: A Study in Revolution*, Cambridge, MA: Harvard University Press, 1977, pp. 323–51.

——— *The Volunteer Army and Allied Intervention in South Russia, 1917–1921: A Study in the Politics and Diplomacy of the Russian Civil War*, Notre Dame: University of Notre Dame Press, 1966.

Brinton, Maurice, *The Bolsheviks and Workers' Control: The State and Counter-Revolution*, London: Solidarity, 1970.

Brogan, Hugh, *The Life of Arthur Ransome*, Hamish Hamilton, 1984.

Broido, Vera, *Lenin and the Mensheviks: The Persecution of Socialists under Bolshevism*, Aldershot: Gower, 1987.

Brook-Shepherd, Gordon, *The Iron Maze: The Western Secret Services and the Bolsheviks*, London: Macmillan, 1998.

Brovkin, Vladimir, "The Mensheviks' Political Comeback: Elections to the Provincial City Soviets in the Spring of 1918," *Russian Review*, vol. 42, no. 1 (1983), pp. 1–50.

——— "The Mensheviks under Attack: The Transformation of Soviet Politics, June–September 1918," *Jahrbücher für Geschichte Osteuropas*, vol. 32, no. 3 (1984), pp. 378–91.

BIBLIOGRAPHY

————— "On the Internal Front: The Bolsheviks and the Greens," *Jahrbücher für Geschichte Osteuropas*, vol. 37, no. 4 (1989), pp. 541–68.

Brovkin, Vladimir N. (ed.), *The Bolsheviks in Russian Society: The Revolution and the Civil Wars*, New Haven: Yale University Press, 1997.

Brower, Daniel R., "'The City in Danger': The Civil War and the Russian Urban Population," in Diane Koenker, William G. Rosenberg, and Ronald G. Suny (eds), *Party, State and Society in the Russian Civil War: Explorations in Social History*, Bloomington: Indiana University Press, 1990, pp. 58–80.

————— *Turkestan and the Fate of the Russian Empire*, London: Routledge Curzon, 2002.

Broxup, Marie B., "The Basmachi," *Central Asian Survey*, vol. 2, no. 1 (1983), pp. 57–81.

Brüggermann, Karsten, *Die Gründung der Republik Estland und das Ende des "Einem und unteilbaren Rußland": Die Petrograder Front des Russischen Bürgerkrieges, 1918–1920*, Wiesbaden: Otto Harrassowitz Verlag, 2004.

Bryant, F. Russell, "Lord D'Abernon, the Anglo-French Mission, and the Battle of Warsaw, 1920," *Jahrbücher für Geschichte Osteuropas*, vol. 38 (1990), pp. 526–47.

Bubnov, A.S., S.S. Kamenev, and R.P. Eidman (eds), *Grazhdanskaia voina, 1918–1921*, Moscow: Voennyi Vestnik, 1928.

Budnitskii, Oleg, *Den'gi russkoi emigratsii: kolchakovskoe zoloto, 1918–1957*, Moscow: Novoe Literaturnoe Obozrenie, 2008.

————— *Rossiiskie evrei mezhdu krasnymi i belymi, 1917–1920*, Moscow: ROSSPEN, 2005.

————— "Shot in the Back: On the Origins of the Anti-Jewish Pogroms of 1918–1921," in Eugene M. Avrutin and Harriet Murav (eds), *Jews in the East European Borderlands: Essays in Honor of John D. Klier*, Boston: Academic Studies Press, 2012, pp. 187–90.

Buldakov, V.P., *Krasnaia smuta: Priroda i posledstviia revolutsionnogo nasiliia*, Moscow: ROSSPEN, 1997.

Bullock, David, *The Russian Civil War, 1918–22*, Oxford: Osprey, 2008.

Burdzhalov, E.N., *Russia's Second Revolution: The February 1917 Uprising in Petrograd*, Bloomington: Indiana University Press, 1987.

Burevoi, K.S., *Kolchakovshchina*, Moscow: Gosizdat, 1919.

Buttino, Marco, "Ethnicité et politique dans la Guerre Civile: À propos des Basmačestvo au Fergana," *Cahiers du Monde Russe*, vol. 38, nos 1–2 (1997), pp. 195–222.

Cadiot, Juliette, "Searching for Nationality: Statistics and National Categories at the End of the Russian Empire (1897–1917)," *Russian Review*, vol. 64, no. 3 (2005), pp. 440–55.

Carley, Michael J., *Revolution and Intervention: The French Government and the Russian Civil War, 1917–1919*, Kingston: McGill University Press, 1983.

Carlton, David, *Churchill and the Soviet Union*, Manchester: Manchester University Press, 2000.

Castagné, Joseph, *Les Basmatchis. Le mouvement national des indigènes d'Asie Centrale depuis la Révolution d'octobre 1917 jusqu'en 1924*, Paris: Ernest Leroux, 1925.

Chabanier, Colonel Jean, "L'Intervention alliée en Russie méridionale, décembre 1918—mars 1919," *Revue Historique de l'Armée*, vol. 16, no. 4 (1960), pp. 74–92.

Chamberlain, Lesley, *The Philosophy Steamer: Lenin and the Exile of the Intelligentsia*, London: Atlantic Books, 2006.

Chamberlin, William H., *The Russian Revolution, 1917–1921*, 2 vols, London: Macmillan, 1935.

Chambers, Roland, *The Last Englishman: The Double Life of Arthur Ransome*, London: Faber and Faber, 2009.

Chaqueri, Cosroe, "The Baku Congress," *Central Asian Survey*, vol. 2, no. 2 (1983), pp. 89–107.

———— *The Soviet Socialist Republic of Iran, 1920–1921: Birth of the Trauma*, Pittsburgh: University of Pittsburgh Press, 1995.

Chemeriskii, I.A., "Eserovskaia gruppa 'Narod' i ee raspad," in I.I. Mints (ed.), *Bankrotstvo melkoburzhuaznykh partii Rossii, 1917–1922gg.*, Moscow: Nauka, 1977, pp. 77–86.

Ciliga, Ante, *The Kronstadt Revolt*, London: The Freedom Press, 1942.

Clements, Barbara E., "Kollontai's Contribution to the Workers' Opposition," *Russian History*, vol. 2, no. 2 (1975), pp. 191–206.

Cohen, Stephen F., "In Praise of War Communism: Bukharin's 'Economics of the Transition Period'," in Alexander Rabinowitch, Janet Rabinowitch, and Ladis K.D. Kristof (eds), *Revolution and Politics in Russia: Essays in Memory of B.I. Nicolaevsky*, Bloomington: Indiana University Press, 1972, pp. 192–203.

Corney, Frederick C., "Rethinking a Great Event: The October Revolution as Memory Project," *Social Science History*, vol. 22, no. 4 (1998), pp. 389–414.

Cornish, Nik, *The Russian Army and the First World War*, Stroud: Spellmount, 2006.

———— *The Russian Revolution; World War to Civil War, 1917–1921*, Barnsley: Pen & Sword Military, 2012.

Courtois, Stéphane *et al.*, *The Black Book of Communism: Crimes, Terror, Repression*, Cambridge, MA: Harvard University Press, 1999.

Croll, Neil, "The Role of M.N. Tukhachevskii in the Suppression of the Kronstadt Rebellion," *Revolutionary Russia*, vol. 17, no. 2 (2004), pp. 1–48.

Czaplicka, John, "Lviv, Lemberg, Leopolis, Lwów, Lvov: A City in the Crosscurrents of European Culture," *Harvard Ukrainian Studies*, vol. 24 (2000), pp. 13–45.

Dabrowski, Stanisław, "The Peace Treaty of Riga," *Polish Review*, vol. 5, no. 1 (1960), pp. 3–34.

Daly, Jonathan W., "'Storming the Last Citadel': The Bolshevik Assault on the Church, 1922," in Vladimir N. Brovkin (ed.), *The Bolsheviks in Russian Society: The Revolution and the Civil Wars*, New Haven: Yale University Press, 1997, pp. 235–68.

Daniels, Robert V., *The Conscience of the Revolution: Communist Opposition in Soviet Russia*, Cambridge, MA: Harvard University Press, 1960.

Danilov, V. and T. Shanin (eds), *Filipp Mironov: Tikhyi Don, 1917–1921 gg.*, Moscow: Mezhdunarodnaia Fond "Demokratiia," 1997.

Davies, Norman, "Lloyd George and Poland, 1919–1920," *Journal of Contemporary History*, vol. 6, no. 3 (1971), pp. 132–54.

———— "The Missing Revolutionary War: The Polish Campaigns and the Retreat from Revolution in Soviet Russia, 1919–1921," *Soviet Studies*, vol. 27, no. 2 (1975), pp. 178–95.

———— *White Eagle, Red Star: The Soviet–Polish War, 1919–20*, London: Orbis Books, 1983.

Davies, R.W., "Changing Economic Systems: An Overview," in R.W. Davies, Mark Harrison, and S.G. Wheatcroft (eds), *The Economic Transformation of the Soviet Union, 1913–1945*, Cambridge: Cambridge University Press, 1994, pp. 1–23.

Davies, R.W. (ed.), *From Tsarism to the New Economic Policy: Continuity and Change in the Economy of the USSR*, London: Macmillan, 1990.

Deák, František, "Russian Mass Spectacles," *Drama Review*, vol. 19, no. 2 (1975), pp. 7–22.

Debo, Richard K., "Lockhart Plot or Dzerzhinskii Plot?" *Journal of Modern History*, vol. 43, no. 3 (1971), pp. 413–39.

———— *Revolution and Survival: The Foreign Policy of Soviet Russia, 1917–18*, Liverpool: Liverpool University Press, 1979.

———— *Survival and Consolidation: The Foreign Policy of Soviet Russia, 1918–1921*, Montreal and Kingston: McGill–Queen's University Press, 1992.

Deutscher, Isaac, *The Prophet Armed: Trotsky, 1879–1921*, London: Oxford University Press, 1954.

Diakin, V.S., "The Leadership Crisis in Russia on the Eve of the February Revolution," *Soviet Studies in History*, vol. 23, no. 1 (1984–5), pp. 10–38.

Dmitriev, P.N. and K.I. Kulikov, *Miatezh v Izhevsk-Votkinskom raione*, Izhevsk: Udmurtiia, 1992.

Dobson, Christopher and John Miller, *The Day We Almost Bombed Moscow: The Allied War in Russia, 1918–1920*, London: Hodder & Stoughton, 1986.

Döring, Falk, *Organisationsprobleme der russischen Wirktschaft in Revolution und Bürgerkrieg (1918–1920)*, Hanover: Verlag für Literatur und Zeitgeschehen, 1970.

Dowling, Timothy C., *The Brusilov Offensive*, Bloomington: Indiana University Press, 2009.

Draper, Hal, *The Adventures of the Communist Manifesto*, Berkeley: Center for Socialist History, 1998.

DuGarm, Delano, "Peasant Wars in Tambov Province," in Vladimir N. Brovkin (ed.), *The Bolsheviks in Russian Society: The Revolution and Civil Wars*, New Haven: Yale University Press, 1997, pp. 177–98.

Duguet, Raymond, *Moscou et la Géorgie martyre. Préface de C. B. Stokes*, Paris: Tallandier, 1927.

Dukes, Paul, "The Changchun Conference: 4–28 September 1922," in A.L. Litvin (ed.), *Rossiiskaia istoricheska mozaika: sbornik nauchnykh statei*, Kazan': Izdatel'stvo Kazanskogo Matematicheskogo Obshchestva, 2003, pp. 228–51.

———— *The USA in the Making of the USSR: The Washington Conference, 1921–1922 and "Uninvited Russia,"* London: Routledge, 2004.

Dumont, Paul, "L'Axe Moscou–Ankara: Les relations turco-soviétiques de 1919 à 1922," *Cahiers du Monde Russe et Soviétique*, vol. 18, no. 3 (1977), pp. 165–93.

Dumova, N.G., *Kadetskaia kontrrevoliutsiia i ee razgrom*, Moscow: Nauka, 1982.

Dunscomb, Paul E., *Japan's Siberian Intervention, 1918–1922: "A Great Disobedience Against the People"*, Lanham: Lexington Books, 2011.

Duvakin, Viktor N., *Rosta-Fenster: Majakowski aus Dichter und bildender Künstler*, Dresden: Verlag der Kunst, 1975.

Duval, Charles, "Yakov M. Sverdlov and the All-Russian Central Executive Committee of Soviets (VTsIK)," *Soviet Studies*, vol. 31, no. 1 (1979), pp. 3–22.

Dziewanowski, Marian K., *Joseph Pilsudski: A European Federalist, 1918–1922*, Stanford: Stanford University Press, 1969.

"Dzunaid-khan, 'King of the Karakum Desert,'" *Central Asian Survey*, vol. 13 (1965), pp. 216–26.

Edmondson, Charles M., "An Enquiry into the Termination of Soviet Famine Relief Programmes and the Renewal of Grain Exports, 1922–1923," *Soviet Studies*, vol. 33, no. 3 (1981), pp. 370–85.

———— "The Politics of Hunger: The Soviet Response to Famine, 1921," *Soviet Studies*, vol. 29, no. 4 (1977), pp. 506–18.

Efimov, A.G., *Izhevtsy i Votkintsy, 1918–1920*, Moscow: Airis Press, 2008.

Eikhe, G.Kh., *Oprokinutyi tyl*, Moscow: Voenizdat, 1966.

———— *Ufimskaia avantiura Kolchaka (mart–aprel' 1919g.): pochemu Kolchak ne udalas' prorvat'sia k Volge na soedinenie s Denikinym*, Moscow: Voenizdat, 1960.

Eley, Geoff, "Remapping the Nation: War, Revolutionary Upheaval and State Formation in Eastern Europe, 1914–1923," in Peter J. Potichnj and Howard Aster (eds), *Ukrainian–Jewish Relations in Historical Perspective*, Edmonton: Canadian Institute of Ukrainian Studies, 1988, pp. 205–46.

Elkin, Boris, "The Doom of the Russian Monarchy," *Slavonic and East European Review*, vol. 47 (1969), pp. 514–24.

Ellis, C.H., *The Transcaspian Episode, 1918–1919*, London: Hutchinson, 1963.

El'tsin, V., "Krest'ianskoe dvizhenie v Sibiri v periode Kolchaka," *Proletarskaia revoliutsiia*, no. 49 (1926), pp. 5–48; no. 50 (1926), pp. 51–82.

Erickson, John, "The Origins of the Red Army," in Richard Pipes (ed.), *Revolutionary Russia*, Cambridge, MA: Harvard University Press, 1968, pp. 224–56.

Erlikhman, V.V., *Poteri narodonaseleniia v XX veke: spravochnik*, Moscow: Russkaia Panorama, 2004.

Estep, Raymond, "John F. Stevens and the Far Eastern Railways, 1917–1923," *Explorer's Journal*, vol. 48, no. 1 (1970), pp. 13–24.

Evain, Emmanuel, *Le problème de l'indépendance de l'Ukraine et la France*, Paris: F. Alcan, 1931.

Ewing, T.E., "Russia, China and the Origins of the Mongolian People's Republic, 1918–1921: A Reappraisal," *Slavonic and East European Review*, vol. 58, no. 3 (1980), pp. 399–421.

Fainsod, Merle, *International Socialism and the War*, Cambridge, MA: Harvard University Press, 1935.

Fay, Victor (ed.), *La Révolution d'octobre et le mouvement ouvrier européen*, Paris: Études et Documentation Internationales, 1967.

Fedorovskii, Iu.O., "O vziamootnosheniiakh atamana Grigor'eva i bat'ki Makhno v 1919 godu," *Voprosy istorii*, no. 9 (1998), pp. 169–71.

Fedyshyn, Oleh S., "The Germans and the Union for the Liberation of Ukraine, 1914–1917," in Taras Hunczak (ed.), *The Ukraine, 1917–1921: A Study in Revolution*, Cambridge, MA: Harvard University Press, 1977, pp. 305–22.

——— *Germany's Drive to the East and the Ukrainian Revolution*, New Brunswick, NJ: Rutgers University Press, 1971.

Feist, Joe M., "Theirs Not to Reason Why: The Case of the Russian Railway Service Corps," *Military Affairs*, vol. 42, no. 1 (1978), pp. 1–6.

Ferguson, Harry, *Operation Kronstadt*, London: Hutchinson, 2008.

Fic, Victor M., *The Bolsheviks and the Czechoslovak Legion: The Origin of their Armed Conflict, March–May 1918*, New Delhi: Abhinav Publications, 1978.

Fiddick, Thomas C., *Russia's Retreat from Poland, 1920: From Permanent Revolution to Peaceful Coexistence*, London: Macmillan, 1990.

Figes, Orlando, *Peasant Russia, Civil War: The Volga Countryside in Revolution, 1917–1921*, Oxford: Clarendon, 1989.

——— *A People's Tragedy: The Russian Revolution 1891–1924*, London: Pimlico, 1997.

——— "The Red Army and Mass Mobilization during the Russian Civil War, 1918–1920," *Past and Present*, no. 129 (1990), pp. 168–211.

——— "The Russian Peasant Community in the Agrarian Revolution, 1917–1918," in Roger Bartlett (ed.), *Land Commune and Peasant Community in Russia*, London: Macmillan, 1990, pp. 237–53.

Figes, Orlando and Boris Kolonitskii, *Interpreting the Russian Revolution: The Language and Symbols of 1917*, New Haven: Yale University Press, 1999.

BIBLIOGRAPHY

Fischer, Fritz, *Griff nach der Weltmacht. Der Kriegszielpolitik des kaiserlichen Deutschland, 1914/18*, Düsseldorf: Droste Verlag, 1961.

Fischer, Lars, "The 'Pogromshchina' and the Directory: A New Historiographical Synthesis?" *Revolutionary Russia*, vol. 16, no. 2 (2003), pp. 47–93.

———— "Whither *Pogromshchina*—Historical Synthesis or Deconstruction?" *East European Jewish Affairs*, vol. 38, no. 3 (2008), pp. 303–20.

Fisher, H.H., *The Famine in Soviet Russia, 1919–1923: The Operation of the American Relief Administration*, New York: Macmillan & Co., 1927.

Fisher, John, "'On the Glacis of India': Lord Curzon and British Policy in the Caucasus, 1919," *Diplomacy and Statecraft*, vol. 8, no. 2 (1997), pp. 50–82.

Fitzpatrick, Sheila, "Civil War as Formative Experience," in Albert Gleason, Peter Kenez, and Richard Stites (eds), *Bolshevik Culture: Experiment and Order in the Russian Revolution*, Bloomington: Indiana University Press, 1985, pp. 57–76.

———— "The Legacy of the Civil War," in Diane Koenker, William G. Rosenberg, and Ronald G. Suny (eds), *Party, State and Society in the Russian Civil Wars: Explorations in Social History*, Bloomington: Indiana University Press, 1990, pp. 385–9.

———— "Origins of Stalinism: How Important was the Civil War?" *Acta Slavica Iaponica*, vol. 2 (1984), pp. 105–16.

———— *The Russian Revolution, 1917–1932*, Oxford University Press, 1982.

Fitzpatrick, Sheila, Alexander Rabinowitch, and Richards Stites (eds), *Russia in the Age of NEP: Explorations in Soviet Society and Culture*, Bloomington: Indiana University Press, 1991.

Fleishchauer, Ingeborg, "The Agrarian Program of the Russian Constitutional Democrats," *Cahiers du Monde Russe et Soviétique*, vol. 20, no. 2 (1979), pp. 173–201.

Fontaine, André, *Histoire de la Guerre froide, Vol. 1: De la révolution d'octobre à la guerre de Corée*, Paris: Fayard, 1965.

Footman, David, "The Beginnings of the Red Army," in David Footman, *Civil War in Russia*, London: Faber & Faber, 1961, pp. 135–66.

———— "The Civil War and the Baltic States, Part 1: Von der Goltz and Bermondt-Avalov," *St Antony's Papers on Soviet Affairs*, Oct. 1959.

———— "Murmansk and Archangel," in David Footman, *Civil War in Russia*, London: Faber & Faber, 1961, pp. 167–210.

Forbes, Andrew, *Warlords and Muslims in Chinese Central Asia: A Political History of Republican Sinkiang, 1911–1949*, Cambridge: Cambridge University Press, 1986.

Forest, Benjamin and Juliet Johnson, "Unravelling the Threads of History: Soviet-Era Monuments and Post-Soviet National Identity in Moscow," *Annals of the Association of American Geographers*, vol. 92, no. 3 (2002), pp. 48–72.

Foust, Clifford, *John Frank Stevens: Civil Engineer*, Bloomington: Indiana University Press, 2013.

Fraser, Glenda, "Basmachi," *Central Asian Survey*, vol. 6 (1987), no. 1, pp. 1–71; no. 2, pp. 7–42.

———— "Enver Pasha's Bid for Turkestan, 1920–1922," *Canadian Journal of History*, vol. 22, no. 2 (1988), pp. 197–211.

Frenkin, Mikhail, *Russkaia armiia i revoliutsiia, 1917–1918*, Munich: Logos, 1978.

———— *Tragediia krest'ianskikh vosstanii v Rossii, 1918–1921 gg.*, Jerusalem: Leksikon, 1987.

———— *Zakhvat vlasti Bols'shevikami v Rossii i rol' tylovykh garizonov armii: podgotovka i provedenie oktiabr'skogo miatezha 1917–1918 gg.*, Jerusalem: Stav, 1982.

Freund, Gerald, *Unholy Alliance: Russo-German Relations from the Treaty of Brest-Litovsk to the Treaty of Berlin*, London: Chatto & Windus, 1957.

Friedman, Saul S., *Pogromchik: The Assassination of Simon Petliura*, New York: Hart, 1976.

Fuller Jr, William C., *Civil–Military Conflict in Imperial Russia, 1881–1914*, Princeton: Princeton University Press, 1985.

Gagkuev, R.G. and V.Zh. Tsetkov, *General Kutepov*, Moscow: Posev, 2009.

Ganin, A.V., *Ataman A.I. Dutov*. Moscow: Tsentropoligraf, 2006.

——— *Chernogorets v russkoi sluzhbe: General Bakich*, Moscow: Russkii Put', 2004.

——— "O roli ofitserov General'nogo shtaba v grazhdanskoi voine," *Voprosy istorii*, no. 6 (2004), pp. 98–111.

——— "Posledniaia poludennaia ekspeditsiia Imperarorskoi Rossii: Russkaia armiia na podavlenii turkestanskogo miatezha, 1916–1917 gg.," in O.R. Airapetov *et al.* (eds), *Russkii sbornik: Issledovaniia po istorii Rossii XIX–XX vv.*, Moscow: Modest Kolerov, 2008, pp. 152–214.

——— "Workers and Peasants Red Army 'General Staff Personalities' Defecting to the Enemy Side in 1918–1921," *Journal of Slavic Military Studies*, vol. 26, no. 2 (2013), pp. 259–309.

Ganz, A. Harding, "The German Expedition to Finland, 1918," *Military Affairs*, vol. 44, no. 2 (1980), pp. 84–9.

Garvy, George, "The Origins of Lenin's Views on the Role of Banks in the Socialist Transformation of Society," *History of Political Economy*, vol. 4, no. 1 (1972), pp. 252–63.

Gatrell, Peter, *Russia's First World War: A Social and Economic History*, London: Longman, 2005.

——— "War after the War: Conflicts, 1919–23," in John Horne (ed.), *A Companion to World War I*, Oxford: Wiley-Blackwell, 2010, pp. 558–75.

——— "War, Population Displacement and State Formation in the Russian Borderlands, 1914–1924," in Nick Baron and Peter Gatrell (eds), *Homelands: War, Population and Statehood in Eastern Europe and Russia, 1918–1924*, London: Anthem Press, 2004, pp. 10–34.

——— *A Whole Empire Walking: Refugees in Russia during World War I*, Bloomington: Indiana University Press, 1999.

Geifman, Anna (ed.), *Russia under the Last Tsar: Opposition and Subversion, 1894–1917*, Oxford: Blackwell, 1999.

Geldern, James von, *Bolshevik Festivals, 1917–1920*, Berkeley: University of California Press, 1993.

Genis, V.L., "Les bolcheviks au Guilan. La chute du gouvernement de Koutchek Khan (juin–juillet 1920)," *Cahiers du Monde Russe*, vol. 40, no. 3 (1999), pp. 459–96.

——— "Pervaia Konnaia armiia: za kulisami slavy," *Voprosy istorii*, no. 12 (1994), pp. 64–77.

——— "Raskazachivanie v Sovetskoi Rossii," *Voprosy istorii*, vol. 1 (1994), pp. 42–55.

Gērmanis, Uldis, *Oberst Vācietis und die lettischen Schützen im Weltkrieg und in der Oktoberrevolution*, Stockholm: Almqvist & Wiksell, 1974.

Gerson, Lennard D., *The Secret Police in Lenin's Russia*, Philadelphia: Temple University Press, 1976.

Gerwarth, Robert and John Horne, "Vectors of Violence: Paramilitarism in Europe after the Great War," *Journal of Modern History*, vol. 83, no. 3 (2011), pp. 489–512.

——— (eds), *War in Peace: Paramilitary Violence in Europe after the Great War*, Oxford: Oxford University Press, 2013.

Getzler, Israel, "The Communist Leaders' Role in the Kronstadt Tragedy of 1921 in the Light of Recently Published Archival Documents," *Revolutionary Russia*, vol. 15, no. 1 (2002), pp. 24–44.

—— *Kronstadt, 1917–1921: The Fate of a Soviet Democracy*, Cambridge: Cambridge University Press, 1983.

—— *Nikolai Sukhanov: Chronicler of the Russian Revolution*, London: Palgrave, 2002.

Gill, Graham, "Changing Symbols: The Renovation of Moscow Place Names," *Russian Review*, vol. 64, no. 3 (2005), pp. 480–503.

—— "'Lenin Lives": Or Does He? Symbols and the Transition from Socialism," *Europe–Asia Studies*, vol. 60, no. 3 (2008), pp. 173–96.

Gilley, Christopher, "Volodymyr Vynnychenko's Mission to Moscow and Kharkov," *Slavonic and East European Review*, vol. 84, no. 3 (2006), pp. 508–37.

Gimpel'son, E.G., *Voennyi kommunizm: politika, praktika, ideologiia*, Moscow: Mysl', 1973.

Gleason, Abbott, Peter Kenez, and Richard Stites (eds), *Bolshevik Culture: Experiment and Order in the Russian Revolution*, Bloomington: Indiana University Press, 1985.

Gleason, William E., *Alexander Guchkov and the End of the Russian Empire*, Philadelphia: The American Philosophical Society, 1983.

Glenny, Misha V., "The Anglo-Soviet Trade Agreement, March 1921," *Journal of Contemporary History*, vol. 5, no. 2 (1970), pp. 63–82.

Gökay, Bülent, "The Battle for Baku (May–September 1918): A Peculiar Episode in the History of the Caucasus," *Middle Eastern Studies*, vol. 34, no. 1 (1998), pp. 30–50.

—— *A Clash of Empires: Turkey between Russian Bolshevism and British Imperialism, 1918–1923*, London: I.B. Tauris, 1996.

—— "Turkish Settlement and the Caucasus," *Middle Eastern Studies*, vol. 32, no. 2 (1996), pp. 45–76.

Golczewski, Frank, "Polen, Ukrainer und Juden in Lemberg, 1918," *Slavica Gandensia*, vol. 20 (1993), pp. 177–92.

Goldin, V.I., *Interventsiia i antibol'shevistckoe dvizhenie na Russkom Severe, 1918–1920*, Moscow: Izd-vo Moskovskogo Universiteta, 1993.

Goldin, V.I. and John W. Long, "Resistance and Retribution: The Life and Fate of General E.K. Miller," *Revolutionary Russia*, vol. 12, no. 2 (1999), pp. 19–40.

Golovine, N.N., *The Russian Army in the World War*, New Haven: Yale University Press, 1931.

Golub, P.A., *V zastenkakh Kolchaka: pravda o Belom admirale*, Moscow: Izdatel'stvo Patriot, 2010.

Golubev, A.V., *Vrangelevskie desanty na Kuban, avgust–sentiabr' 1920 goda*, Moscow–Leningrad: Gosizdat, 1920.

Gor'kii, Maksim *et al.* (eds), *History of the Civil War in the USSR*, 2 vols, London: Lawrence & Wishart, 1937–47.

Grabowicz, George G., "Three Perspectives on the Cossack Past: Gogol', Ševčenko, Kuliš," *Harvard Ukrainian Studies*, vol. 5 (1981), pp. 135–70.

Graziosi, Andrea, *The Great Soviet Peasant War: Bolsheviks and Peasants, 1917–1933*, Cambridge, MA: Harvard University Ukrainian Research Institute, 1996.

Grebing, Helga, "Österreich-Ungarn und die 'Ukrainische Aktion' 1914–1918. Zur Österreichisch-Ungarischen Ukraine-Politik im ersten Weltkrieg," *Jahrbücher für Geschichte Osteuropas*, vol. 7 (1959), pp. 270–96.

BIBLIOGRAPHY

Gritskevich, A.P., *Zapadnyi Front RSFSR, 1918–1920: Bor'ba mezhdu Rossiei i Pol'shei za Belorossiiu*, Minsk: Kharvest, 2010.

Guthier, Steven L., "The Popular Base of Ukrainian Nationalism in 1917," *Slavic Review*, vol. 38, no. 1 (1979), pp. 30–47.

——— "Ukrainian Cities during the Revolution and Interwar Era," in Ivan L. Rudnytsky (ed.), *Rethinking Ukrainian History*, Edmonton: Canadian Institute of Ukrainian Studies, 1981, pp. 156–79.

Gutman, A.Ia., *The Destruction of Nikolaevsk-on-Amur*, Kingston, Ontario: Limestone Press, 1993.

Haapala, Pertti and Marko Tikka, "Revolution, Civil War, and Terror in Finland in 1918," in Robert Gerwarth and John Horne (eds), *War in Peace: Paramilitary Violence in Europe after the Great War*, Oxford: Oxford University Press, 2013, pp. 72–84.

Häfner, Lutz, *Die Partei der linken Sozialrevolutionäre in der Russischen Revolution von 1917–1918*, Cologne: Böhlau, 1994.

Hagen, Mark von, "The Dilemmas of Ukrainian Independence and Statehood, 1917–1921," *The Harriman Institute Forum*, vol. 7 (1994), pp. 7–11.

——— "I Love Russia but Want Ukraine: How a Russian Imperial General became Hetman Pavlo Skoropadsky of the Ukrainian State," in Frank Sysyn and Serhii Plokhii (eds), *Synopsis: A Collection of Essays in Honor of Zenon E. Kohut*, Edmonton: Canadian Institute of Ukrainian Studies Press, 2005, pp. 115–48.

——— *Soldiers in the Proletarian Dictatorship: The Red Army and the Soviet Socialist State, 1917–1930*, Ithaca: Cornell University Press, 1990, pp. 67–182.

——— *War in a European Borderland: Occupation and Occupation Plans in Galicia and Ukraine, 1914–1918*, Seattle: Herbert J. Ellison Center for Russian, East European and Central Asian Studies, University of Washington, 2007.

Haimson, Leopold H. (ed.), *The Mensheviks: From the Revolution of 1917 to the Second World War*, University of Chicago Press, 1974.

——— "The Problem of Social Stability in Urban Russia, 1905–1917," *Slavic Review*, vol. 23, no. 4 (1964), pp. 619–42; vol. 24, no. 1 (1965), pp. 1–22.

Hamalainen, Pekka Kalevi, *In Time of Storm: Revolution, Civil War and the Ethnolinguistic Issue in Finland*, Albany: State University of New York Press, 1979.

Hamm, Michael F., "The Breakdown of Urban Modernization: A Prelude to the Revolution of 1917," in Michael F. Hamm (ed.), *The City in Russian History*, Lexington: Kentucky University Press, 1976, pp. 182–210.

Hardeman, Hilda, *Coming to Terms with the Soviet Regime: The "Changing Signposts" Movement among Russian Émigrés in the Early 1920s*, Dekalb: Northern Illinois University Press, 1994.

Harding, Neil, *Lenin's Political Thought*, 2 vols, London: Macmillan, 1983.

Harvey, A.D., "Trotsky at Halifax, April 1917," *Archives*, vol. 22, no. 97 (1997), pp. 170–74.

Hasegawa, Tsuyoshi, *The February Revolution: Petrograd 1917*, Seattle: University of Washington Press, 1981.

Haupt, Georges, *Socialism and the Great War: The Collapse of the Second International*, Oxford: Clarendon Press, 1972.

Hayit, Baymirza, *Basmatschi. Nationaler Kampf Turkestans in den Jahren 1917 bis 1934*, Cologne: Dreisam-Verlag, 1993.

——— *Turkestan im XX. Jahrhundert*, Darmstadt: Leske, 1956.

Heenan, Louise E., *Russian Democracy's Fatal Blunder: The Summer Offensive of 1917*, New York: Praeger, 1987.

Heretz, Leonid, "The Psychology of the White Movement," in Vladimir N. Brovkin (ed.), *The Bolsheviks in Russian Society: The Russian Revolution and the Civil Wars*, New Haven: Yale University Press, 1997, pp. 105–21.

Herwig, Holger H., "German Policy in the Eastern Baltic Sea in 1918: Expansion or Anti-Bolshevik Crusade?" *Slavic Review*, vol. 32, no. 2 (1973), pp. 339–57.

Heyman, Neil M., "Leon Trotsky: Propagandist to the Red Army," *Studies in Comparative Communism*, vol. 10, nos 1–2 (1977), pp. 34–43.

——— "Leon Trotsky's Military Education: From the Russo-Japanese War to 1917," *Journal of Modern History*, vol. 45, no. 2 (microfiche supplement) (1973), pp. 71–98.

Hillman, Tom, *The Trans-Dnepr Operation: Wrangel's Last Operation in the Russian Civil War*, n.p.: Gauntlet International, 2004.

Hogenhuis-Seliverstoff, Anne, *Les relations franco-soviétiques, 1917–1924*, Paris: Institut d'Histoire des Relations Internationales Contemporaines, 1981.

Holmes, Larry E., *For the Revolution Redeemed: The Workers' Opposition in the Bolshevik Party, 1919–1921*, Pittsburgh: University of Pittsburgh, Center for Russian and East European Studies, 1990.

Holquist, Peter, "'Conduct Merciless Mass Terror': Decossackization on the Don in 1919," *Cahiers du Monde Russe*, vol. 38, nos 1–2 (1997), pp. 127–62.

——— *Making War, Forging Revolution: Russia's Continuum of Crisis, 1914–1921*, Cambridge, MA: Harvard University Press, 2002.

Holubko, Viktor, *Armiia Ukrainskoi Narodnoi Respubliky, 1917–1918: Utvorennia na borot'ba za derzhavu*, Lviv: Kal'variia, 1997.

Hopkirk, Peter, *Setting the East Ablaze: Lenin's Dream of an Empire in Asia*, Oxford: Oxford University Press, 1986.

Horak, Stephan M., *The First Treaty of the First World War: Ukraine's Treaty with the Central Powers of February 9, 1918*, Boulder: East European Monographs, 1988.

Horak, Volodymyr, *Povstantsi Otamana Hryhor'ieva (serpen' 1918—serpen' 1919 rr.) Istorychne doslidzhennia*, Fastiv: Polifast, 1998.

Hosking, Geoffrey, *The Russian Constitutional Experiment: Government and Duma, 1907–1914*, Cambridge: Cambridge University Press, 1973.

——— *Russia: People and Empire, 1552–1917*, London: Fontana, 1997.

Hovannisian, Richard G., "Armenia and the Caucasus in the Genesis of the Soviet–Turkish Entente," *International Journal of Middle East Studies*, vol. 4, no. 2 (1973), pp. 129–47.

Hovannisian, Richard G. (ed.), *The Armenian Genocide in Perspective*, New Brunswick, NJ: Transaction Books, 1986.

——— *The Republic of Armenia*, 4 vols, Berkeley: University of California Press, 1971–96.

Hovey, Tamara, *John Reed: Witness to Revolution*, Los Angeles: George Sand Books, 1975.

Hovi, Kalervo, *Alliance de Revers: The Stabilization of France's Alliance Policies in East Central Europe, 1919–1921*, Turku: Turun Yliopisto, 1984.

——— *Cordon Sanitaire or Barrière de l'Est? The Emergence of the New French Eastern European Policy, 1917–1919*, Turku: Turun Yliopisto, 1975.

Hunchak, Taras, "Sir Lewis Namier and the Struggle for Eastern Galicia, 1918–1920," *Harvard Ukrainian Studies*, vol. 1, no. 2 (1977), pp. 198–210.

Hunczak, Taras, *Symon Petlura et les Juifs*, Bibliothèque Ukrainienne Symon Petlura, 1987.

———— "The Ukraine under Hetman Pavlo Skoropadskyi," in Taras Hunczak (ed.), *The Ukraine, 1917–1921: A Study in Revolution*, Cambridge, MA: Harvard University Press, 1977, pp. 61–81.

Husband, William B., *"Godless Communists": Atheism and Society in Soviet Russia, 1917–1932*, DeKalb: Northern Illinois University Press, 2000.

———— "Workers' Control and Centralization in the Russian Revolution: The Textile Industry of the Central Industrial Region, 1917–1920," *Carl Beck Papers in Russian and East European Studies*, no. 403, Pittsburgh: University of Pittsburgh Press, 1985.

Ianchevskii, N.L., *Grazhdanskaia bor'ba na Severnom Kavkaze*, Rostov-on-Don: Sevkavkniga, 1927.

Iarov, S.V., *Krest'ianin kak politik. Krest'ianstvo Severo-Zapada Rossii v 1918–1919gg: politicheskie myshlenie i massovyi protest*, Saint Petersburg: Dmitrii Bulanin, 1999.

Iazykov, G.L., "Evakuatsiia Chenomorskogo flota iz Kryma v Bizertu v 1920 godu," *Novyi chasovoi*, no. 4 (1996), pp. 160–66.

Ioffe, G.Z., *Kolchakovskaia avantiura i ee krakh*, Moscow: Mysl', 1983.

———— *Krakh rossiiskoi monarkhicheskoi kontrrevoliutsii*, Moscow: Nauka, 1977.

Iskhakov, S.M. (ed.), *Krym. Vrangel'. 1920 god*, Moscow: Izdatel'stvo "Sotsial'no-politicheskaia MYSL'," 2006.

Isono, Fujiko, "Soviet Russia and the Mongolian Revolution of 1921," *Past and Present*, no. 83 (1979), pp. 116–40.

Issit, Benjamin, *From Victoria to Vladivostok: Canada's Siberian Expedition, 1917–19*, Vancouver: University of British Columbia Press, 2010.

Ivanov, V.D. and O.I. Sergeev, *Ussuriiskoe Kazachestvo v revoliutsiakh 1917 goda i v grazhdanskoi voine na Dal'nem Vostoke*, Vladivostok: DVO RAN, 1999.

Iz istorii Dal'nevostochnoi respubliki. Sbornik nauchnykkh trudov, Vladivostok: Izd-vo Dal'nevostochnogo Universiteta, 1992.

Jahn, Huburtus F., "The Housing Revolution in Petrograd, 1917–1920," *Jahrbücher für Geschichte Osteuropas*, vol. 38, no. 2 (1990), pp. 212–27.

Janke, Arthur E., "The Don Cossacks on the Road to Independence," *Canadian Slavonic Papers*, vol. 12, no. 3 (1970), pp. 273–94.

Jansen, Marc, "International Class Solidarity or Foreign Intervention? Internationalists and Latvian Rifles in the Russian Revolution and Civil War," *International Review of Social History*, vol. 31, no. 1 (1986), pp. 68–79.

———— *A Show Trial under Lenin: The Trial of the Socialist Revolutionaries, Moscow, 1922*, The Hague: M. Nijhoff, 1982.

Jeffreys-Jones, Rhodri, "W. Somerset Maugham: Anglo-American Agent in Revolutionary Russia," *American Quarterly*, vol. 28, no. 1 (1976), pp. 90–106.

Jones, David R., "The Imperial Army in World War I," in Frederick W. Kagan and Robin Higham (eds), *The Military History of Tsarist Russia*, London: Palgrave, 2002, pp. 227–48.

———— "Imperial Russia's Forces at War," in Allan R. Millett and Williamson Murray (eds), *Military Effectiveness, Vol. 1: The First World War*, Boston: Allen and Unwin, 1988, pp. 249–329.

———— "Nicholas II and the Supreme Command: An Investigation of Motives," *Study Group on the Russian Revolution: Sbornik*, no. 11 (1985), pp. 47–83.

———— "The Officers and the October Revolution," *Soviet Studies*, vol. 28, no. 2 (1976), pp. 207–23.

BIBLIOGRAPHY

Jones, Stephen, "The Establishment of Soviet Power in Transcaucasia: The Case of Georgia, 1921–1928," *Soviet Studies*, vol. 40, no. 4 (1988), pp. 616–39.

Kadishev, A.V., *Interventsiia i Grazhdanskaia voina v Zakavkaz'e*, Moscow: Voenizdat, 1960

Kakurin, N.E., *Kak srazhalas' revoliutsiia, 1917–21*, 2 vols, Moscow: Gosizdat, 1925.

Kaminskii, V.V., "Brat protiv brat: ofitsery-genshtabisty v 1917–1920gg.," *Voprosy istorii*, no. 11 (2003), pp. 115–26.

——— "Russkie genshtabisty v 1917–1920: Itogi izucheniia," *Voprosy istorii*, no. 12 (2002), pp. 40–51.

——— "Vypuskniki Akademii gereral'nogo shtaba na sluzhbe v Krasnoi Armii," *Voenno-istoricheskii zhurnal*, no. 8 (2002), pp. 54–61.

Kaplan, Frederick I., "The Origins and Function of the Subbotniks and Voskreniks," *Jahrbücher für Geschichte Osteuropas*, vol. 13, no. 1 (1965), pp. 30–9.

Kappeler, Andreas, *The Russian Empire: A Multi-Ethnic History*, Harlow: Pearson, 2001.

Karmann, Rudolf, *Der Freiheitskampf der Kosaken. Die Weiße Armee in der russischen Revolution 1917–1920*, Puchheim: IDEA, 1985.

Karolevitz, Robert F. and Ross S. Fenn, *Flight of the Eagles: The Story of the American Kościuszko Squadron in the Polish Russian War, 1919–1920*, Sioux Falls: Brevet Press, 1974.

Karpenko, V.V., *Komkor Dumenko*, Saratov: Privolzhckoe Knizhnoe izd.-vo, 1976.

Karpov, N.D., *Miatezh glavkoma Sorokina: pravda i vymysli*, Moscow: Russkaia Panorama, 2006.

Katkov, George, *Russia, 1917: The February Revolution*, London: Longmans, Green & Co., 1967.

Katouzian, Homayoun, "Nationalist Trends in Iran, 1921–1926," *International Journal of Middle Eastern Studies*, vol. 10, no. 4 (1979), pp. 533–51.

Kavtaradze, A.G., *Voennye spetsialisty na sluzhbe Respubliki Sovetov 1917–1920 gg.*, Moscow: Nauka, 1998.

Kazemzadeh, Firuz, *The Struggle for Transcaucasia, 1917–1921*, New York: Philosophical Library, 1951.

Kellogg, Michael, *The Russian Roots of Nazism: White Émigrés and the Making of National Socialism, 1917–1945*, Cambridge: Cambridge University Press, 2005.

Kenez, Peter, *The Birth of the Propaganda State: Soviet Methods of Mass Mobilization, 1917–1929*, Cambridge: Cambridge University Press 1985.

——— *Civil War in South Russia, 1918: The First Year of the Volunteer Army*, Berkeley: University of California Press, 1971.

——— *Civil War in South Russia, 1919–20: The Defeat of the Whites*, Berkeley: University of California Press, 1977.

——— "The Ideology of the Don Cossacks in the Civil War," in R. Carter Elwood (ed.), *Russian and East European History: Selected Papers from the Second World Congress of Soviet and East European Studies*, Berkeley: Berkeley Slavic Specialists, 1984, pp. 160–84.

——— "The Ideology of the White Movement," *Soviet Studies*, vol. 32, no. 1 (1980), pp. 58–83.

——— "Pogroms and White Ideology in the Russian Civil War," in John D. Klier and Shlomo Lambroza (eds), *Pogroms: Anti-Jewish Violence in Modern Russian History*, Cambridge: Cambridge University Press, 1992, pp. 293–313.

——— "A Profile of the Pre-Revolutionary Officer Corps," *Californian Slavic Studies*, vol. 7 (1973), pp. 128–45.

———— "The Relations between the Volunteer Army and Georgia, 1918–1920: A Case Study in Disunity," *Slavonic and East European Review*, vol. 48 (1970), pp. 403–24.

———— "The Russian Officer Corps before the Revolution: The Military Mind," *Russian Review*, vol. 31, no. 3 (1972), pp. 226–37.

Kettle, Michael, *Russia and the Allies, 1917–1920: Vol. 1, The Allies and the Russian Collapse, March 1917—March 1918*, London: Deutsch, 1979.

———— *Russia and the Allies, 1917–1920: Vol. 2, Road to Intervention, March–November 1918*, London: Routledge, 1988.

———— *Russia and the Allies, 1917–1920: Vol. 3, Churchill and the Archangel Fiasco, November 1918—July 1919*, London: Routledge, 1992.

Khalid, Adeeb, "Nationalizing the Revolution in Central Asia: The Transformation of Jadidism, 1917–1920," in Ronald Grigor Suny and Terry Martin (eds), *A State of Nations: Empire and Nation-Making in the Age of Lenin and Stalin*, New York: Oxford University Press, 2001, pp. 145–64.

———— *The Politics of Muslim Cultural Reform: Jadidism in Central Asia*, Berkeley: University of California Press, 1998.

King, David, *Red Star over Russia: A Visual History of the Soviet Union from 1917 to the Death of Stalin*, London: Tate Publishing, 2009.

———— *Russian Revolutionary Posters: From Civil War to Socialist Realism, from Bolshevism to the End of Stalinism*, London: Tate Publishing, 2012.

Kinvig, Clifford, *Churchill's Crusade: The British Invasion of Russia, 1918–1920*, London and New York: Hambledon Continuum, 2006.

Kirby, David G., "Revolutionary Ferment in Finland and the Origins of the Civil War, 1917–1918," *Scandinavian Economic History Review*, vol. 26, no. 1 (1978), pp. 15–35.

———— *War, Peace and Revolution: International Socialism at the Crossroads, 1914–1918*, Aldershot: Gower, 1986.

Klante, Margarete, *Von der Wolga zum Amur. Die tschechische Legion und der russische Bürgerkrieg*, Berlin: Ost-Europa Verlag, 1931.

Kliatskin, S.M., *Na zashchite Oktiabria: Organizatsiia reguliarnoi army i militsionnoe stroitel'stvo v Sovetskoi respublike, 1917–1920*, Moscow: Nauka, 1965.

Knollys, Lt Col. D.E., "Military Operations in Transcaspia, 1918–1919," *Journal of the Central Asian Society*, vol. 13, no. 2 (1926), pp. 88–110.

Kochan, Lionel, "Kadet Policy in 1917 and the Constituent Assembly," *Slavonic and East European Review*, vol. 45 (1967), pp. 183–93.

Koenker, Diane, "Urbanization and Deurbanization in the Russian Revolution and Civil War," *Journal of Modern History*, vol. 57, no. 3 (1985), pp. 424–50.

Kolonitskii, Boris, "Fevral'skaia revolutsiia kak simbolicheskii perevorot: Otrazenie v russkoi onomastike," *Russian Studies: Ezhekvartal'nik russkoi filologii i kultury*, vol. 3, no. 3 (2000), pp. 92–101.

———— *Simboly vlasti i bor'ba za vlast': k izucheniiu polititicheskoi kultura rossiiskoi revoliutsii 1917 goda*, St Petersburg: Liki Rossii, 2012.

Kolupaev, V.E., "Russkii flot v Afrike," *Voenno-istoricheskii arkhiv*, no. 8 (2002), pp. 3–36.

Kondakov, A.A., *Razgrom desantov Vrangelia na Kubani*, Krasnodar: Krasnodarnoe Knizhnoe izd.-vo, 1960.

Kondrashin, V.V., *Krest'ianskoe dvizhenie v Povolzh'e, 1918–1922*, Moscow: Izd-vo Ianus-k, 2001.

BIBLIOGRAPHY

Koo, Ja-Jeong, "Universalising Cossack Particularism: 'The Cossack Revolution' in Early Twentieth-Century Kuban," *Revolutionary Russia*, vol. 25, no. 1 (2012), pp. 1–29.

Kornatovskii, N.A., *Bor'ba za Krasnyi Petrograd, 1919*, Leningrad: Izd-vo "Krasnoi Gazety," 1929.

Korsakova, N.A., "Otnoshenie P.N. Vrangelia k Kubanskomu kazachestvu (po materialam dnevnikov B.G. Naumenko)," in Iskhakov (ed.), *Krym. Vrangel'. 1920 god*, Moscow: Izdatel'stvo "Sotsial'no-politicheskaia MYSL'," 2006, pp. 56–62.

Kosyk, Wolodymyr, "Première agression de la Russie soviétique contre l'Ukraine (1917–1918)," *L'Est Européen*, no. 230 (Apr.–June 1993), pp. 59–62; no. 231 (Oct.–Dec. 1993), pp. 37–45; no. 233 (Jan.–Mar. 1994), pp. 56–8.

Kowalski, Ronald I., *The Bolshevik Party in Conflict: The Left Communist Opposition of 1918*, London: Macmillan, 1991.

Krammer, Arnold, "Soviet Propaganda among German and Austro-Hungarian Prisoners of War in Russia, 1917–1921," in Samuel R. Richardson and Peter Pastor (eds), *Essays on World War I: Origins and Prisoners of War*, New York: Brooklyn College Press, 1983, pp. 249–64.

Krawchenko, Bohdan, "The Social Structure of the Ukraine at the Turn of the Twentieth Century," *East European Quarterly*, vol. 16, no. 2 (1982), pp. 171–81.

——— "The Social Structure of Ukraine in 1917," *Harvard Ukrainian Studies*, vol. 14, nos 1–2 (1990), pp. 97–112.

Krepp, Endel, *The Estonian War of Independence, 1918–1920*, Stockholm: Estonian Information Bureau, 1980.

Kritsmann, L.N., *Die heroische Periode der Grossen Russischen Revolution. Ein Versuch der Analyse des sogenannien "Kriegskommunismus"*, Vienna and Berlin: Verlag für Literatur und Politik, 1929.

Krivosheeva, G.F. (ed.), *Grif sekretnosti sniat: Poteri vooruzhennykh sil SSSR v voinakh, boevykh deistviiakh i voennykh konfliktakh*, Moscow: Voenizdat, 1993.

Krivoshein, A.K., *Aleksandr Vasil'evich Krivoshein: Sud'ba rossiiskogo reformatora*, Moscow: Moskovskii Rabochii, 1993.

Kröner, Anthony, *The White Knight of the Black Sea: The Life of Peter Wrangel*, The Hague: Leuxenhoff, 2010.

Kruchinin, A.S., *Admiral Kolchak: zhizn podvig, pamiat'*, Moscow: AST, 2010.

——— "P.N. Vrangel' i Ia.S. Slashchov: konflikt lichnostei ili konflikt strategii?" in S.M. Iskhakov (ed.), *Krym. Vrangel'. 1920 god*, Moscow: Izd. "Sotsial'no-politicheskaia MYSL'," 2006, pp. 39–55.

Kuchabsky, Vasyl, *Western Ukraine in Conflict with Poland and Bolshevism, 1918–1923*, Edmonton and Toronto: Canadian Institute of Ukrainian Studies Press, 2011.

Kudinov, O.A., *Konstitutsionnye proekty Belogo dvizheniia i konstitutsionno-pravovye teorii rossisskoi beloemigratsii (1918–1940 gg.), ili Za chto ikh rasstrelivali i deportirovali (dlia tekh, kto khochet poniat' smysl prava). Monografiia*, Moscow: Os'-89, 2006.

Kvashonkin, A.V., "Sovetizatsiia Zakavkaz'ia v perepiske bol'shevistskogo rukovodstva 1920–22gg.," *Cahiers du Monde Russe*, vol. 38, nos 1–2 (1997), pp. 163–94.

Lageard, Helene A. de, "The Revolt of the Basmachi according to Red Army Journals (1920–1922)," *Central Asian Survey*, vol. 6, no. 3 (1987), pp. 1–35.

Landis, Erik C., *Bandits and Partisans: The Antonov Movement in the Russian Civil War*, University of Pittsburgh Press, 2008.

BIBLIOGRAPHY

———— "Between Village and Kremlin: Confronting State Food Procurement in Civil War Tambov, 1919–20," *Russian Review*, vol. 63, no. 1 (2004), pp. 70–88.

———— "A Civil War Episode: General Mamontov in Tambov, August 1919," *Carl Beck Papers in Russian and East European Studies*, no. 1,601, Center for Russian and East European Studies/University Center for International Studies, Pittsburgh: University of Pittsburgh, 2002.

———— "Who Were the "Greens"? Rumor and Collective Identity in the Russian Civil War," *Russian Review*, vol. 69, no. 1 (2010), pp. 30–46.

Lang, David M., *A Modern History of Georgia*, London: Weidenfeld & Nicolson, 1962.

Laqueur, Walter, *Russia and Germany*, London: Weidenfeld and Nicolson, 1965.

Latawski, Paul (ed.), *The Reconstruction of Poland, 1914–23*, London: Macmillan, 1992.

Latsis, Martin, *Dva goda bor'by na vnutrennem fronte. Populiarnyi ozbor dvukhgodichnoi deiatel'nosti ChK*, Moscow: Gosizdat, 1920.

Lazarski, Christopher, "How the Whites Blew Their Chances," *Canadian–American Slavic Studies*, vol. 47, no. 2 (2013), pp. 137–69.

———— *Lost Opportunity: Attempts at Unification of the Anti-Bolsheviks, 1917–1919: Moscow, Kiev, Jassy, Odessa*, Lanham: University Press of America, 2008.

———— "White Propaganda Efforts in the South during the Russian Civil War, 1918–1919 (the Alekseev–Denikin Period)," *Slavonic and East European Review*, vol. 70, no. 4 (1992), pp. 688–707.

Leggett, George, *The Cheka: Lenin's Political Police*, Oxford: Clarendon, 1981.

Lehto-Hoogendorn, Mandy, "The Persistence of a Painful Past: The Finnish Civil War of 1918," *The Masaryk Journal*, vol. 3, no. 1 (2000), pp. 83–94.

Lensen, George A., *Japanese Recognition of the USSR: Soviet–Japanese Relations, 1921–1930*, Tokyo: Sophia University, 1979.

Lesčius, Vytautas, *Lietuvos kariuomenė nepriklausomybės kovose 1918–1920*, Vilnius: Generolo Jono Žemaičio Lietuvos Karo Akademija, 2004.

Letkemann, Peter, "Mennonite Victims of Revolution, Anarchy, Civil War, Disease and Famine, 1917–1923," *Mennonite Historian*, vol. 24, no. 2 (1998), pp. 1–9.

Liebich, André, *From the Other Shore: Russian Social Democracy after 1921*, Cambridge, MA: Harvard University Press, 1997.

Lieven, Dominic, *Nicholas II: Emperor of All the Russias*, London: Pimlico, 1994.

Lih, Lars T., "The Bolsheviks, Razverstka and War Communism," *Slavic Review*, vol. 45, no. 4 (1986), pp. 673–88.

———— "The Bolshevik Sowing Committees of 1920: Apotheosis of War Communism?" *Carl Beck Papers in Russian and East European Studies*, no. 803, Pittsburgh: University of Pittsburgh Press, 1990.

———— *Lenin*, London: Reaktion Books, 2011.

———— *Lenin Rediscovered: "What is to be Done?" in Context*, Boston: Brill, 2005.

Lincoln, W. Bruce, *Passage through Armageddon: The Russians in War and Revolution*, New York: Simon and Schuster, 1986.

———— *Red Victory: A History of the Russian Civil War*, New York: Simon and Schuster, 1989.

Lindemann, Albert S., *The "Red Years": European Socialism versus Communism, 1919–1921*, Berkeley: University of California Press, 1974.

Liulevicious, Gabriel Vejas, *War Land on the Eastern Front: Culture, National Identity and German Occupation in World War I*, Cambridge: Cambridge University Press, 2000.

Lodder, Christina, "Lenin's Plan for Monumental Propaganda," in Matthew C. Bown and Brandon Taylor (eds), *Art of the Soviets: Painting, Sculpture and Architecture in a One-party State, 1917–1992*, Manchester: Manchester University Press, 1993, pp. 16–32.

Lohr, Eric, "The Russian Army and the Jews: Mass Deportation, Hostages and Violence during World War I," *Russian Review*, vol. 60, no. 3 (2001), pp. 404–19.

——— "War and Revolution, 1914–1917," in Dominic Lieven (ed.), *The Cambridge History of Russia, Volume 2: Imperial Russia, 1689–1917*, Cambridge: Cambridge University Press, 2006, pp. 655–69.

Long, John W., "General Sir Alfred Knox and the Russian Civil War: A Brief Commentary," *Sbornik of the Study Group on the Russian Revolution*, no. 9 (1983), pp. 54–64.

——— "Searching for Sydney Reilly: The Lockhart Plot in Revolutionary Russia, 1918," *Europe–Asia Studies*, vol. 47, no. 7 (1995), pp. 1,225–43.

Lorenz, Richard, "Economic Bases of the Basmachi Movement in the Ferghana Valley," in Andreas Kappeler, Gerhard Simon, and Edward Allworth (eds), *Muslim Communities Reemerge: Historical Perspectives on Nationality, Politics, and Opposition in the Former Soviet Union and Yugoslavia*, Durham, NC: Duke University Press, 1994, pp. 277–303.

Lorimer, Frank, *The Population of the Soviet Union: History and Prospects*, Geneva: League of Nations, 1946.

Łossowski, Piotr, *Konflikt polsko-litewski 1918–1920*, Warsaw: Książka i Wiedza, 1995.

——— *Stosunki polsko-litewskie w latach 1918–1920*, Warsaw: Książka i Wiedza, 1966.

Luukanen, Arto, *The Party of Unbelief: The Religious Policy of the Bolshevik Party, 1917–1929*, Helsinki: Suomen Historiallinen Seura, 1994.

Lukov, E.V. and D.N. Shevlev, *Osvedomitel'nyi apparat beloi Sibiri: struktura, funktsii, deiatel'nost' (iiun' 1918—ianvar' 1920 g.)*, Tomsk: Izdatel'stvo Tomskogo Universiteta, 2007.

Lunacharsky, A.V., *Revolutionary Silhouettes*, London: Penguin, 1967.

Lundgreen-Nielsen, Kay, *The Polish Problem at the Paris Peace Conference: A Study in the Policies of the Great Powers and the Poles, 1918–1919*, Odense: Odense University Press, 1979.

Lyandres, Semion, "The 1918 Attempt on the Life of Lenin: A New Look at the Evidence," *Slavic Review*, vol. 48, no. 3 (1989), pp. 432–48.

——— *The Bolsheviks' "German Gold" Revisited: An Inquiry into the 1917 Accusations*, Pittsburgh: University of Pittsburgh Press, 1995.

McCann, James M., "Beyond the Bug: Soviet Historiography of the Soviet–Polish War of 1920," *Soviet Studies*, vol. 36, no. 4 (1984), pp. 475–93.

Macfarlane, L.J., "Hands off Russia: British Labour and the Russo-Polish War, 1920," *Past and Present*, no. 38 (1967), pp. 126–52.

McKean, Robert B., *Between the Revolutions: Russia, 1905–1917*, London: The Historical Association, 1998.

McNeal, Robert H., "The Conference of Jassy: An Early Fiasco of the Anti-Bolshevik Movement," in John S. Curtiss (ed.), *Essays in Russian and Soviet History*, New York: Columbia University Press, 1963, pp. 221–36.

——— *Tsar and Cossack, 1855–1914*, London: Macmillan, 1987.

Main, Steven J., "Pragmatism in the Face of Adversity: The Bolsheviks and the Academy of the General Staff of the Red Army during the Russian Civil War, 1918–1921," *Journal of Slavic Military Studies*, vol. 8, no. 2 (1995), pp. 333–55.

Majstrenko, Iwan, *Borot'bism: A Chapter in the History of Ukrainian Communism*, New York: Praeger, 1954.

Malet, Michael, *Nestor Makhno in the Russian Civil War*, London: Macmillan, 1982.

Malle, Silvana, *The Economic Organization of War Communism, 1918–1921*, Cambridge: Cambridge University Press, 1985.

Manninen, Ohto, "Red, White and Blue in Finland, 1918: A Survey of Interpretations of the Civil War," *Scandinavian Journal of History*, vol. 3, no. 3 (1978), pp. 229–49.

Manusevich, A.Ia., *Internatsionalisty: uchastie trudiashchikhsia stran Tsentral'noi i Iugovostochnoi Evropy v bor'be za vlast' Sovetov v Rossii, 1917–1920 gg.*, Moscow: Nauka, 1987.

Markevich, Andrei and Mark Harrison, "Great War, Civil War, and Recovery: Russia's National Income 1913 to 1928," *Journal of Economic History*, vol. 71, no. 3 (2011), pp. 672–703.

Marot, John E., "Class Conflict, Political Competition and Social Transformation: Critical Perspectives on the Social History of the Russian Revolution," *Revolutionary Russia*, vol. 7, no. 2 (1994), pp. 111–63.

——— "A 'Postmodern' Approach to the Russian Revolution: A Comment on Suny," *Russian Review*, vol. 54, no. 2 (1995), pp. 260–64.

Marshall, Alex, *The Caucasus under Soviet Rule*, London: Routledge, 2010.

——— "The Terek People's Republic, 1918: Coalition Government in the Russian Revolution," *Revolutionary Russia*, vol. 22, no. 2 (2009), pp. 203–21.

Martin, Terry, "The Origins of Soviet Ethnic Cleansing," *Journal of Modern History*, vol. 70, no. 4 (1998), pp. 813–61.

Marwat, Fazal-ur-Rahim Khan, *The Basmachi Movement in Soviet Central Asia: A Study in Political Development*, Peshawar: Emjay Books International, 1985.

Masayuki, Yamauchi, *The Green Crescent under the Red Flag: Enver Pasha in Soviet Russia, 1919–1922*, Tokyo: Institute for the Study of Languages and Cultures of Asia and Africa, 1991.

Masianov, L.L., *Gibel' Ural'skogo kazach'ego voiska*, New York: Vseslavianskoe Izd.-vo, 1963.

Massell, Gregory J., *The Surrogate Proletariat: Moslem Women and Revolutionary Strategy in Soviet Central Asia, 1919–1929*, Princeton: Princeton University Press, 1974.

Matveyev, A.M., "Foreign Prisoners of War in Turkestan, 1917–1918," *Central Asian Review*, vol. 9, no. 3 (1961), pp. 240–50.

Mawdsley, Evan, "The Baltic Fleet and the Kronstadt Mutiny," *Soviet Studies*, vol. 24, no. 4 (1972–3), pp. 506–21.

——— *The Russian Civil War*, Boston: Allen & Unwin, 1987.

Maximoff, G.P., *The Guillotine at Work, Vol. 1: The Leninist Counter-Revolution*, Orkney: Cienfuegos Press, 1979.

Mayer, A.J., *The Furies: Violence and Terror in the French and Russian Revolutions*, Princeton: Princeton University Press, 2000.

Mayzel, Matitahu, *Generals and Revolutionaries: The Russian General Staff during the Revolution—A Study in the Transformation of a Military Elite*, Osnabrück: Biblio-Verlag, 1979.

Medvedev, Roi, *Russkaia revoliutsiia 1917 goda: Pobeda i porazhenie bol'shevikov (k 80-letiu Russkoi revoliutsii 1917 goda)*, Moscow: Izd-vo "Prava Cheloveka," 1997.

Medvetskii, A.F., *General ot infanterii General N.N. Iudenich v gody obshchenatsional'nogo krizisa v Rossii (1914–1920 gg.): monograficheskoe issledovanie*, Samara: PGATI, 2005.

Melancon, Michael, "Rethinking Russia's February Revolution: Anonymous Spontaneity or Socialist Agency?" *Carl Beck Papers in Russian and East European Studies*, no. 1,408, Center for Russian and East European Studies, Pittsburgh: University of Pittsburgh, 2000.

BIBLIOGRAPHY

Melgounov, S.P., *The Red Terror in Russia*, London: J.M. Dent & Sons, 1925.

Mel'gunov, S.P., *Na putiak k dvorstovomu perevorotu. Zagovory pered revoliutsiei 1917 goda*, Paris: Knizhnoe delo "Rodnik," 1931.

Melograni, Piero, *Lenin and the Myth of World Revolution: Ideology and Reasons of State*, Atlantic Highlands, NJ: Humanities Press International, 1989.

Menteshashvili, Avtandil, "An Assessment of the 1920 Uprising in South Ossetia," *Political History of Russia*, vol. 5, no. 1 (1995), pp. 47–56.

Mett, Ida, *La commune de Cronstadt: crépuscule sanglant des Soviets*, Paris: Spartakus, 1938.

Miliukov, P.N., *The Russian Revolution*, 3 vols, Gulf Breeze, FL: Academic International Press, 1978.

Millman, Brock, "The Problem with Generals: Military Observers and the Origins of the Intervention in Russia and Persia, 1917–1918," *Journal of Contemporary History*, vol. 33, no. 2 (1988), pp. 291–320.

Minassian, Taline Ter, *Reginald Teague-Jones: Au service secret de l'Empire britannique*, Paris: Bernard Grasset, 2012.

Mitrovkin, L.V., *Failure of Three Missions: British Diplomacy and Intelligence Efforts to Overthrow the Soviet Government in Central Asia*, Moscow: Progress Publishers, 1987.

Molodtsygin, M.A., *Krasnaia armiia: rozhdenie i stanovlenie, 1917–1920 gg.*, Moscow: RAN, 1997.

———— *Raboche-krest'ianskii soiuz, 1918–1920*, Moscow: Nauka, 1987.

Mommsen, W.J. and G. Hirschfeld (eds), *Social Protest, Violence and Terror in Nineteenth- and Twentieth-Century Europe*, London: Macmillan/Berg, 1982.

Morgan, Kenneth O., *Consensus and Disunity: The Lloyd George Coalition Cabinet, 1918–1922*, Oxford: Clarendon, 1979.

Moskovskii, V.V., "Vosstanie krest'ian v Zapadnoi Sibiri v 1921 godu," *Voprosy istorii*, no. 6 (1998), pp. 46–63.

Mosse, W.E., "Stolypin's Villages," *Slavonic and East European Review*, vol. 43 (1965), pp. 257–74.

Movchin, N.N., *Komplektovanie Krasnoi armii*, Moscow: Gosizdat, 1926.

Mukhamedyarov, Sh.F. and B.F. Sultanbekov, "Mirsaid Sultan-Galiev: His Character and Fate," *Central Asian Survey*, vol. 9, no. 2 (1990), pp. 109–17.

Munholland, J. Kim, "The French Army and Intervention in Ukraine," in Peter Pastor (ed.), *Revolutions and Interventions in Hungary and its Neighbor States, 1918–1919*, Boulder: East European Monographs, 1988, pp. 335–56.

Murdered by Moscow: Petlura, Konovalets, Bandera, London: Ukrainian Publishers, 1958.

Murphy, Brian, "The Don Rebellion, March–June 1919," *Revolutionary Russia*, vol. 6, no. 2 (1993), pp. 315–50.

Murray, Kenneth A., *Wings over Poland: The 7th (Kociuszko) Squadron of the Polish Air Service, 1919, 1920, 1921*, New York: Appleton, 1932.

Musialik, Zdzisław, *General Weygand and the Battle of the Vistula, 1920*, London: J. Pilsudski Institute of Research, 1987.

Myer, William, *Islam and Colonialism: Western Perspectives on Soviet Asia*, London: RoutledgeCurzon, 2002.

Neiberg, Michael S. and David Jordan, *The Eastern Front, 1914–1920: From Tannenberg to the Russo-Polish War*, London: Amber, 2008.

Neilson, Keith, *Strategy and Supply: The Anglo-Russian Alliance, 1914–1917*, London: Allen and Unwin, 1984.

Nenarkov, A.P. (ed.), *Revvoensovet Respubliki (6 sent. 1918 g.—28 avg. 1923 g.)*, Moscow: Politizdat, 1991.

Neumann, J. "A Note on the Winter of the Kronstadt Sailors' Uprising in 1921," *Soviet Studies*, vol. 44, no. 1 (1992), pp. 153–4.

Nilsson, Nils Å. (ed.), *Art, Society, Revolution: Russia, 1917–21*, Stockholm: Almqvist & Wiksell International, 1979.

Norton, Henry K., *The Far Eastern Republic of Siberia*, London: Allen & Unwin, 1923.

Nove, Alec, *An Economic History of the USSR, 1917–1991*, London: Penguin, 1992.

Novikova, Liudmila G., "Northerners into Whites: Popular Participation in the Counter-Revolution in Arkhangel'sk Province, Summer–Autumn 1918," *Europe–Asia Studies*, vol. 60, no. 2 (2008), pp. 277–93.

———— "A Province of a Non-Existent State: The White Government in the Russian North and Political Power in the Russian Civil War, 1918–20," *Revolutionary Russia*, vol. 18, no. 2 (2005), pp. 121–44.

———— *Provintsial'naia "kontrrevoliutsiia": Beloe dvizhenie i Grazhdanskaia voina na russkom Severe, 1917–1920*, Moscow: Novoe Literaturnoe Obozrenie, 2011.

Oberländer, E., "Nationalbolschewistische Tendenzen in der russischen Intelligenz. Die "Smena Vech"-Diskussion, 1921–22," *Jahrbücher für Geschichte Osteuropas*, vol. 16, no. 2 (1968), pp. 194–211.

O'Connor, Timothy E., *Diplomacy and Revolution: G.V. Chicherin and Soviet Foreign Affairs, 1918–1930*, Ames: Iowa State University Press, 1988.

Okhotnikov, J. and N. Batchinsky, *La Bessarabie et la Paix européenne*, Paris: Association des Émigrés Bessarabiens, 1927.

Olcott, Martha B., "The Basmachi or Freemen's Revolt in Turkestan, 1918–1924," *Soviet Studies*, vol. 33, no. 3 (1981), pp. 352–69.

Olikov, S.P., *Dezertirstvo v Krasnoi armii i bor'ba s nim*, Moscow: Izdanie Voennoi tipografii Upravleniia delami Narkomvoenmor i RVS SSSR, 1926.

Oppenheim, Samuel A., "The Supreme Economic Council, 1917–1921," *Soviet Studies*, vol. 25, no. 1 (1973), pp. 3–27.

Orzell, Laurence J., "A 'Hotly Disputed' Issue: Eastern Galicia at the Paris Peace Conference, 1919," *Polish Review*, vol. 25, no. 1 (1980), pp. 49–68.

Osipova, T.A., "Krest'ianstvo v grazhdanskoi voiny: bor'ba na dva fronta," in I.N. Afanasev (ed.), *Sud'by rossiiskogo krest'ianstva*, Moscow: Rosskii Gos.gumanitarnyi Universitet, 1996, pp. 90–161.

———— "Peasant Rebellions: Origin, Scope, Dynamics and Consequences," in Vladimir N. Brovkin (ed.), *The Bolsheviks in Russian Society: The Revolution and Civil Wars*, New Haven: Yale University Press, 1997, pp. 154–70.

———— *Rossiiskoe krest'ianstvo v revoliutsii i grazhdanskoi voine*, Moscow: Izd.-vo Strelets, 2001.

Ostryzniuk, Evan, "The Ukrainian Countryside during the Russian Revolution, 1917–1919: The Limits of Peasant Mobilization," *Ukrainian Review*, vol. 44, no. 1 (1997), pp. 54–63.

Page, Stanley, *The Formation of the Baltic States*, Cambridge, MA: Harvard University Press, 1959.

Palij, Michael, *The Anarchism of Nestor Makhno, 1917–1921: An Aspect of the Ukrainian Revolution*, Seattle: Washington University Press, 1976.

—— *The Ukrainian–Polish Defensive Alliance, 1919–1921: An Aspect of the Ukrainian Revolution*, Edmonton and Toronto: Canadian Institute of Ukrainian Studies Press, 1995.

Palmer, James, *The Bloody White Baron*, London: Faber and Faber, 2008.

Park, Alexander G., *Bolshevism in Turkestan, 1917–1927*, New York: Columbia University Press, 1957.

Parrott, Andrew "The Baltic States from 1914 to 1923: The First World War and the Wars of Independence," *Baltic Defence Review*, vol. 2, no. 8 (2002), pp. 131–58.

Patenaude, Bernard M., *The Big Show in Bololand: The American Relief Expedition to Soviet Russia in the Famine of 1921*, Stanford: Stanford University Press, 2002.

—— "Peasants into Russians: The Utopian Essence of War Communism," *Russian Review*, vol. 54, no. 4 (1995), pp. 552–70.

—— *Stalin's Nemesis: The Exile and Murder of Leon Trotsky*, London: Faber & Faber, 2009.

Patterson, K. David, "Typhus and its Control in Russia," *Medical History*, vol. 37, no. 4 (1993), pp. 361–81.

Pavliuchenkov, S.A., *Krest'ianskaia Brest: ili predistoriia bol'shevistkogo NEPa*, Moscow: Russkoe Knigoizdatel'skoe Tovarishchestvo, 1996.

—— *Voennyi kommunizm: vlast' i massy*, Moscow: RKT-Istoriia, 1997.

Pavliuk, Oleksandr, "Ukrainian–Polish Relations in Galicia, 1918–1919," *Journal of Ukrainian Studies*, vol. 23 (1998), pp. 1–23.

Pearce, Brian, "The 26 Commissars," *Sbornik of the Study Group on the Russian Revolution*, nos 6–7 (1981), pp. 54–66.

—— "A Falsifier of History," *Revolutionary Russia*, vol. 1, no. 1 (1988), pp. 20–23.

—— "More about the 26 Commissars," *Sbornik of the Study Group on the Russian Revolution*, no. 9 (1983), pp. 83–5.

—— "On the Fate of the 26 Commissars," *Sbornik of the Study Group on the Russian Revolution*, nos 6–7 (1981), pp. 83–95.

Pelenski, Jaroslaw, "Hetman Pavlo Skoropadsky and Germany (1917–1918) as Reflected in His Memoirs," in Hans-Joachim Torke and John-Paul Himka (eds), *German–Ukrainian Relations in Historical Perspective*, Edmonton: Canadian Institute of Ukrainian Studies Press, 1994, pp. 69–83.

Pereira, Norman G.O., "Regional Consciousness in Siberia before and after October 1917," *Canadian Slavonic Papers*, vol. 30, no. 1 (1988), pp. 2–21.

Peters, Victor, *Nestor Makhno: The Life of an Anarchist*, Winnipeg: Echo Books, 1970.

Pethybridge, Roger, "The Bolsheviks and Technical Disorder, 1917–1918," *Slavonic and East European Review*, vol. 49 (1971), pp. 410–24.

—— *The Spread of the Russian Revolution: Essays on 1917*, London: Macmillan/St Martin's Press, 1972.

Petricioli, Marta, "L'occupazione italiana del Caucaso: 'nun ingrato servizio' da rendere a Londra," *Il Politico*, vol. 37 (1972), pp. 99–141.

Petroff, Serge P., *Remembering a Forgotten War: Civil War in Eastern European Russia and Siberia, 1918–1920*, Boulder, CO: Eastern European Monographs, 2000.

Petrusheva, L.I., "'Groza tyla i liubimets fronta': General Ia.A. Slashchov v 1919–1921 gg.," in S.V. Karpenko (ed.), *Novyi istoricheskii vestnik: izbranooe 2000–2004*, Moscow: Izdatel'stvo Ippolitova, 2004, pp. 245–66.

Piltz, Georg (ed.) *Russland wird Rot. Satirische Plakate 1918–1922*, Berlin: Eulenspiegel, 1977.

Pipes, Richard E., "The First Experiment in Soviet National Policy: The Bashkir Republic, 1917–1920," *Russian Review*, vol. 9, no. 4 (1950), pp. 303–19.

――― *The Formation of the Soviet Union, 1917–1923*, Cambridge, MA: Harvard University Press, 1954.

――― "The Russian Military Colonies, 1810–1831," *Journal of Modern History*, vol. 12, no. 3 (1950), pp. 205–19.

――― *The Russian Revolution, 1899–1919*, London: Collins Harvill, 1990.

――― *Russia under the Bolshevik Regime, 1919–1924*, New York: A.A. Knopf, 1993.

Pirani, Simon, "The Moscow Workers' Movement in 1921 and the Role of Non-Partyism," *Europe–Asia Studies*, vol. 56, no. 1 (2004), pp. 143–60.

Pliutto, P.A., "Aleksandr Bogdanov on the Period of War Communism," *Revolutionary Russia*, vol. 5, no. 1 (1992), pp. 46–52.

Poliakov, Iu.A., "Grazhdanskaia voina v Rossii: vozniknovenie i eskalatsiia," *Otechestvennaia istoriia*, no. 6 (1992), pp. 32–41.

――― (ed.), *Naselenie Rossii v XX veke, Tom 1: 1900–1939*, Moscow: ROSSPEN, 2000.

――― *Sovetskaia strana posle okonchania grazhdanskoi voiny: territoriia i naselenie*, Moscow: Nauka, 1986.

Polikarpov, V.D., "Tragediia komkora Dumenko," *Don*, no. 1 (1988), pp. 142–8.

Ponting, Clive, *Churchill*, London: Sinclair-Stevenson, 1994.

Procyk, Anna, *Russian Nationalism and Ukraine: The Nationality Policy of the Volunteer Army during the Civil War*, Edmonton: Canadian Institute of Ukrainian Studies, 1995.

Prusin, Alexander V., *Nationalizing a Borderland: War, Ethnicity and Anti-Jewish Violence in East Galicia, 1914–1920*, Tuscaloosa: University of Alabama Press, 2005.

Prymak, Thomas M., *Mykhailo Hrushevsky: The Politics of National Culture*, Toronto: University of Toronto Press, 1987.

Quenoy, Paul du, "Warlordism *à la russe*: Baron von Ungern Sternberg's Anti-Bolshevik Crusade, 1912–1921," *Revolutionary Russia*, vol. 16, no. 2 (2003), pp. 1–27.

Rabinowitch, Alexander, *The Bolsheviks Come to Power: The Revolution of 1917 in Petrograd*, New York: W.W. Norton, 1976.

――― *The Bolsheviks in Power: The First Year of Soviet Rule in Petrograd*, Bloomington: Indiana University Press, 2007.

――― "Early Disenchantment with Bolshevik Rule: New Data from the Archives of the Extraordinary Assembly of Delegates from Petrograd Factories," in Kevin Mcdermott and John Morison (eds), *Politics and Society under the Bolsheviks*, London: Macmillan, 1999, pp. 37–46.

――― *Prelude to Revolution: The Petrograd Bolsheviks and the July 1917 Uprising*, Bloomington: Indiana University Press, 1968.

Radkey, Oliver H., *The Agrarian Foes of Bolshevism: Promise and Default of the Russian Socialist-Revolutionaries, February–October 1917*, New York: Columbia University Press, 1958.

――― *The Unknown Civil War in Russia: A Study of the Green Movement in the Tambov Region, 1920–1921*, Stanford: Stanford University Press, 1976.

Radzinsky, Edvard, *The Last Tsar: The Life and Death of Nicholas II*, London: Hodder & Stoughton, 1992.

――― *Rasputin: The Last Word*, London: Weidenfeld & Nicolson, 2000.

Raleigh, Donald J., "Co-Operation amid Repression: The Revolutionary Communists in Saratov Province, 1918–20," *Cahiers du Monde Russe*, vol. 40, no. 4 (1999), pp. 625–56.

———— *Experiencing Russia's Civil War: Politics, Society and Revolutionary Culture in Saratov, 1917–1922*, Princeton: Princeton University Press, 2002.

———— "A Provincial Kronstadt: Popular Unrest in Saratov at the End of the Civil War," in Donald J. Raleigh (ed.), *Provincial Landscapes: Local Dimensions of Soviet Power, 1917–1953*, Pittsburgh: University of Pittsburgh Press, 2001, pp. 82–104.

Rappaport, Helen, *Ekaterinburg: The Last Days of the Romanovs*, London: Windmill Books, 2009.

Rat'kovskii, I.S., *Krasnyi terror i deiatel'nost' VChK v 1918 gode*, St Petersburg: izd-vo S.-Peterburgskogo univ., 2006.

Rauch, Georg von, *The Baltic States: The Years of Independence, 1917–1940*, London: C. Hurst, 1974.

Read, Christopher, *From Tsar to Soviets: The Russian People and their Revolution, 1917–1921*, London: Routledge, 1996.

———— *War and Revolution in Russia, 1914–22*, Basingstoke: Palgrave, 2013.

Ree, Erik van, "Lenin's Conception of Socialism in One Country, 1915–17," *Revolutionary Russia*, vol. 23, no. 2 (2010), pp. 159–81.

Reshetar, John S., *The Ukrainian Revolution, 1917–1920: A Study in Nationalism*, Princeton: Princeton University Press, 1952.

Rethmann, Petra, "The Discreet Charm of Lenin," *Journal of Historical Sociology*, vol. 26, no. 4 (2013), pp. 576–94.

Retish, Aaron B., *Russia's Peasants in Revolution and Civil War: Citizenship, Identity and the Creation of the Soviet State, 1914–1922*, Cambridge: Cambridge University Press, 2008.

Reynolds, Michael A., "Native Sons: Post-Imperial Politics, Islam, and Identity in the North Caucasus, 1917–1918," *Jahrbücher für Geschichte Osteuropas*, vol. 56, no. 2 (2008), pp. 221–47.

———— *Shattering Empires: The Clash and Collapse of the Ottoman and Russian Empires, 1908–1918*, Cambridge: Cambridge University Press, 2011.

Rhoer, Edward van der, *Master Spy: A True Story of Allied Espionage in Bolshevik Russia*, New York: Charles Scribner's Sons, 1981.

Richardson, R. Dan, "The Defense of Madrid: Mysterious Generals, Red Front Fighters, and the International Brigades," *Military Affairs*, vol. 43, no. 4 (1979), pp. 178–85.

Rigby, Thomas H., *Lenin's Government: Sovnarkom, 1917–1922*, Cambridge: Cambridge University Press, 1979.

Riha, Thomas, "1917—A Year of Illusions," *Soviet Studies*, vol. 19, no. 1 (1967), pp. 115–22.

Ritter, William S., "The Final Phase in the Liquidation of Anti-Soviet Resistance in Tadzhikistan: Ibrahim Bek and the *Basmachi*, 1924–1931," *Soviet Studies*, vol. 37, no. 4 (1985), pp. 484–93.

Roberts, Paul C., "War Communism: A Re-Examination," *Slavic Review*, vol. 29, no. 2 (1970), pp. 238–62.

Robinson, Paul, "'Always with Honour': The Code of the White Russian Officers," *Canadian Slavonic Papers*, vol. 41, no. 2 (1999), pp. 121–41.

———— *The White Russian Army in Exile, 1920–1941*, Oxford: Clarendon, 2002.

Rodgers, Murdoch, "The Anglo-Russian Military Convention and the Lithuanian Community of Lanarkshire, Scotland, 1914–1920," *Immigrants and Minorities*, vol. 1, no. 1 (1982), pp. 60–88.

Rogger, Hans, *Russia in the Age of Modernization and Revolution, 1881–1917*, London: Longman, 1983.

Romero Salvadó, F.J. "The European Civil War: Reds Versus Whites in Russia and Spain, 1917–1939," in Jeremy Black (ed.), *European Warfare, 1815–2000*, Basingstoke: Palgrave, 2002, pp. 104–25.

Rose, John D., "Batum as Domino, 1919–1920: The Defence of India in Transcaucasia," *International History Review*, vol. 2, no. 2 (1980), pp. 266–87.

Rosenberg, William G., *A.I. Denikin and the Anti-Bolshevik Movement in South Russia*, Amherst: Amherst College Press, 1961.

——— *Liberals in the Russian Revolution: The Constitutional Democratic Party, 1917–1921*, Princeton: Princeton University Press, 1974.

——— "Paramilitary Violence in Russia's Civil Wars, 1918–1920," in Robert Gerwarth and John Horne (eds), *War in Peace: Paramilitary Violence in Europe after the Great War*, Oxford: Oxford University Press, 2013, pp. 21–39.

——— "Russian Labor and Bolshevik Power after October," *Slavic Review*, vol. 44, no. 2 (1985), pp. 212–38.

Rosenberg, William G. (ed.), *Bolshevik Visions: The First Phase of the Cultural Revolution in Soviet Russia*, Ann Arbor: Ardis Publishers, 1984.

Roshwald, Aviel, *Ethnic Nationalism and the Fall of Empires: Central Europe, Russia and the Middle East, 1914–1923*, London: Routledge, 2001.

Ross, Nikolai, *Vrangel' v Krymu*, Frankfurt am Main: Posev, 1982.

Rowney, Don K., "Narrating the Russian Revolution: Institutionalism and Continuity across Regime Change," *Comparative Studies in History and Society*, vol. 47, no. 1 (2005), pp. 79–105.

Rozental', Reigo, *Severno-zapadnoi armiia: khronika pobed i porazhenii*, Tallinn: Argo, 2012.

Rucker, R.D., "Workers' Control of Production in the October Revolution and Civil War," *Science and Society*, vol. 43, no. 2 (1979), pp. 158–85.

Rukkas, Andriy, "Georgian Servicemen in the Polish Armed Forces (1922–39)", *Journal of Slavic Military Studies*, vol. 14, no. 3 (2001), pp. 93–106.

Russell, Robert, "The Arts and the Russian Civil War," *Journal of European Studies*, vol. 20, no. 79 (1990), pp. 219–40.

Rutych, N., "Iudenich Nikolai Nikolaevich: General ot infanterii," in N. Rutych, *Belyi front general Iudenicha: Biografii chinov Severno-Zapadnoi armii*, Moscow: Russkii Put', 2002, pp. 18–118.

Ryan, James, *Lenin's Terror: The Ideological Origins of Early Soviet State Violence*, London: Routledge, 2012.

Samoilo, A.A. and M.I. Sboichakov, *Pouchitel'nyi urok: Boevye deistviia Krasnoi Armii protiv interventov i belogvardeitsev v Severe Rossii v 1918–1920 gg.*, Moscow: Voenizdat, 1962.

Sanborn, Joshua A., *Drafting the Russian Nation: Military Conscription, Total War and Mass Politics, 1905–1925*, DeKalb: Northern Illinois University Press, 2003.

——— "The Genesis of Russian Warlordism: Violence and Governance in the First World War and the Civil War," *Contemporary European History*, vol. 19 (2010), pp. 195–13.

——— "Unsettling the Empire: Violent Migrations and Social Disaster in Russia during World War I," *Journal of Modern History*, vol. 77, no. 2 (2005), pp. 290–324.

Saparov, Arsene, "From Conflict to Autonomy: The Making of the South Ossetian Autonomous Region, 1918–1922," *Europe–Asia Studies*, vol. 62, no. 1 (2010), pp. 99–123.

BIBLIOGRAPHY

Sapir, Jacques, "La guerre civile et l'économie de guerre: origines du système soviétique," *Cahiers du Monde Russe et Soviétique*, vol. 38, nos 1–2 (1997), pp. 9–28.

Sareen, T.R., *British Intervention in Central Asia and Trans-Caucasia*, New Delhi: Anmol Publications, 1989.

Saunders, David, "Britain and the Ukrainian Question, 1912–20," *English Historical Review*, vol. 103, no. 406 (1988), pp. 40–68.

———— *Russia in the Age of Modernization and Reform, 1801–1881*, London: Longman, 1992.

Savchenko, V.A., "Glavnokommanduiushchii Murav'ev: '... Nash lozung—byt' besposhchadnymi,'" in V.A. Savchenko, *Avantiuristy grazhdanskoi voiny: istoricheskoe issledovanie*, Khar'kov: Folio, 2000, pp. 44–64.

———— "'Pogromnyi' ataman Grigor'ev," in V.A. Savchenko, *Avantiuristy grazhdanskoi voiny: istoricheskoe issledovanie*, Khar'kov: Folio, 2000, pp. 87–128.

Schapiro, Leonard, *The Origins of the Communist Autocracy: Political Opposition in the Soviet State—The First Phase, 1917–1922*, London: Macmillan, 1955.

Scheibert, Peter, "Deutsche Kolonien an der Wolga in den Jahren der Revolution, 1918–1921," *Forschungen zur Osteuropäischen Geschichte*, vol. 25 (1978), pp. 308–18.

Schleifman, Nurit, "Moscow as Victory Park: A Monumental Change," *History and Memory*, vol. 13, no. 2 (2001), pp. 5–34.

Schnell, Felix, *Räume des Schreckens. Gewalt und Gruppenmilitanz in der Ukraine 1905–1933*, Hamburg: Hamburger Edition, 2012.

Senn, Alfred E., "The Bolsheviks' Acceptance of Baltic Independence, 1919," *Journal of Baltic Studies*, vol. 26, no. 2 (1995), pp. 145–50.

———— *The Emergence of Modern Lithuania*, New York: Columbia University Press, 1959.

———— *The Great Powers, Lithuania and the Vilna Question, 1920–1928*, Leiden: E.J. Brill, 1966.

Sennikov, B.V., *Tambovskoe vosstanie 1918–1919 gg. i raskrest'ianivanie Rossii 1929–1933 gg.*, Moscow: Posev, 2004.

Service, Robert, *The Bolshevik Party in Revolution: A Study in Organizational Change, 1917–1923*, London: Macmillan, 1979.

———— (ed.), *Society and Politics in the Russian Revolution*, London: Macmillan, 1992.

———— *Spies and Commissars: Bolshevik Russia and the West*, London: Macmillan, 2011.

Share, Michael, "The Russian Civil War in Chinese Turkestan (Xinjiang), 1918–1921: A Little Known and Explored Front," *Europe–Asia Studies*, vol. 62, no. 3 (2010), pp. 389–420.

Shereshevskii, B.M., *Razgrom semenovshchiny, aprel'–noiabr' 1920 g.: o roli Dal'nevostochnoi respubliki v bor'be za likvidatsiiu "chitinskoi probki" i ob"edinenie Dal'nego Vostoka*, Novosibirsk: Nauka, 1966.

Shikanov, L.A., "K voprosu o kronologicheskikh ramkakh 'demokraticheskoi' kontrrevoliutsii v Sibiri," in Iu.V. Korablev and V.I. Shishkin (eds), *Iz istorii interventsii i grazhdanskaia interventsiia na Sovetskom Dal'nem Vostoke, 1917–1922 gg.*, Novosibirsk: Nauka, 1985, pp. 62–7.

Shimkin, Michael and Mary Shimkin, "From Golden Horn to Golden Gate: The Flight of the Siberian Russian Flotilla," *Californian History*, vol. 64, no. 4 (1985), pp. 290–4.

Shishkin, V.A. (ed.), *Interventsiia na Severo-Zapade Rossii v 1917–1920 gg.*, St Petersburg: Nauka, 1995.

Shishov, A.V., *Iudenich: general suvorovskoi shkoly*, Moscow: Veche, 2004.

Shubin, A., *Anarkhii-mat' poriadka: Mezhdu krasnymi i belymi. Nestor Makhno kak zerkalo Russkoi revoliutsii*, Moscow: Eksmo "Iauza," 2005.

BIBLIOGRAPHY

Shukman, Harold, *War or Revolution? Russian Jews and Conscription in Britain, 1917*, London: Vallentine Mitchell, 2006.

Shumov, S.A. and A.R. Andreev, *Basmachestvo*, Moscow: Algoritm, 2005.

Sibul, Eric A., "Logistical Aspects of the Estonian War of Independence, 1918–1920," *Baltic Security and Defence Review*, vol. 12, no. 2 (2010), pp. 108–33.

Sicher, Efraim, "The Jewish Cossack: Isaac Babel in the First Red Cavalry," *Studies in Contemporary Jewry*, vol. 4 (1988), pp. 113–34.

Siegelbaum, Lewis H., *The Politics of Industrial Mobilization in Russia, 1914–1917: A Study of the War-Industries Committees*, London: Macmillan, 1983.

——— *Soviet State and Society between Revolutions, 1918–1929*, Cambridge: Cambridge University Press, 1992.

Simonova, T.M., "Strategicheskie zamysly nachal'nika pol'skogo gosudarstva Iuzefa Pilsudskogo: Prometeizm vo vneshnei politiki Pol'shi v 1919–1923gg.," *Voenno-istoricheskii zhurnal*, no. 11 (2008), pp. 42–8.

Singleton, Seth, "The Tambov Revolt (1920–1921)," *Slavic Review*, vol. 25, no. 3 (1966), pp. 497–512.

Skirda, Alexandre, *Nestor Makhno, Anarchy's Cossack: The Struggle for Free Soviets in Ukraine, 1917–1921*, Edinburgh: AK Press, 2004.

Slater, Wendy, *The Many Deaths of Nicholas II: Relics, Remains and the Romanovs*, London: Routledge, 2007.

Slavin, M.M., *Revvoensovety v 1918–1919 gg: Istoriko-iuridicheskiï ocherk*, Moscow: Nauka, 1974.

Slonim, Ilya, *Stillborn Crusade: The Tragic Failure of Western Intervention in the Russian Civil War, 1918–1920*, New Brunswick, NJ: Transaction Publishers, 1996.

Smele, Jonathan D., "A Bolshevik in Brixton Prison: Fedor Raskol'nikov and the Origins of Anglo-Soviet Relations," in Ian D. Thatcher (ed.), *Reinterpreting Revolutionary Russia: Essays in Honour of James D. White.*, Basingstoke: Palgrave, 2006, pp. 105–29.

——— *Civil War in Siberia: The Anti-Bolshevik Government of Admiral Kolchak, 1918–20*, Cambridge: Cambridge University Press, 1996.

——— "'*Mania Grandiosa*' and 'The Turning Point in World History': Kerensky in London in 1918," *Revolutionary Russia*, vol. 20, no. 1 (2007), pp. 1–34.

——— *The Russian Revolution: From Tsarism to Bolshevism*, Frederick, MD: The Modern Scholar/Recorded Books, 2009.

——— "War and Revolution in Russia: The Eastern Front, 1914–1921," http://www.bbc.co.uk/history/worldwars/wwone/eastern_front_01.shtml

——— "'What Kolchak Wants!': Military Versus Polity in White Siberia, 1918–1920," *Revolutionary Russia*, vol. 4, no. 1 (1991), pp. 52–110.

——— "White Gold: The Imperial Russian Gold Reserve in the Anti-Bolshevik East, 1918–? (An Unconcluded Chapter in the History of the Russian Civil War)," *Europe–Asia Studies*, vol. 46, no. 8 (1994), pp. 1317–47.

Smele, Jonathan D. and Anthony Heywood (eds), *The Russian Revolution of 1905: Centenary Perspectives*, Oxford: Routledge, 2005.

Smirnov, A.P., "'Peterburgskii mif' Grigoriia Zinov'ev," *Istoriia Peterburga*, no. 4 (2006), pp. 9–12.

Smirnov, N.N. *et al.* (eds), *Rossiia i pervaia mirovaia voina*, St Petersburg: D. Bulanin, 1999.

Smith, C. Jay, *Finland and the Russian Revolution, 1917–1922*, Athens: University of Georgia Press, 1958.

Smith, Canfield F., "Atamanshchina in the Russian Far East," *Russian History*, vol. 6 (1979), pp. 57–67.

——— "The Ungernovshchina: How and Why," *Jahrbücher für Geschichte Osteuropas*, vol. 28 (1980), pp. 590–5.

——— *Vladivostok under Red and White Rule: Revolution and Counter-Revolution in the Russian Far East, 1920–1922*, Seattle: University of Washington Press, 1975.

Smith, Jeremy, *The Bolsheviks and the National Question*, Basingstoke: Macmillan, 1999.

——— "The Georgian Affair of 1922—Policy Failure, Personality Clash or Power Struggle?" *Europe–Asia Studies*, vol. 50, no. 3 (1998), pp. 519–44.

Smith, Kathleen E., *Mythmaking in the New Russia: Politics and Memory during the Yeltsin Era*, Ithaca: Cornell University Press, 2002.

Smith, Michael G., "Anatomy of Rumor: Murder Scandal, the Musavet Party and the Narrative of the Russian Revolution in Baku, 1917–1920," *Journal of Contemporary History*, vol. 36, no. 2 (2001), pp. 211–40.

——— "Cinema for the 'Soviet East': National Fact and Revolutionary Fiction in Early Azerbaijani Film," *Slavic Review*, vol. 56, no. 4 (1997), pp. 645–78.

——— "The Russian Revolution as a National Revolution: Tragic Deaths and Rituals of Remembrance in Muslim Azerbaijan (1907–1920)," *Jahrbücher für Geschichte Osteuropas*, vol. 49, no. 3 (2001), pp. 363–88.

Smith, Scott, *Captives of Revolution: The Socialist Revolutionaries and the Bolshevik Dictatorship, 1918–23*, Pittsburgh: University of Pittsburgh Press, 2011.

——— "The Socialists-Revolutionaries and the Dilemma of Civil War," in Vladimir N. Brovkin (ed.), *The Bolsheviks in Russian Society: The Revolution and Civil Wars*, New Haven: Yale University Press, 1997, pp. 83–104.

Smolii, V.A. (ed.), *Istoriia Ukrainy*, Kiev: Al'ternatyvy, 1997.

Smolin, A.V., *Beloe dvizhenie na severo-zapade rossii, 1918–1920 gg.*, St Petersburg: Dmitrii Bulanin, 1999.

Snyder, Timothy, *Bloodlands: Europe Between Hitler and Stalin*, London: The Bodley Head, 2010.

——— *The Red Prince: The Fall of a Dynasty and the Rise of Modern Europe*, London: The Bodley Head, 2008.

Sodatenko, B.F., *Grazhdanskaia voina v Ukraine (1917–1920 gg.)*, Moscow: Novyi Khronograf, 2012.

Sokol, Edward D., *The Revolt of 1916 in Russian Central Asia*, Baltimore: Johns Hopkins University Press, 1954.

Sokolov, B.N., *Mikhail Tukhachevskii: zhizn' i smert' "Krasnogo marshala"*, Smolensk: Rusich, 1999.

Sonevytsky, Leonid C., "The Ukrainian Question in R.H. Lord's Writings on the Paris Peace Conference of 1919," *Annals of the Ukrainian Academy of Arts and Sciences in the United States*, vol. 10, no. 1 (29) (1962–3), pp. 65–84.

Sonin, V.V., *Stanovlenie Dal'nevostochnoi respubliki (1920–1922)*, Vladivostok: Izd-vo Dal'nevostochnogo Universiteta, 1990.

Sonyel, Salahi R., "Enver Pasha and the Basmaji Movement in Central Asia," *Middle Eastern Studies*, vol. 26 (1990), pp. 52–64.

Spector, Ivar, *The Soviet Union and the Muslim World, 1917–1958*, Seattle: University of Washington Press, 1959.

Spector, Sherman D., *Rumania at the Paris Peace Conference: A Study of the Diplomacy of Ioan C. Bratianu*, New York: Bookman Associates, 1962.

Spence, Richard B., *Boris Savinkov: Renegade on the Left*, Boulder: East European Monographs, 1991.

———— "Interrupted Journey: British Intelligence and the Arrest of Leon Trotskii, April 1917," *Revolutionary Russia*, vol. 13, no. 1 (2000), pp. 1–28.

———— "Useful Brigand: 'Ataman' S.N. Bulak-Balakhovich, 1917–1921," *Revolutionary Russia*, vol. 11, no. 1 (1998), pp. 17–36.

Spirin, L.M., *Razgrom armii Kolchaka*, Moscow: Voenizdat, 1957.

Stachiw, Matthew and Jaroslaw Sztendera, *Western Ukraine at the Turning Point of Europe's History, 1918–1923*, 2 vols, New York: Shevchenko Scientific Society, 1969–71.

Starikov, Sergei and Roy Medvedev, *Philip Moronov and the Russian Civil War*, New York: Knopf, 1978.

Stepun, Fedor, *Byvshee i nesbyvsheesia*, 2 vols, London: Overseas Publications Interchange, 1990.

Stites, Richard, *Revolutionary Dreams: Utopian Vision and Experimental Life in the Russian Revolution*, London: Oxford University Press, 1989.

Stone, David R., "The Russian Civil Wars," in Robin Higham and Frederick W. Kagan (eds), *The Military History of the Soviet Union*, Basingstoke: Palgrave, 2002, pp. 13–33.

Stone, Norman, *The Eastern Front, 1914–17*, London: Hodder & Stoughton, 1975.

———— *World War One: A Short History*, London: Allen Lane, 2007.

Strachan, Hew, *The First World War*, New York: Viking, 2004.

Subtelny, Orest, *Ukraine: A History*, Toronto: University of Toronto Press, 1994.

Suny, Ronald G., *The Baku Commune, 1917–1918*, Princeton: Princeton University Press, 1972.

———— *The Making of the Georgian Nation*, London: I.B. Tauris, 1989

———— *The Revenge of the Past: Nationalism, Revolution and the Collapse of the Soviet Union*, Stanford: Stanford University Press, 1993.

Survenirov, O.F., *Tragediia RKKA, 1937–1938*, Moscow: Terra, 1998.

Suvorova, L.N., "Behind the Façade of 'War Communism': Political Power and the Market Economy," *Russian Studies in History*, vol. 33, no. 1 (1994), pp. 72–88.

Swain, Geoffrey, "Before the Fighting Started: A Discussion of 'The Third Way'," *Revolutionary Russia*, vol. 4, no. 2 (1991), pp. 210–34.

———— "The Democratic Counter-Revolution Reconsidered" (forthcoming).

———— "The Disillusioning of the Revolution's Praetorian Guard: The Latvian Riflemen, Summer–Autumn 1918," *Europe–Asia Studies*, vol. 51, no. 4 (1999), pp. 667–86.

———— "'An Interesting and Plausible Proposal': Bruce Lockhart, Sidney Reilly and the Latvian Riflemen, Russia, 1918," *Intelligence and National Security*, vol. 14, no. 3 (1999), pp. 81–102.

———— "Maugham, Masaryk and the 'Mensheviks'," *Revolutionary Russia*, vol. 7, no. 1 (1994), pp. 78–97.

———— *The Origins of the Russian Civil War*, London: Longman, 1996.

———— *Russia's Civil War*, Stroud: Tempus, 2000.

———— "Russia's Garibaldi: The Revolutionary Life of Mikhail Artemevich Muraviev," *Revolutionary Russia*, vol. 11, no. 2 (1998), pp. 54–81.

———— *Trotsky*, Harlow: Pearson, 2006.

———— "Trotsky and the Russian Civil War," in Ian D. Thatcher (ed.), *Reinterpreting*

Revolutionary Russia: Essays in Honour of James D. White, Basingstoke: Palgrave, 2006, pp. 86–104.

Swan, Jane, *A Biography of Patriarch Tikhon*, Jordanville, NY: Holy Trinity Monastery, 1964.

Swietochowski, Tadeusz, *Russian Azerbaijan, 1905–1920: The Shaping of National Identity in a Muslim Community*, Cambridge: Cambridge University Press, 1985.

Szamuely, László, "Major Features of the Economy and Ideology of War Communism," *Acta Oeconomica*, vol. 7, no. 2 (1971), pp. 143–60.

Szporluk, Roman, "Lenin, 'Great Russia,' and Ukraine," *Harvard Ukrainian Studies*, vol. 28, nos 1–4 (2006), pp. 611–26.

Takach, Arthur, "In Search of Ukrainian National Identity, 1840–1921," *Ethnic and Racial Studies*, vol. 19, no. 3 (1996), pp. 640–59.

Tapp, J. "The Soviet–Persian Treaty of 1921," *International Law Quarterly*, vol. 4 (1951), pp. 511–14.

Tarkhova, N.S., "Trotsky's Train: An Unknown Page in the History of the Civil War," in Terry Brotherstone and Paul Dukes (eds), *The Trotsky Reappraisal*, Edinburgh: Edinburgh University Press, 1992, pp. 27–40.

Taylor, A.J.P., *The Origins of the Second World War*, London: Hamish Hamilton, 1961.

Thaden, Edward C., *Russia since 1801: The Making of a New Society*, New York: Wiley-Interscience, 1971.

Thatcher, Ian D., "The St Petersburg/Petrograd Mezhraionka, 1913–1917: The Rise and Fall of a Russian Social Democratic Workers' Party Unity Faction," *Slavonic and East European Review*, vol. 87, no. 2 (2009), pp. 284–321.

——— *Trotsky*, London: Routledge, 2003.

Thompson, John M., *Russia, Bolshevism and the Versailles Peace*, Princeton: Princeton University Press, 1966.

Thunig-Nittner, Gerburg, *Die Tschechoslowakische Legion in Russland. Ihre Geschichte und Bedeutung bei der Entsethung der 1. Tschechoslowakischen Republik*, Wiesbaden: Breyer, 1970.

Toews, John B., "No Songs were Sung at the Graveside: The Blumenort (Russia) Massacre (10–12 November 1919)," *Journal of Mennonite Studies*, vol. 13 (1995), pp. 51–70.

——— "The Origins and Activities of the Mennonite *Selbstschutz* in the Ukraine (1918–1919)," *Mennonite Quarterly Review*, vol. 46 (1972), pp. 5–40.

Tolstoy, Nikolai, *Victims of Yalta*, London: Hodder & Stoughton, 1977.

Tolstoy, Vladimir, Irina Bibikova, and Catherine Cooke (eds), *Street Art of the Revolution: Festivities and Celebrations in Russia, 1918–1933*, London: Thames and Hudson, 1990.

Traub, Rainer, "Lenin and Taylor: The Fate of 'Scientific Management' in the (Early) Soviet Union," *Telos*, vol. 37 (1978), pp. 82–92.

Treadgold, Donald W., "The Ideology of the White Movement: Wrangel's 'Leftist Policy from Rightist Hands," *Harvard Slavic Studies*, vol. 4 (1957), pp. 481–97.

——— *Lenin and his Rivals: The Struggle for Russia's Future, 1898–1906*, London: Methuen, 1955.

Troebst, Stefan, "'Intermarium' and 'Wedding to the Sea': The Politics of History and Mental Mapping in East Central Europe," *European Review of History*, vol. 10, no. 2 (2003), pp. 293–321.

Tsipkin, Iu.N. and T.A. Ornatskaia, *Vneshnaia politika Dalnevostochnoi respubliki (1920–1922 gg.)*, Khabarovsk: Otdel Nauchnykh izdanii Khabarovskogo Kraevogo Kraevedcheskogo Muzeiia im. N.I. Grodedova, 2008.

BIBLIOGRAPHY

Tsuji, Yoshimasa, "The Debate on Trade Unions, 1920–21," *Revolutionary Russia*, vol. 2, no. 1 (1989), pp. 31–100.

Tsvetkov, V.Zh., *General Diterikhs*, Moscow: Posev, 2004.

Tucker, Robert C., *Stalin as Revolutionary*, New York: Norton, 1974.

Tumarkin, Nina, *Lenin Lives! The Lenin Cult in Soviet Russia*, Cambridge, MA: Harvard University Press, 1997, pp. 64–111.

—— "The Myth of Lenin during the Civil War Years," in Albert Gleason, Peter Kenez, and Richard Stites (eds), *Bolshevik Culture: Experiment and Order in the Russian Revolution*, Bloomington: Indiana University Press, 1985, pp. 77–92.

Tursunov, Kh.T., *Vosstanie 1916 goda v Srednei Azii i Kazakhstane*, Tashkent: Gos. izd-vo Uzbekskoi SSR, 1962.

Turuk, Fiodar, *Belorusskoe dvizhenie: ocherk istorii natsional'nogo i revoliutsionnogo dvizheniia Belorussa*, Minsk: Otpechatana na Minskoi Kartograficheskoi Fabrike Belgeodezii, 1994.

Uldricks, Teddy J., *Diplomacy and Ideology: The Origins of Soviet Foreign Relations, 1917–1930*, London: Sage, 1979.

Ullman, Richard H., *Anglo-Soviet Relations, 1917–1921*, 3 vols, Princeton: Princeton University Press, 1961–72.

Üngör, Uğur Ümit, "Paramilitary Violence in the Collapsing Ottoman Empire," in Robert Gerwarth and John Horne (eds), *War in Peace: Paramilitary Violence after the Great War*, Oxford: Oxford University Press, pp. 164–83.

Upton, Anthony F., *The Finnish Revolution, 1917–1918*, Minneapolis: University of Minnesota Press, 1980.

Urevich, B., "The End of Ataman Annenkov," *Far Eastern Affairs*, vol. 6 (1990), pp. 92–103.

Ustinov, V.M., *Turar Ryskulov: ocherki politicheskoi biografii*, Almaty: Kazakhstan, 1996.

Vaidyanath, R., *The Formation of the Soviet Central Asian Republics: A Study in Soviet Nationalities Policy, 1917–1936*, New Delhi: People's Publishing House, 1967.

Vakar, Nicholas P., *Belorussia, the Making of a Nation: A Case Study*, Cambridge, MA: Harvard University Press, 1956.

Vaksberg, Arkady, *Stalin's Prosecutor: The Life of Andrei Vyshinsky*, New York: Grove Weidenfeld, 1990.

Vasetskii, N.A., "Zinov'ev: strannitsy zhizni i politicheskoi deiate'nost'," *Novaia i noveishaia istorii*, no. 4 (1989), pp. 111–39.

Vendrykh, G.A., *Dekabr'sko-ianvarskii boi 1919–1920 gg. v Irkutske*, Irkutsk: Gosizdat, 1957.

Venkov, A.V., *Veshenskoe vosstanie*, Moscow: Veche, 2012.

Verstiuk, Vladyslav, "Conceptual Issues in Studying the History of the Ukrainian Revolution," *Journal of Ukrainian Studies*, vol. 24, no. 1 (1999), pp. 5–20.

Veryha, Wasyl, "Famine in Ukraine in 1921–1923 and the Soviet Government's Counter Measures," *Nationalities Papers*, vol. 12, no. 2 (1984), pp. 265–86.

—— "Looting the Churches in Ukraine in 1922," *Ukrainian Quarterly*, vol. 46, no. 3 (1990), pp. 233–45.

Vishnevskii, A.G. (ed.), *Demograficheskaia modernizatsiia Rossii, 1900–2000*, Moscow: Novoe Izdatel'stvo, 2006.

Voline, *The Unknown Revolution*, Montreal: Black Rose Books, 1975.

Volodarsky, Mikhail, *The Soviet Union and its Southern Neighbours: Iran and Afghanistan, 1917–1933*, London: Frank Cass, 1994.

Vorobev, V.K., *Chapannaia voina v Simbirskoi gubernii: mify i realnost'. Zametki kraeveda*, n.p.: Vector-C, 2008.

Wade, Rex A., "Argonauts of Peace: The Soviet Delegation to Western Europe in the Summer of 1917," *Slavic Review*, vol. 26, no. 3 (1967), pp. 453–67.

———— *The Bolshevik Revolution and Russian Civil War*, Westport, CT: Greenwood Press, 2001.

———— "The October Revolution, the Constituent Assembly, and the End of the Russian Revolution," in Ian D. Thatcher (ed.), *Reinterpreting Revolutionary Russia: Essays in Honour of James D. White*, Basingstoke: Palgrave, 2006, pp. 72–85.

———— *The Russian Revolution, 1917*, Cambridge: Cambridge University Press, 2000.

———— *The Russian Search for Peace, February–October 1917*, Stanford: Stanford University Press, 1969.

Waldron, Peter, *Between Two Revolutions: Stolypin and the Politics of Renewal in Russia*, London: UCL Press, 1998.

———— *The End of Imperial Russia, 1855–1917*, Basingstoke: Macmillan, 1997.

Wandycz, Peter S., "General Weygand and the Battle of Warsaw of 1920," *Journal of Central European Affairs*, vol. 19, no. 4 (1959), pp. 357–65.

———— "Poland on the Map of Europe in 1918," *Polish Review*, vol. 35, no. 1 (1990), pp. 19–25.

———— "Secret Soviet–Polish Peace Talks in 1919," *Slavic Review*, vol. 24, no. 3 (1965), pp. 425–49.

———— *Soviet–Polish Relations, 1917–1921*, Cambridge, MA: Harvard University Press, 1969.

Warvariv, Constantine, "America and the Ukrainian National Cause, 1917–1920," in Taras Hunczak (ed.), *The Ukraine, 1917–1921: A Study in Revolution*, Cambridge, MA: Harvard University Press, 1977, pp. 352–81.

Watrous, Stephen D., "The Regionalist Conception of Siberia, 1860–1920," in Galya Diment and Yuri Slezkine (eds), *Between Heaven and Hell: The Myth of Siberia in Russian Culture*, New York: St Martin's Press, 1993, pp. 113–32.

Wedziagolski, Karol, *Boris Savinkov: Portrait of a Terrorist*, Clifton, NJ: The Kingston Press, 1988.

Weeks, Theodore R., "Russification: Word and Practice, 1863–1914," *Proceedings of the American Philosophical Society*, vol. 148 (2004), pp. 471–89.

Wehner, Markus, "Golod 1921–1922 gg. v Samarskoi gubernii i reaktsiia Sovetskogo pravitel'stva," *Cahiers du Monde Russe*, vol. 38, nos 1–2 (1997), pp. 223–42.

———— "Le soulèvement géorgien de 1924 et la réaction des bolcheviks," *Communisme*, nos 42–4 (1995), pp. 155–70.

Werth, Nicolas, "Crimes and Mass Violence of the Russian Civil Wars (1918–1921)," Online Encyclopedia of Mass Violence: http://www.massviolence.org/Crimes-and-mass-violence-of-the-Russian-civil-wars-1918

Wheatcroft, Stephen, "Famine and Epidemic Crises in Russia, 1918–1922: The Case of Saratov," *Annales de Démographie Historique* (1983), pp. 329–51.

Wheeler-Bennett, John W., *The Forgotten Peace: Brest-Litovsk, March 1918*, London: Macmillan, 1938.

White, James D., "The Kornilov Affair—A Study in Counter-Revolution," *Soviet Studies*, vol. 20, no. 2 (1968), pp. 187–205.

———— "Lenin, Trotsky and the Art of Insurrection: The Congress of Soviets of the Northern

Region, 11–13 October 1917," *Slavonic and East European Review*, vol. 77, no. 1 (1999), pp. 117–39.

———— "Lenin, the Germans and the February Revolution," *Revolutionary Russia*, vol. 5, no. 1 (1992), pp. 1–22.

———— "National Communism and World Revolution: The Political Consequences of German Military Withdrawal from the Baltic Area, 1918–19," *Europe–Asia Studies*, vol. 46, no. 8 (1994), pp. 1,349–69.

———— *The Russian Revolution, 1917–1921: A Short History*, London: Edward Arnold, 1994.

———— "Scottish Lithuanians and the Russian Revolution," *Journal of Baltic Studies*, vol. 6, no. 1 (1975), pp. 1–8.

———— "Vincas Kapsukas and the Scottish Lithuanians," *Revolutionary Russia*, vol. 17, no. 1 (2004), pp. 67–89.

White, Stephen, "Communism and the East: The Baku Congress, 1920," *Slavic Review*, vol. 33, no. 3 (1974), pp. 492–514.

———— *The Bolshevik Poster*, New Haven: Yale University Press, 1988.

———— *The Origins of Détente: The Genoa Conference and Soviet Western Relations, 1921–22*, Cambridge: Cambridge University Press, 1985.

———— "Soviet Russia and the Asian Revolution, 1917–1924," *Review of International Studies*, vol. 10, no. 3 (1984), pp. 219–32.

Wildman, Allan K., *The End of the Russian Imperial Army*, 2 vols, Princeton: Princeton University Press, 1980–7.

Williams, Christopher, "The 1921 Famine and Periphery Responses," *Revolutionary Russia*, vol. 6, no. 1 (1993), pp. 277–314.

Williams, Robert C., *The Other Bolsheviks: Lenin and his Critics, 1904–1914*, Bloomington: Indiana University Press, 1986.

Wilson, Michael, *For Them the War Was Not Over: The Royal Navy in Russia, 1918–1920*, Stroud: The History Press, 2010.

Wollenberg, Erich, *The Red Army: A Study of the Growth of Soviet Imperialism*, Westport, CT: Hyperion Press, 1973.

Wood, Alan, *The Romanov Empire, 1613–1917*, London: Hodder Arnold, 2007.

Woytak, Richard, "The Promethean Movement in Interwar Poland," *East European Quarterly*, vol. 18, no. 3 (1984), pp. 273–8.

Wrangel, Alexis, *General Wrangel, 1878–1929: Russia's White Crusader*, London: Leo Cooper, 1987.

Wright, Alistair S., "'Stemming the Flow': The Red Army Anti-Desertion Campaign in Soviet Karelia (1919)," *Revolutionary Russia*, vol. 25, no. 2 (2012), pp. 141–62.

Wrigley, Chris, *Lloyd George*, Oxford: Blackwell, 1992.

Yamauchi, Masayuki, *The Green Crescent under the Red Star: Enver Pasha in Soviet Russia*, Tokyo: Institute for the Study of Languages and Cultures of Asia and Africa, 1991.

Ybert-Chabrier, Edith, "Les Délégués au Premier Congrès des Peuples d'Orient (Bakou, 1-er–8 septembre 1920," *Cahiers du Monde Russe et Soviétique*, vol. 26, no. 1 (1985), pp. 21–42.

Yekelchyk, Sergei, "Bands of Nation Builders? Insurgency and Ideology in the Ukrainian Civil War," in Robert Gerwarth and John Horne (eds), *War in Peace: Paramilitary Violence in Europe after the Great War*, Oxford: Oxford University Press, 2013, pp. 107–25.

———— *Ukraine: Birth of a Modern Nation*, Oxford: Oxford University Press, 2007.

BIBLIOGRAPHY

Yilmaz, Harun, "An Unexpected Peace: Azerbaijani–Georgian Relations, 1918–20," *Revolutionary Russia*, vol. 22, no. 1 (2009), pp. 37–67.

Yilmaz, Şuhnaz, "An Ottoman Warrior Abroad: Enver Paşa as an Expatriate," *Middle Eastern Studies*, vol. 35, no. 4 (1999), pp. 40–69.

Ylikangas, Heikki, *Der Weg nach Tampere. Die Niederlage der Roten im finnischen Bürgerkrieg 1918*, Berlin: Berliner Wissenschafts-Verlag, 2002.

Zaitsov, A., *1918 god: ocherki po istorii russkoi grazhdanskoi voiny*, Paris, 1934.

Zamoyski, Adam, *Stolypin: Russia's Last Great Reformer*, Princeton, NJ: Kingston Press, 1986.

—— *Warsaw, 1920: Lenin's Failed Conquest of Europe*, London: HarperCollins, 2008.

Zbarsky, Ilya and Samuel Hutchinson, *Lenin's Embalmers*, London: The Harvill Press, 1998.

Zeman, Z.A.B., *Pursued by a Bear: The Making of Eastern Europe*, London: Chatto & Windus, 1989.

Zenkovsky, Serge A., "The Tataro-Bashkir Feud of 1917–1920," *Indiana Slavic Studies*, vol. 2 (1958), pp. 37–62.

Zhulikova, E., "Povstancheskoe dvizhenie na Severnom Kavkaze v 1920–25 godakh (dokumental'nye publikatsii noveishaia otchestvennaia istoriografiia," *Otchestvennaia istoriia*, no. 2 (2004), pp. 159–69.

Zhuralev, V.V., "'Prisoiv takovomu litsu naimenovanie verkhovnogo pravitelia': K voprosu o titule, priniatom admiralom A.V. Kolchakom 18 noiabria 1918 g.," *Antropologicheskii forum*, no. 8 (2008), pp. 353–86.

Zürrer, Werner, *Kaukasien, 1918–1921. Der Kampf der Grossmächte um die Landbrücke zwischen Schwarzem und Kaspischem Meer*, Düsseldorf: Droste Verlag, 1978.

Unpublished Secondary Works

Berk, Stephen M., "The Coup d'État of Admiral Kolchak and the Counter-Revolution in Siberia and East Russia, 1917–1918," Columbia University PhD Thesis, 1971.

Croll, Kirsteen Davina, "Soviet–Polish Relations, 1919–1921," University of Glasgow PhD Thesis, 2009.

Croll, Neil Harvey, "Mikhail Tukhachevsky in the Russian Civil War," University of Glasgow PhD Thesis, 2002.

Drujina, Gleb, "The History of the North-West Army of General Iudenich," Stanford University PhD Thesis, 1950.

Henderson, Robert, "Vladimir Burtsev and the Russian Revolutionary Emigration: Surveillance of Foreign Political Refugees in London, 1891–1905," Queen Mary, University of London PhD Thesis, 2008.

Long, John W., "Civil War and Intervention in North Russia, 1918–1920," Columbia University PhD Thesis, 1972.

Main, Steven J., "The Creation, Organization and Work of the Red Army's Political Apparatus during the Civil War, 1918–20," University of Edinburgh PhD Thesis, 1990.

Watrous, Stephen D., "Russia's 'Land of the Future': Regionalism and the Awakening of Siberia, 1819–1894," University of Washington PhD Thesis, 1970.

Wells, Benjamin, "The Union of Regeneration: The Anti-Bolshevik Underground in Revolutionary Russia, 1917–1919," Queen Mary, University of London PhD Thesis, 2004.

BIBLIOGRAPHY

Internet Resources

http://www.hrono.ru/: An invaluable historical encyclopedia with particular focus on Russia (in Russian).

http://www.mochola.org/: Encyclopedia of materials on the emigration (in Russian).

http://www.istorypedia.com/: Historical encyclopedia with special focus on things military and the Cossacks (in Russian).

http://www.worldstatesmen.org/Russia_war.html: A detailed guide to Russian (and other) civil-war polities (in English).

http://rusk.ru/voinstvo.php: Military history site with extensive coverage of the civil war (in Russian).

http://www.marxists.org/: The Marxist Internet Archive (in English).

http://www.marxists.org/glossary/index.htm: Encyclopedia of Marxism (in English).

http://militera.lib.ru/: Collection of texts on military history, including many key sources on the Russian Civil War (in Russian).

http://pygmy-wars.50megs.com/: A site devoted to conflicts in Eastern Europe and Russia, 1918–23 (in English).

http://www.onwar.com/: General military history site (in English).

http://www.nivestnik.ru/index.html: All issues of the *Novyi istoricheskii vestnik*, with many articles on the civil wars (in Russian).

http://slovari.yandex.ru: A portal to a collection of encyclopedias (in Russian).

http://www.historyofwar.org/index.html: Encyclopedia of Military History (in English).

http://www.rkka.ru/maps1940.htm: Maps detailing military activity during the civil wars (in Russian).

http://www.eleven.co.il/: Encyclopedia of Jewish affairs (in Russian).

http://www.jewishvirtuallibrary.org/index.html: Huge library of materials on Jewish affairs (in English).

http://www.rusrevolution.info/index.shtml?about: Diverse collection of materials on the Russian Revolution and Civil Wars (in Russian).

http://eng.plakaty.ru/: Russian posters site, with many military and propaganda works from the civil wars (in English).

http://www.sobiratel.net/zasluga/Russia/Russia.htm: Russian/Soviet medals, including sections on the RSFSR and the Whites (in English and Russian).

http://wwi.lib.byu.edu/index.php/Main_Page: The World War One Document Archive (in English).

http://revsoc.org/: Site of the Union of Revolutionary Socialists, including many historical documents (in English, Russian, and other languages).

http://swolkov.narod.ru/books.htm: Home page of the prolific military historian Sergei Volkov, with texts of many of his books on the imperial Russian Army and the civil wars (in Russian).

http://www.grwar.ru/manifest/manifest.html: Multi-faceted collection of materials on the Russian Army in the First World War (in Russian).

http://www.regiment.ru/index.htm: Huge library of materials relating to the imperial Russian Army (in Russian).

http://www.firstworldwar.com/: An extensive, multi-media, general site on the First World War, with judicious coverage of the Eastern Front.

http://www.knowbysight.info/index.asp: A reference guide to the history of the Bolsheviks (in Russian).

BIBLIOGRAPHY

http://web.mit.edu/fjk/Public/Glossary/: A guide to the history of Marxism in Russia (in Russian).

http://www.rkka.ru/index.htm: Encyclopedic site on the history of the Red Army (in Russian).

http://www.marxists.org/history/ussr/government/red-army/contents.htm: Branch of a popular site that includes Trotsky's writings of the civil-wars era (in English).

http://www.rusnavy.ru/ussr.htm: History of Soviet naval forces (in Russian).

http://kdkv.narod.ru/WW1/index.html#ABC: Lists of recipients of the Order of the Red Banner and other Soviet military honors (in Russian).

http://eugend.livejournal.com/84777.html: Lists almost 1,300 officers of the old army (from full generals to captains) who served in the Red Army.

http://www.cossackdom.com: Collection of materials on the history of the Cossacks (in Russian, Ukrainian, and English).

http://www.whiterussia1.narod.ru/index.html: Massive collection of materials on the Whites (in Russian).

http://www.antibr.ru/index.html: Extensive site devoted to the anti-Bolshevik movement during the civil wars and after (in Russian).

http://www.rovs.narod.ru/: Site devoted to the history of the Russian All-Military Union, ROVS (in Russian).

http://www.bonistikaweb.ru/KNIGI/nikolaev.htm: A work devoted to monetary issues of the White governments (in Russian).

http://cosaques-emchane.skynetblogs.be/: Site devoted to the Cossacks with many photographs (in French).

http://belrussia.ru/: Site devoted to the White movement (in Russian).

http://ricolor.org/history/bldv/: Huge site devoted to the Whites (in Russian).

http://rovs.atropos.spb.ru/index.php: The official site of the Russian All-Military Union (in Russian).

http://www.dk1868.ru/: Huge collection of materials on the Volunteer Army (in Russian).

http://admiral-kolchak.narod.ru/index.htm: Archive of materials relating to Admiral A.V. Kolchak (in Russian).

http://orenbkazak.narod.ru/: A site devoted to the Orenburg Cossack Host and other White formations during the civil wars, edited by historian Andrei Ganin (in Russian).

http://www.zaimka.ru/white/: A huge collection of materials relating to the Whites in Siberia (in Russian).

http://www.carpatho-rusyn.org/: Carpatho-Rusyn Knowledge Base (in English).

http://www.encyclopediaofukraine.com/default.asp: Encyclopedia of Ukraine (in English).

http://www.ukrstor.com/index.html: Collection of materials on the Ukrainian national movement (in Russian).

http://www.armenian-history.com/index.htm: Encyclopedia of Armenian history with extensive coverage of the civil-wars era (in English).

http://www.eng.kavkaz-uzel.ru/: "Caucasian Knot": general site on the Caucasus, including a useful encyclopedia (in English or Russian).

http://libcom.org/: Libertarian site with extensive coverage of anarchism and anarchists in Russia (in English).

http://militants-anarchistes.info/?lang=fr: Biographical dictionary of anarchists (in French).

http://socialist.memo.ru/: An immense site devoted to Russian socialists and anarchists and their fates post-October (in Russian).

BIBLIOGRAPHY

http://www.chernov.h12.ru/: A site devoted to the life and work of V.M. Chernov (in Russian).

http://www.makhno.ru/makhno/: Huge archive of materials on Nestor Makhno and the *Makhnovtsy* (in Russian).

http://www-personal.umich.edu/~mhuey/HOME.html: Translation of a 1921 anarchist publication, *Pravda o Kronshtadt* ("The Truth About Kronstadt!") and other materials relating to the rebellion (in English).

http://www.yivoencyclopedia.org: The YIVO Encyclopedia of Jews in Eastern Europe, the most complete reference work on its subject.

Fiction

Babel, Isaac, *The Collected Stories*, London: Methuen & Co., 1957.
Blok, Aleksandr, "Twelve" (1918).
Bulgakov, Mikhail, *The Heart of a Dog* (1925).
———— *White Guard* (1926).
Grossman, Vasily, *Life and Fate* (1980).
Sholokhov, Mikhail, *Quiet Don* (1926–40).

Films

1920 Bitwa Warszawska ("The Battle of Warsaw, 1920," dir. Jerzy Hoffman, 2011).
Admiral ("The Admiral," dir. Andrei Kravchuk, 2008).
Arsenal ("The Arsenal," dir. A.P. Dovzhenko, 1929).
Chapaev (dir. G.N. and S.D. Vasil'ev, 1934).
Oktiabr' ("October," dir. Sergei Eisenstein, 1927).

INDEX

INDEX